Editing Data in Table Form View

ACTION	KEYS
Binary field (open)	Double-click, Alt-F5, or Ctrl-F
Delete character	Backspace
Delete current record	Delete (Del)
Delete field contents	Ctrl-Backspace
Ditto (Repeat previous entry)	Ctrl-D
Down one screenful (Table view only)	PgDn
End Field view	↵, or F2 in memo field
Field view	Alt-F5, or Ctrl-F, or double-click
First field	Ctrl-Home
First record	Home
Form view/Table view toggle	F7
Insert new record	Insert (Ins)
Last field	Ctrl-End
Last record	End
Left one screenful	Ctrl-←
Memo field (open)	Double-click, Alt-F5, or Ctrl-F
Move to field	Click, →, ←, Tab, or Shift-Tab
Next field	→, Tab, or ↵
Next record	↓ (Table view), Ctrl-PgDn (Form view)
Previous field	← or Shift-Tab
Previous record	↑ (Table view), Ctrl-PgUp (Form view)
Right one screenful	Ctrl-→
Rotate column	Ctrl-R
Save changes	F2
Undo most recent changes	Ctrl-U
Up one screenful (Table view)	PgUp

For every kind of computer user, there is a SYBEX book.

All computer users learn in their own way. Some need straightforward and methodical explanations. Others are just too busy for this approach. But no matter what camp you fall into, SYBEX has a book that can help you get the most out of your computer and computer software while learning at your own pace.

Beginners generally want to start at the beginning. The **ABC's** series, with its step-by-step lessons in plain language, helps you build basic skills quickly. Or you might try our **Quick & Easy** series, the friendly, full-color guide.

The **Mastering** and **Understanding** series will tell you everything you need to know about a subject. They're perfect for intermediate and advanced computer users, yet they don't make the mistake of leaving beginners behind.

If you're a busy person and are already comfortable with computers, you can choose from two SYBEX series—**Up & Running** and **Running Start**. The **Up & Running** series gets you started in just 20 lessons. Or you can get two books in one, a step-by-step tutorial and an alphabetical reference, with our **Running Start** series.

Everyone who uses computer software can also use a computer software reference. SYBEX offers the gamut—from portable **Instant References** to comprehensive **Encyclopedias**, **Desktop References**, and **Bibles**.

SYBEX even offers special titles on subjects that don't neatly fit a category—like **Tips & Tricks**, the **Shareware Treasure Chests**, and a wide range of books for Macintosh computers and software.

SYBEX books are written by authors who are expert in their subjects. In fact, many make their living as professionals, consultants or teachers in the field of computer software. And their manuscripts are thoroughly reviewed by our technical and editorial staff for accuracy and ease-of-use.

So when you want answers about computers or any popular software package, just help yourself to SYBEX.

For a complete catalog of our publications, please write:
SYBEX Inc.
2021 Challenger Drive
Alameda, CA 94501
Tel: (510) 523-8233/(800) 227-2346 Telex: 336311
Fax: (510) 523-2373

SYBEX is committed to using natural resources wisely to preserve and improve our environment. As a leader in the computer book publishing industry, we are aware that over 40% of America's solid waste is paper. This is why we have been printing the text of books like this one on recycled paper since 1982.

This year our use of recycled paper will result in the saving of more than 15,300 trees. We will lower air pollution effluents by 54,000 pounds, save 6,300,000 gallons of water, and reduce landfill by 2,700 cubic yards.

In choosing a SYBEX book you are not only making a choice for the best in skills and information, you are also choosing to enhance the quality of life for all of us.

Mastering Paradox 4.5 for DOS

Mastering Paradox® 4.5 for DOS®,
Special Edition

Second Edition

ALAN SIMPSON

San Francisco • Paris • Düsseldorf • Soest

SYBEX®

Acquisitions Editor: Joanne Cuthbertson
Developmental Editor: David Peal
Editor: Marilyn Smith
Project Editor: Valerie Potter
Technical Editor: Peter Stokes
Book Series Designer and Production Artist: Suzanne Albertson
Screen Graphics: John Corrigan and Cuong Le
Typesetter: Ann Dunn
Proofreaders/Production Assistants: Rhonda Holmes, Stephen Kullmann, Sarah Lemas
Indexer: Matthew Spence
Cover Designer: Ingalls + Associates
Cover Photographer: Mark Johann

Screen reproductions produced with Collage Plus.

Collage Plus is a trademark of Inner Media Inc.
SYBEX is a registered trademark of SYBEX Inc.

TRADEMARKS: SYBEX has attempted throughout this book to distinguish proprietary trademarks from descriptive terms by following the capitalization style used by the manufacturer.

SYBEX is not affiliated with any manufacturer.

Every effort has been made to supply complete and accurate information. However, SYBEX assumes no responsibility for its use, nor for any infringement of the intellectual property rights of third parties which would result from such use.

First edition copyright ©1992 SYBEX Inc.
Copyright ©1994 SYBEX Inc., 2021 Challenger Drive, Alameda, CA 94501. World rights reserved. No part of this publication may be stored in a retrieval system, transmitted, or reproduced in any way, including but not limited to photocopy, photograph, magnetic or other record, without the prior agreement and written permission of the publisher.

Library of Congress Card Number: 93-86871
ISBN: 0-7821-1439-3

Manufactured in the United States of America
10 9 8 7 6 5 4 3 2 1

To Alec Fraser Simpson

ACKNOWLEDGEMENTS

LIKE all books, this one was a team effort, and much credit, along with my sincere appreciation, goes to the many people on the team.

Many thanks to James A. Rock, who revised the book from the previous edition, and to Elizabeth Olson, Martha Mellor, Virginia Andersen, Marilyn Smith, and Valerie Potter, all of whom contributed material, time, and effort to the writing of this book.

Many thanks to the people at SYBEX who brought this book from its original home on my hard disk to the finished book in your hands—especially to Developmental Editor David Peal for his many suggestions, and of course to the full production team for their hard work over the course of an ever-shortening schedule.

Many thanks to the gang at Waterside Productions, my literary agents, for managing the "business and opportunity" aspects of my writing career.

And of course, thanks to Susan, Ashley, and Alec, for being patient and supportive while Daddy was, once again, locked away pounding the keyboard for many long hours.

Contents AT A GLANCE

Introduction — xxxvii

PART ONE — THE BASICS
1. What Can Paradox Do for Me? — 3
2. Getting Started with Paradox — 21
3. Creating a Paradox Table — 39
4. Entering and Editing Table Data — 59
5. Viewing and Validating Your Data — 85
6. Sorting Your Tables — 121
7. Querying Your Tables — 139
8. Printing Formatted Reports — 187
9. Creating Custom Forms — 273
10. Graphing Your Data — 305
11. Simplifying Your Work with Scripts — 365
12. Managing Your Files — 389

PART TWO — MANAGING YOUR FILES
13. Database Design with Multiple Tables — 455
14. Advanced Queries and Calculations — 491
15. Advanced Report and Form Techniques — 549
16. Automatic Updating with Multiple Tables — 631
17. Using Advanced Script Techniques — 661

PART THREE — DEVELOPING PARADOX APPLICATIONS
18. Designing an Application — 711
19. Creating an Application — 749
20. Testing and Fine-Tuning Your Application — 805
21. Learning to Use PAL — 831

APPENDICES

A	Installing Paradox	889
B	What's New in Paradox 4.5	909
C	Networks, SQL Link, and Interoperability	919
D	Customizing Paradox	951
E	Sample Table Structures	999
	Index	1003

CONTENTS

Introduction — xxxvii

PART ONE — THE BASICS

1 What Can Paradox Do for Me? — 3
Organize, Access, and Display All Types of Information — 5
    Working with Tables — 5
    Using Forms for Data Entry — 6
    Organizing Your Information with Reports — 7
    Creating Graphs — 11
    Finding Information with Queries — 11
Manage Multiple Tables — 14
    Keeping Related Data in Separate Places — 14
    Combining Data from Separate Tables — 16
Build Custom Applications — 17
Summary — 18

2 Getting Started with Paradox — 21
Starting Paradox — 24
The Paradox Desktop — 25
    Working with a Mouse — 26
    Using the Menus — 26
    Backing Out of Menu Selections — 28
    Using the Speedbar and the Status Bar — 28
Getting Help — 29
    Working within the Help System — 30
    Using the Help Index — 30
    Exiting Help — 32
Choosing a Working Directory — 32
Choosing an Interface — 35
    Switching to the Full Screen User Interface — 35
    Switching to the Standard User Interface — 37

Exiting Paradox	37
Summary	38

3 Creating a Paradox Table — 39

Planning a Table	42
Planning the Fields to Include	44
Rules for Defining Field Names	46
Defining the Data Type of Fields	47
Defining Memo Fields	49
Table Structure Limitations	50
Creating a Directory for Tables	52
Creating a Table	53
Borrowing Another Table's Structure	56
Choosing a File Format	57
Saving the Table Structure	57
Summary	57

4 Entering and Editing Table Data — 59

Opening a Table	62
Switching to Edit Mode	64
Choosing a View	66
Entering Data in a Table	67
Adding and Saving Records	67
Entering Dates	67
Entering Negative Numbers	68
Entering Data in Memo and Binary Fields	68
Typing Special Characters	70
Data-Entry Shortcuts	70
Using Data Entry to Enter Data	73
Editing a Table	74
Moving through Fields and Records	75
Editing the Contents of a Field	76
Undoing Changes to a Record	78
Editing a Memo Field	79
Inserting Records	79

Deleting Records	80
Using the Modify Menu to Edit Data	81
Saving or Canceling Your Changes	81
Closing a Table	82
Summary	82

5 Viewing and Validating Your Data — 85

Managing Windows on the Desktop	88
Choosing a Window	89
Moving a Window	90
Sizing a Window	90
Maximizing and Restoring a Window	91
Tiling and Cascading Windows	91
Closing a Window	91
Using Dialog Boxes	93
Searching for a Field, Record, or Value	93
Finding a Field or Record	94
Searching for a Value in a Record	95
Searching for Text in Memo Fields	97
Customizing Table View	97
Changing the Table Size	98
Changing the Column Width	99
Formatting Numeric Fields	101
Formatting Date Fields	103
Rearranging Columns	104
Saving and Restoring Image Settings	105
When You See Stars, or When the Data Doesn't Fit	107
Ensuring the Validity of Data	107
Defining the Lowest or Highest Acceptable Value	109
Entering Default Values	110
Defining Picture Formats	110
Defining Required Values	114
Advancing Automatically to the Next Field	115

	Clearing Validity Checks	117
	Getting Unstuck When Validity Checks Fail	118
	Summary	118

6 Sorting Your Tables — 121

Sorts within Sorts	124
Sorting to the Same Table versus Sorting to a Different Table	126
Sorting in Ascending or Descending Order	127
Sorting a Table	128
Rearranging Fields to See the Sort Order	132
Other Techniques for Sorting a Table	133
Uppercase and Lowercase in Sorting	135
Summary	137

7 Querying Your Tables — 139

An Overview of Using Query By Example	142
Opening a Query Form	143
Selecting Fields and Running the Query	145
Using Check-Plus, Plain Check, or Check-Descending Marks	145
Adding the Check Marks	148
Performing the Query	149
Using the Answer Table	150
Working with the Answer Table	150
Controlling the Order of Fields in the Answer Table	151
Using Queries to Select Specific Records	155
Searching for Exact Values	158
Searching for Inexact Values	161
Searching for Ranges of Values	166
Searching for Everything Except Some Value	168
Searching for Blank Fields	168
Searching for Relative Dates	169

Performing AND and OR Searches	170
AND Relationships across Several Fields	171
AND Relationships in a Single Field	171
OR Relationships across Several Fields	172
OR Relationships in a Single Field	174
Avoiding AND/OR Confusion	175
Searching for Punctuation Marks and Symbols	176
Using Queries as Editing Tools	177
Finding Information	177
Making Global Edits	179
Making Global Deletions	182
Summary	184

8   Printing Formatted Reports   187

Printing an Instant Report	190
Getting Paradox and Your Printer in Sync	192
Determining Page Length and Width	193
Determining a Left Margin	194
Determining the Page Ejection Method	195
Changing the Printer Defaults	195
Keeping Pages Vertically Aligned	197
Testing Your New Printer Settings	197
Designing Formatted Reports	198
Getting to the Report Design Screen	199
Understanding Field Masks	201
Report Design Screen Indicators	202
Basic Skills for Controlling Report Text and Lines	203
Understanding Report Design Bands	206
Managing the Table Band	209
Using the Mouse versus Using the Keyboard	210
Deleting a Column	211
Inserting a Column	211
Resizing a Column	211
Moving a Column	213

Copying a Column	213
Managing Field Masks	214
Placing a Field Mask	214
Placing Calculated Fields	219
Deleting a Field Mask	220
Reformatting a Field Mask	220
Word-Wrapping a Field Mask	222
Justifying (Aligning) a Field Mask	224
Changing the Page Layout for a Report	224
Changing the Paper or Printer Settings for a Report	225
Sending Predefined Setup Strings	226
Taking Advantage of the Page and Print Size	227
Choosing a Printer for the Current Report	228
Temporarily Changing the Printer Port	229
Pausing the Printer for Each Page	230
Special Techniques for Free-Form Reports	230
Squeezing Out Blank Spaces	231
Squeezing Out Blank Lines	232
Printing Multicolumn Labels and Reports	233
Using Group Bands to Sort and Group Records	237
Inserting and Deleting Group Bands	239
Grouping on a Field Value	239
Grouping on a Range	240
Grouping on a Record Count	243
Choosing a Sort Direction for a Group	243
Changing a Group Specifier	243
Inserting a Page Break or Blank Line	244
Printing Formatted Reports	245
Printing a Report from the Desktop	246
Printing a Report from the Report Design Screen	246
Printing a Range of Pages	247
Previewing a Printed Report	248
Printing a Report from a Query	249

Printing a Report from a Sorted Copy of a Table	251
File Names for Report Formats	252
Changing an Existing Report Format	252
Sample Tabular Reports	253
Phone List	253
Phone and Fax List	255
Wide Tabular Report	257
Sample Free-Form Reports	260
Directory Listing	260
Form Letter	262
Three-Across Laser Printer Labels	264
Envelopes	267
Report with a Memo Field	270
Summary	271

9 Creating Custom Forms   273

The Standard Form	276
Designing a Custom Form	277
Getting to the Form Design Screen	279
Working in the Form Design Screen	281
Placing Fields on the Form	283
Word-Wrapping Alphanumeric and Memo Fields	287
Reformatting Fields on the Form	289
Moving Items on the Form	290
Erasing Fields and Areas	292
Adding Borders and Lines	293
Drawing Borders	294
Drawing Lines	295
Erasing a Border or Line	296
Coloring and Highlighting a Form	296
Changing Form Colors	296
Changing a Form's Video Attributes	297

Tips on Adding Colors and Video Attributes	298
Showing Field Names during Form Design	299
Using a Form	300
Changing the Default Form	300
Using Word-Wrapped Fields	301
Changing a Form	302
Summary	302

10   Graphing Your Data   305

An Overview of Graphing with Paradox	308
How Paradox Graphs Data	310
Graph Types	312
Viewing an Instant Graph	312
Changing the Graph Type	315
Stacked Bar Graphs	316
Regular Bar Graphs	316
3-D Bar Graphs	317
Rotated Bar Graphs	318
Line Graphs	319
Markers Graphs	320
Combined Lines and Markers Graphs	321
X-Y Graphs	321
Pie Charts	322
Area Graphs	323
Combined Graphs	324
Limiting the Duration of a Graph Display	326
Customizing the Overall Features of Graphs	327
Elements of a Graph	328
Working in Customize Graph Screens	328
Customizing Graph Titles	329
Modifying Graph Colors	332
Modifying Graph Axes	333
Changing the X-Axis Labels for a Keyed Table Graph	338
Modifying Graph Grids	339

Customizing Graph Series	340
Modifying Legends and Labels	340
Modifying Markers and Fill Patterns	343
Customizing Pie Charts	344
Modifying the Label Format	345
Customizing the Pie Slices	346
Saving and Reusing Graph Settings	347
Saving Custom Graph Settings	347
Using Custom Graph Settings for Other Graphs	348
Modifying Existing Custom Graph Settings	350
Using One Custom Graph to Create Another	350
Printing Graphs	351
Customizing the Printed Graph Layout	352
Printing Graphs to a File	353
Summarizing Data with Cross Tabulations	355
Understanding Cross Tabulation	357
Generating a Crosstab Table	358
Graphing a Crosstab Table	359
Arranging Fields for CrossTabs	360
A Shortcut for CrossTabs	362
Summary	364

11 Simplifying Your Work with Scripts   365

Preparing for Recording a Script	368
Recording a Script	370
Playing Back a Script	371
Playing Back a Script at Maximum Speed	372
Watching a Script Play Back Its Keystrokes	373
Playing Back a Script Repeatedly	373
When Things Go Wrong with a Script	375
A Sample Script: Automating Form Letters	376
Creating the Form Letter Script	377

Creating the Label or Envelope Script	380
Using Your New Scripts	380
Creating and Using Instant Scripts	381
Recording and Playing Back an Instant Script	382
Saving an Instant Script	382
Making an Existing Script an Instant Script	383
Making One Script Play Back Another	384
Playing Back a Script Automatically at Startup	385
Summary	386

12 Managing Your Files   389

Managing Objects	392
Renaming Objects	393
Copying Objects	395
Tips on Backing Up a Large Database	399
Deleting Objects	402
Copying and Moving Records	403
Copying Records from One Table to Another	404
Moving Records to Another Table	406
Removing Records from a Table	406
Developing Applications with the Tools Options	409
Recovering Disk Space from Deleted Records	410
Emptying a Table	410
Protecting Data	411
Adding Password Protection	411
Using a Password-Protected Table or Script	413
Reactivating (Clearing) Passwords	414
Changing or Removing a Password	414
Write-Protecting a Table	415
Getting Information about Files	416
Viewing Table Structures	416
Viewing the File Inventory	417

Viewing a Table's Family	419
Viewing Field Names for a Secondary Index	419
Restructuring a Table	420
Changing a Field Type	423
Saving the New Structure	424
Using the Problems or Keyviol Table	425
Converting between Older and Newer Versions of Paradox	426
Fixing Corrupted Objects	427
Speeding Up Queries	428
Interfacing with Other Programs	429
An Overview of Exporting and Importing Data	430
Exporting to Spreadsheets	432
Importing Data from a Spreadsheet	433
Transferring Data between Paradox and dBASE	434
Storing Data in PFS Format	435
Transferring Data between Paradox and Reflex	435
Transferring Data between Paradox and VisiCalc	436
Transferring ASCII Delimited Files	436
Transferring ASCII Text Files	439
Transferring Data between Nonsupported Programs	439
Exporting a WordPerfect Merge File to Paradox	445
Using a Word Processor to Embellish Reports	448
Shelling Out to DOS	449
Summary	450

PART TWO — MANAGING YOUR FILES

13 Database Design with Multiple Tables — 455

Types of Multiple Table Links	458
One-to-One Database Design	459
One-to-Many Database Design	459

Many-to-Many Database Design	465
Normalizing a Database	471
Removing Repetitive Groups of Fields	472
Removing Redundant Data	472
Removing All Partial Dependencies	472
Removing Transitive Dependencies	473
The Fully Normalized Database	474
Using Indexes to Speed Your Work	475
Specifying Primary Key Fields for a Primary Index	476
Defining Keys in Multiple-Table Designs	477
Entering and Editing Records in a Keyed Table	481
How Paradox Handles Duplicate Entries	481
Creating Secondary Indexes	484
Summary	489

14 Advanced Queries and Calculations   491

Sample Tables	494
The Mastinv Table	494
The Invoices Table	495
The Accounts Table	496
The Orders Table	496
The Purchase Table	498
Combining Data from Multiple Tables	499
Understanding Example Elements	499
Combining Data from More than Two Tables	503
Using Query Criteria with Multiple Tables	508
AND and OR Queries with Multiple Tables	509
Displaying Nonmatching Records	514
Using Queries to Perform Calculations	516
Using CALC to Display Calculation Results	517
How Paradox Calculates Blank Fields	518
Renaming Calculated Fields	519
Calculations Using Fields from Multiple Tables	521

Using Calculations to Increase or Decrease Values	522
Performing Summary Calculations in Queries	523
Summarizing All Records	525
Calculations on Groups of Records	526
Frequency Distributions	527
Selecting Records Based on Summary Information	529
Complex Calculations with Multiple Tables	531
Asking about Sets of Records	534
Defining a Set	535
Using the GroupBy Operator	540
Comparing Records to Summary Values	542
Calculating Percentages	543
Saving Queries	546
Replaying a Saved Query	547
Summary	548

15 Advanced Report and Form Techniques 549

Calculating Data in Reports	552
Printing Subtotals and Totals in Reports	555
Formatting Groups	561
Groups of Tables versus Tables of Groups	561
Hiding or Displaying Repetitive Data	562
Formatting Group Headers	564
Starting Each Group on a New Page	566
Positioning Items with BLANKLINE	567
Nesting Groups	567
Omitting the Details	569
Displaying Running Totals	572
Printing Reports from Multiple Tables	573
Looking Up Data from a Related Table	573
Using Queries to Print Reports from Multiple Tables	582

Recovering Lost Report Formats	587
Sprucing Up Reports with Special Printer Attributes	588
Inserting a Printer Code in a Report Format	589
Using Compressed Print	590
Choosing a Font and Print Size	590
Using PAL Functions in Calculated Fields	592
Using a PAL Function to Calculate a Percentage	596
Creating Multipage Forms	599
Using Display-Only Fields to Identify the Current Record	601
Using a Multipage Form	602
Using Calculated Fields in Forms	602
Multiple Table Validation and Automatic Fill-in	604
Defining Validity Checks	605
Using a Table with Multiple Table Validity Checks	608
Looking Up State Abbreviations	610
Displaying Multiple Records on a Custom Form	611
Creating a Multi-record Form	612
Modifying a Multi-record Form	613
Editing Multiple Tables with a Single Form	614
Creating Multi-table Forms with Unlinked Tables	615
Using a Multi-table Form	618
Managing Subforms	619
Using Multi-table Forms with Linked Tables	620
Using the Invoices Master Form	626
Taking Advantage of Referential Integrity	627
Summary	628

16	**Automatic Updating with Multiple Tables**	**631**
	Copying Fields from One Table to Another	635
	Copying Incompatible Records from One Table to Another	638
	Using INSERT and Multiple Queries on a Single Form	639
	Creating an Auto-Execute Query	642
	Calculating with INSERT Queries	644
	Changing the Values in One Table Based on Another Table	645
	Creating an Order History File	645
	Subtracting Quantities Sold from In Stock Quantities	646
	Moving Posted Orders to the History Table	649
	Adding Items Received to In Stock Quantities	651
	Using the Recorded Scripts	656
	Correcting Updated Transactions	657
	Printing a Reorder Report	658
	Summary	659
17	**Using Advanced Script Techniques**	**661**
	Getting to the Editor	664
	Using the Editor with Memo Fields	665
	Using the Editor with Scripts	666
	Using the Editor for ASCII Text Files	667
	Working in Editor Windows	668
	Moving to a Specific Row/Column Position	671
	Inserting and Deleting Text	671
	Selecting Text	672
	Cutting, Copying, and Pasting Text in an Editing Window	674
	Deleting Selected Text	674
	Cutting and Pasting between Windows	675
	Viewing the Clipboard	676

Making Changes in the Clipboard	676
Using Word-Wrap in the Editor	678
Specifying Tab Stop Distance	680
Auto-Indenting Text	680
Working with Files in the Editor	681
"Quick-Saving" Your Changes	681
Copying the Current Editing Window to a File	681
Reading an External File into Current Text	682
Copying Selected Text to a File	683
Transferring Text between Programs	683
Printing the Current File	684
Opening an Existing File while Editing	685
Starting a New File while Editing	685
Finding and Replacing Text	685
Searching for Text	686
Controlling Case Sensitivity in Editor Searches	687
Replacing Text	688
Leaving the Editor	690
Editing an Existing Script	691
Elements of a Recorded Script	691
Editing a Saved Query	692
Using PAL Commands in Scripts	693
Adding Programmer Comments	693
Placing Objects on the Desktop	694
Displaying a Custom Message	696
Using Sound to Get Attention	697
Creating a Script from Scratch	697
About {Scripts} and {End-Record} in Scripts	699
Pausing for User Input	699
Combining and Embellishing Scripts	700
Combining the Automatic Update Scripts	703

Tips on Scripts	705
About the .SC2 File	706
Cautions on Using Go from the Editor	707
Summary	707

PART THREE DEVELOPING PARADOX APPLICATIONS

18 Designing an Application — 711

What Is an Application?	714
What Is Workshop?	716
An Overview of Designing an Application	717
Defining the Goals of the Application	718
Designing the Menu Structure on Paper	719
Designing and Testing the Database Objects	721
Testing and Refining the Application	724
Documenting and Distributing the Application	724
The Design of the Membership Application Database	725
Custom Forms for the Membership Application	727
Membership Application Reports	728
Membership Application Mailing Label Format	731
Membership Application Menu Structure	732
Understanding the Update Renewals Process	734
Testing the Completed Membership Application	738
Tips on Using the Membership Application	745
Summary	747

19 Creating an Application — 749

An Overview of Application Creation	752
Starting Workshop	753
Selecting Options in Workshop	754
Creating or Selecting the Application Directory	758
Creating a New Application	759
Defining Application Attributes	760

Creating the Menu Structure	763
Creating Action Objects	769
Creating Actions before Attaching Them to Menus	769
Creating and Attaching Action Items to Menu Options	771
Attaching Utility Objects to Menu Options	773
Attaching an Existing Action Object to a Menu Option	773
Creating an Action Object by Borrowing	774
Changing an Existing Action Object	775
Defining Edit Session Objects	775
Adding Tables to the Edit Session	778
Assigning Key Actions to the Edit Session	782
Assigning Event Procedures to the Edit Session	783
Defining Report Print Objects	786
Defining the Printer Settings	789
Defining Query Objects	790
Defining the Query	793
Defining Multi-Action Objects	794
Defining Help Text Objects	795
Adding Help Text Objects to Menu Options	796
Completing a Help Text Object	797
Defining Execute Objects	801
Defining OK/Cancel Objects	801
Summary	803

20   Testing and Fine-Tuning Your Application   805

Testing an Application	808
Modifying an Application	809
Closing an Application	811
Removing an Application	811

Editing Paradox Objects	812
Managing Paradox and Application Objects	813
Finishing the Application	815
Documenting the Application	815
Selecting a Printer for Documentation	816
Changing the Style of Boxes and Lines in the Documentation	818
Using a Word Processor to Embellish Your Documentation	819
Packaging the Application	820
Anatomy of an Application	820
Putting Applications Together for the End-User	821
Using BACKUP and RESTORE for Large Applications	823
Starting a Completed Application	824
Starting an Application from Paradox	824
Starting an Application from the DOS Command Line	824
Starting an Application from Windows	825
Creating Closed Applications	827
Summary	828

21 Learning to Use PAL   831

Some Basic PAL Concepts	834
Interactive Paradox versus PAL-Controlled Paradox	835
PAL Script Types and Creation	835
PAL Script Format and Structure	839
Using Scripts Together	840
An Overview of PAL Commands and Functions	841
Types of PAL Commands	841
Using Arguments and Parameters in PAL Commands	843
Types of PAL Functions	844

Using Arguments and Parameters in PAL Functions	846
Using Values and Expressions	847
Using Variables	848
Using Arrays	850
Controlling PAL Script Execution	851
Branching in a PAL Script	851
Looping in a PAL Script	854
Using the PAL Menu	855
Playing Back Scripts	855
Repeating Script Playback	856
Beginnning and Ending Script Recording	856
Debugging Scripts	856
Evaluating Expressions	859
Creating Miniscripts	860
Using PAL Functions for Instant Field Summaries	861
Instant Field Summaries Using Value	862
Instant Field Summaries Using Miniscripts	862
Defining Hotkeys	863
Creating Multiple Hotkey Macros	866
Creating GetRecord and PasteRecord Keys	867
Loading Hotkeys and Scripts Automatically	869
Creating Key Assignment Scripts	869
Playing a Script Automatically on Startup	871
Creating Pop-Up Calculators	871
Controlling the PAL Canvas	872
Creating the Squares Calculator	873
Creating the Loan Payments Calculator	877
Creating New Paradox Menu Choices	881
About Paradox.ADD	882
Adding Options to Menus	884
Summary	887

APPENDICES

A Installing Paradox — 889

Single-User Hardware Requirements — 890
Installing Paradox — 891
Installing Workshop and Sample Files — 894
Running Paradox 4.5 under Windows 3 or 3.1 — 895
How Paradox 4.5 Manages Memory — 897
    Compatibility Issues — 897
Paradox Command-Line Configuration — 898
    Video Options — 900
    Memory Options — 901
    Mouse Option — 904
    Share Option — 904
    Query Options — 904
    BIOS Option — 905
    Compatibility Mode Options — 905
Using Command-Line Options in a Batch File — 905
Using Command-Line Options in Windows 3 or 3.1 — 906
    Autoexecuting Scripts at Startup — 907

B What's New in Paradox 4.5 — 909

Changes for End-Users — 910
    User Interface — 910
    Expanded Mouse Support — 911
    Other New Report Designer Enhancements — 912
    File Management and Directory Support Enhancement — 913
    Enhancements in the Paradox Editor — 913
    Enhancements and Changes to the Custom Configuration Program (CCP) — 914
    Other End-User Features — 916
Improvements for Advanced Users and Application Developers — 916

Improvements for Advanced Users and Application Developers	916
Adding User Defined-Choices to Paradox Menus	917
The Miniscript Window	917
Just for Developers	917

C Networks, SQL Link, and Interoperability — 919

About Network Installation	920
Network Hardware Requirements	921
Locking	922
Family Locks	924
Record Locks	924
Group Locks and Write-Record Locks	925
Explicit Locks	928
Avoiding Waits for Busy Tables	930
Using Paradox on a Network	931
Private Directories	932
Network User Names	933
Refreshing the Screen	933
Changing Default Network Settings with CCP	934
Getting Network Information	936
Creating a Table on a Network	937
Data Entry on a Network	937
Viewing Data on a Network	938
Editing on a Network	939
Sorting on a Network	939
Querying on a Network	940
Reports on a Network	940
Forms on a Network	941
Graphs on a Network	941
Scripts on a Network	941
Update Queries on a Network	942
Tools on a Network	942
Security and Protection	942

Creating Owner and Auxiliary Passwords	943
Paradox SQL Link	948
Interoperability	949
Interoperability in DOS	950
Interoperability in Windows	950

D Customizing Paradox   951

Running the Custom Configuration Program	952
Basic Skills for Using CCP Dialog Boxes	953
Getting Information about Your Computer	956
Machine Information Menu Options	957
Changing the Screen Display	958
Video Settings	958
Changing the Color Settings	960
Changing the Report Defaults	968
Changing the Report Settings	969
Defining Printer Setup Strings	971
Changing the Graph Defaults	974
Choosing the Instant Graph Defaults	975
Choosing a Printer for Graphs	975
Choosing a Screen Mode for Graphs	978
Customizing the Standard Settings	979
Working Directory	980
Interface Mode	980
Mouse Use	980
Disable Break	980
Query Order	981
Blank = Zero	981
Autosave	982
File Format	982
Maintain Indexes	983
Maximum Table Size	983
Formatting Data	984

Setting Editor Defaults in Text Files and Memo Fields	985
Changing the Default Format of Numbers and Dates	985
Changing the Network Defaults	986
User Name	987
Private Directory	987
Refresh Interval	987
When Data Changes	988
Setting the PAL Defaults	988
Showing or Hiding Calculation Field Errors	989
Setting Editor Defaults in Script Files	989
Using an External Script Editor	990
Specifying a BLOB Editor	992
Changing the BLOB Editor Screen Swap Default	994
Setting ASCII File Defaults	995
Saving or Canceling CCP Changes	997
Saving CCP Changes on a Network	997

E Sample Table Structures   **999**

Index   1003

INTRODUCTION

SIMPLY stated, Paradox is a powerful database management system that anyone can use. Historically, database management systems have been programming-language oriented and thus best used as tools by programmers and sophisticated computer users. The need to remember numerous commands, functions, data types, syntax rules, file structures, and so on made the older database management systems unwieldy for the neophyte and casual computer user.

Then came Paradox—a new approach to database management that freed the user from needing to memorize complex commands. With Paradox, even the casual computer user can effectively store, retrieve, sort, print, change, and ask questions about data by selecting options from the menus and "filling in the blanks" on standardized questionnaires.

So what's so paradoxical about Paradox? The paradox is that even though it's easy to use, it does not compromise on power or flexibility. You can still ask complex questions about several interrelated tables of data without any programming.

Who Should Read This Book?

This book is designed for the users who are new to Paradox or who are upgrading from an earlier version of the program. As long as you've had some experience in using computers, you will be able to follow the instructions in this book. Even if you're not exactly sure what a database management system *is*, or what it's used for, you're in good hands. The first chapter in this book will get you acquainted with what database management with Paradox is all about.

Like all books in the SYBEX *Mastering* series, we do want to stick with the topic at hand, namely Paradox. So we won't be spending lots of pages teaching you how to use a mouse and keyboard. Prior experience with any kind of program that's taught you enough to feel comfortable with the keyboard and mouse will be helpful. You should also already be comfortable with how information is organized on your hard disk into *files*, *directories*, and *drives*. If you are not already familiar with such concepts, you can get a quick introduction from any small book on DOS, such as my own *Up and Running with DOS 5* or *Up and Running with DOS 6*, also published by SYBEX.

On the other hand, you may be at the opposite end of the spectrum, and already be familiar with database management and earlier versions of Paradox. If so, you might want to refer to Appendix B near the back of this book for a quick summary of what's new in Paradox 4.5 for DOS, and then go to the chapter that contains the information of interest to you.

Which Version of Paradox?

This book is specifically written for version 4.5 of *Paradox for DOS*. If you're using version 4.0, you'll be able to follow along for the most part. However, you'll notice references to user interface changes and new functionality incorporated into version 4.5. If you're using an earlier version of Paradox, such as 3.0 or 3.5, this book won't help you much, because of significant changes and improvements in this newer version.

If you would like to upgrade your earlier version of Paradox to version 4.5 for DOS, you can do so for a nominal upgrade cost.

If you're a Windows fan, you should be aware that *Paradox for DOS* and *Paradox for Windows* are two entirely different products, and this book is specifically written for the DOS version. While Paradox for DOS sports a "Windows-like" interface and can certainly be used on a computer that has Windows on it, only the Paradox for Windows product takes full advantage of the graphical interface that Windows offers.

For minimum hardware and memory requirements, refer to Appendix A.

Features of This Book

This book is designed both as a tutorial and as a reference to the many features of Paradox 4.5 for DOS. Special features of the book, designed to simplify and speed your mastery of Paradox and to provide easy access to information, include the following:

- **Endpapers:** Inside the front and back covers, you'll find a quick reference to the techniques for performing common tasks.

- **In-Text Notes:** Notes provide cross-references to where related features are covered in the book, tips for added insight on creative ways to use features, and cautions about problems that can occur when using a feature.

- **Fast Tracks:** The Fast Tracks at the beginning of chapters provide a quick summary of techniques for using specific features and the page number of the in-depth discussion.

- **Optional Companion Disk:** You can purchase a copy of the various sample tables, reports, and forms, as well as the membership management application presented in this book, in ready-to-use form on a disk. The disk is not required to use this book, but it may come in handy if you want to use some of the examples as a

INTRODUCTION

starting point for your own work, without having to key in everything from scratch. See the coupon near the back of the book if you're interested.

Structure of This Book

This book is designed to supplement the densely packed and somewhat technical manuals that came with your Paradox package. The purpose of the Paradox manual is to document every available feature in great detail. The purpose of this book is to show you how to use Paradox and put it to work for your own purposes, whatever they may be.

To make things easier for you and to help you focus on information that's relevant to your own use of Paradox, the book is divided into three parts:

- **Part One, The Basics:** Teaches you what Paradox is all about, and how to create tables, forms, reports, and graphs for viewing and printing your data. Techniques for sorting and querying (asking questions about) your data, simplifying your work with scripts, and managing your files are also presented in this part. The focus here is on managing a single table, since this is the easiest way to learn to use these various features.

- **Part Two, Managing Related Tables:** Focuses on managing data in separate, related tables. One of the real advantages that a relational database management system, like Paradox, offers over word processors and spreadsheets is the ability to efficiently store information in multiple related tables and then "mix and match" that information as necessary. Working with multiple tables is useful for managing the business of running a business, such as managing orders, inventory, accounts, and so forth.

- **Part Three, Developing Paradox Applications:** Covers the development of custom applications to automate and simplify all aspects of managing data stored in Paradox tables. Paradox offers two tools for creating applications: Workshop, designed for total nonprogrammers, and the Paradox Application Language (PAL). This part focuses first on the Workshop, then presents an introduction to PAL. If this introduction whets your appetite for more

PAL power, you might want to "graduate" to a more advanced book that focuses on PAL.

The appendices at the back of the book present somewhat more technical information about Paradox for installers, network administrators, and those who need to change some of Paradox's many configurable default settings. Appendix B presents a discussion of what's new in Paradox 4.5 for experienced Paradox users.

Conventions Used in This Book

As with most modern programs, you can use a mouse or the keyboard to interact with Paradox. We'll get into specific techniques in detail starting in Chapter 2, but for now, suffice it to say that this book uses the following conventions to present keys, combination keys, and menu selection sequences:

- **↓, →, ←, PgUp, PgDn:** Arrow and other special keys such as Ins (sometimes marked Insert), Delete (sometimes marked Del), and ↵ (Enter) are shown with the symbol commonly displayed on the key. If your keyboard is designed so that these keys are only on the numeric keypad, remember that the Num Lock key must be turned off for these keys to work properly.

- **Combination Keys:** Combination keystrokes, starting with Ctrl, Alt, or Shift, are separated with a hyphen. To press these keys, hold down the first key while pressing the second. For instance, to press Ctrl-z, hold down the Ctrl key, type a z, then release both keys.

- **Menu Sequences:** A series of selections that you make from the menus are displayed in an abbreviated sequence with a ➤ symbol separating each selection. For instance, **Tools** ➤ **More** ➤ **Add** means "Choose Tools from the menu bar, then choose More from the pull-down menu that appears, then choose Add from the submenu that appears." You can use either the mouse or keyboard to choose menu options, as described in Chapter 2.

A Tip for Tyros

One of the more troublesome aspects of learning to use any new program is inadvertently choosing the wrong set of menu options, and ending up in totally unfamiliar territory.

In most cases, you can simply "back out" to more familiar territory simply by pressing the Escape key (labeled Esc on some keyboards, Cancel on others) until you get to more familiar territory.

If you're using a mouse, clicking any "neutral" area or the [Cancel] button (if it's available) serves the same purpose.

PART ONE

The Basics

What Can Paradox Do for Me?

PARADOX 4.5 for DOS is a *relational database management system*. A database is simply a collection of data. The data may be collected into computer files, or it may be kept on cards or paper, as on a Rolodex or in a file cabinet. A relational database management system, often referred to as a RDBMS, lets you work with a database that's stored on a computer disk. The advantage to using a computer rather than paper is perhaps obvious: tasks that may take several minutes, hours, or even days to perform with a paper database usually take only a few seconds or minutes to complete with a computer. A relational database management system lets you combine data from various "tables" of information.

Common tasks you would expect a database management system to handle include the following:

- Adding new data
- Editing—changing and deleting data to keep your database up to date
- Sorting the data into some meaningful order, such as alphabetically
- Searching for specific types of information (*querying*)
- Printing data in various report formats, such as lists, mailing labels, and form letters
- Graphing data using bar charts, line charts, pie charts, and other common business formats

Organize, Access, and Display All Types of Information

Paradox is an extremely flexible program, giving you virtually unlimited options for storing and managing information. The type of information to be stored is limited only by your needs and your imagination. Here are just a few of the things you can do with Paradox:

- Keep mailing lists and telephone directories up to date.
- Manage customer, sales lead, and membership information files.
- Handle bookkeeping and accounting, such as general ledger and accounts payable and receivable.
- Track orders and control inventory.
- Manage a personal or professional library of books, journal articles, video tapes, or CDs.
- Build and keep track of schedules.
- Store and analyze statistical and research data.

Paradox provides all the tools you'll need for organizing and accessing virtually any information you can lay your hands on. These tools let you create a variety of *objects* that you can use over and over again to organize and access the same or different information. To give you an overview of what's available and a preview of what's to come, we'll describe some of the more common objects here.

Working with Tables

You can store your information in one or more tables. A *table* is simply a collection of information organized into rows and columns. Figure 1.1 shows an example of how a portion of a Paradox table might appear on the screen.

A Paradox table might contain much more information than can fit on one screen. But you can easily scroll around the screen to find whatever information you need. For example, although you can see only people's names and their departments or titles in Figure 1.1, the actual table might

What Can Paradox Do for Me?

FIGURE 1.1

A Paradox table on the screen. If there are more rows and columns in the table than can fit on the screen, you can easily scroll the other information into view.

```
=[■]===================== Custlist =====================[↕]=
CUSTLIST| Last Name | Mr/Mrs | First Name | M.I. | Department/Title
    1   | Adams     | Mr.    | Andy       | A.   | President
    2   | Miller    | Miss   | Maria      | N.   | Accounts Receivable
    3   | Zastrou   | Dr.    | Ruth       |      | Internal Medicine
    4   | Rosiello  | Mr.    | Richard    | L.   | Accounts Payable
    5   | Gladstone | Miss   | Tara Rose  |      | Vice President
    6   | Schumack  | Dr.    | Susita     | M.   | Neurosurgeon
    7   | Kenney    | Mr.    | David      | E.   | Attorney at Law
    8   | Newell    | Mr.    | John       | J.   |
    9   | Mohr      | Mrs.   | Mary       | M.   |
   10   | Adams     | Miss   | Anita      | Q.   | Microcomputer Consultant
   11   | Smith     | Dr.    | Savitha    | V.   |
   12   | Ramirez   | Mr     | Rigoberto  | R.   | Author
   13   | Eggo      | Ms.    | Sandy      |      | Owner
   14   | Smith     | Mr.    | John       | Q.   |
   15   | Zeepers   | Mr.    | Zeke       | A.   | Chief Engineer
   16   | Jones     | Ms.    | Alma       | R.   | Account Executive
   17   | Smythe    | Ms.    | Janet      | L.   |
   18   | Clavell   | Miss   | Wanda      | T.   | Mother Superior
   19   | Wilson    | Dr.    | Ted        |      | Psychology Department
   20   | Watson    | Mr.    | Frank      | R.   | Greenskeeper
    1 of 25
```

include each person's address, phone number, and other pertinent information. The table might also contain hundreds or even thousands of names and addresses that you can scroll into view.

NOTE You'll learn how to create a Paradox table in Chapter 3.

Using Forms for Data Entry

You can add new information and change existing information directly in the tabular format shown in Figure 1.1. A Paradox *form* lets you work with all the information for a single row on one screen. Forms are especially useful for tables with many columns. You can even create custom forms. For example, Figure 1.2 shows a form for entering and editing customer information.

NOTE You'll learn how to create custom forms in Chapter 9.

FIGURE 1.2

A custom form for entering and editing data in a table. You can create forms to match the paper forms that contain the original information.

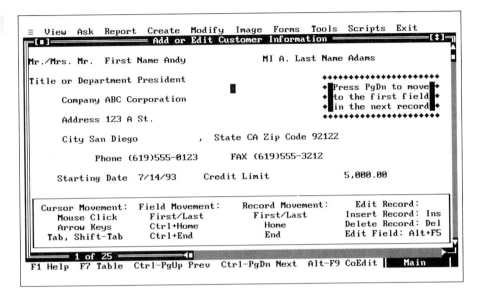

Organizing Your Information with Reports

Whereas the term *form* refers to information that's displayed on the screen, the term *report* generally refers to printed information. There's virtually no limit to the ways in which you can organize information into a report. You can print simple lists, mailing labels, invoices, packing slips, and many other types of reports. For example, Figure 1.3 shows information from a table of names and addresses printed in a customer directory format.

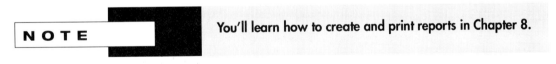

NOTE You'll learn how to create and print reports in Chapter 8.

Figure 1.4 shows information from the same table printed on mailing labels. In this example, labels are printed two-across on a page. You can set up your own labels to print in just about any format.

Figure 1.5 shows a form letter containing data for one customer in a table. Of course, you could print the same letter for every customer in the table.

8   **CHAPTER 1**   **WHAT CAN PARADOX DO FOR ME?**

FIGURE 1.3

A report is any information printed from one or more tables. This report shows a single page of information printed as an alphabetized directory listing.

```
                            Customer Directory
    _____

    Adams, Mr. Andy A.                              (1)
            President
            ABC Corporation
            123 A St.
            San Diego, CA    92122
            Phone:  (619)555-0123    FAX:  (619)555-3212
            Start Date: 7/14/93         Credit Limit: 5,000.00

    Adams, Miss Anita Q.                            (2)
            Microcomputer Consultant
            5434 Oceanic Way
            Silver Spring, MD    20910
            Phone:  (678)555-4354    FAX:  (678)555-3058
            Start Date: 11/13/93        Credit Limit: 2,500.00

    Cherub, Miss Sky R.                             (3)
            Oneness Well-Being
            985 Enlightenment Way
            Jefferson, SD    57038
            Phone:  (605)555-3232    FAX:
            Start Date: 3/30/94         Credit Limit: 10,000.00

    Clavell, Miss Wanda T.                          (4)
            Mother Superior
            Westridge Convent
            452 Reposo Alto
            Tiverton, RI    02878
            Phone:  (432)555-0323    FAX:  (432)555-0394
            Start Date: 2/02/94         Credit Limit: 2,500.00

    Dewey, Mr. Frank R.                             (5)
            Senior Partner
            Dewey, Cheatham, and Howe
            1121 Cass St. Suite 33
            Bothell, WA    98011
            Phone:  (206)555-4323    FAX:  (206)555-4323
            Start Date: 3/11/94         Credit Limit: 5,000.00




    August 19, 1993                                    Page    1
```

ORGANIZE, ACCESS, AND DISPLAY ALL TYPES OF INFORMATION

FIGURE 1.4

Data from a sample table printed on two-across mailing labels. Paradox can print labels in just about any format.

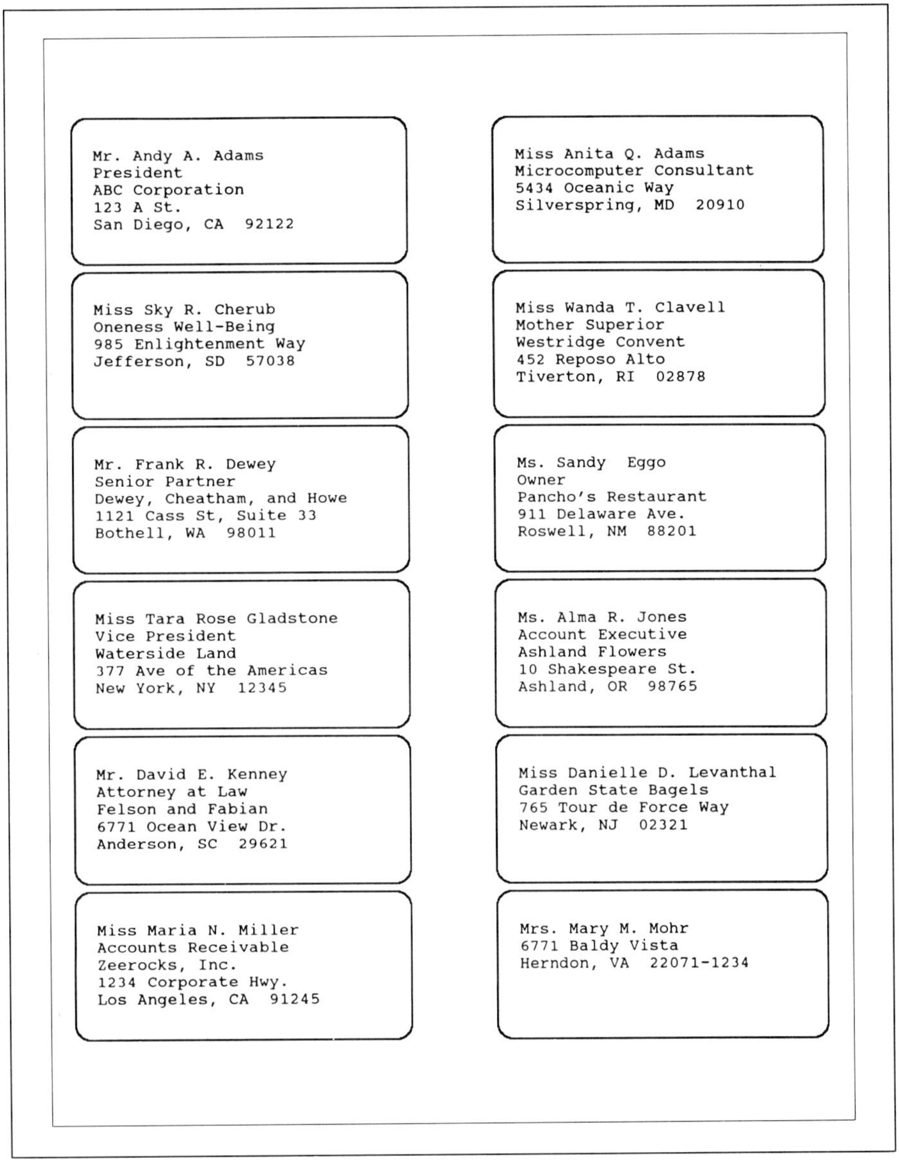

```
Mr. Andy A. Adams                    Miss Anita Q. Adams
President                            Microcomputer Consultant
ABC Corporation                      5434 Oceanic Way
123 A St.                            Silverspring, MD  20910
San Diego, CA  92122


Miss Sky R. Cherub                   Miss Wanda T. Clavell
Oneness Well-Being                   Mother Superior
985 Enlightenment Way                Westridge Convent
Jefferson, SD  57038                 452 Reposo Alto
                                     Tiverton, RI  02878


Mr. Frank R. Dewey                   Ms. Sandy  Eggo
Senior Partner                       Owner
Dewey, Cheatham, and Howe            Pancho's Restaurant
1121 Cass St, Suite 33               911 Delaware Ave.
Bothell, WA  98011                   Roswell, NM  88201


Miss Tara Rose Gladstone             Ms. Alma R. Jones
Vice President                       Account Executive
Waterside Land                       Ashland Flowers
377 Ave of the Americas              10 Shakespeare St.
New York, NY  12345                  Ashland, OR  98765


Mr. David E. Kenney                  Miss Danielle D. Levanthal
Attorney at Law                      Garden State Bagels
Felson and Fabian                    765 Tour de Force Way
6771 Ocean View Dr.                  Newark, NJ  02321
Anderson, SC  29621


Miss Maria N. Miller                 Mrs. Mary M. Mohr
Accounts Receivable                  6771 Baldy Vista
Zeerocks, Inc.                       Herndon, VA  22071-1234
1234 Corporate Hwy.
Los Angeles, CA  91245
```

10 CHAPTER 1 WHAT CAN PARADOX DO FOR ME?

FIGURE 1.5

A form letter created with Paradox, using customer information from a table. (The letterhead is from preprinted stock, not printed by Paradox.)

MEGA TECH Int'l.
1234 Xandu Lane
Ponto, CA 92007
(619)555-7750
Fax (619)555-FAX1

September 1, 1994

Mr. Andy A. Adams
President
ABC Corporation
123 A St.
San Diego, CA 92007

Dear Mr. Adams:

Welcome aboard! Megatech International is pleased to have you as one of our new credit customers. Your credit limit of $5,000.00 is available as of March 20, 1994.

Please let us know if there is any way that you can be of further service to you. And once again, MegeTech extends to you the warmest welcome as one of our newest customers.

Sincerely,

Wanda Bea Granolabar
Accounts Supervisor

NOTE: The letterhead shown in Figure 1.5 is preprinted. Paradox for DOS does not have the ability to print the logo graphic or the fancy text. If you have a laser printer, however, it's simple enough to feed your letterhead paper into the printer.

Creating Graphs

Paradox lets you print information in a variety of business graph formats, including bar, line, pie, area, and 3-D. Figure 1.6 shows a few graphs created with data from various tables.

NOTE: You'll learn how to create various types of graphs in Chapter 10.

Finding Information with Queries

A *query* is a basically a question. Queries provide a means of finding or isolating specific types of information in one or more tables. For example, with queries you can perform the following tasks:

- Quickly locate the name and address of a particular person in a table.
- Print letters and labels for individuals in a particular city, state, or zip code region.
- Print a reorder report for items that have slipped below a certain level in your inventory database.
- Print a summary of all sales, subtotaled by product or date.
- Print reminder letters for customers whose accounts are a certain number of days overdue.

With Paradox, you can pick and choose data from a table to isolate only the information you need.

FIGURE 1.6

Sample graphs created by Paradox, using data from various tables

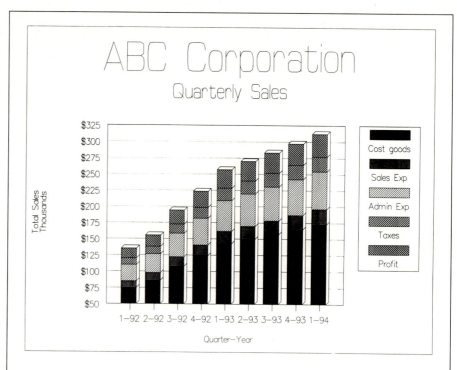

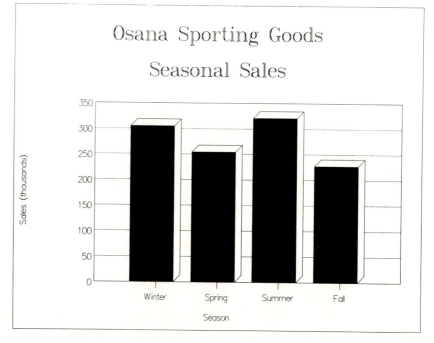

FIGURE 1.6

Sample graphs created by Paradox, using data from various tables (continued)

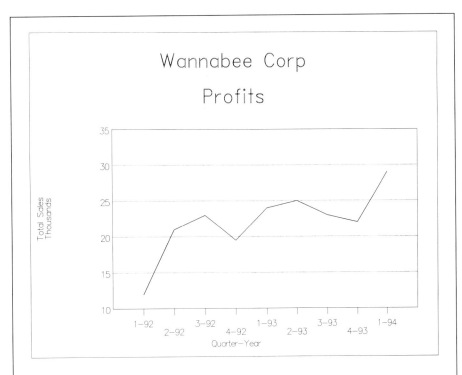

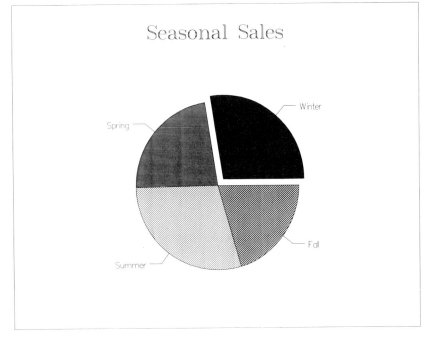

> **NOTE** You'll learn how to query your tables in Chapter 7.

Manage Multiple Tables

At this point, you may be thinking that your word processing or spreadsheet program can handle just about everything described so far. For many such programs, you would be somewhat correct. Some programs can handle all these tasks, but only to a limited extent. Paradox, as a relational database management system, offers capabilities that are not easily duplicated in word processors or spreadsheets. One is the ability to create custom applications, as described in the next section. Another is the ability to mix and match information from multiple tables.

A relational database management system lets you store information in separate tables and combine that information on an as-needed basis to get answers to questions and print complex reports. This brings to the microcomputer the power and flexibility that has traditionally been the domain of large, mainframe computers.

Keeping Related Data in Separate Places

Let's say you want to manage an entire mail-order business, keeping track of inventory, customer accounts, and orders. All this information won't fit neatly into a single table. Although you could combine just the orders and the customer accounts, it is more convenient to keep the data separate. Therefore, it would be best to create three separate tables.

You would need one table to keep track of what you have in inventory. Figure 1.7 shows an example of a table that contains inventory data. Each item in the inventory has a product ID (part number), description, and unit price. The quantity of that item currently in stock is also recorded in this table. As indicated by *etc...* in the figure, you could add any other information about each product as pertains to your business, such as the reorder point, manufacturer information, or whether or not the product is taxable.

MANAGE MULTIPLE TABLES

FIGURE 1.7

A table containing information about the current inventory

Inventory Table

Product ID	Description	Unit Price	In Stock	etc...
HP-123	HP Deskjet Cartridge	16.95	10	
HP-234	HP Paintjet Cartridge	27.95	5	
HP-235	HP Colorjet Cartridge	33.95	3	
HP-291	HP LaserJet Letter Tray	67.97	15	
HP-292	HP Laserjet Legal Tray	71.95	20	
HP-300	HP III Envelope Tray	78.95	25	
HP-500	HP Lower Cassette Tray	139.95	10	

A second table would contain information about customers. In the example in Figure 1.8, the name and company of each customer are stored in a table. Again, the *etc...* in the figure indicates that you can include any other information you want about each customer. For example, you may want to add addresses or credit limits. Notice that each customer has been assigned a unique customer ID (in the first column of the table).

Finally, the third table would keep track of orders. In the example shown in Figure 1.9, each row identifies who placed the order (by the customer's ID number) and what was ordered (by the product ID number). It also shows the quantity ordered and the date each order was placed. The *etc...* indicates that you could add any other pertinent information to each row.

FIGURE 1.8

A table of customers, where each customer is assigned a unique customer ID number (account number)

Customer Table

Cust ID	Last Name	Title	First Name	M.I.	Company	etc...
1001	Adams	Mr.	Andy	A.	ABC Corporation	
1002	Miller	Miss	Maria	N.	Zeerocks, Inc.	
1003	Zastrow	Dr.	Ruth		Scripts Clinic	
1004	Rosiello	Mr.	Richard	L.	Raydontic Labs	
1005	Gladstone	Miss	Tara Rose		Waterside Land	
1006	Schumack	Dr.	Susita	M		
1007	Kenney	Mr.	David	E.	Felson and Fabian	
1008	Newell	Mr.	John	J.	Newell Construction	
1009	Mohr	Mrs.	Mary	M.		
1010	Adams	Miss	Anita	Q.	Microcomputer Consultant	

16 CHAPTER 1   WHAT CAN PARADOX DO FOR ME?

FIGURE 1.9

A table containing information about orders. The customer ID and product ID numbers indicate who placed the order and what was ordered.

```
Orders Table

Cust ID    Product ID    Quantity    Date Ordered    etc...

1001       HP-292        2           7/01/93
1001       HP-300        2           7/01/93
1001       HP-500        1           7/01/93
1003       HP-234        5           7/01/93
1004       HP-300        2           7/01/93
1010       HP-123        1           7/01/93
```

Notice how compact the table in Figure 1.9 is. It doesn't waste a lot of disk space by repeating information that's already stored in the other tables. Instead, it stores only the customer ID, product ID, quantity, and date of each order. This is one reason for assigning each customer and product their own IDs in their respective tables.

Combining Data from Separate Tables

Paradox will let you combine information from these three separate tables, giving you total flexibility in managing that information and presenting it in whatever format you wish. For example, using the information from these three tables, you could have Paradox perform any or all of the following tasks:

- Print invoices, such as the one shown in Figure 1.10, and packing slips for current orders.

The sample invoice in Figure 1.10 is printed on the same preprinted letterhead stock as the form letter in Figure 1.5.

FIGURE 1.10

An invoice including information from three separate tables

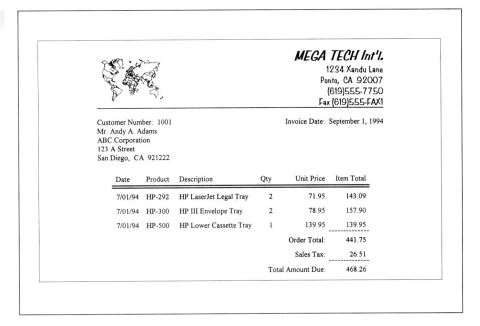

- As orders are filled, automatically subtract the quantity of each item shipped from the inventory database, so your table of inventory information is always up to the minute.
- Check the table containing order information to make sure there is a sufficient quantity of items in stock to fill the order, and if not, place the order on a backorder list to be filled when the stock is replenished.

In fact, you could mix and match the information from these tables however you wish, to manage and gain access to whatever information you need. Setting up and managing multiple related tables is described in Part Two of this book. Learning to manage multiple related tables is much easier *after* you've learned how to manage a single table effectively.

Build Custom Applications

In addition to letting you manage information from multiple tables simultaneously, Paradox offers you the ability to develop custom applications.

With a custom application, you can reduce complex tasks to simple menu options. You can develop applications to automate virtually all the tasks involved in managing a database.

The advantage here is that workers who have little or no knowledge of database management can still use the database to enter or keep track of information and get the information they need when they want it. However, even though the person who's using the custom application doesn't need to know a lot about Paradox and database management, the person who creates the application does need to understand all the underlying basics. Therefore, you won't see much mention of applications in this book until Part Three. By the time you get to that part of the book, you'll be well armed with the knowledge you need to develop applications.

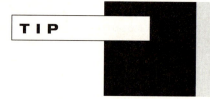

TIP You can also limit access to information by assigning passwords to confidential or sensitive information in a database. You'll learn how to assign passwords in Chapter 12.

But we're getting way ahead of ourselves; let's get back to square one. The first step to doing anything in Paradox is to start the program and get a feel for how to use it. So that's where we'll begin our Paradox journey in Chapter 2. But first, take a moment to review some of the information presented in this chapter.

Summary

This chapter has provided an overview of some of the many features that Paradox has to offer. The main terminology and concepts are summarized below:

- Paradox is a *relational database management system* (RDBMS), designed to help you manage large volumes of information stored in a computer.

- The information that you manage with Paradox is stored in *tables*, with data neatly organized into rows and columns.

SUMMARY

- You can use or create custom *forms* to ease the task of entering and editing information in a table.
- You can create *reports* to display selected information from one or more tables in whatever format you wish.
- You can use *queries* to look up information in a table or to isolate specific types of information.
- You can create *custom applications* to automate aspects of managing your database.

CHAPTER 2

Getting Started with Paradox

fast TRACK

- **To start Paradox**   24

    from the DOS command prompt, switch to the drive and directory in which Paradox is stored, and type the command **PARADOX**.

- **To pull down a menu from the Paradox desktop menu bar**   26

    use any of these methods: (1) click on the menu name with your mouse; (2) press the Menu key, F10 to move the highlight to the menu bar, then type the highlighted letter in the menu name; or (3) press F10, use the arrow keys to move the highlight to the menu name, and then press ↵.

- **To select an option from a menu**   27

    click on the option with your mouse, type its highlighted letter, or use the arrow keys to highlight it and press ↵. Some menus display submenus with more options. In this book, the ➤ symbol separates a series of menu selections, as in **T**ools ➤ **M**ore ➤ **D**irectory (the boldfaced letter is the one you can press to select the option).

- **To "back out" of a series of menu selections**   28

    click on a "neutral" area of the screen, press Esc until you're in more familiar territory, or press F10 to return to the main menu. When Cancel is available, you can also choose that option.

- **To access a feature listed on the Speedbar**   29

    click on the key or feature name on the Speedbar, or press the key that is highlighted on the Speedbar (for example, press F1 for Help information).

To get context-sensitive help while in Paradox　　29

    press the Help key, F1, or click on the F1 Help option on the Speedbar.

To switch to the Help Index from a Help screen　　30

    press F1 again, or click on the F1 Index option on the Speedbar.

To exit the Help system and return to the desktop　　32

    choose **H**elp ➤ **P**aradox, or press Esc a sufficient number of times to return to the desktop.

To choose a working directory for your Paradox files　　32

    select **T**ools ➤ **M**ore ➤ **D**irectory. In the Directory dialog box, you can type in a new directory name or edit the existing entry. You can also press Tab or Alt-t to see a directory tree and select a directory from the tree.

To switch to the Full Screen User Interface　　35

    which automatically opens your tables and forms in the largest possible window, pull down the System menu (represented by the ≡ at the left side of the menu bar), and choose **I**nterface. Then select **Y**es from the submenu that asks if you are sure you want to switch interfaces.

To exit Paradox　　37

    choose **DO-IT!** from the menu bar, or press the Do-It! key, F2, to save any work in progress. Then choose **E**xit ➤ **Y**es from the menu bar.

NOW that you have a basic idea of what database management is all about, it's time to get Paradox up and running on your computer and get a feel for the way it works. In this chapter, you'll learn about the Paradox desktop and Help system. You'll also learn how to choose a working directory and a user interface.

Starting Paradox

With Paradox installed on your hard disk, you can start up the program and get to work. If you don't have Paradox installed already, refer to Appendix A for installation instructions.

The basic procedure for starting Paradox from the DOS command prompt is as follows:

1. Start your computer in the usual manner to get to the DOS command prompt. If a shell (such as Microsoft Windows) appears, exit that shell. If the Paradox directory is included in the PATH statement of your AUTOEXEC.BAT file, you can skip steps 2 and 3.

2. Switch to the drive on which you installed Paradox. For example, if Paradox is stored on drive C:, type **C:** and press ↵.

3. Switch to the Paradox directory, typically PDOX45. For example, type **CD\PDOX45** and press ↵ to get to that directory.

4. Type **PARADOX** and press ↵ to run Paradox.

NOTE You can also start Paradox from Microsoft Windows, after creating a program group and item for it. See Appendix A for more information.

When you start Paradox, the Paradox *desktop* appears on your screen, as shown in Figure 2.1.

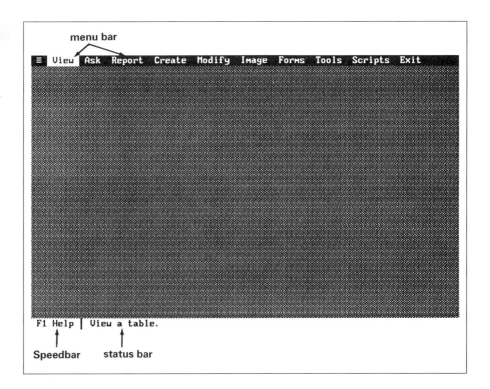

FIGURE 2.1

The Paradox desktop includes the main menu bar across the top and the Speedbar and status bar across the bottom.

The Paradox Desktop

All your work with Paradox takes place at the Paradox desktop. In many ways, the Paradox desktop follows the Common User Access (CUA) guidelines that Windows applications use. So if you're currently working with Windows applications, you'll find that many of the techniques you use in those applications work the same in Paradox for DOS.

Working with a Mouse

Although a mouse is not required to work with Paradox, it can certainly speed up many operations. Paradox 4.5 offers expanded mouse support. Throughout this book, we'll use standard mouse terminology, as summarized below:

- **Mouse pointer:** The mouse pointer appears as solid square on the screen, and it moves in whatever direction you roll the mouse.

- **Click:** To click on an option, move the mouse pointer to that option, then press and release the active mouse button. (The active button is the left button unless you've set up the mouse for left-handed use by specifying the right button as the active button.)

- **Double-click:** To double-click on an option, move the mouse pointer to that option, then press and release the active mouse button twice in rapid succession.

- **Drag:** To drag with the mouse, move the mouse pointer to where you want to start dragging. Then hold down the active mouse button while you move the mouse pointer. When the mouse pointer is where you want it to be, release the mouse button.

> **NOTE** As you'll learn in this book, you can also use special keyboard keys to move around in the desktop and to perform various operations. These keys are often displayed on the Speedbar or the menus themselves.

Using the Menus

The menus are your main tool for interacting with Paradox. When you're at the desktop, the names of the menus appear in a horizontal bar across the top of the screen (View, Ask, Report, and so forth). To pull down, or view, a menu, use any of the following techniques:

- Click on the menu name with your mouse.

- Press the Menu key (F10) to activate (move the highlight to) the menu bar, then type the highlighted letter (usually the first letter) in the menu name.

THE PARADOX DESKTOP

- Press F10 to move the highlight to the menu bar, use the arrow keys to move the highlight to the menu name, and then press ↵.

After you have pulled down a menu, you can choose one of the displayed options in the same ways that you chose the menu: by clicking on it, by typing its highlighted letter, or by using the arrow keys to highlight it and pressing ↵.

NOTE A brief description of the currently highlighted menu option appears in the status bar near the bottom of the screen.

You'll notice a ➤ symbol to the right of some options on the pull-down menus. This symbol means that choosing that option will lead you to another menu, called a *submenu*. You can choose options from submenus in the same ways that you make selections from the pull-down menus.

For some operations, you'll need to select a series of options before anything happens. Throughout this book, we'll use the following technique to identify a series of menu selections:

   Tools ➤ **M**ore ➤ **D**irectory

This format lets you see at a glance the sequence of menu options that you need to choose to access a particular feature. Each option is separated by the ➤ symbol, and the letter you can press to select the option is shown in boldface.

The sample sequence **T**ools ➤ **M**ore ➤ **D**irectory is simply a shortcut way of saying "Pull down the Tools menu, then choose the More option, then choose the Directory option." You can use any of the menu selection techniques to choose these options. That is, you can use your mouse to click on Tools, then More, and then Directory. Or you can press F10, then **T**, then **M**, then **D**. Or use the arrow keys to highlight the first option, press ↵, highlight the second option, press ↵, and so on. Use whatever method you prefer.

Backing Out of Menu Selections

In some situations, particularly when you're first learning to use Paradox, you may inadvertently choose menu options that lead you into unfamiliar territory. You can easily back out of, or *cancel*, your selections by using any of these techniques:

- Press the Esc (Escape) key a sufficient number of times to return to more familiar territory.
- Click on any "neutral" area in the desktop, such as outside the menu or dialog box that appears.
- Click on the Cancel button if one is available in the current dialog box.
- Choose **C**ancel from the menu bar at the top of the screen, if it's available. If this pulls down a submenu with Yes/No options, choose Yes to exit without saving any changes you may have made.
- Press F10 to back out all the way to the main menu in one stroke.

Keep this simple rule in mind for when you find yourself lost in Paradox:

> If in doubt, Escape key out

When Esc doesn't do the trick, choose the Cancel option, which will appear on the menu bar or within a dialog box.

We'll talk more about specific techniques for using dialog boxes and various Paradox windows in the next two chapters. For now, it's sufficient to know how to choose menu options and how to back out when you find yourself in unfamiliar territory.

Using the Speedbar and the Status Bar

At the bottom of the Paradox desktop are the Speedbar and the status bar, divided by a vertical line. The status bar, located to the right of the vertical line, displays helpful information relevant to whatever you're doing at the moment. For example, as you highlight different menu options at the top of the screen, the status bar displays a brief description of the current option. In Figure 2.1, the View menu is highlighted, and the status bar displays

> View a table.

The Speedbar, to the left of the vertical line, provides quick access to some of the options that are currently available. For example, in Figure 2.1, the Speedbar shows

> F1 Help

This indicates that Help information is available for the current operation.

You can access Speedbar items with either a mouse or the keyboard:

- With your mouse, click on the item on the Speedbar. For example, clicking on F1 Help activates the Help feature.
- With the keyboard, press the named key. For example, press F1 to bring up Help text.

Getting Help

You can display Help information on your screen at any time by using the Help key (F1). Paradox offers two types of Help:

- Context-sensitive Help provides information that is relevant to whatever you happen to be doing at the moment.
- The Help Index lets you look up information on any Paradox topic.

For example, if you choose **M**odify from the menu bar and then press F1, you'll see a Help screen providing information about the options on the Modify menu, as shown in Figure 2.2. Notice that the menu bar at the top of the screen now provides general Help system options, and the Speedbar now displays F1 Index.

FIGURE 2.2

A context-sensitive Help screen. This screen provides information about the options on the Modify menu.

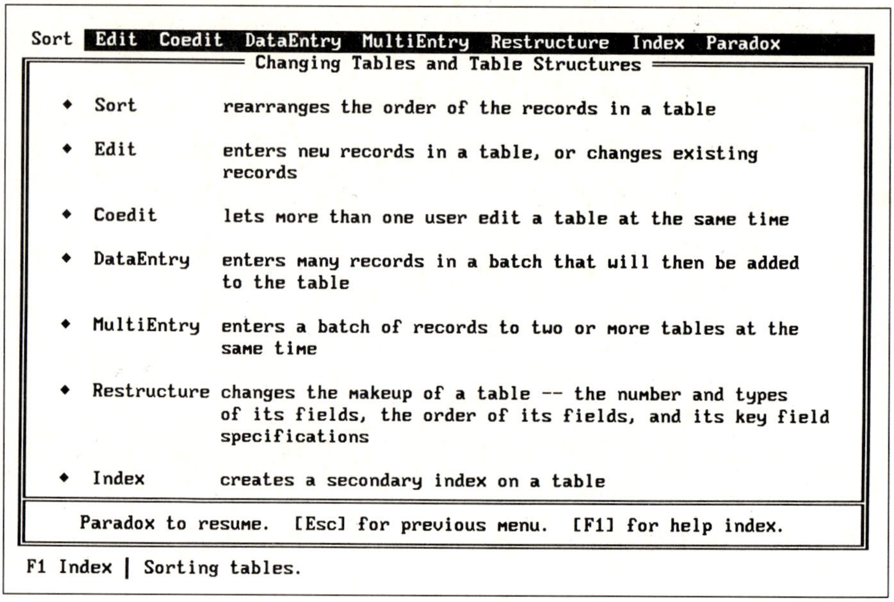

```
Sort  Edit  Coedit  DataEntry  MultiEntry  Restructure  Index  Paradox
            ========== Changing Tables and Table Structures ==========

   ♦ Sort          rearranges the order of the records in a table

   ♦ Edit          enters new records in a table, or changes existing
                   records

   ♦ Coedit        lets more than one user edit a table at the same time

   ♦ DataEntry     enters many records in a batch that will then be added
                   to the table

   ♦ MultiEntry    enters a batch of records to two or more tables at the
                   same time

   ♦ Restructure   changes the makeup of a table -- the number and types
                   of its fields, the order of its fields, and its key field
                   specifications

   ♦ Index         creates a secondary index on a table

       Paradox to resume.   [Esc] for previous menu.   [F1] for help index.

F1 Index | Sorting tables.
```

Working within the Help System

When a Help screen is displayed, you can work within the Help system as follows:

- Choose any available option from the menu bar to get Help with that topic.
- Press Esc to back up to the previous Help screen (if any) or to return to Paradox.
- Choose **P**aradox from the menu bar to return to Paradox.
- Press F1 or click on F1 Index on the Speedbar to switch to the Help Index.

Using the Help Index

If the context-sensitive Help and menu options that appear when you first activate Help don't provide the information you need, switch to the Help Index by pressing the Help key (F1) again or clicking on F1 Index on the Speedbar. The Help Index appears, as shown in Figure 2.3.

GETTING HELP

FIGURE 2.3

The Help Index appears when you press F1 from a context-sensitive Help screen.

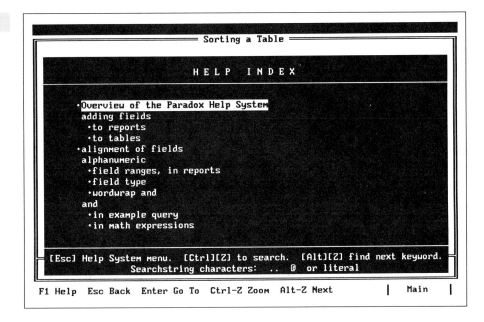

Except for the first item, Overview of Paradox and the Help System, the topics and subtopics in the index are listed in alphabetical order. You can press ↓ and ↑ to scroll line by line, or press PgUp and PgDn to scroll a screenful at a time through the index. When the topic you want help with is highlighted, press ↵ to view its Help information.

You don't need to scroll to search for specific words or phrases that may be included in Help Index topics. You can "zoom" immediately to the word you want. The basic technique is as follows:

1. Press Ctrl-z while the Help Index is displayed. You'll see a Zoom dialog box:

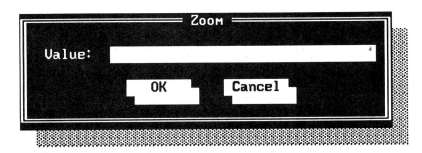

2. Type the word or phrase you want to look up. You can include any combination of the .. and @ wildcard characters (described after these steps).

3. Press ↵ or click on OK.

4. If the first word or phrase found is not the one you're looking for, press Alt-z to search for the next occurrence of that word or phrase.

5. When the highlight is on the Help topic you want, press ↵.

If Paradox can't find the word you specified, the highlight does not move, and the message "Match not found" appears near the lower-right corner of the Help window.

When you're entering the word or phrase in the Zoom dialog box, you can use the .. (double-dot) and @ (at sign) wildcard characters to broaden your search. The .. character matches any series of characters. The @ character matches any single character.

For example, if you just type **key** as the word to search for, Paradox will find only the topic consisting of the single word *key*. However, if you enter **..key..**, Paradox will find topics that have *key* embedded within them, such as *arrow keys* and *Backspace key*.

Exiting Help

You can exit the Help system and return to Paradox at any time by using one of these methods:

- Choose **P**aradox from the menu bar at the top of the Help screen (if it's available).
- Press the Esc key a sufficient number of times to back entirely out of the Help system.

Choosing a Working Directory

When you first start Paradox, its *working*, or *current*, *directory* will be whatever directory you were in when you entered the command to start Paradox. This is the directory that Paradox will use automatically when it

CHOOSING A WORKING DIRECTORY

searches for tables, reports, and other objects that you've previously created. (You can also set a default working directory through the Custom Configuration Program, described in Appendix D.)

You can switch to a different directory at any time by following these steps:

1. Choose **T**ools ➤ **M**ore ➤ **D**irectory. You'll see a dialog box like the one below:

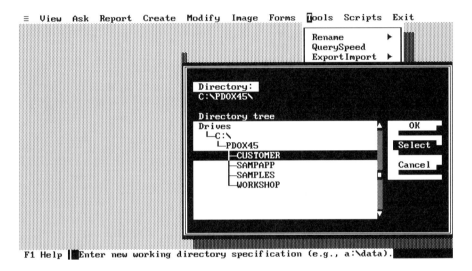

2. To switch to a different directory, use any of these techniques:

   - Type a complete new entry or edit the existing entry. If you just start typing, the existing entry will disappear. To edit or add to the existing entry, press the End key or an arrow key before you begin typing.
   - To change to a subdirectory of the existing directory (for example, to change C:\PDOX45\ to C:\PDOX45\Sample\), click on the words Directory Tree or in the directory tree area of the dialog box to display the tree for the current drive, directory, and all subdirectories. You can also press Tab or Alt-t to see the tree. Double-click on the desired subdirectory name (Sample\ in this example) or click once on a subdirectory name and press ↵. Alternatively, you can use the ↑ or ↓ keys to highlight a subdirectory name and press ↵.

- To change to a directory on another drive, double-click on the word Drive at the top of the directory tree, press Alt-s, or click on the Select button. The directory tree will display a list of drives available on your system. Double-click on the desired drive or use the ↑ and ↓ keys to highlight it and press ↵. The directories on the chosen drive will be displayed. Choose a directory or subdirectory using any of the selection methods. To see a directory's subdirectories, double-click on the directory name, or highlight it and press ↵.

3. Choose OK or move to the Directory name box, which displays the current selection, and press ↵.

If you specify an existing directory name, you'll see the message

> Working directory is now *(name of directory)*

near the lower-right corner of the screen. The message remains until you perform some other action.

If the directory you specify does not exist, you'll see the message

> No such directory as *(name of nonexistent directory)*

You'll either need to change your entry and try again, or choose Cancel (or press Esc or F10) to return to the existing current directory.

> **NOTE** You can't create a directory using Tools ➤ More ➤ Directory. You must either go to DOS and use the MKDIR or MD command or use the Paradox Workshop Applications ➤ Directory command, as described in Chapter 18.

Be aware that changing the working directory automatically closes and saves any work in progress. For this reason, you should store all the objects (such as tables, reports, forms, and so on) for any given project in the same directory. You'll learn more about using directories to organize files in later chapters. For now, just keep in mind that if it seems that Paradox has "lost" work that you've saved, chances are that you are simply in the wrong directory. Use **Tools** ➤ **More** ➤ **Directory** to get to the correct directory.

Choosing an Interface

All the techniques described so far assume you are using the Standard User Interface (Standard UI). However, Paradox 4.5 also offers an entirely separate user interface, called the Full Screen User Interface (Full Screen UI).

When you use the Full Screen UI, tables appear in windows that are the width of the entire screen. The height of the windows is adjusted to show as many records as possible. These table windows are resizable.

Windows for filling in and designing forms are full-screen size, without borders. Windows for designing, previewing, and changing reports are full-screen size, with normal window borders and scroll bars. None of these form or report windows are resizable.

Switching to the Full Screen User Interface

If you prefer to switch to the Full Screen UI, so your tables and forms automatically open in the largest possible window, you should first save all your work in progress. That's because Paradox will close all open windows on the desktop, sometimes without saving changes, before switching interfaces. You can usually save any work in progress by choosing **DO-IT!** from the menu bar (if it's available) or by pressing the Do-It! key, F2. Then follow these steps to choose the Full Screen UI:

1. Display the System menu, represented by the stack of three small, horizontal bars (≡) at the left side of the menu bar, by using one of these methods:

   - Click on the ≡ with your mouse.
   - Press F10 (if the highlight isn't already in the menu bar), use the ← or → key to highlight the ≡, and then press ↵.
   - Press Alt-spacebar.

2. In the System menu, shown in Figure 2.4, choose **I**nterface. You'll see a submenu asking if you are sure you want to switch interfaces.

36 CHAPTER 2   GETTING STARTED WITH PARADOX

FIGURE 2.4

The Paradox System menu is on the left side of the menu bar. Its name is represented by a stack of three short, horizontal bars (≡).

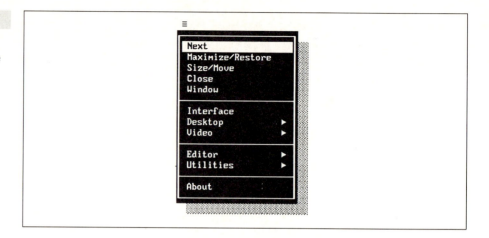

3. If you are sure all your work in progress is saved, or you do not mind abandoning the work, choose **Yes**.

The screen changes to the Full Screen UI, as shown in Figure 2.5. The desktop appears the same as in the Standard UI, but your windows will open as described earlier. The only options available in the System menu in the Full Screen UI are **I**nterface and **A**bout. See Appendix B for a description of the Full Screen UI and the other features new to Paradox version 4.5 for DOS.

FIGURE 2.5

Use the Full Screen UI if you want table, form, and report windows to open full screen. When the Full Screen UI is active, your only choices in the System menu are Interface and About.

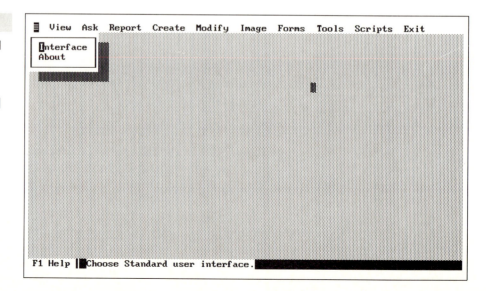

NOTE: In scripts, Paradox 4.5 interprets the version 4.0 COMPATIBLE command as the SETUIMODE command to switch to the Full Screen UI. Version 3.5 and earlier menus display as pop-up menus in the Full Screen UI.

Switching to the Standard User Interface

Throughout this book, we'll assume you're using the Standard UI. To switch from the Full Screen UI to the Standard UI, save any work in progress and then choose Interface from the System menu. As when you switched to the Full Screen UI, you'll see a submenu asking if you are sure you want to switch interfaces. If you are sure that all work in progress has been saved, choose Yes. If you're not sure, choose No to stay in the Full Screen UI and save your work before repeating this procedure.

If you changed directories while in the Full Screen UI, the directory you switched to will remain the current directory. You can use **T**ools ➤ **M**ore ➤ **D**irectory to switch to another directory once you're back in the Standard UI.

Exiting Paradox

You should *always* exit Paradox before you turn off (or reboot) your computer. This ensures that any new data or changes to existing data will be properly stored on disk. If you do not properly exit Paradox before turning off your computer, you will likely lose or corrupt data and any other work you've accomplished in the current Paradox session.

Before you exit Paradox, save any work in progress by choosing **DO-IT!** from the menu bar (if it's available) or by pressing the Do-It! key, F2. Then choose **E**xit ➤ **Y**es. You'll be returned to the DOS command prompt (or wherever you started Paradox from). When only the DOS command prompt appears on the screen, you can safely turn off your computer.

Summary

This chapter has provided a general overview of starting Paradox, interacting with it, and exiting Paradox. In the next chapter, you'll learn how to start putting Paradox to work by designing and creating tables. But first, take a moment to review the basic skills you've learned in this chapter:

- To start Paradox from the DOS command prompt, switch to the drive and directory that it's stored on, type **PARADOX**, and press ↵.

- You can choose an option from a menu by clicking on the option you want with your mouse. You can also use the keyboard to choose menu options. Press F10 to activate the menu bar, then either type the letter that's highlighted in the option you want, or use the arrow keys to move to the option you want and press ↵.

- To back out of an inadvertent menu selection or a dialog box, press Esc (the Escape key) or F10, or choose Cancel if this option is available from the dialog box or menu bar.

- To activate a feature listed in the Speedbar near the bottom of the screen, press the named key or click on the item on the Speedbar.

- To see on-screen Help information at any time, press the Help key, F1, or click on the F1 Help option on the Speedbar. Press F1 again if you want to get to the Help Index. You can exit Help and return to Paradox by choosing **P**aradox from the **H**elp menu or by pressing Esc a sufficient number of times to return to the desktop.

- To specify a directory for storing and retrieving objects in the current session, choose **T**ools ➤ **M**ore ➤ **D**irectory.

- You should always exit Paradox before turning off your computer. Choose **E**xit ➤ **Y**es to do so.

CHAPTER 3

Creating a Paradox Table

fast TRACK

- **In a Paradox table**   42

    each row of information is called a *record*, and each column is called a *field*.

- **When designing a Paradox table**   44

    divide the information you want to store into as many separate meaningful units of information (fields) as possible.

- **The names you give to fields in a table structure**   46

    can be up to 25 characters in length, and they can contain blank spaces.

- **The types of fields you can define include**   47

    alphanumeric (text up to 255 characters long), memo (larger bodies of text), numeric (numbers with decimal places), currency (numbers with two decimal places), short numeric (whole numbers in the range of $-32{,}767$ to $32{,}767$), date (such as 12/31/94), and binary (any data, including pictures and sound files, created and edited with an external program).

To use DOS to create a directory for storing a new table   52

"shell out" to DOS using **T**ools ➤ **M**ore ➤ **T**oDOS. Use the DOS MKDIR (or MD) command to create the directory, then enter the command **EXIT** to return to Paradox.

To switch to the directory in which you want to store the table   53

choose **T**ools ➤ **M**ore ➤ **D**irectory before creating the table.

To create a table structure   53

Choose **C**reate from the menu bar, type in a valid DOS file name without an extension, then choose OK or press ↵. In the Create screen, define the fields by typing each field name followed by the one-letter abbreviation for the field type. You must also provide a length for alphanumeric, memo, and binary fields.

To save the completed table structure   57

choose **D**O-IT! from the menu bar or press the Do-It! key, F2.

IN this chapter, you'll learn how to organize information into a Paradox table. Although Paradox's full power lies in its management of multiple tables, the focus in this part of the book is on handling a single table. The information presented here will start you out with your applications that require only one table. Once you've learned the basics of working with Paradox and how to manage a single table, you'll be ready to tackle multiple tables for more advanced applications.

Planning a Table

A table is a collection of information organized into a tabular format of rows and columns. In database terminology, each column of information in the table is a *field* and each row of information is a *record*. Figure 3.1 shows a small list of names and telephone numbers organized into a table. The table contains three fields, and each field has a unique *field name* (Last Name, First Name, and Phone). The table contains seven records, with the first and last names and phone numbers of seven people.

If the information you plan on storing is not in a tabular format already, you need to decide how you will organize it in a Paradox table. For example, suppose you want to store the information in your Rolodex file. As illustrated in Figure 3.2, the Rolodex card has four lines of information: (1) name, (2) street address, (3) city, state, and zip code, and (4) phone number. To put this information into a Paradox table, think of each Rolodex card as representing one record (row) of information. Each unique item on the card represents one field (column).

Figure 3.3 shows how information from several Rolodex cards might look in a Paradox table. Notice that the name information is divided into several fields: Title, First Name, M.I. (middle initial), and Last Name. The

PLANNING A TABLE

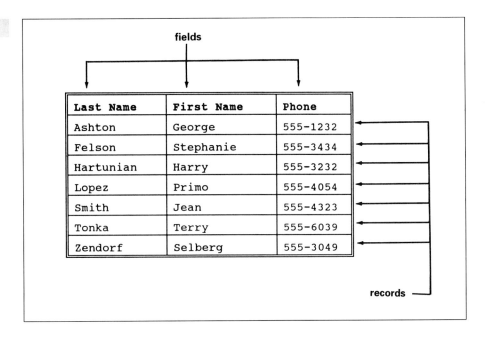

FIGURE 3.1

A sample table with three *fields* and seven *records*. The fields (columns) are the categories. Each row of information constitutes a record.

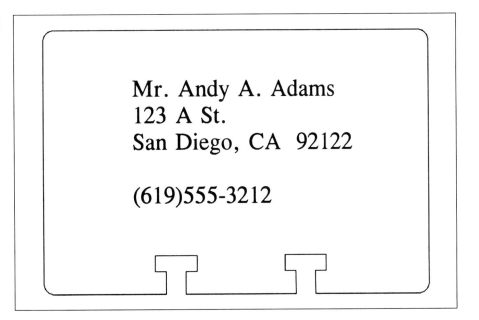

FIGURE 3.2

A sample Rolodex card. Think of each card in this file as one record in a Paradox table.

FIGURE 3.3

An example of information from several Rolodex cards stored in a Paradox table.

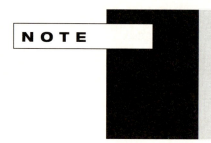

Title	First Name	M.I.	Last Name	Address	City	State	Zip	Phone
Mr.	Andy	A.	Adams	123 A St.	San Diego	CA	92122	(619)555-3212
Miss	Sari	U.	Fell	234 B St.	Azusa	CA	92123	(213)555-4039
Mrs.	Sandy		Beech	P.O. Box 12	Encinitas	CA	92024	(619)555-5928
Dr.	Willie	B.	Goode	755 Oak Ln.	Bonsall	CA	92043	(619)555-2323
Ms.	Wanda	B.	Cruzen	12 Elm St.	Borrego	CA	92323	(619)555-3049

next section explains why you should split your information into as many fields as possible.

NOTE Keep in mind that regardless of the *type* of information—inventory, bookkeeping, accounts payable, accounts receivable, or whatever—it must be organized in Paradox in a tabular format. Some types of information might be spread across several tables, as discussed in Part Two.

Planning the Fields to Include

In your Paradox tables, you need to store each "meaningful" item of information in a separate field. A *meaningful* piece of information is one that you might need to work with separately. You also want to be sure to include enough fields to store all the information you might need.

For example, suppose you're keeping track of information about customers, including each person's name, address, phone number, fax number, credit limit, and perhaps the starting date of the customer's credit account. You might want to break the information for each customer into 14 fields:

    Last Name   City
    Mr/Mrs   State
    First Name   Zip Code

M.I.	Phone
Department/Title	FAX
Company	Credit Limit
Address	Start Date

But why bother to split people's names into four fields (Mr/Mrs, Last Name, First Name, and M.I. for the middle initial)? Because the more fields you break the information into, the easier it will be later to organize and use only the data that is meaningful to your purposes at the time. For example, storing each person's last name in its own field makes it easier to later tell Paradox to "put the information into alphabetical order by last name" or to "find the people whose last name is Smith."

Separating the information also makes it easier to determine exactly how to print it later. For example, if you want to print an alphabetical customer list, you could tell Paradox to list the last name followed by a comma and then the first name:

Adams, Andy

Beech, Sandy

Cruzen, Wanda

Fell, Sari

Goode, Willie

Then, when you want to use the same table to print formal correspondence, you can tell Paradox to arrange the names in a different format, with the honorific followed by first name, middle initial, and then last name:

Mr. Andy A. Adams

Mrs. Sandy Beech

Ms. Wanda B. Cruzen

Miss Sari U. Fell

Dr. Willie B. Goode

Your letter salutations could be formal:

> Dear Mr. Adams:

or informal:

> Dear Andy:

Isolating each meaningful item in a separate field gives you the most flexibility for printing information later. And as you'll discover in later chapters, separating your information also makes it easier to sort your tables and to search for information.

Rules for Defining Field Names

Each field in your table must have a unique name. When you're naming your fields, keep in mind the following rules and suggestions:

- The maximum width of a field name is 25 characters, including spaces.
- To avoid confusing yourself and other users, don't use characters that Paradox itself uses for specific purposes. Your field names should not contain " " (quotation marks), [ ] (brackets), { } (braces), ( ) (parentheses), or -> (a hyphen followed by a greater-than sign). Although a field name can contain the number symbol (#), the # should not be used alone.
- No two fields in the same table can have the same name.
- Don't use any of the reserved temporary table names as the name of a field:

Answer	Keyviol
Changed	Kvtemp
Chantemp	List
Crosstab	Passtemp
Deleted	Password
Deltemp	Problems
Entry	Probtemp
Family	Resttemp

PLANNING A TABLE

Inserted   Sortques
Instemp   Struct

NOTE: The roles played by the Paradox temporary tables are explained in later chapters.

Defining the Data Type of Fields

Paradox stores different types of information in different formats. This means that you also need to decide what type of information you will store in each field of your table. Paradox offers seven different field types:

- **Alphanumeric:** An alphanumeric field can contain letters, numeric characters, spaces, and other characters. Alphanumeric data consists of textual information, such as names, addresses, titles, or any other information that you will not be using mathematically. An alphanumeric field can contain anywhere from 1 to 255 characters.

- **Memo:** Like an alphanumeric field, a memo field contains textual data. However, instead of a maximum of 255 characters, a memo field can hold up to 64MB, or about 67 million characters. For example, a memo field can store entire résumés or job performance reviews in a table of personnel data, or abstracts of books or articles in a table used to manage a library.

- **Numeric:** A numeric field stores "true" numbers, such as quantities, and allows for mathematical operations, such as addition, subtraction, multiplication, and division. Numeric fields accept only numeric characters (0–9), decimal points, commas, parentheses, and minus signs (a hyphen will also work as a minus sign). Alphabetic characters are not allowed in numeric fields. The range of values possible for a numeric field is $\pm 10^{-307}$ to $\pm 10^{308}$ with 15 significant digits.

- **Currency:** A currency field stores numeric data representing dollar amounts. Currency data is like numeric data, except that all numbers are automatically rounded to two decimal places of accuracy and negative values are enclosed in parentheses.

CREATING A PARADOX TABLE

- **Date:** A date field stores dates in *MM/DD/YY*, *DD/MM/YY*, or *DD-Mon-YY* format and allows for date arithmetic. With date arithemetic, you can calculate the number of days between two dates, add or subtract days from a date, and perform other date-related calculations. Paradox automatically validates any entry, rejecting a date such as 04/31/94 (April only has 30 days).

- **Short Numeric:** A short numeric field stores integers (whole numbers) in the range of –32,767 to 32,767. Unlike currency and numeric fields, short numeric fields can't be formatted. Therefore, you might want to avoid using this data type until you learn about developing applications (the topic of Part Three of this book).

- **Binary:** A binary field stores what Paradox calls BLOBs (Binary Large OBjects) from external programs. Because Paradox does not include an editor for creating, changing, or viewing the contents of these fields, all you see is the word *BLOB* in your table. To work with BLOBs, you need to specify an external BLOB editor using the Custom Configuration Program, as described in Appendix D.

If your table contains any alphanumeric or memo fields, you also need to plan how much space each of those fields is likely to require. Paradox automatically determines how much storage space other types of fields, such as currency and numeric, will require. You need to size only alphanumeric and memo fields.

You don't want to shortchange yourself when making these decisions. For example, if you allotted 10 characters for the Last Name field, you wouldn't be able to store a long last name like *Livingston-Gladstone* in that field. On the other hand, you wouldn't want to allot 100 characters for Last Name, since nobody's last name is that long. You would just be wasting disk space to reserve that much space for every last name in the table.

Referring back to our sample customer table, we might assign the following field types to the fields and lengths to the alphanumeric fields:

FIELD NAME	FIELD TYPE	FIELD LENGTH
Last Name	Alphanumeric	20
Mr/Mrs	Alphanumeric	4
First Name	Alphanumeric	20
M.I.	Alphanumeric	2

PLANNING A TABLE

FIELD NAME	FIELD TYPE	FIELD LENGTH
Department/Title	Alphanumeric	30
Company	Alphanumeric	30
Address	Alphanumeric	30
City	Alphanumeric	20
State	Alphanumeric	2
Zip Code	Alphanumeric	10
Phone	Alphanumeric	13
FAX	Alphanumeric	13
Credit Limit	Currency	
Start Date	Date	

Now you may be thinking, "Wait a minute—you just said that the numeric field type is for numbers. Yet you just defined Zip Code, Phone, and FAX as the alphanumeric field type." That's true; they were made alphanumeric because neither zip codes nor phone numbers are "true" numbers. Defining any of these fields as numeric would prevent you from putting letters, leading zeros, and most punctuation into the entries.

For example, if you defined Zip Code as a numeric field, you woudn't be able to enter a hyphenated zip code (such as 92067-3384), a foreign zip code (such as MJ3 OH4), or one with a leading zero (such as 01234) into that field. If you made Phone a numeric field, you wouldn't be able to store phone numbers with a hyphen, as in (510)555-1212. Remember, use numeric, currency, and short numeric fields only to store true numbers—those you want to use in math operations—such as quantities, dollar amounts, and the like.

Defining Memo Fields

Although a memo field can contain millions of characters, you must still define a length within the range of 1 to 240 characters for this type of field. This length determines how much of the memo field is stored within the table and readily visible on the screen. Paradox stores the complete contents of each memo field outside the table (in a file with the extension .MB, as discussed in Chapter 12).

Here's an example of the structure of a table used to manage a library, which includes a memo field to store journal article abstracts:

FIELD NAME	FIELD TYPE	FIELD LENGTH
Author	Alphanumeric	40
Title	Alphanumeric	40
Journal	Alphanumeric	40
Date	Date	
Volume	Numeric	
Number	Numeric	
Pages	Alphanumeric	8
Keywords	Alphanumeric	40
Abstract	Memo	10

In the regular Table view, only ten characters will appear in the memo field. But when you move to the memo field and switch to Field view (by doubling-clicking with your mouse or by pressing Alt-F5 or Ctrl-F), you open a window that contains the entire contents of the field. In this window, you can view, add to, and change the contents of the memo field. Figure 3.4 shows an example of a window with the contents of the sample Abstract field (in the table structure outlined above). The table is displayed on a custom form, with the memo field in Field view.

Entering and editing memo information is discussed in Chapter 4.

Table Structure Limitations

Here are couple of limitations to keep in mind when designing your Paradox tables:

- A single table can contain a maximum of 255 fields. A database, however, can join more than 50 tables in a single query. With Paradox, you can create a query that accesses many more fields than are available in a single table.

PLANNING A TABLE

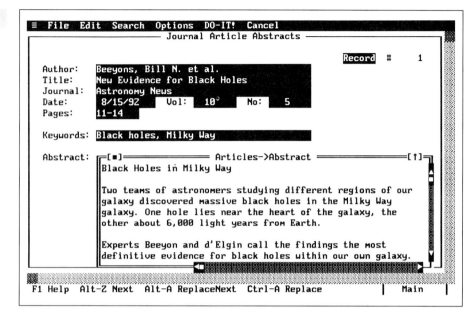

FIGURE 3.4

A sample custom form for a table that includes a memo field. A window for the memo field, named Abstract, is currently open on the screen.

- A single record can contain a maximum of 4000 characters, including the length assigned to any memo fields. That is, even though any memo field can actually contain several million characters, if you assign a length of 10 to a memo field, that counts as 10 characters in the record.

 Indexed tables, discussed in Chapter 13, can contain a maximum of 1350 characters per record.

Remember that it's not necessary to store *all* the information you need in a single table. Paradox is capable of handling multiple related tables, and you should plan to take advantage of this capability once you have mastered the skills and concepts prerequisite to working with single tables. (Managing multiple tables is the topic of Part Two of this book.)

Creating a Directory for Tables

You can store your Paradox tables in any directory you wish. But in general, it's best to store all the tables, reports, forms, and other files that make up a particular project in one special directory for that project only. For example, suppose Paradox is stored in C:\PDOX45. If you're creating a database to manage customer information, you might want to create a subdirectory named C:\PDOX45\Customer and store all your customer data in that directory. Having all your project-related files in a single directory will make it easier to back up, copy, and restructure the various objects that make up your customer database.

If you want several network users to share data in a table, you must create the table in a shared directory. See Appendix C for more information about using Paradox on networks.

To create a new directory, you can temporarily "shell out" to DOS. Follow these steps:

1. From the Paradox desktop, choose **T**ools ➤ **M**ore ➤ **T**oDOS to get to the DOS command prompt.

2. Use the MD command to make a new directory, in the form MD *drive\directory-path*. For example, if Paradox is stored on C:\PDOX45 and you want to create a subdirectory named C:\PDOX45\Customer, you would type this command:

    MD C:\PDOX45\Customer

3. Press ↵ to enter the command. Assuming you've entered a valid path name, you'll be returned to the DOS command prompt. (See your DOS documentation if you need additional help with creating directories.)

CREATING A TABLE

Never turn off the computer while temporarily "shelled out" to DOS. See Chapter 12 for more information about this topic.

4. Type **EXIT** and press ↵ to return to the Paradox desktop.

When you return to Paradox, you can make the new directory your working directory by choosing **T**ools ➤ **M**ore ➤ **D**irectory, as described in the previous chapter.

As mentioned in Chapter 2, you can also create a new directory from the Application – Directory menu in the Paradox Workshop. You'll learn how to do this in Chapter 18.

Creating a Table

After you've planned the structure of a table, you can create it. Start Paradox (as described in Chapter 2), and then follow these steps from the desktop:

1. If you want to store the table in a directory other than the current directory, choose **T**ools ➤ **M**ore ➤ **D**irectory and change to that directory (see Chapter 2 for detailed instructions).

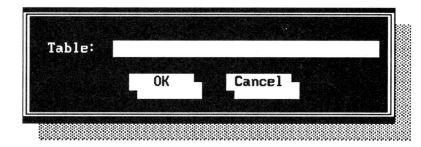

CHAPTER 3

CREATING A PARADOX TABLE

2. Select **C**reate from the Paradox main menu bar. You'll see this dialog box:

3. Type a valid DOS file name for your table, using up to eight characters. Follow these rules in naming your table:

   - Don't include any blank spaces, slashes, commas, or question marks.
   - Don't use any of the reserved temporary table names listed earlier in this chapter.
   - Don't include a file name extension; Paradox will automatically add the extension .DB to whatever name you provide.

4. Choose OK or press ↵. You'll see the screen for defining your table, as shown in Figure 3.5.

5. Type a field name, then press Tab or ↵ or click on the Field Type column to move the cursor to that column.

6. When the highlight is in the Field Type column, use any of the abbreviations listed on the right side of the screen to define the field

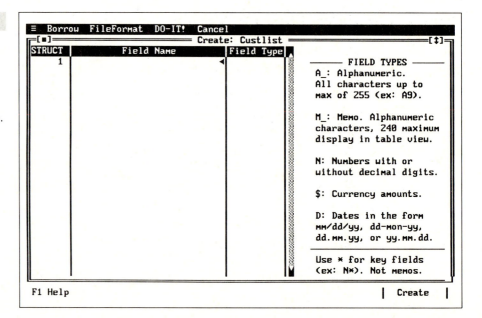

FIGURE 3.5

A Create screen for defining the structure of a Paradox table. Abbreviations for field types are listed on the right side of the screen.

type. The underscores next to A and M (A_ and M_) are just to remind you that you need to assign a length to alphanumeric and memo fields. You don't actually type the underscore.

NOTE Two other field types, short numeric (S) and binary (B), are also available, but they are less commonly used. These field types, which require special treatment, are discussed later in this book. As noted on the Create screen, you can also define a field as a key field by typing an asterisk at the end of the field type description. Key fields are covered in Chapter 13.

7. If you've defined the current field as alphanumeric, memo, or binary, type in a size. Remember that the size of an alphanumeric field limits the amount of text you can actually put into that field. The size you assign to a memo or binary field controls only what portion of the field is actually stored and displayed within the table.

8. Press ↵ or Tab to move down to the next row.

9. Repeat steps 5 through 8 until you've defined all the fields for your table. If you need to make changes and corrections along the way, you can use any of the following techniques:

    - To delete a field, move the cursor to it and press Del.
    - To change an existing entry, double-click on it with your mouse, or use the arrow keys to move the cursor to it and press Alt-F5 or Ctrl-f. Then move within the field, again using the mouse or ← or →, and type your changes. Use the Backspace key to erase text.
    - To insert a field between existing fields, move the cursor to wherever you want to place the new field and press Ins. Paradox inserts a blank row above the current cursor position, and you can type the new field name and field type into that row.

- If you want to start all over from scratch, choose **C**ancel from the menu bar.

Figure 3.6 shows how the sample customer table described in this chapter, which we've named Custlist, might look after entering all the field names, types, and sizes.

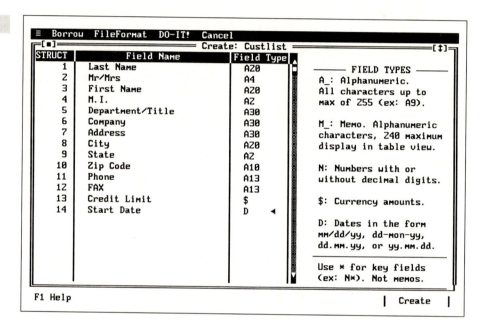

FIGURE 3.6

A sample table structure for customer information

Borrowing Another Table's Structure

If the table you're creating at the moment will use the same field names and types as some other table you've created in the past, you can use the Borrow option to simplify your work. This option copies field definitions from an existing table into the current table structure.

To use another table's structure, choose **B**orrow from the menu bar at the top of the Create screen. In the dialog box that appears, enter the name of the table that has the structure you want to borrow (including its drive and directory if it's not in the current working directory), then choose OK or press ↵. Paradox inserts a copy of that table's structure at the current cursor position within your table. You can then add or delete individual fields as necessary.

Choosing a File Format

Paradox 4.5 is *downwardly compatible* with earlier versions of Paradox. This means that Paradox 4.5 can use tables created with version 4.0 and earlier. But versions earlier than 4.0 can't use tables that you create with version 4.5 of Paradox. In particular, versions before 4.0 cannot interpret memo and binary fields.

If you need to ensure that the table you're creating can be read by Paradox 3.5, you can choose FileFormat ➤ Compatible from the menu bar at the top of the Create screen. But keep in mind, if you choose the Compatible format, you won't be able to define memo or binary fields in your table.

Saving the Table Structure

When you're satisfied with your table structure, choose **DO-IT!** from the menu bar or press the Do-It! key, F2. You'll see a brief message indicating that Paradox is creating the table, then you'll be returned to the desktop. You'll learn how to open your new table and add data to it in the next chapter.

You can still change the structure of a table after you've saved it by using Modify ➤ Restructure. This option is described in Chapter 12.

Summary

In the next chapter, you'll learn how to add data to a table and make changes and corrections as needed. Before moving on to that chapter, take a moment to review some of the main topics presented in this chapter:

- It's a good idea to plan the field names, field types, and sizes of alphanumeric fields before you actually create a table.
- To store your table in a unique directory, use the DOS MD or MKDIR command to create the directory, then use **Tools** ➤ **More** ➤ **Directory** in Paradox to switch to that directory.

CREATING A PARADOX TABLE

- To create a table, start at the Paradox desktop and choose **Create**. Enter a valid DOS file name and choose OK.

- In the Create screen, type in the name and type of each field. Also enter a size for each alphanumeric, memo, and binary field you're including in the table.

- When you've finished defining your table structure, choose **DO-IT!** from the menu bar, or press the Do-It! key, F2.

CHAPTER 4

Entering and Editing Table Data

fast TRACK

● **To open an existing table**   62

use **Tools** ➤ **More** ➤ **Directory** to switch to the table's directory, if necessary. Then choose **View** from the menu bar. In the dialog box that appears, type the name of the table you want to view and press ↵, or just click on OK and then double-click on the name of the table you want to open.

● **To add new data or edit existing data**   64

first switch to Edit mode by pressing F9, or switch to CoEdit mode (if you're sharing data on a network) by pressing Alt-F9.

● **To switch between Table view and Form view**   66

press the F7 key (which toggles between the views) or click on the F7 Form or F7 Table indicator on the Speedbar.

● **To add new data to a table**   67

make sure the table is open and in Edit or CoEdit mode, then press End to move to the last record. Press ↓ in Table view or Ctrl-PgDn in Form view to insert a new blank record at the end of the table. Type the contents of a field, and then press the ↵ or Tab key, or click with your mouse to move to another field.

● **To add or edit data in a memo field**   68

make sure you're in Edit or CoEdit mode. Then double-click on the memo field, or move the cursor to the memo field and press Alt-F5 or Ctrl-f. When you're finished typing or editing the memo, choose **DO-IT!** from the menu bar or press the Do-It! key, F2, to save your work.

CHAPTER 4 61

- **To edit the contents of a field**   76

    make sure you're in Edit or CoEdit mode, then switch to Field view by double-clicking on the field with your mouse, or by pressing Alt-F5 or Ctrl-f. In this view, the arrow keys and other special keys allow you to move within the field to make changes. Press ↵ or click the mouse button to exit Field view after making your changes.

- **To undo recent changes to a record or restore a deleted record**   78

    choose **Undo** ➤ **Y**es or press the Undo key, Ctrl-u.

- **To insert a new record at the current cursor position**   80

    press the Ins (Insert) key on the record below where you want to add the new record. Then fill in the new blank record that appears.

- **To delete the current record from the table**   80

    press the Delete (Del) key.

- **To save your changes after adding or changing table data**   81

    choose **DO-IT!** or press the Do-It! key, F2. You'll be returned to View mode.

- **To close a table**   82

    click on the Close button in the upper-left corner of the window, or press the Close Active Window key, F8. To close all the open windows on the desktop, press the Close All Windows key, Alt-F8.

IN the previous chapter, you created the structure of a Paradox table. Now you need to know how to put data into it, as well how to change and correct the table. This chapter explains how to open a Paradox table, add data to it, edit it, save your work, and close the table.

Opening a Table

To add data to a table or make changes to any existing data, the table must be open (displayed on the screen). To open a table, start from the Paradox desktop. If the table you want to open is not in the current working directory, choose **Tools ➤ More ➤ Directory**, and type in or select the name of directory that contains the table. Then choose OK (see Chapter 3 for details on changing the working directory).

Next, choose **View** from the main menu bar. You'll see a dialog box requesting the name of the table to open. Type the name of the table you want to open and choose OK or press ↵. The table will open immediately.

If you want to select the table you want to open from a list of tables, just press ↵ or choose OK in the View dialog box. You'll see a list of the tables on the current working directory, as shown in Figure 4.1. Any subdirectories to the current directory are indicated by a backslash in front of the subdirectory name. If the current directory is not the root directory, you will see a \.., which represents the current directory's parent directory.

When the table name and directory list appear in the dialog box, you can do any of the following to open a table:

- Double-click on the name of the table you want to open.

OPENING A TABLE

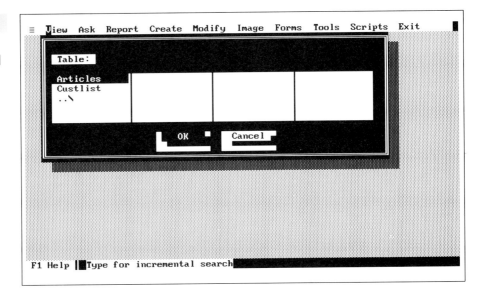

FIGURE 4.1

The View dialog box shows the names of all the tables in the current directory.

- Use the arrow keys to move the highlight to the name of the table you want to open and press ↵ or choose OK.
- Type the first few letters of the name of the table you want to open. Paradox moves the highlight to the first name containing those letters. Press ↵ or choose OK when the name of the table you want to open is highlighted.
- Double-click on a subdirectory name or the parent directory symbol (\..). The names of the tables in the selected directory appear. You can open one of them using any of the techniques described here.

 Some networks do not support the \.. directory indicators, so a \.. won't appear in file lists on those networks.

The table you selected will then be displayed. If the table already contains some data, you'll see whatever amount of information will fit in the current window. If you have not already added data to the table, only the field

ENTERING AND EDITING TABLE DATA

names at the top of the table appear on an otherwise empty table. Only the field names that fit in the current window appear across the top of the table. Other field names will scroll into view as you add data. Figure 4.2 shows the table structure we created in the previous chapter.

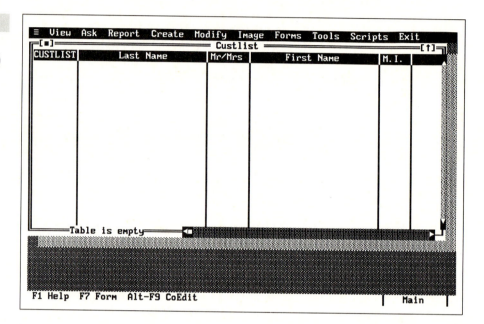

FIGURE 4.2

The Custlist table (created in Chapter 3) open on the desktop

Switching to Edit Mode

When you first open a table, you can only view its contents. If you attempt to type data into a field or make changes, Paradox displays the message

Press Edit F9 or CoEdit Alt-F9 if you want to make changes

As indicated by the message, you can press F9 or Alt-F9 to switch to a mode in which you can edit your table. Use the Edit key, F9, if you're running Paradox on a single-user computer. Use the CoEdit key, Alt-F9, if you're running Paradox on a network and want other users to have access to this table.

SWITCHING TO EDIT MODE

See Appendix C for information about using Paradox on networks and the differences between Edit and CoEdit modes.

Once you're in the Edit mode, the screen changes as follows:

- A ◀ symbol appears at the right side of the current field.
- The menu bar at the top of the screen changes.
- The status bar displays the word *Edit*.
- The options on the Speedbar change.

Figure 4.3 shows the Custlist table after changing to Edit mode.

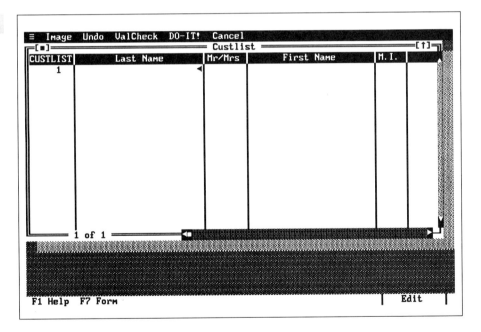

FIGURE 4.3

In Edit mode, the options on the menu bar and Speedbar change, the status bar displays Edit, and a ◀ symbol appears in the current field (Last Name).

Choosing a View

With your table opened on the desktop, you can switch between two views by pressing F7:

- Table view shows the table in tabular format, with as many rows and columns as will fit into the current window. The empty table in Figure 4.3 is shown in Table view.
- Form view displays a single record at a time, as shown in Figure 4.4.

FIGURE 4.4

A table record displayed in Form view. In this view, you can enter and edit data in one record at a time.

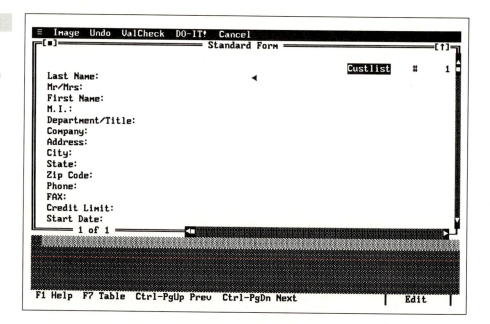

The F7 key acts as a *toggle*, which switches back and forth between two settings. As an alternative to pressing the key, you can click on F7 Form or F7 Table on the Speedbar.

Entering Data in a Table

You can add data to your table in either Form or Table view, as long as you're in Edit or CoEdit mode (the word *Edit* or *CoEdit* appears on the status bar). You can add as many records as you wish at any time using the techniques described in the following sections.

Adding and Saving Records

If you've just created the table structure and the table is empty, you can begin filling in the first record. Enter the contents of the current field (or leave it blank). Move to the next field by clicking on it with your mouse, or by pressing ↵, Tab, or →. Continue entering information and moving to each field in the new record. To move back one field in the record, click on it with your mouse, or press Shift-Tab or ←.

If the table already has records filled in, add your new entries to the end of the table. Press End to move to the last record in the table. If you're in Table view, press ↓ to insert a new blank record below the current record. If you are in Form view, press PgDn or Ctrl-PgDn, or click on Ctrl-PgDn Next on the Speedbar to insert a new blank record.

To save your work, simply choose **DO-IT!** from the menu bar or press the Do-It! key, F2, to return to View mode. The main menu bar reappears on the screen, and the word *Main* reappears on the status bar. In this mode, you can only view data. But you can still toggle between Table view and Form view by pressing F7 or clicking on the Speedbar indicator.

Entering Dates

When entering data into a date field, you can use any of the following formats:

FORMAT	EXAMPLE
mm/dd/yy	2/5/93
dd-Mon-yy	5-Feb-93
dd.mm.yy	5.2.93

Regardless of the format you use to type in dates, Paradox automatically *displays* all the dates in the table in the currently defined format. You'll learn how to change the appearance of dates in Chapter 5.

Entering Negative Numbers

You can enter a negative number into a field in either of two formats:

- Precede the number with a minus sign (or hyphen).
- Enclose the number in parentheses.

For example, both −500 and (500) are interpreted as negative 500. Regardless of which format you use to type in the negative number, Paradox shows it in whatever format (and color) is currently defined for the display of negative numbers. You'll learn how to change the appearance of numbers in Chapter 5.

Entering Data in Memo and Binary Fields

To enter data into a memo field, you need to switch to Field view. The basic steps are as follows:

1. Move the cursor to the memo field (it doesn't matter if you're in Table view or Form view).
2. Press the Field view key, Alt-F5, or Ctrl-f, or double-click the mouse button. A small window appears, as shown in the left half of Figure 4.5.
3. Enter the contents of the memo field, following the guidelines described after these steps.
4. Choose **DO-IT!** or the press the Do-It! key, F2, to return to Table or Form view.

When typing data into a memo field, you use the same basic techniques that you use with word processors. Press ↵ only to end a paragraph, a short line, or to insert a blank line. In other words, type the body of a paragraph as though it were one long line, and let Paradox automatically wrap each line within the window.

ENTERING DATA IN A TABLE

FIGURE 4.5

Pressing Alt-F5 or Ctrl-f or double-clicking while the cursor is in a memo field opens a window for entering and editing data in a memo field.

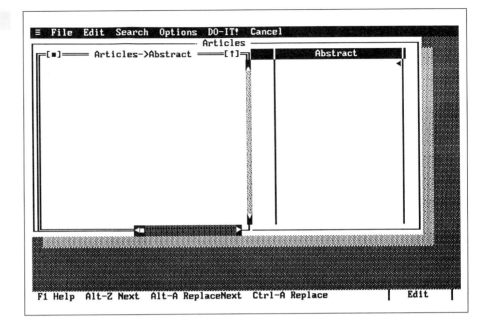

For example, if you were typing the sample memo field entry shown in Figure 4.6, you would press ↵ to end the first short line, and again to insert the blank line beneath it. Then you would type the entire first paragraph, press ↵ at the end of the last line, and press ↵ again to insert the blank line beneath. Finally, type the second paragraph, and press ↵ at the end.

FIGURE 4.6

When you enter text into a memo field, Paradox automatically wraps words from one line to the next. Press ↵ to insert fixed line breaks to create blank lines or to end a paragraph.

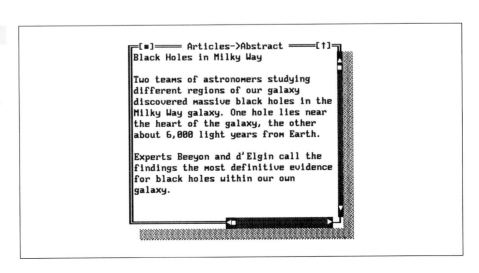

If you've defined a BLOB editor for binary fields, you can enter data into a binary field in Field view (move the cursor to the field, and then press Alt-F5 or Ctrl-f, or double-click on the field with your mouse). Defining a BLOB editor is described in Appendix D.

Typing Special Characters

When typing text into an alphanumeric or memo field, you can use any character on your keyboard. In addition to these characters, you can type foreign and other special characters from the IBM PC Extended Character Set. Table 4.1 lists these special characters. Note that you cannot type a foreign currency symbol into a numeric or currency field.

To type one of the special characters shown in Table 4.1, hold down the Alt key while typing the character's three-digit code on the numeric keypad. You must use the numbers on the numeric keypad, not the numbers at the top of the keyboard. For example, if you want to type a Yen character (¥) into an alphanumeric or memo field, hold down the Alt key, type 157 on the numeric keypad, then release the Alt key.

CAUTION Your printer will print the characters that appear on the screen only if it is capable of printing them and is set to the same symbol set. For instance, to have an Hewlett Packard LaserJet print the characters shown in Table 4.1, the printer must be set to the PC-8 symbol set. See your printer manual for information about choosing a symbol set.

Data-Entry Shortcuts

You can type the complete entry for each field and fill in as many records as you wish following the basic techniques described in the previous sections. But Paradox also offers various shortcuts to speed the process of adding records to a table.

TABLE 4.1: Special Characters from the IBM PC Extended Character Set

CODE	CHAR	CODE	CHAR	CODE	CHAR	CODE	CHAR
128	Ç	160	á	192	└	224	α
129	ü	161	í	193	┴	225	ß
130	é	162	ó	194	┬	226	Γ
131	â	163	ú	195	├	227	π
132	ä	164	ñ	196	─	228	Σ
133	à	165	Ñ	197	┼	229	σ
134	å	166	ª	198	╞	230	μ
135	ç	167	º	199	╟	231	τ
136	ê	168	¿	200	╚	232	Φ
137	ë	169	⌐	201	╔	233	Θ
138	è	170	¬	202	╩	234	Ω
139	ï	171	½	203	╦	235	δ
140	î	172	¼	204	╠	236	∞
141	ì	173	¡	205	═	237	∞
142	Ä	174	«	206	╬	238	ε
143	Å	175	»	207	╧	239	∩
144	É	176	░	208	╨	240	≡
145	æ	177	▒	209	╤	241	±
146	Æ	178	▓	210	╥	242	≥
147	ô	179	│	211	╙	243	≤
148	ö	180	┤	212	╘	244	⌠
149	ò	181	╡	213	╒	245	⌡
150	û	182	╢	214	╓	246	÷
151	ù	183	╖	215	╫	247	≈
152	ÿ	184	╕	216	╪	248	°
153	Ö	185	╣	217	┘	249	·
154	Ü	186	║	218	┌	250	·
155	¢	187	╗	219	█	251	√
156	£	188	╝	220	▄	252	n
157	¥	189	╜	221	▌	253	2
158	₧	190	╛	222	▐		
159	ƒ	191	┐	223	▀		

Duplicating Data from the Previous Record

You can copy the data from one field in the previous record to the same field in the current record by pressing the Ditto key, Ctrl-d. For example, if the City field for the previous record was Los Angeles, and the City field for the current record should also be Los Angeles, you can just press Ctrl-d instead of typing the field entry in the current record. Paradox will fill in the information from the previous record in that field.

Shortcuts for Entering Dates

In addition to typing dates in any of the date formats described eariler, you can also use the following shortcuts to enter a date in a date field:

- Omit the month and year at the end of the field if they are the current month and year. Paradox will automatically fill in the current month and year when you press ↵, Tab, or → or click with the mouse to move to the next field.

- Press the spacebar at the beginning of the day, month, or year part of the field to have Paradox automatically fill in the current day, month, or year. Pressing the spacebar three times at the beginning of a date field automatically fills the field with the entire current system date (as determined by the DOS DATE command).

- Type just the first letter (or two) for the three-letter month abbreviation and then press the spacebar. Paradox automatically fills in the rest of the abbreviation. (Of course, this shortcut isn't much use for Mar, May, Jun, and Jul, since you would need to type all three letters to identify the month.)

Shortcuts for Entering Numbers

You can also use several shortcuts to enter numbers into numeric and currency fields:

- When typing numbers that are greater than or equal to 1000, omit the comma. Paradox will fill it in automatically when you leave the field.

- Press the spacebar rather than type a period to enter a decimal point.

- If you omit the cents portion of a number in a currency field, Paradox automatically fills in the .00 for you when you leave the field.
- Omit the closing parenthesis when entering a negative number. For example, just type **(500** rather than **(500)**.

Using Data Entry to Enter Data

As an alternative to adding new records directly to your original table, you can use **M**odify ➤ **D**ataEntry to add new records to a temporary table. The advantage of using this option is that it eliminates the possibility that you might accidentally modify or delete existing records. In fact, no records from the original table even appear in the temporary table.

To use the DataEntry feature, follow these steps:

1. If the table you want to modify isn't in the current directory, use **T**ools ➤ **M**ore ➤ **D**irectory to switch to the table's directory.
2. Choose **M**odify ➤ **D**ataEntry. The DataEntry dialog box appears.
3. Specify the table to which you want to add data, in the same way that you specify which table you want to view (as described in the section about opening a table, at the beginning of this chapter). A temporary table named Entry, containing only the fields from the table you specified, appears.
4. Add new data using any of the techniques described in this chapter.
5. When you're finished typing in new records, choose **DO-IT!** or press the Do-It! key, F2, to save your new records (or choose **C**ancel ➤ **Y**es if you change your mind and want to abandon the new records).

As soon as you save the new records, Paradox copies them from the Entry table to the end of the table you specified.

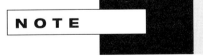

You can still switch between Form view and Table view using F7 when you use the DataEntry feature.

Editing a Table

Few of us can type a bunch of new records into a table without making a mistake. You usually need to make changes and corrections as you go along. You'll also probably need to edit the information in a table just to bring it up to date. For example, if one of your customers moves to a new address, you'll need to replace the old address in your table with the new one.

You can easily change the contents of any field, in any record, at any time. The following sections describe how to move to the field you want to edit and the techniques you can use to make changes. Table 4.2 summarizes the techniques for moving the cursor and making changes.

TABLE 4.2: Keyboard Techniques in Table View and Form View

ACTION	KEYPRESS
Next field	→, Tab, or ↵
Previous field	← or Shift-Tab
First field	Ctrl-Home
Last field	Ctrl-End
Previous record	↑ (Table view); Ctrl-PgUp (Form view)
Next record	↓ (Table view); Ctrl-PgDn (Form view)
First record	Home
Last record	End
Left one screenful	Ctrl-← (Table view)
Right one screenful	Ctrl-→ (Table view)
Up one screenful	PgUp
Down one screenful	PgDn
Insert new record	Insert (Ins)
Delete character	Backspace

TABLE 4.2: Keyboard Techniques in Table View and Form View (continued)

ACTION	KEYPRESS
Delete field contents	Ctrl-Backspace
Delete current record	Delete (Del)
Undo most recent changes	Ctrl-u
Toggle Form/Table view	F7
Save changes	F2 (or **DO-IT!** from menu bar)

Moving through Fields and Records

You can move through fields and records using the arrow and other special keys listed in Table 4.2. If you attempt to scroll past the extreme end (or beginning) of the table, Paradox will beep. In fact, if you hold down one of those keys for too long, you'll hear lots of beeping. But no need to panic; the beeping will stop in a moment and everything will be just fine.

With a mouse, you can also use the scroll bars at the right side and bottom of the table to scroll through your table. Figure 4.7 summarizes the basic scroll-bar techniques in Table view.

Scroll bars also appear in Form view, and you can use the same basic techniques to scroll up and down, left or right within a single form. However, unlike Table view, in Form view the scroll bars won't move you to a new record. Instead, use PgDn to move to the first field in the next record, or PgUp to move to the last field in the previous record. You can also use Ctrl-PgDn and Ctrl-PgUp to move to the current field in the next or previous record. Optionally, you can click on the description of these keys on the Speedbar.

You can also use Image ➤ Zoom to quickly locate a particular field, record, or value in a table. This feature is described in the next chapter.

FIGURE 4.7

Using the scroll bars to scroll through fields and records in Table view

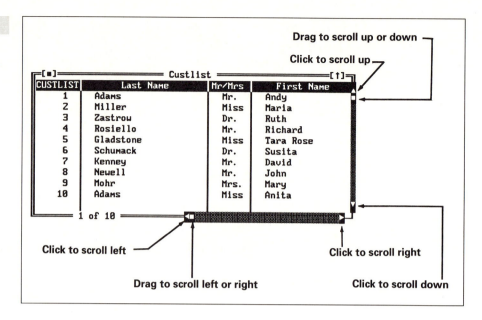

As you scroll through records, you'll notice that the indicator near the lower-left corner of the Table view or Form view window changes to reflect the current record number, which indicates the record's position in the table. For instance, *1 of 100* means that the cursor is currently on the first record of a table that contains 100 records.

Editing the Contents of a Field

After you get the cursor into the field you want to change, you can press Backspace to erase each character of the existing text, or press Ctrl-Backspace to erase all the text in the field, then type the new text.

 Remember that you need to be in Edit mode (F9) or CoEdit mode (Alt-F9) to make any changes to a record.

If you want to make changes to the existing text, you need to switch to *Field view*. In this view, the ←, →, and other cursor-movement keys move the cursor within the field, rather than moving the cursor from field to field.

To switch to Field view, move the cursor to the field you want to edit and press the Field view key, Alt-F5, or press Ctrl-f, or double-click the mouse. The blinking cursor becomes a small box, indicating that you are in Field view. Now you can use the keys listed in Table 4.3 to make changes to the current field.

TABLE 4.3: Keyboard Techniques in Field View

ACTION	KEYPRESS
Start Field view	Alt-F5 or Ctrl-f (also double-click)
One character left	←
One character right	→
First character in field	Home
Last character in field	End
One word left	Ctrl-←
One word right	Ctrl-→
Up one line in memo field	↑
Down one line in memo field	↓
Toggle Insert/Overwrite mode	Insert (Ins)
Delete character at cursor	Delete (Del)
Delete character to left of cursor	Backspace
Exit Field view	↵ (also single click); F2 in memo field

While you're in Field view, you can press the Insert (Ins) key to toggle between Insert and Typeover modes. In Insert mode, any new text you type is inserted at the current cursor position. In Typeover mode, any new text you type replaces existing text. A small box is displayed above the blinking cursor bar when you are in Typeover mode.

When you're finished making changes, press ↵ (except in memo fields press F2) or click the mouse to exit Field view. You'll be back in the normal Edit mode. The arrow and other special keys return to their normal functions to allow you to move through fields and records.

Undoing Changes to a Record

If you make some changes to a record, then change your mind, you can undo your changes by choosing **Undo ➤ Y**es from the menus, or by pressing the Undo key, Ctrl-u. Note that if you're in Field view, you must press ↵ or click the mouse to leave Field view before using the Undo feature.

Undo "undoes" all the changes you've made to the current record. For example, if you change the City and State fields in a given record without making changes to another record between those changes, Undo will undo both those changes. If, on the other hand, you do change another record between the changes to the first record, Undo only undoes the most recent change. For example, if you change the City field in Record 2, then make changes to another record, then go back and change the State field in Record 2, Undo will only undo the change to the State field in Record 2.

Undo operates differently in the Edit and CoEdit modes. In Edit mode, you can use Undo repeatedly to undo a series of changes, back to the last time you saved by choosing DO-IT! or pressing the F2 key. For example, if you change Record 1, then Record 2, then Record 3, Undo will first undo the changes to Record 3. Using Undo again would undo the changes to Record 2. Using Undo a third time would then undo the changes to Record 1.

In CoEdit mode, you can only undo the most recent changes to one record. For example, if you make changes to Record 2, then to Record 3, Undo will only allow you to undo the changes you made to Record 3. Using Undo a second time would have no effect.

EDITING A TABLE

NOTE

Undo only allows you to undo the most recent change in CoEdit mode because Paradox saves your changes to disk each time you move to a new record. There's really no way for Paradox to keep track of all the changes when several users are coediting a table on a network. For example, if you make some changes to a record, which are saved to disk, then another user deletes that record, you won't be able to undo your changes at all, since the record will no longer exist. See Appendix C for more information about the differences between Edit and CoEdit modes.

Editing a Memo Field

To edit text in a memo field, move the cursor to the field and switch to Field view (Alt-F5 or Ctrl-f, or double-click the mouse). You'll be taken to the same window you used for entering the memo, which is actually the Paradox Editor. There you can select, cut, copy, delete, and move large blocks of text. Working with text in the Editor is covered in Chapter 17.

When you're finished editing the memo, choose **DO-IT!** or press the Do-It! key, F2, to save your changes. Optionally, you can choose **C**ancel ➤ **Y**es from the menu to abandon your changes.

Inserting Records

You need not be too concerned about the order in which you enter records into a table, because you can easily sort the records into any order you wish at any time. Furthermore, if your table structure includes key fields, Paradox instantly repositions a new record into its proper sort order as soon as you finished entering the record. Therefore, it's common practice to just keep adding new records to the bottom of the table as the need arises.

NOTE

Chapter 6 describes techniques for sorting tables. Key fields are covered in Chapter 13.

ENTERING AND EDITING TABLE DATA

If, however, you do want to insert a new record between two existing records, just move the highlight to the record that's *below* the place where you want to insert a new record and press Ins. Paradox inserts a new, blank record above the current record, as shown in Figure 4.8. In that figure, the cursor was in the record for Schumack before pressing Ins to insert a new record, so the new blank record appears above Schumack. Paradox moves the cursor to that new blank record, so you can start entering its contents immediately.

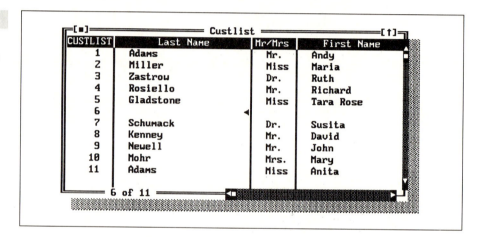

FIGURE 4.8

Pressing Ins with the cursor in the Schumack record inserts a blank record above Schumack.

Deleting Records

If you want to delete an entire record from the current table, move the highlight to the record you want to delete and press Delete (Del). The entire record is removed from the table, and Paradox instantly closes the gap between existing records.

If you inadvertently delete a record and want to "undelete" it, choose **Undo ▶ Yes** or press Ctrl-u to restore the record. If you're in the standard Edit mode, you can choose **Edit ▶ Undo** or press Ctrl-u repeatedly to restore multiple deleted records.

EDITING A TABLE

Keep in mind that you cannot undelete multiple records in CoEdit mode, because CoEdit only allows you to undo the most recent change to a table. Exercise extra caution when deleting records in the CoEdit mode.

Using the Modify Menu to Edit Data

If you know for certain that you'll want to make changes to a table as soon as you open it, you can open it in the Edit or CoEdit mode directly (by-passing View mode) by following these steps:

1. If the table you want to modify isn't in the current directory, use **T**ools ➤ **M**ore ➤ **D**irectory to switch to the table's directory.

2. Choose **M**odify ➤ **E**dit, or **M**odify ➤ **C**oEdit if you want to coedit the table with other users on a network. The Edit or CoEdit dialog box appears.

3. Specify the table that you want to edit (use any of the techniques that you use to specify the table you want to open, as described at the beginning of this chapter). The table appears on the screen, already in Edit or CoEdit mode, so you don't need to press F9 or Alt-F9 before making changes.

4. Make whatever changes you wish, using any of the techniques described earlier in this chapter.

5. When you're finished making changes, choose **DO-IT!** or press the Do-It! key, F2, to save your new records (or choose **C**ancel ➤ **Y**es if you change your mind and want to abandon the changes).

After you save your changes, you'll return to View mode, and the main menu bar will reappear at the top of the desktop.

Saving or Canceling Your Changes

After changing one or more records in a table, you can either save all those changes or abandon them. To save all the current changes to the table, choose **DO-IT!** or press the Do-It! key, F2. In Edit mode (not CoEdit mode), you can abandon all the current changes to the table by choosing **C**ancel ➤ **Y**es.

After you save or cancel your changes, you'll be returned to View mode, and the main menu bar will reappear at the top of the desktop.

Closing a Table

You must close a table in order to remove it from the desktop. If you're still in Edit or CoEdit mode, first either save or cancel your current changes as described in the preceding section. Then use any of the following methods to close the table:

- Click on the Close button in the upper-left corner of the window you want to close.
- Press the Close Active Window key, F8, to close the current window only.
- Press the Close All Windows key, Alt-F8, to close all the windows on the desktop.

You'll learn more about closing, sizing, and moving windows in the next chapter.

Summary

In this chapter, you learned about adding new data to a table and editing data in a table. Here's a quick summary of the most important techniques covered:

- If the table you want to open is not in the current directory, use **T**ools ➤ **M**ore ➤ **D**irectory to switch to the table's directory before opening it.
- To open a table, choose **V**iew, enter the name of the table, and then press ↵ or click on OK. Alternatively, click on OK, then double-click on the name of the table you want to open.

SUMMARY

- To add new data to a table or edit its contents, switch to Edit mode (F9). If you want to coedit the table with other users on a network, switch to CoEdit mode (Alt-F9).

- To switch between Table view (multiple records) and Form view (one record at a time), press the F7 key.

- To add new data to the bottom of the table in Edit or CoEdit mode, press End to move to the last record, then insert a new blank record by pressing ↓ (in Table view) or by pressing PgDn or Ctrl-PgDn (in Form view). Then fill in the record. Press ↵, Tab, or → after typing the contents of each field.

- To enter or edit data in a memo field, press Alt-F5 or Ctrl-f when the cursor is on the memo field, or double-click on the memo field. After typing the field's entry, choose **DO-IT!** or press the Do-It! key (F2) to save it and return to Table or Form view.

- To make changes to the contents of a field, switch to Field view (press Alt-F5 or Ctrl-f, or double-click). After making your changes, press ↵ (or press F2 in a memo field) to leave Field view and restore the normal function of the arrow keys and other special keys.

- To insert a new blank record above the current record, press Ins.

- To delete the current record from a table, press Del.

- To undo a recent change or deletion, choose **Undo ➤ Yes** or press the Undo key (Ctrl-u).

- To save your new or modified records, choose **DO-IT!** or press the Do-It! key (F2).

- To close a table, click on the Close button in the upper-left corner of the window, or press the Close Active Window key (F8). To close all the open windows on the desktop, press the Close All Windows key (Alt-F8).

CHAPTER 5

Viewing and Validating Your Data

fast TRACK

- **To choose the active window**   89

    click anywhere within that window. If the window is totally obscured, choose ≡ (System menu) ➤ **W**indow then choose the name of the window you want, or choose ≡ ➤ **N**ext (or press Ctrl-F4) to cycle through the windows on the desktop.

- **To resize the active window**   90

    drag the lower-right corner of the window in whatever direction you wish, then release the mouse button. Or choose ≡ ➤ **S**ize/Move (or press Ctrl-F5), hold down the Shift key, then use the ↑, ↓, →, and ← keys to size the window. Press ↵ when you're finished.

- **To maximize or restore the active window**   91

    click on the Maximize/Restore button in the upper-right corner of the window. Or choose ≡ ➤ **M**aximize/Restore (or press Shift-F5).

- **To arrange multiple windows on the desktop**   91

    choose ≡ ➤ **D**esktop ➤ **T**ile or ≡ ➤ **D**esktop ➤ **C**ascade.

- **To close the active window**   91

    save any changes (if you wish) by choosing **DO-IT!** or pressing F2. Then click on the Close button or press F8. To close all open windows, press Alt-F8.

- **To choose a button in a dialog box**   93

    press ↵ to choose the default (highlighted) button. To choose another button, click on it, or press Tab or Shift-Tab until the button you want is highlighted, then press ↵. You can press Esc to choose the Cancel button.

CHAPTER 5 87

- **To zoom to a specific field or record** 94

    choose Image ➤ Zoom ➤ Field or Image ➤ Zoom ➤ Record and select a field name or enter a record number.

- **To zoom to a record with a particular value** 95

    press Ctrl-z (if the cursor is in the field you want to search), or choose Image ➤ Zoom ➤ Value, then press → or ← to move to the field you want to search and press ↵. Type a value into the Zoom dialog box (using the .. and @ wildcards if desired) and press ↵. To search for the next occurrence of that value, press Alt-z.

- **To use the Image menu to customize the appearance of a table in Table view** 97

    choose TableSize to temporarily adjust the length of the table, ColumnSize to change the width of a column, Format to set a display format, or Move to rearrange columns. To save the ColumnSize, Format, or Move settings, choose Image ➤ KeepSet.

- **To define validity checks for data entry** 109

    switch to Edit mode (press F9 or choose Modify ➤ Edit from the main menu bar), and then use ValCheck ➤ Define. Move the cursor to the appropriate column and press ↵. From the submenu, select the type of validity check you want to define: LowValue, HighValue, Default, TableLookup, Picture, Required, or Auto. To save validity checks, choose DO-IT! from the Edit menu or press F2.

THIS chapter focuses on techniques for viewing your data and making data entry faster and more accurate. You'll learn how to manage windows and dialog boxes on your desktop and how to quickly move the cursor to a specific record, field, or value. You'll also discover how to customize the appearance of a table without changing its actual structure. And finally, you'll explore validity checks, which speed data entry and help prevent mistakes.

Managing Windows on the Desktop

Tables, the Paradox Editor, memo field entries, and many other Paradox objects are displayed in *windows*. You can have many windows open on the desktop at the same time. However, only one of the windows is *active*.

The active window is always in the forefront, and may overlap or completely obscure other windows. An active window also has these indicators:

- Scroll bars and double lines around the borders
- The blinking cursor
- A Close button and a Maximize/Restore button (↑)

There are many techniques that you can use to choose, move, size, and close windows, as described in the sections that follow. Figure 5.1 shows an active window and the elements you can use to manipulate the window.

MANAGING WINDOWS ON THE DESKTOP

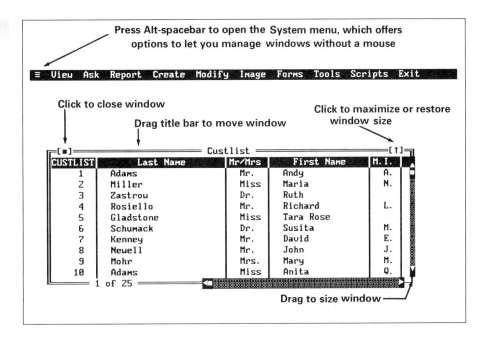

FIGURE 5.1

An active window, with a Close button, a Maximize/Restore button, double lines on the left and upper borders, and scroll bars on the right and lower borders

Windows are displayed somewhat differently in Paradox 4.5's new Full Screen User Interface (described in Chapter 2). Also, the System menu (≡) includes only the choices Interface and About; it doesn't include the window-manipulation commands.

Choosing a Window

When two or more windows are open on the desktop, you can use any of the following techniques to make one of them the active window:

- Click anywhere within the window you want to make active.
- If the window you want is totally obscured, choose ≡ (System menu) ➤ **W**indow, then choose the name of the window.

To open the System menu, click on the ≡ symbol in the menu or press Alt-spacebar.

- Press F3 to cycle backward through the open windows, or press F4 to cycle forward. The windows cycle in the order they were opened.
- Choose ≡ ➤ **N**ext or press Ctrl-F4 to cycle through the windows currently on the desktop.

Moving a Window

You can move a window to a new location on the screen by using either of the following techniques:

- Put the mouse pointer anywhere on the title bar and drag the window to where you want it to appear.
- Choose ≡ ➤ **S**ize/Move or press Ctrl-F5, then use the arrow keys to move the window. Press ↵ when the window is where you want it.

Sizing a Window

To change the size of the active window, use either of these methods:

- Drag the lower-right corner of the window to reduce or enlarge the window, then release the mouse button. If you drag the corner up or down, the window changes size in the vertical plane only. Drag it left or right to change the size in the horizontal plane. To resize the window in both planes, drag its corner in or out diagonally.
- Choose ≡ ➤ **S**ize/Move or press Ctrl-F5, then hold down the Shift key while using the arrow keys to size the window. Press ↵ when the window is sized as you want it.

Maximizing and Restoring a Window

You can expand the active window to full-screen size (*maximize* it) using any of these techniques:

- Click on the Maximize/Restore button (↑) near the upper-right corner of the window, or double-click anywhere on the top of the window's border.
- Choose ≡ ➤ **M**aximize/Restore.
- Press the Maximize/Restore key, Shift-F5.

When the window is maximized, the Maximize/Restore button changes to a double-headed arrow to indicate that it can now be used to *restore* the window to its previous size. To restore a window, click on the button, use ≡ ➤ **M**aximize/Restore or press Shift-F5.

Tiling and Cascading Windows

Besides arranging windows individually by sizing and moving them yourself, you can have Paradox arrange multiple windows on the desktop. Paradox can arrange the windows in either a *tiled* or a *cascading* display. When the windows are tiled, each is sized and arranged so that none of them overlap. When you cascade windows, the windows overlap, but you can see the title bar at the top of each window.

To tile or cascade windows, choose ≡ ➤ **D**esktop, then choose either **T**ile or **C**ascade.

Closing a Window

If you no longer need a particular window and want to unclutter the desktop, you can close the active window using any of these four techniques:

- Click the Close button in the upper-left corner of the window.
- Choose ≡ ➤ **C**lose.
- Press the Close Active Window key, F8, to close the current window only.
- Press the Close All Windows key, Alt-F8, to close all the windows on the desktop.

CHAPTER 5
VIEWING AND VALIDATING YOUR DATA

NOTE Before you close a window that shows a table or record in Edit or CoEdit mode, save your changes (choose DO-IT! or press F2) or cancel your changes to return to View mode.

When you close a window that shows a table in Table view, Paradox automatically closes any open form or memo field editing windows associated with that table. For example, if you opened a table, switched to Form view, and then double-clicked on a memo field, you would see three windows on the screen, like those in Figure 5.2. If you then made the Table view window active and closed it, all three windows would disappear from the screen.

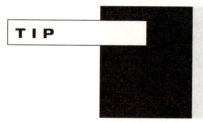

TIP If you share data with other users on a network, or have TSR (terminate and stay resident) programs running while you're using Paradox, other users or programs might occasionally display messages on your screen. To remove these messages, choose ≡ ➤ Desktop ➤ Redraw.

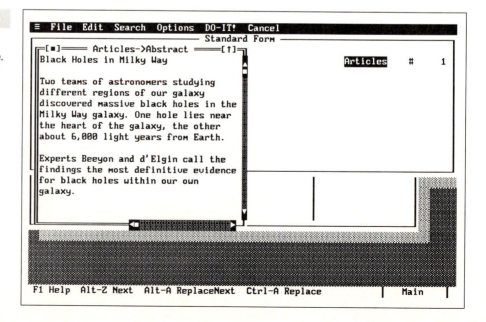

FIGURE 5.2
Three open windows from the Articles table. Switching to the Table view window and clicking on the Close button removes all three windows from the screen at once.

Using Dialog Boxes

A dialog box appears whenever you choose an option that requires more information from you. For example, when you select View to open a table, the View dialog box appears.

If you don't like where Paradox has placed a dialog box on your screen, you can move it. Position the mouse pointer on the top border of the dialog box and drag it to a new location on the screen.

You can select buttons in a dialog box by using any of the following methods:

- Click on the button with your mouse.
- Press ↵ to choose the *default button* (indicated by a brightened name on a color screen or arrows on a monochrome screen).
- Press Tab (to move forward) or Shift-Tab (to move backward) until the button you want is highlighted, then press ↵.
- Press the Esc key to choose the Cancel button.

Figure 5.3 shows the ways you can work with a dialog box.

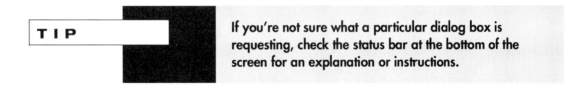

TIP If you're not sure what a particular dialog box is requesting, check the status bar at the bottom of the screen for an explanation or instructions.

Searching for a Field, Record, or Value

In a large table, it can take time to scroll around to find a particular record. Instead, you can use Paradox's Zoom feature to search for a specific field, record, or value.

VIEWING AND VALIDATING YOUR DATA

FIGURE 5.3

Moving a dialog box and choosing command buttons

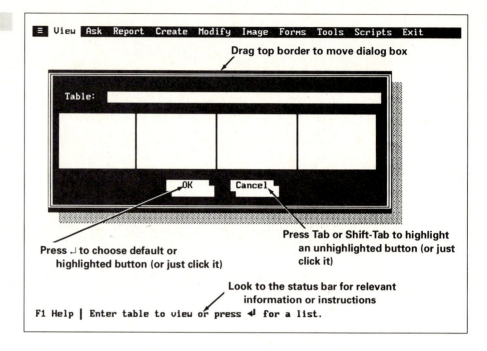

Finding a Field or Record

To search for a record or field, choose **I**mage ➤ **Z**oom. You see this submenu:

Choose **F**ield if you want to move to a particular field in the current rec-ord. Paradox displays a list of field names. Select the field by double-clicking on its name. Alternatively, you can highlight a field name (by clicking the mouse, using the arrow keys, or typing the first few letters of the name), then press ↵ or choose OK. The cursor moves to the field you selected.

If you know the position number of a record, you can move to it by choosing **R**ecord from the Zoom submenu. Enter the record number, then press ↵ or choose OK. The cursor moves to the record you selected.

NOTE You can also use queries to help narrow the search for data that you want to locate. This is especially handy when you're editing large tables. See Chapter 7 for information about using queries.

Searching for a Value in a Record

Another way to find a particular record in your table is to search for a value in any field in that record. The term *value* simply refers to the contents of a field. For example, the Last Name field might contain the value "Smith" in one record and the value "Adams" in another record. You can search for values in Table or Form view, and in either View or Edit mode.

The basic technique for searching for a particular value in a field is as follows:

1. Choose **I**mage ➤ **Z**oom ➤ **V**alue. You'll see the prompt:

   Move to the column you want to search in, then press ↵...

2. Press ← or → to move the cursor to the field or column in which you want to search, then press ↵. You'll see the Zoom dialog box:

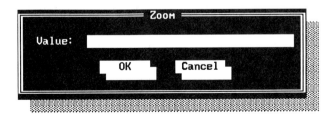

VIEWING AND VALIDATING YOUR DATA

> **T I P**
>
> As a shortcut for steps 1 and 2, you can first position the cursor to the field you want to search (excluding the leftmost column, which contains record numbers), then press the Zoom key (Ctrl-z) to see the Zoom dialog box.

3. Type the value you want to find. You can include text and any combination of the .. and @ wildcards, as described after these steps. If you have already entered a search value for this particular field, that text will appear in the dialog box. In this case, you can use one of these techniques to enter the search value:

    - To use the same search value, press ↵ or choose OK.
    - To clear all the existing text, press Ctrl-Backspace. Then type a new search value.
    - To edit the value, use the ← and → keys or your mouse to position the cursor. Then you can type in additional text, erase characters using the Backspace key, or replace text by pressing Ins before typing.

4. Press ↵ or choose OK. The cursor moves to the next record with a matching field value. If you're searching the Field view of a memo field, the cursor moves to the next matching word in that same memo field. (The next section provides details on searching memo fields.)

5. If this record or word isn't the one you're looking for, you can press Alt-z to search for the next occurrence of that search value. You can continue to search for the next occurrence by pressing Alt-z repeatedly until you've seen all the records in the table that match the search value.

If the value you're looking for isn't found, the cursor doesn't move, and the message

   Match not found

appears near the lower-right corner of the screen.

When entering a value in the Zoom dialog box, you can use the .. and @ wildcards. A .. matches any series of characters. A @ matches any single character. When you use wildcards, uppercase and lowercase characters are treated the same.

For example, if you type **Smith** as the value to search for, your search will find only the word *Smith*. However, if you enter **..Smith..**, Paradox will find *Smith, SMITH, smithy, sMiTh, goldsmith, Smithsonian*, and so on. A search value of **Sm@th** (using a single-character wildcard) will find *Smith, smith, smyth, SMITH,* and probably little else. A search for a value such as **J..n** (using the series wildcard in the middle of a word) will find *Johnson, Jan, Jordan, jargon, Jackson,* and any other word or phrase beginning with *J* and ending with *n*.

Searching for Text in Memo Fields

To search through records to find text in a memo field, move the cursor to the memo field, then press Ctrl-z. Using the .. wildcard, type the word or phrase you want to find. For example, type **..galaxy..** to search for the word *galaxy*. Then choose OK or press ↵. The cursor moves to the first record that has that word or phrase in its memo field. Press Alt-z to repeat the search and locate the next record that contains that word or phrase.

If you want to search for the next occurrence of a term within the same record, you must first open the memo field for viewing by double-clicking on it or pressing Alt-F5 or Ctrl-f. With the memo field editing window on the screen, pressing Ctrl-z and Alt-z has Paradox search for a word or phrase within that memo field only. If you want to search through additional records, you must first close the memo field window by pressing F2 or by clicking on its Close button.

Customizing Table View

Paradox offers many ways to customize the appearance of of your table on the screen without changing the actual structure or contents of the table. For example, you can change the table's size or column width; customize the appearance of numbers, currency, and dates; and rearrange the columns on the screen. The following sections describe the changes you can make to Table view.

> **NOTE** You can also change the appearance of a record in Form view. See Chapter 9 for information about designing custom forms.

Before you can change the appearance of a table, that table's window must be active and in Table view. The changes you make to the table display last only while the window remains on the desktop (or until you change Table view again), unless you save them by using the **Image** **KeepSet** option, as discussed later in this chapter.

Changing the Table Size

When several tables are displayed simultaneously on the screen, you may want to alter the size of some of them to make it easier to view them. Along with changing the window's size (using the techniques described earlier in this chapter), you can also lengthen or shorten a table.

Increasing or decreasing the table length does not change the number of records in the table. It just changes the number of records that you can see at once. For example, if you shorten the display to two records, only two records at a time will appear on the screen.

To lengthen or shorten a table, use the following procedure:

1. Choose **Image** from the menu bar to see the Image menu:

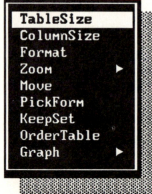

CUSTOMIZING TABLE VIEW

2. Choose **T**ableSize. You'll see the prompt

    Use ↑ and ↓ to change table size, then press ↵.

3. Press ↑ to remove one row from the display, or press ↓ to add one row. Each time you press ↑ or ↓ the table will shorten or lengthen another row.

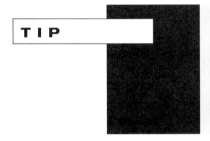

TIP As a shortcut for shortening the table to two records, the minimum that can appear in Table view, press Home. To quickly lengthen the table to the maximum height that your monitor allows, press End. And remember, you can always press Esc to cancel the resizing for the table and return to the Image menu.

4. When the table is the size you want, press ↵.

After you've changed the table's size this way, you can still use the arrow or PgUp and PgDn keys, or the scroll bars on the window, to scroll through all the records in the table.

Changing the Column Width

The default display width of a field in Table view depends on the type of field and the name of the field. Changing the column width is easiest if you have a mouse. Simply drag the field's right vertical border, as shown in Figure 5.4.

You can also use Image ➤ **C**olumnSize to change a column's width. When you select this option, you see the prompt

   Move to the column you want to resize, then press ↵...

Use the → or ← key to move the cursor to the column you want to resize, then press ↵. The prompt changes to

   Now use → and ← to change width, then press ↵.

Use the → or ← keys to change the column size one character at a time. To make the column the minimum width of one character, press Home. To make the column its maximum width (as set in the table structure), press End.

FIGURE 5.4

Resizing a column with the mouse

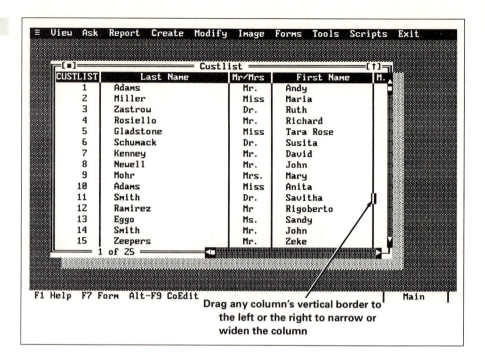

Drag any column's vertical border to the left or the right to narrow or widen the column

If you press Esc, Paradox cancels the resizing for the current column. You can then press → or ← to resize a different column, or press Esc again to return to the Image menu.

You can change the width of any column on the screen. However, there are a few limitations to changing the column sizes:

- The minimum width of a column is 1 character.
- The width of a numeric or currency field is limited to the width of the field name, to a maximum of 25 characters.
- The maximum width of a date field is 14 characters, unless the field name itself is longer.
- The maximum width of an alphanumeric field is limited to the width defined in the table structure, to a maximum of 73 characters.

CUSTOMIZING TABLE VIEW

When you resize a column or table, Paradox will beep if you reach the maximum or minimum limits. If you make a numeric or currency column too narrow for its numbers, asterisks appear in place of the numbers in the column (until you widen the column).

Formatting Numeric Fields

You can modify the display of all the numbers within a column in Table view by following these steps:

1. Choose **Image** ➤ Format. You'll see the prompt

   Move to the field you want to reformat, then press ↵...

2. Press the → or ← key to move to the numeric field (the column) you want to change, then press ↵. You'll see this submenu:

3. Select the format you want from the submenu:

   - **General**: Each number in the column appears with as many decimal places as accuracy requires (within the limits of the number of decimal places you specify). For example, with two decimal places defined, 4747.123 appears as *4747.12*, but 4747, with no decimal portion, appears as *4747*.

   - **Fixed:** Sets a fixed number of decimal places for the numbers in the column, even if the value does not need that many decimal places. If you specify five decimal places, for example, the number 4747 appears as *4747.00000*. Similarly, the number 4747.0004 appears as *4747.00040*.

   - **Comma:** Displays commas to separate every third power of ten (thousands, millions, billions, and so on). For example, if you choose two decimal places, the value 4747 appears as *4,747.00*.

VIEWING AND VALIDATING YOUR DATA

- **Scientific:** Displays numbers in exponential format. For example, if you choose two decimal places, 4747.0004 appears as *4.75e+03*. Paradox can store very large numbers in the range of $\pm 10^{-307}$ to $\pm 10^{308}$, with up to 15 significant digits.

4. After you choose a format, you'll see this dialog box:

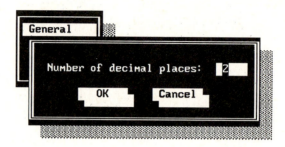

Press ↵ or click on OK to accept the number of decimal places shown, or type a number between 0 and 15, then press ↵ or choose OK.

Table 5.1 presents several numbers and their corresponding appearance in each numeric format after specifying two decimal places or five decimal places.

TABLE 5.1: Examples of Numeric Formats

VALUE: 4747				
DECIMALS	GENERAL	FIXED	COMMA	SCIENTIFIC
2 Places:	4747	4747.00	4,747.00	4.75e+03
5 Places:	4747	4747.00000	4,747.00000	4.74700e+03
VALUE: 4747.123				
DECIMALS	GENERAL	FIXED	COMMA	SCIENTIFIC
2 Places:	4747.12	4747.12	4,747.12	4.75e+03
5 Places:	4747.123	4747.12300	4,747.12300	4.74712e+03

TABLE 5.1: Examples of Numeric Formats (continued)

VALUE: 4747.0004				
DECIMALS	GENERAL	FIXED	COMMA	SCIENTIFIC
2 Places:	4747	4747.00	4,747.00	4.75e+03
5 Places:	4747.0004	4747.00040	4,747.00040	4.74700e+03
VALUE: −4747.0004				
Decimals	General	Fixed	Comma	Scientific
2 Places:	−4747	−4747.00	(4,747.00)	−4.75+e03
5 Places:	−4747.0004	−4747.00040	(4,747.00040)	−4.74700e+03

If a column is too narrow to display a number, the number appears as a series of asterisks (*****). To remedy this, widen the column, as described earlier in this chapter. A number might also appear as asterisks if any portion of it lies off the edge of the screen. Scrolling the screen will bring the number onto the display.

Formatting Date Fields

To choose another format for a date field, use **Image ➤ Format**. Move to the date field (the column) that you want to reformat and press ↵. You'll see this submenu:

Choose an option, and the dates will now appear in the format you selected.

Rearranging Columns

Rearranging the order of the columns displayed on the screen is often handy when you want to focus on just a few columns of a wide table. For example, suppose you need to update the Start Date and Credit Limit fields in the Custlist table we've used as an example in previous chapters. In this case, it would be convenient to display the Last Name, First Name, Start Date, and Credit Limit columns next to each other.

You can't change the position of the column containing the table name and record numbers.

Here are the steps for rearranging columns in Table view:

1. Choose **I**mage ➤ **M**ove. You'll see a list of fields from the current table:

2. Select the field that you want to move. You'll see the prompt

   Now move to the new position for the field, then press ↵.

3. Press the → or ← key to move the cursor to the field's new column position, and then press ↵.

The column containing the field you chose will appear just to the left of where you positioned the cursor. You can repeat this procedure for each column that you want to reposition. After you finish reorganizing the screen, you might want to adjust the widths of the columns.

NOTE Remember that rearranging the columns only affects the current display, not the structure of the table. Also, unless you specifically save these changes to the image (through a procedure we'll discuss in a moment), they are lost when you close the window or exit Paradox.

Quick Moves with the Rotate Key

The Rotate key, Ctrl-r, provides a quick way to move a field to the rightmost column position. To use this technique, simply position the cursor in the column you want to move and press Ctrl-r.

For example, if you position the cursor in the Mr/Mrs field of the Custlist table and press Ctrl-r, that field will disappear off the right edge of the screen, and all fields to the right will "rotate" to the left. Each time you press Ctrl-r, another field will move to the rightmost column. If you press Ctrl-r once for each field in the table (14 times for the Custlist table), the field will rotate back to its original position.

Saving and Restoring Image Settings

Unless you save them, any changes you make to the appearance of your table are lost when you close the Table view window or exit Paradox. To save the current Table view settings for the column size, data display format, or column position within the table, choose **Image ➤ KeepSet**.

NOTE Image ➤ KeepSet does not save the settings for the table size.

The new settings will overwrite the old ones, and you'll see the message

> Settings recorded ...

in the lower-right corner of the screen. The display settings are saved, but the actual structure and contents of the table remain unchanged.

If you later decide that you don't like the display settings you saved for a table, you can easily erase them and return to the original display by following these steps:

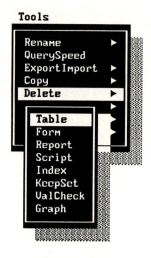

1. Choose **T**ools ➤ **D**elete. You'll see this submenu:

2. Choose **K**eepSet. The KeepSet dialog box appears.

3. Press ↵ or choose OK, then select the table that you want to restore to its original appearance (or just type in the name of the table).

4. Press ↵ or choose OK.

If the current image doesn't change immediately, close the Table view (by clicking on the Close button or pressing F8), then choose **V**iew and select the table that you just restored. The table should appear with its original display settings.

NOTE: The image settings are stored in a file with the same name as the table, but with the extension .SET (for example, Custlist.SET). Therefore, you can also erase the image settings by using the command ERASE Custlist.SET from the DOS prompt, outside Paradox.

When You See Stars, or When the Data Doesn't Fit

Occasionally, the data in a field won't fit into a column on the screen (most likely because you narrowed the column). You will see either a group of asterisks (***) or only a portion of a field, with the rest off the screen.

In a field of asterisks, the cursor will land at the start of the field when you are editing rather than at the end. To view the entire field so that you can see what you're editing, switch to Field view by pressing Alt-F5 or Ctrl-f, or by double-clicking the mouse. You can also widen the column using the techniques described earlier in this chapter.

Ensuring the Validity of Data

Paradox automatically checks the data that you enter into a table, such as ensuring that dates are valid and that numeric fields contain only numeric values. By using the **V**alCheck option on the Edit mode menu bar (and also available under **M**odify ➤ **D**ataEntry), you can set up the additional checks presented in the following sections. These help keep erroneous data from being stored in the table, which in turn reduces the need to make corrections later on.

To enter validity checks, follow this general procedure:

1. To switch to Edit mode from Table view, press F9 or click on the key notation on the Speedbar. From the main menu bar, choose **M**odify ➤ **E**dit or **M**odify ➤ **D**ataEntry to change to Edit mode.

2. Choose **V**alCheck from the menu bar. You'll see a submenu offering two choices: Define and Clear.

VIEWING AND VALIDATING YOUR DATA

3. Choose **D**efine. You'll see the prompt

   Move to the field you want to validity check, then press ↵.

4. Use the arrow keys to move the the field for which you want to define a validity check, and then press ↵. You'll see this submenu of validity checks:

5. Choose the validity check you want to use for this field. The options are described in the following sections.

6. Enter appropriate values for the validity check you chose. If you specify a value that's not the correct type, Paradox will reject your entry and prompt you to enter the correct type. For example, you cannot enter text (such as *ABC*) as a default value for a numeric field.

After you make your selections, you'll see a message at the lower-right corner of the screen indicating that the validity check was set for the field you selected. If you want to make your validity checks permanent, choose DO-IT! or press F2 to save them. Otherwise, the validity checks you defined will be erased when you exit Edit mode and will not be active the next time you use the table.

NOTE Paradox stores all validity checks on disk in a file with the same name as the table and the extension .VAL.

If you find that a validity check won't let you exit a field during data entry, see the section about getting unstuck, later in this chapter, for how to solve this problem. Getting stuck this way usually occurs either because you don't know how to enter data that's appropriate for the field or because you've specified a validity check that doesn't make sense for that field.

The following sections describe the options on the Valcheck ➤ Define submenu, with the exception of TableLookup. The TableLookup option compares the value entered into a table against a value in another table. This option is covered in Part Two, which focuses on managing multiple tables.

Defining the Lowest or Highest Acceptable Value

Selecting **ValCheck** ➤ **Define** ➤ **LowValue** allows you to set the minimum acceptable value for a field. You might want to use this option to control entries in numeric or currency fields. For example, if you want the minimum credit limit entered into a table to be $500, specify **500** as the lowest acceptable value for the field.

You can also use the LowValue option to ensure that numbers are not inadvertently typed into alphanumeric fields. For example, if you define the letter *A* as the low value for the Last Name and First Name fields, it would be impossible to enter a number into either of these fields. (Note that it would also be impossible to enter many punctuation marks, which have lower ASCII Values than A.)

After you set a LowValue validity check for a field, if someone enters a value that's too low, Paradox will reject that entry and display the following message on the status bar:

   Value no less than (*value*) is expected

To correct the entry, press Ctrl-Backspace to erase it. Then type in a value that equals or exceeds the low value indicated in the message.

Selecting **ValCheck** ➤ **Define** ➤ **HighValue** allows you to define the highest acceptable value for a field. For example, if you want the maximum credit limit entered into a table to be $15,000, specify **15000** as the highest acceptable value for the field.

After you set a HighValue validity check for a field, if someone enters a value that's too high, Paradox will reject the entry and display a message indicating the highest acceptable value for the field. Use Ctrl-Backspace to erase the entry and type in an acceptable value.

To set up a range of acceptable values for a field, define both LowValue and HighValue validity checks for that field. If you've specified both and you enter a value that's not in the proper range, you'll see this message:

Value between (*lowvalue*) and (*highvalue*) is expected

You can correct the problem by entering a new value that's within the indicated range.

Entering Default Values

Default values are those that will automatically appear in a field if the field is left blank. For example, suppose that the majority of your customers are California residents. You could set up a default value that automatically fills in the State field with the letters *CA* unless you enter something else.

To set default values, choose **ValCheck ➤ D**efine. Move the cursor to the field in which you want to set the default and press ↵. Choose **D**efault from the submenu, and then type the entry you want to appear when that field is skipped. Finally, press ↵ or choose OK.

Defining Picture Formats

A *Picture* format is a template that ensures that a consistent pattern is used for the data being entered. The most common uses of Picture formats are for social security numbers and phone numbers. For example, the Picture format ###-##-#### ensures that a social security number will be entered with hyphens in the appropriate places. The Picture format (###)###-#### is useful for phone numbers with area codes.

Other characters used in Picture formats act as default values that are automatically added to typed data. For example, the format (###)###-#### accepts only numeric digits and automatically inserts the parentheses and the hyphen.

ENSURING THE VALIDITY OF DATA

When you select **V**alCheck ➤ **D**efine ➤ **P**icture, you see this dialog box:

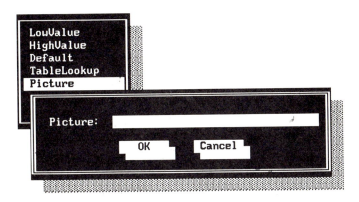

You'll also see the following prompt:

Enter a PAL picture format, (e.g., ###-##-####).

PAL stands for Paradox Application Language, which is covered in Part Three of this book.

Type the format you want to use for this field, using the following symbols:

SYMBOL	RESTRICTION
# (number sign)	Numeric digit
? (question mark)	Any letter A–Z or a–z
& (ampersand)	Any letter, automatically converting it to uppercase
@ (at sign)	Any character (no exclusions)
! (exclamation point)	Any character, automatically converting all letters to uppercase
* (asterisk)	Repeats the next symbol either indefinitely or the number of times specified by the following number (for example, *4- repeats the hyphen character four times)

SYMBOL	RESTRICTION
; (semicolon)	Interprets the following symbol as a literal character
[ ] (brackets)	Optional item, but must be complete
{ } (braces)	Specifies a group of acceptable entries
, (comma)	Separates acceptable values within a group

Here are some examples of Picture formats and the types of data that they allow (and exclude):

- #####-#### allows only a nine-digit numeric value (such as an extended zip code) into a field.

- ##### [-####] allows a nine-digit number, but the hyphen and the last four digits are optional, so either a five-digit zip code or extended nine-digit zip code will be accepted.

- &??????? requires an eight-character string to be entered into the field. Every character entered must be a letter, and the first character will be converted to uppercase.

- &*@ allows an entry of any length and converts the first letter to uppercase.

- &*19? converts the first letter to uppercase and requires 19 additional letters to be entered into the field.

Including Literal Characters in a Picture Format

To include a symbol as a *literal* character in a field, enter the semicolon character (;) before that symbol. For example, suppose you have an inventory system that uses the # symbol in part codes, as in the part number ABC-#1234. Using the picture &&&-#@ @ @ @ makes an entry such as ABC-1234 incomplete, because Paradox interprets -#@ @ @ @ as five characters to the right of the hyphen. Instead, enter the Picture format as &&&-;#@ @ @ @. Then the # symbol itself is part of the entry. When you type in **ABC1234**, Paradox displays ABC-#1234.

Specifying a Group of Acceptable Entries

By defining a Picture format with a list of acceptable entries, separated by commas and enclosed in curly braces, you can provide a list of acceptable choices in the field. For example, the Picture format {Yes,No,Maybe} permits only the letter *Y*, *N*, or *M* to be entered into an alphanumeric field, and converts the entry to *Yes*, *No*, or *Maybe*.

The formats that offer alternative choices can be *nested* to allow multiple choices with the same first letter. For example, if you define a format as

{Mon,Tue,Wed,Thu,Fri}

entering the letter *T* automatically always fills in the field as *Tue*, because *Tue* comes before *Thu* in the list of alternatives. To provide these choices, you can nest the Tuesday and Thursday options to allow the choice *ue* or *hu* within the common *T* entry:

{Mon,T{ue,hu},Wed,Fri}

Translated to English, this format specifies, "Accept *M*, *T*, *W*, or *F* entries. If a *T* is entered, accept either *u* or *h* before filling in the rest of the field."

To allow Saturday or Sunday to be entered into the field as well, you can specify that Paradox should wait for an *a* or *u* before completing an *S* entry:

{Mon,T{ue,hu},Wed,Fri,S{at,un}}

Make sure that you enter an equal number of open and closed curly braces in your Picture formats. Otherwise, they won't work properly.

Forcing an Entry

You can also use curly braces to force the entry of a particular character instead of automatically filling in the character. For example, if you use the Picture format ###-##-#### for a social security number field, Paradox will automatically fill in the two hyphens when you later enter the number. If you prefer to type in the hyphens yourself (but still want Paradox to reject any other character), you can enter the format ###{-}##{-}####. In a sense, {-} means, "The only option allowed here is a hyphen."

Cautions on Using Picture Formats

While Picture formats can be extremely helpful, you should be careful to set them up correctly. When defining Picture formats, remember to avoid using symbols that conflict with the data type of the field. For example, don't use the ? or & symbol in a numeric or currency field, since these symbols require alphabetic characters and numeric and currency fields allow only numbers. Also keep in mind that for formatting the display of numbers and dates rather than performing validity checks, you can use the Image ➤ Format options from the main and Edit mode menu bars, as described earlier in the chapter.

Once a field is defined with a Picture format, you must fill in that field exactly and completely during data entry. If you try to enter a value that doesn't match the defined Picture format during data entry, Paradox beeps and prevents you from continuing until you type in a value that does match the format. Furthermore, if you try to leave the field before the Picture format is complete, you'll see the message

> Incomplete field

You won't be able to advance to the next field until you finish typing the data or exit the field by leaving it blank. In fact, if you've also defined the field as a Required field (described next), you can't even leave it blank!

So the moral is: Be careful when defining Picture formats so that no one gets stuck while entering data. If you are having a problem getting past a field with a Picture format, see the section about getting unstuck when validity checks fail, at the end of this chapter, for ways to bail out.

Defining Required Values

A field that is assigned the Required validity check *must* have data entered into it; you can't leave it blank. For example, you can ensure that no record in a table is entered without a last name by assigning the Required validity check to the Last Name field.

ENSURING THE VALIDITY OF DATA

When you select **V**alCheck ➤ **D**efine ➤ **R**equired, the status bar informs you of the status of the current field by displaying

>Field can be left blank

or

>Field must be filled in

Select the **Y**es option so that the field must be filled in.

After you've set the Required validity check, if you try to leave this field blank during data entry, Paradox will display the message

>A value must be provided in this field; press [F1] for help

You won't be able to move to the next field until you supply a value.

Advancing Automatically to the Next Field

You can set the Auto (short for Auto Confirm) validity check for a field in order to advance the cursor to the next field as soon as the current field has received a complete and valid value during data entry. This saves you the trouble of pressing the ↵ or Tab key or clicking the mouse, and it's especially helpful when you're entering data into fields with a fixed length, such as a two-character State field, or with a specific Picture format, such as a Social Security field.

When you select select **V**alCheck ➤ **D**efine ➤ **A**uto, you see a submenu offering three choices:

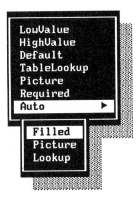

The Filled and Picture options are described in the following sections. The Lookup option is covered in Part Two of this book.

Advancing as Soon as the Field Is Filled

The Filled option on the Auto submenu allows you to have the cursor automatically advance to the next field when the current field is filled. This option is for fields that are of fixed length, either because their field type consists of a specific number of characters or because they have a fixed-length Picture format.

For example, setting **Auto ➤ Filled** to **Yes** can speed data entry for two-character fields that contain state name abbreviations. With this option set, the cursor automatically advances to the next field in the table when you type an abbreviation such as CA, NJ, or NH.

Setting the Auto Filled option to Yes has no effect on a numeric or date field unless you have also defined a fixed-length Picture format for that field.

Advancing When the Field's Picture Format Is Complete

If you select **ValCheck ➤ Define ➤ Auto ➤ Picture ➤ Yes**, the cursor automatically advances to the next field when the current field is filled with data that satisfies its Picture format (defined with **ValCheck ➤ Define ➤ Picture**). For example, you could define the Picture format for the M.I. (middle initial) field of a table as &. and also set **Auto ➤ Picture** to Yes. The &. format specifies a letter, which Paradox converts to uppercase, followed by a period, which Paradox supplies automatically. Then when you enter data into this field, you can just type the one-character middle initial. Paradox will automatically supply the period and advance the cursor to the next field. To leave the field blank during data entry, you can just press ↵, Tab, or click the mouse in the next field, as usual.

You might also want to advance the cursor to the next field after the user's entry satisfies the Picture format for a day name (Mon, Tue, Wed, and so on). Suppose you've defined a Day of Week field with a field type of A3 (three alphabetic characters), a Picture format of {Mon,T{ue,hu},Wed,Fri,S{at,un}}, and **Auto ➤ Picture** set to Yes. When you type *M* into this field,

Paradox automatically fills in *Mon* and advances the cursor to the next field. When you type *Tu* into the field, Paradox fills in *Tue* and advances the cursor.

You can also use this option for fields that require a Yes/No (Y or N) or True/False (T or F) entry. For instance, you can define a Paid field with a field type of A5 and a Picture format of {True,False}, and then set Auto ➤ Picture to Yes. As soon as you type in a T or F during data entry, Paradox will automatically fill in the remaining letters from the Picture format and advance the cursor to the next field.

As convenient as the Auto validity check can be, it can cause problems when used in combination with optional items in a Picture format. Consider, for example, what happens if you use it with a Zip Code field that has a Picture format of #####[- ####]. Here, the first five digits are required, and the hyphen and remaining four digits are optional. If you set Auto ➤ Picture to Yes for this field, the Picture format is satisfied and the cursor advances to the next field as soon as you type the first five digits. After all, the hyphen and remaining four digits are optional. Whoops! This doesn't give you much of a chance to finish typing a nine-digit zip code, does it? In this case, you would need to move the cursor back to the Zip Code field (by pressing ←) and fill in the remaining part of the zip code. After you type the last digit, the cursor again advances to the next field.

Clearing Validity Checks

If you want to remove previously defined validity checks, choose **Val-Check** ➤ **Clear**. You'll see a submenu with two choices: Field and All. Choose **F**ield to clear the validity checks from a single field. You'll see the prompt

> Move cursor to field from which to remove checks, then press ↵

Use the ← or → key to move to the field and press ↵.

To clear the validity checks from all fields in the table, choose **A**ll.

After you clear the validity checks from a field or all the fields, select **DO-IT!** or press F2. The status bar will then indicate that the validity checks have been removed.

NOTE You can also clear validity checks from a table by choosing Tools ➤ Delete ➤ ValCheck from the main menu bar and specifying the name of the table. When you remove validity checks using either this option or Valcheck ➤ Clear, Paradox removes the .VAL file from the disk.

Getting Unstuck When Validity Checks Fail

If you ever get stuck in a field because your entry doesn't pass the validity check, you can use several techniques to get unstuck:

- First, try using the Backspace key to edit the value to one that passes the validity check.

- If you have trouble editing the value, use Ctrl-Backspace to delete the entire entry. Then either leave the field by pressing ↵ or enter a new value.

- If all else fails, press Ctrl-u or Del to delete the entire record.

If it's necessary to delete an entire record, there may be something wrong with your validity check. In this case, clear the validity check (as described in the previous section) or replace it with a new one.

Summary

In this chapter, you learned how to manage windows on the desktop; zoom directly to a field, record, or value; change the appearance of Table view; and set up validity checks. Here's a quick summary of these techniques:

- To choose an active window, click anywhere within that window. If the window you want is totally obscured, choose ≡ ➤ **W**indow then choose the name of the window you want, or choose ≡ ➤ **N**ext (or press Ctrl-F4) to cycle through the windows on the desktop.

SUMMARY

- To use your mouse to move a window, drag the window by its title bar. To move a window without the mouse, choose ≡ ➤ **S**ize/Move (or press Ctrl-F5), use the arrow keys to position the window, and press ↵ when its where you want it.

- To resize the active window using a mouse, drag the lower-right corner of the window. To resize the window without the mouse, choose ≡ ➤ **S**ize/Move (or press Ctrl-F5), hold down the Shift key, use the arrow keys to size the window, and press ↵ when it's sized as you want it.

- To maximize or expand the active window to full-screen size using a mouse, click on the Maximize/Restore button (↑) near the upper-right corner of the window. To maximize or expand a window without a mouse, choose ≡ ➤ **M**aximize/Restore or press Shift-F5. To restore the window to its original size, click on the Maximize/Restore button or use the Maximize/Restore option again.

- To arrange multiple windows on the desktop as tiled or cascading, choose ≡ ➤ **D**esktop ➤ **T**ile or **C**ascade.

- To close the active window, save any changes by choosing **DO-IT!** or pressing F2. Then click on the Close button in the upper-left corner of the window or press F8. To close all windows on the desktop, press Alt-F8.

- To zoom to a specific field, choose **I**mage ➤ **Z**oom ➤ **F**ield and select a field name. To zoom to a specific record, choose **I**mage ➤ **Z**oom ➤ **R**ecord and enter a record number.

- To zoom to a record with a particular value, press Ctrl-z (if the cursor is in the field you want to search), or choose **I**mage ➤ **Z**oom ➤ **V**alue, then press → or ← to move to the field you want to search and press ↵. Type the value into the Zoom dialog box (using .. and @ wildcards if desired) and press ↵ or choose OK. To search for the next occurrence of that value, press Alt-z.

- To customize a Table view, use the options on the **I**mage menu: **T**ableSize to lengthen or shorten the table, **C**olumnSize to change the width of a column, **F**ormat to set a display format, or **M**ove to rearrange columns (you can also press Ctrl-r to quickly rotate the current column to the end of the table). To save the image settings, choose **I**mage ➤ **K**eepSet.

- To define validity checks for use during data entry, switch to Edit mode (press F9 or choose **M**odify ➤ **E**dit or **D**ataEntry from the main menu bar). Choose **V**alCheck ➤ **D**efine and press ← or → to move to the appropriate column, then press ↵. From the submenu, select the type of validity check you want to define: **L**owValue, **H**ighValue, **D**efault, **T**ableLookup, **P**icture, **R**equired, or **A**uto. To save validity checks, choose **DO-IT!** or press F2.

CHAPTER 6

Sorting Your Tables

fast TRACK

- **To sort a table**   128

    choose **M**odify ➤ **S**ort and specify which table you want to sort.

- **To sort to a separate table**   128

    and retain the original record order in the original table, choose **N**ew when given the options **S**ame or **N**ew. Then enter a name for the new table.

- **To fill in the Sort screen**   129

    type a **1** next to the primary sort field, a **2** next to the secondary sort field, and so on, to specify as many fields as you wish.

- **To sort a field in descending order**   129

    type **D** (or **d**) after the number you entered to specify the sort field.

- **To perform the sort**   130

    after defining your sort fields, choose **DO-IT!** or press the Do-It! key, F2.

- **To close the sorted table**   **132**

    click on its Close button on press the Close Active Window key, F8.

- **To make the sort order more apparent in the sorted table**   **132**

    rearrange the fields so that the first sort field is in the leftmost column, the second sort field is in the next column, and so on.

- **To prevent uppercase/lowercase distinctions when sorting text**   **135**

    set Paradox to use the dictionary sort method rather than the ASCII sort method. If you want to change the sorting method, choose the ASCII.SOR or NORDAN.SOR or NORDAN4.SOR file from your original Paradox Disk 1 and copy it to a file named PARADOX.SOR on your Paradox directory.

SORTING in database management terminology means the same thing that it does in plain English—to put things into some kind of order. For example, if your table contains names and addresses, you might want to sort the records so that the last names are in alphabetical order for a directory listing. Or you might want to sort them into zip-code order for a bulk mailing. Sorting is quick and easy, so it's no big deal to, say, sort names and addresses into zip-code order to print form letters and mailing labels, then return to alphabetical order by names to print a directory listing.

Another reason for sorting a table is to group information. For example, suppose you have a table that contains invoice information, including the date that each invoice is due. If you sort the records by date, the bills due in January will be in a group preceding those due in February, which in turn will be in a group preceding those due in March, and so on.

This chapter explains how to use the Modify ➤ Sort option to sort your table. Other ways to sort your table, such as with queries and in formatted reports, are covered in later chapters.

Sorts within Sorts

In many cases, you'll want to sort your table on more than one field, to produce a *sort within a sort*. For example, suppose you have a large table of names and addresses, and there are numerous Smiths. If you were to sort that table by last name, the last names would be in alphabetical order, with all the Smiths together:

LAST NAME	FIRST NAME	M.I.
Smiley	Windsor	J.
Smith	Michael	K.
Smith	Anton	A.
Smith	Wally	P.
Smith	Michael	D.
Smith	Antonio	L.
Smith	Vera	
Smithsonian	Caroline	J.

Within the list, the Smiths are in random order by first names. To order the names alphabetically by first name when the last names are the same, you need to sort on both the Last Name *and* First Name fields. Then the names would be arranged like this:

LAST NAME	FIRST NAME	M.I.
Smiley	Windsor	J.
Smith	Anton	A.
Smith	Antonio	L.
Smith	Michael	K.
Smith	Michael	D.
Smith	Vera	
Smith	Wally	P.
Smithsonian	Caroline	J.

Now the last names are in proper alphabetical order, and the Smiths are all in alphabetical order by first name. What we have just done is use the second sort field as a "tie breaker." That is, when two individuals have the same last name, the secondary sort order, first name, is used to break the tie, enforcing a sort order within the major sort order.

The only "mistake" in this sorted list is that Michael K. Smith comes before Michael D. Smith. But that's easily fixed by sorting on *three* fields: Last Name, First Name, and M.I. (middle initial). Paradox allows you to sort on as many fields as you wish.

Sorting to the Same Table versus Sorting to a Different Table

You can sort your records within the current table or place the sorted records in a separate table. The disadvantage of sorting to the same table is that you won't be able to sort the records back to their original order. That's because each record will be assigned a new sequence number (record number) in the sorted table, based on its new position in the table. If you use record numbers as a means of looking up information, don't sort to the same table. If the table has any key fields, you must sort to another table; you can't sort to the same table (key fields are covered in Chapter 13).

When you sort to a separate table, the original table retains its original order and record numbers. You can use the sorted copy of the table to print reports, labels, form letters, or whatever. When you're finished with the task, delete the sorted version of the table, as discussed later in the chapter. The disadvantage of sorting to a separate table is that it requires disk space to store the sorted copy of the table. If you're pressed for disk storage, sorting to a separate table may not be feasible.

> **TIP**
>
> You can also use indexes to retain the original record order. They don't require sorting to a separate table, and creating them is generally faster than sorting. See Chapter 13 for details on using Paradox indexes.

Sorting in Ascending or Descending Order

You can sort records into either ascending or descending order. Ascending order is smallest to largest: *A* to *Z* for text, smallest number to largest number for numeric fields, and earliest date to latest date for date fields. Descending order is the opposite: *Z* to *A*, largest to smallest number, and latest to earliest date.

You can combine ascending and descending orders in a single sort operation. For example, you could sort the Custlist table, which has been used as an example in the previous chapters, into descending (largest to smallest) order by credit limit (Credit Limit is the primary sort field). Within the same credit limit, you could sort records in ascending alphabetical order by last names (Last Name is the secondary sort field). The records would be arranged like this:

CREDIT LIMIT	LAST NAME	FIRST NAME	M.I.
7,500.00	Gladstone	Tara Rose	
7,500.00	Jones	Alma	R.
7,500.00	Newell	John	J.
7,500.00	Olson	Elizabeth	A.
7,500.00	Ramirez	Rigoberto	R.
7,500.00	Watson	Frank	R.
5,000.00	Adams	Andy	A.
5,000.00	Dewey	Frank	R.
5,000.00	Rosiello	Richard	L.
5,000.00	Schumack	Susita	M.
5,000.00	Smith	Savitha	V.
5,000.00	Wilson	Ted	
5,000.00	Zeepers	Zeke	A.

128 CHAPTER **6** SORTING YOUR TABLES

Sorting a Table

To sort a table, follow these general steps:

1. If the table you want to sort is not in the current working directory, use **T**ools ➤ **M**ore ➤ **D**irectory to switch to the table's directory.

2. Choose **M**odify ➤ **S**ort. You'll see the dialog box for specifying a table.

3. Type in the name of the table you want to sort, or press ↵ or click on OK to choose from a list of table names. Press ↵ or choose OK after specifying the table to sort.

4. If you want to sort to a new, temporary table, choose **N**ew from the submenu that appears next. If you want to sort the original table, choose **S**ame, then skip to step 7.

5. Type the name of the temporary table to hold the sorted records (such as **Tempsort**), then choose OK or press ↵.

TIP

If you prefer to always sort to a separate table, in order to retain the original order in which the records were entered into the table, you might want to always use the same name for the sorted table. This prevents multiple copies of a table, each with a different sort order, from cluttering up the disk. With this method, only the most recent copy is saved. Also, you'll always know that it's safe to overwrite the file with that name, since it's a temporary table.

6. If a table with the name you provided in the preceding step already exists, Paradox will ask if you want to replace it or cancel the creation of the new file. If you're sure you want to overwrite (replace) that table, choose **R**eplace. Otherwise, choose **C**ancel and repeat step 5 using a different file name.

SORTING A TABLE

7. You'll see the Sort screen, as shown in Figure 6.1. Use the arrow keys or mouse to position the cursor next to the primary (main) sort field, and type **1** if you want to sort the field in ascending order, or **1D** (or **1d**) if you want to sort in descending order. (Choose **C**ancel if you change your mind and don't want to sort the table.)

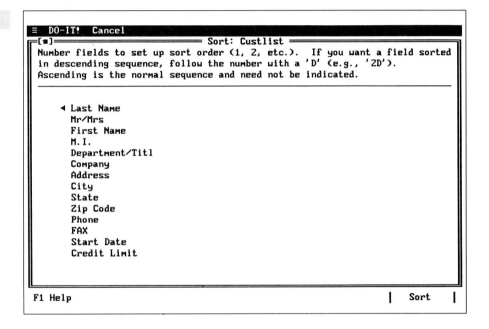

FIGURE 6.1

The Sort screen lets you specify the fields to sort on, as well as ascending or descending order.

8. Use the same basic technique to specify second and third fields, and more if necessary, for sorts within sorts, numbering them 2, 3, 4, and so on. Type **D** (or **d**) after the number of any field you want sorted in descending order. For example, Figure 6.2 shows the Sort screen filled in to sort records by last name, first name, and middle initial.

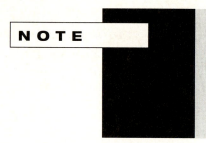

NOTE If you include a memo field as one of the fields to sort on, Paradox sorts *only* on the portion of the memo field that's stored with the table. If you gave a memo field a length of 10 characters when defining the table structure, Paradox will base its sort on the first 10 characters of the memo field.

FIGURE 6.2

The Sort screen to sort records by the Last Name field, then by the First Name and M.I. fields within identical last names. All fields will be sorted in ascending order.

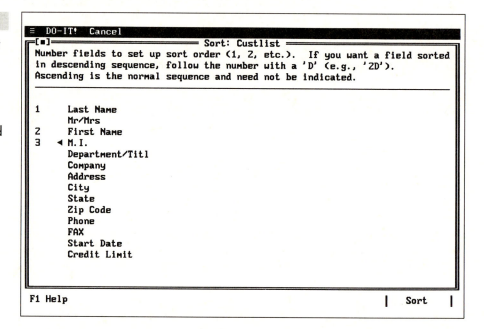

9. After defining your sort fields, choose **DO-IT!** or press F2. If you don't specify any sort fields in the Sort screen but still perform the sort using **DO-IT!**, Paradox uses the first field as the primary sort field, the second field as the secondary sort field, and so on, and sorts the records in ascending order.

After you've completed all the steps, Paradox performs the sort. The time required to complete the sort depends on the size of the table being sorted and the speed of your computer. The sorted records then appear in Table view on the screen, in the temporary table you sorted to or in the original table if you chose to sort to the same table. In Figure 6.3, the records were

SORTING A TABLE

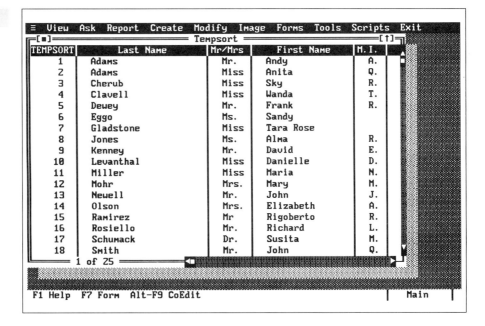

FIGURE 6.3

Results of the sort specified in Figure 6.2. The name of the temporary table, TempSort, appears in the title bar of the window.

sorted to a temporary table named Tempsort. If you switch to Form view while viewing the sorted table and scroll through the records, you'll notice that the records appear in the current sort order.

In some cases, you'll want to use your sorted table data to print a formatted report. For example, you might want to print an alphabetized list of names and addresses, or you might want to print form letters and mailing labels. You'll learn how to create formatted reports in Chapter 8.

CAUTION

Keep in mind that if you sort to a separate, temporary table, the data you see on the screen is a *copy* of the original data. If you happen to notice a mistake in the temporary table, fixing it will *not* fix it in the original table. (Changes to temporary tables are not automatically copied to the original table.) Instead, you should locate the problem in the original table and fix it there.

SORTING YOUR TABLES

When you've finished doing whatever you need to do with your temporary sorted table, you can close its window using the usual techniques: click on its Close button or press F8.

Rearranging Fields to See the Sort Order

Sorting records has no effect on the order of the fields in the table, so the resulting sort order might not be readily apparent. For example, suppose you sort the Custlist table into descending order by the Credit Limit field and ascending order by the Last Name, First Name, and M.I. fields. The Sort screen for this type of sort is shown in Figure 6.4.

When Paradox presents the sorted table, you need to scroll all the way over to the Credit Limit field to see the sort order. To get a better view of the results, you can rearrange the order of fields in Table view, using the techniques described in Chapter 5. You could move the Credit Limit field over to the leftmost column and perhaps move the Mr/Mrs field out of the way (by pressing Ctrl-r) to make the sort order more obvious. This rearrangement is shown in Figure 6.5.

FIGURE 6.4

The Sort screen to sort records in descending order by credit limit, and within each credit limit, alphabetically by name in ascending order

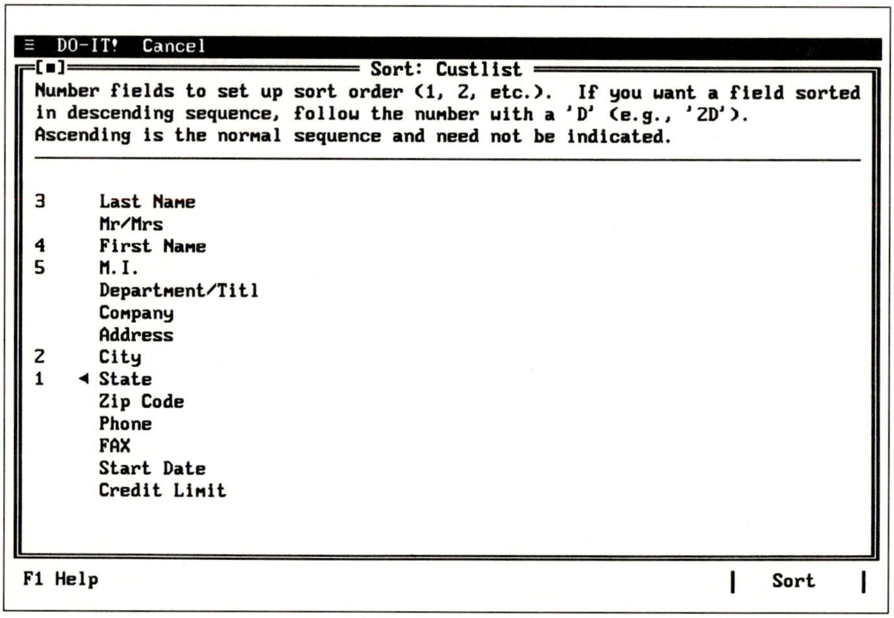

```
≡ DO-IT!  Cancel
┌[■]═════════════════════ Sort: Custlist ═════════════════════┐
│ Number fields to set up sort order (1, 2, etc.).  If you want a field sorted │
│ in descending sequence, follow the number with a 'D' (e.g., '2D'). │
│ Ascending is the normal sequence and need not be indicated. │
│                                                              │
│                                                              │
│     3       Last Name                                        │
│             Mr/Mrs                                           │
│     4       First Name                                       │
│     5       M.I.                                             │
│             Department/Titl                                  │
│             Company                                          │
│             Address                                          │
│     2       City                                             │
│     1    ◄  State                                            │
│             Zip Code                                         │
│             Phone                                            │
│             FAX                                              │
│             Start Date                                       │
│             Credit Limit                                     │
│                                                              │
│                                                              │
│ F1 Help                                        │    Sort    │
└──────────────────────────────────────────────────────────────┘
```

SORTING A TABLE

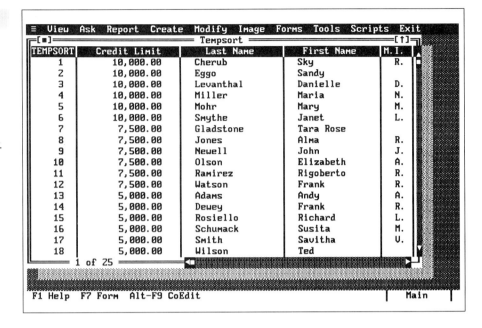

FIGURE 6.5

Results of the sort specified in Figure 6.4. After sorting, the Credit Limit field was moved over to the leftmost column and the Mr/Mrs field was rotated out of the way.

Now suppose that you want to sort the Custlist table into alphabetical order by state. Within each state, records will be sorted by city. Within identical cities and states, records will be sorted by last and first name. Figure 6.6 shows the Sort screen for performing this sort.

Figure 6.7 shows the results of the sort, after moving the State and City fields to the leftmost columns. You can see that the states are in alphabetical order, cities are alphabetized within each state, and names are alphabetized within each city.

Other Techniques for Sorting a Table

The **M**odify ➤ **S**ort option is just one way of sorting records in a table. You can also use the following methods to sort your data:

- Queries enable you to isolate specific records in a table, and simultaneously sort those records into whatever order you wish. Queries are the topic of Chapter 7.

- Report formatting lets you define a sort order for the printed records (by defining group bands in the Report Designer). Formatted reports are covered in Chapter 8.

SORTING YOUR TABLES

FIGURE 6.6

The Sort screen to sort records by state, by city within each state, and by name within each city

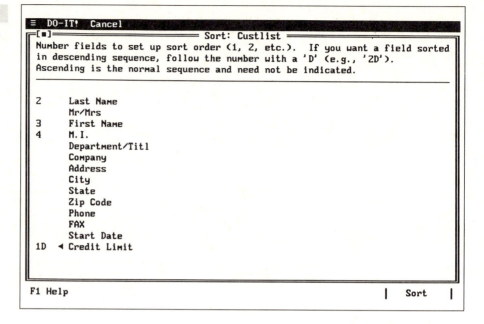

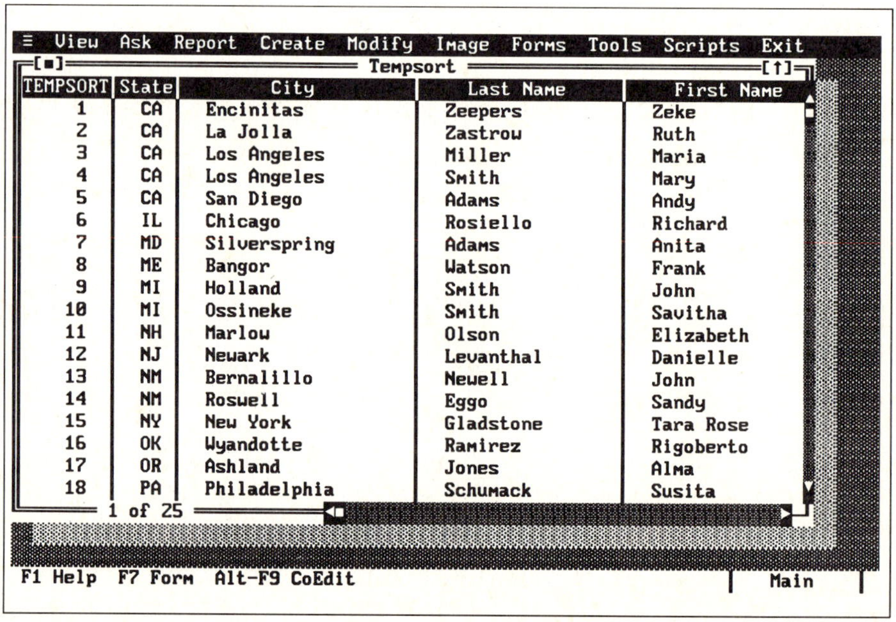

FIGURE 6.7

Results of the sort specified in Figure 6.6. After sorting, the State and City fields were moved to the leftmost columns.

- Key fields provide a means of maintaining an ongoing sort order in a table. They also prevent duplicate records from being entered into the table. Key fields are described in Chapter 13.

Uppercase and Lowercase in Sorting

When you first install Paradox, it gives you the choice of sorting records in ASCII order or in international (NORDAN dictionary) order. In dictionary order, the case of the letters is not considered in the sort. For example, if you were to sort the names Adams, McDonald, d'Elgin, and Zastrow into ascending order, the results would be what you might expect:

Adams

d'Elgin

McDonald

Zastrow

In ASCII order, lowercase letters are considered "greater than" uppercase letters. Any names that begin with a lowercase letter would be at the end of the sorted list, like this:

Adams

McDonald

Zastrow

d'Elgin

If you originally chose ASCII or the dictionary order, and now want to use the other order, you will need to copy a File from one of your original Paradox program disks. Before you proceed, however, you should be aware of the following:

- The instructions that follow are for single-user computers only. If you're using Paradox on a network, contact the network administrator for information about changing the installed sort method.

- You'll need to use the original Disk 1 of your Paradox installation disks to complete the procedure.

- If you've created any tables with key fields, or any secondary indexes, all those indexes will become obsolete after the new sort method is set up. If you try to open a table that was indexed using a different sort order, you'll see an error message. To use the table with the new sort order, choose **M**odify ➤ **R**estructure to view the table's structure, then just choose **DO-IT!** to resave the same structure.

- If you've created any multi-table forms (as described in Chapter 15), use **M**odify ➤ **R**estructure to resave the structure of all the detail tables (those containing subforms) before restructuring the table for the master form. Otherwise, you might lose the subforms.

- If you've upgraded from Paradox 3.5 and you'll be using applications or databases that rely on the dictionary sort order, you'll need to install NORDAN.SOR rather than NORDAN4.SOR.

> **TIP**
>
> You can use the DOS TYPE command to see which sort order is currently specified in the PARADOX.SOR file.

When you're sure it's okay to proceed, here are the steps to follow:

1. If Paradox is currently running, save or abandon any work in progress, then exit Paradox using **E**xit ➤ **Y**es to get to the DOS command prompt.

2. Change to the drive and directory that Paradox is stored in. For example, if Paradox is in C:\PDOX45, enter the command C: then enter the command CD\PDOX45 to get to the correct drive and directory.

3. Put Disk 1 from your original Paradox installation package in drive A or B.

4. Copy the file you want to use to determine sort orders (ASCII.SOR for ASCII order, or NORDAN.SOR or NORDAN4.SOR for dictionary order) from the floppy drive to a file named PARADOX.SOR in the Paradox directory.

5. When the copy is complete, remove the original Paradox Disk 1 and store it in a safe place.

When you sort your tables in future Paradox sessions, Paradox will use whichever file you copied to PARADOX.SOR.

NOTE Disk 1 from your original Paradox installation package contains two other sort order files: INTL.SOR and SWEDFIN.SOR. See your Paradox user manual for a description of the sort order imposed by these and the other .SOR files. To use INTL.SOR or SWEDFIN.SOR, follow the instructions in this section and specify that file in step 4.

Summary

This chapter covered one of several techniques that you can use to sort the records in a table. In the next chapter, we'll talk about ways in which to query, or search, your table. First, take a moment to review the most important techniques and concepts presented in this chapter:

- You can sort on multiple fields to achieve a sort within a sort.
- Sorting to a new table, rather than the original table, preserves the original order of records in the table.
- If you sort to a separate table, remember that the data in that table is a copy of the original data. Any changes you make to that copy will *not* be reflected in your original table.
- To sort a table, choose **M**odify ➤ **S**ort.
- When defining fields to sort on, give the primary sort field the number 1, the secondary sort field the number 2, and so on. To sort any given field in descending order, type the letter **D** (or **d**) after the number.

SORTING YOUR TABLES

- After defining all the sort fields, choose **DO-IT!** or press the Do-It! key, F2, to perform the sort.
- If necessary, you can rearrange fields in Table view to make the current sort order more readily apparent.

CHAPTER 7

Querying Your Tables

fast TRACK

- **To query a table**   142

    first choose **A**sk from the menu bar and specify the name of the table you want to search. You'll be taken to the Query form, where you can define your query.

- **To select fields to display in the results of the query**   145

    mark the fields with a check-plus (Alt-F6) to view all the records, a plain check mark (F6) to disregard duplicates, or a check-descending (Ctrl-F6) to view the records without duplicates in descending sort order.

- **To perform a query after filling in the Query form**   149

    choose F2 Do-It! from the Speedbar, or press F2. The results of the query appear in a temporary table named Answer.

- **To have the Answer table mimic the order of fields in the Query form**   152

    use the Custom Configuration Program to change the **S**tandard Settings ➤ **Q**uery Order setting from Table Order to Image Order.

- **To search for specific records during a query**   155

    type the exact value you're looking for into the appropriate field of the Query form before performing the query.

- **To search for approximate values in a query**   161

    use the .. (match any characters), @ (match a single character), or LIKE (spelled-like) operators in the Query form.

To search for ranges of values — 166

use the < (less than), <= (less than or equal to), > (greater than), or >= (greater than or equal to) operators. Separate the query criteria with a comma to specify an AND relationship that defines both the lower and upper boundaries of the values.

To search for date ranges in relation to the current date — 167

use the TODAY operator to specify a range of dates.

To specify an AND relationship among query criteria — 171

place all the query criteria in the same row of the Query form, or use a comma to separate query criteria in a single field.

To specify an OR relationship among query criteria — 172

place the query criteria in separate rows of the Query form, or use the OR operator to separate query criteria in a single field.

To use a query to locate a record that you want to edit — 177

use the reserved word FIND in the leftmost column of the Query form and enter the criteria you wish to search for in the appropriate fields.

To globally change a table — 179

use the reserved word CHANGETO in your Query form.

To globally delete records in a table — 182

use the reserved word DELETE in the leftmost column of the Query form.

To *query*, or search, a table means to pull out all records that meet some criterion. For example, you might want to view only New York residents or just individuals in California with credit limits over $5,000. Perhaps you'll want to send a form letter to individuals whose starting date was one year ago, or maybe you just want to look up David Kenney's address.

You can also use queries to perform basic calculations, to delete certain types of records, and much more. For example, in a table used to keep track of sales information, you might want to isolate sales for given products. In a table used to manage an inventory, you might use a query to isolate items that need to be reordered.

An Overview of Using Query By Example

Paradox offers a technique referred to as *Query By Example (QBE)* to allow you to search a table. Using Query By Example involves several steps, some required and others optional, which we'll discuss in depth throughout this chapter. But in a nutshell, here's how you go about using QBE:

1. Choose **A**sk from the menu bar, and then specify the name of the table you want to query.

2. Choose the fields that you want to view in the result of your query.

3. Optionally, arrange fields in the Query form to indicate how you want records in the result of the query to be sorted.

4. Optionally, specify the records that you want to include in the result of the query.

5. Optionally, use operators and reserved words to delete or change records during a query.

6. Perform, or *run*, the query by pressing F2 or clicking on the F2 Do-it! indicator on the Speedbar.

The results of the query are displayed in a new, temporary table, which is always named Answer. The Answer table will contain only the fields and records you've requested.

Opening a Query Form

The first step to performing a query is to get to the Query form, as follows:

1. If the table you want to query isn't in the current directory, choose **T**ools ➤ **M**ore ➤ **D**irectory to switch to that table's directory.

2. Choose **A**sk from the main menu bar. You'll see the dialog box for opening a table.

3. Specify the name of the table by typing its name or pressing ↵ and choosing its name from the list. Then choose OK or press ↵.

A blank Query form window appears on the screen, and some new options appear on the Speedbar, as shown in the example in Figure 7.1.

In a Query form window, you can use many of the same techniques that work in a Table view window. You can scroll left and right by using the scroll bar or the arrow keys or click on any visible field to move the cursor to it. After typing text into a column, you can press Backspace to delete characters or Ctrl-Backspace to delete all the text in the column. Table 7.1 summarizes the keystrokes you can use in the Query form window.

144 CHAPTER **7** QUERYING YOUR TABLES

FIGURE 7.1

An empty Query form window. In this example, the Query form displays fields from the sample Custlist table.

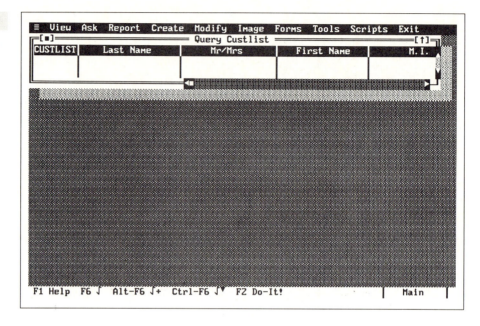

TABLE 7.1: Keyboard Techniques in a Query Form

ACTION	KEYPRESS
Next field	→ or Tab
Previous field	← or Shift-Tab
First field	Ctrl-Home
Last field	Ctrl-End
Left one screenful	Ctrl-←
Right one screenful	Ctrl-→
Delete character	Backspace
Delete field contents	Ctrl-Backspace
Start Field view	Alt-F5 or Ctrl-f (also double-click)
Exit Field view	↵ (also single click); F2 in memo field
Run query	F2 (or click F2 Do-It! on Speedbar)

Selecting Fields and Running the Query

The next step in the query procedure is to tell Paradox which fields you want to see in the Answer table. You also specify whether to include or exclude duplicates and whether to sort in ascending or descending order. Only fields in the Query form that contain a check mark will be displayed in the results of the query. Initially, all the columns are empty, so you need to add the check marks.

Using Check-Plus, Plain Check, or Check-Descending Marks

Paradox provides three types of check marks to determine which fields to include in the Answer table:

- The check-plus check mark displays all the values in the table for that field, including duplicates. It looks like this:

  √+

- The "plain" check mark displays one of each value in a field (no duplicates), sorted in ascending order. It looks like this:

  √

- The check-descending mark acts the same as the plain check mark, except that it displays records in descending sort order. That is, it disregards duplicate values and displays the values in largest-to-smallest (or *Z-to-A*) order. It looks like this:

CHAPTER 7
QUERYING YOUR TABLES

For example, if you marked the the State field from the Custlist table with a check-plus, then performed the query, the Answer table would display the entries in the State field of every record, as shown in Figure 7.2. But if you marked the State field with a plain check, then performed the query, the Answer table would list each state in the table only once, as shown in Figure 7.3. If you put a check-descending check mark in the State field, each state in the table would be listed only once, arranged in descending alphabetical order, as shown in Figure 7.4.

The plain check mark is useful for seeing summary information. In Figure 7.3, you can see at a glance which states are represented in the Custlist table.

FIGURE 7.2

Using a check-plus check mark in the State field displays all the values for that one field, including duplicates, in the Answer table.

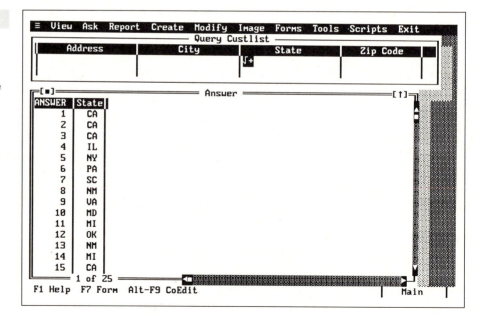

SELECTING FIELDS AND RUNNING THE QUERY

FIGURE 7.3

Using a plain check mark in the State field displays one of each value in that field, with no duplicates, in the Answer table.

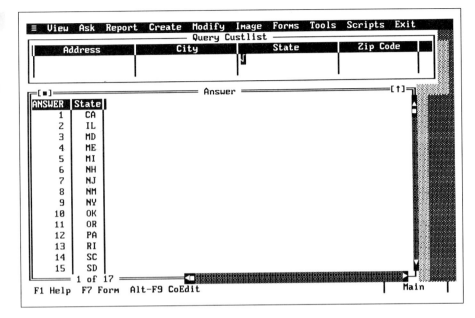

FIGURE 7.4

Using a check-descending mark in the State field displays one of each value, without duplicates, sorted in descending rather than ascending order in the Answer table.

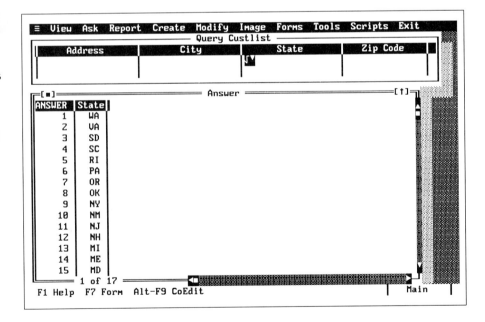

QUERYING YOUR TABLES

If you check more than one field, the Answer table will be sorted on the leftmost of the fields that are checked. Note that when multiple fields are checked, a *duplicate* is defined as any record that has identical values in *all* the checked fields. For example, in Figure 7.5 the Last Name, First Name, and Phone fields are all selected with a plain check mark. The resulting Answer table includes two Adams entries, because Anita Adams is not a full duplicate of Andy Adams.

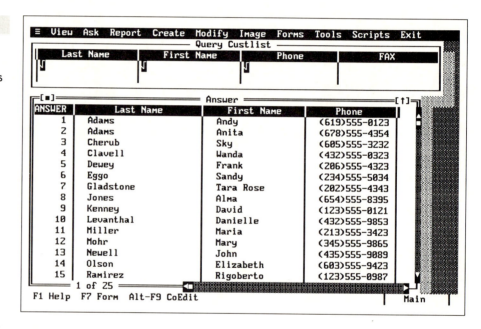

FIGURE 7.5

When you check multiple fields, a duplicate is defined as a record that has identical values in all the checked fields.

Adding the Check Marks

To place a check mark in a field on the Query form, move the cursor to a field you want to view in the Answer table (by clicking with your mouse or using the arrow keys). Then you can add a check mark by clicking on the appropriate check symbol on the Speedbar, or by pressing the key for the type of check mark you want to use:

- Press F6 to add a plain check mark.
- Press Alt-F6 to add a check-plus check mark.
- Press Ctrl-F6 to add a check-descending check mark.

SELECTING FIELDS AND RUNNING THE QUERY

If you want to view all the fields in the table, you can quickly check them all at once. Simply move the cursor to the leftmost column of the Query form, beneath the table name, then choose the type of check mark you want to use. Figure 7.6 shows the results of moving the cursor to the leftmost column of the Query form and marking it with a check-plus.

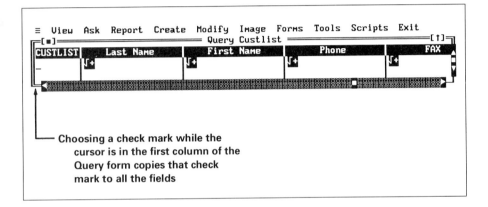

FIGURE 7.6

Choosing a check mark while the cursor is in the leftmost column of the Query form automatically copies that check mark to all the fields in the Query form.

Remember, Paradox doesn't sort records at all when you use the check-plus check mark in the Query form to display duplicate records.

To "uncheck" a field, move the cursor to it and press F6 or click on one of the check symbols on the Speedbar.

Performing the Query

To perform a query, click on the F2 Do-It! indicator on the Speedbar or press F2. The time it takes Paradox to run the query depends on the size of the table and the speed of your computer.

When the query is completed, Paradox displays the results in the temporary Answer table. Figures 7.2 through 7.4 in the preceding sections show examples of Answer tables from different types of queries.

Using the Answer Table

The Answer table contains a copy of records from the original table you used to perform the query. Keep in mind that the Answer table holds just a copy of data from your original table. If you happen to notice a typo or other mistake that needs to be corrected while viewing the Answer table, you could edit it on the spot after you switch to Edit (F9) or Co-Edit (Alt-F9) mode. However, any changes you make to the Answer table will *not* be reflected in your original table. If you need to correct an error, open the original table and make your changes there.

TIP You can save an Answer table by renaming it. If you don't change the table's name, it will be overwritten by the next Answer table produced by a query. Also, any existing table named Answer is automatically deleted when you exit Paradox. See Chapter 12 for information about renaming tables and other objects.

Working with the Answer Table

You can treat the Answer table as you would any other table in Table view:

- To move the Answer table so you can see the underlying query, drag it by its title bar to a new location, or use ≡ ➤ **S**ize/Move, as described in Chapter 5.

- To size the Answer table, drag its lower-left corner with the mouse pointer, or use ≡ ➤ **S**ize/Move, as described in Chapter 5.

- To sort the Answer table, choose **M**odify ➤ **S**ort and specify Answer as the name of the table to sort. Choose **S**ame to sort the original table, then specify your sort fields and perform the sort, as described in Chapter 6. You can also base the sort order on the order of fields in the Query form, as described in the next section.

NOTE If you use the plain or check-descending check mark, Paradox automatically sorts records in the Answer table. It does not sort records when you use a check-plus check mark.

- To rearrange fields in the Answer table, use the Rotate key (Ctrl-r) or any of the options on the **I**mage menu, as described in Chapter 5. (The Rotate key was used to arrange fields in most of the Query forms shown in this chapter.) You can also make the Answer table use the same field order as the Query form, as described in the next section.
- To print the Answer table, press the Instant Report key, Alt-F7, as described in Chapter 8.
- To use the Answer table to print a formatted report, use **T**ools ➤ **C**opy to copy report formats from the original table to the Answer table, then print the report from the Answer table, as described in Chapter 8.
- To close the Answer table, click on its Close button or press F8.
- To close the Query form, click on its Close button or press F8 when the Query form is the active window.

TIP To bring the Query form to the foreground without closing the Answer table, choose ≡ ➤ Desktop ➤ Surface-Queries.

Controlling the Order of Fields in the Answer Table

Normally when you perform a query, Paradox displays the fields in the Answer table in the same order that they were defined in the original table structure. For example, the Query form in Figure 7.7 shows the Custlist table with the Phone field rotated to the leftmost column, the Last Name field to the second column, and the First Name field to the third column. But after performing the query, the Answer table displays those fields in

CHAPTER 7
QUERYING YOUR TABLES

their original table order: with Last Name in the first column, First Name in the next column, and Phone in the third column. Furthermore, the records are sorted based on this order of fields. That is, records are sorted by the Last Name field and by the First Name field within identical last names.

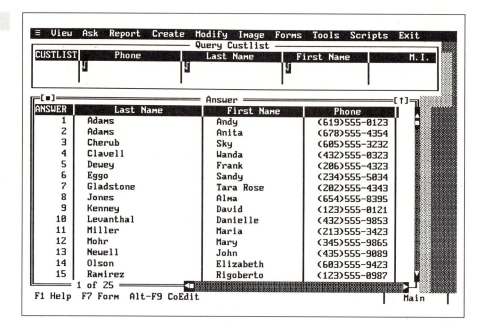

FIGURE 7.7

Paradox displays fields in the Answer table in the same order that they're defined in the table. Even though Phone is in the leftmost column of the Query form, Last Name is in the leftmost column of the Answer table.

Now let's suppose that you would actually prefer to see the phone number in the leftmost column and have all the records sorted by phone number. This arrangement would let you see records grouped by area code, and it might come in handy for a telemarketing campaign.

You could use **M**odify ➤ **S**ort before running the query to sort the Answer table on the Phone field, then rotate the Phone field to the leftmost column. Another way to control the order of the fields is to change Paradox's default setting of using the table order for Answer tables to using the image (Query form) order.

To change the default setting for Answer tables, you use the Custom Configuration Program, as follows:

1. Clear the desktop by pressing the Close All Windows key, Alt-F8.

USING THE ANSWER TABLE

2. Choose ≡ ➤ **U**tilities ➤ **C**ustom from the menus.

3. Choose Color or B&W if prompted.

4. Choose **S**tandard Settings from the menu that appears. You'll see the Standard Settings dialog box:

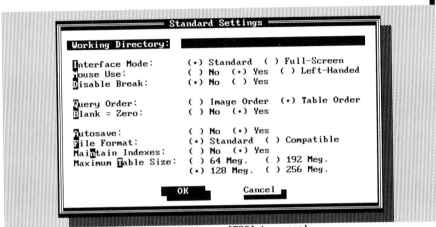

5. Next to Query Order, choose the Image Order option, by clicking on it with your mouse or by pressing Tab until Table Order is highlighted, then pressing ←.

6. Choose OK or press ↵.

7. Choose **DO-IT!** or press F2.

8. If you're working on a single-user computer, choose **HardDisk** from the next menu to appear. If you're using Paradox on a network, choose **N**etwork instead and specify the directory where you want to store the new setting.

Paradox will save your new selection and use it for the remainder of the current session, as well as in all future sessions. If you want to change back to table order as the default for Answer tables, repeat the steps, but choose Table Order in step 5.

QUERYING YOUR TABLES

See Appendix D for more information about using the Custom Configuration Program.

After you change the default setting, the order of fields in the Answer table will be the same as the order of fields in the Query form, and records will be sorted by the leftmost column in that image. For example, repeating the query shown in Figure 7.7 after changing the setting produces the results shown in Figure 7.8.

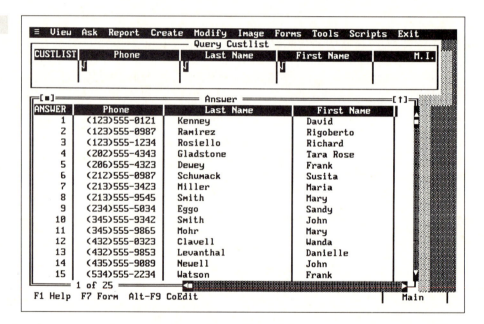

FIGURE 7.8

After changing the default settings, the Answer table displays fields in the same order as the Query form. Records are still sorted by the leftmost column in the Answer table.

In a sense, we've killed two birds with one stone in this example. First, the Answer table displays Phone in the leftmost column. Second, because Phone is in the leftmost column, records are sorted by phone number, which conveniently groups them into area codes.

Most of the sample queries in this chapter were created with the Query Order option set to Image Order, and fields in the Query form rotated with Ctrl-r.

Using Queries to Select Specific Records

So far we've talked about the general techniques for performing a query, controlling which fields are displayed, and so forth. But we have not yet talked about how you can use queries to isolate specific records, such as just the customers in the state of California. When you want to search for specific records, you add one or more *query criteria* (also called *query statements*) to your Query form.

To add a query criterion to the Query form, you simply move the cursor to the field you want to search during the query and type in the criterion. You can query as many fields as you wish and use a variety of techniques to pinpoint the exact information you need, as described in the sections that follow.

Table 7.2 lists all the special operators and reserved words you can use in queries, as well as the purpose of each one. The operators and reserved words used in more advanced queries, such as the summary and set comparison operators, are discussed in detail in Chapter 14.

If you want to treat any of the special operators or reserved words as a *literal* (interpreted as the text you're searching for rather than as a special word or as an operator), you must enclose the text in quotation marks. Otherwise, your query will not be interpreted as you intended.

TABLE 7.2: Symbols and Reserved Words Used in Query Forms

SYMBOL OR WORD	PURPOSE
CHECK MARKS	
✓+	Display all values, including duplicates
✓	Display all values, disregarding duplicates
CM∇	Display all values in descending order, disregarding duplicates
G	Specify group for set operations
COMPARISON OPERATORS	
=	Equal to (optional)
>	Greater than
<	Less than
>=	Greater than or equal to
<=	Less than or equal to
ARITHMETIC OPERATORS	
+	Add numbers or join alphanumeric values
−	Subtract
*	Multiply
/	Divide
( )	Give precedence
INEXACT MATCHES	
@	Match any single character
..	Match any series of characters
LIKE	Match words that "sound like"

TABLE 7.2: Symbols and Reserved Words Used in Query Forms (continued)

SYMBOL OR WORD	PURPOSE
SPECIAL OPERATORS	
NOT	Do not match
BLANK	Contains no value
TODAY	System date
OR	One condition *or* another (or both) must be met
, (comma)	Both conditions must be met (acts as AND operator)
AS	Field name to use in Answer table
!	Display all values, regardless of match
RESERVED WORDS	
CALC	Display result in newly calculated field in Answer table
CHANGETO	Globally change matching values
FIND	Locate matching records within table
INSERT	Insert records with specified value
DELETE	Delete records with specified value
SET	Define set of matching values for set comparisons
SUMMARY OPERATORS	
AVERAGE	Average of values in field
COUNT	Number of unique matching values
MAX	Highest value in field
MIN	Lowest value in field
SUM	Total of values in field
ALL	Calculate summary based on all values in a group, including duplicates
UNIQUE	Calculate summary based on all values in group, disregarding duplicates

TABLE 7.2: Symbols and Reserved Words Used in Query Forms (continued)

SYMBOL OR WORD	PURPOSE
SET COMPARISON OPERATORS	
ONLY	Display only those values that match values in defined set
NO	Display only those values that do not match any members in defined set
EVERY	Display only values that match every member of defined set
EXACTLY	Displays only values that match all members of defined set and no others

Searching for Exact Values

To search for the full and exact value (the entire contents) of a field, type the exact value into the field of interest. For example, Figure 7.9 shows the Query form with CA typed into the State field and several fields selected with check marks. The resulting Answer table (below the Query form), shows only the records that contain CA in the State field.

Be aware that an exact match requires a completely exact match, including the same spacing and uppercase and lowercase letters. The entire contents of the field must be precisely the same as your criteria for a match. For example, if you placed ca rather than CA in the State field of the Query form and then performed the search, the Answer table would be empty, because all the two-letter abbreviations in the State field are in uppercase, not lowercase. Furthermore, the length of the entries must also match for exact searches. A query for Smith will find exactly Smith, but not Smithsonian, BlackSmith, Smith-Jones, Smith & Wesson, or even Igor Smith. Although these longer names *contain* Smith, they do not *equal* Smith.

Searching Numeric, Currency, and Date Fields

When querying numeric and currency fields, don't include commas to separate every third power of ten (thousands, millions, billions, and so on), even if the field is formatted with them. For example, Figure 7.10 shows

FIGURE 7.9

Defining CA as the query criterion in the State field of the Query form displays only records that contain exactly CA in the State field.

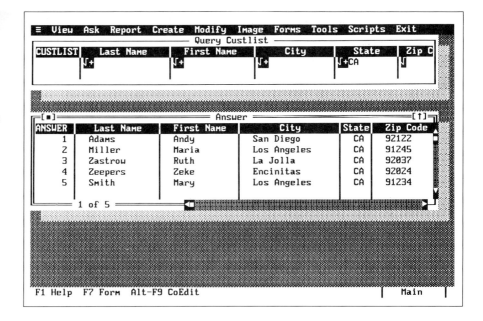

a query that isolates records that have a value of 5,000 in the Credit Limit field. Even though the Answer table displays numbers in the Credit Limit field with a comma after the five, 5000 (without a comma) is specified in the Query form.

See the section about searching for punctuation marks and symbols later in this chapter for limitations on including commas and special words and symbols in your query criteria.

When searching a date field, you can use any of the acceptable date formats. For example, if you want to search for records containing November 13, 1993 in a date field, you can enter the date in one of these formats:

- 11/13/93
- 13-Nov-93
- 13.11.93

160 CHAPTER **7** QUERYING YOUR TABLES

FIGURE 7.10

When searching numeric or currency fields, omit the comma to separate thousands, millions, etc., in numbers. This Query form isolates records with a value of 5000 in the Credit Limit field.

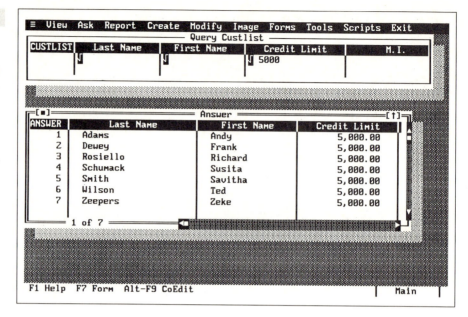

For example, the Query form below will isolate records that have 11/13/93 in the Start Date field.

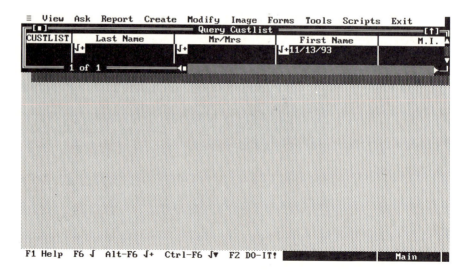

Searching for Inexact Values

In some cases, you might need to view records that match a pattern or contain a certain sequence of characters. For example, in an inventory system, you might want to view all the records that have the sequence J2 embedded somewhere in the part number. Or you might want to look up an individual named Erikson but you're not sure of the spelling. You would need to search for records that are spelled *like* Erikson, such as Erikson, Ericson, Erickson, or Ericksen. You can use the following operators for these types of searches:

..	Matches any sequence of characters (not a case-sensitive search)
@	Matches any single character
LIKE	Matches items similar to the criterion

The use of these operators is explained in the following sections.

Finding Embedded Text

You can use .. to stand for any sequence of characters or numbers in a query criterion. For example, suppose you want to view records for people who live on a particular street. You can't ask for address records by using just a street name, such as Ocean, because the word Ocean will never appear as anyone's complete address; it will be embedded somewhere in the middle of the address, as in 234 Ocean View Dr.

To find the records with Ocean as the street name, you can use the .. operator to indicate the numbers preceding the street name, followed by the word Ocean, followed by .. again to indicate any other characters. Figure 7.11 shows such a query and its results.

In a large table, searching for records with the word Ocean embedded in the Address field might produce a lot of records. To be more specific about the match, you can enter more query criteria in other fields. For example, if you were specifically looking for people on Ocean View Drive in

FIGURE 7.11

A search for records with the word Ocean embedded in the Address field

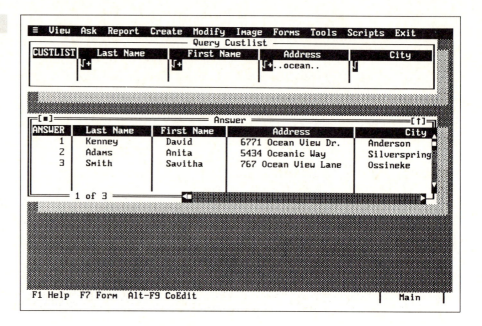

the city of Anderson, you might want to set up the query as shown below. This query isolates records that specifically have Ocean View Dr in the Address field *and* Anderson in the City field:

In the Query form for Ocean View Dr in Anderson, the query criteria are set up for an AND search. You'll learn about AND and OR searches a little later in this chapter.

USING QUERIES TO SELECT SPECIFIC RECORDS

Another example of using the .. operator is shown in the Query form below. In this example, the query criterion A.. will isolate records of people whose last names begin with A (the letter *A* followed by any other characters).

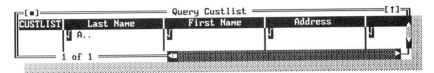

You can also use the .. operator to isolate records for a particular month in a date field. For example, the query below uses .. in place of a specific day in the Start Date field to isolate records with start dates on any day of November 1993:

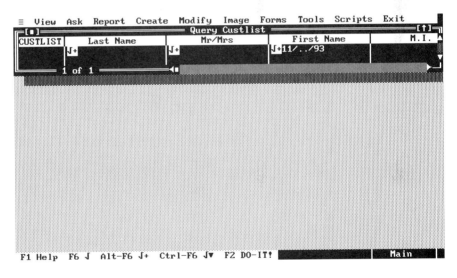

Searching for embedded rather than exact text is a good way to broaden a query should your initial search fail. For example, suppose you perform a search for the name Davis in the Last Name field, and the resulting Answer table is empty. Yet, you know that there is a Davis in the table somewhere. If you change your search criterion to ..Davis.., you just might find the record you're looking for. Perhaps the record you're seeking actually contains Davis, Jr. rather than just Davis.

Finding Text in Memos Fields

The .. operator is also useful for finding records with a word embedded in a memo field. Use .. to stand for any text before and after the word you're searching for. For example, the query below will search the sample Articles table for records that have *milky way* embedded anywhere in the Abstract memo field:

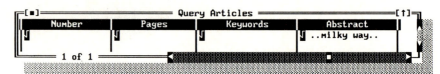

 You cannot search for text embedded in a binary field.

Matching a Single Character

The @ operator is used to match any single character, as opposed to any series of characters. This can be handy when you're not sure of the exact spelling of the word or phrase you're looking for. For example, a search for Sm@th in the Last Name field would isolate records that contain *Sm* followed by any single character followed by *th*. Thus, names such as Smith and Smyth would be included in the Answer table.

The query shown below searches for Sm@th.. in the Last Name field. It will find Smith, Smythe, Smithsonian, Smathers, and other words that have a single letter embedded between the *m* and the *t*, with or without any characters following the *h*.

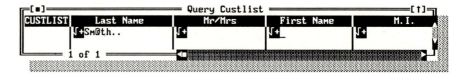

Searching for Inexact Spellings

The use of uppercase and lowercase letters will sometimes mislead a query. As mentioned earlier in the chapter, a query for all ca residents in the State field would display nothing, since CA is stored in uppercase in all records. This could be a problem if you were not absolutely certain of the case in all the records.

The LIKE operator takes care of this by searching for text that "looks like" or "sounds like" the word you provide, regardless of its case. Just type the word LIKE (or like), followed by a blank space, in front of the value you want to search for when specifying your query criterion.

For example, the query below isolates any records that have anything in the State field that looks or sounds like CA, which ensures that records containing CA, ca, and Ca are all included in the Answer table. However, if you have any Colorado residents (CO, Co, or co), this query will display them as well, because they look like CA.

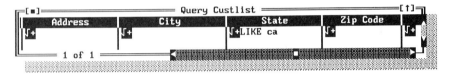

The query shown below uses the query criterion LIKE shoomack in the Last Name field, which will help find last names that are like shoomack in spelling, including Schumack.

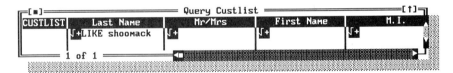

When using the LIKE operator, keep in mind the following points:

- Only records that have the same first letter as the query criterion will be included in the search. For example, the criterion LIKE kwik will not find *Quick* even though they sound alike.
- If a record contains at least half of the letters in the query criterion, in the same order, it will likely be considered a match.
- Remember that you can use .. to match any characters. For example, La .. (La followed by a space, followed by any other characters) in the City field will find La Jolla, even without the LIKE operator. It will also find any other cities starting with *La* and a space.
- You cannot use LIKE to query a memo field. However, you can use .. to search for text embedded in a memo field.

Searching for Ranges of Values

Another type of query you can perform allows you to view records that have a value that is less than or greater than some value. For example, you might want to view records for people who have credit limits of $5,000 or more. You can use the following *comparison operators* to perform such queries:

=	Equal to
<	Less than
>	Greater than
<=	Less than or equal to
>=	Greater than or equal to

If you want a more specific range, such as values that are greater than or equal to one value *and* less than or equal to another value, enter two query criteria, separated by a comma, into the field. For example, the Query form below uses the criteria >=2500,<=5000 in the Credit Limit field. The resulting Answer table will include only records for people with credit limits greater than or equal to $2,500 and less than or equal to $5,000.

CAUTION Do not use commas to separate thousands in numbers on the Query form. In a Query form, commas are interpreted as separators between criteria.

Searching for a Range of Letters

You can use the comparison operators to search alphanumeric fields that fall within a range of letters. Use >= to specify the lowest acceptable letter or < to specify one letter *higher* than the largest acceptable letter. For example, the query below will display records only for people whose last names start with the letters *A* through *M*:

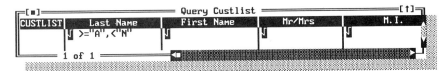

Notice that the second half of the criterion is <N. You can't use <=M because any word starting with M is considered greater than the letter M by itself, so the Answer table wouldn't include any last names beginning with M. The query criterion >=A includes all names from just the letter A by itself up to the end of the range, which is Mzzzzzzzzzzzzzz.

Searching for a Range of Numbers

You can also use the comparison operators to search an alphanumeric field for a range of numbers. For example, to isolate records that have zip codes in the range of 92000 up to and including 92999, use the query criterion >=92000 in the Zip Code field. For nine-digit zip codes, however, you need to account for the extra four digits in your query. You would enter the criteria >=92000,<=92999-9999. You can't search for values starting from 92000-0000 because *any* characters that add to the length of an alphanumeric string, even zeros, increase the sort value of that string. In an alphanumeric field, 92000-0000 is greater than 92000. Thus, if you started your search from 92000-0000, you would not find 92000.

Searching for a Range of Dates

The comparison operators are also useful for searching a date field for records that fall within a range of dates. For example, the query shown below will display records that have dates in the first quarter of 1994 (1/1/94 through 3/31/94) in the Start Date field:

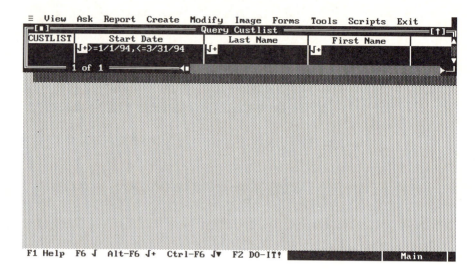

Searching for Everything Except Some Value

The NOT operator reverses the meaning of any query criterion. For example, if you want only non-California residents in your Answer table, you would use the query shown below. The resulting Answer table won't include any records that have CA in the State field.

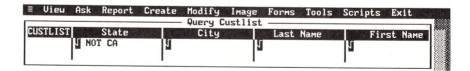

Searching for Blank Fields

If you want to search for records that have no entry in a particular field, use the BLANK operator. For example, this query isolates records that don't have an entry in the Company field:

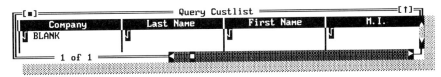

To exclude blank records from the results of a query, use NOT BLANK instead. For example, this query does the exact opposite of the query shown above. Instead of displaying just the records without an entry in the Company field, it displays only records that do have an entry in the Company field:

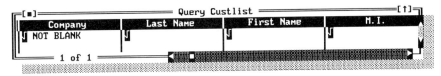

Searching for Relative Dates

The TODAY operator represents the current system date in your computer. Typically, the system date is maintained by a clock within the computer. You can set the current date using the DATE command at the DOS command prompt or the Date/Time option in the Windows Control Panel.

Used alone, the TODAY operator isolates records that match today's date exactly. A more common use of the TODAY operator is to locate records with dates that fall within a range of days relative to today's date. If your table contains accounts payable or accounts receivable data, this type of query can help you isolate records of payables and receivables within certain ranges of dates.

You can use the comparison operators described earlier and the arithmetic operators listed below to help isolate ranges of dates:

+   Add a number of days to the date
−   Subtract a number of days from the date

Here are some examples of query criteria that can be used in a date field to isolate ranges of dates relative to the current system date.

- To find records with today's date and all dates prior to and today, use the criterion <=TODAY.
- To find records with today's date and all dates after today, use the criterion >=TODAY.
- To find records with dates within the last 30 days, including today, use the criteria <=TODAY, >=TODAY–30.
- To find records with today's date and all dates within the next 30 days, use the criteria >=TODAY, <=TODAY+30.
- To find records with dates between 30 and 60 days ago (inclusive), use the criteria >=TODAY–60, <=TODAY–30.
- To find records with dates between 30 and 60 days from today (inclusive), use the criteria <=TODAY+60, >=TODAY+30.

Performing AND and OR Searches

You may need to define queries that produce only records that meet *all* the query criteria. For example, when you are specifically trying to locate information about Andy Adams in San Diego, you need to structure your query to display only records that contain Adams in the Last Name field *and* Andy in the first Name field *and* San Diego in the City field. For this type of query, you specify an AND relationship among multiple fields.

In other situations, you might need to find records that match *any* of the search criteria. For example, if you want to isolate records for individuals in certain states, you need to structure your query to isolate records that have NY *or* NJ *or* PA in the State field. For this type of query, you specify an OR relationship between the criteria.

The following sections describe the techniques you use in the Query form to specify AND and OR relationships among query criteria.

AND Relationships across Several Fields

To specify an AND relationship among multiple fields, place the query criteria on the same row. For example, the query below has Adams in the Last Name field and Andy in the First Name field. Because Adams and Andy are in the same row in the Query form, the Answer table will displays only records that contain both Adams in the Last Name field *and* Andy in the First Name field.

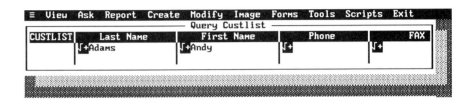

AND Relationships in a Single Field

If you want to specify an AND relationship among query criteria in a single field, separate the criteria with a comma. In most cases, using multiple criteria in a single field makes sense only when you're searching for ranges using comparison operators, as discussed earlier. For example, the query criteria >=2500,<=5000 in the Credit Limit field isolate records that have a number that is greater than or equal to $2,500 *and* less than or equal to $5,000. The query criteria >=1/1/94,<=3/31/94 in a date field isolate records that have dates that are greater than or equal to 1/1/94 *and* less than or equal to 3/31/94.

Paradox does not recognize the word *AND* as an operator; you must use the comma.

You might also want to search for records that contain a combination of words. For example, the query below isolates records that contain both the terms *milky way* and *black hole* in the same field, Abstract, which is a memo field. With this query, you can find records of articles that are about black holes in the Milky Way.

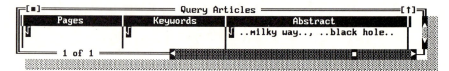

OR Relationships across Several Fields

If you want to search for records that contain either certain values *or* other values, place the query criteria on separate rows in the Query form. To add a row to the Query form, press ↓.

For example, the query below will find records that have *either* San Diego in the City field *or* 92 followed by any other characters in the Zip Code field. Notice how the two query criteria are on separate rows.

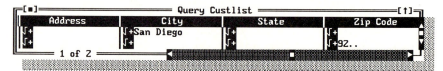

The following query will locate records that have the words *milky way* embedded in either the Keywords field *or* the Abstract field.

PERFORMING AND AND OR SEARCHES

NOTE All rows in a Query form must have the same checked fields. If the same fields are not checked in all rows, Paradox will display the message "Query appears to ask two unrelated questions."

Think of each row in the Query form as representing a single question. For example, the query below searches for people with a last name like Smith who live in California *or* Washington.

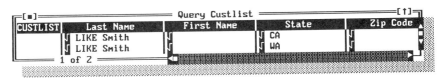

When performing this query, Paradox looks at each record in the table and asks the following questions:

- Does this record have a name like Smith in the Last Name field *and* contain CA in the State field?

- Does this record have a name like Smith in the Last Name field *and* contain WA in the State field?

If it can answer Yes to *either* of those questions, it displays that record in the Answer table.

The following query will produce an Answer table that contains Smiths in California and *all* Washington residents, regardless of last name.

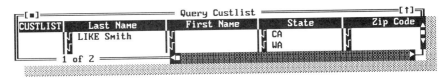

Why? Because this query asks these two questions when deciding whether or not to display a record in the Answer table:

- Does this record have a name like Smith in the Last Name field *and* contain CA in the State field?

- Does this record have WA in the State field?

For Paradox to be able to answer Yes to the second question, and thereby display the record in the Answer table, a record need only have WA in the State field. That's because there is no query criterion in the Last Name field in the second row.

OR Relationships in a Single Field

If you want to search for one of several given values in a field, you can either stack the values in separate rows or use the OR operator to separate the values you want to find. For example, if you want to isolate records that have NY or PA or NJ in the State field, you could set up the Query form like this:

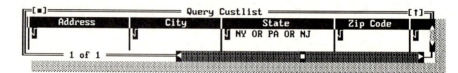

or like this:

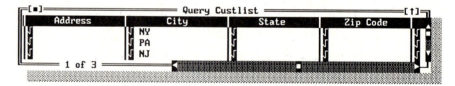

Either way, the results are the same. The Answer table displays records with NY, PA, or NJ in the State field.

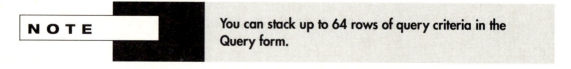

NOTE You can stack up to 64 rows of query criteria in the Query form.

If you want to locate records containing either the words *milky way* or *black hole* in the Abstract field, you can either stack the query criteria or separate them with the OR operator, like this:

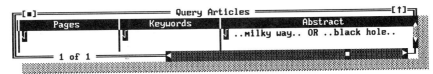

This differs from the example in the section about AND relationships in a single field, which limits the Answer table to records that contain both the terms *milky way* and *black hole*. The query above uses an OR relationship to broad the search so that records containing either the term *milky way* or *black hole* are found.

Avoiding AND/OR Confusion

When building criteria that use AND and OR logic, remember that the way you might think about the query in plain English might *not* be the way to express it in a query. For example, you might think to yourself, "I want to view all the California and Texas residents." Accordingly, you might define the query criterion as CA,TX in the State field of the Query form. When you run this query, however, the Answer table will be empty, regardless of how many CA and TX residents are actually in the table. Why? Because it is impossible for the State field in any single record in the table to contain both CA *and* TX. Therefore, Paradox cannot answer Yes when it asks itself, "Does this record have CA in the State field *and* TX in the State field?"

To isolate records for California and Texas residents, you need to structure the query so that it looks for records that have either CA *or* TX in the State field: CA OR TX. Then Paradox will ask two questions as it checks each record:

- Does this record have CA in the State field?
- Does this record have TX in the State field?

If it can answer Yes to either question, the record is displayed in the Answer table.

Searching for Punctuation Marks and Symbols

Paradox interprets certain punctuation marks, such as commas and exclamation points, and some operators, such as NOT, BLANK, OR, and TODAY, as special symbols in a query. If you fail to remember this, the results of your query can be quite misleading.

For example, suppose you want to search for a record that has Davis, Jr. in the Last Name field. If you simply enter the query criterion as Davis, Jr., the resulting Answer table will be empty. Why? Because Paradox interprets the comma as the AND operator, rather than as a literal comma. And a single field cannot logically consist only of Davis *and* only of Jr.

If you want to include an operator or special word in a query criterion and have it treated as a literal character rather than as an operator, you need to enclose the query criterion in quotation marks ("").

Thus, if you change the query criterion to "Davis, Jr.", Paradox will know to look for Davis, Jr., not for records that match both Davis and Jr. Hence, the Answer table will contain whatever records have Davis, Jr. in the Last Name field. Similarly, if you wanted to isolate records for people living in California, Oregon, and Washington, you would need to structure your query criterion carefully. The two-letter abbreviation for Oregon is OR, the same as the operator, so you need to enclose it in quotation marks, as on the Query form shown below. This query will isolate records that have CA *or* OR *or* WA in the State field:

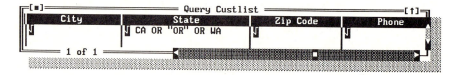

You may be thinking, "What if the value I want to search for *contains* quotation marks?" For example, suppose you want to look up the phrase *"hello there"*, including the quotation marks. In that case, you need to precede the quotation marks with a backslash (\) and enclose the entire expression in quotation marks to indicate that the second set are literal characters, in this format:

"\"hello there\""

Using Queries as Editing Tools

Queries are also useful as editing tools. By using some of Paradox's reserved words, you can perform the following editing tasks:

- Locate information that needs editing by using FIND in the original table (not in the Answer table).
- Perform *global edits* to change all matching records to a new value in one fell swoop by using CHANGETO.
- Delete specified records from the table by using DELETE.

Another useful reserved word is INSERT, which inserts selected fields from the records of one table into another table. Its uses are covered in Chapter 14.

Finding Information

FIND is one of the most useful reserved words. It displays the results of the query in the original table, rather than in the temporary Answer table. This allows you to make permanent changes to a record immediately. Rather than displaying only records that match the query criteria, FIND displays all the records in the table and moves the cursor to the first record that matches the criteria. Although Paradox doesn't display the Answer table when you use FIND, it does create one. You can view this table in the same way that you open other tables: choose **V**iew from the menu bar, and specify the table (Answer) as the table to view.

CHAPTER 7: QUERYING YOUR TABLES

NOTE: You cannot check any fields in the Query form when using FIND, because it always displays all the fields in the table.

To use FIND, simply type the word under the leftmost column of the Query form, beneath the table name. As an example of using FIND, suppose you need to change the address for a person named David Kenney in a large table of names and addresses. You're not exactly sure of the spelling, however, so you want to use a query rather than the Zoom feature to locate his record. To look for the record, you could set up the Query form as shown in the top of Figure 7.12:

- The word FIND appears under the table name (Custlist in this example) in the leftmost column.

- The LIKE operator in the Last Name field specifies that this might be an inexact spelling.

- The .. operator is used in the First Name field (Dav..), since it might be David or Dave.)

FIGURE 7.12

The FIND reserved word displays the original table rather than the Answer table, and includes all the records in the table. It also moves the cursor to the first record in the table that matches the query criteria.

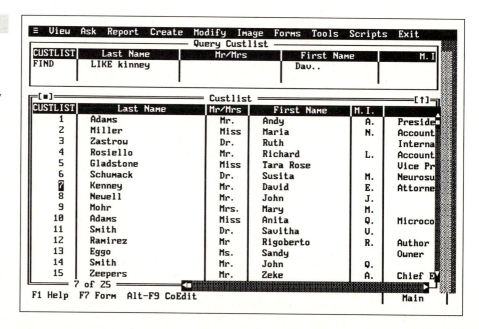

After you run this query, the cursor moves to the first field that matches the query criteria, which is David Kenney in the example in Figure 7.12. If the cursor is indeed on the record you want to edit, you merely need to switch to Edit (F9) or CoEdit (Alt-F9) mode and make your changes.

On the other hand, if the cursor didn't land on the record you're looking for, you could open the Answer table to see which other records match the search criteria. If you find the record you're looking for in the Answer table, you can close the Answer table and the original table, modify the query to pinpoint the record you need, then perform the query again.

Making Global Edits

Global editing is a technique that may someday save you many hours of tedious work. Through the global editing process, you can automatically change the contents of a field to a new value in records that meet a certain criterion.

For example, suppose you have two different people entering data into your table. One types in *Los Angeles* for all Los Angeles residents, and the other types in *L.A.* This creates problems, because queries that search for Los Angeles records miss those with L.A., and queries that search for L.A. miss those with Los Angeles. Even though an OR search could take care of this, it would be even better to have a consistent entry. You might prefer to have all the Los Angeles records changed to L.A. in the original table. For this type of global editing, you can use CHANGETO, which allows you to change a value in multiple records in one easy operation.

You need to exercise great caution when using CHANGETO, because it makes its changes globally and quickly. If you make a mistake, there may not be any easy way to undo the changes you made. To play it extra safe, you might want to make a backup copy of your original table before you run a CHANGETO query. That way, if you do make a mistake, you can replace the newly modified table with the backup copy you created just before performing the query.

As an example, suppose that you decide you want to change all the records with Los Angeles in the City field to L.A. You want to make a backup copy first, so you proceed as follows:

1. Choose **T**ools ➤ **C**opy ➤ **T**able, specify the name of the table you want to copy (Custlist in this example), and choose OK or press ↵.

NOTE The Tools ➤ Copy ➤ Table option allows you to make a backup copy of a table, as well as to replace the changed version of a table with the original backup copy. See Chapter 12 for more information about copying tables.

2. Enter a name for the backup copy of the table (**Custback** in this example) and choose OK. Custlist and Custback are identical copies of the same table.

3. Choose **A**sk and specify the name of the table you want to edit globally (**Custlist** in this example). A Query form appears on your screen.

4. Move the cursor to the field you want to change, and type the query criterion specifying which records you want to change (**Los Angeles** in this example), followed by a comma, followed by the reserved word CHANGETO, followed by a blank space and the new value you want to put into the field (**L.A.** in the example). The Query form to change Los Angeles to L.A. looks like this:

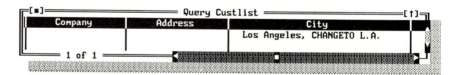

CAUTION If you don't specify which records you want to change, Paradox will change *all* the records!

5. Run the query by choosing F2 Do-It! from the Speedbar or by pressing F2.

Paradox displays a temporary table, named Changed, which includes a list of records that have been changed as the result of the global edit. However, it doesn't display the changes that were made; instead, it displays the original records, as shown in Figure 7.13. If you open the original table,

USING QUERIES AS EDITING TOOLS

you'll see that those records have been changed as you specified, as shown in Figure 7.14.

FIGURE 7.13

Whenever you perform a CHANGETO query, Paradox displays a list of records that were modified during the query in a temporary table named Changed. This table does not show the changes themselves.

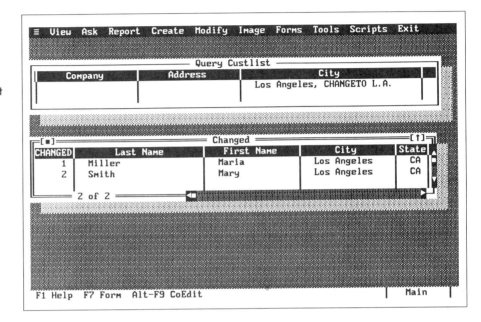

FIGURE 7.14

The global changes that were made are apparent in the original table (Custlist). The City fields that formerly contained Los Angeles now show L.A.

Now, should you change your mind and want to undo this change, you could either create and perform another query that changes L.A. to Los Angeles or, since you made a backup copy of the original table, you could use **T**ools ➤ **C**opy ➤ **T**able to copy the backup table (Custback in this example) to the original table name (Custlist in this example).

The CHANGETO query can also be used to increase or decrease a value in a numeric or currency field by a percentage or an amount, as you'll learn in Chapter 14. That chapter also explains how to use Tools ➤ More ➤ Add ➤ Update to undo a CHANGETO query on a indexed table.

Making Global Deletions

You can globally delete a group of records from a table by putting the DELETE reserved word in the leftmost column of the Query form. When performing a global deletion, you most certainly want to make a backup copy of the table first. That way, if you make a mistake or change your mind and want to recover the records you've deleted, you can simply copy the backup copy of the table to the original table (using **T**ools ➤ **C**opy ➤ **T**able, as described in the previous section).

After you've made your backup, select **A**sk and specify your original table as the table to query. Then enter a query criterion that specifies the records you want to delete, and enter DELETE under that table name in the leftmost column of the Query form. For example, the Query form below specifies that all records that have CA in the State field are to be deleted. (Perhaps, heaven forbid, because of annexation by Arizona!)

USING QUERIES AS EDITING TOOLS

When you perform the query, Paradox displays a temporary table named Deleted, which shows which records were deleted from the original table. Figure 7.15 shows the records deleted using CA in the State field as the criterion.

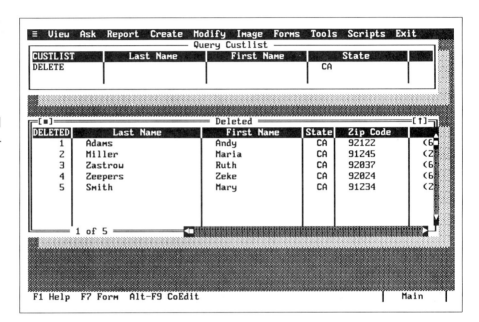

FIGURE 7.15

After using a DELETE query, Paradox displays a temporary table (named Deleted) listing all the records that have been deleted from the original table.

If you don't like the results of the query, and want to put all those deleted records from the Deleted table back into the original table, you can choose **T**ools ➤ **M**ore ➤ **A**dd, specify Deleted as the name of the source table, and then choose the original table as the target table. Paradox will copy the records from the temporary Deleted table right back into the original table.

Keep in mind that the Deleted table is a temporary one, which will be erased as soon as you exit Paradox or perform another DELETE query. At that point, the only way to recover the deleted records would be to use Tools ➤ More ➤ Copy to copy the backup of your original table back to the original table name.

> **NOTE**
>
> Even though a DELETE query removes records from a table, Paradox does not immediately reduce the disk space consumed by the table. See Chapter 12 for tips on reclaiming the disk space left by deleted records.

Summary

In this chapter, we've covered queries in considerable depth, focusing on the types of queries you're most likely to use for day-to-day work when managing a single table. Here's a quick recap of the most important techniques and concepts:

- To search (query) a table, select **A**sk from the main menu bar and specify a table name. A Query form appears.

- Place a plain check mark (F6) in a field of the Query form so that it will be included in the query, but only once for each different entry. The leftmost checked field determines the sort order of the display.

- Place a check-plus (Alt-F6) in each field if you wish to find duplicates with the query.

- To display records in descending order in the Answer table, use the check-descending mark (Ctrl-F6).

- To search for particular records, put the data that you want to search for in the appropriate field in the Query form.

- To perform a query after filling in the Query form, choose F2 Do-It! from the Speedbar or press F2. The results of the query (other than editing queries) are displayed in a temporary table named Answer.

- To search for inexact matches, use the .. (any characters), @ (any single character), and LIKE (spelled-like) operators in the Query form.

- To search for relative values, use the <, >, <=, and >= operators in the Query form.

- To search for ranges, place two values (with < or <=, and > or >= operators) in a single field, separated by a comma.
- To search for nonmatches, use the NOT operator in your criterion.
- To search for blank values in a field, use the BLANK operator.
- To specify an AND relationship among several criteria in different fields, place all items in the same row on the Query form.
- To specify an OR relationship among criteria in different fields in the Query form, place the criteria on different rows.
- To locate a record to edit using a query, use the FIND reserved word in the leftmost column of the Query form and enter the search criteria in the appropriate column(s).
- To back up a table before globally changing or deleting records, use **T**ools ➤ **C**opy ➤ **T**able.
- To globally change a table, use the CHANGETO reserved word in your criterion.
- To globally delete records on a table, use the DELETE reserved word in the leftmost column of the Query form.

CHAPTER 8

Printing Formatted Reports

fast TRACK

- **To print an Instant Report**   **190**

    display the table from which you want the report on the screen (using the View option on the menu bar) and press the Instant Report key, Alt-F7.

- **To get Paradox and your current printer settings in sync**   **192**

    use the Custom Configuration Program to change the Report Settings to the page length, width, and margins that work best with your printer.

- **To design a new, formatted report**   **198**

    choose **R**eport ➤ **D**esign from the desktop menu bar. Specify the table from which you want to print a report, choose an Unused report, enter a brief description of the report, then choose either **T**abular or **F**ree-form as the initial report format. To save a completed report design, choose **DO-IT!** or press F2.

- **To insert and edit literal text and lines in the report design**   **205**

    use the mouse or arrow keys to place the cursor. Use Ins, Delete, and other special keys to make your changes.

- **To insert blank lines in the printed report**   **205**

    press ↵ while in Insert mode. Use Ctrl-Home, followed by Ctrl-y to delete blank lines. (Any blank lines in the report format print as blank lines in the final, printed report.)

To work with columns in a tabular report format 211

use the options on the **T**ableBand menu in the Report Design screen. The options allow you to insert, delete, resize, move, and copy columns in the report design.

To work with field masks in a report format 214

use the options on the **F**ield menu in the Report Design screen. The options allow you to insert, delete, and format field masks.

To change page layout settings for the current report only 225

choose options from the **S**etting menu in the Report Design screen while you're designing the report.

To define a sort order and, optionally, groups for a report 237

use options on the **G**roup menu to insert, define, and delete Group bands.

To print a formatted report from the desktop 246

choose **R**eport ➤ **O**utput from the menu. Specify the name of the table and report you want to print, then choose a destination from the menu that appears.

To print, save on disk, or preview a report from the Report Design screen 246

choose **O**utput from the menu bar. Then choose a destination from the submenu that appears. Select **P**rinter to send the report to the printer, **S**creen to preview the report on the screen, or **F**ile to send the report to a file on disk.

THIS chapter focuses on the techniques for printing data from your table in whatever format you wish. Paradox provides the Report Design screen for designing formatted reports. As you'll learn, the Report Design screen offers a huge selection of tools and features to help you print data in exactly the format you want. Near the end of this chapter, you'll find sample report formats, which illustrate how you can "mix and match" the many features Paradox offers to present data in a wide variety of formats.

We'll begin this chapter with the simplest report of all to print: the Instant Report you can print from any table that's currently on your desktop.

Printing an Instant Report

An Instant Report prints every field in your table in a tabular format. You can print an Instant Report of the current table with a single keypress. Just open the table in Table view (by using **T**ools ➤ **M**ore ➤ **D**irectory to switch to the table's directory if necessary, then choosing **V**iew and specifying the table). With the table on your screen, press the Instant Report key, Alt-F7, to get a quick printout.

If the last printed page is not fully ejected from the printer, send a *form feed* code to your printer. On most printers, you need to press a button on the printer to take the printer off line, then press the form feed (or FF) button, then press a button to put the printer back on line. See your printer manual for instructions.

PRINTING AN INSTANT REPORT **191**

If your table has more columns than can fit across a single page, Paradox prints as many columns as it can on one page, and prints remaining columns on the next pages (called *spillover* pages). You can lay the pages side-by-side to see the whole table. Figure 8.1 shows an example, with the right side of the first printed page next to the left side of the second printed page.

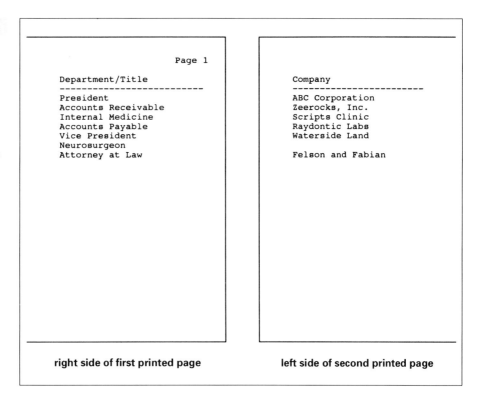

FIGURE 8.1

Paradox prints as many columns as will fit on a page. Any additional columns are printed on spillover pages. This example shows the first and second pages of a sample printed report.

If the rows don't line up across spillover pages, Paradox is not set up properly to print with your printer. For example, Figure 8.2 shows the first and second pages from a sample printed report in which the rows clearly don't line up across the pages. In the example, there are six lines between the Department/Title heading and the Company heading. This means that Paradox is printing six lines too many per page for this printer. If Paradox isn't printing the correct amount of lines for your printer, before you do any more printing, you need to synchronize Paradox and your printer, as described in the next section.

FIGURE 8.2

If the rows across a printed Instant Report don't line up across the pages, Paradox is not set up correctly to print with your printer.

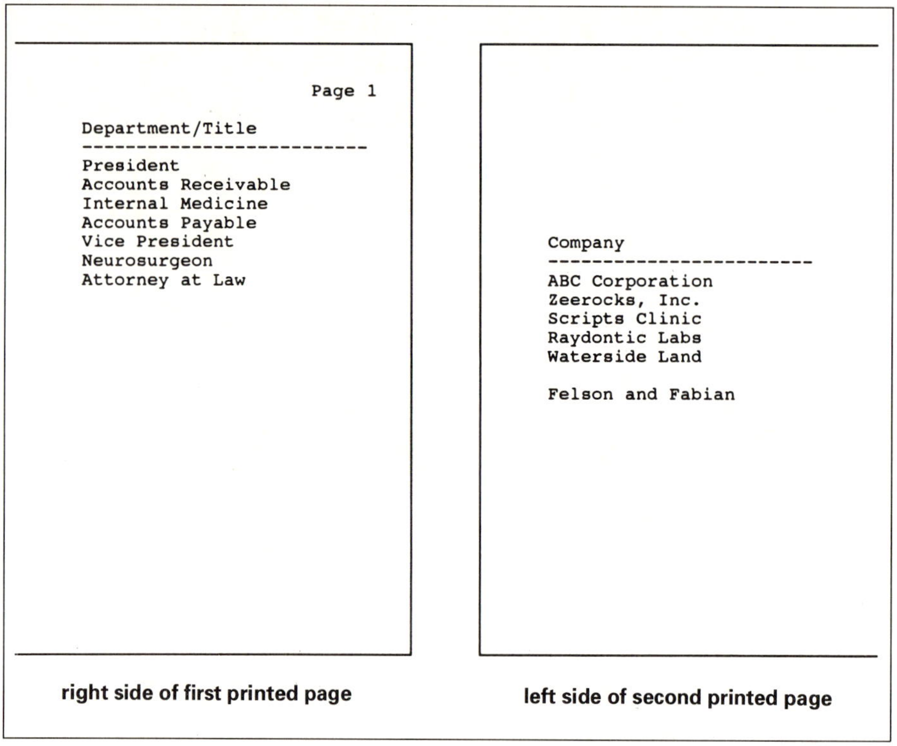

```
                          Page 1
Department/Title
-------------------------
President
Accounts Receivable
Internal Medicine
Accounts Payable
Vice President
Neurosurgeon
Attorney at Law
```

```
Company
-------------------------
ABC Corporation
Zeerocks, Inc.
Scripts Clinic
Raydontic Labs
Waterside Land

Felson and Fabian
```

right side of first printed page   **left side of second printed page**

Getting Paradox and Your Printer in Sync

The first step to getting any of your printed reports to look the way you want is to get Paradox and your printer in sync. Doing so can be a little tricky because Paradox measures everything in characters and lines, and we usually think of the space on a page in terms of inches. Figure 8.3 illustrates how Paradox measures page width and margins.

FIGURE 8.3

Paradox measures the page width and margins in units of characters (not inches) and the page length in units of lines.

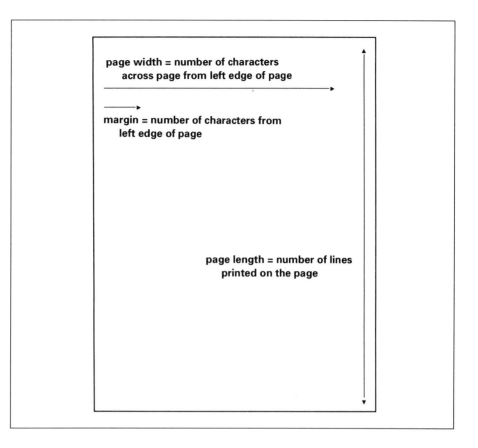

Determining Page Length and Width

Most printers can print at either 6 lines to the inch (60 lines per page) or roughly 6.5 lines to the inch (66 lines to a page). To ensure that Paradox vertically aligns the pages correctly, you need to either change the settings on your printer, as per instructions in your printer manual, or change the default settings in Paradox, as described shortly, so that both are printing either 60 or 66 lines per page.

By default, Paradox attempts to print 80 characters across each page, which is the same width that most screens display. Most printers, by default, print at about 10 characters per inch (cpi). Thus, in most cases, Paradox will print lines that are about 8 inches across, leaving about $\frac{1}{2}$ inch total for the margins at the left and right sides of the page ($\frac{1}{4}$ inch on each side).

If Paradox can't print 80 characters across the page, some text at the right side of the page might be truncated (not printed at all), or the extra characters will wrap down to the next line. In an Instant Report, you might even find that Paradox prints a blank page between each printed page.

One way to fix this problem is to change your printer settings so that the printer prints at a smaller size, such as 12 cpi. Alternatively, you can change Paradox so that it prints fewer characters per line. For example, you might want Paradox to print about 75 characters per line (roughly a $7\frac{1}{2}$-inch line across the page), leaving room for about $\frac{1}{2}$-inch left and right margins.

Determining a Left Margin

By default, Paradox starts printing at the left edge of the page. If you want to set a left margin for your printed reports, remember that Paradox deals with the margin width in terms of characters, not inches. For example, if your printer prints at 10 cpi, a left margin of 10 would be roughly equivalent to 1 inch.

On tractor-fed paper, it's really the location of the paper on the platen that determines where printing begins on each line. If you set the left margin to 10 characters, you will get a 1-inch margin only if the print head initially aligns with the left edge of the page. See your printer manual for additional information about aligning the paper in your printer.

On a laser or other page-fed printer, you might need to take into consideration the $\frac{1}{4}$- to $\frac{1}{2}$-inch "dead zone" when calculating the margin. The dead zone is the space all around the edge of printed page where rollers in the printer touch the paper to move it through the printer. Text is never printed within the dead zone. For example, a left margin setting of 8 might give you a more exact 1-inch margin than a setting of 10, since the dead zone adds another $\frac{1}{4}$ inch to the eight characters you've allotted.

NOTE The margin setting does not affect spillover pages, which are always printed with text aligned at the left edge of the page.

Determining the Page Ejection Method

When Paradox determines that the current page has been fully printed, it ejects that page from the printer before printing the next page. It can use either of two methods to eject a page:

- By sending *line feeds* to print the amount of blank lines needed to reach the predetermined page length
- By sending a *form feed code* to the printer

By default, Paradox uses the form feed method. Sending a form feed code ensures that the page is fully ejected from the printer and printing starts at the top of the next page. The line feed method is less reliable. It can cause some reports to start printing at the middle (or elsewhere) of the page, particularly if the page length isn't set correctly. Unless your printer can't understand a form feed code (which is highly unlikely), leave Paradox set to use the form feed method.

Changing the Printer Defaults

As noted earlier, to get Paradox and your printer in sync, you change either your printer's settings or Paradox's default settings for printing. If you want to change the settings directly on the printer, see your printer manual for instructions. To modify Paradox's printing settings, use the Report Settings option in the Custom Configuration Program. Follow these steps to run the program and adjust the settings for printing reports:

1. If necessary, save any work in progress with the Do-It! key (F2), then close all the windows on the desktop (press Alt-F8).
2. Choose ≡ ➤ **U**tilities ➤ **C**ustom. You should see the opening screen for the Custom Configuration Program.
3. Choose **R**eports ➤ **R**eport Settings. You'll see a dialog box like the one shown in Figure 8.4.
4. Adjust the settings as necessary to suit your printer. Click with your mouse or press Tab and Shift-Tab to move from one set of options to the next. To change the setting, type in a new one, or choose an option within a set by clicking with your mouse or by pressing the ↑ and ↓ keys.
5. After you're finished adjusting the settings, choose OK or press ↵.

196 CHAPTER 8   PRINTING FORMATTED REPORTS

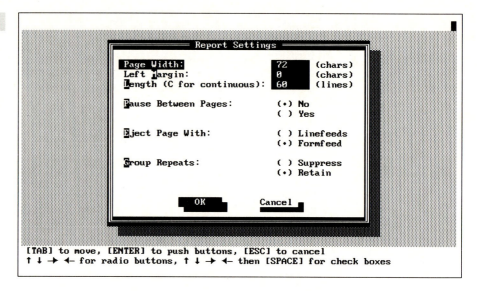

FIGURE 8.4

The Report Settings dialog box in the Custom Configuration Program. The settings shown in this example leave 1-inch margins at the left and right edges of the page and work well with most laser printers.

6. Choose **DO-IT!** or press F2.

7. If you're working with a single-user computer, choose **HardDisk** to save your settings. If you're working on a network, choose **Network**.

The Custom Configuration Program automatically restarts Paradox, and your new settings will now be used for any reports you print.

 See Appendix D for details on using the Custom Configuration Program.

Now let's take a moment to review some of the settings displayed in Figure 8.4. These settings were used to print most of the sample reports in this chapter to a Hewlett Packard (HP) LaserJet printer.

- The page width of 72 characters assumes text is being printed at 10 cpi. Thus, text should extend to about 7.2 inches from the left edge of the page. However, because the LaserJet printer gives a .25-inch dead zone, text actually extends about 7.5 inches across the page, leaving a 1-inch right margin on a page that is 8.5 inches wide.

- The left margin setting of 8 characters (.8 inch at 10 cpi), added to the .25-inch dead zone, leaves a left margin of about 1 inch.
- The length of 60 lines is the default for most laser printers. You can usually choose between 60 and 66 lines per page. Just be sure that both Paradox and the printer are set to print the same number of lines per page.
- Because the LaserJet can certainly interpret a form feed code, that method is chosen for page ejection.

You'll learn about the other printing options in this chapter and in later chapters that discuss more advanced printing features.

Keeping Pages Vertically Aligned

If you have a tractor-fed, dot-matrix printer, when you first turn on the printer, the computer (and Paradox) assumes that the print head is aligned at the top of a new page. Any report you start printing begins wherever the print head happens to be.

When Paradox has finished printing a report, you should eject the last page from the printer using the form feed (or equivalent) button. Don't "crank" the page manually out of the printer. If you do, Paradox will lose track of where the top of each page is.

If you want to be absolutely sure that Paradox starts each page of a report at the top of a page, turn off the printer, manually position the top of the first page right at the print head, then turn on the printer again. Doing so not only aligns all the pages, but also resets the "top of form" setting that tells Paradox where the top of the current page is.

Testing Your New Printer Settings

Before you can test your new settings by printing another Instant Report, you need to delete the Standard Report that Paradox automatically creates the first time you use the Instant Report feature. This is necessary because the new printer settings are only applied to new report formats. Follow these steps to delete the original Standard Report and print an Instant Report with your new settings:

1. As usual, choose **Tools** ➤ **More** ➤ **Directory** if you need to switch to the directory that contains the table you want to print.

2. Choose **T**ools ➤ **D**elete ➤ **R**eport.

3. Type or choose the name of the table you want to print.

4. Choose **R**-Standard Report (it may be the only option), then choose OK.

5. Open the table and press the Instant Report key, Alt-F7.

If the settings don't work as you intended, you can return to the Custom Configuration Program's Report Settings dialog box and try different ones. Getting Paradox and your printer in sync isn't so crucial for your Instant Reports, but it is important to set up defaults that will work with the formatted reports you will create.

Designing Formatted Reports

The Instant Report method is a quick and easy way to print a "data dump" of information in a table. But in many cases, you'll want your data printed in more refined formats, for mailing labels, form letters, neatly arranged lists, and other types of reports. Paradox allows you to design up to 15 reports per table (including the Standard Report, which you can customize or replace like any other report).

You can define two basic types of reports with Paradox:

- Tabular reports, which print data in tabular columns. The Instant Report you get when you press Alt-F7 is a tabular report. Examples of tabular reports are shown in Figures 8.14 through 8.17 in this chapter.

- Free-form reports, which print data in any arrangement you wish. The directory listing, form letters, mailing labels, and envelopes presented in Figures 8.18 through 8.22 are all examples of free-form reports.

Regardless of which type of report you want to print, you use the Paradox Report Designer to do it.

Getting to the Report Design Screen

To design a free-form or tabular report, you first need to get to the Report Design screen. Here's how:

1. From the Paradox desktop, choose **R**eport ➤ **D**esign. You'll see a dialog box for choosing a table.

2. Type or choose the name of the table for which you want to design the report. (As usual, if the table you want to design a report for isn't in the current directory, use **T**ools ➤ **M**ore ➤ **D**irectory to get to the appropriate directory first.) You'll see a list of existing and available (Unused) reports:

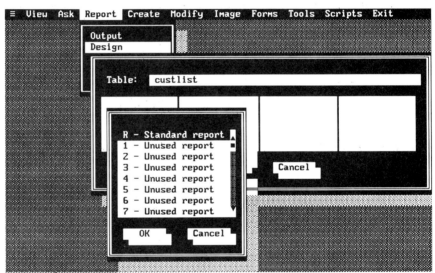

3. If you're designing a new report, choose the first unused report in the list, either by double-clicking on it with the mouse or by highlighting its name with the arrow keys and pressing ↵.

(You can also use the scroll bar or the ↑, ↓, PgUp, and PgDn keys to scroll through the list.) You'll see this dialog box:

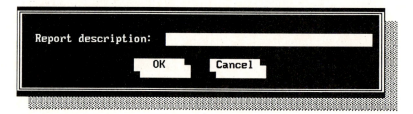

4. Type a brief description of the purpose of the report, such as **Directory Listing** or **Mailing Labels**. Then choose OK or press ↵. You'll see a submenu of the two report types.

5. From the submenu, choose either **T**abular or **F**ree-Form, depending on which type of report you want to create.

The Report Design screen appears. If you chose to create a tabular report, all the fields are listed horizontally across the middle of the screen, as shown in Figure 8.5. If you selected to create a free-form report, all the fields in a single record are listed vertically near the center of the screen, as in Figure 8.6.

FIGURE 8.5

When you create a tabular report, the field names appear across the center of the Report Design screen.

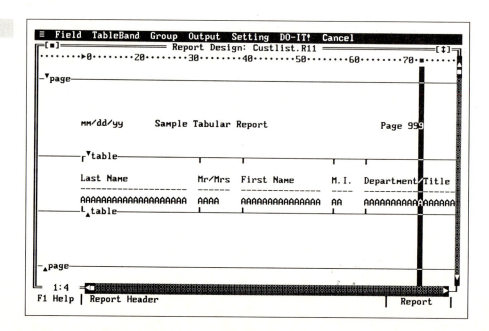

FIGURE 8.6

When you create a free-form report, the field names are arranged vertically in the Report Design screen.

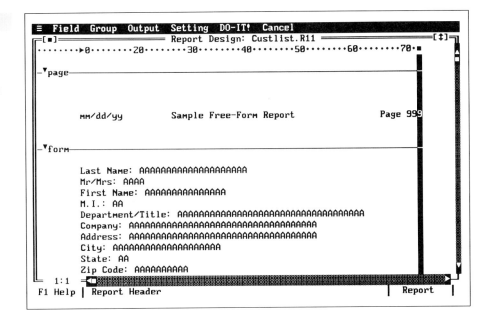

You can now design the format for your report, using the options and techniques described in this chapter. When your design is complete, save it by choosing **DO-IT!** from the menu bar or by pressing F2.

If you close the Report Design window using its Close button, your work will not be saved. You must choose DO-IT! or press the Do-It! key (F2) to save a report format.

Understanding Field Masks

The *field masks* on the Report Design screen show where data from the table (or elsewhere) will appear on the printed report and how much space is allotted to each field. For example, the row of *A*'s below Last Name in Figure 8.5 and next to Last Name: in Figure 8.6 shows where the contents of the Last Name field from each record will appear in the printed report. The *A* itself indicates that the field is alphanumeric. In this example, the field mask is 20 characters wide, which is the size assigned to the field in the table structure.

Different types of data are represented by different field masks:

- A numeric field is represented by a series of 9's, with the number of decimal places defined for that field. For example, the field mask 999999.99 might print the field as 123.45.

- A currency field is represented by a series of 9's, with two decimal places and commas for thousand separators. For example, the field mask (999,999.99) might print the field as 1,234.56.

- A date field is represented by its date format. For example, the field mask mm/dd/yy might print the date as 5/31/94.

- A time field is represented by its time format. For example, the standard format field mask hh:mm pm might print the time as 12:00 pm.

Report Design Screen Indicators

The Report Design screen displays several indicators to help you design reports:

- The horizontal ruler across the top of the screen indicates character positions on the page. Heavy dots mark the "fives" positions (5, 15, 25, 35, and so on), and smaller dots mark the "ones" positions in between. Numbers mark the "tens" positions, with the 0 in 10 at position 10, the 0 in 20 at position 20, and so on. When you press Ctrl-Home to move to the beginning of the line, the cursor moves to the left margin position of that line. Home to move to the beginning of the line, the cursor moves to the left margin position of that line.

- The left margin indicator appears as a triangle (▶) on the horizontal ruler. This triangle indicates the position of the leftmost character in the report, and it is always one character position greater than the actual left margin setting.

- The right margin indicator appears as a solid bar down the right edge of the window, with a small solid box at the top of the bar. Any text on or to the left of this bar will print on the first printed page. Any text or fields beyond that vertical bar will print on a spillover page.

- The vertical ruler indicates which line the cursor is on. You can turn this vertical ruler on and off by pressing Ctrl-v.

DESIGNING FORMATTED REPORTS

- The current/total page-width indicator, in the lower-left corner of the window, shows which "page width" the cursor is currently on, as well as the total number of page widths in the report. This is useful for keeping track of which data will print on a spillover page. For example, 2:4 indicates that the cursor is on the second (second-from-the-left) page width, and that there are a total of four page widths in the report (that is, three spillover pages to the right of the right margin setting).

Figure 8.7 illustrates these indicators on the Report Design screen.

Basic Skills for Controlling Report Text and Lines

A report format basically consists of two types of information: field masks and literal text and lines, which are to be printed on the report exactly as they appear on the Report Design screen. This section describes the basic

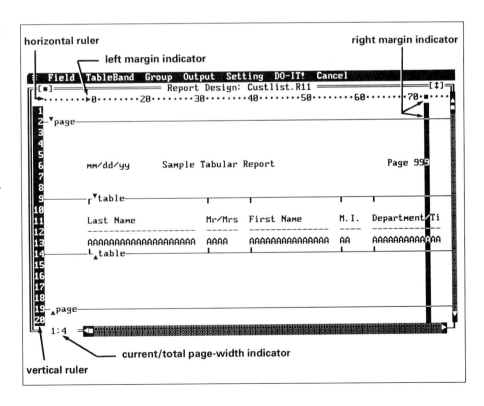

FIGURE 8.7

Report Design screen indicators help you design your reports. Note that the left margin in this example is set to 8, which places the left margin (▶) indicator on the horizontal ruler at position 9. You cannot place text or fields to the left of the ▶.

PRINTING FORMATTED REPORTS

techniques for managing literal text and blank lines. Field masks require different handling, as explained a little later in the chapter.

You can move around the Report Design screen using the standard techniques: by clicking with your mouse or using the scroll bars at the right and bottom borders of the window. You can also size the window by dragging its lower-left corner and move it by dragging its title bar.

The keys that you can use to position the cursor and to insert and delete text and lines are summarized in Table 8.1.

TABLE 8.1: Keyboard Techniques in a Report Design Screen

ACTION	KEYPRESS
Up one line	↑
Down one line	↓
Left one character	←
Right one character	→
Top line	Home
Bottom line	End
Beginning of line	Ctrl-Home
End of line	Ctrl-End
Up one screen	PgUp
Down one screen	PgDn
Left one screen	Ctrl-←
Right one window	Ctrl-→
Toggle Insert/Typeover mode	Insert (Ins)
Delete character at cursor	Delete (Del)
Delete character to left of cursor	Backspace
Vertical ruler on/off	Ctrl-v
Delete to end of line	Ctrl-y
Insert a line	↵ (in Insert mode)

Inserting and Overwriting Text

The Ins (Insert) key acts as a toggle between Insert and Overwrite modes, just as it does when you are editing a field of a table in Field view. When Insert mode is active, the cursor appears as a small blinking underline, and any text you type is inserted into the line without replacing existing text. Pressing Ins again toggles to Overwrite mode, and the cursor appears as a blinking rectangle. Any text you type overwrites (replaces) any existing text at the cursor position.

Inserting and Deleting Lines

If you want to insert a blank line into the report format, make sure you are in Insert mode. Then simply press ↵ to add the line.

To delete an entire line, first move the cursor to the left margin by pressing Ctrl-Home. Then press Ctrl-y to delete the whole line.

Moving Text and Fields Left and Right

You can "push and pull" text and field masks left and right across the Report Design screen by inserting and deleting spaces. For example, to push text toward the right margin, move the cursor to the left of the field mask or text you want to move, make sure you're in Insert mode, and press the spacebar to insert blank spaces.

To move text or a field mask to the left, again place the cursor to the left of the text or field mask. Then press Backspace or Delete to delete blank spaces to the left of the item you want to move.

Deleting and Inserting Spillover Pages

The current/total page-width indicator shows whether your report has spillover pages. If you don't want the spillover pages in your report, you can remove them. Choose **S**etting ➤ **P**ageLayout ➤ **D**elete to delete the rightmost spillover page. To ensure that no spillover pages appear, repeat these menu selections until the indicator shows 1:1. Any column which is even partly in the deleted spillover page and any literal text in the deleted spillover page will be removed from the report design.

If you want to add a spillover page, choose **S**etting ➤ **P**ageLayout ➤ **I**nsert. The first text on a spillover page appears just to the right of the right margin indicator.

Understanding Report Design Bands

The Report Design screen is divided into several *bands*. As you move the cursor up and down through the screen, the status bar near the lower-left corner indicates which band currently contains the cursor. Understanding the role of each band is essential to good report design.

Figure 8.8 summarizes the position and role of the various bands, which are described in the following sections. Sample reports in this chapter (and in Chapter 15) show how and when to use the various bands to get precisely the effect you want in your formatted reports.

FIGURE 8.8

The various bands that appear in the Report Design screen

```
                This is the Report Header band: Text and/or fields here are printed
                         once at the beginning of the report.
──▼page────────────────────────────────────────────────────

                 This is the Page Header band: Text and/or fields here are printed
                            once at the top of each page.

──▼form or ▼table──────────────────────────────────────────

                This is a Form or Table band: Text and/or fields here are printed once
                                 for each record.

──▲form or ▲table──────────────────────────────────────────

                 This is a Page Footer band: Text and/or fields here are printed once
                             at the bottom of each page.

──▲page────────────────────────────────────────────────────

                This is the Report Footer band: Text and/or fields here are printed
                            once at the end of the report.
```

Report Header Band

The Report Header band appears at the top of the Report Design screen, above the ▼ page indicator. Any text or fields placed in this area are printed once at the top of the report.

When you first create a new report, the Report Header band contains one blank line. You can type any text that you want to appear at the top of the first printed page, such as a report title, into the Report Header band. If you don't want to print a report header on the first page of the report, you might want to delete the blank line in the Report Header band, so you don't end up with an extra blank line at the top of the first page.

Page Header Band

The second band in the Report Design screen, beneath the ▼ page indicator, is the Page Header band. Text and any blank lines in this band are printed once at the top of each printed page.

When you first create a new report format, the Page Header band consists of six lines, including a line with a field mask for the current date (*mm/dd/yy*), the report description (if any), and the word *Page* followed by a field mask for the page number (*999*). You can change the text and fields in the Page Header band and add or delete blank lines to increase or decrease the size of the top margin on each page.

Most printers print six lines to the inch. So the six lines in the Page Header band leave about a 1-inch margin at the top of each printed page.

Table Band

If you created a tabular report, the Table band appears near the middle of the screen, between the ▼ table and ▲ table indicators, as in the example shown below.

The Table band represents the main body of a tabular report. The field names and underlines (and any blank lines above them) appear once at the top of each page. They print below the Page Header band text but above the first printed record. The field masks indicate data to be printed from the table. Any blank lines beneath the field masks are printed as blank lines between records in the report.

For example, using the sample Table band, the printed report might look like this:

Adams	Mr.	Andy	A.
Miller	Miss	Maria	N.
Zastrow	Dr.	Ruth	
Rosiello	Mr.	Richard	L.

You could insert one blank line beneath the field masks in the Table band, like this:

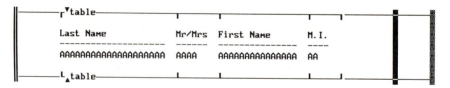

Then each printed record would have a blank line beneath it, like this:

Adams	Mr.	Andy	A.
Miller	Miss	Maria	N.
Zastrow	Dr.	Ruth	
Rosiello	Mr.	Richard	L.

Techniques for changing the Table band are covered in more detail a little later in this chapter.

Form Band

If you're designing a free-form report, a Form band appears in the Report Design screen, between the ▼ form and ▲ form indicators (see Figure 8.6).

Like the Table band in a tabular report, the Form band contains the text and fields that make up the main body of a free-form report. Any blank lines within the Form band are printed as blank lines in or between records. You'll see examples of setting up the Form band to print a directory list, form letters, and mailing labels later in the chapter.

Page Footer Band

Beneath the Table or Form band but above the ▲ page indicator on the screen lies the Page Footer band. Any text and blank lines in this section of the Report Design screen are printed once at the bottom of each page. Initially, this part of the report consists of four blank lines, without any text or fields. This leaves about a ³⁄₄-inch margin at the bottom of each page.

Report Footer Band

Beneath the ▲ page indicator on the Report Design screen lies the Report Footer band. Any text or fields you enter in this area will be printed once at the end of the report. As you'll learn in Chapter 15, this band is particularly useful for printing a grand total at the end of a report that includes subtotals.

Managing the Table Band

When you're designing a tabular report, you can manipulate the columns that appear in the Table band. If you selected to create a tabular report, **T**ableBand appears on the Report Design screen's menu bar. When you select **T**ableBand, you see this menu:

PRINTING FORMATTED REPORTS

The following sections describe how to use the TableBand menu options to manage the columns in your report. Once you have the columns arranged as you want them to print, you can place field masks within those columns to control the format of your printed data, as described later in this chapter.

Using the Mouse versus Using the Keyboard

Many of the operations described in the following sections can be performed by using either a mouse or the keyboard. In most cases, using the mouse requires fewer steps and is faster. For example, with the mouse you can delete a column with one click; the keyboard method requires using the arrow keys to position the cursor and then pressing ↵. In some cases, the only difference between the mouse and keyboard methods is that you move the mouse pointer and click, rather than position the cursor and press ↵.

You may prefer to use the less abrupt keyboard method at first, graduating to the mouse when you're sure of the steps involved. The messages that Paradox places at the top of the screen during many of the column operations refer to the keyboard method.

> **TIP**
>
> Even when you're using the keyboard method, if you click on the column or field mask you want to work with before choosing a menu option, you won't need to bother with the arrow keys to position the cursor.

You can also combine the keyboard and mouse methods for most operations. However, if you're using the keyboard, in the final steps, usually you'll need to move the cursor with the arrow keys not by clicking the mouse, since clicking the mouse is the equivalent of moving the cursor and pressing ↵.

Deleting a Column

By pressing Alt-F7, you can quickly print every field in your table in a tabular format. But when you're designing your own tabular reports, you'll probably want to print only certain fields, if only to avoid dealing with spillover pages. The simplest way to remove a field from a tabular report is to delete its column in the Table band.

To remove a column, choose **TableBand ➤ Erase**. Then move the mouse pointer to the column you want to erase and click. Be careful; the column will be deleted with one click. With the keyboard, use the arrow keys to move the cursor to the column you want to delete, then press ↵. The column, including its contents, is deleted. All columns to the right are shifted to the left to fill in the void.

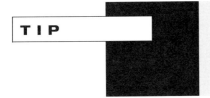

You can delete all the columns in the last spillover page using Setting ➤ PageLayout ➤ Delete. Remember, even columns that are only partially in the spillover page will be deleted.

Inserting a Column

To insert a new, empty column into the table band, choose **TableBand ➤ Insert**. Move the mouse pointer to where you want to insert the column and click the left mouse button. With the keyboard, use the arrow keys to move the cursor to where you want the new column inserted, and then press ↵.

The new column appears at the cursor position, shifting the field under the cursor and all fields to the right of the cursor further right. You can then resize the column to suit the data that will print in it.

Resizing a Column

To narrow or widen a column in the Table band, choose **TableBand ➤ Resize**. Move the mouse pointer to an empty space in the column you want to resize (usually toward the right end of the column), then hold down the left mouse button and drag to resize the column.

With the keyboard, use the arrow keys to move the cursor to the column you want to resize (preferably to the right edge of that column) and press ↵ to select the column. Then, as indicated by the instructions on the screen, use the → key to widen the column or the ← key to narrow it. When the column is the desired size, press ↵.

TIP If you plan to place a field mask in a newly inserted column, resize the column to an appropriate width before adding the field mask.

You can narrow or widen any column in the Table band, but you can't make a column any narrower than the width required by its current text or field masks. Also, you can only widen a column as far as the combined page widths in the report format will allow. Here are some other points to keep in mind while resizing a column in the Table band:

- If you see the message "Cannot split field during column resize," it's because the mouse pointer or cursor is currently on (or above) a field mask. Reposition the mouse pointer or cursor to an empty portion of the column, then proceed. If there is no empty space in the column, press Esc three times to cancel the operation. Then change the width of the text or field mask, as described next, to make some room within the column.

- You can only narrow a column to the width currently occupied by text and/or a field mask plus one. If you want to narrow a column more than that, you must first delete some text using Backspace or Delete, and/or reduce the size of the field mask (using **Field ➤ Reformat**, as described later in this chapter).

- Always start resizing from just inside the column boundary. If there's empty space to the right of the mouse pointer or cursor when you start resizing, you may run into the edge of the column, existing text, or a field mask before you've narrowed the column to your liking. If this happens, release the mouse button (or press ↵ if you're using the keyboard) and repeat the resizing operation to narrow the column even more.

- As you widen a column, columns to the right are pushed out toward the end of the last page width. If the rightmost column reaches the end of the last page width, you won't be able to widen the column any further. You'll need to either narrow or delete another column to make room (or use **S**etting ➤ **P**ageLayout ➤ **I**nsert to insert another spillover page at the right edge of the report).

Resizing columns helps you fit as much of your data as possible across a page. We'll explore other ways of fitting information on a page throughout the rest of this chapter.

Moving a Column

To move a column to a new location in the Table band, choose **T**able-Band ➤ **M**ove. Using the mouse, click on the column you want to move, move the mouse pointer to where you want the column to appear, and click. With the keyboard, follow the instructions on the screen: use the arrow keys to position the cursor on the column you want to move, press ↵, use the ← or → key to move the cursor to the column's new location, and press ↵.

When you click the mouse or press ƒ to designate where the column should go, the column appears at the current mouse pointer or cursor position, and the columns to the right shift further to the right to make room for it.

You can also move columns in the Table band using the Rotate key (Ctrl-r), just as you can in Table view.

Copying a Column

If you want the same field to be printed in two or more separate columns in the report, you can copy an existing column to a new location. To copy a column, choose **T**ableBand ➤ **C**opy. With the mouse, click on the column you want to copy, move the mouse pointer to wherever you want the copy to appear, and click. With the keyboard, follow the instructions on the screen to make a copy: position the cursor, press ↵, move the cursor to wherever you want the copy of the column to appear in the Table band, and press ↵.

When you click the mouse or press ↵ to complete the copy operation, the column is copied to the current mouse pointer or cursor position, and the columns to the right shift to the right to make room for it.

Managing Field Masks

Unlike the techniques for managing columns in the Table band, which apply only to tabular reports, the techniques for managing field masks are relevant to both tabular and free-form reports. The options for managing field masks on tabular and free-form reports are available on the **Field** menu on the Report Design screen's menu bar:

Placing a Field Mask

You use **Field ▶ Place** to insert a new field. Remember, before you insert a new field into the Table band of a tabular report, you first need to use the **Insert** and **Resize** options on the **TableBand** menu to create a new column of the appropriate size to contain the field mask.

MANAGING FIELD MASKS

The general steps for placing a field mask into your report are as follows:

1. Choose **Field ➤ P**lace. You'll see this submenu:

2. Select the type of field you want to place:

   - **Regular:** Inserts a field for displaying data from the table. You'll see a menu containing field names from the current table, as in this example:

   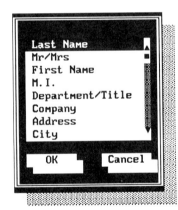

   - **Summary:** Inserts a field for calculating and displaying subtotals and totals in a printed report. See Chapter 15 for more information.
   - **Calculated:** Inserts a field for printing values incorporated from different fields or the results of a calculation of values from different fields. See the next section for more information about using calculated fields.

- **Date:** Inserts a field that prints the current date from your computer's system clock when the report is printed. This type of field is often used in a Page Header or Page Footer band. If you're placing a field mask that displays a date (either a regular one from your table or by choosing **D**ate as the type), you'll see this submenu:

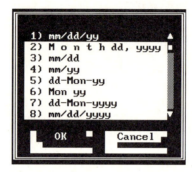

Table 8.2 shows examples of dates in these formats.

- **Time:** Inserts a field that displays the system time when the report is printed. You can choose between the standard format *hh:mm pm* (for example, 2:30 pm), or military format *hh:mm:ss* (for example, 14:30:00).

- **Page:** Inserts a field for printing the current page number on the printed report. Place this mask in the Page Header or Page Footer band when you want to number pages in the report. You can control report page numbering by using the PAGEBREAK command, discussed later in this chapter.

- **#Record:** Numbers the records in the report. You'll be given the options Overall and Per-Group. Select **O**verall to number each record consecutively from the beginning of the report. **P**er-Group numbers records consecutively within groups. (Group bands are discussed later in this chapter.)

CAUTION #Record always displays the record's position in the report, which may not be the same as the record's original position in the table if records are sorted or grouped.

3. Move the mouse pointer to wherever you want to place the field mask (usually at the beginning of a blank Table band column) and click. With the keyboard, use the arrow keys to position the cursor where you want to place the field mask, then press ↵.

If there isn't enough empty space to the right of the cursor to accommodate the field you want to place, you'll see the message

Not enough space here for the field.

You'll need to move the mouse pointer or cursor elsewhere and then click or press ↵ again. You can also or press Esc a few times to back out of the menu selections that got you to this point, then start over.

After the field mask is placed, you'll see instructions for sizing the mask. The exact instructions that appear depend on the type of field you're inserting, as explained in the following sections. If you don't want to resize the field mask, just press ↵.

TABLE 8.2: Date Formats for Printed Reports

FORMAT	EXAMPLE
mm/dd/yy	12/31/94
Month dd, yy	December 31, 1994
mm/dd	12/31
mm/yy	12/94
dd-Mon-yy	31-Dec-94
Mon yy	Dec 94
dd-Mon-yyyy	31-Dec-1994
mm/dd/yyyy	12/31/1994
dd.mm.yy	31.12.94
dd/mm/yy	31/12/94
yy-mm-dd	94-12-31
yy.mm.dd	94.12.31

Sizing Alphanumeric and Memo Field Masks

If the field mask you're placing is to display alphanumeric or memo field data, it will appear as a row of *A*'s. Initially, the mask is equal to the width of its defined width in the table, or the maximum width available in the current column or line. To accept the suggested width, just click on the last *A* in the mask or press ↵.

To shorten or widen the mask, use any of the following methods:

- With the mouse, drag the last *A* in the mask to the left or right. When the mask is the desired size, release the mouse button.

- Click on the *A* that you want to be the last one in the mask, and all the *A*'s to the right of it will be deleted.

- With the keyboard, use ← or → to narrow or widen the mask. When it is the desired size, press ↵.

Sizing Date Fields

When you place a field mask that displays a date, you select from a menu of date formats (see Table 8.2 for examples of the date formats). The field mask will appear in the format you chose. You won't be given an option to size it, because the format defines the width of the mask.

Sizing Numeric and Currency Fields

If the field you're placing is numeric, the field mask will appear on the screen as a series of 9's. If you're placing a currency field, the nines are separated by commas (for example, 999,999,999,999). With the mouse, you can drag the last 9 to the left or right. When the mask is the desired size, release the mouse button. With the keyboard, use the ← key or → key to shorten or widen the number, and press ↵ when it's the desired size. Repeat the process, as prompted, to adjust the number of decimal places.

The maximum width of a numeric field is 12 digits to the left of the decimal point and 8 digits to the right. Once the field mask is placed and sized, you can use **Field ➤ R**eformat to reformat the number according to a variety of international standards.

Placing Calculated Fields

A calculated field is one that incorporates values from other fields in the table. It might simply include data from one or more fields, or it might perform operations with the data and display the result. Each data type uses slightly different calculation rules. This section describes techniques for performing calculations with alphanumeric fields. See Chapter 15 for details on using mathematical calculations with other field types.

To create a calculated field with alphanumeric data types, choose **Field** ➤ **Place** ➤ **Calculated**. You'll see the dialog box shown below:

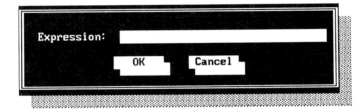

The expression you enter here must follow a few simple rules:

- Field names must be enclosed in square brackets ([ ]).
- Literal text must be enclosed in quotation marks (" ").
- You must use a plus sign (+) to separate the field's text from the field you want to incorporate.

For example, in the sample calculated field below, the literals "Dear " and ":" are both enclosed in quotation marks. Both are joined to the contents of the First Name field using the + operator:

   "Dear "+[First Name]+":"

Note that there is a blank space after the word *Dear* but inside the quotation marks. When creating your own calculated fields, be sure to include blank spaces within quotation marks where you want the spaces to appear in the printed report.

After entering the expression for the calculated field, choose OK or press ↵.

If Paradox cannot interpret the expression, the error message

   Syntax error in expression

appears on the screen, and the dialog box remains. You'll need to fix the expression, then choose OK or press ↵ again. Optionally, you can choose Cancel or press Esc to work your way back to the previous menu.

Later in this chapter, you'll see an example of using a calculated field to print names in a phone list.

Changing a Calculated Field

If you want to change a field mask for a calculated field after you've placed it, use **Field ➤ CalcEdit**. Then click on the mask you want to edit or use the arrow keys to move the cursor to the mask and press ↵.

A dialog box containing the original expression appears. To replace the expression, just type in a new one. To edit the existing text, press an arrow key or click the mouse on the entry before you begin typing. Make your changes, then choose OK or press ↵.

Deleting a Field Mask

To delete an entire field mask from the Report Design screen, choose **Field ➤ Erase**. Place the mouse pointer on any character in the field mask you wish to delete and click. With the keyboard, use the arrow keys to move the cursor to the field mask you want to remove and press ↵.

Reformatting a Field Mask

You can reformat field masks as follows:

- Change the width of any alphanumeric or memo field mask.
- Change the format of any date field mask.
- Change the format and size of any numeric, currency, or short numeric field mask.

To change a field mask's format, choose **Field ➤ Reformat**. Next, click on the mask you want to reformat or use the arrow keys to move the cursor to the desired mask and press ↵. Then you can reformat the field mask, as described in the following sections.

Reformatting Alphanumeric and Memo Fields

If the field mask you chose to reformat is for an alphanumeric or a memo field, you can drag the last character of the mask to resize the mask, or click on any character in the mask to delete the characters to the right of that character. With the keyboard, use the → and ← keys, per the instructions at the top of the screen, to widen or narrow the field, then press ↵.

Remember that in a Table band, you can widen the field only to the width of the current column. If you need to widen the field mask more than that, first use **T**ableBand ➤ **R**esize to widen the column.

Reformatting Date Fields

When you're reformatting a date field mask, you'll see the menu of date formats available for reports, shown earlier in the chapter. Choose the new format you want to use from the menu.

As with other types of fields, if the date field is in the Table band and the column is too narrow to accommodate the new format, you'll see an error message indicating that there's not enough room for the new format. You'll need to choose Cancel, press Esc a few times, then use **T**ableBand ➤ **R**esize to widen the column before reformatting the field mask.

Reformatting Numeric and Currency Fields

When you choose to reformat a numeric, currency, or short numeric field, you'll see this submenu:

Select the option for the format you want to use:

- **Digits:** Lets you change decimal and non-decimal digits displayed in the report. Just as when you first place a numeric field on the Report Design screen, you can use the mouse or keyboard to size the field mask.

- **Sign-Convention:** Displays a submenu with three choices:

  - **N**egativeOnly places a minus sign in front of negative numbers, as in –123.45, and no sign in front of positive numbers, which is the default display for numeric fields.
  - **P**arenNegative displays negative numbers in parentheses, as in (123.45), and positive numbers with no sign, which is the default display for currency fields.
  - **A**lwaysSign places a minus sign in front of negative numbers and a plus sign in front of positive numbers, as in +123.45.

- **Commas:** Displays a submenu with the choices Commas or NoCommas. Commas separates thousands with a comma, as in 123,456.78. NoCommas displays the number without commas, as in 123456.78.

- **International:** Displays a submenu with the choices **U**.S.Convention or **I**nternationalConvention. U.S.Convention displays the number in United States format, where commas are used to separate thousands and a period is used as the decimal point, as in 123,456.78. InternationalConvention displays the number with periods used to separate thousands and a comma as the decimal separator, as in 123.456,78.

NOTE Keep in mind that regardless of whether you choose U.S.Convention or InternationalConvention for your number format, three-digit groups are separated only if the Commas option is chosen from the Commas submenu.

Word-Wrapping a Field Mask

When you place a field mask for an alphanumeric or memo field but make the field mask narrower than the full width of the field in the table, you can choose between having Paradox truncate the field or having it word-wrap the field when printing the report. For example, suppose you place

MANAGING FIELD MASKS   223

a field mask like this for a memo field in a report format:

Abstract:
AAAAAAAAAAAAAAAAAAAAAAAAAAAAAAAAAAAAAAAAA

When you print the report, only the first line of the memo field will be printed within the field mask. However, if you choose to word-wrap the contents of the field, any text that is too wide to print within the field mask will wrap onto additional lines, like this:

Abstract: Black Holes in Milky Way
(blank)
Two teams of astronomers studying different
regions of our galaxy discovered massive
black holes in the Milky Way galaxy. One hole
lies near the heart of the galaxy, the other
about 6,000 light years from Earth.
(blank)
Experts Beeyon and d'Elgin call the findings
the most definitive evidence for black holes
within our own galaxy.

CAUTION — Memo field text will not wrap properly within the field mask if you pressed ↵ after each line, rather than just at the end of short lines and paragraphs.

To have the contents of an alphanumeric field word-wrap within the field, use **Field ➤ WordWrap**. Click on the field mask or move the cursor to the mask and press ↵. You'll see this dialog box:

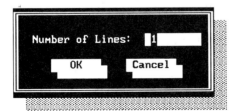

Enter a number indicating the maximum lines to display in the field. Entering **V** (for Variable) means that all the text in the field will be displayed, regardless of how many lines it takes. You can also enter any fixed number to specify the amount of lines you want to print. For example, type **5** to allow a maximum of five lines to be printed on the report. After you enter the number of lines, press ↵ or choose OK.

If you change your mind and decide you want a different word-wrap setting or don't want text in the field to word-wrap at all, choose **Field ➤ WordWrap** again. Replace the number of lines to change the word-wrap. Entering **0** or **1** means that text won't wrap at all.

Justifying (Aligning) a Field Mask

The default alignment for the contents of alphanumeric and word-wrapped fields is left-justified. For numeric, currency, and date fields, the default alignment is right-justified.

Use left justification to align zip code fields so that extended zip code suffixes (the last four digits) align.

You can use **Field ➤ Justify** to specify how you want the contents of a field to be aligned within the column. After you select this option, click on the field mask you want to align, or move the cursor to the mask and then press ↵. You'll see a submenu offering the choices **L**eft, **C**enter, **R**ight, or **D**efault.

After you set the alignment, you won't see any change to the field mask on the screen. However, when you print the report, the data within the field will be justified accordingly.

Changing the Page Layout for a Report

Earlier in this chapter we discussed getting Paradox and your printer "in sync" by changing the default report settings via the Custom Configuration Program. After you change the default page length, margin, and other settings, any new reports that you create with the **R**eport ➤ **D**esign options automatically inherit those same settings.

In some cases, you might want to change those defaults just for the report you happen to be working on at the moment. For example, when you're designing a report to print mailing labels, you may need to change the margins or page length.

You can set the page layout for a single report by choosing options from the Setting menu on the Report Design screen's menu bar, as follows:

- To change the page length for the current report, choose **S**etting ➤ **P**ageLayout ➤ **L**ength. Enter the number of lines to be printed on each page of this particular report, then choose OK or press ↵.

You can set the page length to C (for Continuous), which is useful for certain types of labels and for exporting reports to other programs.

- To change the page width for the current report, choose **S**etting ➤ **P**ageLayout ➤ **W**idth, type in the new page width (in characters), and choose OK or press ↵.

- To change the margin for the current report, choose **S**etting ➤ **M**argin, type in a new left margin measurement (in characters), then choose OK or press ↵.

Usually, you will need to change the margin, page length, or page width for a particular report because you chose a unique page size or print size for that report, as described next.

Changing the Paper or Printer Settings for a Report

Unless you tell it otherwise, Paradox will print your report using the default printer settings and whatever settings you've defined via the Custom

Configuration Program. If you want to change the print size or the paper orientation for a particular report, you can tell Paradox to send the appropriate special code to your printer. You can also choose a printer for the current report, temporarily change the printer port, and pause the printer afer each page. These printing controls are described in the following sections.

Sending Predefined Setup Strings

The code that Paradox sends to the printer is called a *setup string*, which simply tells the printer to switch to another mode. The setup string itself is never actually printed on the page. For example, you might have Paradox send a code to tell the printer to use smaller characters (12 or 16 cpi rather than 10 cpi), or you might send the printer a code telling it to print in landscape mode (sideways on the page).

Unfortunately, there are no standards among printer manufacturers for switching modes. Different printers require different setup strings to perform equivalent functions. The codes you use to get a particular printer to switch modes are usually listed in the owner's manual that came with that printer.

To simplify matters, Paradox comes with a predefined selection of setup strings that you can use without knowing the codes. To use a predefined setup string, from the Report Design screen, choose **Setting** ➤ **Setup** ➤ **Predefined**. You'll see this submenu:

Use the scroll bars or arrow keys to scroll through the menu. The various Small and Condensed options set the print size to about 16.66 cpi. To select an option, double-click on it, or choose OK or press ↵ when the option is highlighted.

NOTE If your printer is not included in the list of predefined setup strings, see Chapter 15 for information about sending custom setup strings to the printer.

You won't notice any immediate change on your screen, other than the message

    Setup information recorded

If you want to see how the setup string will affect the final outcome, you can print a quick copy of the report directly from the Report Design screen by choosing **O**utput ➤ **P**rinter.

Choosing a setup string to define a new page or print size does not change the page length, margin, or page width settings that the report currently uses. Therefore, the same amount of text will still be printed on the page, regardless of the page or print size. To take advantage of a smaller print size or landscape paper size, you need to adjust the page layout settings accordingly, as described in the next section.

Taking Advantage of the Page and Print Size

When you change the paper or print size for a particular report, you usually will also want to change the page layout settings for that report using the options on the Report Design screen's Setting menu, as described earlier. In a nutshell, if you switch to a smaller print size or to a landscape paper size, you want to increase the page width to take advantage of the extra number of characters that can fit across the page.

Table 8.3 shows suggested page lengths, page widths, and margin settings that you might want to try with the various setup strings provided for the HP LaserJet printer.

TABLE 8.3: Predefined Setup Strings for HP LaserJet Printers, with Suggested Page Length, Page Width, and Margin Settings

PREDEFINED SETUP STRING	PAGE LENGTH	PAGE WIDTH	MARGIN
HPLaserJet	60	72	8
HP-Portrait-66lines	66	72	8
HP-Landscape-Normal	45	98	8
HP-Compressed	60	120	12
HP-Landscp	45	166	12

Choosing a Printer for the Current Report

If you're using Paradox on a network or you have more than one printer attached to your computer, you might want the report that you're designing at the moment to always be sent to a particular printer. To choose a printer for the current report, follow these steps:

1. Choose **S**etting ➤ **S**etup ➤ **C**ustom. You'll see this dialog box:

2. Choose the printer port that you want to always send this report to in the future. Next, you'll see this dialog box:

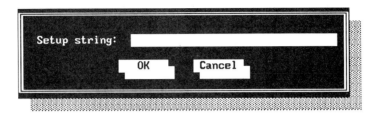

3. Enter a custom setup string to send to the printer before the report prints or leave the box blank to avoid sending a setup string. (See Chapter 15 for more information about setup strings.) Then choose OK or press ↵.

4. When prompted for a reset string, type a custom string to send to the printer after the report prints (or leave the box blank). Then choose OK or press ↵.

Whenever you print the report in the future, it will automatically be sent to whatever port you chose in step 2.

Temporarily Changing the Printer Port

If you're printing on a network (or you have multiple printers attached to your computer), you can temporarily override any previous settings you defined in a particular report format to redirect the report to another printer. Any changes you make affect only your current Paradox session, not the defaults you may have defined in the Custom Configuration Program nor any options you specified from the Report Design screen.

To temporarily override printer defaults, choose **R**eport ➤ **S**etPrinter from the Paradox desktop menu bar. You'll see a submenu with the options Regular and Override. Choose **O**verride, then **P**rinterPort, then whichever port you want to use. Any reports you print during the current session will be sent to that port. If you want to return to the original port during the current session, choose **R**eport ➤ **S**etPrinter ➤ **R**egular.

Report ➤ SetPrinter ➤ Override also lets you send custom setup and reset strings to the printer. You'll learn more about setup strings in Chapter 15.

Pausing the Printer for Each Page

In some situations, you might want Paradox to pause after printing a single page of a report. For example, if you need to hand-feed letterhead stock into a tractor-fed printer one page at a time, you'll want Paradox to pause after each printed page.

To make Paradox pause between pages when printing the report that you're currently designing, from the Report Design screen, choose **Setting ➤ Wait**, then choose **Yes**. When you actually print the report later, Paradox will display the message

   Insert next page in printer. Press any key to continue.

on the screen before printing each page.

If you're hand-feeding paper into a dot-matrix printer, turn off the printer and insert a page so that it's aligned where you want printing to start. Then turn the printer back on and click the mouse or press the spacebar, ↵, or any letter or number key to start printing. You'll need to repeat this process for each printed page in the report.

In general, it's not a good idea to crank the platen manually while the printer is turned on.

Special Techniques for Free-Form Reports

When you're designing a free-form report, field names and field masks are arranged vertically in the Form band. You can insert and delete text, lines, and field masks by using any of the techniques described earlier in this chapter.

A couple of the options on the Report Design screen's Setting menu are available only for free-form reports:

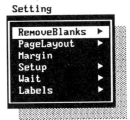

The additional choices are RemoveBlanks and Labels. These options are described in the sections that follow.

Squeezing Out Blank Spaces

Normally, when Paradox prints the contents of a field, it pads (inserts blank spaces into) any field that is narrower than its field mask. In a tabular format, this makes sense, since it ensures that text in the columns lines up. However, padding field contents with blank spaces isn't always appropriate in a free-form report.

For example, Figure 8.9 shows an arrangement of field masks based on fields from the sample Custlist table. The first field mask (AAAA) is for the Mr/Mrs field, the second field mask is for the First Name field, and so on.

If you were to print a report based on this arrangement of field masks, a sample name and address might come out looking something like this:

```
Mrs. Mary       M.      Mohr
(blank)
(blank)
6771 Baldy Vista
Herndon   ,   VA 22071-1234
```

The blank spaces used to pad the fields are certainly not appropriate.

FIGURE 8.9

Field masks in a free-form report arranged to print names and addresses in the customary name and address format: name, department/title, company, address, and so on

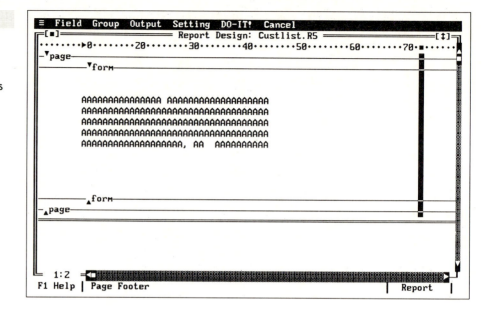

To remove extra blank spaces, from the Report Design screen, choose **S**etting ▶ **R**emoveBlanks ▶ **F**ieldSqueeze ▶ **Y**es. You won't see any changes on the screen. However, the next time you print the report, the blank spaces that usually pad the fields will be omitted. Only blank spaces between field masks remain. Therefore, the name and address shown above would print like this:

```
Mrs. Mary M. Mohr
(blank)
(blank)
6771 Baldy Vista
Herndon, VA 22071-1234
```

This is better, but it might not be quite what you want. You might also want to remove extra blank lines, as explained in the next section.

Squeezing Out Blank Lines

If a particular field in a table is empty when you print a report, Paradox normally will print a blank field, which appears as an extra blank line in the report. For example, the blank lines under the name shown in the previous section are printed because the Department/Title Company fields for that particular record happen to be empty.

To have Paradox omit extra blank lines, from the Report Design screen, choose **S**etting ➤ **R**emoveBlanks ➤ **L**ineSqueeze ➤ **Y**es. The submenu that appears offers two choices:

- **Fixed:** Moves the squeezed-out blank lines to the bottom. This is appropriate for printing labels or for any multicolumn report where each record needs to be printed with the same number of lines to maintain a constant alignment.

- **Variable:** Eliminates the extra blank lines completely, without moving them. This is appropriate for form letters or for single-column reports where each printed record doesn't need to contain the same number of lines.

After choosing either option, the sample address would look like this when printed:

Mrs. Mary M. Mohr
6771 Baldy Vista
Herndon, VA 22071-1234

The blank lines initially printed by the empty Department/Title and Company fields no longer appear.

Printing Multicolumn Labels and Reports

The Labels option, which is available on the Setting menu only when you're designing a free-form report, lets you print text in multiple columns. When you choose **S**etting ➤ **L**abels, you get to choose from a confusing pair of options:

- **No:** Prints any text to the right of the right margin indicator on a separate spillover page. This is the default setting.

- **Yes:** Prints text to the right of the right margin in the next column of the same page (if space permits).

After you make your choice, the message

Label status has been recorded

briefly appears (and that's the only change you'll see on the screen).

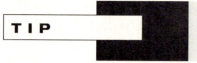

Think of the Labels option as the Multicolumn option, since it's not necessary for printing single-column labels.

To actually print in columns, you first need to change the page width to the width of each column, rather than the width of each page. Also, if you're printing on multicolumn label stock, you'll probably want to reduce the left margin, since labels rarely have much margin space at the left edge of the page.

For example, if you want to print two-across labels, you might begin by choosing **S**etting ➤ **M**argin and reducing the left margin to 0 or some small number, so you won't have a full 1-inch margin when printing labels. Next, choose **S**etting ➤ **P**ageLayout ➤ **W**idth and set the page width equal to the width (in characters) of each label or column.

Perhaps the easiest way to determine the width is to divide the full printable width of the page by the number of columns you need. For example, at 10 cpi, you can get a maximum of 80 characters across the page. So to print two columns, set the page width to 40. To print three columns, set the page width to about 26 (80 divided by 3), and so on. Table 8.4 lists other suggested column widths in relation to different print sizes.

TABLE 8.4: Suggested Column Widths for Various Print Sizes (across 8½" Paper)

PRINT SIZE	SUGGESTED WIDTH		
	2 COLUMNS	3 COLUMNS	4 COLUMNS
10 cpi	40	26	20
12 cpi	48	32	24
16.66 cpi	66	45	33

There is one catch, however. If you try to narrow the page width to less than the widest text or field mask currently on the screen, you'll see the error message

Erase text and delete fields in page width 2 and higher

Paradox will refuse to accept the new page width. You'll need to cancel the operation, press Esc to work your way back to the Report Design screen, then delete text (using Backspace and Del) and/or field masks (with **Field ➤ Erase**), or change the widths of field masks (with **Field ➤ Reformat**) so that no line is wider than the columns you want to print in. Then you can go back and change the page width to the width of a column.

After you set the page width appropriately, you can use **Setting ➤ PageLayout ➤ Insert** or **Delete** to determine the number of columns to print across the page. The number to the right of the colon in the indicator in the lower-left corner of the Report Design screen indicates the number of columns across the page. For example, 1:2 indicates that there are two columns and that the cursor is currently in the first one.

You also need to make sure the Form band contains exactly enough lines to fill one label. If your printer prints six lines per inch, and each label is 1.5 inches tall, each label would need to contain exactly nine lines, as in Figure 8.10.

Notice in the figure that only one set of field masks is used to define the format of the label. The first line of field masks is for the First Name and Last Name fields from a table. This line is followed by the line for Department/Title, then the line for Company, and so on. The last line of field

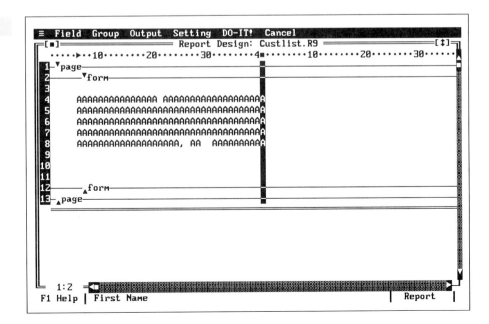

FIGURE 8.10

A report format designed to print two-across labels, where each label is 1.5" tall masks shows the masks for the City, State, and Zip Code fields. You need only define the field masks once, because when the Labels option is set to Yes, Paradox automatically uses the same field masks to print information in each column.

The vertical bar down the center of the screen is the right margin indicator, set at 40 in this example. The 1:2 indicator near the lower-left corner of the screen indicates that this format will print two columns of labels.

The Form band contains exactly nine lines (lines 3 through 11), so each label is 1.5 inches tall. The Report Header, Page Header, Page Footer, and Report Footer bands are all completely empty; they don't even include blank lines. Thus, they don't cause any blank lines to be printed.

If the labels will be printed on pages with a laser or other sheet-fed printer, use **S**etting ➤ **P**ageLayout ➤ **L**ength to set the page length to the normal page length for your printer (such as 60 or 66 lines). If there's any blank space at the top and bottom of each page of labels, add blank lines in the Page Header and Page Footer bands to accommodate that space. For example, Figure 8.11 shows a report designed to print a sheet of two-across labels on a laser printer. The Page Header and Page Footer bands each contain three blank lines, which are included to accommodate the $\frac{1}{2}$ inch (or so) of extra space at the top and bottom of each page of labels. Each label, however, is still nine lines ($1\frac{1}{2}$ inches) tall.

Here are some other points to keep in mind when designing reports for multicolumn reports or labels:

- Use **S**etting ➤ **R**emoveBlanks ➤ **L**ineSqueeze ➤ **Y**es ➤ **F**ixed to squeeze out blank lines on the labels.

- Use **S**etting ➤ **R**emoveBlanks ➤ **F**ieldSqueeze ➤ **Y**es to squeeze out blank spaces.

- If the labels will be printed on a dot-matrix or other tractor-fed type of printer, use **S**etting ➤ **P**ageLayout ➤ **L**ength to set the page length to continuous (C).

- To print one-across labels, use **S**etting ➤ **L**abels ➤ **N**o to prevent multicolumn printing.

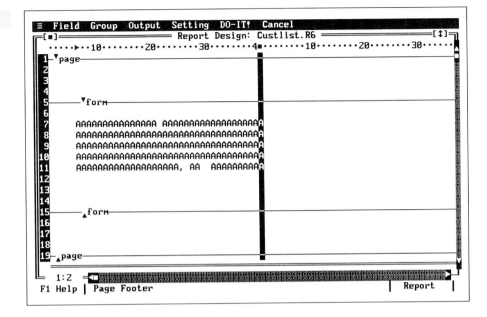

FIGURE 8.11

A report format designed for printing two-across laser printer labels, each label being 1½" tall. The blank lines in the Page Header and Page Footer bands accommodate an extra ½" of blank space at the top and bottom of each page of labels.

Using Group Bands to Sort and Group Records

In addition to the various bands described earlier in this chapter, you can define Group bands for a report. Group bands are useful for several purposes:

- To define the order in which records are to be sorted each time the report is printed
- To print blank spaces between groups of similar records
- To print group headings and footings (including subtotals)

TIP If you want to be able to determine a sort order "on the fly," don't define any Group bands. Instead, use a query or sort procedure to arrange the table in whatever order you want, then print the report using the current sort order. Printing reports from queries and sorts is discussed later in the chapter.

You can define up to 16 levels of grouping. The outermost group specifies the main (primary) sort order, the next group in specifies the secondary sort order, and so on. For example, Figure 8.12 shows a Report Design screen with several grouping levels. The outermost group band is based on the Last Name field. Within that Group band is another group band based on the First Name field. This arrangement of Group bands tells Paradox to print records in Last Name order, with names alphabetized by First Name within groups of identical last names (for example, *Smith, John* comes before *Smith, Mary*).

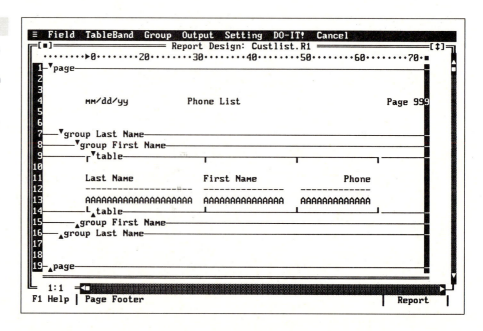

FIGURE 8.12

When defining Group bands, the outermost band defines the main (primary) sort order, the next Group band defines the secondary sort order, and so on.

Inserting and Deleting Group Bands

To insert a Group band into a report, choose **Group ➤ Insert**. With the keyboard, move the cursor to the Page Header band before selecting the menu option. (If you want to insert a Group band within an existing Group band, move the cursor inside that band instead.) The Insert submenu lists three options: Field, Range, and NumberRecords. These options are discussed in the sections that follow.

Each group you insert actually consists of a Group Header, which is bordered by ▼ group above the Table or Form band, and a Group Footer, bordered by ▲ group beneath the Table or Form band. Initially, Paradox puts a blank line in the Group Header and Group Footer bands within each Group band you create. These blank lines (and any text you type inside the Group Header) will appear between groups in the printed report.

Keep in mind that it's the blank lines in the Group Header and Group Footer bands that are printed to create the groupings. If both of these bands are empty, the records are still sorted, but there are no blank lines between the groups. Therefore, you can use Group bands to sort the records without grouping simply by deleting the blank lines that Paradox automatically places in the Group Header and Group Footer bands.

If you change your mind about a Group band and want to remove it, choose **Group ➤ Delete**. Click on the band you want to delete, or move the cursor to that band and press ↵, then choose OK from the submenu that appears. The Group indicator and the Group Header and Group Footer bands are removed from the display.

Grouping on a Field Value

When you choose **Group ➤ Insert ➤ Field** to insert a Group band, you'll see a menu of all the fields in the current table. You can choose a field name in the usual manner: by scrolling, double-clicking, or highlighting and pressing ↵ or choosing OK. Instructions to position the cursor appear, and you can use either the keyboard method and press ↵ to finish the job or position the mouse pointer at the desired location and click.

Grouping on a field sorts all the records by that field. If there are any blank lines or text in the Group Header or Group Footer bands, they appear between nonidentical values in the field. For example, if you group on the State field, and there's a blank line in the group header or footer band, records will be displayed in alphabetical order by state, with blank lines between each state:

AK
AK
AK
(blank)
AL
AL
(blank)
AZ
AZ
AZ

Grouping on a Range

If you choose **Group ➤ Insert ➤ R**ange to insert a Group band, you'll be given the option to choose which field to sort on. After you choose a field, you'll be prompted to define a grouping range. This lets you separate groups in the printed report by some range within that group. The ranges available to you depend on the type of field you use to define the group.

Defining Alphanumeric Ranges

If you chose to sort on an alphanumeric field, you'll see this dialog box:

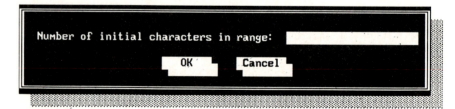

You define the range by specifying how many leading characters make up a group. For example, if you choose Last Name as the field to group on and then enter 1 as the number of initial characters, all the names beginning with *A* will be in one group, all the names beginning with *B* will be in the next group, and so on, like this:

Abzug
Adams

USING GROUP BANDS TO SORT AND GROUP RECORDS

Alinsky
Azimuth
(blank)
Baker
Boorish
Bucolic
(blank)
Carlson
Christianson
Cleaver

Similarly, if you choose the Phone field (an alphanumeric field) as the field to sort on and enter 5 as the number of initial characters in the range, the phone numbers will sorted and grouped like this:

(101)555-1234
(101)555-2345
(101)555-3456
(blank)
(102)555-1029
(102)555-2323
(blank)
(103)555-1212
(103)555-9483

The two parentheses and three-digit area code make up the first five digits of the Phone field, so defining the range as the first five characters groups the numbers by area code.

See the Phone and Fax lists in Figures 8.14 and 8.15 for examples of using Group bands to group and sort records.

Defining Numeric, Currency, or Short Numeric Ranges

If you choose a numeric, currency, or short numeric field after selecting **Group ➤ Insert ➤ Range**, you'll see this dialog box:

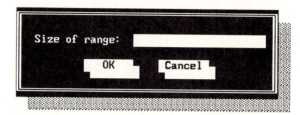

Enter a number indicating the range of values used for grouping. For example, if you choose Credit Limit as the field to group on and specify 2500 as the size of the range, the records will be sorted by the Credit Limit field, with 0–2499 in the first group, 2500–4999 in the second group, 5000–7499 in the next group, and so on.

Defining Date Ranges

If you're defining a range for a date field sort, you'll see this submenu:

Choose one of the options to define the date range:

- **Day:** Groups records with identical dates. For example, all records with 1/1/94 are in one group, all records with 1/2/94 are in the next group, and so forth.

- **Week:** Groups records by week (Sunday to Saturday). For example, records with dates from 12/26/93 (a Sunday) to 1/1/94 (a Saturday) are in one group, records with dates from 1/2/94 (a Sunday) to 1/8/94 (a Saturday) are in the next group, and so on.

- **Month:** Groups records by month. For example, all the January 1994 dates are in one group, February 1994 dates are in the next group, and so on. Records with January 1995 dates would follow records dated in December of 1994.
- **Year:** Groups records by year. For example, records with 1993 dates are in one group, records with 1994 dates are in the next group, and so on.

Grouping on a Record Count

When you choose **G**roup ➤ **I**nsert ➤ **N**umberRecords, you see this dialog box:

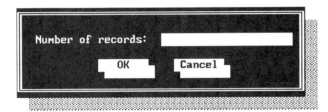

This option does not really sort records at all. Instead, it organizes records into equal-size groups in the printed report. For example, entering 5 as the number of records places one or more blank lines between groups of five records.

Choosing a Sort Direction for a Group

By default, a Group band sort is in ascending order. To sort records in descending order, choose **G**roup ➤ **S**ortDirection. Then click on the Group band that you want to rearrange, or move the cursor into the Group band and press ↵. Choose **D**escending from the submenu that appears.

You can reverse the sort direction for the Group band you've put in descending order by selecting **G**roup ➤ **S**ortDirection again and choosing **A**scending from the submenu.

Changing a Group Specifier

If you want to change the field, range, or number of records you've defined for a Group band, choose **G**roup ➤ **R**egroup. Then click in the Group band or move the cursor to the group you want to change and press ↵. You'll be presented with the same menu of grouping options you saw when you inserted the Group band. Choose a new grouping to redefine the Group band.

Inserting a Page Break or Blank Line

Paradox offers two commands that you can use to ensure that printing starts on a new page or on a new line of your report: PAGEBREAK and BLANKLINE. These two commands are unique in that you type them directly onto the Report Design screen; you can't insert them with menu options.

The PAGEBREAK command tells Paradox where to start printing on a new page. Use this command with Group bands to print each group on a separate page, or with form letters to ensure that each letter is printed on a separate page.

Optionally, you can designate a new page number with which to restart page numbering each time the PAGEBREAK command is encountered during report output. For example, the command PAGEBREAK 1 placed in a Group Header or Group Footer band would force each subsequent group to start printing on a new page and also force Paradox to start numbering each new group's pages with the number 1.

Designating a new page number with PAGEBREAK won't print any numbers on your report pages unless you've placed a page number in the Page Header or Page Footer band, as described earlier in this chapter.

The BLANKLINE command ensures that a blank line will be printed even when you're using LineSqueeze to prevent blank lines within a printed record. This command is particularly useful beneath a word-wrapped field mask when you want to ensure that a blank line is printed between records. BLANKLINE followed by a space and a number inserts blank lines until the page line number specified is reached. You can use this command in a header or to force lines of text to begin printing at a certain place in the page.

There are three rules for using the PAGEBREAK and BLANKLINE commands:

- The command must start at the left margin.
- The command must be alone on the line; no text or field masks can follow it.
- The command must be typed in all uppercase letters.

You must be especially careful where you place the PAGEBREAK command. For example, if you place the PAGEBREAK command within a Table band, each record of the report will be printed on a separate page, which is probably not what you want. On the other hand, if you put the PAGEBREAK command at the bottom of a Form band in a report to print form letters, it will ensure that each letter is printed on a separate page, which probably is what you want.

The sample report formats presented a little later in this chapter show some practical examples of using PAGEBREAK and BLANKLINE, as well as the proper placement of the commands.

Printing Formatted Reports

You can print a formatted report either from the desktop or from the Report Design screen. You can also print just a range of pages and preview a report.

Another way to "print" a report is to a file. This is useful when you want to incorporate the information from the report into a word processed document or use your word processor to embellish the report. Exporting reports to other programs is covered in Chapter 12.

Printing a Report from the Desktop

To print a formatted report from the Paradox desktop, follow these steps:

1. Choose **R**eport ➤ **O**utput. You'll see the dialog box for choosing a table.

2. Type or choose the name of the table you want to print the report from. You'll see a list of formatted reports that you've created for that table, as in the example below:

3. Choose the report you want to print. You'll see a submenu listing the options Printer, Screen, and File.

4. Choose **P**rinter to send the report to the printer.

Printing a Report from the Report Design Screen

Printing your report from the Report Design screen is a handy way to check your progress while you're designing the report. To print from the Report Design screen, choose **O**utput ➤ **P**rinter from the menu bar. Paradox prints a copy of the report, including all the records in the table.

The disadvantage to this approach is that it might waste paper. For example, if you're designing a form letter and just want to take a look at a printed copy, you really don't need to print a letter for every name and address in the table. Instead, you should save the report format, then print selected pages from the desktop, as described next.

Printing a Range of Pages

If you just want to see a single sample page of your printed report, or need to print a few pages that somehow got messed up in the first printing, you can use the **R**eport ➤ **R**angeOutput. Here's how:

1. From the Paradox desktop, choose **R**eport ➤ **R**angeOutput.
2. Choose the table that you want to print the report from.
3. Choose the report that you want to print.
4. Choose the destination for the report (Printer in this case). You'll see this dialog box:

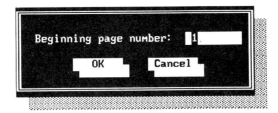

5. Type the page number of the first page you want to print, then choose OK or press ↵. Next you'll see this dialog box:

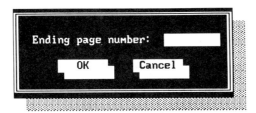

6. Type the ending page number, or leave it blank to print up to the last page of the report. Then choose OK or press ↵. Enter the same page number in both the beginning and ending RangeOutput dialog boxes to print a single page of a report.

Paradox prints only the pages you requested.

Previewing a Printed Report

You can also "print" a copy of your report to the screen. This is handy for checking the format of your report without wasting any paper. To print to the screen, follow the same steps listed above for printing from either the desktop or the Report Design screen, but when Paradox asks for the destination, choose **S**creen.

A copy of the printed report appears in a window named Report Preview, as shown in Figure 8.13. You can move, size, maximize, and close this window as you would any other window. You can also scroll through the report with the scroll bar or cursor-movement keys.

The Report Preview screen's menu bar includes two special menus: Goto and Search. The Goto menu offers the choices Page and EndofReport. Choosing Page from this menu lets you specify a specific page to go to in the printed report. Choosing EndofReport moves the cursor to the last page of the report. The Search menu provides options to let you type some text or a number to search for, starting at the current page position.

FIGURE 8.13

A sample report displayed in the Report Preview screen on the desktop

```
 Goto  Search  Cancel
              Report Preview

    4/17/92         Phone List              Page    1


    Last Name         First Name             Phone
    ---------         ----------             -----
    Adams             Andy                   (619)555-0123
    Adams             Anita                  (678)555-4354
    Cherub            Sky                    (605)555-3232
    Clavell           Wanda                  (432)555-0323
    Dewey             Frank                  (206)555-4323
    Eggo              Sandy                  (234)555-5034
    Gladstone         Tara Rose              (202)555-4343
    Jones             Alma                   (654)555-8395
    Kenney            David                  (123)555-0121
    Levanthal         Danielle               (432)555-9853
    Miller            Maria                  (213)555-3423
    Mohr              Mary                   (345)555-9865

 F1 Help                                              Preview
```

Searching for Values in a Report Preview

After you choose **S**earch ➤ **F**ind from the Report Preview screen's menu bar, type the value you want to find. As with Zoom in Table view, Search is normally case-sensitive. For example, searching for Smith will find only Smiths with the first letter capitalized. But also like Zoom, Search supports the .. and @ wildcards, which make searches non-case-sensitive. Searching for ..smith will find any Smith, regardless of capitalization.

If the first record that Search finds is not the one you're looking for, press Alt-z or choose **S**earch ➤ **N**ext to find the next match (if any).

> **NOTE** You can only search through the copy of the report on the screen. You can't make any changes to the text, since this is simply a preview of your printed report.

When you're finished previewing your report, you can click on the Close button in the upper-left corner of its window or choose **C**ancel ➤ **Y**es to close the window.

Printing a Report from a Query

Normally, Paradox prints a report from all the records in a table. In some situations, however, you might want it to print only specific records. For example, you might want to print form letters and envelopes for residents of a particular state or for people in a specific zip code range.

To print a report for only certain records, you first need to query the table to isolate the records you want (Chapter 7 covers running queries). Then you can copy the report format from the original table to the Answer table and print the report from that table. In order for this to work, you must check all the table's fields in the Query form, because the resulting Answer table must contain all the fields that the report prints. Here are the exact steps:

1. From the desktop, Choose **A**sk and specify the name of the table from which you want to print the report (the table that contains the report format).

2. When the Query form appears, press F6 (or Alt-F6) to check all the fields in the Query form.

3. Define your query criteria, as described in Chapter 7, then choose **DO-IT!** to perform the query. The Answer table appears.

4. If the records in the Answer table are not in the sort order you want, and if you haven't previously defined Group bands in the report format to specify a sort order, you can use **M**odify ➤ **S**ort to sort the Answer table to the same table.

5. Choose **T**ools ➤ **C**opy ➤ **R**eport ➤ **D**ifferentTable.

6. When prompted for the name of the source table, specify the name of the original table (the one you created the report format for), then choose OK or press ↵.

7. Choose the name of the report that you want to print.

8. When prompted for the target table, specify **Answer** as the name of the table (you can just click on OK twice to select this table).

9. Choose any unused report.

10. Select **R**eport ➤ **O**utput and specify **Answer** as the name of the table. (Again, you can just click on OK twice to do so.)

11. Choose the report you want to print, then the destination (Printer).

You can repeat steps 5 through 11 to copy and print additional reports from the Answer table. Note that if the report format includes a #Record field to display record numbers, the printed record number will be the one that appears in the Answer table, not the record number in the original table.

When you've finished, you can close the Answer table by clicking on its Close button or by pressing F8.

> **TIP**
>
> If you will often need to print a report from an Answer table, you can record the necessary steps in a script and save yourself a lot of repetitive work. See Chapter 11 for information about recording scripts.

Printing a Report from a Sorted Copy of a Table

Printing a report from a sorted copy of a table requires the same general steps as printing a report from a query (described in the previous section). This will work, *unless* you've used Group bands to define a sort order within the report format.

Use **M**odify ➤ **S**ort (rather than Ask) from the desktop menu bar, to sort all the records in the table to a temporary table. Then copy the report format to that temporary table and print from that table. Here are the steps:

1. Choose **M**odify ➤ **S**ort and specify the name of the table from which you want to print.
2. Choose **N**ew, enter a name for the temporary sort table (such as **Tempsort**), and then choose OK.
3. Define your sort fields, as described in Chapter 6, then choose DO-IT! The temporary table appears on the screen with records in sorted order.
4. Choose **T**ools ➤ **C**opy ➤ **R**eport ➤ **D**ifferentTable.
5. When prompted for the name of the source table, specify the name of the original table (the one you created the report format for), then choose OK or press ↵.
6. Choose the name of the report that you want to print from the list that appears.
7. When prompted for the target table, specify the name of the temporary sort table (for example, **Tempsort**).
8. Choose any unused report.
9. Choose **R**eport ➤ **O**utput and specify the name of the temporary sort table again.
10. Choose the report you want to print, then choose the destination (**P**rinter).

As when you print from an Answer table, you can repeat steps 4 through 10 to copy and print additional reports from the temporary sorted table.

Also, if the report format contains a #Record field, the record number printed is the record's position in the temporary sort table, not the record number from the original table.

When you're finished, you can close the temporary sort table by clicking on the Close button or by pressing F8.

File Names for Report Formats

All the report formats for a given table are stored in files with an extension beginning with .R. The Instant Report that is created automatically when you press Alt-F7 (named Standard Report) has the same name as the table but with a .R extension. For example, Custlist.R is the file name assigned to the Standard Report for the Custlist table.

Any additional reports you create are given the extensions .R1, .R2, .R3, ..., up to .R14. Therefore, the first custom report that you create for a table named Custlist will be given the file name Custlist.R1.

Changing an Existing Report Format

You may need to change a report format after you've saved it and returned to the desktop. Here are the steps for displaying the existing format:

1. From the desktop, choose **Report ➤ Change**. You'll see the dialog box for choosing a table.

2. Specify the table for which you originally designed the report. You'll see a list of all the reports saved for that table.

3. Choose the report format that you want to change. You'll see the description of the report in a dialog box.

4. If you want to change the report description, edit the text in the dialog box.

5. Choose OK or press ↵.

The report format appears in the Report Design screen. You can use all the techniques described in this chapter to make changes. When you've finished, choose **DO-IT!** or press F2 to save your changes.

Sample Tabular Reports

Now let's take a look at some examples of various printed reports, the report formats used to print those reports, and the techniques used to create each format. The examples illustrate how you can take advantage of the many features Paradox offers to get exactly the format you want in your printed reports.

Each of the three sample tabular reports was created by first choosing **R**eport ➤ **D**esign and specifying a Tabular format.

Phone List

Figure 8.14 shows a fairly simple phone list and the report format used to print the report.

Here's a summary of options and features used to create the phone list report format:

- **S**etting ➤ **M**argin to set the left margin to 8.
- Ctrl-r to rotate the Last Name, First Name, and Phone fields to the first three column positions in the Table band.
- **S**etting ➤ **P**ageLayout ➤ **D**elete three times to delete the three spillover pages that the Standard Report format inserts when you create the initial report.
- **F**ield ➤ **J**ustify to right-justify the contents of the Phone field.
- **G**roup ➤ **I**nsert ➤ **F**ield to insert Group bands for the Last Name and First Name fields. (Last Name is the outermost Group band.)
- Ctrl-y to delete blank lines from the Report Header, Report Footer, Group Header, and Group Footer bands to prevent blank lines from being printed on the report.
- Blank spaces in front of the word *Phone* to right-justify it within its column, to match the right justification of phone numbers.

254 CHAPTER **8**   **PRINTING FORMATTED REPORTS**

FIGURE 8.14

Top: A phone list printed from the Custlist table. This is a tabular report that prints only the Last Name, First Name, and Phone fields, so there are no spillover pages. Bottom: The report format used to print the phone list.

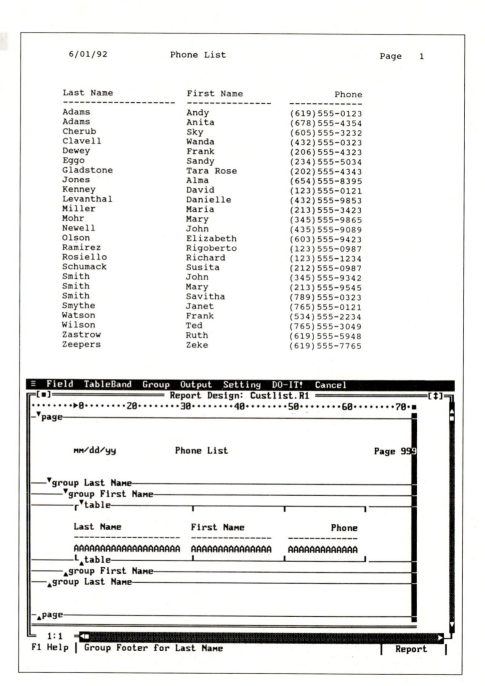

Phone and Fax List

Figure 8.15 shows a modified phone list that uses a calculated field to display each person's name. The calculated field saves some space, leaving room for both the phone and fax numbers.

Here's a summary of options and features used to create the phone and fax list report format:

- **S**etting ➤ **M**argin to set the left margin to 8.
- Ctrl-r to rotate the Phone and FAX columns to the left margin so they are the first two columns in the Table band.
- **S**etting ➤ **P**ageLayout ➤ **D**elete three times to delete all the spillover pages.
- **T**ableBand ➤ **E**rase to delete the Start Date and Credit Limit columns from the Table band.
- **T**ableBand ➤ **I**nsert, then **T**ableBand ➤ **R**esize to insert a blank column to the left of the Phone field and widen it as much as possible (until the FAX column reached the right margin).
- The title **Name** and the underline (hyphens on the line below) typed into the new column, **F**ield ➤ **P**lace ➤ **C**alculated to insert a calculated field containing the expression below into this new column, and the field mask resized to be slightly narrower than the column:

  [Last Name]+", "+[Mr/Mrs]+" "+[First Name]+" "+[M.I.]

- **F**ield ➤ **J**ustify to right-justify the Phone and FAX field masks.
- Blank lines in front of the words *Phone* and *FAX* to align these column titles with the data within each column.
- Ctrl-y to delete the default line in the Page Header band and some blank lines, and the title **Customer Phone and FAX Numbers** typed in this band.
- In the Page Footer band, the underscore (Shift-hyphen) typed across row 17, **F**ield ➤ **P**lace ➤ **D**ate to insert the field mask for the current date at the left margin of line 18, **P**age typed near the right margin, and **F**ield ➤ **P**lace ➤ **P**age to insert a field mask for the page number.

FIGURE 8.15

Top: A phone list that uses a calculated field to display names and includes both the phone number and Fax number for each record. Bottom: The report format used to print the modified phone list. The cursor is currently in the field mask used to print names, so you can see the expression used in that calculated field in the status bar.

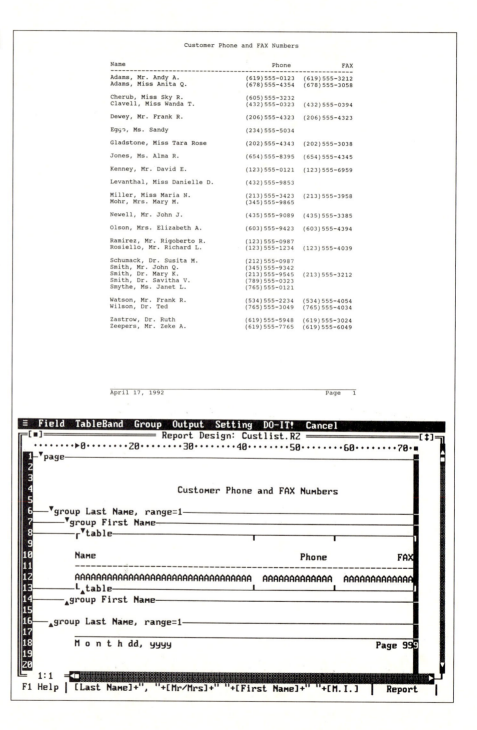

SAMPLE TABULAR REPORTS 257

- **G**roup ➤ **I**nsert ➤ **R**ange to insert the outermost Group band based on the first letter of the last name (Range = 1). Ctrl-y to delete the blank line in the Group Header band (but not the Group Footer band) so that one blank line separates last names that begin with the same letter.

- **G**roup ➤ **I**nsert ➤ **F**ield to insert a Group band for the First Name field. Ctrl-y to delete blank lines in the First Name Group Header and Group Footer bands, since First Name is used for sorting purposes only.

Wide Tabular Report

Figure 8.16 shows a report that takes advantage of the HP LaserJet's ability to print in compressed size in landscape mode.

The report format used to print this report is wider than what a single screen can show, but Figure 8.17 shows the first two screen widths used to print the report.

FIGURE 8.16

A report printed in landscape mode, using compressed print size, on an HP LaserJet

```
                              Customer Names and Addresses
                              ==============================

Last Name    First Name    Department/Title      Company                    Address                     City              State  Zip Code

Adams        Andy          President             ABC Corporation            123 A St.                   San Diego         CA     92122
Adams        Anita         Microcomputer Consultant                         5434 Oceanic Way            Silversprings     MD     20910
Cherub       Sky                                 Oneness Well-Being         985 Enlightenment Way       Jefferson         SD     57038
Clavell      Wanda         Mother Superior       Westridge Convent          452 Reposo Alto             Tiverton          RI     02878
Dewey        Frank         Senior Partner        Dewey, Cheatham, and Howe  1121 Cass St, Suite 33      Bothell           WA     98011
Eggo         Sandy         Owner                 Pancho's Restaurant        911 Delaware Ave.           Roswell           NM     88201
Gladstone    Tara Rose     Vice President        Waterside Land             377 Ave of the Americas     New York          NY     12345
Jones        Alma          Account Executive     Ashland Flowers            10 Shakespeare St.          Ashland           OR     98765
Kenney       David         Attorney at Law       Felson and Fabian          6771 Ocean View Dr.         Anderson          SC     29621
Levanthal    Danielle                            Garden State Bagels        765 Tour de Force Way       Newark            NJ     02321
Miller       Maria         Accounts Receivable   Zeerocks, Inc.             1234 Corporate Hwy.         Los Angeles       CA     91245
Mohr         Mary                                                           6771 Baldy Vista            Herndon           VA     22071-1234
Newell       John                                Newell Construction        212 Riverside Way           Bernalillo        NM     88004
Olson        Elizabeth     Vice President        Precision Computer Arts    80486 Mill Street           Marlow            NH     03456
Ramirez      Rigoberto     Author                                           4323 Moonglow Dr.           Wyandotte         OK     74370
Rosiello     Richard       Accounts Payable      Raydontic Labs             P.O. Box 77112              Chicago           IL     60606
Schumack     Susita        Neurosurgeon                                     P.O. Box 1121               Philadelphia      PA     23456
Smith        John                                                           65 Overton Hwy, Box 112     Holland           MI     49423
Smith        Mary          Graduate School of    Cal State L.A.             P.O. Box 1234               Los Angeles       CA     91234
                           Business
Smith        Savitha                                                        767 Ocean View Lane         Ossineke          MI     49766
Smythe       Janet                                                          P.O. Box 3384               Seattle           WA     98762
Watson       Frank         Greenskeeper          Whispering Palms Golf      8775 Concha de Golf         Bangor            ME     01876
                                                 Club
Wilson       Ted           Psychology Department Pine Valley University     P.O. Box 463                Seattle           WA     98103
Zastrow      Ruth          Internal Medicine     Scripts Clinic             4331 La Jolla Scenic Dr.    La Jolla          CA     92037
Zeepers      Zeke          Chief Engineer        Virtual Reality Designs    5409 Crest Dr.              Encinitas         CA     92024


                                         Page 1
```

FIGURE 8.17

First two screen-widths of report format used to print the report shown in Figure 8.16

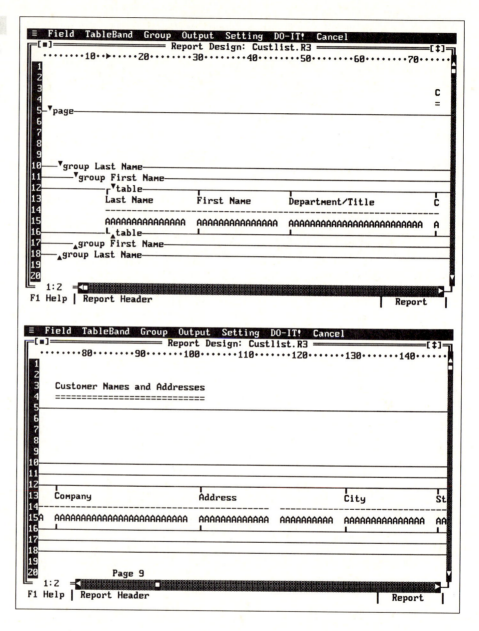

The general techniques to create this wide tabular report are summarized below:

- **S**etting ➤ **S**etup ➤ **P**redefined ➤ HP-LandscpCompressed to choose landscape printing with a small print size.
- **S**etting ➤ **P**ageLayout ➤ **W**idth to set the page width to 166 characters.
- **S**etting ➤ **P**ageLayout ➤ **L**ength to set the page length to 45.
- **S**etting ➤ **M**argin to set the left margin to 12.
- **T**ableBand ➤ **E**rase to delete the Mr/Mrs, M.I., Phone, FAX, Start Date, and Credit Limit columns in the Table band.
- **F**ield ➤ **R**eformat to reduce the Department/Title, Company, and Address field masks each by 10 characters. Ctrl-y to delete left-over hyphens in each of these columns.
- **F**ield ➤ **J**ustify ➤ **R**ight to right-justify the Zip Code field mask.
- **F**ield ➤ **W**ordWrap ➤ **V** to word-wrap the Last Name, Department/Title, Company, Address, and City fields to variable lengths.
- Ctrl-y to delete the original entry in the Page Header band.
- A new title, **Customer Names and Addresses**, typed in the Report Header band.
- In the Page Footer band, **Page** typed, then **F**ield ➤ **P**lace ➤ **P**age to insert a field mask for the page number.
- **G**roup ➤ **I**nsert ➤ **F**ield to insert Group bands for the Last Name and First Name fields. (Basing the Group band on the complete Last Name field ensures that records will be alphabetized by the entire name, rather than just the first letter.) Then Ctrl-y to delete blank lines in the Group Header and Group Footer bands to prevent printing blank lines between groups.
- Ctrl-y to delete the blank line above the column headings.

Sample Free-Form Reports

The remaining sample reports were all created as free-form reports. As mentioned, Paradox initially places field names and masks for each field in a vertical format within the Form band. In most of these examples, the field name and colon were deleted and the field masks were modified.

Directory Listing

The directory listing in Figure 8.18 shows virtually all the information for each customer in the customer table without using spillover pages, because fields are arranged vertically.

Here's a summary of the basic techniques used to create the directory listing report format:

- **S**etting ➤ **M**argin to set the left margin to 8.
- In the Page Header band, the title **Customer Directory** typed and a separating rule added below.
- In the Page Footer band, **F**ield ➤ **P**lace ➤ **D**ate to insert a field mask for a date field; then **F**ield ➤ **P**lace ➤ **P**age to insert a field mask for a page number, then **Page** typed. Also, a separating rule added above.
- **G**roup ➤ **I**nsert ➤ **F**ield to insert Group bands for the Last Name and First Name fields, so records would be sorted by last and first name. Ctrl-y to delete blank lines from the Group Header and Group Footer bands to prevent printing extra blank lines between records.
- The Delete key to delete most of the field names. **F**ield ➤ **E**rase to delete most of the field masks. Then **F**ield ➤ **P**lace to place field masks in the order shown.
- Each of the lines beneath the first field mask indented five spaces by pressing the spacebar five times.
- **F**ield ➤ **P**lace ➤ **#**Record ➤ **O**verall to insert the record number for each person, which appears next to each person's name in parentheses. The parentheses surrounding the field mask were typed in; they are not part of the field mask.

SAMPLE FREE-FORM REPORTS

FIGURE 8.18

Top: A directory listing report, created as a free-form report. Bottom: The format used to print the report.

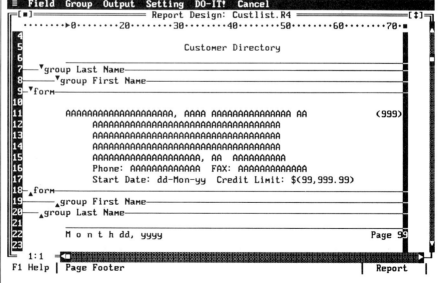

- **S**etting ➤ **R**emoveBlanks ➤ **L**ineSqueeze ➤ **Y**es ➤ **V**ariable, and **S**etting ➤ **R**emoveBlanks ➤ **F**ieldSqueeze ➤ **Y**es to remove field padding in the Form band.
- **F**ield ➤ **J**ustify to left-justify the Credit Limit field mask, to close the potential gap between the dollar sign and the number that follows.
- The underscore characters and the word **Page** typed into the Page Footer band.
- **F**ield ➤ **P**lace ➤ **D**ate to place the system date in the *Month dd, yyyy* format in line 22. **F**ield ➤ **P**lace ➤ **P**age to place the field mask for the page number at the right margin of line 22.

Form Letter

The printed form letter shown at the top of Figure 8.19 was printed with the format shown at the bottom of that figure.

Here's a summary of the basic techniques used to create the form letter report format:

- **S**etting ➤ **P**ageLayout ➤ **W**idth to set the page width to 72 characters.
- **S**etting ➤ **P**ageLayout ➤ **L**ength to set the page length to 60. The page layout settings ensure a 1-inch margin at the left and right sides of each letter.
- **S**etting ➤ **M**argin to set the left margin to 8.
- Ctrl-y to delete the blank line in the Report Header band.
- Ctrl-y to delete the default report title from the Page Header band. A new, blank line inserted in its place, leaving six blank lines in the Page Header band for a 1-inch top margin.
- **F**ield ➤ **P**lace ➤ **D**ate ➤ Month dd, yyyy to place the system date at the top of the report (line 9, just inside the Form band).
- Ctrl-y to delete existing field names. Field masks for the Mr/Mrs, First Name, M.I., Last Name, Company, and other fields arranged in the standard name-and-address format used at the start of a letter.

SAMPLE FREE-FORM REPORTS

FIGURE 8.19

Top: A form letter printed for one record from the Custlist table. Bottom: A portion of the report format used to print the form letter.

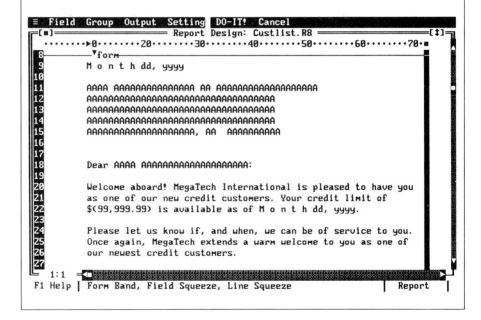

- The salutation **Dear** typed at line 18. **F**ield ➤ **P**lace ➤ **R**egular to place masks for the Mr/Mrs and Last Name fields. A colon typed after the Last Name field mask.

- The body of the letter beginning at line 20. **F**ield ➤ **P**lace ➤ **R**egular to insert field masks directly into the body of the letter (*99,999.99* is the Credit Limit field and *M o n t h dd, yyyy* is the Start Date field).

- **S**etting ➤ **R**emoveBlanks ➤ **L**ineSqueeze ➤ **Y**es ➤ **V**ariable and **S**etting ➤ **R**emoveBlanks ➤ **F**ieldSqueeze ➤ **Y**es to squeeze out blank lines and spaces.

- A PAGEBREAK command at the bottom of the Form band to ensure that each form letter is printed on a separate page, as shown below (it isn't visible in Figure 8.19):

- Ctrl-y to delete blank lines from the Page Footer and Report Footer bands.

CAUTION When you're designing form letters and mailing labels or envelopes, keep in mind that all these report formats should have the same Group bands (or no Group bands). Otherwise, your letters, labels, and envelopes won't be printed in the same order, and you'll need to manually match each printed letter with its appropriate label or envelope later.

Three-Across Laser Printer Labels

Figure 8.20 shows examples of some three-across labels, printed on an HP LaserJet, and the format used to print them. Each label is 2⅝ inches wide and 1 inch tall. Compressed print is required to print on such small

SAMPLE FREE-FORM REPORTS

FIGURE 8.20

Top: Three-across labels printed with an HP LaserJet. Each label is 1" tall by 2⅝" wide. Compressed print is required to print such small labels. Bottom: The report format used to print the labels. The 1:3 in the lower-left corner of the window indicates that there are three page widths in the report format. Note that the right margin bar appears at the 45th character position.

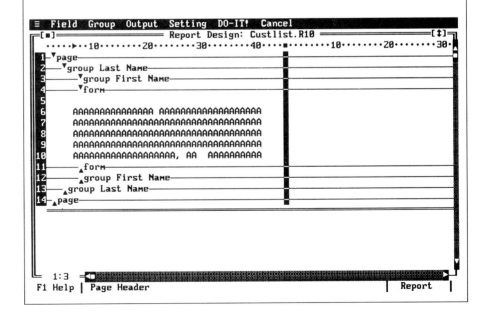

labels, so the predefined setup string for the HP-Compressed print mode was used in the report format.

Here's a summary of the techniques used to create the three-across label report format:

- **G**roup ➤ **I**nsert ➤ **F**ield twice to group the report by Last Name and then by First Name.
- Ctrl-y to delete the existing field masks and text. **F**ield ➤ **P**lace ➤ **R**egular to arrange the fields in a normal name-and-address format.
- **F**ield ➤ **R**eformat to narrow the Last Name and City field masks by one character each.
- **S**etting ➤ **S**etup ➤ **P**redefined ➤ HP-Compressed to print in compressed print size (16.66 cpi).
- **S**etting ➤ **M**argin to set the left margin to 5 characters.
- **S**etting ➤ **P**ageLayout ➤ **W**idth to set the page width for each label to 45 characters.
- **S**etting ➤ **P**ageLayout ➤ **L**ength to set the page length to 60 (with the printer also set to print 60 lines per page).
- **S**etting ➤ **L**abels ➤ **Y**es to ensure multicolumn printing.
- **S**etting ➤ **P**ageLayout ➤ **I**nsert to print three columns. (The indicator near the lower-left corner of Report Design screen should show 1:3 when the cursor is in the first column.)
- **S**etting ➤ **R**emoveBlanks ➤ **L**ineSqueeze ➤ **Y**es ➤ **F**ixed to squeeze out blank lines to maintain an even number of printed lines per label. **S**etting ➤ **R**emoveBlanks ➤ **F**ieldSqueeze ➤ **Y**es to squeeze out blank spaces.
- The Page Header, Page Footer, Report Header, and Report Footer bands are empty (contain no blank lines), because each sheet of labels in this example has only $\frac{1}{4}$-inch top and bottom margins, which equal the "dead zone" at the top and bottom of each page.

- The Group bands are for sorting purposes only, and therefore all the Group Header and Group Footer bands are empty (contain no blank lines).
- The Form band contains exactly six lines, to print 1-inch labels (6 lines = 1 inch).

See the section about printing multicolumn labels and reports earlier in this chapter for more information about printing labels.

Envelopes

If you have a laser printer with an envelope feeder, you can create a report format to print directly to envelopes. Figure 8.21 shows an example of a printed envelope and a portion of the report format used to print it.

Here's a summary of the techniques used to create the envelope report format:

- **G**roup ➤ **I**nsert ➤ **F**ield twice to group the report by Last Name and then by First Name.
- Ctrl-y to delete the existing field masks and text. **F**ield ➤ **P**lace ➤ **R**egular to arrange the fields in a normal name-and-address format.
- **S**etting ➤ **S**etup ➤ **P**redefined ➤ HP-Landscape-Normal to define the paper size.
- **S**etting ➤ **P**ageLayout ➤ **L**ength to set the page length to 45 (the length of a standard landscape page). For printers that do not feed the envelope down the center of the page path, you need to set the page length to about 24.
- **S**etting ➤ **P**ageLayout ➤ **W**idth to set the page width to 98 (the width of a standard landscape page).
- **S**etting ➤ **M**argin to set the left margin to 45 (for envelopes with a preprinted return address).
- **S**etting ➤ **W**ait ➤ **Y**es to pause before printing each envelope (for a printer that must be manually fed one envelope at a time).

268 CHAPTER 8 — PRINTING FORMATTED REPORTS

FIGURE 8.21

Top: An envelope printed from one record in a table. This example was printed with an HP LaserJet that includes a manual feed for printing on envelopes. Bottom: A report format for printing envelopes that have a preprinted return address. The screen is scrolled down to the bottom of the report format, but only blank lines and empty bands appear above the field masks.

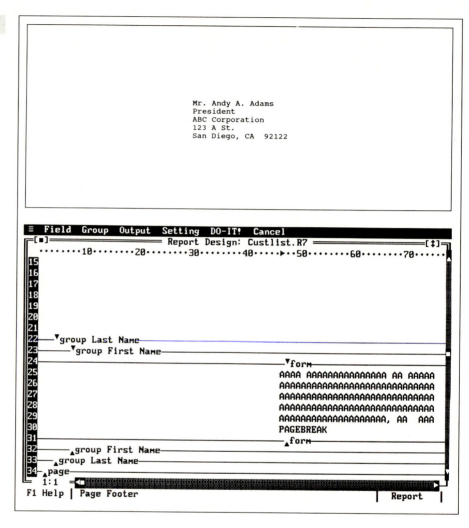

- **S**etting ➤ **R**emoveBlanks ➤ **L**ineSqueeze ➤ **Y**es ➤ **F**ixed to squeeze out blank lines to maintain an even number of printed lines per envelope.

- **S**etting ➤ **R**emoveBlanks ➤ **F**ieldSqueeze ➤ **Y**es to squeeze out blank spaces.

- The Report Header, Page Footer, Report Footer, and all Group bands are empty (contain no blank lines).
- The PAGEBREAK command inserted at the bottom of the Form band, aligned at the left margin, to ensure that each name and address is printed on a separate envelope.

If your envelopes don't have a preprinted return address, Paradox can print the return address on each envelope for you. You'll need to set the left margin to about 15 (rather than 45) and type the return address at about line 13 (or line 2, if your envelopes aren't fed down the center of the page path) in the Page Header band. Then you'll need to indent the field masks for the recipient's name and address manually, to about column 45, using the spacebar. However, make sure the PAGEBREAK command at the bottom of the Form band begins at the left margin. Figure 8.22 shows an example of an envelope report format that includes a return address.

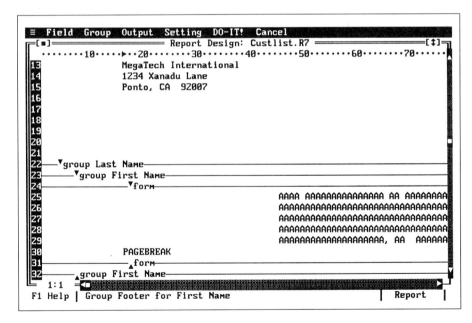

FIGURE 8.22

A report format for printing envelopes that do not have a preprinted return address. The company name and address near the upper-left corner in this example constitute the return address.

270 CHAPTER 8

PRINTING FORMATTED REPORTS

Report with a Memo Field

Figure 8.23 shows a printed report that includes a memo field and the report format to print the report.

FIGURE 8.23

Top: A printed report that includes all the text in a memo field. Bottom: The report format used to print the report. In the report format, the field mask next to Abstract is the memo field, with word-wrap turned on and set to a variable length.

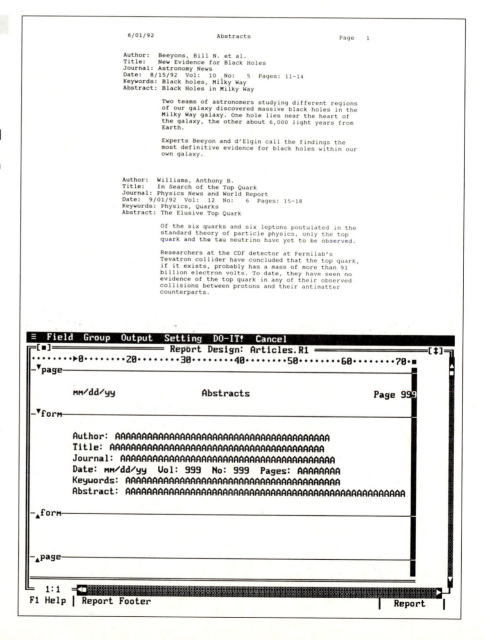

Here's a summary of the techniques used to create the format for the report with a memo field:

- The Delete key to delete field names. **Field** ➤ **Erase** to delete most of the field masks. Then **Field** ➤ **Place** ➤ **Regular** to reinsert deleted field masks at new locations.
- **Field** ➤ **Reformat** to widen the memo field mask to almost the right margin.
- **Field** ➤ **WordWrap** ➤ **V** to set the length of the memo field.
- All the other settings for page length, width, and margin are the standard settings for printing on $8\frac{1}{2}$-by-11-inch paper in portrait mode.

Summary

This chapter covered most of Paradox's features and capabilities for designing reports. For more information about different types of reports, see Chapter 10, which describes how to graph your data. Also read the section about using advanced report and form techniques in Chapter 15. Here's a quick review of the major points covered in this chapter:

- To print an Instant Report of the table currently on the screen in Table view, press Alt-F7.
- To get Paradox and your printer in sync, use the Custom Configuration Program (CCP) to change the default report settings (see Appendix D).
- To design a new, formatted report, choose **Report** ➤ **Design** from the menu bar, choose the table for which you want to design the report, and select Unused report from the list that appears.
- When designing a report, choose between a **T**abular (columnar) and **F**ree-form format.
- The mouse, along with the arrow, Ins, Delete, and other special keys let you insert and edit literal text in the Report Design screen.
- When designing a tabular report, options on the **T**ableBand menu let you insert, delete, and resize tabular report columns.

- Field masks indicate where data from the table and other information, such as the current date and page number, will appear on the printed report.

- Options on the **F**ield menu let you place, delete, and reformat field masks in the report design.

- Report and page bands let you define what text appears in the Report Header, Page Header, Page Footer, and Report Footer in the printed report.

- Group bands, which you can create and delete with options on the **G**roup menu, let you define sort orders and groups in the printed report.

- When designing free-form reports, you can use **S**etting ➤ **R**emoveBlanks to remove the blank spaces and lines that Paradox normally pads field contents with. You can also use **S**etting ➤ **L**abel to design multicolumn reports.

- Options on the **S**etting menu let you change the page layout and other characteristics of the report you are currently designing.

- To save the current report format, choose **DO-IT!** or press F2.

- To print a report, choose **R**eport ➤ **O**utput from the desktop menu bar, or **O**utput from the Report Design screen's menu bar.

- To change an existing report format, choose **R**eport ➤ **C**hange from the desktop menu bar.

CHAPTER 9

Creating Custom Forms

fast TRACK

- **To create a custom form** — 279

    choose **F**orms ➤ **D**esign from the desktop menu bar and select a table. Choose one of the Unused forms from the submenu, then type in a description for the form.

- **To place text on the form** — 283

    position the cursor and type the text. You can add text anywhere on the form.

- **To place a field on the form** — 283

    choose **F**ield ➤ **P**lace from the Form Design screen's menu bar, then choose a field type from the submenu: **R**egular, **D**isplayOnly, **C**alculated, or **R**ecordNumber.

- **To word-wrap a memo or alphanumeric field** — 287

    place the field as usual, then choose **F**ield ➤ **W**ordWrap from the Form Design screen's menu bar, move to the field you want to wrap, and specify the maximum number of lines the field should occupy.

- **To move items on the form** — 290

    choose **A**rea ➤ **M**ove from the Form Design screen's menu bar. Mark the area to be moved, then drag the area to a new position and press ↵.

- **To delete a field or area** — 292

    choose **F**ield ➤ **E**rase or **A**rea ➤ **E**rase. Then mark the area to be removed, and release the mouse button (if you're using a mouse) or press ↵ (if you're using the keyboard).

CHAPTER 9   **275**

To place borders around text on a form   **294**

choose **B**order ➤ **P**lace from the Form Design screen's menu bar and select a border type, then mark the opposite corners for the border.

To add color or other highlighting to a form   **296**

choose **S**tyle from the Form Design screen's menu bar, choose **C**olor or **M**onochrome, and then select **A**rea or **B**order. Mark the area or border, use the mouse or arrow keys to select the enhancement you want, and press ↵.

To display field names during form design   **299**

choose **S**tyle ➤ **F**ieldnames ➤ **S**how from the Form Design screen's menu bar.

To use a form for entering or editing data   **300**

choose **V**iew from the desktop menu bar and select the table whose form you want to display. Then choose **I**mage ➤ **P**ickForm and select a form by number or by double-clicking on its name.

To make a custom form the default   **300**

which will appear when you use F7, display the custom form on your screen, then choose **I**mage ➤ **K**eepSet from the desktop menu bar.

To change an existing form   **302**

choose **F**orms ➤ **C**hange from the desktop menu bar, select a table and form to edit, then change the form using the same techniques you used to create it.

IN Form view, you can enter or edit data a single record at a time. You can use the form that Paradox creates for you, or you can develop your own custom forms. Custom forms are useful when you need to provide on-screen instructions for data entry, or when you want the screen to resemble the paper forms already used in your business. For example, you can design a custom form that looks like a purchase requisition, a sales order, or even a check. Each table can have up to 14 custom forms.

In this chapter, you'll learn how to design your own forms for a table, using the options and features of the Form Design screen. The Form Design screen menus allow you to arrange the fields on the form, as well as add other text, borders, and lines. You can also enhance your forms with colors and video attributes, such as blinking and reverse video.

The Standard Form

When you press F7 or click on F7-Form on the Speedbar, Paradox displays a Standard Form screen, as shown in Figure 9.1. This is the form that Paradox automatically generates for your table.

The Standard Form has a specific format, with the following features:

- The table name appears highlighted in the upper-right corner of the form, followed by a number sign (#) and the current record number.
- Each field is on a separate line, preceded by its field name.

FIGURE 9.1

A Standard Form generated by Paradox

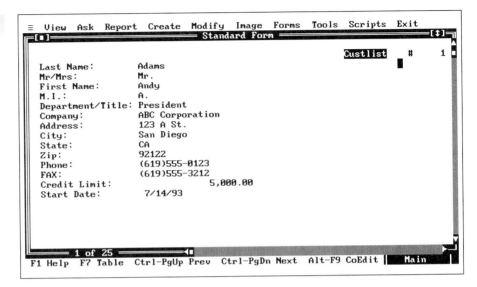

- Each page of the form can hold up to 19 fields, and Paradox generates additional pages as needed. Hence, the Standard Form for a 30-field table has two pages, the Standard Form for a 50-field table has three pages, and so on.

Designing a Custom Form

For many purposes, using a custom form is preferable to using the Standard Form. Figure 9.2 shows an example of a custom form designed for the sample Custlist table. Notice that the highlights and custom borders improve the appearance of the form. Some of the field prompts (such as Starting Date) are spelled out, rather than abbreviated as in the field names. The boxes at the bottom and to the right of the screen contain useful reminders about managing the cursor.

Along with displaying only one record at a time, there are other ways that a custom form differs from a table in Table view:

- In a custom form, you can arrange information in many different ways, not just in rows and columns.

FIGURE 9.2

A custom form for the Custlist table

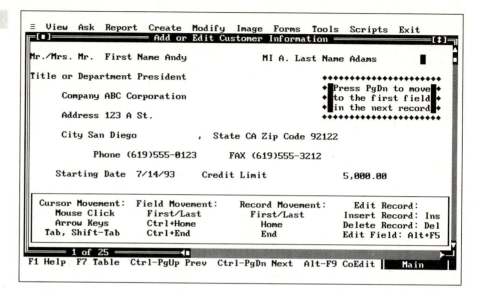

- Excess fields in a form are displayed on separate pages. (In a form, a page is actually one screenful of text and fields.) You can scroll from page to page by pressing PgUp and PgDn.

- You can include calculated fields that aren't actually in the table in a form (see Chapter 15 for details).

- In a custom form, a single memo or alphanumeric field can wrap across two or more lines.

- A custom form can be no wider than a maximized window.

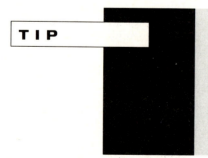

TIP

As an alternative to creating custom forms from scratch, you can begin with a copy of an existing form. If you've already developed a custom form that looks almost like a new form you plan to create, or if you prefer to use a Standard Form as a starting point, you can easily copy that form to either the same table or a different table. See Chapter 12 for more information.

DESIGNING A CUSTOM FORM

Getting to the Form Design Screen

To create a custom form, you first need to get to the Form Design screen. Here's how:

1. Choose **Forms ➤ D**esign from the desktop menu bar. You'll see the standard dialog box for choosing a table.

2. Type or specify the name of the table for which you want to create a form. You'll see a list of forms, as in the example shown below:

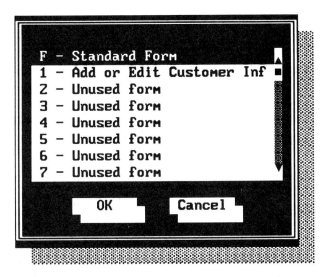

3. Choose the first Unused form in the list, either by double-clicking on it with the mouse or by highlighting its name with the arrow keys and pressing ↵. (You can also use the scroll bar or the ↑, ↓, PgUp, and PgDn keys to scroll through the list.) You'll see this dialog box:

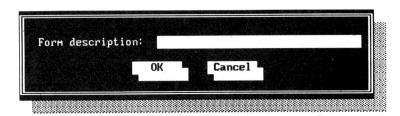

NOTE If you choose an existing form name, such as the Standard Form (F) or a numbered form that you've defined earlier, you'll see a menu with the choices Cancel and Replace. In most cases, you should choose Cancel and select a different form number. If you really intend to replace the existing form completely—clearing all current information in that form and reusing only the form number—choose Replace. (If you want to change rather than replace an existing form, choose Forms ➤ Change, rather than Forms ➤ Design, from the desktop menu bar, as described later in this chapter).

4. Type a description for the form and press ↵ or choose OK. You can enter up to 40 characters. The description will be displayed later when you're selecting forms to use.

After you've entered the description, Paradox displays a blank Form Design screen on which to design your form, as shown in Figure 9.3.

Near the lower-left corner of the Form Design screen is the cursor-position indicator (1, 1 in the figure), which displays the current row and column position of the cursor. Immediately to the right of the cursor-position indicator is the page indicator, which displays the current page number and the total number of pages in the form. In Figure 9.3, the indicator (1:1) shows that the cursor is on the first page of a one-page form. The word *Form* appears in the right corner of the status bar to indicate that you're using the Form Design screen.

Unlike the Report Design screen, the Form Design screen does not appear with field names and field masks. Instead, you start with a blank screen, on which you can place text and place field masks where you want them.

When you're finished designing your form, be sure to save it by pressing the Do-It! key, F2. You'll be returned to the Paradox desktop. If you want to abandon an edited form without saving any of your changes, choose Cancel ➤ Yes instead (or click on the Close button and confirm that you want to close without saving).

FIGURE 9.3

The Form Design screen and menu bar

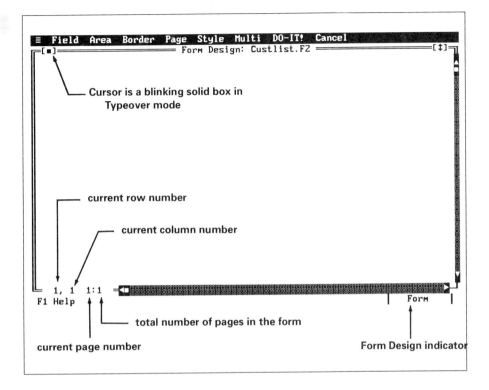

Paradox stores your forms in files with the same name as the table, but with an .F extension. The Standard Form (the one that Paradox creates automatically for the table) has the extension .F, the first custom form has .F1, the second has .F2, and so on, up to .F14.

Working in the Form Design Screen

Managing the cursor and inserting and deleting text in the Form Design screen is similar to doing so in a Report Design screen. The arrow keys move the cursor about the screen. You can also click the mouse anywhere on the screen to move the cursor to that position. The Delete and Backspace keys erase any text that you've already entered onto the form. The Ins key toggles the Insert mode on and off. However, unlike Insert mode in the Report Design screen, pressing ↵ in Insert mode does not insert a new blank line. If you want to move existing text or fields down, you must use **Area ➤ M**ove, as described a little later in this chapter.

Table 9.1 summarizes the keys to use in the Form Design screen.

CREATING CUSTOM FORMS

TABLE 9.1: Keyboard Techniques in a Form Design Screen

ACTION	KEYPRESS
Up one line	↑
Down one line	↓
Left one column	←
Right one column	→
Top of screen	Home
Bottom of screen	End
Beginning of line	Ctrl-Home
End of line	Ctrl-End
Up one page in a multipage form	PgUp
Down one page in a multipage form	PgDn
Toggle Insert/Typeover mode	Ins
Delete character at cursor	Delete (Del)
Delete character to left of cursor	Backspace
Save the current form	F2

> **TIP**
>
> When you use the arrow keys to move the cursor beyond the borders of a maximized Form Design window, the cursor wraps to the opposite side of the form instead of scrolling the form vertically or horizontally. You can take advantage of this seemingly odd behavior to zip quickly to the opposite edge of the screen when you're designing forms. For example, if the cursor is at the left edge of the screen and you want to get to the right edge of the screen, just press ←.

DESIGNING A CUSTOM FORM

You can type text anywhere on the Form Design screen. Just position the cursor where you want to start typing (using the mouse or keyboard), then type your text.

Chapter 15 covers advanced form design for multiple tables.

Placing Fields on the Form

Fields on the Form Design screen are similar to the field masks that you use in the Report Design screen, in that they show where data from the table will appear. However, unlike field masks, fields in the Form Design screen appear as the actual field name or as underscores.

Paradox lets you place four different types of fields on the form: Regular, DisplayOnly, Calculated, and Record Number. The following sections describe how to add Regular, DisplayOnly, and Record Number fields. Calculated fields are covered in Chapter 15.

As when you're placing field masks in the Report Design screen, the quickest way to place a field is with a mouse click, although Paradox's prompts are for the keyboard methods. If you use the keyboard method, you may want to position the cursor before choosing menu options so you won't need to reposition the cursor with the arrow keys after you've made a menu selection.

Placing a Regular Field

Regular fields come directly from the table. To place a Regular field, choose **F**ield ➤ **P**lace ➤ **R**egular from the Form Design menu bar. Paradox will display a list of fields from the table, as in the example shown below for the Custlist table:

Field names appear in the same order as in the table structure. After you've placed a Regular field, however, its name is removed from the list (because there's no need to enter data into the same field more than once). Choose a field name using the usual techniques of highlighting and pressing ↵, double-clicking the mouse, or typing the first few letters of the field you want and pressing ↵.

After you select a field, Paradox will ask you to position the cursor at the start of the field. With the mouse, move the mouse pointer to where you want the field to start, then click. To place the field at its full length, click anywhere on the form to the right of the end of the field. To size the field, place your mouse pointer on the field at the position you want to end the field display and click. The field will be shortened to the point at which you clicked. Alternatively, you can place the mouse pointer on the highlighted last position in the field, hold down the left mouse button, drag until you have sized the field as you desire, and then release the mouse button.

If you are using the keyboard method and haven't already positioned the cursor, use the arrow keys to do so after selecting the field. Otherwise, just press ↵. Then follow the instructions on the screen: use the ← and → keys to adjust the field width and press ↵ when you're satisfied with the width of the field.

Usually, you'll want the full field size, so you can just press ↵ to use the suggested size or click on, or to the right of, the last position in the field.

However, if you're placing a memo field, you might want to widen it, especially if you plan to add word-wrapping (described later in this chapter). You may also want to narrow numeric or currency fields that are never going to require the full length provided by the default Paradox field placement. Paradox will beep and display an error message if you try to make the field too wide or too narrow.

After placing the field, you'll notice that the field position appears as underscores, equal to the size of the field, as in Figure 9.4. If you move the cursor to any of the underscore characters in that field, the status bar at the bottom of the screen will indicate the field type (Regular in this case) and the field name (Mr/Mrs).

Paradox won't let you place a field over an existing field. If you try to do so, you'll see the message

    A field has already been placed here

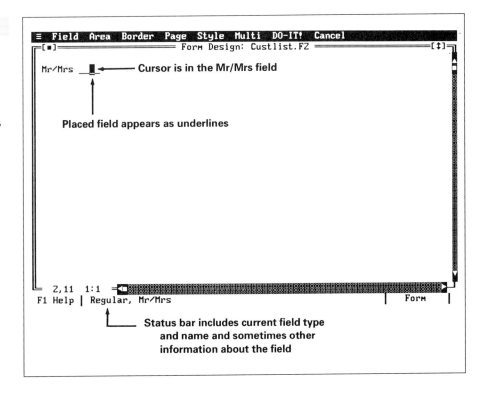

FIGURE 9.4

A field prompt and field placed on the screen. When you place the cursor anywhere in the field, the status bar displays the information about that field.

CREATING CUSTOM FORMS

However, Paradox won't stop you from placing a field over existing *text* (but you should be careful when doing so). If you're in Insert mode, the text that's on and to the right of the starting position for the field is pushed over to the right; if you're in Typeover mode, the text to the right is overwritten.

NOTE The Area ➤ Move option provides another way to rearrange parts of the form, as described later in this chapter.

Placing a DisplayOnly Field

You might want to display a field on your form without allowing the user to change it during data entry. This is when you place a DisplayOnly field on your form. For example, an order form might display a customer's credit limit during data entry but not allow the user to change that information. DisplayOnly fields can also provide handy reminders on multipage forms, as described in Chapter 15. Unlike Regular fields, DisplayOnly fields can be repeated on a form as often as you like.

Defining a DisplayOnly field is a lot like defining a Regular field. Choose **Field** ➤ **Place** ➤ **DisplayOnly** from the Form Design screen's menu bar and select a field name from the list that appears, as described in the previous section. Then use the same positioning and field-width adjustment techniques that you use for placing a Regular field.

If you move the cursor to any of the underscores in a DisplayOnly field, the status bar shows *DisplayOnly*, followed by the name of the field.

Placing the Record Number

As mentioned earlier, the Standard Form includes a field that displays the current record number during data entry. You can add a record number to a custom form as well by placing a #Record field.

Choose **Field** ➤ **Place** ➤ **#Record**. Then use the same positioning and field-width adjustment techniques that you use to place the other types of fields.

Word-Wrapping Alphanumeric and Memo Fields

If your table includes long alphanumeric or memo fields that don't fit on a single line, you can wrap the fields onto two or more lines on a form. During data entry, lines in word-wrapped fields break at a blank space or at a hyphen. However, if the word is too long to fit into the field, Paradox will break it at the end of a line.

Word-wrapping affects only how much of the field is visible on the form, not the amount of data you can put into the field. For example, if you don't word-wrap a memo field, only the first line of the field will appear on the screen when you use the form. But you will still be able to enter, view, or edit as many lines as you want by switching to Field view when you're using the form.

Before defining a word-wrapped field, you must place it on the form using **Field ➤ P**lace. You might also want to widen or narrow the field.

To wrap long fields, choose **Field ➤ W**ordWrap from the Form Design screen's menu bar. Click on the field you want to wrap or use the arrow keys to position the cursor in the field and press ↵. Paradox will display the dialog box shown below:

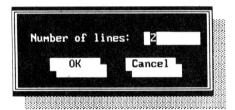

Type in the number of lines you want to use for the field, and then press ↵. The default is 0, or off. The value you choose sets the total number of lines displayed. You must enter a value of at least 2 to have any visible effect. Setting word-wrap to 1 displays the field on one line, the same as the default 0 setting.

288 CHAPTER 9 CREATING CUSTOM FORMS

NOTE Unlike reports, with forms you cannot set the number of lines for a word-wrapped field to V (for variable). That's because a field might require more lines than will fit on the screen.

Figure 9.5 shows a sample form in the Form Design screen. In this example, the cursor is resting in the Abstract field, and the status bar shows

Regular, Abstract wrap:10

The wrap:10 notation indicates the total number of lines that will be displayed (ten). The figure also illustrates another point: Word-wrapped lines look just like unwrapped lines on the Form Design screen. Although Paradox doesn't display the wrap continuation lines on the screen, it places them in the area immediately under the field you're wrapping. The wrap continuation lines start the same distance from the left edge of the form as the wrapped field, and they are the same width.

You must leave enough blank lines beneath the word-wrapped field to accommodate the continuation lines. For example, the form design in Figure 9.5 requires nine continuation lines. Even though you can't see the

FIGURE 9.5

Keywords and Abstract are word-wrapped fields on this sample form. Blank lines below these fields are necessary for the continuation lines.

continuation lines, Paradox will not let you save a form if you've placed any text, fields, or borders in their way.

If you do try to save a form (by choosing **DO-IT!** or pressing F2) that contains continuation lines that bump into other data, Paradox displays the message

> The area designated for the word wrap must be clear

just above the status bar, and moves the cursor into the wrapped field that's causing the problem. If this happens, look at the status bar to see how many lines this field occupies on the form. You can then reduce the number of continuation lines for the field, move (or erase) the wrapped field, or move whatever is beneath the wrapped field to make room for the continuation lines. Later sections in this chapter explain how to move and erase fields.

To turn off wrap-wrapping for a field, follow the same steps used to wrap it, but set the number of lines to 0.

Reformatting Fields on the Form

To change the width of a field on the form, choose **Field ▶ Reformat**. Click on the field you want to reformat or use the arrow keys to position the cursor in the field and press ↵. Then use the mouse or the → and ← keys to increase or decrease the width of the field, and press ↵.

You can quickly reformat a selected field to maximum size by clicking the mouse anywhere on the form to the right of the maximum field length.

If you're using the keyboard method, you can cancel the sizing so you can start over again. Press the End key to revert the field to its original length when you started resizing. The cursor appears at the end of the field, so you can start resizing again.

Moving Items on the Form

You can move existing text or fields on a custom form by using **Area ➤ Move**. You define the item you want to move as an area on the form, using either the mouse or keyboard method.

As long as there's room on the line, you can move text and fields horizontally by adding or deleting spaces while in Insert mode.

Moving an Item with the Mouse

After you select **Area ➤ Move** from the Form Design screen's menu bar, you'll see the prompt

> Move to a corner of the area to be moved, then press ↵ ...

Move the mouse pointer to a corner of the area you want to move, hold down the left mouse button, and drag diagonally to the opposite corner of the area, which will be highlighted as you move the mouse pointer.

When the area to be moved is highlighted, release the mouse button. Place the mouse pointer anywhere in the highlighted area, hold down the left mouse button, and drag the area to the desired location. Release the mouse button to complete the move. The highlight will disappear, and the area you moved will jump to the new location.

Moving an Item with the Keyboard

To move an item on a custom form using the keyboard, follow these steps:

1. Choose **Area ➤ Move** from the Form Design screen's menu bar.
2. Use the arrow keys to position the cursor in a corner of the area to be moved, then press ↵. You'll see the instructions:

   Now move to the diagonal corner of the area, then press ↵ ...

3. Use the arrow keys to expand and highlight the area to be moved, as in the example shown in Figure 9.6.

DESIGNING A CUSTOM FORM

FIGURE 9.6

The highlighted area expands as you move the cursor to the opposite (diagonal) corner.

```
Now move to the diagonal corner of the area, then press ↵...
┌─[■]══════════════ Form Design: Articles.F1 ══════════════[↕]─┐
│                                              Record  #_____ │
│   Author:  _____               │
│   Title:   _____               │
│   Journal: _____               │
│   Date:    _____  Vol: _____  No: _____              │
│   Pages:   ██████████                                        │
│                                                              │
│   Keywords: _____                          │
│                                                              │
│                                                              │
│   Abstract: _____                  │
│                                                              │
│                                                              │
│                                                              │
│                                                              │
│                                                              │
│                                                              │
│  ▙ 7,21  1:1  ═▆▆▆▆▆▆▆▆▆▆▆▆▆▆▆▆▆▆▆▆▆▆▆▆▆▆▆▆▆▆▆▆▆▆▆▆▆▆▆▆▆▆▆▶  │
│    F1 Help │                                                 │
└──────────────────────────────────────────────────────────────┘
```

4. Press ↵ when the entire area you want to move is highlighted. You'll see the prompt

   Use ↑ ↓ → ← to drag the area, then press ↵ ...

5. Use the arrow keys to drag the highlighted area to its new location on the screen. Although the highlight moves to the new area, the item you're moving still appears in its original position, as shown in Figure 9.7.

6. Press ↵ to complete the move. The highlight will disappear, and the area you moved will jump to the new location.

NOTE Moving a word-wrapped field is the same as moving any other field. You don't need to include the continuation lines when you're highlighting the area to move; they automatically move along with the wrapped field.

FIGURE 9.7

Although the highlight moves as you drag it to a new position with the arrow keys, the item you're moving remains in its original position until you press ↵.

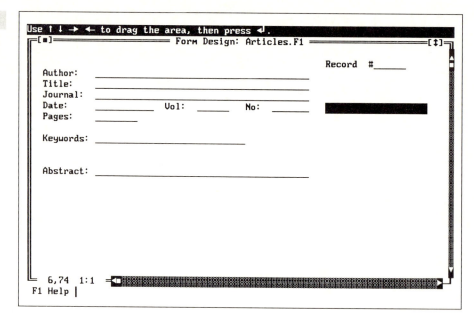

Erasing Fields and Areas

To erase characters on a form, use the usual Backspace and Delete keys. To remove larger portions of the screen, use **Field ➤ Erase** or **Area ➤ Erase**.

To remove a field from a custom form with the mouse, choose **Field ➤ Erase** from the Form Design screen's menu bar and click on the field you want to remove. With the keyboard, use the arrow keys to move the cursor to the appropriate field either before or after you select the menu option (you can also use the mouse to move the cursor if you do so before selecting Erase), then press ↵.

To erase a larger area of the screen using the mouse, choose **Area ➤ Erase**. Move the mouse pointer to one corner of the area you want to remove, hold down the left mouse button, and drag to the diagonal corner of the area, which will be highlighted as you move the mouse pointer. When you release the mouse button, the highlighted area is erased.

CAUTION Paradox removes the area from the form immediately after you stop dragging with the mouse or press ↵ when an area is highlighted. It's a good idea to save your form design immediately before you choose Area ➤ Erase, so you can return to the saved version if you make a mistake.

To erase an area with the keyboard, use the arrow keys to move the cursor to one corner of the area, either before or after you select **Area** ➤ **Erase** (as with other operations, you can also use the mouse to position the cursor before selecting the option), and press ↵. Use the arrow keys to extend the highlight to the opposite corner of the area you want to erase and press ↵.

Note that the area you define cannot contain a partial field. If there is a field (or fields) within the area to be erased, *all* the underscores that represent that field must be enclosed within the area to be erased.

NOTE Erasing a word-wrapped field is the same as erasing any other field. As when you define an area to move, you don't need to include the continuation lines; they'll be erased automatically.

Adding Borders and Lines

Borders and lines are a great way to enhance custom forms. For example, you can use borders to set help text off from the data-entry portion of your form (see Figure 9.2 for an example). Vertical and horizontal lines can be used in a similar way.

CHAPTER 9 · CREATING CUSTOM FORMS

TIP If you wish to make your form easier for a novice to use, you can develop your own Help box (as in Figure 9.2, earlier in this chapter). Adding help is simply a matter of typing text and adding borders and lines, and possibly some color or highlighting to make the Help text stand out. All these techniques are covered in this chapter.

Drawing Borders

You can draw borders with single or double thin lines, or with any character you specify. To add a border on a custom form, use your mouse or keyboard to position the cursor at one corner of the area that you want to draw a border around and choose **B**order ➤ **P**lace. You'll see this submenu:

Choose **S**ingle-line to draw a border with a single thin line or double **D**ouble-line to draw with double thin lines.

If you want to specify another character to use for the border, choose **O**ther. You'll see this dialog box:

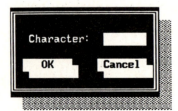

You can enter any keyboard character by typing that character and choosing OK or pressing ↵. To use any ASCII or extended character set character, type a backslash (\) and the character's three-digit ASCII code, using the numbers on the numeric keypad then choose OK or press ↵.

For example, enter \219 to create a thick-line border, \003 to create a border of hearts, or \004 to create a border of diamonds (see Figure 9.2 for an example of a diamond border).

After you select the type of border, you can designate where you want to place it with either the mouse or keyboard. With the mouse, move the mouse pointer to the place on the form where you want to start one corner of the border, hold down the left mouse button, and drag to where you want the diagonal corner of the border to appear. A highlighted border outline will appear as you drag the mouse pointer. When you release the mouse button, the border will be placed.

To place a border using the keyboard, use the arrow keys to position the cursor at one corner of where you want the border to appear and press ↵. You'll see the instructions

> Now move to diagonal corner, then press ↵.

Use the arrow keys to start drawing a border on the screen. As you move the cursor, you'll see the border expand (or reduce) on the screen. Press ↵ when the border is the desired size.

If you attempt to draw a border through a field, you'll see the message

> A border can't intersect a field or multi-record region

You'll need to expand or reduce the border outline until none of the lines intersect a field. Or you can just start over by pressing Esc five times to back out of your previous selections.

Drawing Lines

To draw a horizontal or vertical line, position the cursor where you want to start drawing the line and choose **Border** ➤ **P**lace. Select a line style from the submenu that appears. With the mouse, place the mouse pointer at one end of the desired line, hold down the left mouse button, and drag across or down. Release the mouse button when you reach the desired line endpoint.

To draw a horizontal line with the keyboard, use the ← and → keys. If you want to draw a vertical line, use only ↓ and ↑. When the line is the desired length, press ↵.

Erasing a Border or Line

To remove a border or line after you've added it to a form, choose **B**order ➤ **E**rase. With the mouse, drag the mouse pointer until the highlight covers the border. When you release the mouse button, the border is erased.

With the keyboard, use the mouse or arrow keys to move the cursor to one corner of the border that you want to erase, choose **B**order ➤ **E**rase, and press ↵. Then, following the instructions on the screen, use the arrow keys again to move the cursor to the opposite (diagonal) corner of the border and press ↵.

Coloring and Highlighting a Form

If you have a color monitor, you can change the color of any border, text, field, or area of the screen. You can also control video attributes such as blinking, intensity, and reverse video. Later, when you use the form, the video attributes or colored areas will make it easier to distinguish between the prompts and the data from the table.

You change the colors and video attributes of a form using the options on the Style menu. Choose **S**tyle from the Form Design screen's menu bar to see this menu:

Changing Form Colors

To color an area or border, choose **S**tyle ➤ **C**olor. You'll see a submenu offering the choices Area and Border. Choose **A**rea to define a style for an entire area. Choose **B**order to define a style for an outlined area. Typically, this outlined area is an existing border, but it can be any area on the screen that doesn't intersect a field mask.

Place the mouse pointer on the corner of the area for which you want to define a color, hold down the left mouse button, drag to highlight the area, and then release the button. To define the area with the keyboard, place the cursor with the arrow keys, press ↵ to mark the one corner, use the arrow keys to highlight the area, and press ↵ to mark the opposite corner.

Next, you'll be presented with a palette of possible color combinations. The current color selection will blink in the palette. If you know which combination you want to use, click on the specific foreground/background location on the palette to select it immediately.

To see how the palette choices look, press ← and → to change the foreground color, and ↑ and ↓ to change the background color. The color will change on your screen as you move through the palette. If the palette covers up the area you're coloring, you can press Alt-c to turn it off. Press Alt-c (a toggle key) again to redisplay the palette. You can change colors by pressing arrow keys even if the palette isn't displayed on your screen. When the color combination is just right, press ↵.

Changing a Form's Video Attributes

To change the video attributes of an area or border, choose **Style ➤ Monochrome**. As when you're changing colors, you can choose to define a style for an area or a border. Next, define the area or border using the techniques described in earlier sections.

When you're finished marking the area, you'll see the prompt

> Use → ← to switch between monochrome styles, then press ↵ to select the one you want.

Use the → and ← keys to experiment with different video attributes:

- **Normal:** No special video attributes are assigned.
- **Intense:** The foreground text is brightened.
- **Reverse:** The foreground and background shades are reversed.

CREATING CUSTOM FORMS

NOTE See Figure 9.2 earlier in this chapter for an example of the Reverse style. That style was used to highlight the fields and text titles in the form.

- **Intense-Reverse:** The foreground and background shades are reversed; foreground is brightened.
- **Blink:** The foreground blinks against the background.
- **Non-Blink:** The foreground does not blink.

The name of the current monochrome attribute appears in the status bar as you press ← and →.

NOTE If you are running Paradox in a DOS window under Microsoft Windows 3.1, the blinking characteristic will take effect but will not be visible unless you run Paradox in full-screen mode in Microsoft Windows or from DOS.

You can easily reset all monochrome video attributes. Choose **S**tyle ➤ **M**onochrome ➤ **A**rea and mark the area you want to restore as usual. After marking the area, press ← or → until Normal appears on the status bar, and then press ↵.

Tips on Adding Colors and Video Attributes

Here are some tips on coloring and adding video attributes to your forms:

- Use blinking areas sparingly; they can be distracting over long periods of data entry.
- Select pleasing color combinations that provide good contrast between the text or field data and its background.

- Choosing a color option displays all previous monochrome settings, but not vice-versa. Thus, if you want to combine color and monochrome options (such as a blinking color foreground), set the color first, then use the monochrome option to set blinking.

Showing Field Names during Form Design

When defining forms, it's easy to lose track of where each field is actually located, especially in a table with many fields. To help you with this, Paradox provides the Fieldnames option on the Style menu.

To display the field names while you're creating a form, choose **S**tyle ➤ **F**ieldnames ➤ **S**how. The field names will now appear highlighted in place of some (or all) of the underscores that normally mark the field locations on the form. If the field width you've defined is too narrow to hold the entire name of the field, Paradox will truncate the right end of the name. Figure 9.8 shows a sample form with the field names displayed.

FIGURE 9.8

A form with field names after choosing Style ➤ Fieldnames ➤ Show. The Mr/Mrs, M.I., and State field names are truncated because they're too long to fit into the allotted field width on the form.

```
≡ Field  Area  Border  Page  Style  Multi  DO-IT!  Cancel
┌[■]═══════════════ Form Design: Custlist.F2 ═══════════════[↕]┐
│                                                              │
│  Mr/Mrs Mr/M  First Name First Name__  M.I. M.  Last Name Last Name_____  │
│                                                              │
│  Title or Department Department/Title_____          │
│                                                              │
│           Company Company_____               │
│                                                              │
│           Address Address_____               │
│                                                              │
│       City City_____    State St  Zip Code Zip Code__  │
│                                                              │
│          Phone Phone_____      FAX FAX_____            │
│                                                              │
│    Starting Date Start Date_   Credit Limit Credit Limit__    │
│                                                              │
│  ┌─────────────────┬─────────────────┬─────────────────┬──────────────────┐ │
│  │ Cursor Movement │ Field Movement  │ Record Movement │ Edit Record      │ │
│  │   Mouse Click   │   First/Last    │   First/Last    │ Insert Record: Ins│ │
│  │   Arrow Keys    │   Ctrl+Home     │   Home          │ Delete Record: Del│ │
│  │   Tab, Shift+Tab│   Ctrl+End      │   End           │ Edit Field: Alt+F5│ │
│  └─────────────────┴─────────────────┴─────────────────┴──────────────────┘ │
└  1, 1  1:1 ═══════════════════════════════════════════│ Form  │────────────┘
  F1 Help
```

Keep in mind that field names appear only on the Form Design screen, not during data entry. This is why you need to provide text labels that clearly indicate which information needs to go into each field.

If you want to turn off the field name display, choose **S**tyle ➤ **F**ieldnames ➤ **H**ide. The names will disappear from the Form Design screen.

Using a Form

To use a custom form to view, enter, or edit data, follow these steps:

1. Choose **V**iew from the desktop menu bar, and then choose the table you want to edit or view.

2. Press F9 if you want to switch to Edit mode.

3. Choose **I**mage ➤ **P**ickForm. You'll see a menu of existing form descriptions, as in this example:

4. Double-click on the form description or highlight it and press ↵.

After you've selected a form, you can press F7 or click on the indicator in the Speedbar to switch between Form view and Table view.

Changing the Default Form

Often, a custom form is the form that you most often want to work in when viewing or editing a table. You can make any custom form the default form. Then that form will be the one that appears when you switch to Form view.

USING A FORM

To make one of your custom forms the default, open that form and choose **I**mage ➤ **K**eepSet. From now on, when you open the table for viewing and press F7 (or select it from the Speedbar), the custom form you've chosen will open instead of the Standard Form screen. Like all KeepSet settings, this setting will remain in effect until you either select another default form with **I**mage ➤ **K**eepSet or until you delete the table's KeepSet file by using **T**ools ➤ **D**elete ➤ Keepset.

Deleting a table's KeepSet file deletes all custom settings you have saved for the table. If you just want to change the default form, open the desired form, make your changes, and then save the new setting with Image ➤ KeepSet.

All the special Paradox keys work the same way on a custom form as they do on the Standard Form. See Table 4.2 in Chapter 4 for a list of the keys and functions.

Using Word-Wrapped Fields

Word-wrapped fields behave somewhat differently from other fields when you use a custom form to edit or view data. Here are the techniques for working with word-wrapped fields:

- To position the cursor at the beginning of any word-wrapped field, use the arrow keys or click the mouse on any line of the wrapped field.

- To display parts of a word-wrapped field that aren't currently visible, press Alt-F5 or Ctrl-f or double-click in the field to switch to Field view. In Field view, you can use ↑ and ↓ to move from line to line in non-memo fields. Use the usual techniques to move through memo fields (see Chapter 4).

- To end Field view in a word-wrapped alphanumeric field, just press ↵. To end Field view in a memo field, choose **DO-IT!** or press F2.

Changing a Form

Few forms are perfect the first time through. Fortunately, custom forms are very easy to change. You can change the form even if you're currently using it to enter table data. After you save all the changes, your form will change to match the updated form.

Here are the steps for modifying an existing form:

1. Choose **Forms ➤ Change** from the desktop menu bar.
2. Specify the table for which you designed the form.
3. Select the appropriate form from the menu of existing forms, either by typing its form number and pressing ↵ or by double-clicking the form name.
4. Change the description of the form as you wish. Then press ↵.

The form will appear on the Form Design screen, ready for editing. You can use all the techniques described in this chapter to make whatever changes you want. Choose **DO-IT!** or press F2 to save your changes.

Summary

As you have seen, designing useful and attractive forms for data entry is easy in Paradox. The Form Design screen's menu bar includes several options for designing more sophisticated forms that involve multiple tables and calculated fields. Those options are covered in Chapter 15. For now, let's review the most important procedures for creating and using custom forms:

- To create a custom form, choose **Forms ➤ Design** from the desktop menu bar. Then, from the Form Design screen, you can design the form using the following techniques:

    - To place fields on a form, choose **Field ➤ Place**.

SUMMARY

- To wrap memo or alphanumeric fields on the form, place the field as usual, then choose **F**ield ➤ **W**ordWrap and move to the field you want to wrap. Then specify the maximum number of lines the field should occupy.
- To place borders or lines on a form, choose **B**order ➤ **P**lace.
- To move items on the form, choose **A**rea ➤ **M**ove.
- To erase parts of a form, choose **F**ield ➤ **E**rase or **A**rea ➤ **E**rase.
- To display portions of the form in color or with highlighting, choose **S**tyle, then choose **C**olor or **M**onochrome followed by **A**rea or **B**order. Mark the area or border, then select the enhancement you want.
- To save a form, press F2 or choose **DO-IT!** from the menu after designing the form. To abandon an edited form, choose **C**ancel ➤ **Y**es or click the Close button and answer **Y**es.

- To use a form for entering or editing data, choose **I**mage ➤ **P**ick-Form on the desktop menu bar, and choose a form by number or by double-clicking the mouse. Use F7 to switch from Table view to Form view.
- To make a custom form the default form (the one that appears when you use F7), open it on the desktop and choose **I**mage ➤ **K**eepSet.
- To change an existing form, choose **F**orms ➤ **C**hange from the desktop menu bar.

CHAPTER 10

Graphing Your Data

fast TRACK

- **To display an Instant Graph with default settings** — 312

    open the table, move the cursor to the first numeric field that you want to graph, and press the Instant Graph key, Ctrl-F7. The table's leftmost column will provide X-axis labels.

- **To change the graph type** — 315

    choose **I**mage ➤ **G**raph ➤ **M**odify, choose a graph type, and choose **DO-IT!** to return to the desktop. Then press Ctrl-F7 to view the graph.

- **To limit the duration of a graph display** — 326

    choose **O**verall ➤ **W**ait, then select **K**ey**S**troke (to require a keypress to exit the graph display) or **D**uration (to display the graph for a specified number of seconds).

- **To customize the current graph** — 327

    choose **I**mage ➤ **G**raph ➤ **M**odify, then use the various options on the Customize Graph screen's menu bar to change the settings. Choose **DO-IT!** to return to the desktop, then press Ctrl-F7 to view the graph with its current settings.

- **To save custom graph settings for future use** — 347

    choose **I**mage ➤ **G**raph ➤ **S**ave from the desktop menu bar and enter a file name.

● **To load previously saved custom graph settings**   348

  choose **I**mage ➤ **G**raph ➤ **L**oad from the desktop menu bar, and enter or choose the name of a previously saved graph settings file. Then press Ctrl-F7 to view the current table data with those current graph settings.

● **To modify existing custom graph settings**   350

  load the custom graph settings, make any desired changes using **I**mage➤ **M**odify ➤ **G**raph, and choose **DO-IT!**. Then choose **I**mage ➤ **G**raph ➤ **S**ave and enter a new file name.

● **To print a graph**   351

  first run the Custom Configuration Program to define the printer for printing graphs. Then preview the graph (press Ctrl-F7). From the desktop, choose **I**mage ➤ **G**raph ➤ **V**iewGraph ➤ **P**rinter, or choose **V**iewGraph ➤ **P**rinter from the Customize Graph screen's menu bar.

● **To print a graph to a file**   353

  for printing later or importing into another program, choose **I**mage ➤ **G**raph ➤ **M**odify ➤ **O**verall ➤ **D**evice ➤ **F**ile from the Customize Graph screen's menu bar, then select **C**urrentPrinter, **EPS**, or **PIC**. Then choose **V**iewGraph ➤ **F**ile and enter a file name.

● **To cross tabulate data for graphing**   358

  display the table on your screen, then choose **I**mage ➤ **G**raph ➤ **C**rossTab. From the submenu, choose **S**um, **M**in, **M**ax, or **C**ount. Then mark the columns to be used for the row labels, column labels, and cross tabulation values.

PARADOX lets you display data from your tables in a variety of common business graphs, such as bar charts, pie charts, and line graphs. In this chapter, you'll learn how to plot data from tables and customize graphs to suit your own requirements.

This chapter also describes the uses of cross tabulations, which let you quickly summarize data in a table. You can then create a meaningful graph of the summarized data from that table.

An Overview of Graphing with Paradox

Paradox offers many tools for designing and printing graphs in exactly the format you want. Here's the general procedure for graphing your data:

1. Open the table that contains the data you want to graph. If you're in Form view, switch to Table view.

2. If necessary, use the Rotate key (Ctrl-r) or **Image ➤ Move** to move the field that contains X-axis labels to the first column position in the table, just to the right of the record numbers.

The only time the X-axis labels don't come from the first column is when you're graphing data from keyed tables, as explained later in this chapter.

AN OVERVIEW OF GRAPHING WITH PARADOX

3. Move the cursor to the numeric, currency, or short numeric field that you want to graph. You can rotate up to five more numeric fields to the right of that column to include in the graph, except when you're creating an X-Y graph or a pie chart. X-Y graphs plot the data in the leftmost and rightmost columns. Pie charts plot only one column's data.

4. Press the Instant Graph key, Ctrl-F7 (or choose **I**mage ➤ **G**raph ➤ **V**iewGraph ➤ **S**creen) to view the graph on the screen.

5. After viewing the graph, press any regular key (such as a letter, ↵, or the spacebar) to return to the desktop.

6. To customize the current graph or use a different graph type, choose **I**mage ➤ **G**raph ➤ **M**odify and choose new settings for the graph. You can check your progress from time to time without returning to the desktop by pressing Ctrl-F7 to preview the graph on the screen.

7. After customizing the graph settings, choose **DO-IT!** to return to the desktop. If you want to save the current graph settings for future use, choose **I**mage ➤ **G**raph ➤ **S**ave, and enter a valid file name. You can later use those settings for a new graph by choosing **I**mage ➤ **G**raph ➤ **L**oad.

8. To print the current graph, choose **I**mage ➤ **G**raph ➤ **V**iewGraph ➤ **P**rinter.

NOTE Before you can print a graph, you must install a graphics printer using Paradox's Custom Configuration Program, as described in Appendix D.

For the examples in this chapter, we'll use a table named Finsum (short for Financial Summary). Figure 10.1 shows the structure of the Finsum table and sample data for that table.

GRAPHING YOUR DATA

FIGURE 10.1

Top: The structure of the Finsum table, which is used in many of the graphing examples. Bottom: Sample data for the Finsum table.

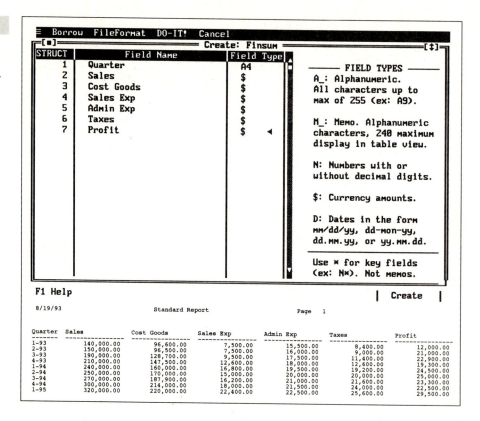

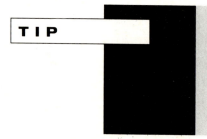

If the table contains many records, you may want to use a query to isolate records, or a cross tabulation to summarize the data you want to graph. Queries are covered in Chapter 7. Using the CrossTab option to generate cross tabulations is described near the end of this chapter.

How Paradox Graphs Data

The way Paradox translates data from the current table into graph elements is determined by the field order in Table view and the location of the cursor when the graph is created. Here's how Paradox sets up your graph:

- The graph title at the top of the graph is the same as the table name.
- The X-axis labels come from the first field in Table view.
- The X-axis title is the name of the field that contains the X-axis labels.

NOTE In a keyed table, the X-axis titles will come from the least significant key field, as described later in this chapter.

- Only numeric values (those from numeric, short numeric of currency fields) are displayed.
- On all graphs except pie charts, Paradox uses the field in which the cursor is positioned as the first series of values to plot, the next numeric field to the right (if any) as the second series, the next one (if any) as the third series, and so on.
- The legend labels are field names from the table. The first label is the name of the field containing the cursor, the second label is the next field to the right, and so on.

You can use the Rotate key (Ctrl-r) to rotate fields in Table view to determine which fields to include and which to exclude from the graph. You can change any of the titles on the graph, as well as the type of graph, graph colors, and other features. In addition, you can plot graphs using data from the Answer table that appears after you perform a query. This is an extremely handy feature that allows you to isolate specific records to plot.

NOTE You can also use Image ➤ Move from the desktop menu bar to move a field to any position in Table view. See Chapter 5.

Graph Types

The purpose of a graph is to display information in a form that is easy to understand. This requires more than a bit of creativity on your part and a lot of capability from the graphic tools you use. Paradox allows you to create, modify, display, and print ten different types of graphs:

Stacked bar	Marked graph
Regular bar	Combined lines and markers graph
3-D bar	X-Y graph
Rotated bar	Pie chart
Line graph	Area graph

By default, Paradox creates a stacked bar graph. You can easily change to any of the other types by modifying a graph's settings, as described shortly.

Viewing an Instant Graph

Like an Instant Report, an Instant Graph is automatically created for you by Paradox, using the current default settings, and can be displayed with a single keypress (Ctrl-F7). Follow these steps to view an Instant Graph:

1. Before you generate this type of graph, make sure that the fields in Table view are arranged so that the field that contains the X-axis labels for the graph is the first column. For example, if you were using the contents of the Quarter field in the sample Finsum table for the X-axis labels, you wouldn't need to move fields, because Quarter is already in the first column in Table view.

2. Move the cursor to the numeric, currency, or short numeric field that contains the data you wish to graph. Up to six numeric fields from the cursor position can be graphed. For example, if you wanted to graph the cost of goods data, you would move the cursor to the Cost Goods field in the Finsum table, as shown in Figure 10.2.

FIGURE 10.2

The Finsum table on the desktop. Some fields are scrolled off the right edge of the screen.

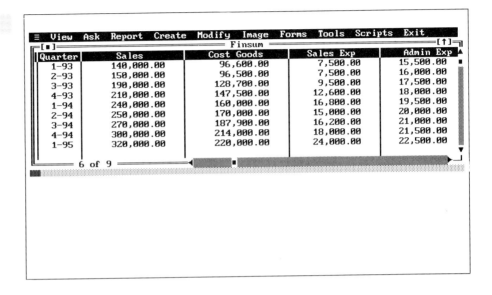

3. Press Ctrl-F7 to see the graph on the screen. Alternatively, you can use **I**mage ➤ **G**raph ➤ **V**iewGraph ➤ **S**creen. After a brief pause, a stacked bar graph will appear, as in the example shown in Figure 10.3. (If you didn't place the cursor in a numeric field prior to pressing Ctrl-F7, Paradox will display a message letting you know that the active field is not numeric.)

4. After viewing the graph, press any key to return to the desktop.

The graph in Figure 10.3 was created with Paradox's default settings. The graph title at the top of the graph, FINSUM, is the same as the table name. The X-axis labels (1-93, 2-93, 3-93, and so on) come from the first field in Table view, and the X-axis title is the name of that field in the table, Quarter. Paradox used the field in which the cursor was positioned (Cost Goods) as the first series of values to plot, the next field (Sales Exp) as the second series, and so on. The Sales field is excluded from the graph in Figure 10.3 because it was to the left of the cursor in Table view. The legend labels are the field names from the table: Cost Goods, Sales Exp, Admin Exp, and Profit.

314 CHAPTER **10** GRAPHING YOUR DATA

FIGURE 10.3

An Instant Graph uses the default settings provided by Paradox.

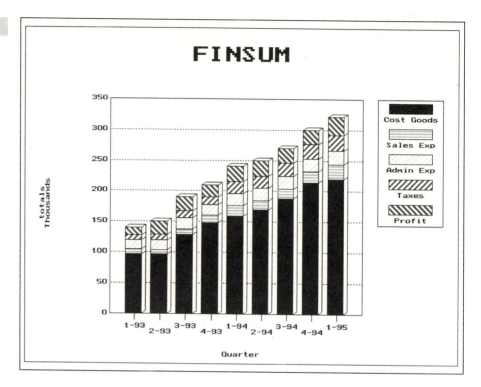

TIP

When you display an Instant Graph, the graph that appears on the screen uses defaults that were defined when you first installed Paradox. You can change the default settings used to create new Instant Graphs with the Custom Configuration Program, as explained in Appendix D.

Changing the Graph Type

To select a graph type other than the default type, follow these steps:

1. Choose **I**mage ➤ **G**raph. You'll see the submenu below:

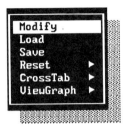

2. Choose **M**odify. The Customize Graph Type screen appears, as shown in Figure 10.4.

3. Select the appropriate graph type by typing in its first character, which is shown in parentheses. For example, type **B** for Bar graph or **3** for 3-D Bar graph. The graph types are described in the following sections.

FIGURE 10.4

The Customize Graph Type screen appears when you choose Image ➤ Graph ➤ Modify from the desktop menu bar.

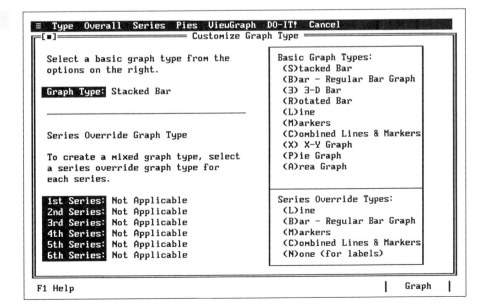

GRAPHING YOUR DATA

4. Press F2 or choose **DO-IT!** to save your selection and return to the desktop.

5. If you didn't do so already, use the Rotate key (Ctrl-r) or **Image ➤ Move** to rearrange fields.

6. Position the cursor on the first numeric field you want to graph.

7. Press Ctrl-F7 or choose **Image ➤ Graph ➤ ViewGraph** to view the graph.

8. Press any key after viewing the graph to return to the desktop.

By studying the examples of graphs presented in the following sections, you'll get an idea of how the various graph types show table data. You'll also see how the order of fields and the cursor's position in Table view determine which fields are plotted on the graph.

Stacked Bar Graphs

A stacked bar graph shows the value of selected series relative to the total by representing the series elements as ranges in their respective categories. In the earlier example (Figure 10.3), you can see the relative impact of all the various expense items on total sales for each quarter.

Paradox automatically displays a stacked bar graph if you do not specify a different graph type.

Regular Bar Graphs

A regular (vertical) bar graph uses a single bar for each data element. This can be useful for comparing values over a period of time. The example in Figure 10.5 was produced by defining the graph type as Bar (B). Then the Sales field was rotated to the rightmost column of the table and the cursor was moved into the Sales field. The graph shows values from the Sales field only, because there were no numeric fields to the right of the Sales field.

FIGURE 10.5

A regular bar graph based on the Sales field in the Finsum table

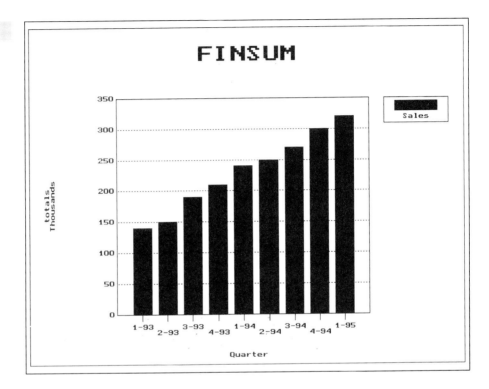

3-D Bar Graphs

A 3-D bar graph is visually appealing and easy to read when just a few values are plotted. This type of graph is useful for comparing values over time. In Figure 10.6, the 3-D graph displays only the Profit field for quarterly data in 1993.

To create this graph, the following procedure was used:

- Set the graph type to 3-D (3) and choose **DO-IT!** to return to the desktop.
- Select **A**sk from the desktop menu bar and specify Finsum as the table to query.
- Place the criterion ..93 in the Quarter field of the Query form to isolate records that have 93 as the last two characters in that field.
- Place check marks (using the F6 key) in the Quarter and Profit fields of the Query form.

FIGURE 10.6

A 3-D bar graph based on the Profit field of the Finsum table, after using a query to isolate records with 1993 dates in the Quarter field.

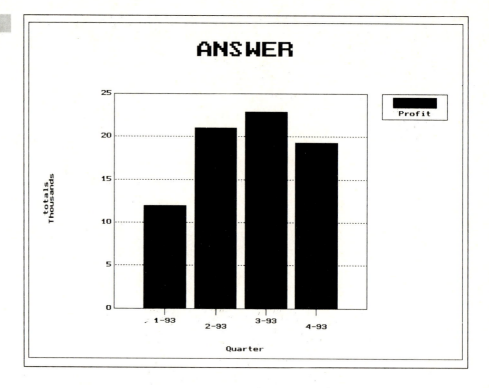

- Press F2 to perform the query and create an Answer table with only 1993 data in it.
- Move the cursor to the Profit field in the Answer table, press Ctrl-F7 to view the graph, and then press a key to return to the desktop.
- Close the Answer table and Query form to return to the original table.

Rotated Bar Graphs

In a rotated bar graph, the X- and Y-axes are reversed, and the bars are laid out horizontally. In the example shown in Figure 10.7, profit per quarter is illustrated. The graph type was defined as Rotated (R). Then the Profit field was rotated to the far right column and the cursor was placed in that column.

FIGURE 10.7

A rotated bar graph based on the Profit field in the Finsum table

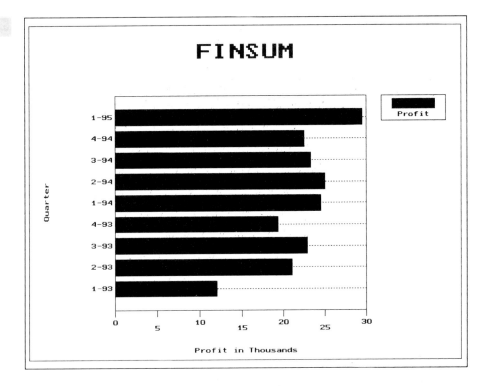

The axis label at the bottom of the rotated bar graph was modified to add the words *in thousands* to the field name from the table. You'll learn how to customize titles a little later in this chapter.

Line Graphs

A line graph is often used to show the changes in a value (or values) over time, so that you can easily see the dips and rises in your data. Although the X-axis on a line graph is usually a progression of time, this type of graph can plot any series of values.

For the graph shown in Figure 10.8, Line (L) was chosen as the type, and then the Sales and Cost Goods fields were rotated to become the right-most columns. With the cursor in the Sales field, pressing Ctrl-F7 produced a line graph of the sales and cost of goods data.

FIGURE 10.8

A line graph based on the Sales and Cost Goods fields of the Finsum table

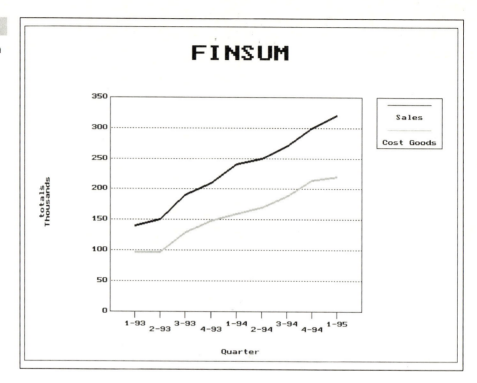

Markers Graphs

A markers graph represents values in the same way as a line graph, except that the values are marked with symbols rather than with a line. This type of graph emphasizes individual values rather than changes over time.

Using the same settings and cursor position as the line graph in Figure 10.8 and changing the graph type to Markers (M) produced the graph shown in Figure 10.9.

CHANGING THE GRAPH TYPE

FIGURE 10.9

A markers graph of the Sales and Cost Goods field from the Finsum table

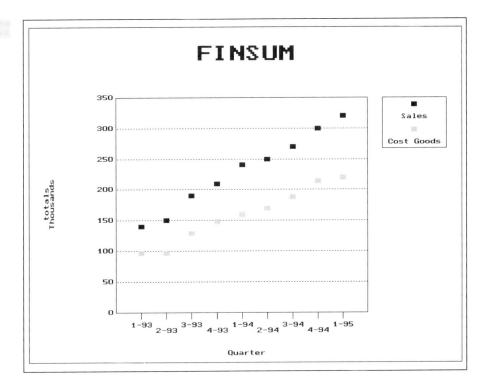

Combined Lines and Markers Graphs

As its name implies, a combined lines and markers graph displays both lines and markers. This type of graph is useful for showing progressions of changes while emphasizing discrete points. The graph shown in Figure 10.10 was produced with the same settings as the ones in Figures 10.9 and 10.10, but with the graph type changed to Combined Lines and Markers (C).

X-Y Graphs

Paradox always uses the numeric fields in the far left and right columns of Table view to plot data on an X-Y graph. The example shown in Figure 10.11 uses the graph type X-Y (X) to show how sales and profit are

FIGURE 10.10

A combined lines and markers graph of the Sales and Cost Goods fields from the Finsum table

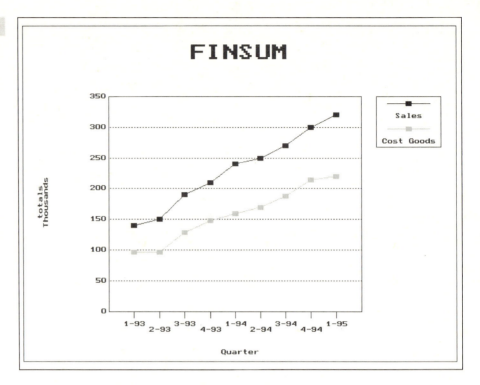

related. The Sales field was rotated to the leftmost column of Table view, and the Profit column was rotated to the rightmost column before pressing Ctrl-F7.

Pie Charts

A pie chart is a good choice when you want to display a proportional breakdown of the values that make up a whole. In a sense, the pie chart is one-dimensional. It plots data only from the numeric field that contains the cursor, ignoring all fields to the right. Each pie slice represents only one value from each record of the table.

The sample pie chart shown in Figure 10.12 shows how each quarter's profit contributed to total profits for the year. To create this chart, the graph type was set to Pie (P). Then a query (as discussed in the example of the 3-D bar graph) was used to isolate records from 1993. The check

CHANGING THE GRAPH TYPE

FIGURE 10.11

An X-Y graph based on the Sales and Profit fields of the Finsum table. In Table view, Sales was rotated to the leftmost column, and Profit was rotated to the rightmost column.

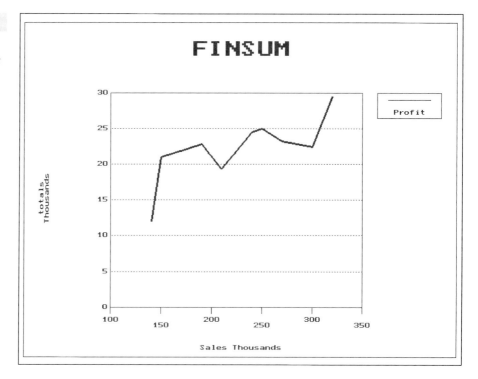

marks went in the Quarter and Profit fields of the Query form. In the resulting Answer table, the cursor was placed in the Profit field prior to pressing Ctrl-F7. (The pie label format was changed to currency, a customization discussed later in this chapter.)

Area Graphs

An area graph combines the multiple bands of a stacked bar graph with the smoothness of a line graph. This type of graph is useful for showing changes in values over time.

In Figure 10.13, the graph type was set to Area (A). Then the fields were placed back into their original, "unrotated" order. The cursor was placed in the Cost Goods field before pressing Ctrl-F7 to view the graph.

FIGURE 10.12

A pie chart based on the Profit field of the Finsum table after isolating records with 1993 dates in the Quarter field

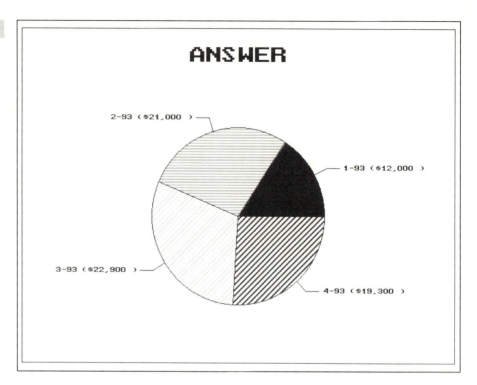

TIP An easy way to "unrotate" fields in a table is to simply close the table (click on its Close button or press F8 or Alt-F8), then reopen it using the View menu on the desktop menu bar.

Combined Graphs

Mixing graph types can be an effective way of displaying distinctions between the series or types of data being plotted. Usually, the various line, markers, and bar types are combined in a graph. The Customize Graph Type screen provides Series Override Types options that let you combine graph types.

CHANGING THE GRAPH TYPE 325

FIGURE 10.13

An area graph based on the Cost Goods, Sales Exp, Admin Exp, Taxes, and Profit fields of the Finsum table

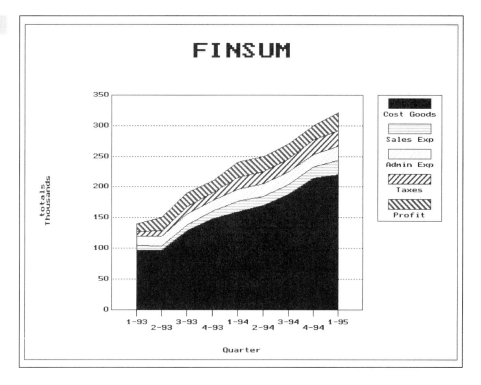

To create the graph in Figure 10.14, the graph type was first changed to Bar (with Image ➤ Graph ➤ Modify), and then the 1st Series option on the Customized Graph Type screen was changed to Combined Lines and Markers (C). The Sales and Cost Goods fields were rotated to the rightmost columns of the table, to graph their values only. Placing the cursor in the Sales field and pressing Ctrl-F7 produced the sample combined graph.

NOTE The first series plotted in a graph is always the field with the cursor. The progression for the remaining series is left to right, starting from the field that contains the cursor.

FIGURE 10.14

A combined graph based on the Sales and Cost Goods fields of the Finsum table. The basic graph is a bar graph with the first series set to the Combined Lines and Markers graph type.

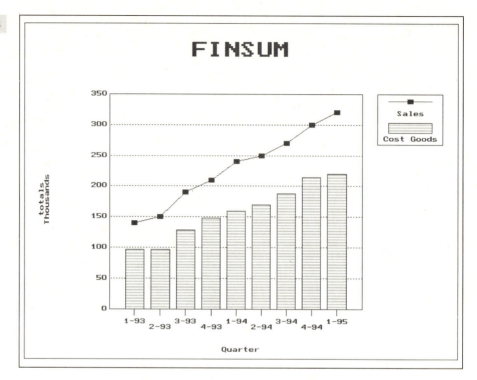

Limiting the Duration of a Graph Display

When you view a graph on your screen (with Ctrl-F7 or Image ➤ Graph ➤ ViewGraph ➤ Screen), Paradox displays the graph until you press any key to return to the desktop. As an alternative to displaying the graph indefinitely, you can specify how long the graph is to appear on the screen. To set or change the duration, choose Image ➤ Graph ➤ Modify from the desktop menu bar, then choose Overall ➤ Wait from the Customize Graph screen's menu bar. You will see a submenu with the options Keystroke and Duration.

NOTE Displaying graphs for a specified period of time can be useful for creating scripts that display multiple graphs. You'll learn about scripts in Chapter 11.

The Keystroke option allows a graph to remain displayed on the screen until a key (any key) is pressed. This is the default setting.

If you select Duration, you will see this dialog box:

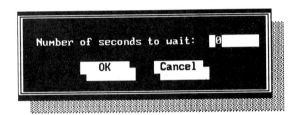

Type in the number of seconds you want Paradox to display the graph before returning you to the desktop. If you leave the box blank, Paradox returns you to the desktop as soon as it can. Note that the default setting, 0, is not the same as a blank. A setting of 0 sets the duration to infinite; the graph is still displayed until you press a key.

Customizing the Overall Features of Graphs

Along with the graph type, you can change many other settings for your graphs, such as screen colors, titles, and the format of the numbers. You use **I**mage ➤ **G**raph ➤ **M**odify to customize your graphs, as explained in the following sections. You can save your custom settings in a file by using **I**mage ➤ **S**ave. Later, you can load those settings with **I**mage ➤ **G**raph ➤ **L**oad and reuse them to plot other graphs.

Before getting into the details of customizing graphs, take a moment to review the terms used to describe the various elements that make up the graph.

Elements of a Graph

Depending on the type of graph or chart, Paradox will include any or all of the following elements:

- **Titles**: The text that appears at the top of the graph and along the axes. By default, Paradox uses the table name as the graph title and field names for axis titles.
- **Axes:** The horizontal (X) and vertical (Y) lines that establish the range of values plotted on the graph. Normally, the X-axis categorizes the data, and the Y-axis measures the values. The exceptions are pie charts, which don't have axes, and rotated bar graphs, in which the X- and Y-axes are reversed.
- **Tick marks:** The marks along an axis that divide it into segments are the tick marks. They indicate the scale of the graph.
- **Labels:** The labels are the text placed near the tick marks to identify values on the axes. You can also place labels inside the graph to identify the values of the represented data.
- **Series:** The data in a single field from the table that is plotted on the graph is a series.
- **Legend:** The visual key that identifies the different series within the graph is the legend. Labels within the legend identify each series represented in the graph.
- **Scale:** The range of values assigned in the graph is shown on the scale. This includes the increments used to divide the axis into tick marks.
- **Slice:** On a pie chart, a slice represents one graphed value.

Most of these elements are labeled in Figure 10.3, near the beginning of this chapter.

Working in Customize Graph Screens

The screens for customizing the various elements of your graphs all have the same basic format. The right side of the screen lists the options that you can change, and the left side of the screen lists the choices and the codes you can enter for the options.

CUSTOMIZING THE OVERALL FEATURES OF GRAPHS

You can use any of the following methods to move the cursor to the options on the left side of the screen:

- Click the mouse on the letter that specifies the current setting.
- Press the arrow keys to move the cursor through the screen.
- Press ↵ to move the cursor down to the next option.

If you want to take a quick look at your graph with its new settings, press Ctrl-F7. Then you can press any key to return to the Customize Graph screen. When you're satisfied with the settings, choose **DO-IT!** to return to the desktop. Choose **C**ancel ➤ **Y**es if you want to cancel your current selections.

Customizing Graph Titles

To change the titles on the current graph, starting at the desktop, choose **I**mage ➤ **G**raph ➤ **M**odify. Then select **O**verall ➤ **T**itles. The Customize Graph Titles screen appears, as shown in Figure 10.15.

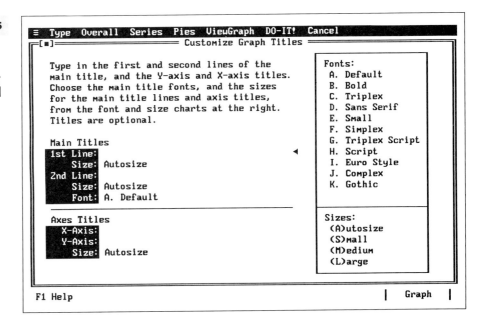

FIGURE 10.15

The Customize Graph Titles screen lets you define custom titles for a graph. It is accessed via Image ➤ Graph ➤ Modify ➤ Overall ➤ Titles.

GRAPHING YOUR DATA

To change one of the titles, move the cursor to that title option on the left side of the screen and type in the title you want to appear on the graph.

The right side of the screen shows options for fonts (type styles) and sizes. To select a font or size, move the cursor to the appropriate Size or Font option on the left side of the screen and type the letter corresponding to the option you want, as listed under the headings Fonts and Sizes on the right side of the screen. The Autosize (A) option automatically selects a size for the title based on the number of characters in the title and the size of the space available.

For example, to make the second line of the title medium size, move the cursor to the Size option beneath 2nd Line and type **M**. To change the font of the title lines to Euro Style, move the cursor to the Font option and type **I**.

Figure 10.16 shows an example of a graph with custom titles. The Customize Graph Titles screen for this example was set as follows:

>   Main Titles
>   1st Line: ABC Corporation
>   Size: Autosize
>   2nd Line: Quarterly Sales
>   Size: Medium
>   Font: Euro Style
>   Axes Titles
>   X-Axis: Quarter-Year
>   Y-Axis: Total Sales
>   Size: Autosize

Examples of various fonts that you can use for titles are presented in Figure 10.17.

NOTE Remember, if you want to take a quick look at your new titles, press Ctrl-F7; then press any key to return to the Customize Graph Titles screen. When you're satisfied with the title settings, choose DO-IT! to return to the desktop. If you want to leave the titles as they were, choose Cancel ➤ Yes.

CUSTOMIZING THE OVERALL FEATURES OF GRAPHS

FIGURE 10.16

A graph with custom titles

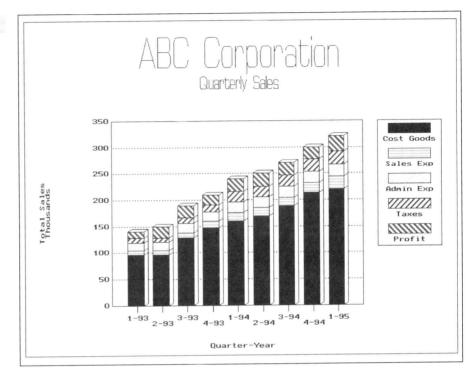

FIGURE 10.17

Examples of fonts for graph titles

GRAPHING YOUR DATA

Modifying Graph Colors

To change the colors used to display the graph on a color monitor, starting from the desktop, choose **I**mage ➤ **G**raph ➤ **M**odify ➤ **O**verall ➤ **C**olors. You'll see a submenu offering the options Screen, Printer, and Copy. Select **S**creen to change only the colors of the screen display of the graph. Select **P**rinter to specify colors for printed copies of the graph. Paradox displays the Customize Graph Colors screen, as shown in Figure 10.18.

> **NOTE** The figure shows how the form looks on a monochrome monitor. On a color monitor, you'll see colors in the box at the right.

The leftmost column in the Customize Graph Colors screen lists the graph elements (the background, frame, and grid) and titles (first and second lines of the main title, the axes titles, and the series titles) that can be colored. To change the graph background color, type in the appropriate color code (B through H). The color codes are listed on the right side of the screen under the heading Background Choices.

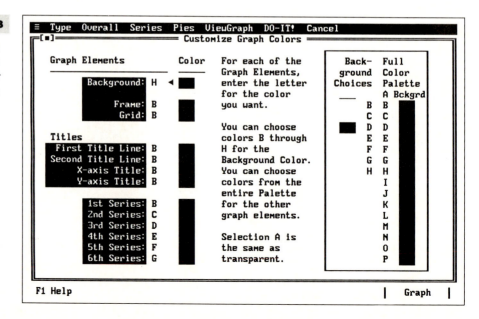

FIGURE 10.18

The Customize Graph Colors screen lets you define graph colors. It is accessed via Image ➤ Graph ➤ Modify ➤ Overall ➤ Colors.

NOTE: Only EGA and VGA (and better) monitors are capable of displaying Paradox graphics in color.

For the Frame, Grid, and Titles colors, enter one of the color codes (A through P) listed under the heading Full Color Palette on the right side of the screen. For example, to make the frame surrounding the graph bright red, type **M** next to the Frame option.

If you are changing screen colors (as opposed to printer colors), you can press Ctrl-F7 to see how the graph looks with the new colors. Then press any key to return to the Customize Graph Colors screen. You can experiment with various color combinations until you find a color scheme that you like.

Matching Screen Colors to Printer Colors

As an alternative to coloring screen and printer graphs separately, you can copy screen colors to the printed graph or vice versa. To copy a color scheme, choose **O**verall ➤ **C**olors ➤ **C**opy from the Customize Graph screen's menu bar. From the submenu, choose **S**creenToPrinter to copy screen colors to the printed graph. If you want to copy the printed graph's colors to the one that appears on the screen, Choose **P**rinterToScreen.

Modifying Graph Axes

All graphs (except pie charts) have two axes: X and Y. The X-axis is the horizontal axis at the bottom of the graph. The Y-axis is the vertical axis on the left side of the graph. (But remember that the X- and Y-axes are reversed on a rotated graph.) You can customize either axis in a variety of ways.

To get to the screen for customizing axes, from the desktop, choose **I**mage ➤ **G**raph ➤ **M**odify. Then choose **O**verall ➤ **A**xes from the Customize Graph screen's menu bar. You'll see the Customize Graph Axes screen, as shown in Figure 10.19. This screen allows you to choose scaling, tick mark formatting, and tick mark display options, as discussed in the sections that follow.

Chapter 10
Graphing Your Data

FIGURE 10.19

The Customize Graph Axes screen lets you customize graph axes. It is accessed via Image ➤ Graph ➤ Modify ➤ Overall ➤ Axes.

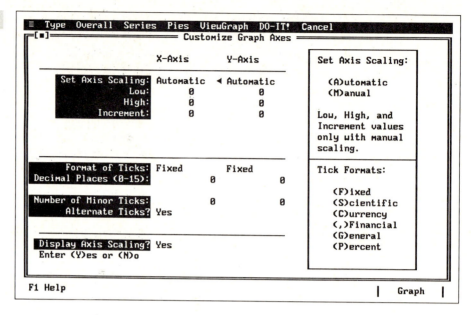

Remember, you can move the cursor to an option on a Customize Graph screen by clicking on the existing setting for that option or by pressing the arrow keys. You can also press ↵ if you just want to move down to the next option.

Scaling

A graph's scaling controls the range of values represented. By default, Paradox determines how to scale the graph axes based on the data being plotted. For example, if the smallest value to be plotted on the graph is 1000 and the largest value to be plotted is 5000, Paradox automatically sets up the Y-axis so it extends from 0 to 6,000.

As an alternative to allowing Paradox to scale the graph automatically, you can change to manual scaling and set the value range yourself. On the Customize Graph Axes screen, change the scaling technique to Manual by typing **M** for the Set Axis Scaling option. Changing the X-axis scaling to Manual affects only the X-Y graph type. Changing the Y-axis affects all graphs (except pie charts).

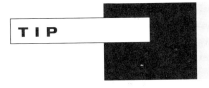

TIP Setting your own minimum and maximum values for a graph's scale allows you to refine the graph display or accentuate a trend or value.

After you set the scaling to Manual, enter the lowest value you want to appear for the Low option and the highest value next to the Low option. Make sure the range you select includes all the values to be graphed, or the resulting graph may show inaccurate results. For example, if you set the High option for the Y-axis to 2000 and there are values larger than 2000 in the table, those values will only reach the top of the graph; a value of 5000 would appear as 2000.

You can also specify the increment value of tick marks along the Y-axis of a graph by changing the Increment option. By default, if you plot values in the range of 0 to 5000, Paradox will automatically place tick marks at 1000, 2000, 3000, and so on along the Y-axis. However, if you change the tick mark increment value for the Y-axis to 2000, Paradox will place tick marks at 2000, 4000, and 6000 along that axis.

Customizing the X-axis only makes sense on an X-Y graph, because all other graph types automatically receive their X-axis titles from the leftmost field in the table. That is, there is one tick mark along the X-axis for each record in the table. But an X-Y graph can plot data from any numeric field in the table along the X-axis, and therefore you can customize the low and high values displayed on the X-axis, as well as the increment value of the tick marks.

Tick Formats

You can also control the appearance of numbers displayed on the X- and Y-axes. The options for ticks, listed under the Tick Formats heading on the right side of the Customize Graph Axes screen, display the numbers as follows:

- **(F)ixed:** Displays numbers with a fixed number of decimal places.
- **(S)cientific:** Displays numbers in scientific notation.
- **(C)urrency:** Displays numbers in fixed notation with dollar signs.
- **(,)Financial:** Inserts commas as necessary, and displays negative numbers within parentheses.

- **(G)eneral:** Displays numbers as they appear in the table.
- **(P)ercent:** Displays numbers multiplied by 100 and followed by a % sign (for example, 0.2 is displayed as 20%).

You can also set the number of decimal places to display with any type of number except General by entering a value of 0 to 15 for the Decimal Places option. However, keep in mind that there may not be enough room to display any decimal places if your graph is plotting very large numbers.

Minor Tick Mark Labels

A *minor* tick is a tick mark without a label. With automatic scaling, every tick mark along the X- and Y-axes is labeled. The Number of Minor Ticks option on the Customize Graph Axes screen allows you to remove labels from some of the tick marks. If you change the Number of Minor Ticks option to 1, every other tick label is displayed. If you change it to 2, every third tick label is displayed (two successive ticks are left blank), and so on.

TIP: Reducing the numer of minor tick marks can help improve a graph that is too cluttered.

Other Axis Labeling Options

The Alternate Ticks? option is available only for the X-axis. It lets you determine whether or not long X-axis titles will be staggered onto two separate (alternate) lines. Changing this setting to No limits X-axis titles to a single line. Note, however, that if the titles are wider than column space permits, they will run together and be illegible.

The Display Axis Scaling? option determines whether the scaling indicator at the left of the graph is displayed. Back in Figure 10.3, where this option was set to Yes, the word *Thousands* indicates that the Y-axis values are multiples of 1000. Changing the setting to No would remove the indicator.

Sample Custom Axes

Figure 10.20 shows examples of a Customize Graph Axes screen and a stacked bar graph using those settings. The Y-axis setting has been

CUSTOMIZING THE OVERALL FEATURES OF GRAPHS

FIGURE 10.20

Top: The Customize Graph Axes setting for Manual scaling and a Currency format. Bottom: A graph produced with these settings, which control the appearance of its Y-axis.

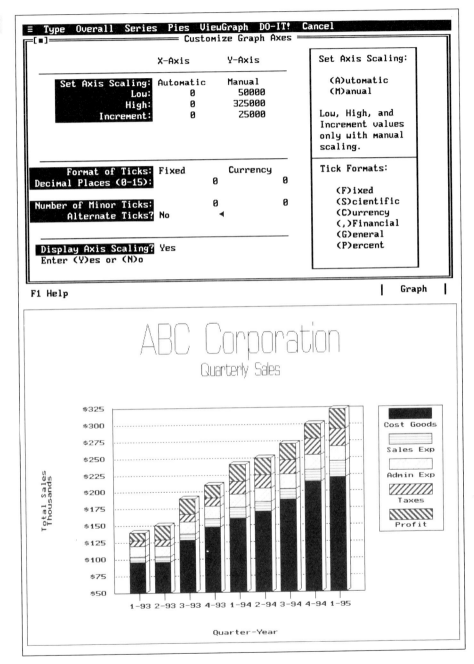

changed to Manual. The Low, High, and Increment settings have been customized, and the Format of Ticks option has been changed to Currency. The Alternate Ticks setting has been changed to No.

> **NOTE** The titles in Figure 10.20 are also customized, using the same settings as for Figure 10.16.

Comparing this figure to the one in Figure 10.3, which is the same graph but with the default axis settings, you can see that values on the Y-axis now range from 50 to 325 (thousand), in increments of 25 (thousand). A dollar sign precedes each Y-axis label because Currency was selected for the Y-axis setting for the Format of Ticks option.

Changing the X-Axis Labels for a Keyed Table Graph

The only case in which Paradox won't use the entries in the first column of the table in Table view for the X-axis labels is when the table has a *primary key*. In that case, Paradox uses the "least significant key" for the X-axis labels, regardless of the order of fields in Table view. If you view a table's structure using **Tools ▶ Info ▶ Structure**, the last field in the table that's marked with an asterisk is the least significant key.

> **NOTE** Primary keys are covered in Chapter 13.

If you don't want to use that least significant key as the X-axis labels in a graph, you can perform a query that includes only the fields you want to plot in the graph. The resulting Answer table is never keyed. Therefore, you can rotate the field that you want to use for X-axis labels to the leftmost column of the Answer table. Then base the graph on the Answer table rather than on the original table.

Modifying Graph Grids

Paradox automatically displays a graph with a pattern of horizontal grid lines at the tick marks. You can control the grid pattern and colors by changing the options on the Customize Grids and Frames screen. To display this screen, starting from the desktop, choose **Image** ➤ **Graph** ➤ **Modify**. Then choose **Overall** ➤ **Grids** from the Customize Graph screen's menu bar. You'll see the screen shown in Figure 10.21. The options on the screen are described in the following sections.

FIGURE 10.21

The Customize Grids and Frames screen lets you change the grid and graph frame. It is accessed via Image ➤ Graph ➤ Modify ➤ Overall ➤ Grids.

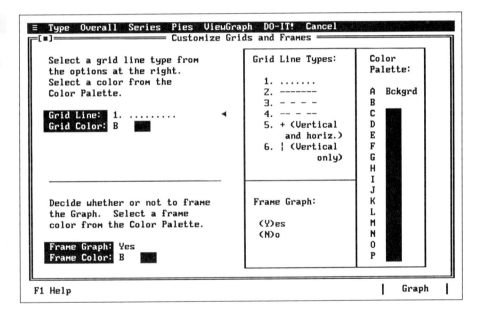

Grid Lines

By default, Paradox uses a series of dots to represent grid lines. The other options for displaying grids are listed under the heading Grid Line Types on the right side of the Customize Grids and Frames screen. To select a new grid line style, type the appropriate number (from 1 to 6) next to the Grid Line option on the left side of the screen.

To change the color of the grid lines, select any of the options listed under the heading Color Palette. Type the appropriate letter next to the Grid Color option.

GRAPHING YOUR DATA

If you want to remove grid lines, select a color that is the same as the background color or A (Bckgrd).

Graph Frames

By default, Paradox places a thin frame around the entire graph (near the edges of your screen). The Frame Graph option on the Customize Grids and Frames screen lets you determine whether to keep this frame (Yes) or remove it (No).

You can also select a color for the frame from the list under the Color Palette heading on the left side of the screen. Changing the Frame Color setting also changes the color used to outline bars and pie segments, as well as the color used to display labels and series outlines in the legend of the graph.

Customizing Graph Series

In addition to customizing the overall features of a graph, you can customize individual series. Choose **Image** ➤ **Graph** ➤ **Modify** from the Paradox desktop menu bar. Then choose **Series** from the Customize Graph screen's menu bar. You'll see the menu shown below:

The **Series** ➤ **Colors** option is the same as the **Overall** ➤ **Colors** option described earlier. The other Series options are described in the following sections.

Modifying Legends and Labels

The LegendsAndLabels option on the Series menu lets you specify how each series is labeled on the graph. Select this option to display the Customize Series Legends and Labels screen, as shown in Figure 10.22.

FIGURE 10.22

The Customize Series Legends and Labels screen. It is accessed via Image ➤ Graph ➤ Modify ➤ Series ➤ LegendsAndLabels.

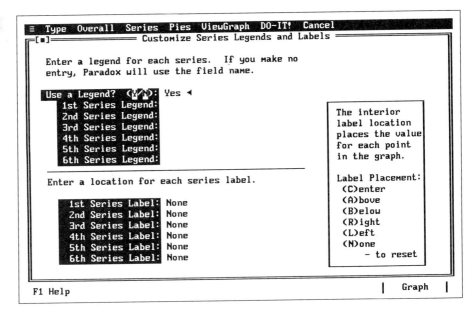

Customizing the Graph Legend

By default, Paradox automatically creates a legend and uses field names from the table as legend labels to identify the pattern or line style representing each series plotted on the graph. To create your own legend labels, make sure that the Use a Legend? option is set to Yes, and type in a legend label for each series (field) on the graph. Be sure to type the legends in the proper order, corresponding to the left-to-right order of fields in Table view.

Series Labels

Series labels can be used to display numeric values directly within a graph. By default, Paradox does not display series labels (it leaves these options set to None).

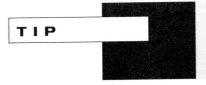

Add series labels when your graph needs to show not only the relationships between values but the actual values as well.

GRAPHING YOUR DATA

You can specify which series you wish to label and where to place each label using the options on the bottom half of the Customize Series Legends and Labels screen. Specify a position in relation to the plotted point by typing one of the codes listed under the heading Label Placement on the right side of the screen:

- **(C)enter:** Places the label in the middle of the point.
- **(A)bove:** Places the label above the point.
- **(B)elow:** Places the label below the point.
- **(R)ight:** Places the label to the right of the point.
- **(L)eft:** Places the label to the left of the point.
- **(N)one:** Omits or resets labels.

Because labels can clutter a graph, you should probably limit your use of these options to graphs that display only a few series. For example, Figure 10.23 shows a relatively simple bar graph with labels displayed above each bar. Also, because the graph only plots one series, the legend was removed changing the Use a Legend? option from Yes to No.

FIGURE 10.23

A graph with series labels above each bar

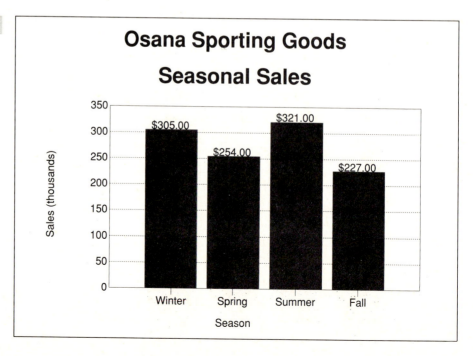

CUSTOMIZING GRAPH SERIES   343

CAUTION If you attempt to display interior labels on graphs that are plotting very large numbers, Paradox will display rows of asterisks (*****) rather than the labels.

Modifying Markers and Fill Patterns

The various forms of bar graphs and area graphs that display more than one series of values use fill patterns, such as stripes, to make it easier to distinguish the different series. Markers graphs and combined lines and markers graphs use markers to display points that are plotted on the graph.

You can customize the fill patterns or markers for a graph by using the Customize Fills and Markers screen. If you're starting at the desktop, choose **I**mage ➤ **G**raph ➤ **M**odify. Then choose **S**eries ➤ **M**arkersAnd-Fills from the Customize Graph screen's menu bar. You'll see the screen shown in Figure 10.24.

FIGURE 10.24

The Customize Fills and Markers screen. It is accessed via Image ➤ Graph ➤ Modify ➤ Series ➤ MarkersAndFills.

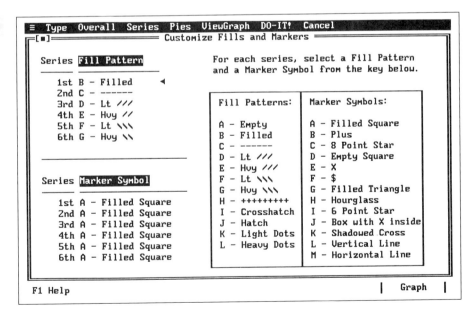

344 CHAPTER 10 GRAPHING YOUR DATA

You can select from 12 fill patterns for each series plotted in the graph by typing the appropriate letter (A through L), as listed under the heading Fill Patterns on the right side of the screen. For markers graphs and combined lines and markers graphs, you can select from up to 13 different marker symbols (A through M), as listed under the heading Marker Symbols.

Customizing Pie Charts

Many of the enhancements that can be added to other types of graphs do not apply to pie charts because they have no axes and can only display a single series (data from a single field). However, Paradox does allow you to customize features that are unique to pie charts.

As an example, Figure 10.25 shows a pie chart for the Profit field of the Finsum table, using the custom titles shown earlier in this chapter. In this

FIGURE 10.25

A pie chart. Numbers that are too large to display on the graph appear as asterisks.

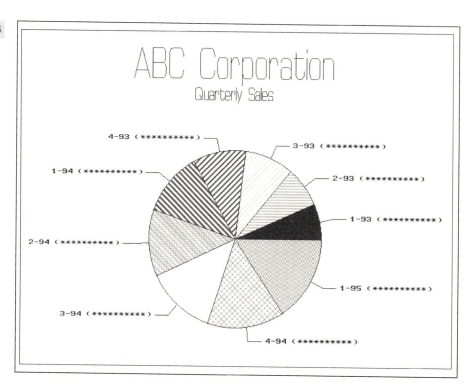

CUSTOMIZING PIE CHARTS

pie chart, Paradox shows asterisks rather than numeric values because the numbers are too large to display. You'll learn how to rectify this problem in a moment.

To customize an existing pie chart, choose **Image** ➤ **Graph** ➤ **Modify** from the Paradox desktop menu bar. Then choose **P**ies from the Customize Graph screen's menu bar. You'll see the Customize Pie Graph screen, as shown in Figure 10.26.

The options on this screen provide ways to control the appearance of your pie charts, as discussed in the sections that follow.

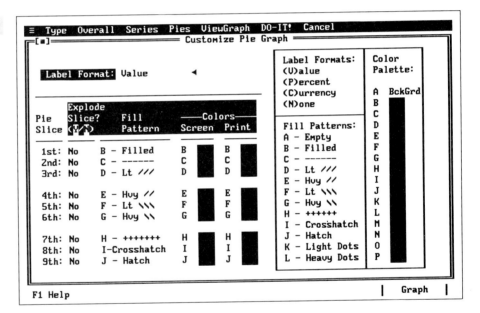

FIGURE 10.26

The Customize Pie Graph screen lets you refine pie charts. It is accessed via Image ➤ Graph ➤ Modify ➤ Pies.

Modifying the Label Format

You have four choices for the format of the slice labels on your pie chart:

- **(V)alue:** Each slice will be labeled with the actual table value, if it fits. (This is the default.)

- **(P)ercent:** Each slice will be labeled with the percentage of the whole it represents.

- **(C)urrency:** Slice labels will be preceded by a dollar sign.
- **(N)one:** No slice labels will be displayed (other than the labels from the leftmost column of Table view).

Simply type the appropriate letter for the Label Format option at the top of the left side of the Customize Pie Graph screen.

Customizing the Pie Slices

You can individually explode, fill, or color each slice in a pie chart by changing settings for that slice on the Customize Pie Graph screen. Each line (1st, 2nd, 3rd, and so on) represents one slice in the pie (the entire pie can have up to nine slices).

To change a slice, move the cursor to the appropriate line for the slice you want to customize and then set its options as follows:

- To explode the slice, change the first option from No to Yes (by typing Y).
- To change the fill pattern for the slice, press Tab or → to move to the Fill Pattern option. Then type a letter, A through L, to choose one of the fill patterns listed under the heading Fill Patterns on the right side of the screen.
- To change the screen color for a slice, press → or Tab to move the cursor to the Screen option, then type the letter that represents the color you want from the Color Palette list near the right edge of the screen.
- To change the printed color for a slice, press → or Tab to move the cursor to the Print option, then type the letter that represents the color you want, as listed under the Color Palette heading.

As usual, you can quickly see the effects of your changes by pressing Ctrl-F7 at any time. Return to the screen by pressing any key. When you're satisfied with your settings, you can choose **DO-IT!** to return to the desktop. Or, to cancel your current selections, choose **Cancel ► Y**es.

Figure 10.27 shows the sample pie chart with the ninth slice exploded and labels displayed in Currency format.

FIGURE 10.27

A pie chart with an exploded slice and values displayed in Currency format

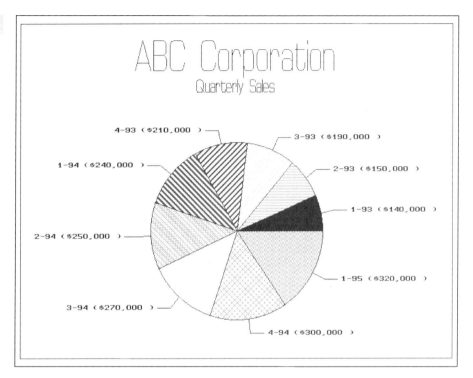

Saving and Reusing Graph Settings

Chances are, after you've customized a graph to get exactly the look you want, you won't want to repeat all the steps later when you want to redisplay that graph with new data. Instead, you can just save the graph settings in a file. Then you can recall that file to use those settings with a graph.

Saving Custom Graph Settings

To save the settings you've defined for a graph, follow these steps:

1. If you're still in a Customize Graph screen, choose **DO-IT!** or press F2 to return to the desktop.

GRAPHING YOUR DATA

2. To make sure you know what you're saving, press F7 to view the graph (or choose **I**mage ➤ **V**iewGraph ➤ **S**creen). Press any key after viewing the graph to return to the desktop.

3. Choose **I**mage ➤ **G**raph ➤ **S**ave. You'll see a dialog box requesting the name of the graph settings file, along with the prompt

   Enter graph file name for current graph specification

4. Type in a valid DOS file name, but without an extension (for example, Mygraph or Barstyle), then choose OK or press ↵.

If a graph settings file with that name already exists, you'll see a warning message and the options to **C**ancel or **R**eplace. Choose **C**ancel to enter a new file name or **R**eplace to overwrite the old settings with the new ones.

You can save any number of graph settings files, as long as each has a different file name. Thus, you could create one file of settings for pie charts, another file for area graphs, and so on.

The settings are stored in a file with the file name you provided in step 4, followed by the .G extension (as in Mygraph.G or Barstyle.G). Keep in mind that *only* the settings are saved, which means that you can use those settings to display new or modified data, or data from a completely different table, at any time in the future. You can also modify the saved settings, or use them as the starting point for developing other graphs.

Using Custom Graph Settings for Other Graphs

Before using your saved graph settings, you must prepare the table as usual. That is, choose **V**iew from the desktop menu bar to open the table, then rotate the fields (if necessary) and position the cursor in a numeric field for displaying a graph.

At this point, rather than simply pressing Ctrl-F7 to view an Instant Graph, you load the custom graph settings that you saved earlier. Select

Image ▶ Graph ▶ Load. You'll see the following dialog box:

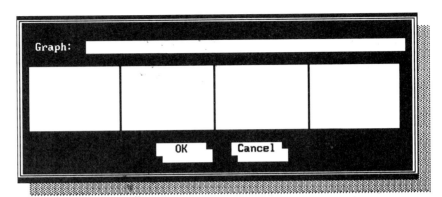

Type in the name of the graph settings file you want to use and press ↵ or choose OK. Or press ↵ or choose OK (without typing a name) to see the names of existing graph settings files; then double-click on the graph file name or highlight the name of the graph that contains the custom settings you want and press ↵.

Now the graph that appears when you press Ctrl-F7 will have all the custom settings (including those for titles, series, and so on) that you stored in the graph settings file. However, the values plotted on the graph will reflect the data stored in the current table.

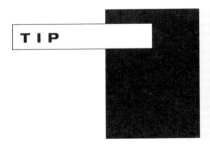

Take advantage of this capability to save a custom graph format and use it repeatedly in the future to display current data. You can experiment with data in the table to try out various what-if scenarios, and then just press the Instant Graph key (Ctrl-F7) to see how your changes look on the graph.

Modifying Existing Custom Graph Settings

If you want to make further changes or additions to a custom graph, you can use the same basic techniques that you used to create the graph. Here are the steps:

1. Load the custom graph settings, as described in the previous section.
2. Choose **I**mage ➤ **G**raph ➤ **M**odify from the desktop menu bar.
3. Choose menu options for further modifying your graph, and make whatever additional changes you wish.
4. To save your new changes to the graph, press F2 or choose **D**O-IT!.
5. When you return to the desktop, choose **I**mage ➤ **G**raph ➤ **S**ave to save your new modifications.

CAUTION If you forget to save the new modifications with Image ➤ Graph ➤ Save, they will be lost when you exit Paradox.

6. When Paradox asks for the name of the graph, use the same name that you used to save the graph the first time, and choose **R**eplace when you're warned that the graph already exists.

Another way that you might want to modify your custom settings is to return them to the default settings by choosing **I**mage ➤ **G**raph ➤ **R**eset ➤ **O**K from the desktop. Of course, if you previously saved the settings for the graph (by choosing **I**mage ➤ **G**raph ➤ **S**ave), you can still retrieve those settings after resetting the defaults. To do so, choose **I**mage ➤ **G**raph ➤ **L**oad, as described previously.

Using One Custom Graph to Create Another

Let's assume you created a stacked bar graph with custom titles. Suppose that now you also want to create a line graph using these same titles.

Rather than creating an entirely new graph and retyping the custom titles, you could use the original graph as a starting point for the new graph. To do so, follow these steps:

1. Make sure that the appropriate table for the graph is displayed on your screen and that the cursor is positioned appropriately for the graph.
2. Choose **I**mage ➤ **G**raph ➤ **L**oad to load the graph settings that you want to use as the starting point.
3. Press Ctrl-F7 to view the current graph (just to make sure you've selected the appropriate one), and then press any key to return to the desktop.
4. Choose **I**mage ➤ **G**raph ➤ **M**odify.
5. Change the graph type or make other kinds of changes. For example, to create a line graph, type the letter **L** on the Customize Graph Type screen. As usual, press Ctrl-F7 when you want to see the effects of your changes.
6. When you are satisfied with the new graph, press F2 or choose **DO-IT!** from the Customize Graph screen's menu bar.
7. To save the new graph without losing the original graph, choose **I**mage ➤ **G**raph ➤ **S**ave and give this graph a new name.

You can also use Tools ➤ Copy ➤ Graph from the desktop to copy an existing graph settings file to a new name. See Chapter 12 for details.

Printing Graphs

Laser printers and many dot-matrix printers can print graphs. Obviously, plotters can produce graphs as well. Before you can print graphs, however, you need to tell Paradox which printer you'll be using for them. You need only do this once, not each time you want to print graphs. For information about setting up a graphics printer, see Appendix D.

To print a graph, follow these steps:

1. View the graph on the screen (Ctrl-F7) to make sure that it's ready for printing, then press any key to return to the desktop.

2. If you've only defined one graphics printer, or already know which printer the graph will be sent to, skip to step 6.

3. Choose **I**mage ➤ **G**raph ➤ **M**odify ➤ **O**verall ➤ **D**evice.

4. Choose **P**rinter. You'll see a submenu with printer options. As you scroll through the options, the printer assigned to each option appears on the status bar (*Undefined* appears if no printer is defined for that option).

5. Click on the option you want, or press ↵ when it's highlighted. Then choose **DO-IT!** to return to the desktop.

6. Select **I**mage ➤ **G**raph ➤ **V**iewGraph ➤ **P**rinter.

NOTE ViewGraph appears on the menu bar (after you choose Image ➤ Graph ➤ Modify) and works the same as Image ➤ Graph ➤ ViewGraph from the desktop.

Most printers will pause for a minute or so as Paradox prepares the graph for printing. You won't have access to Paradox during this pause. When the graph is finally printed, you'll be returned to the Paradox desktop.

If absolutely nothing comes out of the printer, the problem may be that the printer is not installed or connected correctly, the printer isn't on-line, or the page simply needs to be ejected from the printer using the printer's form feed button.

Customizing the Printed Graph Layout

By default, Paradox will print graphs so that they fit well on the page. However, you may want to alter the size or some other features of your printed graph. To customize the printed graph's layout, choose **I**mage ➤ **G**raph ➤ **M**odify from the desktop menu bar. Then select **O**verall ➤ **P**rinterLayout from the Customize Graph screen's menu bar. The Customize Graph Layout for Printing screen appears, as shown in Figure 10.28.

FIGURE 10.28

The Customize Graph Layout for Printing screen lets you define options for printing a graph. It is accessed via Overall ➤ PrinterLayout.

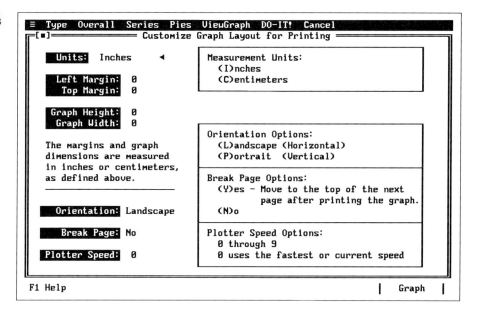

You change the options on the Customize Graph Layout for Printing screen in the same way that you do on other Customize Graph screens. Paradox interprets measurements for the margins and the graph height and width as either inches or centimeters, depending on which one you specify for the Units option near the top of the screen.

Set the Break Page option to No if you want to print more than one graph on a single page. If you are using a plotter, it is recommended that you use a slow speed setting for older pens, and a setting of 2 for transparencies.

As usual, press F2 or choose **DO-IT!** to save the settings for the current Paradox session and return to the desktop. If you want to save these settings for all future printings of this graph, choose **I**mage ➤ **G**raph ➤ **S**ave from the desktop menu bar, as discussed earlier in this chapter.

Printing Graphs to a File

As an alternative to printing graphs immediately, you can "print" them to files. Later, you can import them as graphics into a word processing or desktop publishing program. You can also print them on another computer without using Paradox.

GRAPHING YOUR DATA

Follow these steps to print a graph to a file:

1. Choose **I**mage ➤ **G**raph ➤ **M**odify from the desktop menu bar.
2. Choose **O**verall ➤ **D**evice ➤ **F**ile. You'll see a submenu offering three choices.
3. Choose the **C**urrentPrinter, **E**PS, or **P**IC option, depending on the file format you want to use, as follows:
    - **C**urrentPrinter prints the graph to a file with the extension .GRF, formatted for whatever printer is currently selected.
    - **E**PS stores the graph in Encapsulated PostScript (EPS) format and gives the file name the .EPS extension.
    - **P**IC formats the graph file for use with Lotus 1-2-3. Files saved in this format are given the extension .PIC.
4. Choose ViewGraph ➤ **F**ile from the Customize Graph screen's menu bar. You'll see the usual dialog box for entering a file name, along with the prompt to enter a name for the graph file.
5. Type a valid DOS file name with no extension, then press ↵. As always, you can specify a path before the file name to send the graph to a particular drive or directory.
6. Choose **DO**-IT! to return to the desktop.

Using the Graph File

If you created the graph file by choosing **C**urrentPrinter in step 3 of the previous section, you can use the DOS COPY command with the >PRN option to print the graph outside Paradox. For example, suppose you print a graph to a file named A:\Graph1 so that it is stored on a floppy disk. You could then insert that floppy into any PC that uses DOS, whether it has Paradox on it or not, then print the graph using a command such as

   COPY A:\GRAPH1.GRF >PRN

> **NOTE** See your DOS manual for more information about printing graphic files with the COPY command and the >PRN redirection option.

You can also use the DOS COPY command with the >PRN option to print an EPS file to a PostScript printer without Paradox. The EPS format is widely used for desktop publishing applications that require high-resolution output. Several word processing programs allow you to embed graphs stored in EPS format directly into written documents, such as reports and newsletters. However, few programs can display such graphs on the screen; furthermore, these graphs can only be printed on PostScript printers.

The EPS format is the best choice if you plan to use an outside service to produce high-quality final copies of your graphs. In a typical application, you copy the .EPS files onto a floppy disk or send them via modem to a desktop publishing service bureau, which then outputs the files to a PostScript device, such as a laser printer, typesetter, or 35mm slide production equipment.

If you saved your graph in PIC format, you can use Lotus 1-2-3, Symphony, and many other spreadsheet programs to print them. Many word processing programs can also import graphics stored in PIC format and display them on the screen as well as print them.

Summarizing Data with Cross Tabulations

In Chapter 14, you'll learn techniques for performing calculations on numeric data with Paradox. However, one type of calculation, called a *cross tabulation*, is particularly useful when plotting graphs and is available through the graphing menus. Paradox provides the CrossTab option for performing cross tabulations.

Cross tabulations are most useful for summarizing and arranging data from a large table into a smaller table that's easier to graph, and produces a more meaningful graph. However, getting Paradox's CrossTab option to produce the results that you want can be a little bit tricky at first, because you must be very careful about how you arrange the columns and place the cursor in Table view. But once you learn to adhere to a few rules of thumb, you'll see that using cross tabulation isn't really that difficult.

The examples of using the CrossTab option use a sample table named Salesreg, which stores information about individual salesperson's sales of products by part number. The table structure and the table with some sample data are shown in Figure 10.29.

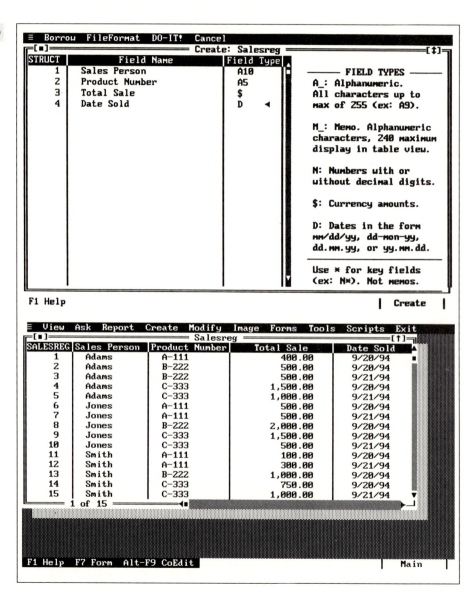

FIGURE 10.29

Top: The structure of the Salesreg table, which will be used in the cross tabulation examples. Bottom: Sample data for the Salesreg table.

Understanding Cross Tabulation

The sample table at the bottom of Figure 10.29 contains data for individual sales transactions. Generating a graph directly from this table would lead to a very cluttered and complicated graph, because there are so many records and no meaningful, summarized (totaled) results.

A better way to graph data in the Salesreg table would be to first summarize the records into a smaller table of total sales. To create this table, you could use CrossTab to determine each salesperson's total sales for each product. Paradox will use the data in the Salesreg table to produce a table named Crosstab. This calculation involves three fields: you want each salesperson's [1] total sales (2) for each product (number) [3]. In fact, a cross tabulation always requires exactly three fields of data to generate a result:

- **Row labels:** One field in the starting table must contain values that will label unique rows in the Crosstab table. The values in this field will be listed down the left side of the Crosstab table. The records will be sorted by the values in this field.

- **Column labels:** A second field in the original table will label unique columns of information in the Crosstab table. The values in the field you select for the column labels will be listed across the top of the Crosstab table once it is generated.

- **Summary values:** A third field, which must be numeric, must contain the values on which the calculation will be performed. The results will appear at the intersection of each row and column in the Crosstab table.

In the Salesreg table, you would make Sales Person the field for row labels, Product Number the field for column labels, and Total Sales the field for summary values. The resulting table would contain the total sales for each salesperson and each product; in other words, the table would show each salesperson's total sales for each product, as intended.

Most likely, you will use the CrossTab option to generate totals, as in the preceding example. However, CrossTab can perform other types of operations on the field used as the summary value, as explained in the next section.

Generating a Crosstab Table

Now that you understand the requirements and capabilities of the Cross-Tab option, you're ready to generate a Crosstab table. Here are the steps:

1. If you haven't done so already, open the table that you want to graph data from, then make sure you are in Table view.
2. Put the cursor in the column containing the row labels.
3. Choose Image ➤ Graph ➤ CrossTab. You'll see a submenu offering the options Sum, Min, Max, and Count.
4. Select one of the options to perform the various crosstab operations:

   - **Sum:** Summary values are totals for each row and column pair. In the Salesreg table, this would be the total sales for each salesperson and each product number. Sum is the operation to choose for this example.
   - **Min:** Summary values for each row and column pair are the smallest of all individual values. In the Salesreg table, this would be the smallest individual sale for each salesperson, for each product number.
   - **Max:** Summary values for each row and column pair are the largest of all individual values. In the Salesreg table, this would be the largest individual sale for each salesperson, for each product number.
   - **Count:** Summary values for each row and column pair indicate how many records refer to that row and column pair. In the Salesreg table, this would be the total number of records for each salesperson, for each product number.

   You'll see the message

   Move to column containing crosstab row labels, then press ↵...

5. With the cursor in the field with the row labels (Sales Person in the Salesreg table), press ↵. You'll see the prompt

   Move to column containing crosstab column labels then press ↵...

SUMMARIZING DATA WITH CROSS TABULATIONS

6. Move the cursor to the field with the column labels (Product Number in the Salesreg table) and press ↵. You'll see the prompt for the summary values

   Move to column containing crosstab values, then press ↵.

7. Move the cursor to the field that contains the summary values (Total Sale in the Salesreg table) and press ↵.

After you specify the third field, Paradox generates the Crosstab table. Figure 10.30 shows the Crosstab table generated from the Salesreg table.

As you can see, the Crosstab table displays exactly the data requested. Each row refers to an individual salesperson, and each column refers to an individual product. At the intersection of each row and column is the total of all sales for the row and column pair.

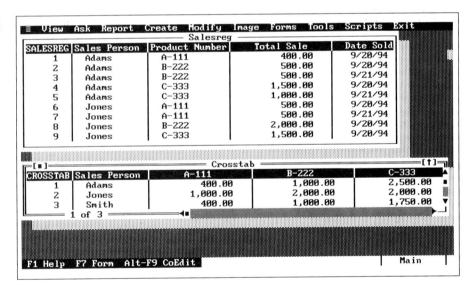

FIGURE 10.30

The Crosstab table generated from the Salesreg table totals the sales of each product for each salesperson.

Graphing a Crosstab Table

To see an instant graphic result of a Crosstab table, place the cursor into the first numeric field. Then choose Image ➤ Graph ➤ Modify and select a graph type that's capable of displaying multiple series, such as stacked bar. Then press Ctrl-F7 to view the graph. As usual, when you are finished viewing the graph, press any key to return to the desktop.

Figure 10.31 shows the graph generated from the Crosstab table created with the sample Salesreg table. The graph plots the total sales for each salesperson, for each product. The stacked bar graph is particularly suitable in this case because it shows both the overall total sales for each salesperson and sales of individual products for each salesperson (as indicated in the graph legend).

FIGURE 10.31

A graph generated from a Crosstab table

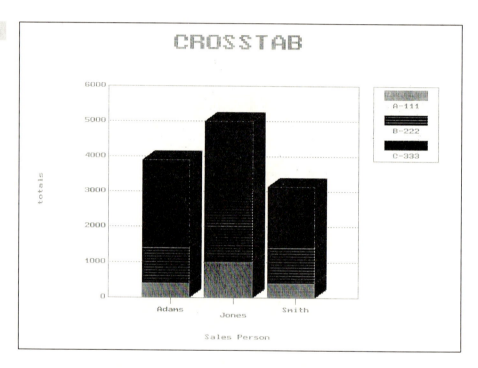

Arranging Fields for CrossTabs

The fields in the Salesreg table were already arranged to make the cross tabulation example easy to follow. However, when using the CrossTab option for your own work, you may need to use the Rotate key (Ctrl-r) or **Image ▶ M**ove to rearrange fields in Table view before you begin. Keep in mind these important points about the order of fields in Table view when generating your own Crosstab tables:

- If the field used for row labels has any fields to the left of it, those fields are combined to create the row labels.

SUMMARIZING DATA WITH CROSS TABULATIONS

- The field used for column labels must be to the right of the field(s) used for row values.

As an example of the first point, suppose that you wanted to produce a Crosstab table using the Salesreg table and the Product Number column as the row labels field. Here are the steps:

1. Clear the existing Crosstab table from the screen by closing its window (click on its Close button or press F8).

NOTE It's not strictly necessary to clear the existing Crosstab table before generating another one. Paradox automatically overwrites any existing Crosstab table the next time it performs a cross tabulation. However, if you skip this step, be sure to position the cursor in the correct table before choosing Image ➤ Graph ➤ CrossTab again.

2. Choose Image ➤ Graph ➤ CrossTab ➤ Sum.
3. When prompted, move the cursor to the field for row labels (Product Number) and press ↵ to mark that field.
4. When prompted, move the cursor to the field for the column labels (Date Sold) and press ↵.
5. Again when prompted, move the cursor to the field containing the summary values (Total Sale) and press ↵ to mark that field and generate the Crosstab table.

Figure 10.32 shows the resulting Crosstab table. Notice that each row no longer uniquely represents an individual salesperson. Instead, each row now represents an individual Salesperson–product number *pair*. That's because Product Number was used as the field for row values and the Sales Person field is to the left of it. Thus, Paradox assumed that you wanted to combine Sales Person and Product Number when generating unique values for the rows in the Crosstab table.

FIGURE 10.32

A Crosstab table with two row label fields

```
≡  View  Ask  Report  Create  Modify  Image  Forms  Tools  Scripts  Exit
┌─────────────────────── Salesreg ────────────────────────┐
│ Sales Person │ Product Number │ Total Sale │ Date Sold  │
│ Adams        │ A-111          │    400.00  │ 9/20/94    │
│ Adams        │ B-222          │    500.00  │ 9/20/94    │
│ Adams        │ B-222          │    500.00  │ 9/21/94    │
│ Adams        │ C-333          │  1,500.00  │ 9/20/94    │
│ Adams        │ C-333          │  1,000.00  │ 9/21/94    │
│ Jones        │ A-111          │    500.00  │ 9/20/94    │
│ Jones        │ A-111          │    500.00  │ 9/21/94    │
┌─[■]─────────────────── Crosstab ───────────────────[↑]──┐
│ CROSSTAB │ Sales Person │ Product Number │ 9/20/94  │ 9/21/94  │
│    1     │ Adams        │ A-111          │   400.00 │     0.00 │
│    2     │ Adams        │ B-222          │   500.00 │   500.00 │
│    3     │ Adams        │ C-333          │ 1,500.00 │ 1,000.00 │
│    4     │ Jones        │ A-111          │   500.00 │   500.00 │
│    5     │ Jones        │ B-222          │ 2,000.00 │     0.00 │
│    6     │ Jones        │ C-333          │ 1,500.00 │   500.00 │
│    7     │ Smith        │ A-111          │   100.00 │   300.00 │
│    8     │ Smith        │ B-222          │ 1,000.00 │     0.00 │
│    9     │ Smith        │ C-333          │   750.00 │ 1,000.00 │
        ═══ 1 of 9 ═══

  F1 Help  F7 Form  Alt-F9 CoEdit                          Main
```

But suppose you wanted to use Product Number as the row labels field, rather than the Product Number and Sales Person field combination. In that case, you would clear the Crosstab table from the screen, then move the cursor to the Sales Person field in the Salesreg table and press Ctrl-r to rotate that field to the rightmost column.

After you repeat the steps to generate the Crosstab table and specify Product Number as the field for row labels, the resulting table will display a single row for each unique part number.

A Shortcut for CrossTabs

If your work requires many cross tabulations, you may want to use the shortcut CrossTab key, Alt-x. When you use the CrossTab key, Paradox will not prompt you for fields to use for row, column, and summary values. Instead, it will assume that you've already ordered the columns in the table and positioned the cursor, informed by the following knowledge:

- The values in the field that the cursor is in and all fields to its left will become the row labels.

- The values in the second from the rightmost field will become the column labels.

SUMMARIZING DATA WITH CROSS TABULATIONS

- The values in the rightmost field will be the values displayed in the Crosstab table. Thus, the field must be numeric. The field is then tabulated for every row and column.
- All other fields in the table are ignored.

You can use the usual Ctrl-r key or **Image ➤ M**ove method to arrange the columns in Table view prior to using the CrossTab key. After you've arranged the order of columns, you must also remember to put the cursor in the row label field prior to pressing Alt-x.

As an example, suppose that you want to use the CrossTab key to generate a table of total sales for each sales person and each product number in the Salesreg table (as in our first example). You would first use Ctrl-r or **Image ➤ M**ove to arrange the fields in the Salesreg table, as shown in Figure 10.33. Then position the cursor in the row label field (Sales Person) and press the CrossTab key, Alt-x. Paradox quickly generates the Crosstab table, without asking any questions. The resulting table looks exactly like the one you saw back in Figure 10.30.

In Figure 10.33, the columns were properly arranged for the instant cross tabulation. That is, the row labels field (Sales Person) is in the leftmost column, the column labels field (Product Number) is in the second-to-last column, and the summary field (Total Sale) is in the rightmost column.

FIGURE 10.33

Columns arranged for an instant Crosstab table

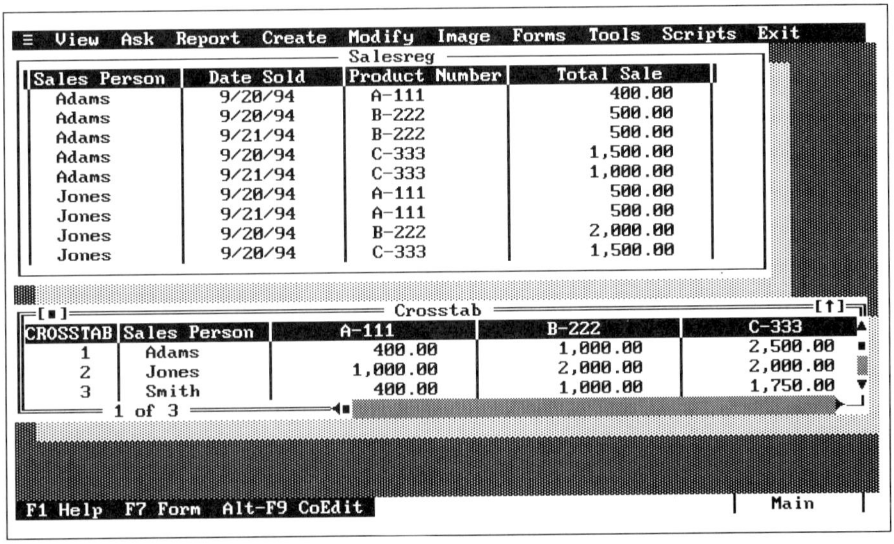

Summary

This chapter introduced you to the rich variety of business graphs available in Paradox for presenting a pictorial view of your data. Here's a quick summary of the most important points:

- To produce an Instant Graph, view your table, move the cursor to a numeric field, and press the Instant Graph key, Ctrl-F7.

- To select a type of graph, select **I**mage ➤ **G**raph ➤ **M**odify from the desktop menu bar.

- To customize a graph, select **I**mage ➤ **G**raph ➤ **M**odify from the desktop menu bar, then choose options from the Customize Graph screen's menu bar. Press F2 or choose **DO-IT!** from the menu to return to the desktop, then press Ctrl-F7 to view the graph with the current settings.

- To save custom graph settings, select **I**mage ➤ **G**raph ➤ **S**ave from the desktop menu bar.

- To load previously saved graph settings, select **I**mage ➤ **G**raph ➤ **L**oad from the desktop menu bar.

- To prepare the printer for graphs, run the Custom Configuration Program (see Appendix D).

- To customize the layout of a printed graph, select **I**mage ➤ **G**raph ➤ **M**odify from the desktop menu bar. Then choose **O**verall ➤ **P**rinterLayout.

- To print a graph, first view it on the screen, then press any key to return to the desktop. Then choose **I**mage ➤ **G**raph ➤ **V**iewGraph ➤ **P**rinter from the desktop menu bar or choose **V**iewGraph ➤ **P**rinter from the Customize Graph screen's menu bar.

- To summarize data in a table for graphing, choose **I**mage ➤ **G**raph ➤ **C**rossTab.

CHAPTER 11

Simplifying Your Work with Scripts

fast TRACK

- **To record a script** — 370

    choose **S**cripts ➤ **B**eginRecord, or press Alt-F10 and choose **B**eginRecord. Enter a valid DOS file name for the script (without an extension), then perform whatever actions you want to record.

- **To stop recording a script** — 371

    choose **S**cripts ➤ **E**nd-Record from the desktop, or press Alt-F10 and choose **E**nd-Record from the PAL menu.

- **To play back a script at maximum speed** — 372

    select **S**cripts ➤ **P**lay from the desktop, or press Alt-F10 and choose **P**lay. Type or choose the name of the script in the usual manner.

- **To play back a script and watch every action** — 373

    choose **S**cripts ➤ **S**howPlay from the desktop. Type or choose the name of the script in the usual manner, and then select either **F**ast or **S**low.

- **To record an Instant Script** — 382

    press the Instant Script Record key, Alt-F3, to begin recording keystrokes. Perform whatever actions you want to record, then press Alt-F3 again to stop recording.

- **To play back an Instant Script** 382

    press the Instant Script Play key, Alt-F4.

- **To play back any script as an Instant Script** 383

    use **T**ools ➤ **C**opy to make a copy of the script and name the copy Instant. Then you can play back the script by pressing Alt-F4.

- **To create a script that plays back another script** 384

    choose **S**cripts ➤ **P**lay, or **S**cripts ➤ **R**epeatPlay, and type or choose the name of the script to play.

- **To create a script that plays back automatically on startup** 385

    name the script Init and store it in the directory from which you normally start Paradox.

SOME tasks in Paradox require several steps to complete. For example, in order to edit table data using a custom form, you must perform some variation of the following steps: (1) choose **T**ools ➤ **M**ore ➤ **D**irectory to get to the table's directory; (2) choose **M**odify ➤ **E**dit and specify the name of the table you want to edit; then (3) choose **I**mage ➤ **P**ickForm and the name of the form to use.

Instead of manually repeating all the required steps each time you need to perform a task, you can record all the required keystrokes in a *script*. Then you can play back the recorded script to automatically perform all the steps needed to complete the task. When you begin performing complex tasks requiring dozens or perhaps hundreds of keystrokes, you'll really begin to appreciate the power of Paradox scripts.

NOTE A recorded script performs the function of a *macro* in other programs.

Preparing for Recording a Script

Before you begin recording a script, you need to consider how you'll use the script later. When you play back a script by using the menus (**S**cripts ➤ **P**lay), Paradox searches only the current directory for the script file. Therefore, if that is the way you are going to play back the script, and you'll always be using the script with a particular set of files, you might want to use **Tools ➤ More ➤ D**irectory to switch to the directory that stores those files before you start recording keystrokes.

NOTE Later in this chapter and in Chapter 21, you'll learn how to run a script from any directory. Chapter 21 also explains the uses of the PAL menu, which you can access from almost anywhere in the program to begin or end script recording.

You also need to keep in mind that when you play back the script in the future, it will repeat *exactly* the keystrokes you recorded (you can't record mouse actions). Thus, you need to decide where you'll be within Paradox when you play back the script and get to that place before you start recording. For example, if you'll always be starting the script at the desktop, you should be at the desktop before you start recording keystrokes. However, if you think you'll be using the script in Form Design screens, you should already be in one of those screens when you start recording. Whenever possible, start recording from a blank desktop and record the keystrokes that take you to the context needed to perform the rest of the task that you want to record in the script.

Here are some other points to keep in mind when you're recording a script:

- Since you can't use the mouse when recording keystrokes, you must use the keyboard alternative for every action you want to record. For example, in a dialog box, press ↵ to choose the default OK button, or press Esc to choose the Cancel button. To close a window, press F8. To size or move a window, use the System menu (≡), which you must open by pressing Alt-spacebar.

- If you "shell out" to DOS or Windows, keystrokes you type in either of those products will not be recorded. However, as soon as you return to Paradox, any additional keystrokes will be recorded.

- Paradox stops recording keystrokes as soon as you activate a utility that plays another script, such as the Paradox Custom Configuration Program or Workshop utilities.

See the inside front and back covers of this book for lists of special keys available in various Paradox screens. All these keystrokes can be recorded in a script.

Recording a Script

When you're ready to begin recording (you're at the same place you intend to play back the recorded script), follow these steps:

1. If you're at the desktop, choose **S**cripts ➤ **B**eginRecord. If the Scripts option isn't available on the current menu bar, press the PAL Menu key, Alt-F10, then choose **B**eginRecord. You'll see this dialog box:

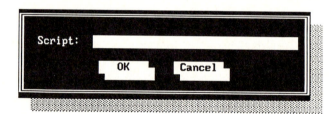

2. Type in a valid DOS file name for the script (up to eight characters, no spaces, and no extension) then press ↵ or choose OK. The letter *R* appears at the far right end of the status bar near the bottom of the screen, as a reminder that your actions are being recorded.

If you enter the name of an existing script, Paradox will ask for permission to replace the old script with the new one. Select Cancel to rename the new script, or Replace to replace the old script with the new one.

3. If you want to make sure you begin your script with a blank Paradox desktop, press Alt-F8 to close all windows as the first recorded keystroke in the script.

4. Perform whatever keystrokes and/or menu selections you want to record. Remember that you can't record mouse actions, so you'll need to use the arrow and other cursor-movement keys to move around the screen. Use the F10 key to access the menu bar when necessary, and so on. Other restrictions on recording are described in the previous section.

5. When you want to stop recording your keystrokes, if you're at the desktop, press F10 (if necessary) and choose **S**cripts ➤ **E**nd-Record. If you're not at the desktop, press Alt-F10 and choose **E**nd-Record. The *R* will disappear from the status bar, and your keystrokes will no longer be recorded into the script.

Paradox will save the script with the file name you provided in step 2 and the extension .SC, in whatever directory was current when you started recording the script.

If while recording a script you decide you don't want to save those keystrokes after all, press the PAL Menu key, Alt-F10, then choose **C**ancel. Paradox stops recording keystrokes, and it won't create a script from the keystrokes you recorded up to that point.

See Appendix C for more information about using scripts on the network.

Playing Back a Script

Once you have recorded a script, you can play it back at any time. But before you do, review these three points, which relate to how you recorded the script:

- If you try to play back a script that isn't in the current directory, Paradox will tell you that it can't find the script. You'll need to specify the directory with the script name (as in \PDOX45\Myscript) or choose Cancel and then use **T**ools ➤ **M**ore ➤ **D**irectory to get to the appropriate directory before recording the script.

> **TIP** You can record the Tools ➤ More ➤ Directory menu selections in a script if you want the script to always switch to a certain directory during playback.

- You should get to whatever screen or mode you were in when you recorded the keystrokes, so that they can be played back within that same context. For example, if you recorded the keystrokes in Table view and Edit mode, you should be in that view and mode before playing back the script. If you recorded the script starting from a blank desktop, you can close all open windows (Alt-F8) and then play back the script.

- The keystrokes in the script are played back, starting at the cursor position. If keystrokes to position the cursor aren't included in the script, you may need to place the cursor properly before playing back the script. For example, if you recorded the keystrokes to type your name and address at the top of a form letter in a Report Design screen, you should move the cursor to where you want your name and address in the new letter in the Report Design screen before playing back the script.

Once you're ready to play back the script, you can use any of the techniques described in the following sections. These are the simplest ways to play back a script. Chapter 21 covers a number of more flexible and sophisticated techniques for running scripts, as well as the options on the PAL menu that you see when you press Alt-F10.

Playing Back a Script at Maximum Speed

If you want the script to do its job as quickly as possible, play it back by choosing **S**cripts ➤ **P**lay from the Paradox desktop (if that's where you want to start from), or press the PAL Menu key, Alt-F10, and choose **P**lay. You'll see a dialog box and prompt requesting the name of the script you want to play back.

Type in the name of the script you want to play and choose OK. To select from a list instead, just choose OK (or press ↵) without entering a name. You'll see a list of scripts available on the current directory. Choose the name of the script to play back by double-clicking on it or highlighting it and pressing ↵.

Paradox will attempt to play back all the keystrokes stored in the script, but you won't see any of this activity on the screen. Instead, you'll only see the end results of all the completed keystrokes, then be returned to normal Paradox operation.

In Chapter 21, you'll learn about the PAL canvas that Paradox uses to hide operations performed during script playback.

Watching a Script Play Back Its Keystrokes

If you can start playing your script from the desktop, and you want to watch it play back its keystrokes, choose **S**cripts ➤ **S**howPlay. Then type (or choose) the name of the script you want to play. You'll see the options Fast and Slow.

Choose **F**ast to watch the macro play back its keystrokes at a rapid speed, or **S**low to have the script played back very slowly. The Slow option is especially helpful when you're developing more complex scripts that need to be analyzed for changes and enhancements.

There is no ShowPlay option on the PAL menu. However, the PAL Debugger on the PAL menu offers sophisticated tools for programmers to trace the progress of a script.

Playing Back a Script Repeatedly

The RepeatPlay option lets you specify the number of times to play a script. This is handy when you record a script that makes a change to a field in

SIMPLIFYING YOUR WORK WITH SCRIPTS

a record and then moves down to the same field in the next record. By playing back that script several times, you can make the same change to any number of records in the table. To play back a recorded script multiple times, follow these steps:

1. Choose **S**cripts ➤ **R**epeatPlay from the desktop, or press the PAL Menu key, Alt-F10 and choose **R**epeatPlay.

2. Type or choose the name of the script you want to play from the dialog box that appears. You'll see this dialog box:

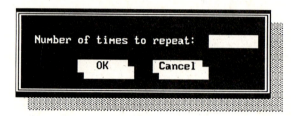

3. Type a number to indicate how many times you want to play back the script. For continuous playback, enter the letter **C**. Then choose OK or press ↵.

The script will be repeated as many times as you've specified, or continuously if you entered C, or until you press Ctrl-Break.

To interrupt the playback of any script, press Ctrl-Break—hold down the Ctrl key and press the key labeled Break (the Break key may have Break written on the side and Pause written on top). You may need to press Ctrl-Break more than once. After you press Ctrl-Break, you'll see this submenu:

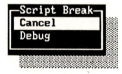

Choose **C**ancel to stop the script playback.

When Things Go Wrong with a Script

If Paradox encounters a keystroke it simply cannot play back in the current context, it stops playing back the script and displays the Cancel and Debug options, as shown in the previous section.

If you simply want to stop the script now, choose Cancel, and you'll return to normal Paradox operation. Chances are, if you get to the appropriate context, then play the script again, it will work just fine.

If you want to get an indication of what went wrong, choose Debug instead. You'll see the PAL Debugger window, as shown in the example in Figure 11.1. This window contains the lines of the script surrounding the place where things went wrong, with an ➤ indicator pointing at the position in the script where playback was suspended. The Debugger window's status bar displays an error message indicating the problem with the script.

From the Debugger window, you can press Ctrl-q to go to the Paradox desktop, in the condition it was left in by the last recorded keystroke executed by your script. You can also press Ctrl-e to open the Editor, with

FIGURE 11.1

When a script stops executing due to an error and you choose Debug, the offending segment of the script is opened in the PAL Debugger window. Press Ctrl-q to exit the Debugger.

```
≣ View  Ask  Report  Create  Modify  Image  Forms  Tools  Scripts  Exit
[■]══════════════════ c:\PDOX45\CUSTOMER\WELCOME.SC ══════════════════[↑]
 1  ;************************************************* Welcome.sc
 2  ;******* Prints welcome letters and envelopes for new customers.
 3  ClearAll        ;Clear the desktop
 4  MESSAGE "Preparing new customers..."
 5
 6  {Ask} {CustList} CtrlEnd   "BLANK, CHANGETO \""
 7  "Y\"" Do_It!
 8  Menu {Tools} {Copy} {Report} {DifferentTable} {CustList} {8}
 9  ▶ {Changed} {1}
10  Menu {Report} {Output} {Changed} {1} {Printer}
11
12  ;********************** Pause to let user load labels.
─Watch─────────────────────────────────────────────────────────────
─MiniScript─────────────────────────────────────────────────────────

                                                  Changed table not found
 F1 Help   Ctrl-Q Quit   Ctrl-S Step   Ctrl-T Trace   Ctrl-G Go   Ctrl-U Suspend   D
```

your script already placed in the Editor window and the cursor at the place where your script stopped running.

While the information in the Debugger window might give you a clue as to why the script failed, it's really intended as an aid to help you debug scripts that you've written from scratch (without recording keystrokes). We'll get to all of that in Chapter 21.

If a script keeps aborting in the same spot, you may have changed something in the Paradox environment since you recorded the script. The simplest way to debug a recorded script is to simply replace it by recording the steps to perform the desired task again. To replace an existing script, choose **Scripts ➤ B**egin**R**ecord, give the name of the script you want to re-record, and choose **R**eplace when prompted. Then record the keystrokes to perform the task.

A Sample Script: Automating Form Letters

One useful application of scripts is to produce form letters. For example, suppose that you have a table of names and addresses, like the sample Custlist table, and you've also created report formats for a form letter and labels (or envelopes). Now suppose that you want to send a copy of the form letter, which welcomes customers, to new customers every month or so.

First, you need to devise a scheme for identifying which customers have already been sent these form letters. One way to do this is to use **M**odify **➤ R**estructure to add a field named Welcomed to the table. Make the field alphanumeric and give it a length of 1, as shown in Figure 11.2.

Now let's say that, as a rule, this Welcomed field is left blank any time you add a new customer to the table. As soon as you print a welcome letter for a new customer, that field is filled with a Y (for Yes). That way, you can use a query to isolate records that have blank Welcomed fields. The same query can then automatically fill that field with a Y to indicate that the welcome letter for that record has been printed.

A SAMPLE SCRIPT: AUTOMATING FORM LETTERS

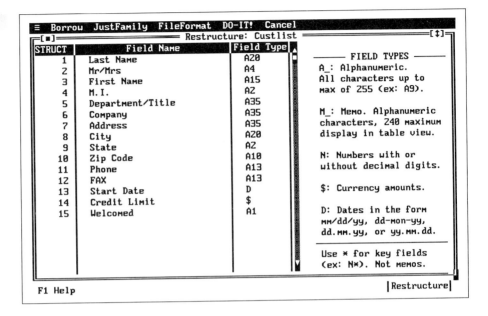

FIGURE 11.2

The Custlist table modified to include a Welcomed field for identifying customers who have been sent welcome letters

Creating the Form Letter Script

To print your first batch of welcome letters and record those keystrokes to automate this task for future letters, follow these steps:

1. Make sure your printer is ready to print letters. You need to actually print the first batch of letters so you can record the keystrokes required to do so.

2. To get yourself to a starting place that will be easy to remember, clear the desktop (press Alt-F8).

3. Use **T**ools ➤ **M**ore ➤ **D**irectory to get to the directory where the table and reports are stored (C:\PDOX45\Customer using our earlier example).

> **NOTE**
>
> Make a mental note that the proper starting place for the script you're about to record is (1) a blank desktop, (2) with C:\PDOX45\Customer (or whatever) as the current directory, and (3) the printer on-line and ready to go.

4. Choose **Scripts ➤ BeginRecord** to start recording the script.
5. Enter a valid name for the script, such as **Welcome**, and choose OK.
6. Choose **A**sk and specify the name of the table you want to query (Custlist in this example).
7. Move the cursor to the Welcomed field and type **BLANK, CHANGETO "Y"**. This tells Paradox that you want to isolate records that have a blank in the Welcomed field and to fill in that field with a Y.
8. Press F2 to perform the query. The Changed table appears, listing records that had blank Welcomed fields, as shown in Figure 11.3.

FIGURE 11.3

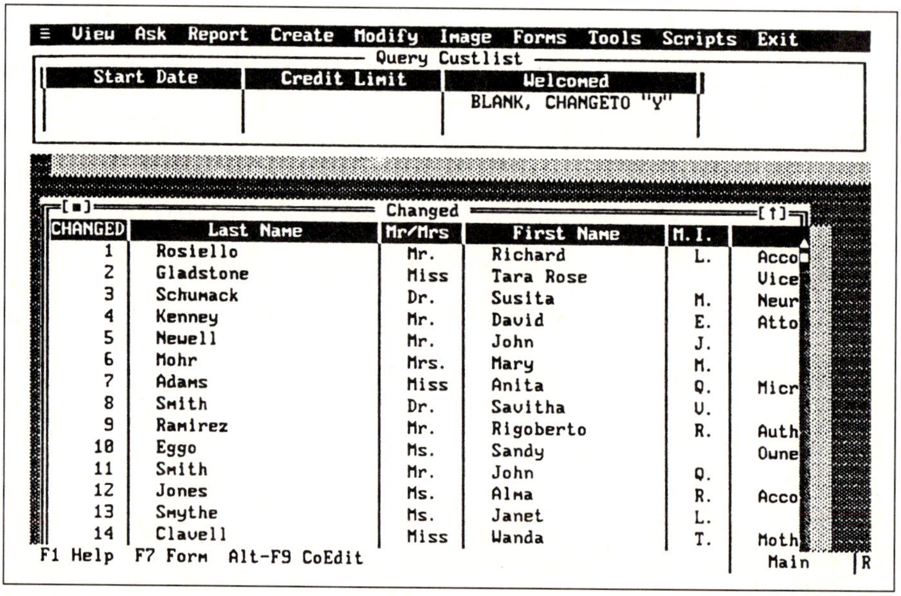

A query to isolate records with blank Welcomed fields and put a Y into those blank fields. The resulting Changed table contains records changed by the query.

A SAMPLE SCRIPT: AUTOMATING FORM LETTERS

NOTE The Changed table that results from a CHANGETO query automatically contains all the fields from the original table. In any other type of query, you need to check all the fields you want to include before performing the query.

9. Press F10 and choose **T**ools ➤ **C**opy ➤ **R**eport ➤ **D**ifferentTable.
10. Type or choose (using the keyboard method) the name of the source table containing the report (Custlist in this example), then press ↵ to choose OK.
11. Use the arrow keys to highlight the name of the report you want to copy, then press ↵.
12. Specify Changed as the name of target table to copy the report to, then press ↵.
13. Choose any Unused report number (by using the arrow keys to highlight it and pressing ↵).
14. Press F10 and choose **R**eport ➤ **O**utput. Type or choose (using the keyboard method) Changed as the name of the table to print from. Then press ↵.
15. Use the arrow keys to move the highlight to the name of the report you want to print and press ↵.
16. Select **P**rinter to print the letters.
17. After the letters are printed, press F10 and choose **S**cripts ➤ EndRecord.

So now you've printed a batch of welcome letters and recorded all the necessary steps to automate that task. You didn't print labels or envelopes, for the simple reason that, when playing back the script in the future, you're going to need some time to load the letters or labels into the printer after the letters have been printed. But since the Changed table is still on the desktop, and these are exactly the records for which you need to print labels or envelopes, you can just record the necessary steps in another script.

Creating the Label or Envelope Script

To continue with our example and record the script for printing labels or envelopes to go with the welcome letters, follow these steps:

1. Choose **S**cripts ➤ **B**eginRecord.
2. Give this script a new name (perhaps **Welcenv** or **Welclab**) and choose OK.
3. Press F10 and choose **T**ools ➤ **C**opy ➤ **R**eport ➤ **D**ifferentTable, and again specify Custlist as the source table for the report. Press ↵ to choose OK.
4. Use the arrow keys to highlight your label or envelope report format and press ↵.
5. Specify Changed as the target table and press ↵.
6. Highlight any Unused report number and press ↵.
7. Press F10 and choose **R**eport ➤ **O**utput and again specify Changed as the table to print the report from.
8. Use the arrow keys to highlight the name of your label or envelope report format and press ↵.
9. Choose **P**rinter.
10. After the labels are printed, press F10 and choose **S**cripts ➤ **E**ndRecord.

Now both of the scripts that you need to produce the form letters and their labels or envelopes are recorded. You can play back these scripts at any time to generate letters for the correct records in your table.

Using Your New Scripts

Say that during the course of the next few days or weeks you add several new records to your Custlist table. Whenever you've typed in a new record, you've left the Welcomed field for that record blank. Now you can follow these steps to produce your next set of welcome letters:

1. Get the printer ready, clear the desktop (Alt-F8), and use **T**ools ➤ **M**ore ➤ **D**irectory to get to the directory where your customer information and script are stored, so you're at the correct starting point.

NOTE: You can record the keystrokes to change directories in your script. However, if you do so, you won't be able to use the script to perform the same task in another directory.

2. From the desktop, choose **S**cripts ➤ **S**howPlay (if you want to watch the script run) or **S**cripts ➤ **P**lay (for top speed).

3. Type or choose Welcome as the name of the script, then choose OK. (If you chose ShowPlay, you can now choose **F**ast from the next menu to appear.)

4. Sit back and relax while Paradox prints the letters.

5. After all the letters have been printed, leave the Changed table on the desktop and load your labels or envelopes into the printer.

6. Choose **S**cripts ➤ **S**howPlay (or **S**cripts ➤ **P**lay) and now run the script for printing labels or envelopes.

After the labels or envelopes are printed, you can just clear the desktop (Alt-F8) and do whatever else you need to do in Paradox.

Creating and Using Instant Scripts

An Instant Script is a temporary script that you can record and play back "on the fly." An Instant Script might come in handy when you find yourself repeating a set of keystrokes during a particular task that you don't perform often. Instead of bothering with a regular script that's saved indefinitely, you can record an Instant Script.

Recording and Playing Back an Instant Script

Here are the steps for recording and playing back an Instant Script:

1. Press the Instant Script Record key, Alt-F3. Paradox starts recording your keystrokes immediately, and the R appears in the status bar as usual.
2. Type the necessary keystrokes and make the required menu selections in the usual manner (but remember, you can't use the mouse).
3. To stop recording keystrokes, press Alt-F3 again.
4. To play back this Instant Script, just press the Instant Script Play key, Alt-F4. Paradox will instantly play back your keystrokes exactly as you recorded them.

As an example of using an Instant Script, suppose you're typing in a bunch of new records into a table, and the address for most (though not all) of the current records is the city of San Pasqual, CA. While entering this batch of records, you could move the cursor to the City field in a new record, then press Alt-F3, type **San Pasqual**, press ↵, type **CA**, press ↵ again, type the zip code for San Pasqual, press ↵, and type the area code for San Pasqual. Then press Alt-F4 again to stop recording the script.

When you get to the City field in another new record that requires this same information, you can just press Alt-F4 to type that information into the current record.

Saving an Instant Script

Paradox stores the Instant Script in a file named Instant.SC, in the current directory. If a script with this name already exists when you start recording a new Instant Script, Paradox automatically overwrites the existing one.

If you create an Instant Script and then decide that you want to save that script for future use, you must rename it to protect it from being overwritten by the next Instant.SC file to be created. Here are the steps:

1. Choose **Tools** ➤ **Rename** ➤ **Script** from the desktop.

2. Type (or choose) Instant, the name of the script to rename, then choose OK.

3. Type any new, valid DOS file name (without spaces or an extension) for the script, and then press ↵.

Now you can play back the renamed script just as you play back any other script you recorded.

See Chapter 12 for more information about renaming and managing files.

Making an Existing Script an Instant Script

To play back any existing script by pressing the Instant Script Play key, Alt-F4, make a copy of that script and name it Instant.SC. Here's how:

1. Use **T**ools ➤ **M**ore ➤ **D**irectory to change to the directory containing the script to be copied.

2. Choose **T**ools ➤ **C**opy ➤ **S**cript to copy the script, using the name Instant as the script name to copy to.

3. If there is an existing script named Instant.SC in the current directory, Paradox will present the usual Cancel or Replace choices, along with the message Instant Script already exists. Choose **R**eplace.

If you have recorded an Instant Script that you want to save for future use, use Tools ➤ Rename to give that current Instant Script a new name before copying a new script file to that name, because the current Instant Script will be overwritten when you choose Replace during the copying process.

Once a script has been copied as Instant, you can play it back by simply pressing Alt-F4. The copied script will remain the Instant Script in its directory until you either use Alt-F3 to record a new Instant Script in the directory or copy another script to the Instant name.

You can have one script file named Instant per directory. When you change to a new working directory, the script file named Instant in that directory will be played by pressing Alt-F4.

Making One Script Play Back Another

A good strategy for recording large, complex scripts is to break the job down into smaller scripts, test each script independently, then record a larger script to play all the smaller successful scripts for you. When recording these smaller scripts, try to start and end each script at the desktop.

When you play back the script to test it, make sure it does its job, starting and ending at the desktop without a hitch. Later, when recording the larger script that plays all these smaller scripts, start recording it from the desktop as well. When you come to a place where you want this larger script to play back one of the smaller scripts, follow these steps:

1. From the desktop menu bar, choose **S**cripts ➤ **P**lay or **S**cripts ➤ **R**epeatPlay.

2. Type or choose the name of the script that you want this larger script to play back, then press ↵.

3. If you chose RepeatPlay in step 1, specify the number of times you want the smaller script to be played back, then press ↵. Paradox executes the smaller script at that moment, but it will be ready to continue recording keystrokes for the current larger script when that smaller script has finished its job.

4. Finish recording the larger script. Then choose **S**cripts ➤ **E**ndRecord or press Alt-F10 and choose **E**ndRecord.

You can repeat steps 1 through 3 as necessary to have the larger script play any number of smaller scripts.

Playing Back a Script Automatically at Startup

Whenever you first start Paradox, it automatically searches the current directory (and only the current directory) for a script named Init.SC. If it finds such a script, it plays it immediately, even before displaying the desktop. This is called *autoexecuting* the script, because Paradox executes (plays back) the script automatically at startup.

One way to have Paradox autoexecute a script is to name that script Init. For example, suppose you want Paradox to ask you for a working directory as soon as it's started. First, follow these steps to create the script:

1. Choose **T**ools ➤ **M**ore ➤ **D**irectory and enter the name of the directory you normally start Paradox from (typically C:\PDOX45), then choose OK.

2. Choose **S**cripts ➤ **B**eginRecord.

3. Type **Init** as the name of the script, then choose OK.

4. Choose **T**ools ➤ **M**ore ➤ **D**irectory once again. The dialog box for specifying a directory appears, as usual.

5. Rather than entering a directory name, press the PAL Menu key, Alt-F10, then choose **E**nd-Record. (When you play back the script in the future, it will stop at the dialog box.)

6. Choose Cancel or OK, since you're finished recording the script.

As long as you start Paradox from the directory in which you stored the Init.SC script, the dialog box for specifying a directory will appear on the desktop as soon as Paradox starts.

Another way to have Paradox autoexecute a script as soon as you start the program is simply to follow the Paradox command with a space and the name of the script you want to play back (include the path if the script isn't in the current directory). For example, if you created a script named Myform, and you're just about to start Paradox from the DOS command prompt, you could start Paradox *and* run your script by entering this command:

    PARADOX Myform

or, if the current directory is not C:\PDOX45, this command:

PARADOX C:\PDOX45\Myform

NOTE Be aware that Paradox will still play back the Init.SC script (if one exists) before it plays back any script you've specified at the DOS command prompt.

Summary

Scripts provide a powerful way to store many keystrokes or PAL commands and play them back later, as many times as you wish. In Chapters 17 and 21, you'll learn how to use more advanced scripting techniques. For now, just keep in mind that any time you find yourself repeating the same keystrokes over and over again, recording those keystrokes in a script will save you a lot of time and tedious work.

Here's a summary of the most important points discussed in this chapter:

- To record a script, choose **S**cripts ➤ **B**eginRecord. If you're not at the desktop, press Alt-F10 and choose **B**eginRecord. Enter a valid DOS file name for the script.

- When recording a script, you cannot use the mouse. You must use the keyboard to position the cursor, make menu selections, and type text or numbers.

- To stop recording a script, choose **S**cripts ➤ **E**nd-Record from the desktop, or press Alt-F10 and choose **E**nd-Record.

- To cancel recording without saving the script, press Alt-F10 and choose **C**ancel.

- To play back a script at maximum speed, choose **S**cripts ➤ **P**lay from the desktop, or press Alt-F10 and choose **P**lay. Then type (or choose) the name of the script.

- To play back a script and watch it perform its keystrokes, choose **S**cripts ➤ **S**howPlay from the desktop, type or choose the name of the script, and then choose either **F**ast or **S**low.

SUMMARY

- To record an Instant Script, press the Instant Script Record key, Alt-F3, to begin recording keystrokes. Type whatever you want to record, then press Alt-F3 again to stop recording. You can have a different Instant Script in each working directory.

- To play back an Instant Script, press the Instant Script Play key, Alt-F4.

- To play back any script as an Instant Script, using the Alt-F4 key, copy the desired script to a new script named Instant by using **T**ools ➤ **C**opy ➤ **S**cript. Press Alt-F4 to play back the script, in the current directory.

CHAPTER 12

Managing Your Files

fast TRACK

- **To rename, copy, or delete a Paradox object** — 393
  choose the appropriate option from the Tools menu.

- **To copy records from one table to another** — 403
  use Tools ➤ More ➤ Add. Specify the table containing the records you want to copy as the source table, and the table to copy records to as the target table.

- **To remove records that match records in another table** — 406
  use Tools ➤ More ➤ Subtract. Specify the table that has the records to subtract as the source table, and the table you actually want to remove the records from as the target table.

- **To empty a table of all records** — 410
  use Tools ➤ More ➤ Empty.

- **To protect data with passwords or write-protection** — 411
  use Tools ➤ More ➤ Protect.

To view general information about files   416

use **T**ools ➤ **I**nfo. From the submenu, choose the type of information you want to see, such as the table structure, file inventory, or objects in a family.

To change the structure of a table   417

choose **M**odify ➤ **R**estructure. Use Ins and Delete to insert, delete, and rearrange fields. To save the modified table structure, choose **DO-IT!** from the menu or press F2.

To speed up frequently used queries   428

choose **T**ools ➤ **Q**uerySpeed after you define the query.

To import and export data   431

use **T**ools ➤ **E**xportImport. Select **E**xport or **I**mport, and then choose the format you want to import from or export to.

To temporarily suspend Paradox to get to the DOS prompt   449

choose **T**ools ➤ **M**ore ➤ **T**oDOS, or press the DOS key, Ctrl-o, or the DOS Big key, Alt-o.

As you develop more Paradox objects (tables, forms, reports, and scripts), you'll need to learn techniques for managing them. The Tools menu includes options for managing your objects. This menu also provides options for importing and exporting data between Paradox and other database or spreadsheet programs, as well as for protecting data.

You've already seen several options from the Tools menu in previous chapters. In this chapter, we'll round out your knowledge of the Tools options and discuss general techniques for managing objects. We'll discuss each of the Tools options in this chapter except for Net, an option for networking that is discussed in Appendix C.

Managing Objects

The Tools menu, available from the desktop menu bar, provides options for renaming, copying, and deleting objects. When you select **T**ools, you'll see this menu:

The following sections describe how to use the Rename, Copy, and Delete options.

MANAGING OBJECTS

Renaming Objects

The Rename option lets you assign a new name to an existing object (or family of objects). You can rename tables, forms, reports, scripts, and graphs. Note that the description of the report is not the report name. The name of a form or report consists of the name of the master table and an extension containing the report or form number, as in Custlist.R1 or Custlist.F2. Renaming a form or report simply assigns a new extension number to the file. If you want to change the description of a form or report rather than its file name, choose **R**eport or **F**orm and then choose **C**hange.

When you rename a table, the renamed table will include all the objects associated with the original table, such as forms, reports, and indexes.

NOTE Indexing is covered in Part Two of this book.

To rename an object, choose **T**ools ➤ **R**ename. You'll see this submenu:

Your next steps depend on the type of object you're renaming.

Renaming a Form or Report

If you're renaming a form or report, follow these steps:

1. Select **F**orm or **R**eport from the Tools menu.
2. Type (or choose) the table that contains the report or form you want to rename and choose OK.

3. From the next menu that appears, select the name of the report or form that you want to rename, then choose OK. You'll be prompted to enter a new name or position for the form or report.

4. Double-click on the new form or report number, or highlight or type the new number for the form or report and press ↵.

If a form or report with that number already exists, you'll see the choices Cancel or Replace. Choose **R**eplace if you want to overwrite the existing form or report file.

Renaming a Table, Script, or Graph

If you're renaming a table, script, or graph, follow these steps:

1. Select **T**able, **S**cript, or **G**raph from the Tools menu.

2. Type (or choose) the name of the table, script, or graph that you want to rename, then choose OK. You'll be prompted to enter a new name or position for the object.

3. Type a new, valid DOS file name (up to eight characters, without spaces, punctuation, or an extension), and then choose OK.

If an object with that name already exists, Paradox will present the Cancel or Replace dialog box. Choose **C**ancel to enter a new name. Select **R**eplace to replace the existing object with the one you're renaming.

Renaming an Answer Table

The Rename option can be especially useful with the Answer table. An Answer table, like all Paradox temporary tables, is really a regular table with a name that Paradox is programmed to delete or overwrite in certain circumstances. Paradox will delete or overwrite any table named Answer, whether it is the result of a query or not. If you rename an Answer table, Paradox will leave it alone.

For example, if you perform a complex query whose results you wish to save for future use, simply rename the Answer table. Then the renamed Answer table will not be overwritten by future queries. You can even query the renamed table to come up with yet another Answer table.

Copying Objects

Copying is useful for several tasks:

- Making backups of important data and other objects
- Creating new forms or reports that are similar to existing forms or reports
- Creating forms and reports for just the records included in an Answer table produced by a query

NOTE Copying report forms from an original table to an Answer table is discussed in Chapter 8, in the section about printing a report from a query.

You can copy tables, forms, reports, scripts, and graphs. When you copy a table using **Tools ➤ Copy**, Paradox automatically copies all the objects associated with that table as well. The objects associated with a table, such as forms, reports, memo field text, BLOB field data, and indexes, have the same file name as the table but different file name extensions. For example, if you choose **Tools ➤ Copy ➤ Table**, enter the table as Custlist, then specify A:\Custlist as the name of the copied table, Paradox will copy the following:

- The table itself (Custlist.DB)
- The memo text and BLOB fields, if any, for that table (Custlist.MB)
- Reports (Custlist.R1, Custlist.R2, and so on)
- Forms (Custlist.F1, Custlist.F2, and so on)
- Primary and secondary indexes (Custlist.PX, Custlist.XG0, Custlist.XG1, and so on)

To begin copying an object, choose **Tools** ➤ **Copy** from the Paradox desktop. You'll see the submenu shown below:

The **JustFamily** option copies all the forms, reports, and other objects associated with a table, but not the table itself.

Your next steps depend on the type of object you're copying. However, all copying operations require you to specify a source and target file name. The following sections describe how to specify those file names and how to copy the different types of objects.

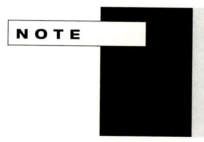

You can't use Tools ➤ Report, Form, or JustFamily to copy the family to or from anything other than an existing table. If you want to copy the family to a floppy disk instead of to another table, you should use DOS or some other file manager, as described later in this chapter.

Specifying Source and Target Files

In a copy operation, the *source* file is the one that currently contains the object that you want to copy. The *target* file is the one that you want to copy the form or report to.

Whenever you're prompted for a source or target file name, you can include the drive and directory if you wish. For example, if you're copying a table named Custlist, and want to copy it to the disk in drive A, you would type A:\Custlist as the target table name.

If the source or target file is in the current directory, you can simply type in the name. Or, if the dialog box that's prompting for the file name has a list area, you can choose OK, press ↵, or click the mouse in the list area to display the list of names. Then choose a name by clicking on it with your mouse, highlighting it with the arrow keys, or typing the first few letters of the name.

To copy an object from another directory or drive to the current working directory, use the directory names or symbols to move to the desired directory and select the source file using one of these techniques:

- If the source file is in a subdirectory of your current directory, the directory name will be listed after all the files shown in the file list box, with a backslash at the end of the name, as in Customer\. Choose the directory name to see a list of all the files of the current type in that subdirectory. Then choose the one that you want to copy.

- If the source file you want to copy is in a directory at the same level or higher on the directory tree, or on another branch of the directory tree in the current drive, select the parent directory symbol (..\) at the end of the file list to see the files and directories in the directory level above the current directory. If the object you want to copy is in one of the parent directory's other subdirectories, select that subdirectory to list the files it contains. When you've found the object you want to use as the source in your copy operation, choose it.

NOTE You can move up and down in the directory tree by choosing a combination of the parent directory symbols (..\) and the subdirectory names in the file list.

- If the object you want to copy is on a different drive, type the drive letter, followed by a colon and backslash (for example, A:\), into the file name box and press ↵. The files and subdirectories of the selected drive will be displayed. Use the techniques described above to move around in the selected drive's directory until you find the object you want to copy, then choose it.

After you've chosen an object to copy, type in the name you want to give to the copy of the object (without a path or extension) and press ↵. The object will be copied to your current working directory.

Copying Forms and Reports

After you choose **F**orm or **R**eport from the Copy submenu, follow these steps:

1. From the submenu that appears, choose **D**ifferentTable if you want to copy the form or report to another table. Choose **S**ameTable to copy the form or report to a new number in the same table.

2. When prompted for the source table (the one that currently contains the form or report you want to copy), type or choose the table name in the usual manner, then choose OK.

3. When prompted for the source form or report, choose the form or report you want to copy, then choose OK.

4. If you chose DifferentTable in step 1, you'll be prompted for the target table (the one you want to copy the form or report to). Type or choose the target table's name, then choose OK.

5. When prompted for the target form or report (the one you want to copy to), choose a form or report, then choose OK.

If an object with the new name already exists, Paradox will prompt you with the choices Cancel or Replace. Choose **R**eplace if you want to replace the existing object with the one being copied. Otherwise, choose **C**ancel and choose a different object.

Copying Tables, Scripts, Graphs, and Just Family Objects

When you choose **T**able, **S**cript, **J**ustFamily, or **G**raph from the Copy submenu, you'll be prompted for the name of the object you want to copy from, which is the name of the source object (table, script, graph, or family name). After you press ↵ or choose OK, you'll be prompted for the name of the object you want to copy to. Type or choose the name of the target object, then choose OK or press ↵.

Remember, to specify a family name, just type the file name of the family's table, without an extension.

As usual, if an object with the new name already exists, Paradox will present the choices Cancel or Replace. Choose **R**eplace if you want to replace the existing object with the one being copied. Otherwise, choose **C**ancel and select a different object.

Copying to a Floppy Disk

To copy a family of files to or from a floppy disk instead of an existing table, use the DOS COPY command, or the appropriate command in another file-management program. If you use DOS to copy a table that has a memo or BLOB field, you must copy both the table (the file with the .DB extension) and the memo or BLOB field file (the one with the .MB extension). If you want to include primary and secondary indexes in the copy, you must also copy their files. You can ensure that you're copying all the necessary files by using the * wildcard with the DOS COPY command. For example, entering the command

    COPY Custlist.* A:

copies the Custlist table and all associated files, forms, reports, and indexes to drive A.

Objects that are not associated with a specific table, such as scripts and graph settings, can have any file name, but they still have preset file name extensions. Table 12.1 lists file name extensions for the various objects.

NOTE Secondary indexes are actually stored in two files: one with an extension beginning with .XG and another with an extension beginning with .YG.

Tips on Backing Up a Large Database

You may need to copy a database (a table and all its associated objects) to one or more floppies but find that the files are too large to fit on one floppy. To get around this, you can use the DOS BACKUP command to copy and compress the files, or you can separate the files onto multiple disks. Both techniques are described in the following sections.

MANAGING YOUR FILES

TABLE 12.1: File Name Extensions for Paradox Objects

TYPE OF OBJECT	EXTENSION	EXAMPLE
Table	.DB	Custlist.DB
Memo/BLOB field	.MB	Custlist.MB
Form	.F, .F1, .F2, ...F14	Custlist.F1
Report	.R, .R1, .R2, ...R14	Custlist.R1
Validity checks	.VAL	Custlist.VAL
Image settings	.SET	Custlist.SET
Primary index	.PX	Custlist.PX
Secondary index	.XG0, .XG1, ...XG9, .XGA, .XGB, ...XGZ	Custlist.XG0
Secondary index	.YG0, .YG1, ...YG9, .YGA, .YGB, ...YGZ	Custlist.YG0
Graph settings	.G	Piechart.G
Script	.SC	Autonum.SC
Temporary object	.T00	(automatically erased after serving its purpose)

Using the DOS BACKUP Command

When you use the DOS BACKUP command, it automatically compresses the files and, if necessary, splits them up across multiple disks. Since the table and all its objects are in the same directory, you can simply exit (not suspend) Paradox to get to the DOS prompt, then use the DOS CD command to switch to the directory that contains the table and all its objects.

Then, with a few formatted floppies on hand, enter a command like

    BACKUP *.* A:

to back up all the files in that directory to the floppy.

If you just want to copy a specific table, such as Custlist, and its family, you could enter this command instead:

BACKUP Custlist.* A:

Later, when you want to copy those backed up files, use the DOS RESTORE command.

NOTE See your DOS manual for more information about using the BACKUP and RESTORE commands.

Using a Query to Copy Selected Records to a Floppy

Another way to split up a large file in order to copy it to several disks is to use a query to copy selected records to the floppy. For example, you could create a query to isolate records with last names that begin with the letters *A* through *M*, then copy those records from the Answer table to a floppy disk. Then create another query that isolates records with last names beginning with the letters *N* through *Z*, and copy those records from the Answer table to a second floppy.

After all the records have been copied, use **T**ools ➤ **C**opy ➤ **J**ustFamily to copy the table's associated objects to any floppy that contains records from the original table. Or, just use the DOS COPY command to copy these objects directly to floppies.

When it comes time to copy the table and its objects to another computer, first use **T**ools ➤ **M**ore ➤ **C**opy on that computer to copy the first part of the table (such as records A through M) to whatever directory you want. Then use **T**ools ➤ **M**ore ➤ **A**dd (as described later in this chapter) to add records from the second floppy (such as records N through Z) to that same table. Finally, use **T**ools ➤ **C**opy ➤ **J**ustFamily to copy the table's objects from the floppy to the table that's now on the hard disk.

NOTE If any of the files containing forms and reports that you've copied with DOS are corrupted, you may be able to repair them. See the section about fixing corrupted objects, later in this chapter, for details.

Deleting Objects

You can use **T**ools ➤ **D**elete to delete objects, as well as image settings and validity checks assigned to a table. When you select the Delete option, you'll see this submenu:

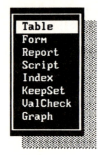

Select the type of object you want to delete and proceed as follows:

- If you choose **T**able, **S**cript, or **G**raph, Paradox will ask you to identify the object you want to delete. Specify the name of the object you want to remove, and then choose OK to confirm the deletion.

CAUTION Deleting a table also deletes all the forms, reports, and objects associated with that table. If you simply want to delete all the records in a table, use Tools ➤ More ➤ Empty.

- If you choose **R**eport or **F**orm, Paradox will prompt you for the name of the table associated with the report or form. Specify the table. Next, you'll be prompted for the report or form number you want to delete. After you specify the number, the report or form is removed. You won't be given a chance to change your mind.

- If you choose **I**ndex, you'll be given the choices Single or All. Choose **S**ingle to delete just a single index for a table. Choose **A**ll to delete all indexes for a table. Next, Paradox will ask for the name of the table whose index you want to delete; if you chose Single, you'll also be asked to select the index to delete. Specify the table and index, if necessary. You won't be given an opportunity to change your mind.

- If you choose **K**eepSet or **V**alCheck, Paradox will ask for the name of the table associated with the image settings or validity checks. Specify the table. You will not be prompted to verify your selection before Paradox deletes the selected items.

Be careful when deleting objects. Once deleted, an object cannot always be recovered. If you inadvertently delete one or more files and want to recover them, you should exit Paradox immediately and use the UN-DELETE command if you have DOS 5 (or use some third-party utility package) to try to recover the deleted files.

Copying and Moving Records

When you choose **T**ools ➤ **M**ore from the Paradox desktop, you'll see this submenu:

These options allow you to copy and move records from one table to another, and to remove all records from a table without deleting the table itself. The next few sections describe the Add, Subtract, and Empty options. Later in this chapter, you'll learn about the Protect and ToDOS options. The MultiAdd and FormAdd options, which are used with multiple tables, are covered in Part Two of this book. The Directory option lets you change to another working directory, as described in Chapter 2.

Copying Records from One Table to Another

Paradox offers a neat technique for copying records from one table to another without requiring you to retype them. This technique can also be used to combine information from several tables into a single table.

You can copy records from one table to another if the tables have the same fields (with the same field types). The fields do not need to be in the same order.

You can't copy records across tables that don't contain the same fields. For example, you can't add records from a table containing Last Name, First Name, and Address fields to a table containing Amount, Qty, and Date fields. If you wish to combine tables with incompatible structures, use multiple-table query forms, then rename the Answer table so that you have a new table with a new structure. See Chapter 14 for more information about multiple-table query forms.

Here are the basic steps for copying records from one table to another:

1. If you want to copy only some of the records (rather than all the records) from the source table, use **A**sk to perform a query that isolates the records you want to copy. The resulting Answer table should contain all the fields of the table but only the records you want to copy to the target table. Be sure to check all the fields in the Query form before performing the query (see Chapter 7 for more information on querying a table).

> **NOTE** Remember, in copy operations, the *source* table refers to the table you're copying records from, and the *target* table refers to the table you're copying records to.

2. Select **Tools ➤ More ➤ A**dd from the desktop menu bar. Paradox will display a dialog box for selecting the source table and prompt you with:

   Enter table with records to add or press ↵ for a list.

3. Specify the name of the source table (if you're copying selected records only, the source table is Answer), then choose OK or press ↵.

4. When prompted for the target table, type or choose the name of the table you want to copy the records to, then choose OK or press ↵.

Paradox adds the records from the source table to the end of the target table, unless the table is keyed. Copying records in keyed tables is described in the next section.

Copying Records in Keyed Tables

If the table you're copying records to is keyed, Paradox will display a submenu after you specify the target table. The submenu offers the options NewEntries and Updates.

In a keyed table, each value in the key field must be unique. You'll learn about keyed tables in Chapter 13.

Select **N**ewEntries to append the source records to the end of an existing table. If a record in the source table has the same key as an existing record in the target table, that record will be stored in a separate Keyviol table. You can edit or delete records in the Keyviol table, then use **T**ools ➤ **M**ore ➤ **A**dd once again to add records from the Keyviol table to the target table. You must do so immediately, however, because the Keyviol table is erased when you exit Paradox. (Optionally, just copy the Keyviol table using **T**ools ➤ **C**opy, then edit the copied table at your convenience, or rename the Keyviol table with **T**ools ➤ **R**ename.)

Choose **U**pdate to replace records in the target table with records that have identical key fields in the source. Paradox then places any updated records from the target table into a separate Changed table, so that you can easily keep track of updated records. (Of course, you'll need to rename Changed if you want to keep a permanent copy.)

Moving Records to Another Table

If you want to move the records from the source to the target table, first copy the records to the new table, as described in the previous sections. Then delete the copied records from the source table.

If you copied all the records from the source table, just use **T**ools ➤ **M**ore ➤ **E**mpty to empty the source table. If you copied only selected records to the target table, you can use **T**ools ➤ **M**ore ➤ **S**ubtract to subtract the records in the Answer table from the original source table, as described in the next section.

Removing Records from a Table

You can remove individual records from a table by simply pressing Delete while in Edit mode. Or, as described in Chapter 7, you can use the DELETE reserved word in a query to delete records that match a query criterion. A third way to delete records from a table is to remove records from one table that match records in another table. For this method, you use **T**ools ➤ **M**ore ➤ **S**ubtract.

When you're using the Subtract option, the *source* table is the table that contains copies of the records that you want to delete. The *target* table is the one that the records are actually deleted from. **T**ools ➤ **M**ore ➤ **S**ubtract does not change the source table in any way.

To subtract records from a table, choose **T**ools ➤ **M**ore ➤ **S**ubtract from the desktop. Type or select the name of the source table (the one containing records that you want to delete from the target table). This can be the Answer table if the records to be deleted have been selected via a query. Choose OK or press ↵. Finally, type or select the table from which you want to subtract the records.

If the target table isn't keyed, it will lose all the records that exactly match any record in the source table. If the target table is keyed, it loses only records with key fields that exactly match the key fields of any record in the source table.

COPYING AND MOVING RECORDS

TIP If you'll be moving and copying selected records across tables on a regular basis, you can save time by storing the steps in a script, and then playing them back as needed. See Chapter 11 for details on recording scripts.

Now let's look at an example. Suppose you have an accounts receivable system in which you bill clients at the end of the month for purchases made during the previous month. You store these charges in a table named Charges, as shown in Figure 12.1.

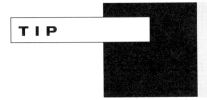

FIGURE 12.1

Charges in a sample Charges table, containing some transactions from October and November

At the end of November, you want to isolate charges for the month of October. You could set up a query like the one in Figure 12.2 to pull out all records with purchase dates in October.

Next, using **T**ools ➤ **R**ename ➤ **T**able, rename the Answer table as Billed. The Billed table contains only transactions for the month of October, as shown in Figure 12.3. Now you can use **T**ools ➤ **C**opy ➤ **J**ust-Family to copy a report format for printing invoices from any other table to the Billed table and print October invoices.

MANAGING YOUR FILES

FIGURE 12.2

A query for charges in the month of October, and the resulting Answer table

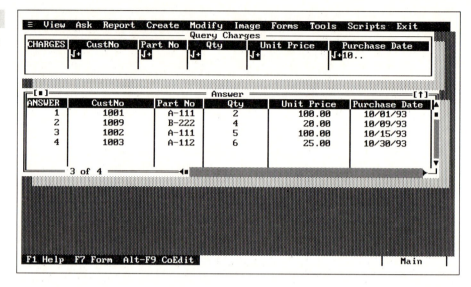

FIGURE 12.3

Charges for the month of October in the Billed table

Once the October transactions have been billed, they should be removed from the Charges table using the **T**ools ➤ **M**ore ➤ **S**ubtract option. When Paradox prompts you for the table names, specify Billed as the table containing the transactions to be subtracted (source table) and Charges as the table from which to subtract these records (target table). The resulting

Charges table will no longer contain charges for the month of October, as shown in Figure 12.4.

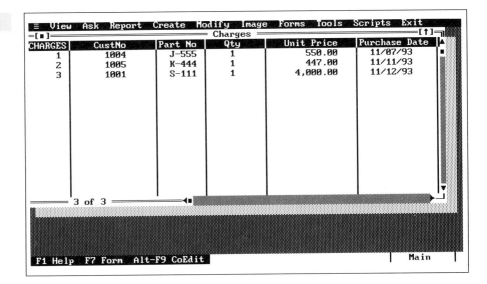

FIGURE 12.4

The Charges table after the October transactions were subtracted

Developing Applications with the Tools Options

Now that you've seen a complete example, it shouldn't be very difficult for you to develop your own applications with the options on the Tools menu. Here's a scenario that will give you an idea of how useful the Tools options can be.

Suppose you're planning a special mailing to introduce an extra-hot, low-priced item that everyone is sure to want. Assuming your inactive client list is stored in a table (perhaps named Inactive), you can perform a query on that table to select customers who haven't ordered within the past year. Rename the resulting Answer table to Pastyear using **T**ools ➤ **R**ename. Then use **T**ools ➤ **M**ore ➤ **A**dd to add the names from Pastyear (the source table) to a master mailing list table named Mailmast.

Next, create a form letter for your Mailmast table (using the techniques described in Chapter 8) to print letters introducing your new product.

After the mailing is complete, you can use **T**ools ➤ **M**ore ➤ **S**ubtract to remove the inactive customers from the master mailing list. In this case, specify Pastyear as the source table and Mailmast as the target table.

Recovering Disk Space from Deleted Records

You may discover a peculiar quirk when deleting records from a Paradox table using **T**ools ➤ **M**ore ➤ **S**ubtract or a DELETE query. The size of the table (as reported by DOS) is the same after you delete the records as it was before you deleted them! That's because Paradox reserves the space that was once occupied by the deleted records in anticipation that you'll probably just add new records later.

If you want to reclaim the disk space left by those deleted records, choose **M**odify ➤ **R**estructure, and specify the name of the table that you want to delete the records from. You need not make any changes to the structure. Instead, just choose **DO-IT!**. If you then use DOS to check the size of the file, you'll see that the file is indeed consuming less disk space.

Emptying a Table

Tools ➤ **M**ore ➤ **E**mpty lets you empty all the records from a table. This is particularly useful in applications that automatically update files, such as when updated transactions are copied to a history file (using Tools ➤ More ➤ Add), then deleted from the current table.

See Chapter 16 for more information about automatically updating tables.

Note that you must use the Empty option with great care. Once you empty all the records from a table, there's no way to recover them!

To empty a table, choose **T**ools ➤ **M**ore ➤ **E**mpty from the Paradox desktop. As usual, Paradox displays a dialog box and prompts for the name of the table. Specify the name of the table you want to empty. Paradox then displays a submenu with Cancel and OK options. If you're absolutely sure you want to remove all the records from the table, choose OK (remember, once you choose OK, there is no way to recover the deleted records). If you change your mind, select Cancel.

Protecting Data

Paradox offers two ways to protect a table or other object:

- If you password-protect a table, other users cannot perform any operation on that table without first supplying the correct password. Similarly, if you password-protect a script, no one can read or modify that script without entering the password.

- If you write-protect a table, it can be viewed at any time, but cannot be changed. Unlike password protection, however, write protection can be removed by anyone (without requiring a password). Therefore, write protection is simply a stopgap measure to prevent accidental changes to a table.

Both protection schemes are available from the Tools menu, as described in the following sections.

Adding Password Protection

To password-protect a table or script, choose **Tools ➤ More ➤ Protect**. You'll see this submenu:

Select **P**assword. Paradox will display the choices Table and Script. Choose one, then specify the name of the table or script to protect. Paradox will display the dialog box shown below, along with a prompt telling you to enter a new password or to leave the password blank to remove the current one.

MANAGING YOUR FILES

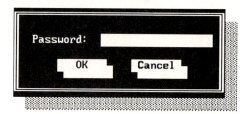

Before typing in your password, note these important points:

- The password can be up to 15 characters long, including spaces.

- Case counts. That is, the password *Hello* is not the same as *hello*. Therefore, pay attention to case as you enter your password.

- The password does not appear on the screen as you type it. Instead, a star character appears for every character you type. This is a safety precaution to prevent others from watching what you enter on the screen. (If you type away expectantly waiting for something other than stars to appear on the screen, you will actually be entering what is considered to be your password as you do so.)

- Once you enter your password, if you do not remember the password, there is no way to change or remove the password or to view the table or script. Therefore, you should write down your password, in matching uppercase and lowercase, and store it in a safe place where you can find it easily.

- If your data is sensitive enough to deserve password protection, you should avoid obvious passwords like your first name, initials, nickname, or the names of pets, spouses, friends, and so on.

- If you decide to bail out now after having read the above, you can just press Esc to do so.

Once you decide on a password, type it in and press ↵. Paradox will display a password verification dialog box. Verify the password by typing it in again, exactly as before. If you don't get it right, Paradox will inform you of this. You can try again, or press Esc to return to the first password dialog box in order to reenter the password from scratch.

If you are setting a password for a script, Paradox will record the password and return you to the desktop. If you're setting a password for a table, you'll see the screen shown in Figure 12.5 for entering auxiliary passwords.

PROTECTING DATA

Unless you are working on a network, auxiliary passwords will probably not be necessary. To bypass the auxiliary passwords and save only the "master" password, press F2 or choose **DO-IT!** from the menu bar. You'll see the message

    Encrypting...

at the bottom-right corner of the screen, and then you'll be returned to the desktop.

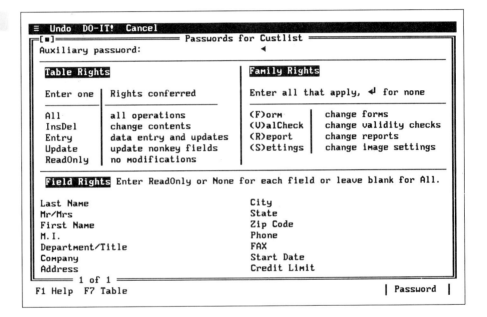

FIGURE 12.5

The screen for entering auxiliary passwords

Using a Password-Protected Table or Script

When you attempt to view or work with a password-protected table, you'll see the password dialog box shown earlier, along with the message

    Enter password for table

before Paradox will allow you any access to the table.

If you attempt to edit a protected script, using **S**cripts ➤ **E**ditor ➤ **O**pen from the desktop menu bar, you'll see the password dialog box, along with a prompt to enter the password for the script.

Obviously, you must type in the correct password to proceed. As when you first defined the password, it will appear only as stars on the screen as you type it, so type carefully. Press ↵ after typing in the password.

If you do not enter the correct password, Paradox will display the error message

    Invalid password

and allow you to try again. If you cannot enter the correct password, your only alternative is to press Esc and return to the earlier screen.

Reactivating (Clearing) Passwords

Once you access a password-protected table or script by entering the appropriate password, Paradox allows you to access that table or script as often as you wish during the current session (that is, until you exit Paradox), without asking you to reenter the password.

This is convenient, as it can become tedious to reenter the password each time you need a table or script, but there is a drawback: If you walk away from your computer during the current session, anybody who sits down at your computer can also access all your password-protected tables and scripts without reentering the passwords.

To work around this problem, choose **Tools ➤ More ➤ Protect ➤ Clear-Passwords** from the Paradox desktop. This clears all the passwords that you've entered in the current session, so that Paradox will require you to reenter the passwords to access the tables or scripts again. (This option also clears the screen, as Alt-F8 does.)

Changing or Removing a Password

If you decide that you no longer want password protection for a table or script, you can easily remove the current password by following these steps (which are similar to adding the password in the first place):

1. Choose **Tools ➤ More ➤ Protect ➤ Password**.
2. Choose **Table** to remove the password from a table, or **Script** to remove the password from a script.
3. Specify the table name or script name when prompted.

4. When Paradox displays the password dialog box and prompt, type the correct password for the table or script and choose OK or press ↲. (This dialog box won't appear if you have already entered a password for the table or script during the current Paradox session.)

5. If you're changing the password for a table, Paradox will display the choices Master and Auxiliary.

    - Choose **M**aster to remove or change both the owner (overall) and auxiliary passwords.
    - Choose **A**uxiliary to remove or change only the auxiliary passwords.

6. When prompted with the password dialog box or the auxiliary form, you can either change or remove the existing password, as follows:

    - To change the master or script password, simply type in a new one and verify it just as you did when setting the original password.
    - To remove the master or script password, leave the password blank and choose OK or press ↲ (you won't be prompted to verify the blank password).
    - To change the auxiliary password, edit it as you wish. To delete the auxiliary password, press the Backspace key until the password is blank, and then delete any specified table, family, and field rights. Finally, choose **DO-IT!** from the menu or press F2 to save your changes.

If you changed the password, you'll see a message indicating that Paradox is encrypting it. If you removed the password, you'll see a message indicating that the password is being decrypted.

Write-Protecting a Table

As mentioned earlier, write-protecting a table prevents users from making any changes to a table, although they can view the table. Write protection is not much of a security measure, since users can easily remove the write protection and make changes. However, it is useful for preventing accidental deletions or other changes.

MANAGING YOUR FILES

To add write protection, choose **T**ools ➤ **M**ore ➤ **P**rotect ➤ **W**rite-protect. When prompted, specify the table to write-protect. You'll see the options Set and Clear. Select **S**et, and the table will now be available for viewing only.

To remove the write protection, select **T**ools ➤ **M**ore ➤ **P**rotect ➤ **W**rite-protect, specify the table, and then choose **C**lear.

Getting Information about Files

The Info option from the Tools menu provides a powerful and convenient way for viewing and printing your Paradox objects. When you select this option, you'll see this submenu:

The Who and Lock options on this submenu apply only to Paradox networks. Who lists users currently running Paradox on the network, and Lock lists the locks for a table. See Appendix C for more information about using Paradox on networks. The remaining options on the Info submenu are explained in the sections that follow.

Viewing Table Structures

You can get information about the structure of a table by selecting **T**ools ➤ **I**nfo ➤ **S**tructure. Paradox will display the table structure you specify, as in the example shown in Figure 12.6. To print a copy of the table structure, press the Instant Report key, Alt-F7.

GETTING INFORMATION ABOUT FILES

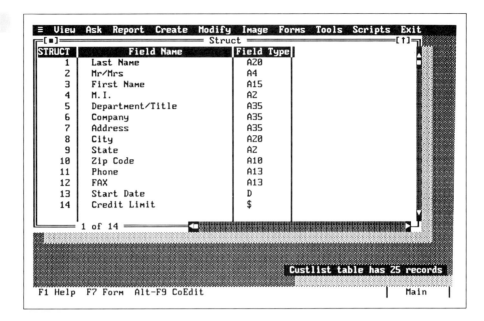

FIGURE 12.6

Tools ➤ Info ➤ Structure shows the structure of the table you specify

The Structure option displays the structure in a temporary table named Struct. Although you can edit this structure using the usual techniques, because it is a temporary table, your changes won't affect the structure or contents of the original table. If you want to make changes and keep the modified table, you must rename the Struct table. In order to actually modify the structure of a table, use **M**odify ➤ **R**estructure, as described later in this chapter.

Viewing the File Inventory

When you select **T**ools ➤ **I**nfo ➤ **I**nventory, you'll see a submenu with a list of tables, scripts, or files associated with a particular directory. If you choose the **T**ables or **S**cripts option, you'll see a Directory dialog box along with the prompt

  Enter directory or leave blank for working directory

Type in the drive letter and the name of the directory of interest (such as C:\PDOX45\Samples) and press ↵, or just leave the dialog box blank and press ↵ to bring up a list of the names of tables or scripts in the working directory.

MANAGING YOUR FILES

Select **F**iles if you want view to any group of files. You'll see this dialog box:

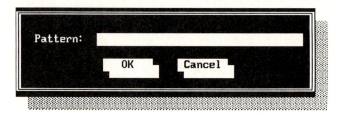

You'll also see the prompt

   Enter DOS pattern, e.g., *.TXT

You can use a question mark as a wildcard for a single character, or an asterisk for a group of characters. If you leave the box empty and just press ↵, Paradox will display all the files in your current working directory.

Each Inventory option shows the name and the date of the last modification, displayed in a special table named List, as shown in Figure 12.7. To print a report of the information on the screen, press the Instant Report key, Alt-F7.

FIGURE 12.7

Choosing Tools ➤ Info ➤ Inventory ➤ Files and then specifying the pattern Charges.* creates a List table showing all the Charges files in the current directory.

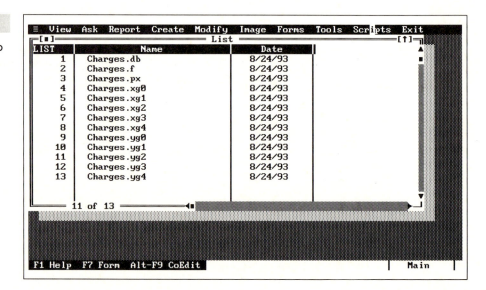

Viewing a Table's Family

When you choose **T**ools ➤ **I**nfo ➤ **F**amily, you must next specify the table whose family you want to view. Paradox will then display the family (the table and all its associated objects), as shown in Figure 12.8. Notice that the Custlist table shown in this figure includes validity checks in a .VAL file (that is, a file named Custlist.VAL), two forms (named Custlist.F and Custlist.F1), and four reports (Custlist.R, Custlist.R1, Custlist.R2, Custlist.R3).

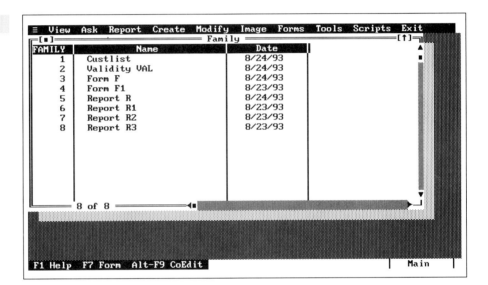

FIGURE 12.8

The family of objects for the Custlist table

Viewing Field Names for a Secondary Index

Secondary indexes are created automatically when you use the **T**ools ➤ **Q**uerySpeed option (described later in this chapter) and when you use the **M**odify ➤ **I**ndex option to add an index to a table. You can see which field names are associated with secondary indexes in a table by choosing the **T**ools ➤ **I**nfo ➤ **T**ableIndex.

After you choose this option, you'll be prompted to specify the name of the table whose secondary index names and field types you want to find out about. You'll see a dialog box, similar to the one shown below, showing the names of secondary indexes associated with the table you selected.

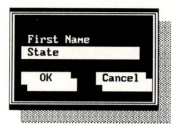

If the table doesn't have any secondary indexes, Paradox displays a message informing you of this, and prompts you again to specify a table name. Use the usual techniques to choose a different table or to cancel the operation.

When you choose the secondary index you're interested in, Paradox will display a structure table named Struct (just as it does when you use Tools ➤ Info ➤ Structure). This table includes each field's name and type in the secondary index you chose.

Restructuring a Table

Once you've created a table, added some data to it, and used it for a while, you may find that you want to change something about its basic structure. For example, after creating a table like Custlist, which is designed to handle addresses within the U.S., you may find that you need to make some changes to store names and addresses for people in other countries. You need to add a field named Country to store the country name. You might also want to change the name of the State field to State/Province, and extend its size to 15 or 20 characters so you're not limited to the two-letter abbreviations used within the U.S.

When modifying the structure of a table, however, there's always the possibility of losing some data in the table. To reduce the risks involved, you might want to first copy the entire table, using **T**ools ➤ **C**opy ➤ **T**able, to some other name. For example, you could copy the Custlist table to a table named Custback. If after restructuring the table you discover that you've lost significant amounts of data, you could recover your losses by using **T**ools ➤ **C**opy ➤ **T**able to copy the Custback table back to Custlist.

RESTRUCTURING A TABLE

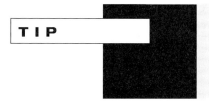

TIP Moving fields to a new position in the table can come in handy when you're specifying multiple fields for a primary index. See Chapter 13 for information about creating and using indexes.

To modify the structure of a table, follow these steps:

1. Make your backup of the original table using **T**ools ➤ **C**opy ➤ **T**able.

2. Select **M**odify from the desktop, which brings up this familiar submenu:

3. Select **R**estructure. Paradox will ask for the name of the table to restructure.

4. Type or choose the name of the table you want to restructure. You'll see the same screen used for creating tables but now it already contains the existing structure, as in the example shown in Figure 12.9.

You can use the arrow keys or mouse, as usual, to move the cursor around and make changes. To change the name of a field, simply move the cursor to the appropriate field name in the structure. Then type in the new name, or switch to Field view (Alt-F5 or Ctrl-f, or double-click) to make minor changes.

To change the length of a field, just type in the new number. Lengthening an alphanumeric field (for example, from A20 to A25) will generally not

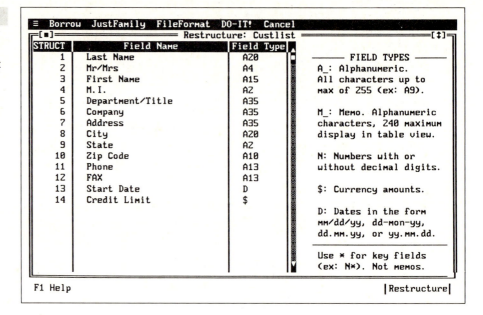

FIGURE 12.9

Choosing Modify ➤ Restructure displays the current structure of a table and lets you change it.

cause any problems, although you might need to change the format of a custom form or report later to accommodate the new width. Be careful when shortening an alphanumeric field (for example, from A25 to A20), because you may lose some data if it is longer than the new width.

The Ins and Delete keys let you insert, delete, and move fields, as follows:

- To add a field, move the cursor to where you want the new field to appear and press Ins. A blank line will appear above the cursor position. Now type the new field name and press ↵, then specify the field type and press ↵.

- To delete a field while the table structure is displayed, move the cursor to that field and press Delete. Keep in mind that when you delete a field, you delete all of its contents as well. Paradox will also delete the field mask for that field from any reports and forms that you've created for that table.

NOTE If you delete a field accidentally, you can choose Cancel from the menu bar to abandon the operation and retain the original table structure. You'll also be given a chance to change your mind about deleted fields when you save the modified table structure.

- To move a field, place the cursor where you want to move the existing field, then press Ins to insert a blank line. Next, type in the field name *exactly* as it is spelled in the original position—same spelling and same uppercase and lowercase. Finally, press ↵. Paradox will move the field from its original position to its new position.

As when you're creating a new table, you can use the **B**orrow option on the menu bar as a shortcut when typing in field names and types that are already defined in another table. See Chapter 2 for more information about borrowing another table's structure.

Changing a Field Type

Changing a field's type is generally not a good idea, since doing so can lead to a great deal of data loss. Nonetheless, if you selected an inappropriate field type at the outset, changing the field type is unavoidable. You can change a field's type by moving the cursor to the Field Type column and entering any valid abbreviation (followed by a length if it's an alphanumeric, BLOB, or memo field).

The following are some important points to keep in mind when you're considering changing a field type:

- If you change a memo field to an alphanumeric field, it's likely that any data from existing memos that won't fit into the length you give to the alphanumeric field will be lost.

- There's no harm in converting a currency ($) field to a number (N) field or vice-versa. But be careful about changing either of these field types to short numeric (S). Numbers outside the acceptable range for short numbers (−32,767 to 32,767), as well as any numbers to the right of the decimal point, will be lost.

- You can convert an alphanumeric or memo field type to a date field (D). But any data in the existing field that's not in date format will be lost.

- Converting any field to binary (B) will change the contents of the field to *BLOB*, and you're likely to lose all the data in that field.

- You cannot change a BLOB field to any other field type.

- Unless an alphanumeric or memo field contains only numbers, converting one of these to a numeric, currency, short numeric, or date field will almost surely cause data loss. For example, converting an alphanumeric zip code field to numeric will lose records that have zip codes like 12345-6789 because of the embedded hyphen.

Saving the New Structure

To save your new table structure, choose **DO-IT!** from the menu or press F2. Depending on what kinds of changes you've made to the table, you'll see some of the prompts described in the following sections.

Confirming a Deleted Field

If you deleted one or more fields from the table structure, the name of each field to be deleted appears near the lower-right corner of the screen while Paradox is restructuring the table, and you'll be given the choice to follow through with the deletion (**D**elete) or to reconsider and back out (**O**ops!). If you choose Oops!, you'll be returned to the table structure screen, where you can either reinsert the field you've deleted or choose Cancel from the menu bar to cancel the entire restructure and keep the deleted field.

Confirming a Shortened Field

If you shortened an alphanumeric field, or converted some other field type to the alphanumeric or short numeric type, you'll see the name of the field in question in the lower-right corner of the screen, and you'll be given three choices:

- **T**rimming is the option you want if you don't care if data that cannot fit within the new field size is permanently truncated (deleted from the end of the field).

- **N**o-Trimming is the option you want if you're not quite sure if truncation is going to cause problems. No-Trimming does truncate data that doesn't fit, but only after it puts a copy of the original records in a temporary table (named Problems, described in a moment).

- **O**ops! cancels the operation and brings you back to the screen for changing the table structure. At that point, you can either increase the field to an acceptable length and choose DO-IT! to try again, or choose Cancel to cancel the entire operation.

Using the Problems or Keyviol Table

If your table restructuring results in any data loss, the records that could not be copied into the new table structure are displayed in a temporary table named Problems, as shown in the example in Figure 12.10.

If you find you need to use the data that has been eliminated in the restructuring, you cannot simply use **T**ools ➤ **M**ore ➤ **A**dd to copy the data into the table, because the records in the Problems table are not compatible with the new table structure. Your best bet might be to use

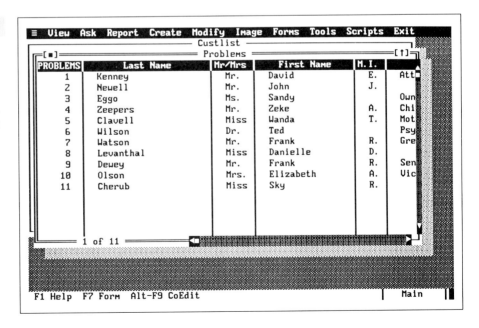

FIGURE 12.10

The Problems table holds records that could not be added to the table after the table was restructured, or records that contain text that was trimmed.

MANAGING YOUR FILES

Tools ➤ Rename to rename the table, so you can refer to it later when trying to get these records back into the new table structure. Or, print a copy of the Problems table (press Alt-F7).

The Keyviol table appears only if you've added a key to an unkeyed table or changed the key fields in the table. This table contains records that break the rule of uniqueness for key fields.

After renaming the temporary Problems or Keyviol table and figuring out what needs to be done to correct the records in them, you can take one of several approaches:

- If the records in the renamed Problems or Keyviol table are easily corrected to match the restructured table, you can edit those records as needed, and then use Tools ➤ More ➤ Add to add the corrected records back to the restructured table.

- If you prefer to return the restructured table to its original state but you didn't make a backup of it before restructuring, you can use Modify ➤ Restructure again to restore the table to its original field structure (assuming the current field types will allow it). Then use Tools ➤ More ➤ Add to add the records from the renamed Problems or Keyviol table back into the restructured table.

- If the Problems or Keyviol table contains more troublesome records than you had anticipated, but you remembered to make a backup of the original table before restructuring it, you're not out of luck. Just use Tools ➤ Copy ➤ Table to copy the backup to the original table name.

Converting between Older and Newer Versions of Paradox

Like the Create screen, the Restructure screen also offers the FileFormat option on the menu bar. Choosing that option presents a submenu with the options Standard and Compatible.

Choose Standard if you want the table to be used in Paradox 4.0 and later only, and support memo and binary fields. Select Compatible if you want the table to be read by Paradox 4.5 *and* earlier versions of Paradox, but without memo or binary fields.

So, let's say you created a table in Paradox 3.5, and now want to add a memo field to that table. First, you would use **M**odify ➤ **R**estructure in Paradox 4.5 to get to the table's structure. Then choose **F**ileFormat ➤ **S**tandard. Next, add your memo field, and save the new table structure with DO-IT!.

Going the other way around, let's suppose you want to convert a Paradox 4.5 table to Paradox 3.5. Again, you would use **M**odify ➤ **R**estructure to change the table's structure, but this time you would choose **F**ileFormat ➤ **C**ompatible. If the table contains memo or BLOB fields, you'll see the message

> WARNING! Structure contains non-compatible field types

You'll need to delete those fields before saving the new table structure. In the case of memo fields, you might instead try to change the data to another type. BLOB fields, on the other hand, cannot be changed to another field type.

If you do try to save a file that contains incompatible field types in Compatible format, as soon as you choose DO- IT!, Paradox will pop up the alternatives Convert and Oops!. Choose **C**onvert to retain the Paradox 4.5 format and return to the desktop. Select **O**ops! to stay in the Restructure screen to change the offending field types and try again.

Fixing Corrupted Objects

If you've used the DOS COPY command to copy just a table, and haven't backed up the other family members such as reports and forms, it's possible to end up with family members whose structures don't match the table structure. (If you use **T**ools ➤ **C**opy or **T**ools ➤ **R**ename in Paradox instead of the DOS COPY command, your tables and associated family files will always be in sync.) When you then try to view or change one of the out-of-sync reports or forms, you may see a message describing the reports as corrupt or out of date. In this case, you can use **M**odify ➤ **R**estructure ➤ **J**ustFamily to bring the family members up to date.

To make the other objects match the structure of a table, choose **M**odify ➤ **R**estructure from the Paradox desktop and specify the name of the table whose family members need updating. Select **J**ustFamily, then OK to restructure the family and return to the desktop.

NOTE: Pressing F2 or choosing DO-IT! from the menu bar automatically restructures a table and its family members, so you'll rarely need to use JustFamily. However, JustFamily is faster than using DO-IT! if your only goal is to bring the table and its family back in sync without modifying the structure of the table itself.

Speeding Up Queries

The QuerySpeed option on the Tools menu speeds up frequently used queries and operations that search the contents of a field, such as Zoom. For example, if you regularly perform an automated update (as discussed in Chapter 16), you can use QuerySpeed to reduce the time required to perform the update.

To use the QuerySpeed feature, choose **A**sk from the desktop and fill out the Query form to perform whatever operation you want the query to perform. If you want, you can choose **DO-IT!** to test the query and make sure it does what you want. When your query is ready to run, choose **T**ools ➤ **Q**uerySpeed.

Paradox will decide whether or not to create a secondary index for the table (it won't create a secondary index if the query operation is based on a key field or an existing secondary index). The index is a copy of the data in just the fields used in the query. The index is maintained in memory, rather than on the disk, whenever the table is open. By operating on the index rather than on the disk, Paradox can speed any operations involving that field.

While indexes do speed up many operations, a couple of costs are associated with them:

- They consume disk space. This is only important if you're pressed for space on your disk.

- They require time to update. If a table is very small, it may very well take more time to update the index and perform the query than it would to perform the query in the first place. Hence, QuerySpeed could actually slow things down. However, for a table containing hundreds or thousands of records, QuerySpeed will probably enhance the speed noticeably.

If you find that secondary indexes are slowing things down rather than speeding them up, use **T**ools ➤ **D**elete ➤ **I**ndex to delete any indexes that are based on fields that you really don't need to search or query very often. To delete a speed-up index, use **T**ools ➤ **D**elete ➤ **I**ndex ➤ **S**ingle, as described earlier in this chapter.

NOTE

You can use Modify ➤ Index to more precisely determine which fields to create secondary indexes for, as explained in Chapter 13. You can also use the PAL option in the Paradox Custom Configuration Program to determine whether secondary indexes are updated incrementally (as you change the table) or when needed, as explained in Appendix D. However, changing this setting only affects secondary indexes in tables that also contain key fields, and it only applies to new secondary indexes that you create after you change the setting.

Interfacing with Other Programs

Paradox provides tools for transferring data to and from other programs via the ExportImport option on the Tools menu. Once you've successfully transferred the data to or from another program, you can use that data just as if you had originally created it in that program. For example, if you import a dBASE database as a Paradox table, you can then use that new Paradox table just as if you had created it and added the data in Paradox. And if you export a Paradox table to a Lotus 1-2-3 spreadsheet, you'll be able to use that spreadsheet in 1-2-3 just as if you had used 1-2-3 to create it from scratch.

However, you may need to tweak the new data somewhat to compensate for assumptions that Paradox made about the data when exporting or importing it. For example, you may need to use **M**odify ➤ **R**estructure in Paradox to change a field name, width, or type for an imported table, or to reorganize the fields. Likewise, you may need to widen or narrow a spreadsheet column after exporting a Paradox table to Quattro Pro, Lotus 1-2-3, or Symphony.

If Paradox cannot interpret the type of data in an imported table, it gives a field type of U, for Unknown. You can use **M**odify ➤ **R**estructure to change that to whatever field type seems reasonable.

Paradox always converts data through *copies* of files. In all cases, your original data is left unchanged, and converted data is copied to a new file with a name you provide.

In the sections that follow, we'll discuss the general steps for transferring data, then we'll explore details for converting to and from each program. Finally, we'll look at some creative ways to import and export data.

An Overview of Exporting and Importing Data

When you're importing or exporting files, it's your responsibility to keep track of the locations of those files. If the file you're importing is not in the current directory, or you want to export a file to another directory, you must specify the path to the file. For example, to import a 1-2-3 spreadsheet named Sales from the directory named 123 on drive C, enter the name of the file to import as C:\123\Sales when prompted for the file name. Whenever you omit the path, Paradox will look for (and save) files in the current working directory.

INTERFACING WITH OTHER PROGRAMS

Here are the general steps for exporting or importing data between Paradox and other programs:

1. Choose **T**ools ➤ **E**xportImport and then either **E**xport or **I**mport. You'll see this submenu:

2. Choose the format you want to export to or import from. If the option you selected is followed by a ➤ symbol (**Quattro** ➤, for example), another submenu will appear, and you can select the appropriate version of that program. Paradox will prompt you for the source table or file name you're exporting to or importing from.

3. If you're exporting data from Paradox to another system, specify the name of the Paradox table you're exporting from. If you're importing data from another system to Paradox, specify the name of the file you're importing from. If the file is not on the current directory, be sure to specify the full path to that file. Paradox will then prompt you for the target table or file name you're exporting or importing to.

TIP Before exporting a Paradox table, you may want to perform a query that selects specific fields or records to export. Then specify Answer, rather than the original table, as the table to export.

4. If you're exporting data from Paradox to another system, specify the name and, optionally, the location of the file you're exporting to. If you're importing data from another system to Paradox, specify the name of the Paradox table you're importing to.

Managing Your Files

As usual, if the table or file you're importing or exporting already exists, Paradox will give you a chance to cancel the operation or to replace the existing table or file.

If you omit the file name extension when prompted for a file name, Paradox will assign it automatically, based on the program you chose in step 2 above. Table 12.2 lists each program supported by Paradox and the file name extensions that Paradox either expects when importing data or automatically assigns when exporting data.

Exporting to Spreadsheets

You might want to export a Paradox table to a spreadsheet program to use that program's more advanced math or graphics capabilities. However, keep in mind that it's not always necessary to do so, since Paradox is also capable of doing a fair amount of math (see Chapter 15) and graphics (see Chapter 10) on its own.

TABLE 12.2: Programs and File Name Extensions for Paradox Data Transfer

PROGRAM	FILE NAME EXTENSION
ASCII Delimited	.TXT
ASCII Text	.TXT
dBASE II, III, III Plus, IV	.DBF
Lotus 1-2-3 Release 1A	.WKS
Lotus 1-2-3 Release 2	.WK1
PFS or IBM Filing Assistant	.PFS
Quattro Release 1.*x*	.WKQ
Quattro Pro	.WQ1
Reflex Release 1.0 and 1.2	.RXD
Reflex Release 2.0	.R2D
Symphony Release 1.0	.WRK
Symphony Release 1.1	.WR1
VisiCalc (and other Data Interchange Format files)	.DIF

TIP Quattro Pro can read Paradox tables directly, so you can usually bypass the Tools ➤ Export Import ➤ Export options if you want to convert a Paradox table to a QuattroPro spreadsheet.

Also, keep in mind that Paradox can manage huge amounts of data because it works with those data on disk. Most spreadsheet programs load all the data for a spreadsheet into memory (RAM). If you export more data than can fit into your computer's memory, your spreadsheet program might not be able to handle all that data.

When you export data to a spreadsheet, the table fields and records are stored in individual columns and rows. The file will have the name you assigned, plus the appropriate extension for your version of the spreadsheet (as listed in Table 12.2).

Once you export the Paradox file, you can exit Paradox and start up the spreadsheet program, then use the usual commands or options within that program to open (or retrieve) the spreadsheet. When you load the exported data into your spreadsheet, chances are that many columns will be too narrow to display the full contents of each field, so you will need to use the appropriate commands within the spreadsheet program to resize columns. Note that although memo and BLOB fields in Paradox will display the correct field names as column headings in the spreadsheet, the data for those fields will be blank.

Importing Data from a Spreadsheet

When importing spreadsheet data, Paradox will look for files with the appropriate extension in the specified directory. For example, if you import a spreadsheet from Release 2 of Lotus 1-2-3, and then you specify C:\LOTUS\Sales as the file to import, Paradox will search the Lotus directory in drive C for a file named Sales.WK1.

Keep in mind that Paradox tables store information in columns (fields) and rows (records). If the Start Date field of a Paradox table is defined as a date field type, the Start Date field in *every* record of that table must always contain a date; formulas, numbers, memos, and BLOB data aren't allowed. The same structure is expected for all fields in a table. Spreadsheets, on the other hand, are more freeform. Although they are defined by columns and rows, spreadsheets let you arrange text, numbers, and formulas in any manner you wish.

Due to the strict column-and-row organization of its tables, Paradox cannot reliably import data that is randomly placed about a spreadsheet. Instead, it needs to import columns and rows, and the top row must contain the field names for the Paradox table.

If your spreadsheet contains labels or formulas which aren't in a consistent row-and-column orientation, or your spreadsheet uses headings, underlines, or other characters to improve the spreadsheet's appearance, do not attempt to import these into a Paradox table. Instead, you should use whatever commands your spreadsheet program offers (such as File ➤ Xtract in Lotus 1-2-3) to extract only the field names and values beneath them into a separate spreadsheet file (perhaps named Temp). Then, use Paradox to import the extracted file only.

CAUTION When extracting portions of the spreadsheet, be sure to extract the data as values, not as formulas.

Paradox will assign data types to the imported data as follows:

- Labels become alphanumeric fields.
- Numbers become numeric fields.
- Numbers formatted as currency or with fixed two decimal places become currency fields.
- Dates formatted as dates become date fields.

Any column storing the results of calculations will be imported as values; Paradox will not import the formulas themselves.

Transferring Data between Paradox and dBASE

Transferring data to and from dBASE is a simple, straightforward process, because Paradox and dBASE store data in records and fields and both fully support memo fields.

To export data to dBASE, select **T**ools ➤ **E**xportImport ➤ **E**xport ➤ **d**BASE. From the submenu, choose dBASE II, dBASE III, or dBASE IV. Paradox will copy data to the file name you provide, adding the usual dBASE .DBF extension (for instance, Partodb4.DBF).

NOTE BLOB fields are exported to dBASE as memo fields. However, dBASE does not directly support BLOB fields or an external BLOB editor. Therefore, you may not be able to edit the exported memo fields.

Importing dBASE data is even easier than exporting: Simply choose **T**ools ➤ **E**xportImport ➤ **I**mport ➤ **d**BASE and specify the database file name to import from and the Paradox table to import to. When importing data, dBASE logical fields are converted to alphanumeric fields with a length of 1 character, and the width of memo fields is initially set to 20 characters.

Storing Data in PFS Format

The PFS option stores data in PFS and IBM Filing Assistant format with the file name extension .PFS. When you're importing data from PFS or IBM Filing Assistant, make sure that the file you are importing has the file name extension .PFS. (If it does not, use the DOS RENAME command to change the file's name before you import it.)

Since PFS does not use data types, Paradox will make reasonable assumptions about data types during the conversion. Attachment pages are converted to memo fields, with the usual initial width of 20 characters.

Transferring Data between Paradox and Reflex

Reflex and Paradox store data in a similar format and both handle memo fields, so transferring data between these programs is usually easy.

When you're exporting a table, Paradox will allow you to choose Reflex Release 1.0, Reflex Release 1.1, or Reflex Release 2.0. When importing, Paradox handles these minor version differences automatically.

Transferring Data between Paradox and VisiCalc

The VisiCalc option on the Export or Import submenu lets you export and import data stored in Data Interchange Format (DIF). A file exported to DIF format is assigned the file name extension .DIF.

VisiCalc, many other spreadsheet programs, and even some word processing programs allow you to store data in DIF format, and any file that you convert to DIF format can be imported into Paradox. Keep in mind that because Paradox stores data in fields and records, the data being imported should have a consistent row-and-column format. Paradox cannot import a spreadsheet that contains data stored randomly throughout the rows and columns. Also, extraneous characters (such as boxes and asterisks) used to enhance the appearance of the spreadsheet on the screen are not converted easily. Remove these before importing the spreadsheet into Paradox.

Note that you can't export Paradox databases containing a memo field to DIF. If you try to do so, Paradox will display the message

> Field of type Memo, Blob, or Unknown not supported

And you will be returned to the desktop.

Transferring ASCII Delimited Files

When you select to export to an ASCII file (with **T**ools ➤ **E**xportImport ➤ **E**xport ➤ **A**SCII), you'll see this submenu:

INTERFACING WITH OTHER PROGRAMS

When you select to import an ASCII file (with **T**ools ➤ **E**xportImport ➤ **I**mport ➤ **A**SCII), you'll see this submenu:

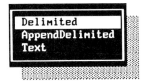

The Delimited option on both the Export and Import submenus and the AppendDelimited option on the Import submenu transfer ASCII delimited files. (The Text option on these submenus transfers files with only one field, as described shortly.)

A *delimited* file (also called a *text* file or a *sequential data* file in some programs) is one in which fields are separated by commas and each record is terminated by a carriage-return/line-feed combination. Usually, character data is enclosed in quotation marks. When you use the DOS TYPE command to view a delimited file, it will look something like the example in Figure 12.11. The carriage-return/line-feed at the end of each record causes each new record to begin on a new line in the screen, as in the figure.

FIGURE 12.11

Records from the sample Custlist table after being exported to an ASCII delimited text file. These were displayed on the screen using the DOS TYPE command.

```
112","Chicago","IL","60606","(123)555-1234","(123)555-4039",12/28/1993,5000.00
"Schumack","Dr.","Susita","M.","Neurosurgeon","","P.O. Box 1121","Philadelphia",
"PA","23456","(212)555-0987","",10/14/1992,5000.00
"Smith","Dr.","Mary","K.","Graduate School of Business","Cal State L.A.","P.O. B
ox 1234","L.A.","CA","91234","(345)555-9342","",10/27/1992,5000.00
"Smith","Dr.","Savitha","V.","","","767 Ocean View Lane","Ossineke","MI","49766"
,"(213)555-9545","(213)555-3212",5/17/1993,5000.00
"Smith","Mr.","John","Q.","","","65 Overton Hwy, Box 112","Holland","MI","49423"
,"(789)555-0323","",10/18/1993,7500.00
"Smythe","Ms.","Janet","L.","","","P.O. Box 3384","Seattle","WA","98762","(765)5
55-0121","",12/27/1992,10000.00
"Watson","Mr.","Frank","R.","Greenskeeper","Whispering Palms Golf Club","8775 Co
ncha de Golf","Bangor","ME","01875","(539)555-2239","(539)555-4054",1/28/1994,75
00.00
"Wilson","Dr.","Ted","","Psychology Department","Pine Valley University","P.O. B
ox 463","Seattle","WA","98103","(765)555-3049","(765)555-4034",11/13/1993,5000.0
0
"Zastrow","Dr.","Ruth","","Internal Medicine","Scripps Clinic","4331 La Jolla Sc
enic Dr.","La Jolla","CA","92037","(619)555-5948","(619)555-3024",2/27/1994,7500
.00
"Zeepers","Mr.","Zeke","A.","Chief Engineer","Virtual Reality Designs","5409 Cre
st Dr.","Encinitas","CA","92024","(619)555-7765","(619)555-6049",2/27/1994,5000.
00

C:\PDOX45\CUSTOMER>
```

When you export a delimited file, Paradox creates a file with the name you provide and the extension .TXT (unless you provide a different extension). The ASCII file shown in Figure 12.11 is a Paradox table exported in delimited format. Because this is such a common format, you can export data from Paradox to just about any program by exporting to a delimited ASCII file, then use the other software to import the delimited file.

When importing delimited ASCII files, Paradox assumes that individual fields are separated by commas. You can, however, use the ASCII option in the Paradox Custom Configuration Program to specify a different delimiter. The imported data will be stored in a new table with the field names Field 1, Field 2, Field 3, and so on. Data types in the imported table are determined on a best-guess basis. As usual, you can use **M**odify ➤ **R**estructure in Paradox to change the field names and data types in the imported table.

The ASCII option in the Custom Configuration Program also lets you define the string delimiter character and specify whether that delimiter is used for text strings only or for all fields. You'll see an example of using this option a little later in the chapter.

The AppendDelimited option lets you import ASCII data into an existing Paradox table. If the table you are importing records into is keyed, you'll be given the options NewEntries and Update. If you select NewEntries, Paradox attempts to append the imported records to the bottom of an existing table. If you select Update, Paradox attempts to replace records in an existing table with imported records that have identical key fields.

Because the ASCII file has no field names, Paradox simply attempts to append records according to the order of the fields. That is, the first field in the ASCII file is imported into the first field in the Paradox table, the second field in the ASCII file is imported into the second field of the Paradox table, and so on.

Any data that cannot be imported, because of nonmatching fields or conflicting data types, is stored in a table named Problems. This table shows the record number of the record that could not be imported, the first 80 characters of that record, and the reason the importation failed. Likewise, any data that cannot be imported because of duplicate key fields are stored in a table named Keyviol. You can use this information, if necessary, to modify the ASCII file (using any DOS text editor with a nondocument mode), and try again later.

Transferring ASCII Text Files

You can import and export text files consisting of single lines of information by choosing **Tools** ➤ **ExportImport** ➤ **Import** or **Export** ➤ **ASCII Text**. When you import text files, the new table will have a single field named Text, containing a single line from the imported file. When you export to a text file, the Paradox table can contain only a single alphanumeric field. Each record in the Paradox table becomes a line in the exported text file.

Using the Text option to export data is not the same as exporting a printed report. We'll explore exporting reports later in this chapter, in the section about using a word processor to embellish reports.

Transferring Data between Nonsupported Programs

Although Paradox offers straight-across import and export options for some programs, you can generally transfer data between any two programs simply by finding an intermediary file format that both programs support.

For example, most programs can import and export files in ASCII delimited and DIF formats. Thus, if both programs support the DIF format, you can export data from one of those programs to a DIF format file. Then, run the other program and import the data from that DIF file.

A perfect example might be the "mail merge" files used with word processors to print form letters, mailing labels, and the like. Even though you can print all these same types of reports using Paradox alone, you might prefer to use some of the fancier fonts and other printing capabilities that your word processing program offers instead.

If your word processing program can merge directly from an ASCII delimited text file, you could simply export your Paradox table to an ASCII delimited text file, and then use that file as your merge file in your word processing program. Or, if you have problems with that method, you could try exporting data from Paradox in DIF format, then importing that DIF file into a merge file for your word processing program.

As an example, suppose that you want to use data from a Paradox table as a secondary merge file in WordPerfect 5.1 for DOS. This requires the following steps:

- Print the structure of the table you're exporting.
- Define the format of the ASCII file.
- Export the Paradox data.
- Prepare WordPerfect for the imported file.
- Create the primary merge file.
- Perform the merge.

The following sections describe each of these steps in more detail.

Printing the Structure of the Paradox Table

You should print a copy of the Paradox table's structure for reference. Follow these steps to print a copy of the table you're about to export:

1. Run Paradox in the usual manner, and use **Tools ➤ More ➤ Directory** to get to the directory that contains the table you want to export.
2. Choose **Tools ➤ Info ➤ Structure**, specify the table you plan to export, and choose OK.
3. When the table structure appears on your screen, press the Instant Report key, Alt-F7, to print it.
4. Close the current window by clicking on its Close button or pressing F8.
5. Grab a pencil and number the fields from top to bottom on the printed copy of the table structure.

Defining the Format of the ASCII File

Next, you need to make sure that WordPerfect will be able to read the file you're exporting. Although WordPerfect can import both DIF and ASCII files, ASCII is a little more direct than DIF. If you use DIF as the intermediary format between WordPerfect and Paradox, you need to use the WordPerfect Convert program to convert the exported DIF file to a merge file.

INTERFACING WITH OTHER PROGRAMS

However, there is one catch to converting your table to ASCII format: although Paradox automatically encloses alphanumeric fields in quotation marks, you want Paradox to enclose *all* the fields in quotation marks, because WordPerfect doesn't differentiate between data types. Fortunately, you can change the ASCII exporting defaults in Paradox to take care of this, as follows:

1. From the Paradox desktop, choose ≡ ➤ **U**tilities ➤ **C**ustom to get to the Paradox Custom Conversion Program.

2. Choose **A**SCII. You'll see the ASCII Export/Import Settings dialog box.

3. Set up the dialog box as shown below, so that all fields in the exported table will be delimited. Then choose OK.

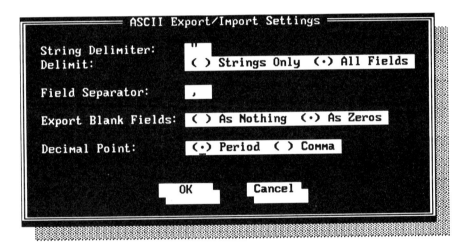

4. From the Custom Conversion Program desktop menu, choose **D**O-IT!, then **H**ardDisk (for a single-user system) or **N**etwork (for a system on a network, as discussed in Appendix D).

You'll be returned to the Paradox desktop. At this point, you may need to use **T**ools ➤ **M**ore ➤ **D**irectory to get back to the directory containing the table you want to export.

Exporting the Paradox Data

Now you can export the data from a table to an ASCII file. Here are the steps:

1. If you want to export only selected records to the ASCII file, choose **A**sk and create a query that defines the records you want to export (see Chapter 7). When you complete the query, the Answer table should contain just the records you want to export.

2. If you want to presort the records before exporting, use **M**odify ➤ **S**ort (see Chapter 6) to sort either the Answer table (if you created a query in the preceding step) to the same table or to sort the original table to a new table (such as Tempsort).

> **CAUTION**
> If you rearrange the order of fields in the Answer table, the order of fields in the exported table may match that new order rather than the order you determined earlier.

3. Choose **T**ools ➤ **E**xportImport ➤ **E**xport ➤ **A**SCII ➤ **D**elimited to begin the exportation.

4. Specify the table you want to export (the original table for all records, the Answer table, or the new, sorted table if you queried or sorted the original table).

5. Specify the location of your WordPerfect document files and a file name. For example, if your WordPerfect documents are stored in C:\WP51, type C:\WP51\Frompdox.SCD (you can use any valid file name), then choose OK or press ↵.

6. Choose **E**xit ➤ **Y**es to leave Paradox and return to the command prompt.

Preparing WordPerfect for the Imported File

The next step is to make sure that WordPerfect knows the format of the exported ASCII file so it can handle it correctly as a secondary merge file. Here's the procedure:

1. Run WordPerfect in the usual manner for your computer.

INTERFACING WITH OTHER PROGRAMS

2. Choose **F**ile ➤ Set**u**p or press Shift-F1.

3. Choose **I**nitial Settings ➤ **M**erge.

4. Define the field delimiters as shown below. Note that each field is defined as starting with a quotation mark and ending with a quotation mark and comma. Each record is defined as ending with a carriage return. (Press Ctrl-M, which WordPerfect will convert to [CR]; don't type [CR]).

```
Setup: Merge DOS Text File

    1 - Field Delimiters   - Begin  "
                             End    ",

    2 - Record Delimiters  - Begin
                             End    [CR]
```

```
Selection: 0
```

5. Press F7 to work your way back to WordPerfect's main editing screen.

Creating the Primary Merge File

Now you can create the primary merge file in WordPerfect with the usual techniques. That is, you can place fields by choosing **T**ools ➤ **M**erge Codes ➤ **F**ield, or by pressing Shift-F9, then F. Specify the number of each field, using your Instant Report printout as reference.

As with any WordPerfect primary merge file, you can use the ? option in the field name to prevent blank lines from being printed where there are empty fields. You can also use the {IF BLANK} {ENDIF} commands to prevent blank spaces within a line. And, of course, you can choose fonts, insert graphics, define a paper size, or do anything else you would normally do in WordPerfect to format your document. Figure 12.12 shows a sample primary merge file formatted as a form letter.

FIGURE 12.12

Sample WordPerfect 5.1 primary merge file. Field numbers assigned to each [FIELD] command match the order of fields in the original Paradox table.

```
November 10, 1993

{FIELD}2~ {FIELD}3~ {FIELD}4~ {FIELD}1~
{FIELD}5~
{FIELD}6~
{FIELD}7~
{FIELD}8~, {FIELD}9~ {FIELD}10~

Dear {FIELD}2~ {FIELD}1~

How do you like getting these fancy form letters from me {FIELD}3~? I'll
bet you're wondering how I was able to print these beautifully
formatted letters with my personal computer.

Well first I exported a Paradox table to an ASCII delimited file
Then I created this form letter in WordPerfect, using all the fancy
printer features that WordPerfect offers. Then I simply merged the
WordPerfect primary merge file with the ASCII file and, voila,
here's the result.

Well, gotta run

Frank Lee Ausom
D:\WP51\MERGE                              Doc 1 Pg 1 Ln 3.83" Pos 3.9"
```

> **NOTE** See your WordPerfect documentation if you need more information about setting up for a merge operation.

After you've defined your primary merge file, follow these steps:

1. Choose **F**ile ➤ E**x**it or press F7.

2. When asked about saving the document, choose **Y**es and provide a file name (such as Letter.PRM). Then press ↵.

3. When asked if you want to exit WP, choose **N**o to clear the screen but stay in WordPerfect.

Performing the Merge

Finally, you can merge your primary and secondary merge files. Here's how:

1. Choose **T**ools ➤ **M**erge or press Ctrl-F9, then M.
2. Type in the name of your primary merge file (for example, Letter.PRM), then press ↵.
3. As prompted, type in the name of the secondary merge file (for example, Frompdox.SCD). Press ↵.

Remember, if the secondary merge file isn't in the directory where WordPerfect expects to find documents, you'll need to specify the path to that file.

4. When WordPerfect detects that the secondary merge file is an ASCII file, it displays a screen asking for the field and record delimiters. Since you've already defined those settings via the Setup option, just press ↵ to proceed.

When the merge is complete, you can scroll through all the letters (or labels, or envelopes, or whatever) on your screen. This is now just a normal WordPerfect document that you can print, edit, and save.

When you're finished with the merge operation, you may want to delete the exported file (Frompdox.SCD in this example), since you probably won't be using it in the future. Besides, if you make any changes whatsoever to the original Paradox table, you'll want to reexport the table before merging in WordPerfect, so that the merge always uses the most up-to-date Paradox data.

Exporting a WordPerfect Merge File to Paradox

Let's assume you've been maintaining your customer list in a WordPerfect secondary merge file for a while, but now that you've purchased Paradox, you decide that the data can be maintained more easily in a Paradox table. Rather than create a new Paradox table from scratch, you can export your existing secondary merge file to a Paradox table. That way, you don't need to reenter all the data that's already in your WordPerfect merge file.

Here again, however, you're faced with the sticky matter of not having a direct interface between Paradox and WordPerfect. Furthermore, because the WordPerfect 5.1 Convert program only offers DIF as the format for exported secondary merge files, you'll need to use DIF as the intermediate format between WordPerfect and Paradox.

For this example, assume that WordPerfect, the WordPerfect Convert program, and the secondary merge file that you want to export to Paradox are all in the C:\WP51 directory. Furthermore, assume that the name of the existing secondary merge file is Customer.SCD. Remember, you're exporting a "regular" WordPerfect secondary merge file here, not an ASCII file.

Here are the steps to follow:

1. Starting at the DOS command prompt, switch to the drive and directory containing the WordPerfect Convert program (C:\WP51 in this example).

2. Type **CONVERT** and press ↵ to run the WordPerfect Convert program.

3. When prompted, type the location and name of the secondary merge file you want to export (Customer.SCD in this example) and press ↵.

4. When prompted, type the location and file name (Customer.DIF in this example) for the output file and press ↵. (Be sure to specify a .DIF extension.)

5. When you see the first screen of the Convert program, type **1** to select WordPerfect to Another Format. You'll see the screen shown in Figure 12.13.

6. Type **8** to select WordPerfect Secondary Merge to Spreadsheet DIF.

INTERFACING WITH OTHER PROGRAMS

FIGURE 12.13

The second screen of WordPerfect's Convert program offers options for exporting from WordPerfect to other programs.

```
Name of Input File? customer.scd
Name of Output File? customer.dif
Confirm Overwrite of customer.dif (Y/[N])

0 EXIT
1 Revisable-Form-Text (IBM DCA Format)
2 Final-Form-Text (IBM DCA Format)
3 Navy DIF Standard
4 WordStar 3.3
5 MultiMate Advantage II
6 Seven-Bit Transfer Format
7 ASCII Text File
8 WordPerfect Secondary Merge to Spreadsheet DIF

Enter number of output file format desired
```

> **NOTE** WordPerfect will convert the program to DIF format and return you to the DOS prompt. At the DOS prompt, you can use the DOS MKDIR (or MD) command to create a directory for the table that you're about to create. For example, you might enter a command such as MD \PDOX45\Custdata if you want to store your new Paradox table in a subdirectory named Custdata.

7. To begin importing the data from the DIF file you created, start Paradox in the usual manner.

8. Choose **T**ools ➤ **M**ore ➤ **D**irectory, and switch to the directory where you want to store your new Paradox table.

9. Choose **T**ools ➤ **E**xportImport ➤ **I**mport ➤ **V**isiCalc.

10. When prompted for the file name, type in the path and file name of the exported DIF file (C:\WP51\Customer.DIF in this example) and press ↵.

11. When prompted, type the name for the new table (Customer in this example) and press ↵.

When conversion is complete, Paradox will display the new Customer table on the screen. From now on, you can manage the data in the table with Paradox. You may want to use **M**odify ➤ **R**estructure to refine the field names, types, and widths in the Paradox table to your liking.

After you've had a chance to work with the data in the new Paradox table and are satisfied with it, you can delete the old WordPerfect secondary merge file, or rename it as a backup file. When you want to use WordPerfect to merge data from the Paradox table in the future, just export a copy to an ASCII file, as described in the preceding section.

Using a Word Processor to Embellish Reports

The previous examples of interacting with a word processor have involved using table data for merging. But in some cases, you may simply want to export a formatted report from Paradox into your word processor. You may want to spruce up the report with fonts and graphics, or perhaps you need to embed the table data into a larger word processed document.

In these cases, you need not bother importing and exporting at all. Instead, just print the report to a file, then read the file into your word processing document. Here are the steps:

1. In Paradox, choose **R**eport ➤ **O**utput, and specify the name of the table that you want to print the report from.

Remember, you can query or sort the table before exporting it to a file, as described in Chapter 8.

2. Choose the formatted report that you want to print.
3. Choose **F**ile as the destination.
4. Specify the path and file name for the report (for example, you could enter C:\WP51\Frompdox.TXT to store the Frompdox file on the C:\WP51 directory).
5. Press ↵ or choose OK.
6. When you're ready to work on the report with your word processor, choose **E**xit ➤ **Y**es.
7. From DOS, just run your word processor in the usual manner.

8. Use the techniques you normally use to retrieve the file you named in step 4 above. For example, in WordPerfect 5.1 for DOS, you could choose **File** ➤ **Text In** ➤ **DOS Text (CR/LF to SRt)** from the menus, or press Ctrl-F5, 1, 3, and specify the path (if necessary) and name of the file (C:\WP51\Frompdox.TXT in this example).

When the imported file comes into your word processing document, you may need to change your margins or reduce the font size to eliminate word-wrapping. You can make these and other changes just as you can in any other word processed document.

Shelling Out to DOS

You can temporarily suspend Paradox and exit back to the DOS command prompt without exiting Paradox altogether. This technique, called *shelling out* to DOS, is handy for using DOS commands such as FORMAT or COPY during a session in Paradox.

Before you shell out to DOS, work back to the desktop if you're not already there. For example, if you happen to be editing a table, form, or report specification, save it by pressing F2. Although this isn't absolutely necessary, it is a safety precaution. If anything should go wrong while Paradox is suspended, any data being edited might be lost. You need not clear any tables from the screen, however.

Next, select **Tools** ➤ **More** ➤ **ToDOS**, or press Ctrl-o. Paradox will display a warning message and the DOS prompt. While Paradox is suspended, and the DOS prompt is showing, you'll need to keep in mind a few rules to protect the suspended Paradox:

- Don't load any RAM-resident programs, such as desktop tools, keyboard enhancers, or memory-resident spelling checkers. Similarly, don't use the DOS PRINT or MODE commands.
- Don't use DOS commands to erase, rename, or change any Paradox objects that were in use when you suspended the current Paradox session.

- If you change floppy disks, be sure to put the original disks back in their drives before returning to Paradox.
- Always return to Paradox and exit properly before turning off the computer.

To return to your Paradox session from DOS, just type the command EXIT at the DOS prompt, then press ↵. Your Paradox session will reappear on the screen as though you never left (assuming you've followed the rules above). If at any time you forget whether or not Paradox is suspended, enter the EXIT command to find out. If Paradox is not in suspension, the DOS prompt will simply reappear—no harm done.

> **TIP** It's a good idea to get in the habit of entering the EXIT command at the DOS command prompt just before turning off your computer, just to see if you left any programs suspended.

While Paradox is suspended, you may not be able to run all your programs, because the suspended Paradox still occupies 420K of memory. If you need more memory, you can shell out to DOS using the DOS Big key, Alt-o. DOS Big leaves only 100K of Paradox in memory while Paradox is suspended, so there's more room for other programs. The only disadvantage to using DOS Big is that it takes a little longer to get back into Paradox from the DOS prompt when you enter the EXIT command.

Summary

This chapter covers the many useful tools provided in Paradox to help you manage files. Here's a summary of the most important points:

- To rename, copy, or delete a Paradox object, use the appropriate option on the **T**ools menu.
- To copy records from one table to another, use **T**ools ➤ **M**ore ➤ **A**dd.

SUMMARY

- To remove records from one table that match records in another table, use **Tools ➤ More ➤ Subtract**.
- To empty a table of all records, use **Tools ➤ More ➤ Empty**.
- To protect data with passwords or write-protection, use **Tools ➤ More ➤ Protect**.
- To view general information about files, use **Tools ➤ Info**.
- To change the structure of a table, select **Modify ➤ Restructure**.
- To speed up often-used queries, choose **Tools ➤ QuerySpeed**.
- To import and export data, use **Tools ➤ ExportImport**.
- You can read a delimited ASCII text file into an existing table using the **Tools ➤ ExportImport ➤ Import ➤ AppendDelimited** option.
- To temporarily suspend Paradox and return to the DOS prompt, choose **Tools ➤ More ➤ ToDOS**, or press Ctrl-o or the DOS Big key, Alt-o.

PART TWO

Managing Your Files

CHAPTER 13

Database Design with Multiple Tables

fast TRACK

- **The one-to-many database design** — 459

   is used when there might be some unknown number of records in one table that refer to a single record in another table. For example, any one credit customer might charge many products.

- **To avoid repetitive fields and redundant data in a table** — 461

   split the data into multiple related tables.

- **When storing related data in separate tables** — 463

   each table needs a common field that relates data in one table to the other. That field should have the same field type and size in both tables.

- **To prevent duplicate entries in a field that uniquely defines each record** — 463

   on the "one" side of a one-to-many relationship, you can define that field as the primary key for the table. You can also use a primary key in any table to maintain an ongoing sort order and to prevent duplicate entries.

- **The many-to-many database design**   **465**

  is used when multiple one-to-many relationships are required among tables. For example, any one student might be enrolled in many courses; and any one course consists of many students.

- **To define a primary key for a table**   **475**

  choose **M**odify ➤ **R**estructure. Move the fields that define the primary key to the top of the structure. Then put an asterisk (*) next to the field type for those fields that make up the key.

- **To define a secondary index for a table**   **484**

  that table must already have a primary key. You can create a secondary index in one of three ways: use **I**mage ➤ **O**rderTable (or the shortcut Alt-s), use **T**ools ➤ **Q**uerySpeed after filling in a Query form, or choose **M**odify ➤ **I**ndex and fill in the Secondary Index screen.

So far, the examples in this book have used single tables to teach and demonstrate the important "nuts-and-bolts" of managing data stored in a single table. In fact, many applications, such as those that manage a mailing list or customer list, only require a single table of information.

But larger business applications typically require several related tables linked by a common field. Determining how to divide data into separate related tables and how to set up the links among them are important elements of database design.

Also involved in more advanced database design is the use of indexes, which are required to create logical relationships between tables. Indexes speed operations involving multiple tables and prevent unnecessary duplication of records. You can also use indexes in single-table databases for a variety of purposes, as you'll learn in this chapter.

Types of Multiple Table Links

In a database with multiple tables, the tables are linked by their common fields. The tables are defined in terms of the logical relationships between matching records, which are the records that contain the same values in their common field or fields. The matching records are commonly referred to as the *master records* and the *detail records*. The table that holds the master records is referred to as the *master table*. The one that holds the detail records is the *detail table*.

Within master and detail tables, four types of links are possible between matching fields: one-to-one, one-to-many, many-to-one, and many-to-many. Each of these relationships is described in the following sections.

One-to-One Database Design

In a one-to-one relationship, each master record is linked to only one detail record. The values in the linking field of both tables must be unique; only one record in each table can have the same value in that field.

For example, suppose that you create a table to contain identifying data about the customers listed in the Custlist table used in the examples in Part One of this book. This new table, named Custdata, includes a BLOB field with a photo of each customer and several memo fields. To link the tables, you include a Customer Code field in the Custdata table and add a Customer Code field to the Custlist table.

In order to link the record in the Custdata table that contains data about a particular customer with that customer's record in the Custlist table, the customer code in that record in each table must be identical. Furthermore, the number must be unique within its table; a customer code cannot be repeated in the table. Thus, the customer record in the Custlist table with customer code 0007 always relates to only one record in the Custdata table: the one with 0007 in that table's Customer Code field.

One-to-one relationships between tables are useful when you need to place a large body of specialized information about each record in the master table in a separate detail table. This is often done in large databases to improve the performance of the master table. Smaller tables with fewer fields are more efficient in Paradox.

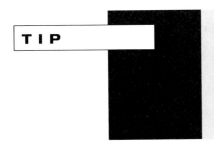

TIP Paradox performs searches, report generation, and other operations more efficiently on a narrow table (one with only a few short fields). Whenever possible, design your tables to be vertical, with many records but few fields, rather than horizontal, with few records and many fields.

One-to-Many Database Design

One-to-many is the most commonly used relationship for multiple tables, because it's the natural relationship for keeping track of business transactions. The one-to-many database design is used in situations where many (usually an unknown number) items of data are associated with another data item. For example, in a billing application, each individual customer might charge several items during the course of the month. In other words, any *one* customer might purchase *many* items during any given month or year.

You could store information about customers and their charge transactions in a single table, but there are problems inherent in such a structure. For example, one way to allow each customer to make multiple charges during a single month might be to store one record for each customer, and have several repetitive groups of fields for charges, as shown in Figure 13.1. This table structure uses repetitive groups of fields—Part #1, Qty #1, Unit Price #1, Date #1, followed by Part #2, Qty #2, Unit Price #2, Date #2, and so on—to allow a given customer to make multiple charges.

FIGURE 13.1

An accounts receivable table structure with repetitive groups of fields to store multiple charge transactions per customer

```
Field Name            Field Type
Last Name             A20
First Name            A20
Address               A25
City                  A15
State                 A2
Zip Code              A10
Part #1               A5
Qty #1                N
Unit Price #1         $
Date #1               D
Part #2               A5
Qty #2                N
Unit Price #2         $
Date #2               D
Part #3               A5
Qty #3                N
Unit Price #3         $
Date #3               D
Part #4               A5
Qty #4                N
Unit Price #4         $
Date #4               D
```

However, this structure is limiting and inefficient. Since a table can't contain more than 255 fields, the number of charges that can be assigned to a particular customer is limited. This structure also makes it virtually impossible to perform queries to get certain information about sales, such as how many charge transactions this month involved part number A-123. Another problem with this type of design is that it creates a wide table,

TYPES OF MULTIPLE TABLE LINKS

which takes more time for Paradox to search through, generate reports for, and perform other operations.

An alternative might be to design the database using a single record per transaction, rather than a single record per customer, as shown in Figure 13.2. But this approach usually leads to a great deal of redundant data in the table.

FIGURE 13.2

A structure with a single record per transaction solves the problem of repetitive groups of fields, but leads to storing redundant data.

```
Field Name          Field Type
Part No             A5
Qty                 N
Unit Price          $
Date                D
Last Name           A20
First Name          A20
Address             A25
City                A15
State               A2
Zip Code            A10
```

For example, even though the Charges table shown in Figure 13.3 contains only three unique customers (Smith, Miller, and Jones), the table uses a lot of disk space because it contains redundant data in the Last Name, First Name, and Address fields (as well as the City, State, and Zip fields, not shown). The person entering data will waste a lot of time retyping the name and address of each customer. Furthermore, if one of the customers moves, that customer's address will need to be changed in many different records.

FIGURE 13.3

Customer names and addresses are repeated each time the customer charges an item, making the table unwieldy to maintain and unnecessarily large.

Part No	Qty	Unit Price	Date	Last Name	First Name	Address
A-111	1	4.99	9/01/93	Smith	Andy	123 A St.
B-222	2	16.98	9/01/93	Smith	Andy	123 A St.
C-333	1	98.99	9/01/93	Smith	Andy	123 A St.
A-111	4	4.99	9/01/93	Miller	Martha	234 B St.
B-222	5	16.98	9/01/93	Miller	Martha	234 B St.
C-333	1	98.99	9/01/93	Miller	Martha	234 B St.
B-222	1	16.98	9/02/93	Jones	Jane	11 Oak Ave.
C-333	2	98.99	9/02/93	Jones	Jane	11 Oak Ave.

DATABASE DESIGN WITH MULTIPLE TABLES

Rather than trying to store customers and their charge transactions in a single table, the data can be stored in two separate tables. Then a single common field can be used to link the two tables.

In a one-to-many design, the common field on the "one" side of the relationship must be unique to each record. Otherwise, there will be no way of matching a given record from the "many" side of the relationship with the appropriate record on the "one" side.

NOTE The common field on the "one" side of a one-to-many relationship is often called the *key field*. The common field on the "many" side is often called the *foreign key*.

Figure 13.4 shows the structures of two tables named Customer and Charges. The Customer table contains a single record for each customer. Each customer is assigned a unique customer number in the field named Cust No. The Charges table stores each individual charge transaction in a separate record. The Cust No field in the Charges table identifies the customer who made the transaction.

FIGURE 13.4

Structures of the Customer and Charges tables

Structure of the Customer Table

Field Name	Field Type
Cust No	N*
Last Name	A20
First Name	A20
Address	A25
City	A15
State	A2
Zip Code	A10

Structure of the Charges Table

Field Name	Field Type
Cust No	N
Part No	A5
Qty	N
Unit Price	$
Date	D

The Cust No field is the common field in the two tables (the asterisk next to the field type code in the Customer table indicates that the field is the primary key, as explained later in this chapter). In this example, the common field has the exact same name and type in both table structures. Although the common fields in each table must be the same type and length, they don't need to have the same field name.

Figure 13.5 shows sample data in the Customer and Charges tables. Notice that, unlike in a one-to-one database design, the detail table in a one-to-many design can repeat the same value in the common field.

FIGURE 13.5

Sample data from the Customer and Charges tables.

```
CustNo  Part No  Qty   Unit Price       Date
------  -------  ----  ---------------  --------
 1001   A-111     1             4.99    9/01/93
 1001   B-222     2            16.98    9/01/93
 1001   C-333     1            98.99    9/01/93
 1002   A-111     4             4.99    9/01/93
 1002   B-222     5            16.98    9/01/93
 1002   C-333     1            98.99    9/01/93
 1003   B-222     1            16.98    9/02/93
 1003   C-333     2            98.99    9/02/93
```

Dividing the information into two separate tables makes handling the database more efficient. The information about each customer fills a single record in the Customer table. Each transaction for each customer requires one record in the Charges table. Only the customer number is repeated in both tables, and there is no limit to the number of transactions that can be assigned to each customer.

Ensuring Uniqueness

Remember that the common field values in the Customer table must be unique to each record. For example, suppose you use the Last Name field rather than Cust No field as the common field. If there were ten people with the last name Smith listed in the Customer table, you would have no way of knowing which Smith made the transaction recorded for Smith in the Charges table. You could link the two tables by both the Last Name and First Name fields, but if you have two customers with the same first and last names—not an unusual occurrence—you won't be able to distinguish between their transactions.

One way to ensure uniqueness in the common field is to assign your own account numbers, as in this example. Businesses that consider that they will have more than 1000 but fewer than 10,000 customers commonly number the first customer 1001, then the next customer 1002, and so forth. In fact, this system limits the table to 9000 customers, but in many cases that is plenty. Assigning these arbitrary numbers in a sequential manner is easy, and it ensures that each record has a unique value in the field.

When you're assigning your own account numbers, try to avoid encoding information into the identifying number. Doing so might make it difficult to ensure uniqueness and consistency in your common field. For instance, suppose you hit on the idea of assigning a customer the number SDC5112, where SD stands for San Diego, C5 stands for a credit rating of 5, and 112 is the customer number. You might have some difficulty in ensuring that your customers in Santo Domingo have their own unique numbers.

Furthermore, if any of your customers move, or you change their credit ratings, their original account numbers are no longer meaningful. If you do change a customer's number on the Customer table, you must make sure that the new number is not already in use. You also must be sure to make the same change to all the Cust No fields in any related tables. This can get to be very confusing and tedious. When assigning identification numbers, it's best to stick to a system of arbitrary numbers.

Another way to ensure uniqueness in a common field is to give each record some value that you know will be unique. For example, your local pizza delivery or video store might use your phone number as the common field that identifies you as a customer. They know that your phone number is unique because no two people in the immediate vicinity will have the same phone number.

On a larger scale, a phone number with area code could also be used to uniquely identify individual records. Similarly, every U.S. taxpayer has a unique social security number, so that field could also be used to identify individuals in a table.

The Master Table/Detail Table Relationship

In a typical database design for keeping track of customer transactions, the master table keeps track of current, ongoing balances, while the detail table records individual transactions that affect those balances. The master table shows the status of things at the moment; the transaction table maintains a history, or *audit trail*, of the events that produced those current balances.

A retail-store inventory database provides a good example. The master table stores one record for each item that is kept in stock and the quantity currently in stock. The detail table keeps track of individual transactions and items sold. Figure 13.6 shows an Inventory table and Sales table with sample data to illustrate the relationship between the master and detail tables in this type of design. Each product in the Inventory table has a unique part number assigned to it in the Part No field. This same field is used to identify the item sold in each transaction of the Sales table. You can clearly see which product is involved in each transaction.

FIGURE 13.6

The Inventory table keeps track of items in the inventory. The Sales table keeps track of individual sales.

```
11/03/93                  Standard Report                  Page   1


Part No   Qty Sold   Unit Price        Date
-------   --------   ----------        --------
A-111        1             4.99        9/01/93
B-222        2            16.98        9/01/93
C-333        1            98.99        9/01/93
A-111        4             4.99        9/01/93
B-222        5            16.98        9/01/93
C-333        1            98.99        9/01/93
B-222        1            16.98        9/02/93
C-333        2            98.99        9/02/93
```

Through a process called updating, Paradox can subtract the quantities of items sold from the appropriate in-stock quantity in the Inventory table. Thus, the master table reflects the true quantity of each item in stock. However, the Sales table (the detail table) continues to track information about individual sales transactions.

Many-to-Many Database Design

In a many-to-many database design, records from one table might be referred to in many records of another table, and vice-versa. In essence, a many-to-many link is like two simultaneous and reciprocal one-to-many links, which define master and detail records in each table.

In a many-to-many relationship, each master table owns its own detail records and each detail table owns its master records. However, in Paradox, a detail table can't own master records, and you cannot nest embedded forms. For these reasons, many-to-many relationships are handled in Paradox through the use of multiple one-to-many relationships, linked through a common linking table. In this way, a many-to-many relationship can be treated as just a collection of two or more one-to-many relationships.

For example, Figure 13.7 shows sample data for Customer, Sales, and Inventory tables. In this example, there is a many-to-many relationship between customers and products in the Inventory table. That is, any given customer might buy *many* products, and any given product will be sold to *many* different customers.

FIGURE 13.7

In this many-to-many relationship, many customers buy many products, and many products are sold to many customers.

```
Cust No    Part No    Qty    Sell Price    Date
--------   -------    ---    ----------    --------
  1001     A-111       1          4.99     9/01/93
  1001     B-222       2         16.98     9/01/93
  1001     C-333       1         98.99     9/01/93
  1002     A-111       4          4.99     9/01/93
  1002     B-222       5         16.98     9/01/93
  1002     C-333       1         98.99     9/01/93
  1003     B-222       1         16.98     9/02/93
  1003     C-333       2         98.99     9/02/93
```

Notice how there are actually two one-to-many relationships in the tables in Figure 13.7. That is, any one customer number might appear in several records in the Sales table, and any one part number might also appear in several records of the Sales table. The Sales table is called a *linking* table, because it acts as a link between customers and products. The only redundant items are the Cust No and Part No fields in the Sales table. But these important fields identify exactly which customer and product are involved in each sales transaction.

A Scheduling Database

Scheduling students and courses in a school is a classic example of the many-to-many relationship. Any given student might be enrolled in many different courses. And any given course contains many students. To schedule students and courses without repeating groups of fields or redundant data, you need to split the information into three separate tables.

TYPES OF MULTIPLE TABLE LINKS

The structure and sample data for a table named Courses are shown in Figure 13.8. This table contains information about each course or each section of each course. Each course has a unique number assigned to it; this is the common field that links specific students to specific courses.

FIGURE 13.8

Top: The structure of the Courses table.
Bottom: Sample data for the Courses table.

Structure of the Courses Table

```
Field Name      Field Type
Course ID       A8*
Course Name     A20
Section         A1
Instructor      A20
Room Number     A5
Hours           A11
```

Sample Courses Data

```
Course ID  Course Name    Section  Instructor   Room  Hours
Alg101-A   Algebra 101    A        Smith        901   1:00-1:50
Alg101-B   Algebra 101    B        Smith        921   2:00-2:50
Bio101-A   Biology 101    A        Jones        123   1:00-1:50
Bio101-B   Biology 101    B        Ramirez      143   2:00-2:50
Chm101-A   Chemistry 101  A        Gomez        534   3:00-3:50
```

The structure and sample data for a table named Students are shown in Figure 13.9. This table contains one record for each student in the school. To identify students, each student is assigned a unique student number.

To link the many students to their appropriate courses, a third table contains one record for each student enrolled in each class. For this example, the linking table is called Sclink, and it has the structure and sample data shown in Figure 13.10.

The Sclink table provides a sort of "map" of which students are enrolled in which courses. This table need only include Student ID and Course ID numbers, because any other information is readily available from the related Students and Courses tables. As you'll learn in the next chapter, Paradox can print the data from these tables however you wish. For example, you could print schedules for individual students or roll sheets for individual courses.

CHAPTER 13 — DATABASE DESIGN WITH MULTIPLE TABLES

FIGURE 13.9

Top: The structure of the Students table.
Bottom: Sample data for the Students table.

Structure of the Students Table

```
Field Name      Field Type
Student ID      A11*
Last Name       A15
First Name      A15
Address         A20
City            A15
State           A2
Zip Code        A10
```

Sample Student Data

```
Student ID    Last Name  First Name  Address              etc...
123-45-6789   Adams      Annie       123 Oak Lane
234-56-7890   Baker      Bobbie      3456 Vista St.
543-54-3418   Edwards    Edie        41 Delaware Ave
555-75-4343   Davis      David       3323 Orange Court
987-65-4321   Carlson    Carla       54 Apian Way
```

FIGURE 13.10

Top: The structure of the Sclink table.
Bottom: Sample contents of the Sclink table.

Structure of the SCLink Table

```
Field Name      Field Type
Student ID      A11*
Course ID       A8*
```

Sample SCLink Data

```
Student ID      Course ID
123-45-6789     Alg101-A
123-45-6789     Bio101-B
123-45-6789     Chm101-A
234-56-7890     Alg101-A
234-56-7890     Bio101-B
234-56-7890     Chm101-A
543-54-3418     Alg101-A
543-54-3418     Chm101-A
555-75-4343     Bio101-B
555-75-4343     Chm101-A
```

An Exploded Inventory Database

Another example of a many-to-many relationship among tables is the *exploded inventory* model. One table, named Products, stores one record for each type of product a company produces. The structure and sample data for the Products table are shown in Figure 13.11. Of course, you can also include other fields, such as the quantity in stock, selling price, and so on. This version of the table just shows some basic information about each product. The field named Needed is designed to store information about the quantities required.

FIGURE 13.11

Top: The structure of the Products table. Bottom: Sample data for the Products table.

Structure of the Products Table

```
Field Name        Field Type
Product Number    A5*
Product Name      A25
Needed            N
```

Sample Products Data

```
Product Number   Product Name         Needed
A-123            Personal Computer    0
B-123            Business Computer    0
C-123            Workstation          0
D-123            Notebook Computer    0
```

A second table, named Componen, contains one record for each component that the manufacturer purchases to create its products. Each component has a unique component number, stored in the field named Component Number. The structure and sample data for the Componen table are shown in Figure 13.12. Again, you might want to include other relevant information, such as purchase price, date of last shipment received, quantity on order, expected date of next shipment, vendor, and so on.

FIGURE 13.12

Top: The structure of the Componen table. Bottom: Sample data for the Componen table.

```
Structure of the Componen Table
Field Name              Field Type
Component Number        A7*
Component Name          A25
In Stock                N

Sample Componen Data

Component Number    Component Name          In Stock
I-80286             80286 processor         500
I-80386             80386 processor         500
I-80486             80486 processor         500
NEC-001             Monochrome Monitor      500
NEC-3D              VGA Monitor             500
NEC-4D              Super VGA Monitor       500
HD-40               40MB Hard Disk          500
HD-80               80MB Hard Disk          500
HD-120              120MB Hard Disk         500
HD-380              380MB Hard Disk         500
FD-350              3.5-inch floppy drive   500
FD-525              5.25-inch floppy drive  500
```

There is a many-to-many relationship between the Products and Componen tables, because each product uses many components, and each component is used in many products. A linking table, named Linker in this example, sets up the relationship between the two tables, describing which products use which components.

Because some products use more than one of a particular component, the Linker table includes the quantity of each component required to produce each product. This information is stored in the Qty Used field. The structure and sample data for the Linker table are shown in Figure 13.13.

Here you can see that personal computers (product A-123) require one I-80286 processor, one NEC-001 monitor, one HD-40 hard disk, and two FD-525 floppy drives. The table also shows component requirements for business computers (product B-123). Using queries, as discussed in Chapter 14, you can use these three tables to answer questions such as the following:

- If I plan to manufacture 75 personal computers and 50 business computers, how many of each component will I need?

- Given that I've manufactured 22 personal computers and 17 business computers today, how many of each component are left in stock?

FIGURE 13.13

Top: The structure of the Linker table. Sample data for the Linker table.

Structure of the Linker Table

```
Field Name          Field Type
Product Number      A5
Component Number    A7
Qty Used            N
```

Sample Linker Data

```
Product Number   Component Number   Qty Used
A-123            I-80286            1
A-123            NEC-001            1
A-123            HD-40              1
A-123            FD-525             2
B-123            I-80386            1
B-123            NEC-3D             1
B-123            HD-80              1
B-123            FD-350             1
B-123            FD-525             1
etc...
```

Normalizing a Database

All the techniques discussed so far for dividing data into separate related tables are collectively referred to as database *normalization*. The goal of normalization is to structure each table so that every field in a table contains some fact about the common field. In other words, if the common field uniquely identifies an individual customer, all the rest of the fields in that record should store information about that single customer, and about that single customer only.

All the sample database designs presented so far are fully normalized. Of course, your particular application might require that you store information that doesn't resemble any of the tables you've seen. No matter what type of data you're managing, you should try to normalize the database by following these four rules of normalization:

- Remove repetitive groups of fields.
- Remove redundant data.

- Remove all partial dependencies.
- Remove all transitive dependencies.

Each rule in this process produces a database design that has achieved one of the *normal forms* of database design. This is a lot of terminology for a procedure that's fairly intuitive. The following sections explain how each rule applies to the examples.

Removing Repetitive Groups of Fields

Using repetitive groups of fields as a means of storing multiple items of information per record makes for a database that's difficult to manage. If you find yourself structuring a table this way, as in the example in Figure 13.1, you need to use one of those groups of fields as the structure for a second table, as shown in Figure 13.4.

Once you've eliminated repeating groups of fields from a table and stored that information in a separate table, you've achieved what's called the *first normal form* of database design.

Removing Redundant Data

Any time a table contains redundant information, such as the repetitive names and addresses in the sample table in Figure 13.3, the table wastes disk space and makes it difficult to make changes to the data. By storing the customer information in a separate table, as in Figure 13.5, you need only change one record if a customer's address changes.

When none of the tables in a database contains redundant data, the database has achieved the *second normal form*. The two-table design in Figure 13.5 has achieved both the first and second normal forms because there are neither repetitive groups of fields nor redundant data outside the common field.

Removing All Partial Dependencies

Partial dependencies may occur in a table that contains more than one common field. In that situation, any information that is not dependent on all the common fields should be removed and placed in a separate table.

For example, the Linker table in the exploded inventory example (Figure 13.13) contains two common fields:

- Product Number, which acts as the link to the Products table
- Component Number, which forms the link to the Componen table

This table also includes the Qty Used field, which is directly dependent on *both* the product number and component number, because it describes how many of each component each product requires.

Any other information given in this example would be dependent on only one of the common fields (either Product Number or Component Number) if stored in this table. For example, the product name would be directly relevant only to the Product Number field. To avoid any such partial dependencies, all information that is specific to individual products is stored in the Products table, and all information that is specific to individual components is stored in the Componen table. When only the data that is directly relevant to all common fields in a table record remains in the table, the database has reached the *third normal form*.

Removing Transitive Dependencies

Finally, the fourth step in normalizing a database design is to remove the *transitive dependencies*: those fields that are occasionally (though not always) dependent on some other non-common field in the same record. For example, in the Componen table (Figure 13.12), where information about components purchased by the manufacturer is listed, you might want to place the name and address of the vendor who supplies the component. However, if a given component were the only component purchased from that vendor, and you later stopped using that component and deleted the record, you would lose the vendor's name and address. Hence, the dependence between the particular component and the vendor was a temporary, or transitive, one.

To avoid this situation, you could store a vendor code in the Componen table and use that to relate each component to a vendor in a separate table of vendors' names and addresses named Vendors. That way, your list of vendors would remain intact, regardless of the components you were using at a particular moment.

An everyday example of avoiding transitive dependencies can be found in the chart of accounts that bookkeepers and accountants use to categorize income and expenses. Rather than making up the chart of accounts as they go along, all the accounts are defined up front, and they are usually assigned their own account numbers.

During the course of the month, individual income and expense transactions are assigned to accounts as appropriate. In any particular month, certain accounts might not be used. But that doesn't mean those accounts no longer exist. In fact, deleting or recategorizing a particular transaction has no effect whatsoever on the existing chart of accounts. Thus, the chart of accounts is not dependent on the transactions that happened to occur in a particular month.

The Fully Normalized Database

Like most theories, database normalization tends to make abstract what is actually intuitively obvious. To paraphrase a somewhat famous quote, the goal of normalization is to have each field in each table contain a fact about "the key, the whole key, and nothing but the key." Multiple-table designs that achieve this goal are designed in such a way that each record in each table contains only fields that describe something about the key (or multiple keys) that identify each record.

When you take away all the fancy terminology, a fully normalized database is one that is easy to manage because the data are grouped into tables of similar information. There's no limit to the number of tables a database might contain, and there are no hard and fast rules that are applicable to all types of applications. A supermarket's needs are different from a video rental store's. A clothing manufacturer's needs are vastly different from those of a mail-order concern.

The noncomputerized, manual system of organizing the information in any one of these businesses is probably already somewhat normalized. The customer information is probably stored in one place, inventory information in another, and sales and purchase transactions in yet another. So don't let a lot of theory confuse you. If you avoid repetitive groups of fields when structuring tables and strive to reduce redundant data in your tables, your data will naturally fall into independent tables that are easy to work with. And that's the goal of normalization.

Using Indexes to Speed Your Work

Dividing information into separate, related tables is one aspect of database design. The basic goal of all this is to make the data as manageable as possible. A second aspect of database design centers around using *indexes* to help a database management system manage data more quickly.

The role that an index plays in a database is similar to the role of an index at the back of a book. When you want to find information about a particular topic in a book, you flip to the index and look up the topic you're interested in. The index, in turn, points you to page numbers where that topic is discussed.

Unlike the index at the back of a book, which you personally use to look up information, you never actually see the contents of a Paradox index. Instead, Paradox uses the index to speed things along on its own.

To understand how Paradox uses an index, you first need to understand how it does things without the aid of an index. When Paradox needs to find a bit of information in a table, it laboriously reads through each record of the table on disk until it happens to find the record you're looking for. This is akin to trying to find information about a topic in a book by flipping through all the pages until you happen upon that topic. Furthermore, on a computer, searching the disk requires moving the drive head, which is a somewhat slow, mechanical job.

A table index, on the other hand, is stored in memory (RAM) when the table is open. It's already sorted into alphabetical or some other order, just like the index at the back of the book. When Paradox needs to find a particular piece of information, it can simply look it up in the index, in memory, without moving the drive head. Once it finds the information in the index, it can move the drive head straight to the appropriate record number on the disk, which reduces disk drive activity and overall processing time considerably.

You can define several indexes for any given table. One of the indexes, called the *primary index*, acts as the main index. Additional indexes, called *secondary indexes*, are used on an as-needed basis to speed queries and sorts. The following sections describe these two different types of indexes and how to create them.

Specifying Primary Key Fields for a Primary Index

To define a primary index for a table, you place an asterisk next to the field type in the table structure. The field (or fields) that you mark with an asterisk make up the *primary key* for that table. The primary key defines which field or fields are stored in the primary index. The primary index for a table is stored in a file that has the same name as the table, followed by the extension .PX.

There are a few rules about primary keys that you need to understand before defining a primary key for a table:

- The key fields that you mark with an asterisk (*) in a table must be grouped together at the top of the table structure.

- All the fields marked with an asterisk in the table structure make up the primary key. In other words, the primary key can consist of one field or several fields. (A key that's composed of more than one field is called a *composite key*).

- Paradox automatically sorts the table based on the primary key, where the first field defines the main sort order, the second field defines the "tie-breaker" order, and so on (see Chapter 6 for information about sort orders).

- Within the primary key field, no two records in a table can contain the same information. If multiple fields are used to define the key, only records that have identical data in *all* the keys are considered duplicates.

The last item, sometimes referred to as the *rule of uniqueness*, can be a real blessing when used correctly, but confusing and frustrating when used incorrectly. The following sections describe defining keys for multiple-table databases and single-table databases, as well as how you can avoid problems with the rule of uniqueness.

Defining Keys in Multiple-Table Designs

In a multiple-table database design, it's always to your advantage to define the common field on the one side of the one-to-many relationship as the primary key, for two reasons:

- The common field that identifies each record must be unique to each record. Therefore, making that field the primary key prevents you from inadvertently entering records that break the rule of uniqueness.

- Queries and other operations that involve multiple tables will go faster if the common field on the one side of the relationship is defined as that table's primary key.

If you look back at a couple of this chapter's previous examples, you'll see that the common field on the one side of one-to-many relationships is indeed the primary key for that table. For instance, in the Customer table (Figure 13.4), Cust No is marked as the primary key, because each customer must have a unique customer number.

So why not also mark the Cust No field in the related Charges table as a key? Because in that table, you *don't* want to enforce a rule of uniqueness. For example, if customer number 1001 charges ten items, you need to enter ten records with 1001 in the Cust No field. You couldn't do that if Cust No were defined as the primary key in the Charges table.

Looking at a many-to-many example, the Course ID field in the Courses table (Figure 13.8) is the key, because each course must have a unique identifying number. The Student ID field in the Students table (Figure 13.9) is the key, because each student must have a unique identifying number.

So you may be wondering why both the Student ID and Course ID fields are the keys in the Sclink table (Figure 13.10). Well, first of all, remember that indexes are entirely optional; it wasn't necessary to make those fields keys. However, building a composite key from these two fields offers two conveniences. For one, it prevents you from inadvertently entering the same Student/Course combination into the table; that is, it keeps you from enrolling the same student in the same course twice. Second, any operations that require getting data from the Sclink table will go a little faster with these fields identified as the primary key.

Defining a Primary Key in Single-Table Design

You can define a primary key for any table, regardless of whether that table contains a single field that uniquely identifies each record. If there is no natural key that uniquely identifies each record, defining a primary key is largely a matter of deciding which sort order you'll use most often and which combination of fields would most likely indicate duplicate records.

For example, the Custlist table used in the examples in Part One doesn't include a customer number to uniquely identify each record. But suppose that you just want to use a primary index to keep records in that table sorted by customers' last and first names, so you don't need to resort the table (using Modify ➤ Sort) after adding new records.

Using **M**odify ➤ **R**estructure, as described in Chapter 12, you could move the Last Name and First Name fields to the top of the table structure, and then mark each with an asterisk to define them as the primary key, as shown in Figure 13.14.

Because Last Name appears before First Name in the table structure, Paradox knows that it should keep records sorted by last name, and then sort them by first name within identical records.

FIGURE 13.14

Marking Last Name and First Name as the primary key fields keeps records sorted by name, but also prevents any two records from having the same value in both the Last Name and First Name field.

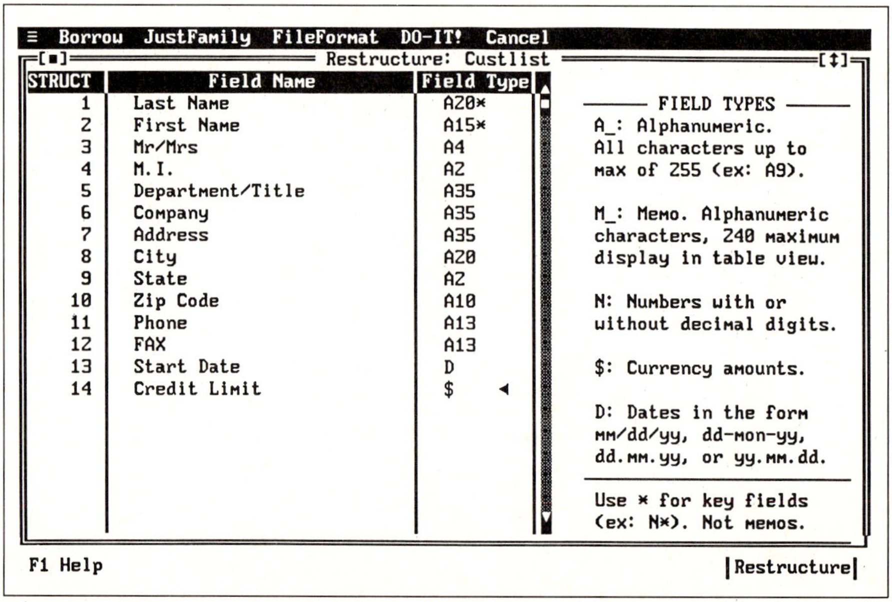

But keep in mind that the design shown in Figure 13.14 will also prevent any two records with the same last and first name from being entered into the table. Thus, you could not have a record for John Doe in Tulsa, and another record for John Doe in Cucamonga within that same table.

So now you need to think in terms of exactly what constitutes a duplicate entry. Perhaps a reasonable assumption would be that any two records that contain the same last name, first name, address, and zip code are indeed duplicates. To maintain your sort order by last and first name, but allow two people with the same name yet different addresses to be entered into the table, you actually need to define the table structure as shown in Figure 13.15.

FIGURE 13.15

Defining Address and Zip Codes as part of the key still maintains the sort order by last and first name, and rejects only those entries that contain identical names and addresses.

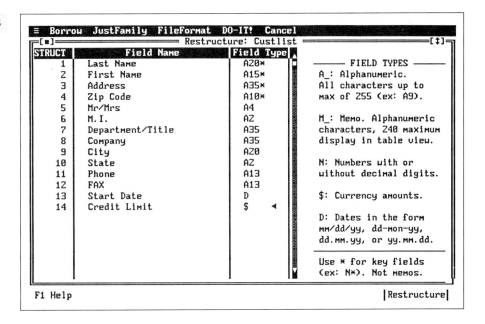

About the only problem with this table structure is that it puts the fields into an order that does not match the order you would naturally use to type information into a record. But that problem is easily resolved by rearranging fields in Table view into a more natural order (see Chapter 5), or by creating a custom form that orders the fields more to your liking (see Chapter 9).

DATABASE DESIGN WITH MULTIPLE TABLES

Now you might think that you can kill two birds with one stone by putting the fields into an order that offers a somewhat natural data-entry sequence yet still maintains the sort order of records you need. For example, in Figure 13.16, the Last Name and First Name fields are at the top of the table structure to maintain that sort order. The Mr/Mrs, M.I., Department/Title, Company, and other fields are in a more natural order beneath Last Name and First Name. All the fields down to Zip Code are marked as keys.

FIGURE 13.16

In trying to ensure a natural field order, this design marks too many fields as keys, and could slow your data entry and editing substantially when the table contains many records.

```
≡  Borrow   JustFamily   FileFormat   DO-IT!   Cancel
=[■]========================= Restructure: Custlist =========================[↕]=
 STRUCT │       Field Name       │ Field Type │
      1 │ Last Name              │ A20*       │     ─────── FIELD TYPES ───────
      2 │ First Name             │ A15*       │
      3 │ M.I.                   │ A2*        │     A_: Alphanumeric.
      4 │ Mr/Mrs                 │ A4*        │     All characters up to
      5 │ Department/Title       │ A35*       │     max of 255 (ex: A9).
      6 │ Company                │ A35*       │
      7 │ Address                │ A35*       │     M_: Memo. Alphanumeric
      8 │ City                   │ A20*       │     characters, 240 maximum
      9 │ State                  │ A2*        │     display in table view.
     10 │ Zip Code               │ A10*       │
     11 │ Phone                  │ A13        │     N: Numbers with or
     12 │ FAX                    │ A13        │     without decimal digits.
     13 │ Start Date             │ D          │
     14 │ Credit Limit           │ $          │     $: Currency amounts.
                                                    D: Dates in the form
                                                    mm/dd/yy, dd-mon-yy,
                                                    dd.mm.yy, or yy.mm.dd.

                                                    Use * for key fields
                                                    (ex: N*). Not memos.
 F1 Help                                                         │Restructure│
```

The disadvantage to making such a large primary key is that it will take Paradox a good deal of time to maintain the resulting index as you add and edit data in the future. Such a large primary key might actually slow things down rather than speed them up.

The structure in Figure 13.15 is better, because it minimizes the number of fields that define a duplicate entry, and thereby reduces the amount of time it takes for Paradox to maintain the index.

Entering and Editing Records in a Keyed Table

As mentioned, the primary key in a table defines the ongoing sort order of a table. When you add new records or modify existing records, Paradox moves the new or modified record to its correct position immediately after you move the cursor off that record. If the proper sorted position for that record is more than a screenful away from the current cursor position, the record may seem to disappear from the table altogether. But you can always use the Zoom option (**I**mage ➤ **Z**oom or Ctrl-z) to quickly locate the record that seemed to disappear.

If you're entering new records rather than editing existing ones, using **M**odify ➤ **D**ataEntry rather than working in Edit mode will prevent this "disappearing act." That's because the DataEntry option stores new records in a temporary table named Entry. When you complete the data entry, the records are then added to the actual table and sorted into their proper positions at the same time.

How Paradox Handles Duplicate Entries

When entering new records into a keyed table, any new record that duplicates the contents of the key fields of an existing record is considered a *key violation*. Exactly how Paradox handles a key violation depends on how you enter the new records into the keyed table, as described in the sections that follow.

NOTE When you use Tools ➤ More ➤ Add to copy new records to a keyed table, or Tools ➤ ExportImport ➤ Import ➤ ASCII ➤ AppendDelimited to import records to a keyed table, any key violations are stored in the temporary Keyviol table. See Chapter 12 for more information.

Key Violations Using Modify ➤ DataEntry

When you use Modify ➤ DataEntry to add new records to a table, Paradox accepts all new records to the temporary Entry table. When you choose DO-IT! to save the new records, key violations are stored in a temporary table named Keyviol.

You can inspect the keyed table and the Keyviol table to see why certain records are being rejected as duplicate entries. Your choices for correcting problems are as follows:

- If the new record is indeed a duplicate, and you entered it a second time by accident, delete the second copy of the record from the Keyviol table.

- If a simple typographical error in the new record is causing the record to be treated as a duplicate, you can correct the record in the Keyviol table.

- If you made a mistake while entering the first record into the original keyed table, you can correct the mistake in that table.

- If the fault lies in how you defined the primary key in the original table, use **M**odify ➤ **R**estructure to redefine which fields make up the primary key.

Once you've resolved the key violations, you can use **T**ools ➤ **M**ore ➤ **A**dd to add the records from the Keyviol table into the original keyed table.

Key Violations in CoEdit Mode

When you are in CoEdit mode (accessed by pressing Alt-F9) and a key violation occurs, Paradox displays this warning as soon as you attempt to move the cursor from the new or modified record:

> Key exists -- press [Alt][L] to confirm or [Alt][K] to see existing record

At this point, you have four choices:

- If you simply made a typographical error in the current record, edit the record to fix the error, then save your change by moving the cursor to another record.

- If the entire record you just added or edited is incorrect, use Undo (Ctrl-u) to undo the change. If you just modified an existing record, pressing Ctrl-u undoes the modification. If you just added the record, pressing Ctrl-u deletes the entry but leaves the record intact. Press Ctrl-u again to delete the record.
- If you're sure that the new record is correct, and want to replace the existing record with the new record, press the LockToggle key, Alt-l. Paradox replaces the existing record with the one you just entered or modified (the original record is deleted).
- If you're not sure which of the duplicate records is the one you want to save, you can press the Keyviol key, Alt-k to switch back and forth between the existing record and the duplicate you just entered. If you decide to replace the existing record with the new one, press Alt-l. If you want to delete the new or modified record, and keep the old one, use Undo (Ctrl-u).

Key Violations in Edit Mode

The standard Edit mode (accessed by pressing F9) is a particularly dangerous one when it comes to adding new records to a keyed table or editing existing records, because if a new record duplicates an existing one, you are given neither a Keyviol table nor any warning of any kind. Instead, the newer record simply replaces the existing record, and the original record is deleted.

Similarly, if you change a key field so that it now duplicates another record, the original record is deleted, and the new record replaces it. Again, you're given no warning that Paradox is deleting the original record.

Allowing Paradox to delete and replace existing records without warning is risky business. So when adding new records to a keyed table, your safest move is to use **M**odify ➤ **D**ataEntry. And CoEdit is the preferred method for editing records in a keyed table, even on a single-user system.

See Chapter 15 for information about entering and editing records in keyed tables via custom forms.

Creating Secondary Indexes

A secondary index is similar to a primary index in that it stores one or more fields from the table and corresponding record positions in memory. However, the role played by a secondary index is much more passive than that of a primary index. Secondary indexes do not check for duplicate entries, nor do they enforce uniqueness. Although secondary indexes do not maintain an ongoing sort order, you can use them to quickly resort a table into a new order via **Image** ➤ **OrderTable** (or Alt-s).

There are basically three ways to create a secondary index: via **Image** ➤ **OrderTable**, via **Tools** ➤ **QuerySpeed**, or directly via **Modify** ➤ **Index**. However, you cannot create a secondary index for a table unless you've already defined a primary index for it.

Creating a Secondary Index Using OrderTable

Image ➤ **OrderTable** (and its shortcut, Alt-s) lets you resort any table that has a primary key. This new sort order can be based on any single field. This option will also automatically create a secondary index to speed up any resorting in the future.

To create a secondary index for resorting, follow these steps:

1. Open the table for which you want to create an index. Remember, this must be a table for which you've already defined a primary index.

2. Choose **Image** ➤ **OrderTable**.

3. Move the cursor to the field that you want to sort the table on, then press ↵. You'll see a list of secondary indexes capable of sorting on the selected field.

As a shortcut to steps 2 and 3, you can first move the cursor to the field you want to sort by, then press Alt-s.

4. If more than one index is available, highlight the one you want. Choose OK. If there isn't already an index for the field, you'll see the options Cancel and OK.

5. Choose OK to build a secondary index.

Building the index might take some time on a large table. When the secondary index is complete, Paradox will display all the records in the table sorted by that field. For example, if you chose the Zip Code field in step 3, records would now appear in zip code order in the table.

Keep in mind that the sort order is only temporary and will be gone when you close the table. The records will appear in their original primary-key sort order the next time you open the table.

When you resort the table again based on the field you chose in step 3, it won't take nearly as long, because Paradox will use the existing secondary index to determine the sort order.

Creating a Secondary Index Using QuerySpeed

If you often need to reuse the same query, you can speed the time it takes to complete the query by using the QuerySpeed option. As explained in Chapter 12, to use QuerySpeed, choose **A**sk from the desktop. Select a table to query, then fill out the Query form to isolate the records or perform the operation that you want the query to perform. Finally, choose **T**ools ➤ QuerySpeed.

If the query searches for a particular value in a field, and there is no index based on the field, Paradox will create a secondary index based on that field. It will then automatically use that index in the future to speed the query or similar queries that search the same field.

If an appropriate index already exists, or if Paradox cannot create an index to help speed up the current query, you'll see the message

    No speedup possible

Creating a Secondary Index using Modify

You can also use **Modify ➤ Index** to create a secondary index. This option gives you more direct control over the secondary index than either OrderTable or QuerySpeed, and is the only approach that lets you define a secondary index that contains more than one field.

To create a secondary index, choose **Modify ➤ Index**, then specify the table for which you want to create a secondary index. The table must be one for which you've already defined a primary index. You'll see the Secondary Index screen, as in the example shown in Figure 13.17.

Fill in the options at the top of the screen as follows:

- **Index Name:** Enter a valid DOS file name (eight characters maximum, no spaces, no extension). Try to provide a name that will make it easy to remember which fields are included in the index.

FIGURE 13.17

The Secondary Index screen appears after you choose Modify ➤ Index.

```
≡ DO-IT!  Cancel
┌─[■]═══════════════════ Secondary Index: Custlist ═══════════════════
│ Index name:                            ◄
│ Maintained: Yes
│ Case Sensitive: No
│─────────────────────────────────────────────────────────────────────
│ Place a number next to the fields to be included in this index.
│ Start with 1 for the first field, 2 for the second, etc.
│─────────────────────────────────────────────────────────────────────
│
│         Last Name
│         Mr/Mrs                        Credit Limit
│         First Name
│         M.I.
│         Department/Titl
│         Company
│         Address
│         City
│         State
│         Zip Code
│         Phone
│         FAX
│         Start Date
│
│ F1 Help                                            |  Index  |
└─────────────────────────────────────────────────────────────────────
```

NOTE Even though the name you give a secondary index must conform to the rules of file names, secondary indexes are actually stored in two tables: one with the extension .XG*n* and the other with the extension .YG*n*, where *n* is a number from 0 to 9 (for example, .XG0 and .YG0 for the first secondary index to create, .XG1 and .YG1 for the next one, and so on). If you have indexes beyond .XG9 and .YG9, the numbers are replaced by letters of the alphabet (.XGA, .XGB, and so on).

- **Maintained:** This option determines whether the index will be maintained as you enter and edit records in the table or only when needed. Choose Yes to maintain the index as records are added and deleted. This can slow down basic data entry and editing operations; however, it speeds up a query or a zoom that uses the secondary index. Choose No to maintain secondary indexes only when needed; such as when using Zoom or a query that searches one of the indexed fields. This choice prevents the secondary index from slowing down basic data entry and editing operations.

- **Case-Sensitive:** This option defines how the index handles uppercase/lowercase differences. Select Yes to sort records based on the current default sort order (see Chapter 6). It also allows for case-sensitive searching within the field (for example, *SMITH* will not be the same as *Smith*). Choose No to ignore uppercase/lowercase distinctions when creating the index. Records are sorted alphabetically without regard to case, and searches are not case-sensitive (for example, *SMITH* will be the same as *Smith*).

Your next step is to deciding which fields to include in the index. This is similar to filling out the Sort screen, as described in Chapter 6. Place a 1 next to the field that determines the main sort order. If you want a "tie-breaker" field, place a 2 next to that field. For a third-level tie-breaker, place a 3 next to the field. You can specify up to 16 fields in this manner, numbered 1 through 16. (You cannot specify a descending sort order in a secondary index.)

Figure 13.18 shows an example of a completed Secondary Index screen. The index, named Zipname, will display records in zip code order (smallest zip code to largest). Within each zip code, names will be alphabetized by last name, first name, and middle initial.

After you've filled in the Secondary Index screen, choose DO-IT! or press F2 to create the secondary index. Now you can use that secondary index at any time without recreating it. After you open the table, move the cursor to the field that the index is based on. If the index is based on several fields, move the cursor to the main field (the one you specified as 1) and press Alt-s. Choose the name of the secondary index, then choose OK to resort the records. For other operations, such as queries and Zoom searches, Paradox will automatically determine if and when a secondary index is helpful.

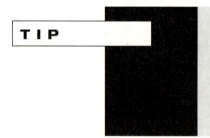

> **TIP**
>
> If you lose track of the secondary indexes you've created for a table, you can use Tools ➤ Info ➤ Family to view a list of all family objects, including secondary indexes, for the table. You can also use Tools ➤ Info ➤ TableIndex to view just the names and contents of secondary indexes for a table. See Chapter 12 for more information.

FIGURE 13.18

A sample Secondary Index screen filled out to create a secondary index named Zipname. This index will sort records by zip code, and alphabetically by name within each zip code.

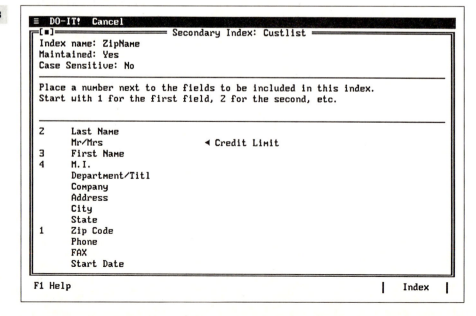

Deleting a Secondary Index

You can create as many indexes for a given table as you wish. However, because indexes need to be maintained, there might actually be more of a performance cost than a benefit to using many secondary indexes. This is particularly true when the table contains thousands of records, and Paradox needs to maintain many secondary indexes as you enter and edit records.

To keep Paradox running at top speed, try to limit your collection of secondary indexes to only those you need most often for resorting the table, looking up a value with Zoom, and speeding up frequently used queries.

To delete any secondary indexes that you don't use often. choose **T**ools ➤ **D**elete ➤ **I**ndex. Choose **S**ingle to delete a single index, or choose **A**ll to delete all the secondary indexes for a given table. Then specify the table that contains the secondary index you want to delete. If you chose Single to delete one index, choose the name of the index you want to delete, then choose OK. If you chose All, Paradox will immediately delete all the secondary indexes for that table.

Summary

In this chapter, you've learned about some of the more advanced aspects of database design. The next chapter presents more advanced queries for managing data in multiple tables and also techniques for using queries to perform mathematical calculations. First, here's a review of the main topics and techniques discussed in this chapter:

- When designing a database, you can avoid repetitive groups of fields and redundant data by splitting the data into two or more tables.

- To relate the data in two or more tables, you need to create common fields that relate data from one table to the appropriate records in the other table.

- In the one-to-many database design, information from one record in one master table might be referred to by many records in another detail table.

DATABASE DESIGN WITH MULTIPLE TABLES

- In a many-to-many design, records from two or more tables might each be referred to by several records in yet another table.

- You can use a primary index in a table on the "one" side of a one-to-many relationship to ensure that each record contains some unique identifying value and to speed operations involving multiple tables.

- You can also use a composite primary key in a table that does not have a field that uniquely identifies each record. In this case, the primary key can help to maintain a sort order and prevent duplicate entries.

- To define a primary index, use **Modify** ➤ **R**estructure to change the table structure, and move the fields that define the primary key to the top of the structure. Then put an asterisk (★) next to the field type for those fields that make up the key.

- You can speed queries, sorts, and other operations that might otherwise take a long time to complete by defining secondary indexes for any table that has a primary index.

- There are three ways to create a secondary index: using **I**mage ➤ **O**rderTable (or the shortcut Alt-s), using **T**ools ➤ **Q**uerySpeed while filling in a Query form, or using **M**odify ➤ **I**ndex and filling out the Secondary Index screen.

CHAPTER 14

Advanced Queries and Calculations

fast TRACK

- **To join data from multiple tables into a single Answer table** — 499

    open a Query form for each table, and use the same *example element* in the common field of each Query form to link the tables.

- **To enter an example element into a Query form** — 500

    position the cursor where you want to type the example element, press F5, then type the example element. To stop typing the example element, move to another column or type a space or punctuation mark.

- **To perform calculations in a query** — 516

    use any combination of the arithmetic operators + (addition), – (subtraction), * (multiplication), and / (division) in an expression. You can control the order of precedence using parentheses, as in standard mathematics.

- **To view the results of a calculation in the Answer table** — 517

    place the reserved word CALC in front of the calculation expression.

- **To use the contents of a field in a calculation** — 518

    place an example element in the field that contains the value you want to use, then place that same example element in the calculation expression.

CHAPTER 14   493

● **To assign a name to a calculated field in the Answer table**   519

follow the keyword CALC and the calculation expression with the AS operator and the name you want to assign to the calculated field.

● **To perform statistical summary calculations on data in a table**   523

use any of the summary operators SUM, AVERAGE, MIN (lowest), MAX (highest), and COUNT.

● **To compare sets of records in one table to sets of records in another table**   535

use a *set query* with any of the SET operators ONLY, NO, EVERY, and EXACTLY.

● **To save a query for future use**   546

choose **S**cripts ➤ **Q**uerySave while the Query form is displayed on the desktop, and assign a valid DOS file name to the query.

● **To redisplay a saved query on the desktop**   547

choose **S**cripts ➤ **P**lay, and specify the name of the query.

Now that you've had a chance to learn some of the conceptual matters of database design, let's look at techniques for getting access to data that's stored in multiple tables. We'll focus on using queries to combine data from multiple tables. This chapter also describes techniques for performing calculations with queries.

Sample Tables

For the examples in this chapter, we'll use a database that consists of five tables, named Accounts, Invoices, Mastinv, Orders, and Purchase. These tables represent a design that a retail or mail-order business with both cash and charge orders might use.

Of course, there are many ways of doing business. So unlike socks and bathrobes, there is no one-size-fits-all database design for every business. But as you look at the sample tables, you'll see that we've stuck to our basic principles of avoiding repetitive groups of fields and redundant data in the various table structures.

The Mastinv Table

The Mastinv (for Master Inventory) table stores information about individual products. Its structure is shown in Figure 14.1, along with a description of what each field stores. The Product Code field is the key field, since each record in this table must have a unique identifying number or code. The bottom half of the figure shows some sample data in the first few fields of the table.

SAMPLE TABLES

FIGURE 14.1

Top: Structure of the sample Mastinv table with brief descriptions of each field. Bottom: Sample data in the Mastinv table. Each product has a unique identifying product code.

```
    Field Name       Field Type  Description
 1  Product Code     A5*         Uniquely identifies each product
 2  Product          A25         Product name
 3  Selling Price    $           Price we sell for
 4  Category         A6          Category of product
 5  In Stock         N           Quantity currently in stock
 6  Reorder          N           Reorder point
 7  On Order         N           Quantity currently on order
 8  Order Date       D           Date last order placed
 9  Purchase Price   $           Our cost to purchase
10  Vendor           A15         Manufacturer's Name
11  Location         A5          Where stored in stock room

Product Code   Product                   Selling Price   Category
------------   -----------------------   -------------   --------
A-100          Gershwin Bicycle                 675.00   BIKE
A-101          Nikono Bicycle                   562.50   BIKE
A-200          Racing Bicycle                   900.00   BIKE
B-100          Nikono Safety Helmet              30.00   HELMET
B-111          Carrera Safety Helmet             60.00   HELMET
B-112          Elsworth Crash Helmet             22.50   HELMET
C-551          Hobie Skateboard                  67.50   SKATE
C-559          Flexie Skateboard                 22.50   SKATE
```

The Invoices Table

For orders that involve invoices, the data is stored in a table named Invoices, which has the structure shown in Figure 14.2. Each invoice must have a unique identifying invoice number, so Invoice Number is the key field. Individual detail items on the invoice are stored with other orders, as you'll see in a moment. Some sample data in the Invoices table is shown in the bottom half of the figure. (The fields not shown are blank in each record.)

FIGURE 14.2

Top: Structure of the sample Invoices table, with brief descriptions of each field. Bottom: Sample data in the Invoices table.

```
   Field Name        Field Type  Description
1  Invoice Number    N*          Uniquely identifies each invoice
2  Account Number    A8          Who billed to
3  Invoice Date      D           Date order was placed
4  Last Printed      D           Date printed (blank until then)
5  Date Paid         D           Date (blank until paid)

Invoice Number   Account Number   Invoice Date
--------------   --------------   ------------
      1001          555-1212         10/01/93
      1002          555-3212         10/01/93
      1003          555-0323         10/01/93
      1004          555-1212         10/01/93
      1005          555-3212         10/15/93
      1006          555-0323         10/15/93
```

The Accounts Table

The Accounts table keeps track of customers who have charge accounts. Each customer must have a unique identifying number, so the Account Number field is the key field. The Account Number field in the Invoices table links each invoice to a customer in the Accounts table. The structure of the Accounts table is shown in Figure 14.3.

FIGURE 14.3

Top: Structure of the sample Accounts table with brief descriptions of each field. Bottom: Sample data in the Accounts table. Each record identifies a single charge-account customer.

```
  Field Name        Field Type  Description
  --------------    ----------  ---------------------------------
1 Account Number    A8*         Uniquely identifies each account
2 Account Name      A25         Person or company name
3 Address           A25         Street address
4 City              A15         City
5 State             A2          State
6 Zip               A13         ZIP code

Account Number    Account Name              Address
--------------    ----------------------    ---------------------
555-0323          RKO Computing             P.O. Box 2212
555-1000          Bob Baker                 P.O. Box 123
555-1212          Rigoberto Martinez        4343 Meadowlark Lane
555-3212          Marsha Riyad              354 Ocean Vista Way
555-3232          Wilma Wangdoodle          P.O. Box 322
555-9999          Andrea Nouveau            333 Third St.
```

The Accounts table could, of course, be divided into more fields, such as Last Name, First Name, and M.I., like the Custlist table. We've minimized the number of fields in this table only so you could see more of the table when we present sample reports, forms, and queries later.

The bottom half of Figure 14.3 shows some sample data in the Accounts table (as much as will fit on the page). We've used phone numbers without area codes as account numbers, on the assumption that all account customers are somewhat localized within the same area code. Over a larger area, you would need to use some other means of uniquely identifying each customer, as discussed in Chapter 13.

The Orders Table

The Orders table tracks individual orders, both for cash and for invoice transactions. The Invoice Number field links each order to an invoice. The

Product Code field links each order transaction to a particular product. The structure of the Orders table is shown in Figure 14.4, along with the first few fields of the table filled in with sample data, to give you an idea of how each order might look in the table. Records that contain no invoice number are cash transactions; that is, they are not associated with any invoice. Some records have identical invoice numbers, because they're individual line items on a single invoice.

FIGURE 14.4

Top: Structure of the sample Orders table, with brief descriptions of each field. Bottom: Sample data in the Orders table. Records with no invoice number are cash transactions.

```
  Field Name       Field Type  Description
1 Invoice Number   N           Which invoice? (blank if none)
2 Product Code     A5          Which product?
3 Qty Sold         N           Quantity sold
4 Selling Price    $           Price sold at
5 Sold By          A3          Salesperson's initials
6 Date Sold        D           Date of transaction
7 Fulfilled        A1          Y if fullfilled, otherwide blank
7 Remarks          A25         General comments


Invoice Number   Product Code   Qty Sold   Selling Price   Sold By
--------------   ------------   --------   -------------   -------
     1001            B-100          1             30.00      JAK
     1001            C-551          2             67.50      JAK
     1001            A-200          1            900.00      JAK
     1001            C-559          5             22.50      BBG
                     A-100          5            675.00      BBG
                     B-100         -1             22.50      BBG
     1002            A-101          1            562.50      JAK
     1002            B-111          2             60.00      JAK
     1002            C-551          1             67.50      JAK
     1003            A-100          3            675.00      BBG
                     A-100          1            675.00      JAK
     1004            C-559          1             22.50      BBG
     1004            B-112          1             22.50      BBG
     1005            A-200          1            900.00      BBG
     1005            B-111          1             60.00      BBG
     1005            C-551          2             67.50      BBG
                     A-101          1            562.00      JAK
                     B-100          1             30.00      JAK
     1006            A-101          1            562.00      BBG
     1006            B-111          1             60.00      BBG
```

One question that might arise with this table is "What do you do with an order once it's filled?" Well, you could just delete the record, but then you wouldn't have a record of the transaction. To avoid this, the table has a field named Fulfilled. As long as the order is still outstanding, you would leave this field blank. But as soon as the order is filled, you can place a value, such as Y for Yes, in that field. So, this table actually keeps a record of both outstanding orders (Fulfilled is blank) and filled orders (Fulfilled is not blank).

The negative value in the Qty Sold field represents a returned item. As you'll see, placing a returned item in the Orders table as a negative sale provides a record of the transaction and also helps keep the In Stock quantities in the Mastinv table accurate during automatic updating (discussed in Chapter 16).

A database purist might argue that invoiced transactions (those with invoice numbers), direct sales (those with no invoice numbers), and adjustments (negative sales) should be stored on separate tables. Indeed, you could create separate tables for each type of transaction; however, there are certain conveniences to storing all these transactions in one table. For one, it's easier to work with one big table of sales and adjustments rather than different types of sales in separate tables. For another, it makes automatic updating a little easier when all the transactions are stored in one table.

The Purchase Table

The Purchase table keeps track of items purchased as they come into the store. Each time a shipment is received, a record of the shipment needs to be stored in this table. This not only helps maintain a history of items received, but also can be used to help automate the process of keeping the In-Stock quantities up to date in the Mastinv table. Figure 14.5 shows the structure of the Purchase table, with brief descriptions of each field. The bottom half of this figure shows some sample data in the Purchase table, indicating that on 10/1/93 we received 50 units of product C-559 and 1 unit of product A-200.

FIGURE 14.5

Top: Structure of the sample Purchase table, with brief descriptions of each field. Bottom: Sample data in the Purchase table, where each record represents an order received into the stock room.

```
      Field Name         Field Type  Description
  1   Product Code       A5          Which product received?
  2   Qty Recd           N           Quantity received
  3   Purchase Price     $           Unit price of item purchased
  4   Date Recd          D           Date shipment received
  5   Remarks            A25         General comments

Product Code   Qty Recd   Purchase Price   Date Recd   Remarks
------------   --------   --------------   ---------   -------
C-559               50             17.50   10/01/93
A-200                1            600.00   10/01/93
```

Now let's start looking at how we can combine data from these various tables to get whatever information we need.

Combining Data from Multiple Tables

Queries are the basic tool required to join (combine) information from multiple related tables. All the techniques covered in Chapter 7 concerning queries still apply here. There are just two additional points to keep in mind when querying multiple tables:

- You must fill out a separate Query form for each individual table.
- You must provide example elements that tell Paradox which field is the common field that links information from one table to the other.

Let's take a moment to discuss exactly what role example elements play in Query forms.

Understanding Example Elements

An *example element* in a Query form plays the same role that a variable, or placeholder, plays in math. The example element holds a value that's likely to change. For example, we can make the general statement:

X * Y = Extended Price

where the example element X stands for any quantity, * means times (multiplication), and the example element Y stands for unit price. Regardless of what particular numbers you substitute for X (the quantity) and Y (the unit price), it stands true that X times Y results in the extended price. If X is 10 and Y is $15.00, the extended price is $150.00.

When used to link multiple tables, example elements play the additional role of looking up data in one table based on the contents of the field containing the same example elements in another table. For example, while performing a query of the Orders table, Paradox might encounter a transaction for product A-100. If the Product Code fields of the Orders and Mastinv tables are linked in a query, Paradox knows that in order to get related information about product A-100 from the Mastinv table, it needs to look up A-100 in the Product Code field of the Mastinv table. You'll see some examples in a moment, but first let's discuss the rules for entering example elements into Query forms.

Entering Examples in a Query Form

Here are the basic steps for entering example elements into a Query form:

1. After positioning the cursor where you want to type the example element in the Query form, press the Example Element key, F5.

2. Type the example element, which can be any combination of letters and numbers and any combination of uppercase and lowercase, but cannot contain blank spaces. For example, X, Y, hello, QUESTION1, and PRODUCT are five valid example elements. Example elements linking common fields in tables in Query forms must be identical, with the exception of case; example elements are not case sensitive.

3. Move the cursor to any other column, or type a space or punctuation mark, after typing the example element.

Here are some ground rules to keep in mind when using example elements:

- You cannot use example elements in memo or binary fields.
- Unlike query criteria and other elements used in Query forms, example elements are always displayed in reverse video or some color scheme that makes them stand out. In the text of this book, we will show them in a special font, as in step 2 in this section.
- You can link up to 24 tables using example elements.

Using Example Elements to Link Tables

Suppose that you want to view a listing of orders from the sample Orders table, but you want to include the part name with each order. The part name is stored in the Mastinv table, not the Orders table, so you'll need to combine data from both tables to get the information you want.

Since you are primarily interested in orders in this example, you need to choose **A**sk from the desktop menu bar, specify Orders as the table to query, then check the fields that you want to see in the resulting Answer table. For this example, assume you're just interested in the Product Code and Qty Sold fields, so you check those fields in the Query form.

Remember, press F6 or click on F6 on the Speedbar to put a check mark in the current field of the Query form.

Because you also want data from the related Mastinv table, you need to put an example element into the Product Code field of the Query Orders form to act as the placeholder for the current Product Code as Paradox performs the query. Remember, you must press F5 to type the example element. We'll use the abbreviation PROD as the example element, so the completed Query form looks like this:

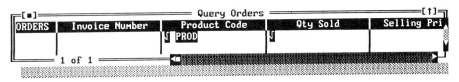

Remember, the example element is just a placeholder; it has no meaning of its own. So you could have used x or abc or HOWDY or prodcode or row1 in place of PROD in the Query form.

Now let's see how you can use the information in the example element PROD to tell Paradox to find matching information in the Mastinv table. First, you need to use **A**sk to open another Query form. In this case, specify Mastinv as the table to query.

Next, you need to put the exact same example element in the Product Code field of the Query form for the Mastinv that you put into the Query form for the Orders table to define the link between the tables. Remember to press F5 before typing the example element. Since you used PROD in the first Query form, you need to use that same example element in the second one. You can check whatever fields in Mastinv you want to see in the resulting Answer table. In this instance, assume that you only want to see the Product (product name) field from Mastinv, so you check that field. The screen now looks like Figure 14.6.

FIGURE 14.6

Query forms for the Orders and Mastinv tables. The example element, PROD, in the Product Code field of both tables defines the common field that links the tables. Check marks indicate fields to display.

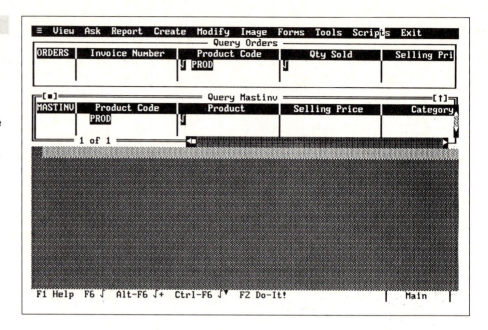

Because PROD is an example element and is identical in both Query forms, Paradox knows that you want matching information in these two fields when you perform the query. For example, if the current record in the Orders table contains product code A-100, Paradox knows that it must find the record that contains A-100 in the Mastinv table when performing the query.

When you press F2 to perform the query, the resulting Answer table includes all nonduplicate records from the Orders table, as well as the name of each product (taken from the Mastinv table), as shown in Figure 14.7.

 We've resized and moved columns in the Query forms and Answer tables in many figures in this chapter so you can better see their contents.

Notice that the Product Code field in the Query form for the Orders table is checked, but that field isn't checked in the Query form for the Mastinv table. This is because there's no need to see the product code twice in the resulting Answer table.

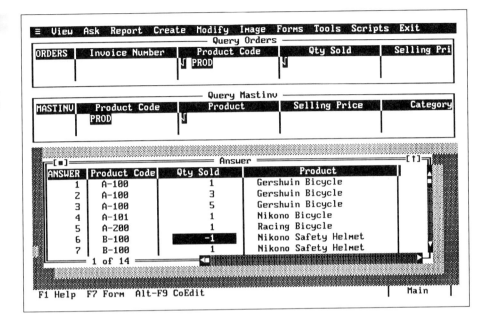

FIGURE 14.7

The resulting Answer table includes all records from the Orders table, with the name of each product "borrowed" from the Mastinv table.

However, there's no harm in checking that field in both tables. For example, in Figure 14.8, the Product Code field is checked in both tables. In the resulting Answer table, the field titled Product Code is the product code from the Orders table. The field titled Product Code-1 is the product code from the Mastinv table. The Answer table in this figure indicates that Paradox did indeed find the product code in Mastinv that matches the product code in Orders, because those codes are identical in each record of the Answer table.

Combining Data from More than Two Tables

You can use the same basic techniques described in the previous sections to query more than 50 tables. For example, Figure 14.9 links four separate tables in a single query.

ADVANCED QUERIES AND CALCULATIONS

FIGURE 14.8

Checking the Product Code field in both the Orders and Mastinv tables displays identical Product Code and Product Code-1 fields in the Answer table, indicating that Paradox has indeed displayed records with matching product codes from both tables.

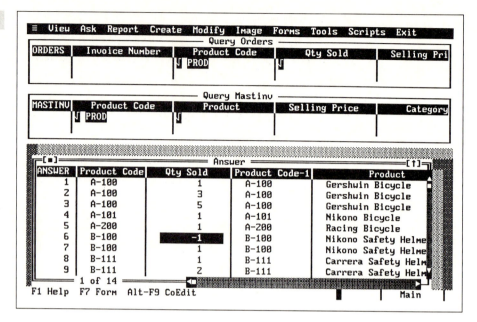

FIGURE 14.9

Sample query that takes data from four different tables. Example elements in each Query form link the common fields among the tables.

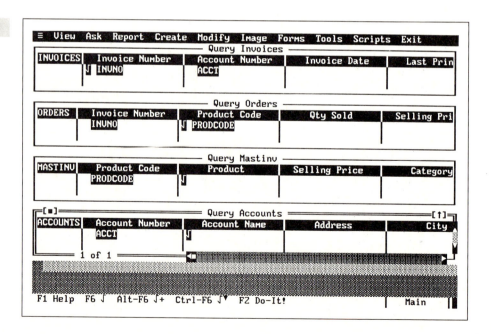

COMBINING DATA FROM MULTIPLE TABLES

The Query form for each table works as follows:

- For the Invoices table query, the Invoice Number field is checked for display. INVNO and ACCT are the example elements.

- For the Orders table query, the Product Code field is checked for display. INVNO is an example element linking the Orders table to the Invoices table. PRODCODE is also an example element.

- For the Mastinv table query, the Product field is checked for display. PRODCODE is the example element linking the Mastinv table to the Orders table.

- For the Accounts table query, the Account Name field is checked for display. The ACCT example element links the Accounts table to the Account Number field of the Invoices table.

When you perform the query, the Answer table contains all the checked fields from all the tables, as shown in Figure 14.10. (The Answer table in this figure covers the bottom two Query forms.) Here you can see which products are included on each invoice, and whom each invoice is billed to.

In Chapter 15, you'll see how to print nicely formatted invoices from these sample tables.

FIGURE 14.10

Results of the query shown in Figure 14.9. All checked fields in all the Query forms are included in the Answer table.

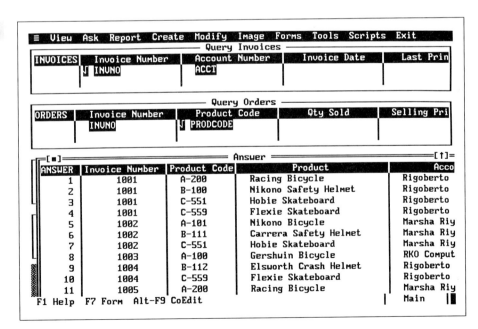

Matching Students to Courses

In Chapter 13, you saw a sample database for scheduling students and courses, with a table named Sclink that lists which students are enrolled in which courses. Using the techniques described so far, you can view a list of student names and the courses each student is enrolled in. The query shown in Figure 14.11 will do the job, as the Answer table in that figure shows.

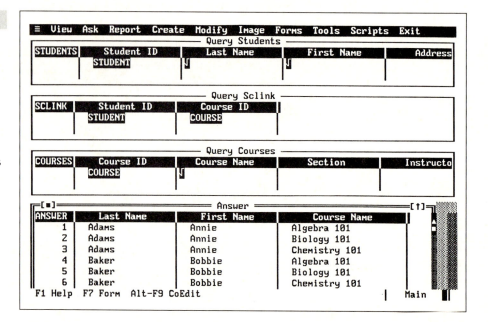

FIGURE 14.11

To list student names and the courses they're enrolled in, use the example element STUDENT to link student numbers, and the example element COURSE to link course ID numbers between the Students, Courses, and Sclink tables.

As you can see, the example element STUDENT links student ID numbers between the Students table and the Sclink table. The example element COURSE links the Course ID fields in the Sclink and Courses tables. Checked fields from the Query forms appear in the Answer table.

When you have multiple Query forms on the screen, the left-to-right and top-to-bottom order of fields in the Query forms determine the order of fields in the Answer table. All Query forms on the desktop are considered part of the current query. It is a good idea to clear all Query form windows before defining a new query. This will help keep Paradox (and you) from getting confused.

For example, if you want to view courses and see which students are enrolled in each course, you need to put the Query form for the Courses table at the top of the screen, then the Sclink table, with the Query form for the Students table below it, as in Figure 14.12. But first clear the current query (using ≡ ➤ **D**esktop ➤ **E**mpty, or Alt-F8); rearranging the Query forms by dragging them into new positions won't do the trick.

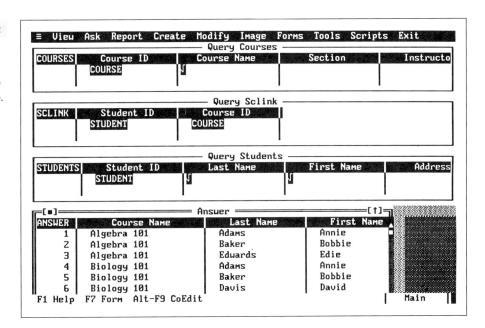

FIGURE 14.12

The same query as in Figure 14.11, but with the Query form for the Courses table at the top.

In the resulting Answer table, Course Name is the first field, Last Name is the second field, and so on. Of course, you can arrange the columns in Table view using the Rotate key (Ctrl-r) or **I**mage ➤ **M**ove (see Chapter 5). Furthermore, if you'll be printing the contents of the Answer table, you can arrange the fields however you wish. So you really don't need to be concerned about the appearance of the Answer table while you're creating your Query forms.

As discussed in Chapter 7, the order of fields in the Answer table depends on whether you've chosen Image Order or Table Order in the Custom Configuration Program.

Using Query Criteria with Multiple Tables

You can add query criteria to any table in a multiple table query, including the various operators such as <, >, LIKE, .., and all the others discussed in Chapter 7. Here are a few points to keep in mind:

- Unlike example elements, you don't press F5 before typing query criteria (that is, unlike example elements, query criteria should not be highlighted).

- If you want to include a query criterion in a field that contains an example element, follow the example element with a comma. This ends the example element. Then type the query criterion for that field.

- If the query criterion is used in a field that's common to two tables, use the same query criterion in the Query form of both tables.

Let's start with a fairly simple query. Suppose you only want to see which courses the student named Adams is enrolled in. You could modify the query shown previously in Figure 14.11 so that the Query form for the Students table displays only those records that contain Adams in the Last Name field, as in Figure 14.13. Because Adams is a query criterion, not an example element, F5 wasn't pressed to type it in; therefore it's not highlighted. As you can see in the resulting Answer table, only records for Adams are listed.

USING QUERY CRITERIA WITH MULTIPLE TABLES

Figure 14.14 shows a slightly more complicated example using the Orders table. Here the query isolates the transactions for invoice number 1001. This is virtually the same query shown in Figure 14.9 earlier, but the query criterion 1001 in the Invoice Number field of the Invoices and Orders tables limits the Answer table to records that contain 1001 in the Invoice Number field. Notice how a comma precedes each query criterion, and the query criteria are not highlighted, to distinguish them from example elements.

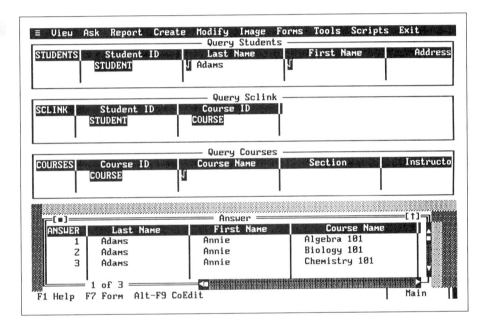

FIGURE 14.13

A query that determines which courses the student named Adams is enrolled in

Figure 14.15 shows the results of the query shown in Figure 14.14. As expected, the Answer table contains information for invoice number 1001 only.

AND and OR Queries with Multiple Tables

AND and OR queries with multiple tables are similar to those with a single table. Their uses are described in the following sections.

ADVANCED QUERIES AND CALCULATIONS

FIGURE 14.14

A multiple table query that limits the Answer table to records that have the number 1001 in the Invoice Number field of the Invoices and Orders tables

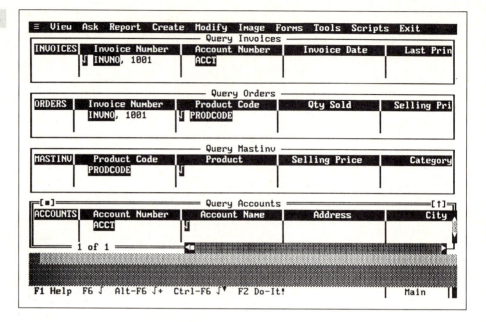

FIGURE 14.15

Results of the query shown in Figure 14.14. Only records for invoice number 1001 are included in the Answer table.

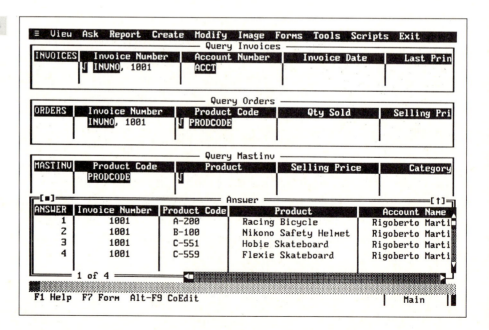

Multiple Table AND Queries

For an AND query, place the query criteria on the same line of the Query form. As with a single table, you can add as many criteria as you want. For example, in Figure 14.15 (shown earlier), the query asks for records that have 1001 in the Invoice Number field of the Invoices table and 1001 in the Invoice Number field of the Orders table.

Even if you use different fields on different Query forms, the relationship among the queries is still treated as an AND. For example, let's suppose you want to know how many bikes salesperson BBG has sold. First, you would use Ask and set up a query to isolate orders for that salesperson, by putting BBG in the Sold By field, as below:

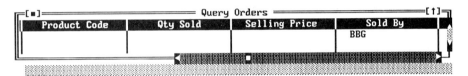

To limit the display of transactions to sales of bikes, open a Query form for the Mastinv table, then set up a link between the two tables, using PROD as an example element in the Product Code field of each table. Also check the fields you want to view, and put the query criterion BIKE in the Category field of the Mastinv table, as shown in Figure 14.16.

Because both BBG and BIKE are on the first row of their respective Query forms, Paradox will interpret the query as requesting records that have BBG in the Sold By field of the Orders table, *and* BIKE in the Category field of the Mastinv table. The Answer table, as you can see in the figure, contains exactly those records.

Multiple Table OR Queries

OR queries involving a single field can be handled with the usual OR operator. For example, the query in Figure 14.17 displays records for salesperson BBG that have either BIKE *or* SKATE in the Category field of the Mastinv table.

FIGURE 14.16

A multiple table query that asks for transactions involving salesperson BBG and products in the BIKE category. PROD is the example element that links the Product Code fields of the two tables.

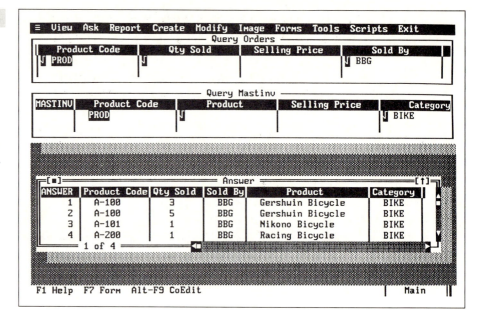

FIGURE 14.17

A multiple table query that asks for transactions involving salesperson BBG *and* products in either the BIKE or SKATE category of the Mastinv table

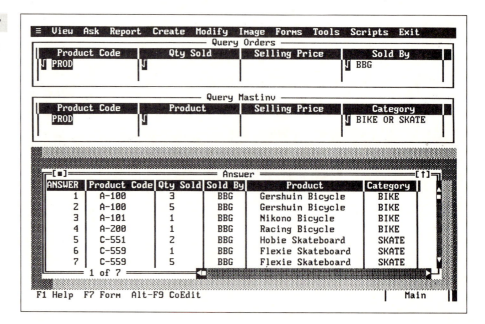

USING QUERY CRITERIA WITH MULTIPLE TABLES

If you need to ask OR questions with separate tables, you need to "stack" them onto separate lines in the Query forms. Keep the following two points in mind:

- Each "question" (row) in each Query form should have its own linking example element. For example, if there are two questions involved, you'll need two pairs of matching example elements.
- The check marks in each row of each Query form should correspond in each Query form.

For example, in Figure 14.18, the example element QUESTION1 links the first row of the top Query form to the first row of the Query form below it. Then a different example element, QUESTION2, links the second row of each Query form. The check marks in both rows of both Query forms correspond.

Because BBG is on the first row of the Query form for the Orders table and BIKE is on the second row of the Query form for the Mastinv table, the two are treated as two separate questions. That is, the resulting Answer table contains records that have BBG in the Sold By field (regardless of category), and also contains records that have BIKE in the Category field (regardless of salesperson).

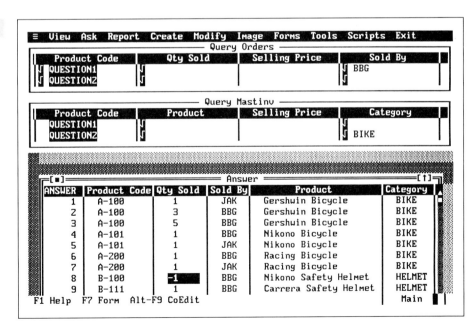

FIGURE 14.18

A query that asks for records with BBG in the Sold By field (regardless of category), or with BIKE in the Category field (regardless of salesperson)

Displaying Nonmatching Records

Usually when you create a query that displays data from two or more tables, Paradox displays only records that have matching values in the two tables. For example, the query in Figure 14.19 displays records from the Orders and Invoices tables. INVNO is the example element linking the two tables; the Invoice Number, Product Code, Qty Sold, and Account Number fields are checked for display. The Answer table contains the results of the query.

As you may recall, the Orders table also contains records of prepaid orders. In those records, the Invoice Number field is left blank. Those records are excluded from the Answer table in Figure 14.19. Why? Because when Paradox is performing the query, the INVNO example element represents a blank when it's processing a record with an empty Invoice Number field. Since there is no corresponding blank value in the Invoice Number field of the Invoices table, Paradox just leaves out the record altogether.

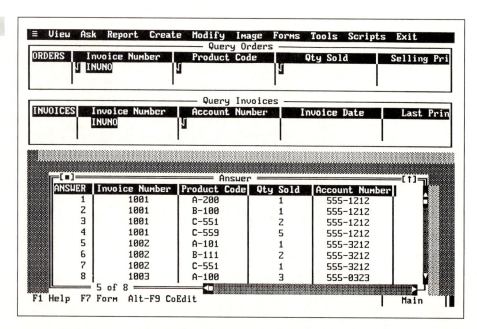

FIGURE 14.19

The Answer table includes invoice number, product code, and other information, but does not include records that have no invoice number.

DISPLAYING NONMATCHING RECORDS

But suppose you do want to see both invoiced and prepaid orders in the Answer table in this query. That is, you want to see the account number if there is an invoice involved, but you also want to see prepaid orders.

To get that information, you need to do what's called an *outer join*. You use the inclusion operator ! (exclamation point) to do so. The inclusion operator must follow the example element, and there should be no blank spaces between the example element and the operator.

Figure 14.20 shows how you would do this. Placing an exclamation point after the INVNO example element in the Orders table tells Paradox that you want every record from the Orders table to be listed in the Answer table, whether or not there's a corresponding invoice number in the Invoices table. As you can see in the figure, the resulting Answer table now includes all the records from the Orders table, including those with blank Invoice Number fields.

Remember, Paradox processes multiple Query forms in the order in which they are placed on the desktop. The inclusion operator works by passing through to the next Query form records which would normally be excluded by query criteria. It is important that you place the inclusion operator in the correct Query form. Placing Query forms on the desktop in

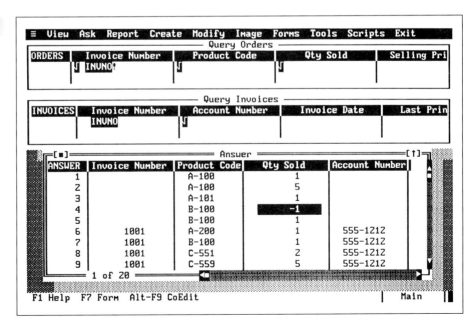

FIGURE 14.20

The inclusion operator (!) tells Paradox to display all the records from the Orders table, even if there are no matching records in the Invoices table.

the correct order is important in many queries, but especially in those involving an outer join.

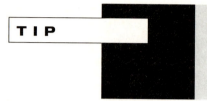

TIP Because the inclusion operator includes records that have no matching records in a linked table, it can help you find any mistakes you may have made while typing data into common fields.

In summary, the basic technique for joining data from multiple related tables into a single table is to link the common fields that relate the tables through identical example elements. As with single-table queries, you can still check the fields you want to view in the Answer table and enter query criteria to define which records to include in the Answer table.

Let's turn our attention away from multiple table queries for a moment, and look at an entirely different aspect of using queries: performing mathematical calculations. As you'll see, this capability is useful both for single table and multiple table queries.

Using Queries to Perform Calculations

There are a few different ways to perform calculations in queries. But all involve typing in some expression using any combination of the following arithmetic operators:

OPERATOR	FUNCTION
+	Addition
–	Subtraction
*	Multiplication
/	Division
( )	Grouping

NOTE You can also use reports and forms to perform calculations, as described in the next chapter.

All Paradox calculations follow the standard order of precedence to calculate a result. That is, multiplication and division are performed before addition and subtraction. As an example, suppose that you used the simple expression

10 + 5 * 2

Because the multiplication is performed before the addition, the result of this expression is 20: five times two, plus ten.

As in standard math, you can use parentheses to override the standard order of precedence. Any portion of a calculation that is enclosed in parentheses always takes place first. Thus, the result of this expression

(10 + 5) * 2

is 30, because the addition within parentheses is calculated first: ten plus five, which is fifteen, times two.

In Chapter 7, you saw how to use arithmetic operators in queries to locate records that fall within a range of dates. By subtracting a number of days from the TODAY operator, you can isolate records that fall within a range of dates in relation to the current date. For example, the query below isolates records in the Invoices table with invoice dates more than 90 days old.

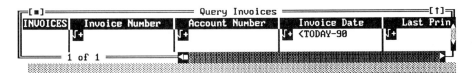

Using CALC to Display Calculation Results

If you want to display the results of a calculation in the Answer table of a query, you need to use the reserved word CALC. CALC displays the result of the expression in a new field in the Answer table. Unless you use the AS operator to name the field (as discussed in a moment), the field takes the calculation expression as its name.

NOTE Although reserved words and operators are shown in all uppercase letters in the text of this book, you can type them in uppercase, lowercase, or a combination of the two.

Using example elements with calculations lets you display the results of calculations of two or more fields, add a constant to a field, or project "what-if" situations. To enter example elements for calculations, use the same basic technique used for linking tables: press F5, type the example element, then type a space or a punctuation mark or move the cursor to another field.

For example, the Orders table has a Qty Sold field and a Selling Price field. To calculate the extended price of each transaction, you need to calculate the quantity times the selling price in each record. To perform the calculations, set up a Query form for the Orders table as in Figure 14.21. QTY and PRICE are example elements, entered with the usual F5 key. Next to the PRICE example element (followed by a comma and blank space) is the expression to multiply the quantity by the price. In this query, a check plus rather than a plain check is used to ensure that records with identical quantities and selling prices are included in the Answer table and not discarded as duplicates.

When you perform the query, Paradox puts the value in the current record's Qty Sold field into the QTY example element, and puts the value in the current record's Selling Price field into the PRICE example element. Then it performs the calculation QTY times PRICE. The end result is a new field that includes the extended price of each transaction, as the Answer table in the figure shows.

How Paradox Calculates Blank Fields

By default, if any field in a calculation is blank in a given record, the calculation will be performed as though that field contained a zero. For example, if either the Qty Sold or Selling Price field were empty in one of the records shown in Figure 14.21, the result of the calculation would

FIGURE 14.21

The total sales price calculated using example elements and CALC

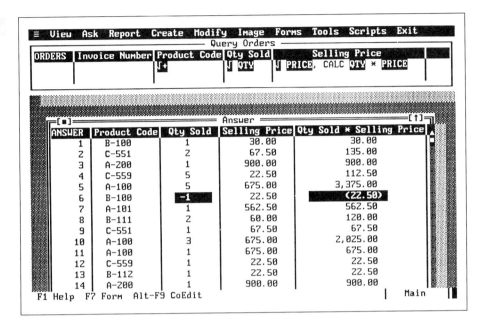

show a zero (since any number times zero is zero). In an addition calculation the blank field will simply add nothing to the total; that is 60 + empty field = 60 + 0 = 60 in the Answer table's calculated field.

If you prefer, you can have Paradox treat blank fields as blanks, in which case any blank field included in a calculation causes the calculated field in the Answer table to be blank. For example, 60 + blank field = blank field. You use the Paradox Custom Configuration Program to change this default, as explained in Appendix D.

Renaming Calculated Fields

Notice in Figure 14.21 that the last column in the Answer table is named Qty Sold * Selling Price. Paradox automatically uses the names of fields involved in the calculation when naming the new field in the Answer table. As an alternative, you can assign your own name to the new calculated field using the AS operator. Giving a calculated field its own name in the Answer table can be useful when you're going to perform another query on the Answer table or use the Answer table to create a report format, as you'll learn later.

Advanced Queries and Calculations

To see how you would use the AS operator in a Query form, take a look at the query in Figure 14.22. In this example, which again uses the Orders table, the example element X has been assigned to the Qty Sold field, and the example element Y has been assigned to the Selling Price field. The Y is then followed by a comma, a space, and the expression

CALC X * Y AS Extended

where X and Y are example elements. That expression is followed by another comma, a space, and the expression

CALC X * Y * 1.0775 AS Total

The result of the first calculation is shown in the field named Extended in the Answer table. The result of the second expression, which adds 7.75 percent sales tax to the quantity times the unit price, is shown in the field named Total in the Answer table.

NOTE If you want to use multiple CALC expressions in a field of the Query form, just separate each CALC expression with a comma, as in this example.

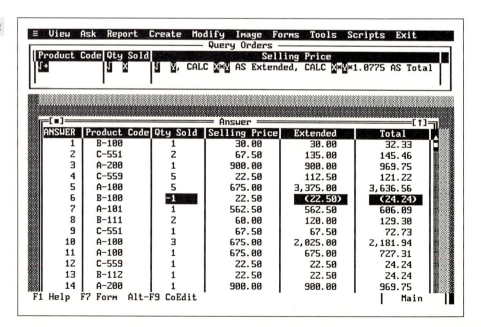

FIGURE 14.22

The extended price (Qty Sold times Selling Price) is displayed in the column named Extended. The extended price with 7.75% sales tax added is displayed in the field named Total in the Answer table.

You can place CALC in any field of the Query form, even one that is not used directly in the calculation. Because the calculated field is always displayed in the results of a query, it need not be checked.

Calculated fields are always placed at the right of the Answer table, after all regular fields checked for inclusion. Multiple calculated fields are placed, from left to right, in the order in which the CALC commands are placed in the Query form. You can rotate these fields to the desired order once the Answer table has been created.

Calculations Using Fields from Multiple Tables

You can also use a field from another table in a calculation. Figure 14.23 shows a sample query where the example element PROD is used to link the Orders and Mastinv tables on the common Product Code field. The example element QTY acts as the placeholder for the Qty Sold field in the Orders table; the example element COST acts the placeholder for the Purchase Price field in the Mastinv table. The expression

    CALC QTY * COST AS Cost Goods

displays the total cost of goods sold.

FIGURE 14.23

A query using two tables to perform a calculation

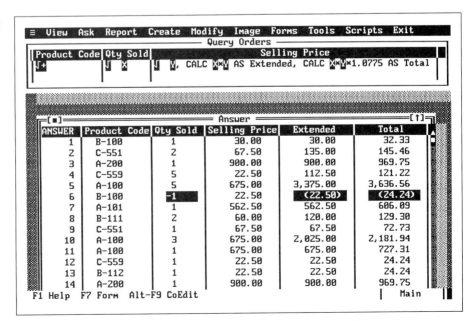

Fields in the Query forms for the Orders and Mastinv tables are resized and rotated in Figure 14.23 so that you can see the contents of the fields used.

Here again you can see that once you've used example elements to link the common fields of two tables, performing the calculation is basically the same as performing the calculation in a single table. That is, even though the COST value comes from the Mastinv table, you can still use that example element in a CALC expression in the Query form for the Orders table.

Using Calculations to Increase or Decrease Values

You can use example elements and arithmetic operators with the reserved word CHANGETO to globally change the value in some field (see Chapter 7 for details on using CHANGETO). For example, suppose you want to increase the selling price of all bikes in the Mastinv table by 15 percent. Here's a query that will do the job:

Notice that the Query form is for the Mastinv table. CURRENT is an example element that holds the current selling price for each record. The calculation

CHANGETO CURRENT * 1.15

multiplies the current price by 1.15 (increases the current price by 15 percent). Because the Category field contains the word BIKE, only records that have the word BIKE in that field will be affected by the query. (Omitting the BIKE query criterion would cause the query to increase the selling price of *every* record in the table by 15 percent.)

As with any CHANGETO query, original copies of records that were changed during the query appear in the temporary Changed table; the actual changes take place in the original table, Mastinv in this example.

Performing Summary Calculations in Queries

You can perform statistical and summary calculations on table data using the summary operators listed in Table 14.1. As with the arithmetic operators, you can use these either with or without CALC in a query.

TABLE 14.1: Summary Operators Used for Performing Calculations in Queries

OPERATOR	CALCULATION	FIELD TYPES	DEFAULT GROUPING
SUM	Total of values	N, $, S	ALL
AVERAGE	Average of values	N, $, S, D	ALL
MAX	Highest value	A, N, $, S, D	UNIQUE
MIN	Lowest value	A, N, $, S, D	UNIQUE
COUNT	Number of values	A, N, $, S, D	UNIQUE

TIP If you need a quick listing of all the Query form operators, just press the Help key, F1, while creating your own queries.

Notice that not all the summary operators can be used with all field types. The SUM operator works only with the typical numeric data types, as these are the only ones that make sense to sum. The AVERAGE operator can handle, in addition to the typical numeric field types, the date field type, since Paradox can determine an average date from a range of dates.

The MAX, MIN, and COUNT operators can additionally handle alphanumeric data, since Paradox can find the smallest (for example, *aardvark*) and largest (for example, *zzyxx*) text values, and can also easily count how many values there are (such as how many Smiths).

The default grouping for a summary operator determines whether it normally includes all values in a field, including duplicates, or whether it weeds out the duplicates. As you'll see in a moment, you can override the default grouping of a summary operator by using the ALL or UNIQUE keywords in the Query form, and by using check marks.

You can't use any of the summary operators with memo or binary fields.

To understand how the default grouping might affect the outcome of a summary calculation, suppose you have a table with 30 records and an Invoice Date field. Of those 30 records, 1 contains the date 1/15/94, 1 contains 1/31/94, and 28 contain 1/1/94.

If you used CALC AVERAGE in a Query form to calculate the "average" date in all those records, the result would be 1/1/94, because the preponderance of 1/1/94 dates would skew the average toward that date. However, if you used CALC AVERAGE UNIQUE, Paradox would treat all the 1/1/94 dates as one unique value; it would not include the 27 duplicates in its calculation. The resulting average date would be 1/15/94. In other words, the average would be the same as if there were only one record with 1/1/94 in the Invoice Date field.

On the other side of the coin, the CALC COUNT operator defaults to a UNIQUE rather than an ALL grouping. For example, suppose you have a large table with thousands of names and addresses in it. If you were to use CALC COUNT in the State field of that table, the result would be no more than 51, since there might be 51 unique states—50 states plus the District of Columbia—in the table. However, if you used CALC COUNT ALL in that field, the result would be in the thousands, since every record, including those with duplicate state entries, would be counted.

Let's take a look at some specific, practical examples of CALC queries.

Summarizing All Records

Summarizing a field for all the records of a table is one of the most common applications of summary operators. When you want to include all the records in a table in summary calculations, just don't check any fields in the Query form.

For example, let's go back to the sample Custlist table. This table, as you may recall, includes a Credit Limit field. Now suppose you want to know just how much total credit you're extending to all your customers by summing all the credit limits. You also want to know what the average, highest, and lowest credit limits are. The query shown in Figure 14.24 gives you the answers to all those questions, as you can see in the Answer table in that figure.

NOTE Some of the columns in the resulting Answer table were narrowed so you could see all of them, but each actually contains the field name Credit Limit fully spelled out.

FIGURE 14.24

The sum, average, lowest, and highest credit limits in the Custlist table

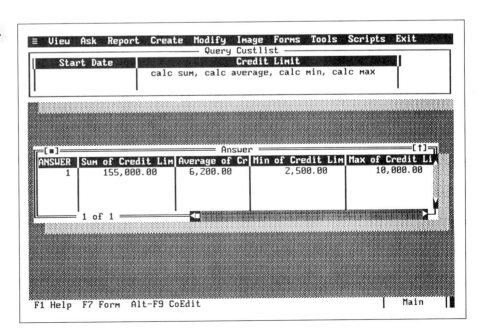

Notice in Figure 14.24 that each CALC expression results in a new field in the Answer table. Each starts with the name of the summary operator followed by *of* and the field name, as in Sum of Credit Limit, Average of Credit Limit, and so on. Even though the Query form contains no checked fields, the summary calculations are still displayed, because CALC always displays its result in the Answer table.

If you had used the COUNT summary operator in the query shown in Figure 14.24, you would need to use the ALL qualifier to get a count of all the customers who have credit limits. CALC COUNT without ALL will count the number of unique values in the field, not all the records that have a value.

The summary operators ignore the setting of Blank=Zero in the Custom Configuration Program. Summary operators always treat a blank value as a blank and do not include it in the summary. This is especially important to note when using the AVERAGE and COUNT summary operators. For example, if a table has four records with the following values: 100, 100, blank, and 100, AVERAGE will average the three records with a nonblank value and report an average value of 100. However, for the same fields with the values: 100, 100, 0, and 100, AVERAGE will average all four records and report an average of 75.

Calculations on Groups of Records

Using check marks in fields of interest with summary operators has a different effect than in other queries. Not only does it ensure that the field is displayed, but it also groups identical values in the checked field (or fields) so that summary calculations are performed separately on each group.

For example, look at the Query form in Figure 14.25, which is based on our sample Orders table. The check mark in the Product Code field tells Paradox that calculations should be based on groups of like products. CALC SUM in the Qty Sold field indicates that the values in the Qty Sold field should be totaled for each product. The resulting Answer table displays the total units sold of each product.

PERFORMING SUMMARY CALCULATIONS IN QUERIES

FIGURE 14.25

The sum of the Qty Sold field for each product

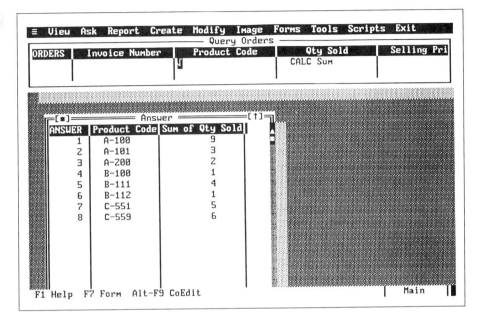

Checking multiple fields in a CALC query will break down the resulting calculations into even more groups. For example, in Figure 14.26, both the Product Code and Sold By fields are checked. CALC SUM is again placed in the Qty Sold field. The resulting Answer table shows the quantity of each item sold by each salesperson. That is, salesperson BBG has sold 8 units of product A-100, salesperson JAK has sold 1 unit of product A-100, and so on.

Frequency Distributions

The CALC COUNT ALL expression combined with a checked field (or fields) provides a quick and easy frequency distribution. For example, the query in Figure 14.27 is based on the Custlist table. The State field is checked for display and grouping. The CALC COUNT ALL expression counts how many records contain each state. ALL is required in this example so that duplicate records with the same state are counted. Omitting ALL would prevent duplicates from being counted, so the COUNT of State field in the Answer table would end up containing 1 for each group.

ADVANCED QUERIES AND CALCULATIONS

FIGURE 14.26

Orders of each part by each salesperson

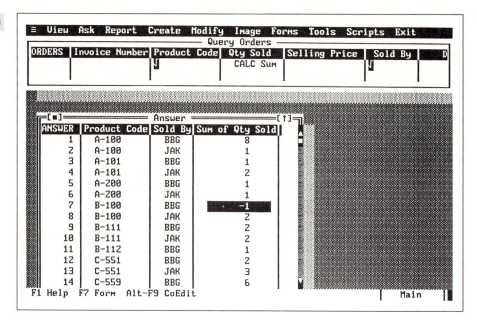

FIGURE 14.27

Frequency distribution of states in the Custlist table

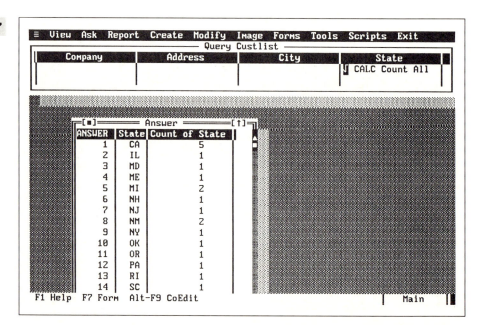

Selecting Records Based on Summary Information

You can also use the summary operators to select records based on a comparison to a summary calculation. To use the summary operators in this manner:

- Omit the reserved word CALC, and use the summary operator in a relational expression, one that uses <, >, =, <=, or >=.
- Check the fields that define the groups you want to compare against the summary calculation.

For example, suppose you want to find out which products in the Orders table have a value of 5 or greater in the Qty Sold field. The query shown in Figure 14.28 gives you that information.

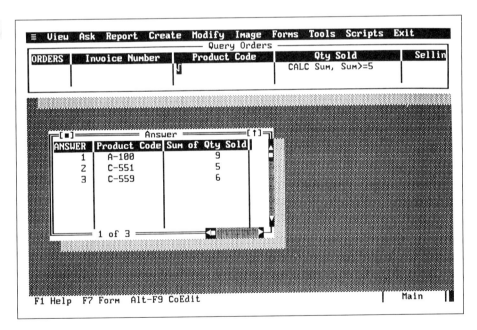

FIGURE 14.28

A query that answers the question "Which products have we sold five or more units of?"

ADVANCED QUERIES AND CALCULATIONS

To better understand this query, you need to break it into its constituent parts:

- The check mark in the Product Code field indicates that you want to perform a calculation on, and view the contents of, values in the Product Code field.

- CALC SUM in the Qty Sold field indicates that you want to sum the units sold for each product. This element is optional.

- SUM >= 5 indicates that you only want to see records for which the total units sold is greater than, or equal to, 5. The Answer table provides just that information.

The CALC SUM in the Qty Sold field is entirely optional in this example. It's used only to display the total units sold in the Answer table. Paradox can make the comparison without displaying the field or using CALC. For example, suppose you want to know which states in the Custlist table have only one customer. Figure 14.29 shows the appropriate query and results.

FIGURE 14.29

A query to isolate states in the Custlist table that are represented by only a single customer

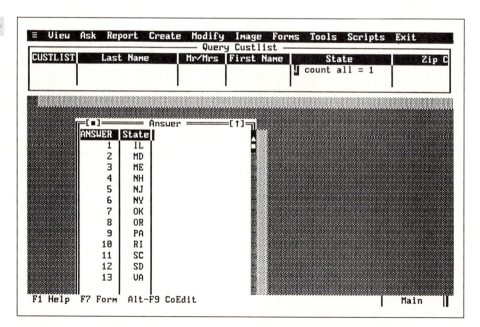

In this sample query, the check mark in the State field indicates that you want to group records by state and display the contents of the State field. The expression COUNT ALL = 1 counts how many customers are in each state, and displays only records in which the count (including duplicate states) is exactly 1.

Here we didn't include a CALC COUNT expression, so there is no field displayed for the count. Nonetheless, the Answer table does display states that are represented by only one customer.

Complex Calculations with Multiple Tables

Chapter 13 presented the basic model for an exploded inventory database, where a manufacturer keeps many different components in stock and produces several different products. The many-to-many relationship is based on the fact that each product manufactured consists of many components, and each component is used in many different products.

To give you an idea of how, with some ingenuity (and patience), you can use calculations to answer difficult questions, suppose you wish to determine the number of each component required to manufacture several of each product. Such a calculation would require several steps.

First, you need to fill the Needed field in the Product table with the number of each product you wish to produce. Figure 14.30 shows an example in which the manufacturer wants to produce 100 personal computers, 50 business computers, 20 workstations, and 20 notebook computers.

Next, you need to create a temporary table that holds all the fields required to perform the calculation. Figure 14.31 shows the queries to create just such a table. The top Query form, based on the Linker table, calculates the number of each component required to produce each product by multiplying the Qty Used field by the number of each product needed. X is the example element for the Qty Used field, and Y is the example element for the number of each product being manufactured, based on the contents of the Needed field in the Products table.

532 CHAPTER 14
ADVANCED QUERIES AND CALCULATIONS

FIGURE 14.30

The Needed field in the Product table indicates how many of each product the manufacturer needs to produce.

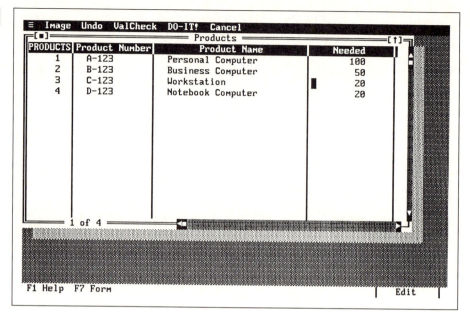

FIGURE 14.31

A query to calculate the number of components required to manufacture several products

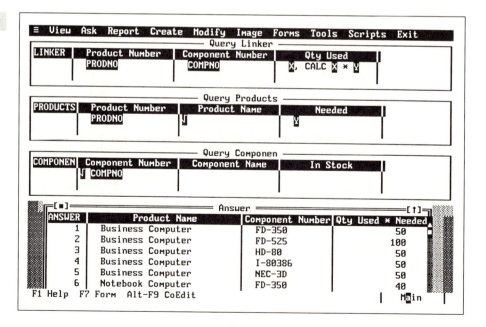

COMPLEX CALCULATIONS WITH MULTIPLE TABLES

The PRODNO example element links the Linker table to the Products table, and the COMPNO example element links the Linker table to the Componen table. Check marks ensure that the appropriate fields will be displayed in the Answer table.

You can see part of the resulting Answer table near the bottom of the figure. The Answer table contains the appropriate data, but it still needs to be summarized a bit to be of real use.

To see the data in the Answer table in a better light, you'll want totals based on individual component numbers. First, you could use **T**ools ➤ **R**ename ➤ **T**able ➤ **A**nswer to rename the Answer table to something such as Step1. Next, clear the desktop (Alt-F8), and use **A**sk to create a Query form for the Step1 table. Then simply place a check mark in the Component Number field to group records by component number, and use a CALC SUM expression to calculate the total of each component required, as in Figure 14.32. The resulting Answer table gives you exactly the information you're looking for: the number of components required to manufacture the various computers (as presented back in Figure 14.30).

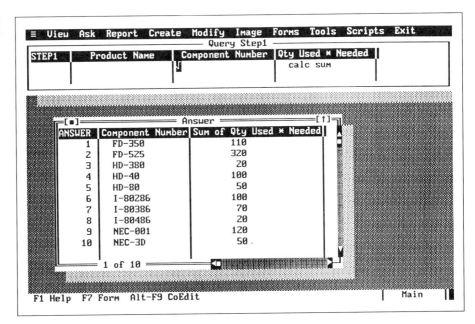

FIGURE 14.32

The totals of components required to manufacture the products listed in Figure 14.30

Asking about Sets of Records

Set queries let you ask questions about categories or sets of records. For example, in the Mastinv table (Figure 14.1), various products are categorized as belonging to the BIKE, HELMET, or SKATE category. With the reserved word SET, you can ask questions about a category as a whole, rather than asking questions about individual products.

To illustrate, suppose that at the end of the year you create a table that contains a record of the quantity of each product purchased by each of your regular customers (those with account numbers). Figure 14.33 shows the query that you would use to create this table and a portion of the resulting Answer table. By year-end, of course, the Answer table might contain many hundreds of records.

After generating the Answer table, you could use **T**ools ➤ **R**ename ➤ **T**able to rename the Answer table to something like YearEnd, to keep its data around for further analysis.

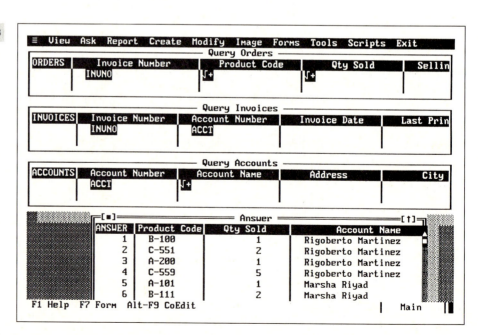

FIGURE 14.33

A portion of the Answer table created by combining fields from the Orders, Invoices, and Accounts tables

ASKING ABOUT SETS OF RECORDS

Once the YearEnd table is created, you could use SET with the SET operators ONLY, NO, EVERY, and EXACTLY to ask questions about which customers did and did not buy products in various categories, as summarized in Table 14.2.

TABLE 14.2: SET Operators Used for Performing Calculations in Queries

OPERATOR	DISPLAYS	SAMPLE QUERY
ONLY	Records that have only values of the defined set	Which customers have bought *only* bicycles?
NO	Records that do not match any values in the defined set	Which customers did not buy *any* bicycles?
EVERY	Records that match every value in the set	Which customers bought *every* product in the BIKE category?
EXACTLY	Records that have exactly the same values as the defined set; no more and no less (a combination of ONLY and EVERY)	Which customers bought *every* product in the BIKE category, but *no* products in any other category?

Figure 14.34 illustrates various SET relationships, using the example of animals rather than products. The group of animals on the left—dog, cat, and duck—could be defined as the set called Pets. The group of animals on the right in each example is another set of animals being compared to Pets. Each example illustrates one of the SET relationships: EVERY, ONLY, EXACTLY, and NO.

Defining a Set

The first step to creating a set query is to define a set. Here is the basic procedure:

1. Open a Query form for the table that contains the records that define the set.

2. Type the word **SET** in the leftmost column of the Query form.

536 CHAPTER **14**   ADVANCED QUERIES AND CALCULATIONS

FIGURE 14.34

An illustration of the various SET relationships: EVERY, ONLY, EXACTLY, and NO

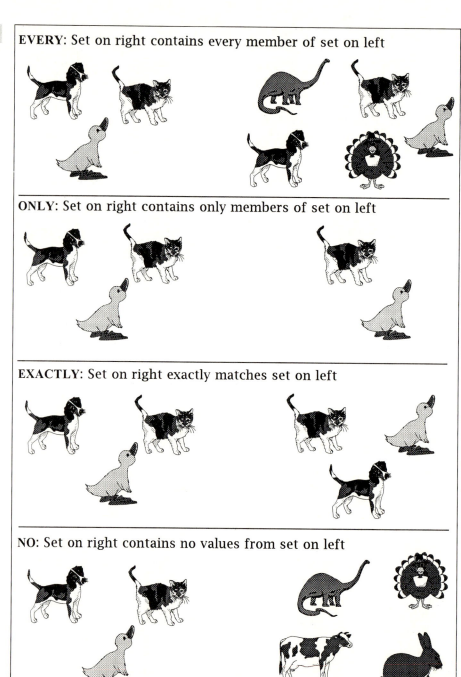

3. Type the value in the field that defines the set. For example, in the Query form below, which is based on the Mastinv table, the word SET is in the leftmost column and the word BIKE is in the Category column. Thus, records that contain the word BIKE are now defined as the set.

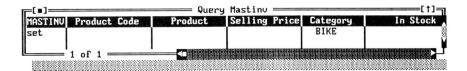

4. Press the F5 key, and then type an example element into the common field that will link this table to records in the table that contains the set to be compared to the BIKE set.

5. Using **A**sk, open a Query form for the table that contains the comparison set: the set to be compared to the BIKE set.

6. Type a SET operator (EVERY, ONLY, EXACTLY, or NO) into the common field that links this new table to the table into the new Query form (from step 5). Follow that operator with a space and the same example element you typed in step 4.

7. Check the field that defines the comparison set (this is also the field that will appear in the Answer table).

Figure 14.35 shows an example, where PROD is the example element that links the two tables, and EVERY is the SET operator that says you want to view customers who bought every product in the BIKE category. The check mark in the Account Name column defines that field as the one to view in the Answer table, and also as the set that you're comparing the BIKE category set to. In other words, the check mark in the Account Name field says "Take all the records with the same account name as a group, then compare that group of records to the set of records in Mastinv that contain the word BIKE in the Category field."

538 CHAPTER **14** ADVANCED QUERIES AND CALCULATIONS

FIGURE 14.35

Sample set query that displays customers who have purchased every product in the BIKE category (and may have purchased products in other categories as well)

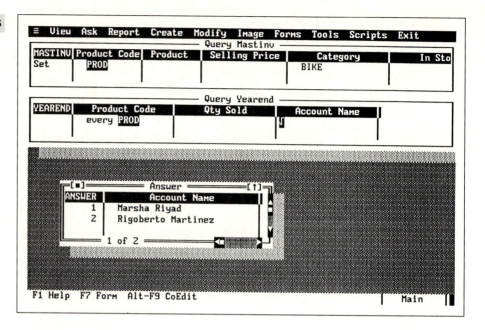

NOTE The results of sample set queries presented in Figures 14.35 through 14.39 are based on a larger hypothetical Yearend table, not one that was created directly from the small collection of sample data presented earlier in this chapter.

The Answer table lists customers who bought every type of bike you sell. (These customers might have also bought products from other categories as well.)

If you wanted to view customers who didn't buy any bikes at all, change the EVERY operator to NO, as in Figure 14.36, and perform the query again. The resulting Answer table displays customers who didn't buy any bikes.

Figure 14.37 shows a modified version of the query that finds customers who bought only bikes, and no other products from any other categories. (These customers may have bought only one type of bike, or several different types of bikes, but they bought *only* bikes.)

ASKING ABOUT SETS OF RECORDS

FIGURE 14.36

A set query using the NO operator to find customer who didn't buy any bikes (but may have bought products in other categories)

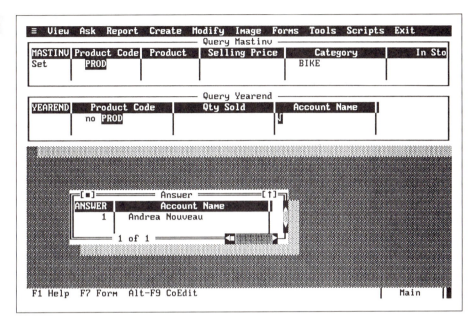

FIGURE 14.37

A set query using the ONLY operator to find people who bought one or more products from the BIKE category, but no products in any other categories

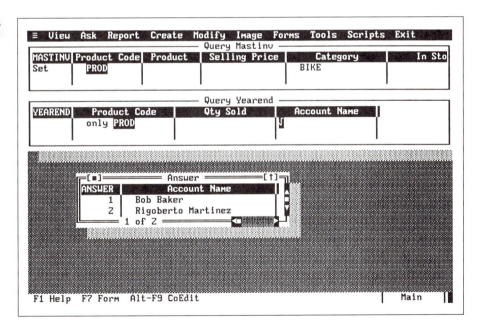

CHAPTER 14
ADVANCED QUERIES AND CALCULATIONS

Finally, suppose you want to see customers who have purchased exactly those products that make up the BIKE category; that is, customers who have bought any type of bike, and no other product. In this case, you would use the EXACTLY operator, as in Figure 14.38.

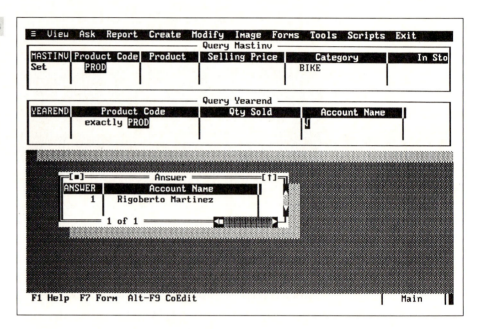

FIGURE 14.38

A set query using the EXACTLY operator to isolate customers who bought every product in the BIKE category, but no products from any other categories

Using the GroupBy Operator

Check marks in set queries with two or more tables play the dual role of defining which field you want to see in the Answer table and defining the group of records for the second set. In some situations, you might not want to perform both operations. That is, you may want to group records by a field, but not display that field. In these situations, you can use the GroupBy operator, G, rather than a check mark in the Query form. Then you can use an example element next to the G to look up data in that field in another table.

NOTE The GroupBy operator can be used only in set queries.

ASKING ABOUT SETS OF RECORDS

To place the GroupBy G into a Query form, press Shift-F6. Figure 14.39 shows an example where GroupBy is used to display the home cities of customers who have not bought bikes, rather than the names of the customers who did not buy any bikes.

You can see the following similarities and differences between the queries in Figures 14.39 and 14.36:

- The first Query form defines products in the BIKE category in the Mastinv table as the first set, exactly as in Figure 14.36 earlier.

- The second Query form, for the Yearend table, contain NO PROD to find individuals who purchased no bikes, just as in Figure 14.36.

- Rather than using a check mark in the Account Name field to define that field for grouping and display it in the Answer table, the field contains the highlighted G for GroupBy. Thus, although Account Name is still the group being compared to the BIKE set, it will not appear in the Answer table.

- The CUSTOMER example element in the Account Name field acts as a placeholder for whatever values would have been displayed in the Answer table had we used the check mark rather than the GroupBy operator in that field.

FIGURE 14.39

Using the GroupBy operator (G) lets you use one field for grouping in a set query, but then display other fields in the resulting Answer table.

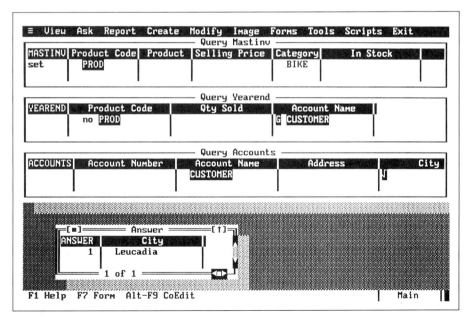

- The bottom Query form, based on the Accounts table, also uses the example element in the Account Name field, linking these two tables by the common Account Name field.
- Also in the bottom Query form, the City field is checked. Hence, that field is displayed in the Answer table.

Comparing Records to Summary Values

In the preceding examples, you saw how set queries can let you compare records in one table to a set of records in another table. You can also use set queries to compare records in a table to a summary calculation within that table, such as an average or sum. You can use any of the summary operators (AVERAGE, COUNT, MAX, and MIN) to perform such an analysis.

Figure 14.40 shows an example using the Custlist table. The first line of the query includes SET in the leftmost column and the example element LIMIT in the Credit Limit field. Because there are no query criteria in the top line of the query, SET defines all records in the table.

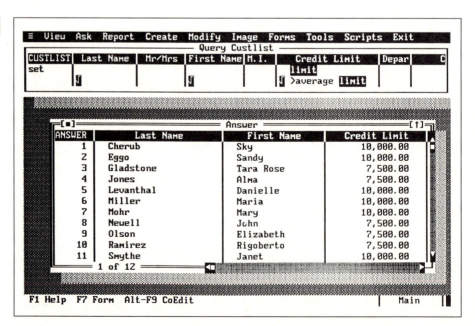

FIGURE 14.40

A set query to find individuals with higher than average credit limits in the sample Custlist table

The second line of the query includes check marks in the Last Name, First Name, and Credit Limit fields, because these are the fields to be displayed in the Answer table. The second line of this query also includes the query criterion > AVERAGE LIMIT, which restricts the records displayed in the Answer table to those that have Credit Limit values that are greater than the average credit limit.

Note that if we had used > MIN LIMIT in place of > AVERAGE LIMIT, the Answer table would display records that have values that are greater than the *smallest* credit limit. Using the criterion = MAX LIMIT instead would display those records containing the *highest* credit limits.

Calculating Percentages

Ironically, with all its powerful calculation capabilities, calculating simple percentages with Paradox can be a complicated task. For example, suppose you want to ask the simple question, "How much does each product in my Orders table contribute to total sales?" You can use a PAL function specifically designed for percentages (see Chapter 15), but there are a couple of techniques you can use without first learning to use PAL.

TIP Remember, you can record any lengthy series of steps in a script, and repeat all those steps in the future simply by playing back the script. See Chapter 11 for information about recording scripts.

One way to find the answer to this question is to create a pie chart, which can calculate percentages automatically. First, use **A**sk to calculate the sum of each unit sold by setting up a Query form for the Orders table, as shown at the top of Figure 14.41. Notice that the Product Code field is checked, and CALC SUM in the Qty Sold field calculates the sum of each product sold. The results appear in the Answer table.

ADVANCED QUERIES AND CALCULATIONS

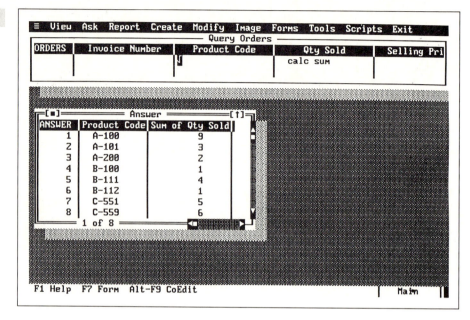

FIGURE 14.41

The Answer table calculates the total units sold of each product from the Orders table.

Next, follow these steps:

1. Move the cursor to the Sum of Qty Sold field in the Answer table.

2. Choose **I**mage ➤ **G**raph ➤ **M**odify then type **P** to choose (P)ie Graph.

3. Choose **P**ies from the Graph Design screen's menu bar, then type **P** once again to choose (P)ercent.

4. Choose **DO-IT!**, then press Ctrl-F7 to see the resulting graph, which includes the percent contribution of each product. Press any key after viewing the graph.

If you need a printed report rather than a pie chart, the task is a bit more complicated. Let's work through the steps, starting with a blank desktop:

1. To find the grand total of units sold, use **A**sk to call up a Query form for the Orders table, and use CALC SUM in the Qty Sold field (and no check marks) to get the grand total. When you perform the query, the grand total appears in the Answer table.

2. Because this Answer table contains only a single field, it won't help much with additional calculations. Instead, just jot down the grand total on a piece of paper, and then press F8 to clear the Answer table.

3. Next, modify the Query form for the Orders table to get a subtotal of units sold for each product. Just check the Product Code field, and perform the query (press F2) to get the results you need in the Answer table.

4. Clear the desktop by pressing Alt-F8.

5. Choose Ask, and specify Answer as the table to query. (Even though you've removed it from the desktop, a copy is still stored on disk.)

6. Place check marks in the Product Code and Sum of Qty Sold fields.

7. Enter a CALC expression in the Sum of Qty Sold field to divide the value in that field by the grand total determined earlier, and multiply that result by 100 to move the decimal place in the answer two digits to the left, as shown below (where UNITS is an example element typed with the usual F5 key):

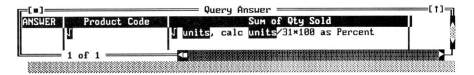

When you perform the query, the resulting Answer table displays the information you want, as shown in Figure 14.42. If you wish, you could press Alt-F7 to print an Instant Report of this table.

Be aware that because the Answer table now contains the data shown in Figure 14.42, you cannot perform additional queries with the data in the previous Answer table you created in step 3. But remember, you can always use **T**ools ➤ **R**ename ➤ **T**able to rename an Answer table, in case you want to use its data for additional calculations or analyses.

ADVANCED QUERIES AND CALCULATIONS

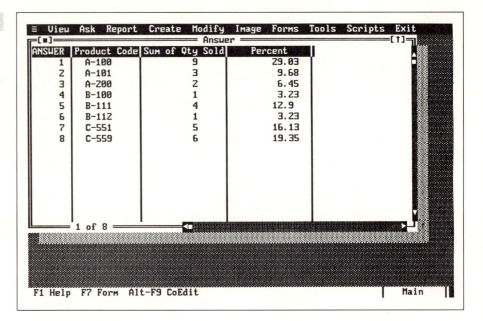

FIGURE 14.42

Each product's contribution to total units sold is displayed as a percentage in the rightmost column.

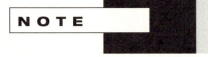

You can also calculate percentages using SET operators in a query to define the sum as a set.

Saving Queries

As you've seen in this chapter, some queries can become quite complex, especially those involving two or more tables. To save yourself the trouble of retyping a query every time you want to use it, you can save it for future use by following these steps:

1. Create the complete query, and test it by pressing F2.

2. Assuming the query works as expected, close the Answer table, either by clicking its Close button or by pressing F8.

3. With the Query form or forms still on the screen, choose **S**cripts ➤ **Q**uerySave. You'll see the dialog box below:

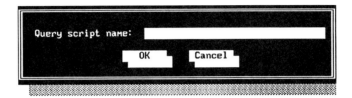

4. Type a valid DOS file name (eight characters maximum length, no spaces or punctuation), with no extension.

5. Choose OK.

Paradox saves the query as a script, adding the extension .SC to whatever file name you provided in step 4. The entire query remains on the screen.

Replaying a Saved Query

To use a saved query, start at the Paradox desktop and follow these steps:

1. If necessary, use **T**ools ➤ **M**ore ➤ **D**irectory to get to whatever directory you were in when you initially saved the query.

2. Choose **S**cripts ➤ **P**lay.

3. Type the name of the script, or choose OK (or press ↵) to view a list of available scripts, then click (or move the highlight to) the name of the query.

4. Choose OK.

The Query form or forms appear on the screen, exactly as they were when you saved the query. You can then modify the query if you wish, or simply perform it by pressing F2.

Summary

In this chapter, you've learned about creating complex queries to join data from multiple tables. You've also learned how to use queries to do math calculations. In the next chapter, you'll see how you can combine data from multiple tables to create sophisticated reports. You'll also see how to view data from multiple tables in a single custom form. But first, let's review some of the basic concepts and techniques presented in this chapter:

- To link multiple tables in a query, enter identical *example elements* into the common field of each table's Query form.

- To enter an example element on a Query form, first press the Example Element key, F5.

- To display the results of calculations in the Answer table of a query, use CALC followed by an expression with any of the operators + (addition), – (subtraction), * (multiplication), and / (division).

- To use the value in a field in a calculation, assign an example element to the field, then use that same example element in a calculation expression.

- The AS operator lets you assign a field name to a calculated field.

- Set queries allow you to ask questions about groups, or categories, of records. Set queries require that you place the word SET beneath the table name in the Query form, and use one of the SET operators: ONLY, NO, EVERY, or EXACTLY.

- To save a query for future use, choose **Scripts** ➤ **QuerySave**, and give the query a valid DOS file name.

- To redisplay a saved query on the desktop, choose **Scripts** ➤ **Play** and enter the name of the saved query.

CHAPTER 15

Advanced Report and Form Techniques

fast TRACK

● **To insert a calculated field into a report**   **553**

    in the Report Design screen, choose **F**ield ➤ **P**lace ➤ **C**alculated, and enter an expression using the arithmetic operators **+** (addition), **−** (subtraction), ***** (multiplication), **/** (division) and **( )** (parentheses used for grouping).

● **To calculate values based on a group of records or all the records in a table**   **555**

    insert a summary operator into the report using **F**ield ➤ **P**lace ➤ **C**alculated.

● **To include data from a related, keyed table in a report design**   **574**

    choose **F**ield ➤ **L**ookup ➤ **L**ink, and choose the table you want to link to. Then use **F**ield ➤ **P**lace ➤ **R**egular to place fields from the linked table into the current report format.

● **To include data from a foreign, linked table in a calculation**   **576**

    choose **F**ield ➤ **P**lace ➤ **C**alculated as usual. When referring to a field from the linked table, precede its field name with the table name, a hyphen, and a greater-than sign (as in [MastInv ->Purchase Price]).

● **To embed code for activating boldface, fonts, or other printer attributes**   **589**

    choose **F**ield ➤ **P**lace ➤ **C**alculated, and type the printer code, in quotation marks, as the field's expression.

- **To create a multipage form**   600

    in the Form Design screen, choose **P**age ➤ **I**nsert, then either **B**efore or **A**fter, depending on whether you want to place the new page above (before) or below (after) the current form page. You can then use the PgUp and PgDn keys to scroll from page to page in the form.

- **To insert a calculated field in a custom form**   603

    choose Field ➤ **P**lace ➤ **C**alculated in the Form Design screen, and enter an expression using one or more of the arithmetic operators +, –, *, /, and ( ).

- **To verify data in one table based upon data in a separate related table**   606

    and to optionally provide automatic help and fill-in, open the table on the desktop and switch to Edit mode (F9). Then choose ValCheck ➤ **D**efine ➤ **T**ableLookup, enter the name of the lookup table, then choose the type of lookup validity check you want.

- **To create a multi-record custom form**   612

    choose **M**ulti ➤ **R**ecords ➤ **D**efine, and follow the instructions on the screen for duplicating fields on the form.

- **To create a multi-table form**   615

    you must first decide which table will be the master table. Next, create a subform for each foreign table. When you then create a master form for the master table, you can choose **M**ulti ➤ **T**ables ➤ **P**lace to place subforms on the master form.

THIS chapter covers advanced techniques that you can use to create custom reports and forms. The techniques for reports include printing reports from multiple tables, using report groups and summary operators to print subtotals and grand totals, and using calculated fields to embed special printer codes within reports. In order to use these techniques, you should already be familiar with the report basics, such as managing table band columns, field masks, blank lines, and text, as discussed in Chapter 8.

The advanced techniques for forms covered in this chapter are similar to those discussed for reports. You'll learn how to access multiple tables with a single form, perform calculations on the screen, and how to handle large tables with multipage forms. Again, you should already be familiar with the basics of creating custom forms, as discussed in Chapter 9.

> **NOTE** In this chapter, the instructions for manipulating fields in report and form design describe the fast and efficient mouse techniques introduced in Paradox version 4.5 (and covered in Chapters 8 and 9). If you need to use the keyboard equivalents, refer to the descriptions of tasks in Chapters 8 and 9. In most cases, the instructions for using the keyboard appear at the top of the screen while you're manipulating fields.

Calculating Data in Reports

You can add calculated fields to a report using the operators used for calculated fields in queries: + (addition), – (subtraction), * (multiplication),

CALCULATING DATA IN REPORTS

/ (division) and parentheses for grouping to override the standard order of precedence. As discussed in Chapter 8, you can also use + in a calculated field to join alphanumeric strings, as in "Dear" + [First Name]. (Remember, literal characters placed in alphanumeric calculations must be surrounded by quotation marks.)

To add a calculated report to a report format, follow these steps:

1. Get to the Report Design screen by choosing **R**eport ➤ **D**esign or **R**eport ➤ **C**hange from the desktop menu bar.

2. Choose **F**ield ➤ **P**lace ➤ **C**alculated. You'll see the dialog box for entering a calculation expression, as shown below.

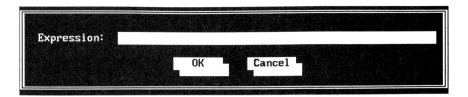

3. Type an expression using any of the arithmetic operators, field names from the current table enclosed in [ ] (square brackets), and any constants (you'll see some examples in a moment). Choose OK after typing the expression.

4. Click the mouse pointer where you want the placed field to begin. A mask of 9's will appear.

5. Place the mouse pointer anywhere on the mask and then hold down the mouse button. Drag to increase or decrease the number of digits to display, then release the mouse button. A decimal point and two decimal place mask characters will appear.

6. If you don't want to include any decimal places, click anywhere on the mask to the left of the decimal point. To change the number of decimal places, position the mouse pointer anywhere on the mask and then hold down the mouse button. Drag to increase or decrease the number of decimal places to display, then release the mouse button.

CHAPTER 15 — ADVANCED REPORT AND FORM TECHNIQUES

NOTE Remember that, as discussed in Chapter 8, you may need to insert, widen, or clear a Table band column in order to be able to display as many digits from your calculated field as you need.

Figure 15.1 shows a sample tabular report format designed from the Orders table presented in the previous chapter. To create this format, we deleted and rearranged fields in the Table band, changed some column titles, and used **TableBand ➤ R**esize to narrow some columns to gain some space.

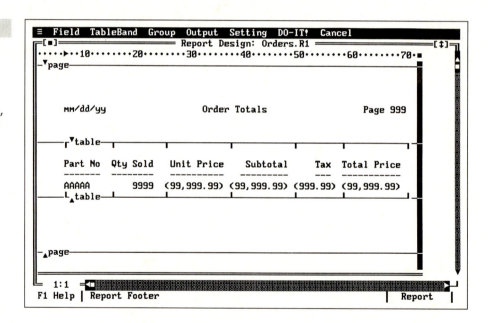

FIGURE 15.1

A sample tabular report format based on the Orders table. The field masks beneath Subtotal, Tax, and Total Price are all calculated fields.

Using **TableBand ➤ I**nsert, we inserted each of the three rightmost columns, and then typed in the column title and underlines (hyphens) as shown in the figure. Each of the field masks in these last three columns contains a calculated field entered with **Field ➤ P**lace ➤ **Calculated**, as follows:

- **Subtotal:** The calculated field beneath subtotal contains the expression [Qty Sold] * [Selling Price], where Qty Sold and Selling Price are names of fields in the current Orders table. Notice that the field names are enclosed in square brackets.
- **Tax:** The field mask beneath the Tax heading contains the expression [Qty Sold] * [Selling Price] * 0.0775, which calculates sales tax at 7.75 percent times the extended price. Note that the constant, 0.0775, is not enclosed in square brackets.
- **Total Price:** The field mask beneath the Total Price heading contains the expression [Qty Sold] * [Selling Price] * 1.0775, which adds the 7.75 percent sales tax to the selling price.

A printed copy of the report is shown in Figure 15.2. Although this sample report isn't fancy, it does perform the necessary calculations.

We changed the column title for the Selling Price field to Unit Price to save some space in the Table band. But the field itself is still named Selling Price in the Orders table structure.

Now let's see how you could spruce up this report a bit to include some subtotals and totals.

Printing Subtotals and Totals in Reports

The Report Design function also lets you insert summary fields, which you can use to print subtotals, totals, counts, and other calculation results. The summary operators for reports are the same as for queries: SUM (addition), AVERAGE, MIN, MAX, and COUNT (quantity).

ADVANCED REPORT AND FORM TECHNIQUES

FIGURE 15.2

Sample printout from the report format shown in Figure 15.1

```
11/04/93                    Order Totals                          Page   1


Part No  Qty Sold  Unit Price    Subtotal       Tax   Total Price
-------  --------  ----------  ----------  --------   -----------
B-100         1        30.00       30.00      2.33         32.33
C-551         2        67.50      135.00     10.46        145.46
A-200         1       900.00      900.00     69.75        969.75
C-559         5        22.50      112.50      8.72        121.22
A-100         5       675.00    3,375.00    261.56      3,636.56
B-100        -1        22.50      (22.50)    (1.74)       (24.24)
A-101         1       562.50      562.50     43.59        606.09
B-111         2        60.00      120.00      9.30        129.30
C-551         1        67.50       67.50      5.23         72.73
A-100         3       675.00    2,025.00    156.94      2,181.94
A-100         1       675.00      675.00     52.31        727.31
C-559         1        22.50       22.50      1.74         24.24
B-112         1        22.50       22.50      1.74         24.24
A-200         1       900.00      900.00     69.75        969.75
B-111         1        60.00       60.00      4.65         64.65
C-551         2        67.50      135.00     10.46        145.46
A-101         1       562.50      562.50     43.59        606.09
B-100         1        30.00       30.00      2.33         32.33
A-101         1       562.50      562.50     43.59        606.09
B-111         1        60.00       60.00      4.65         64.65
B-100         1        30.00       30.00      2.33         32.33
C-551         2        67.50      135.00     10.46        145.46
A-200         1       900.00      900.00     69.75        969.75
C-559         5        22.50      112.50      8.72        121.22
A-100         5       675.00    3,375.00    261.56      3,636.56
B-100        -1        22.50      (22.50)    (1.74)       (24.24)
A-101         1       562.50      562.50     43.59        606.09
B-111         2        60.00      120.00      9.30        129.30
C-551         1        67.50       67.50      5.23         72.73
A-100         3       675.00    2,025.00    156.94      2,181.94
A-100         1       675.00      675.00     52.31        727.31
C-559         1        22.50       22.50      1.74         24.24
B-112         1        22.50       22.50      1.74         24.24
A-200         1       900.00      900.00     69.75        969.75
B-111         1        60.00       60.00      4.65         64.65
C-551         2        67.50      135.00     10.46        145.46
A-101         1       562.50      562.50     43.59        606.09
B-100         1        30.00       30.00      2.33         32.33
A-101         1       562.50      562.50     43.59        606.09
B-111         1        60.00       60.00      4.65         64.65
A-101         2       562.50    1,125.00     87.19      1,212.19
B-100         1        30.00       30.00      2.33         32.33
C-551         2        67.50      135.00     10.46        145.46
A-100         1       675.00      675.00     52.31        727.31
A-101         1       562.50      562.50     43.59        606.09
B-100         1        30.00       30.00      2.33         32.33
```

CALCULATING DATA IN REPORTS

There are two points to consider when you're using summary fields:

- If you want the summary calculation to be based on all the records in a table (such as a grand total), place the field mask for the calculation in the Report Footer band. When given the choice between a PerGroup or Overall calculation, as described in the steps that follow, choose Overall.

- If you want the summary calculation to be based on a particular group of records (such as a subtotal), you must first create a Group band to group those records. Then place the cursor in the Group Footer band before placing the field. Finally, when given the choice between a PerGroup or Overall calculation, choose PerGroup.

You must place summary fields in the Group Footer band rather than the Group Header band, because Paradox groups and then processes sequentially during report output. If you place the summary calculation in the Group Header band, you will get only the first value in the group as the value of your summary.

TIP Using the SUM operator and Overall option within a Group band displays a cumulative (running) total with each group.

Here are the steps for inserting a summary field into a report format:

1. From the Report Design screen, choose **Field** ➤ **Place** ➤ **Summary**. You'll see these options:

   - If the field you're summarizing is a regular field (such as Qty Sold in the Orders table), choose **R**egular, then choose the name of the field you want to summarize from the options that appear.

- If the field you're summarizing is a calculated field (such as Subtotal, Tax, or Total Price in the previous example), choose **C**alculated, then enter the same expression you entered to create the initial calculated field (for example, [Qty Sold] * [Selling Price]).

2. Choose OK or press ↵. You'll see these options:

3. Choose the type of calculation you want the field to perform. You'll see these options:

4. If you want the calculation to be based on all the records in the table, choose **O**verall. If you want the calculation to be based on a group of records (rather than all records), choose **P**erGroup.

5. Place the summary calculation, as described in the previous section.

Figure 15.3 shows a printed report that uses a variety of summary calculations to print a sales report grouped and subtotaled by product code, with a grand total based on total sales. Figure 15.4 shows the report format used to print this report.

FIGURE 15.3

Sample printed report with subtotals and totals, calculated with summary operators

```
11/04/93                    Order Totals                      Page    1

Part No   Qty Sold   Unit Price    Subtotal        Tax    Total Price
-------   --------   ----------    --------     -------   -----------
A-100        1         675.00        675.00       52.31       727.31
A-100        5         675.00      3,375.00      261.56     3,636.56
A-100        3         675.00      2,025.00      156.94     2,181.94
           --------                                        -----------
             9                                               6,545.81

A-101        1         562.50        562.50       43.59       606.09
A-101        1         562.50        562.50       43.59       606.09
A-101        1         562.50        562.50       43.59       606.09
           --------                                        -----------
             3                                               1,818.28

A-200        1         900.00        900.00       69.75       969.75
A-200        1         900.00        900.00       69.75       969.75
           --------                                        -----------
             2                                               1,939.50

B-100       -1          22.50        (22.50)      (1.74)      (24.24)
B-100        1          30.00         30.00        2.33        32.33
B-100        1          30.00         30.00        2.33        32.33
           --------                                        -----------
             1                                                  40.41

B-111        2          60.00        120.00        9.30       129.30
B-111        1          60.00         60.00        4.65        64.65
B-111        1          60.00         60.00        4.65        64.65
           --------                                        -----------
             4                                                 258.60

B-112        1          22.50         22.50        1.74        24.24
           --------                                        -----------
             1                                                  24.24

C-551        2          67.50        135.00       10.46       145.46
C-551        1          67.50         67.50        5.23        72.73
C-551        2          67.50        135.00       10.46       145.46
           --------                                        -----------
             5                                                 363.66

C-559        5          22.50        112.50        8.72       121.22
C-559        1          22.50         22.50        1.74        24.24
           --------                                        -----------
             6                                                 145.46
                                                           ===========
                                              Grand Total:  11,135.96
```

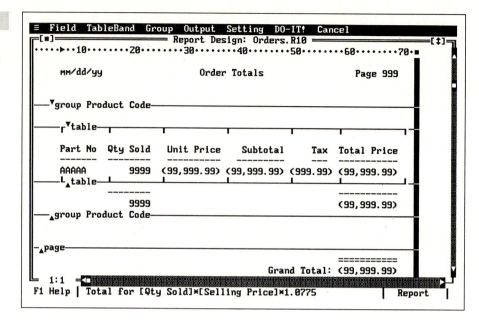

FIGURE 15.4

Report format used to print the report shown in Figure 15.3

Here's a recap of exactly how to create the sample report format:

- Use **G**roup ➤ **I**nsert ➤ **F**ield to insert a Group band based on the Product Code field, just above the Table band.

- In the Group Footer band, aligned with the Qty Sold column, type some underlines (hyphens). Use **F**ield ➤ **P**lace ➤ **S**ummary ➤ **R**egular ➤ **Q**ty Sold ➤ **S**um ➤ **P**erGroup to place a field mask (9999) below those underlines, to sum the Qty Sold field for each group. Size the field mask in the usual manner.

- Also in the Group Footer band, aligned with the Total Price column, type hyphens as underlines. Place the cursor beneath these, and use **F**ield ➤ **P**lace ➤ **S**ummary ➤ **C**alculated to start inserting a summary field for this column. The expression used is [Qty Sold] * [Selling Price] * 1.0775. After entering the expression and choosing OK, choose **S**um ➤ **P**erGroup. Size the field mask in the usual manner.

- In the Report Footer band (not the Page Footer band), aligned with the Total Price column, type a string of equal signs to create an underline, and type the text *Grand Total:*. Next to that text, use **Field ▶ Place ▶ Summary ▶ Calculated** and again the expression [Qty Sold] * [Selling Price] * 1.0775. After entering the expression and choosing OK, choose **Sum ▶ Overall**. Size the field mask in the usual manner.

Formatting Groups

As mentioned in Chapter 8, blank lines in the Group Header and Group Footer bands of a report format also appear as blank lines in the printed report. And as you just saw in the report that includes subtotals, any text and field masks that you place in a Group Footer band also appear at the bottom of each group. The following sections describe some other techniques that you can use to format Group bands.

Groups of Tables versus Tables of Groups

Whenever you're designing a tabular report that contains a Group band, you have the option of displaying the column headings in either of two formats:

- **TableOfGroups:** Displays column headings only at the top of each page, as in Figure 15.3, shown earlier.
- **GroupsOfTables:** Repeats column headings each time the grouping changes, as in Figure 15.5 (only a portion of the report is displayed).

When you're working on a tabular report format that includes a Group band, you can change from one format to another. From the Report Design screen, choose **Setting ▶ Format**. You'll see these options:

FIGURE 15.5

After choosing Setting ➤ Format ➤ GroupsOfTables, column headings appear at the top of each group, rather than just once at the top of the report.

```
11/04/93                    Order Totals                     Page    1


Part No   Qty Sold  Unit Price     Subtotal         Tax   Total Price
-------   --------  ----------   ----------    --------   -----------
A-100            1      675.00       675.00       52.31        727.31
A-100            5      675.00     3,375.00      261.56      3,636.56
A-100            3      675.00     2,025.00      156.94      2,181.94
          --------                                         -----------
                 9                                            6,545.81


Part No   Qty Sold  Unit Price     Subtotal         Tax   Total Price
-------   --------  ----------   ----------    --------   -----------
A-101            1      562.50       562.50       43.59        606.09
A-101            1      562.50       562.50       43.59        606.09
A-101            1      562.50       562.50       43.59        606.09
          --------                                         -----------
                 3                                            1,818.28


Part No   Qty Sold  Unit Price     Subtotal         Tax   Total Price
-------   --------  ----------   ----------    --------   -----------
A-200            1      900.00       900.00       69.75        969.75
A-200            1      900.00       900.00       69.75        969.75
          --------                                         -----------
                 2                                            1,939.50
```

After you choose either **T**ableOfGroups or **G**roupsOfTables, you won't notice any change on the Report Design screen. But the next time you print the report or view it on the screen, the column headings will be displayed in whichever format you chose.

Hiding or Displaying Repetitive Data

Another option available to you when you're designing a tabular report that includes one or more Group bands is the choice to retain or suppress repetitive data within the group. Your options are as follows:

- **Retain:** Repetitive data is displayed within the field, as in the previous examples in Figures 15.3 and 15.5.
- **Suppress:** The value that identifies the group is shown only in the first record of the group, as in Figure 15.6.

When you're working on a tabular report format that includes a Group band, you can change the GroupRepeat setting. From the Report Design

FIGURE 15.6

With GroupRepeats suppressed, only the first record in each group displays the contents of the field that the group is based on (e.g., A-100 appears only in the first record of the records for the product code A-100).

```
11/04/93                   Order Totals                        Page    1


Part No   Qty Sold   Unit Price      Subtotal        Tax    Total Price
-------   --------   ----------    ----------    -------    -----------
A-100            1       675.00        675.00      52.31         727.31
                 5       675.00      3,375.00     261.56       3,636.56
                 3       675.00      2,025.00     156.94       2,181.94
            --------                                          -----------
                 9                                              6,545.81

Part No   Qty Sold   Unit Price      Subtotal        Tax    Total Price
-------   --------   ----------    ----------    -------    -----------
A-101            1       562.50        562.50      43.59         606.09
                 1       562.50        562.50      43.59         606.09
                 1       562.50        562.50      43.59         606.09
            --------                                          -----------
                 3                                              1,818.28

Part No   Qty Sold   Unit Price      Subtotal        Tax    Total Price
-------   --------   ----------    ----------    -------    -----------
A-200            1       900.00        900.00      69.75         969.75
                 1       900.00        900.00      69.75         969.75
            --------                                          -----------
                 2                                              1,939.50
```

screen, choose **S**etting ➤ **G**roupRepeats. You'll see these options:

Again, after you choose either **R**etain or **S**uppress, you won't notice any change on the Report Design screen. However, your selection will be apparent the next time you print the report or view it on the screen.

The default in Paradox 4.5 is to retain group repeats. If you normally want to suppress them in your reports, you can change the default setting in the Custom Configuration Program. Choose ≡ ➤ **U**tilities ➤ **C**ustom ➤ **R**eports ➤ **R**eport Settings ➤ **G**roupRepeats. Use the ↑ key to change the setting to Suppress, choose OK, and then choose **DO-IT!**. Save the new setting to the desired location (usually **H**ardDisk on a stand-alone system). Since the GroupRepeat settings are stored with the report, existing report settings will not be affected.

Formatting Group Headers

As you know, every Group band actually consists of a Group Header band and Group Footer band. When you place a calculated summary field in the Group Header band, it summarizes only the first record in the group, which probably isn't what you want. But you can place text and any regular field in the Group Header band. That information will then be printed at the top of each group.

For example, rather than including the product code in each record of the printed sales report shown earlier in the chapter, you could use **T**able-**B**and ➤ **E**rase to erase the Part No column from the Table band. Then, you could type a title, and use **F**ield ➤ **P**lace ➤ **R**egular to place a field mask for the Product Code field in the Product Code Group Header band, as in Figure 15.7.

While designing the format shown in Figure 15.7, we also chose **S**etting ➤ **F**ormat ➤ **G**roupsOfTables, which is why each group in Figure 15.7 has its own column titles.

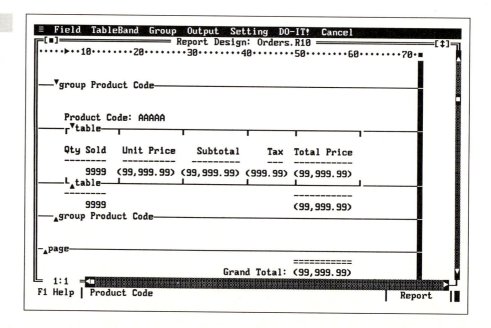

FIGURE 15.7

The text *Product Code:*, followed by a field mask for the Product Code field, placed in the Group Header band of a sample report

Figure 15.8 shows a copy of the report printed from the format shown in Figure 15.7. The two blank lines at the top of the Group Header band in the report format account for the blank lines separating each group of records.

FIGURE 15.8

Report printed from the format shown in Figure 15.7. The product code is printed in the Group Header band (once at the top of each group).

```
11/04/93                  Order Totals                    Page    1

Product Code   A-100

Qty Sold    Unit Price      Subtotal        Tax     Total Price
--------    ----------    ----------    --------    -----------
    1           675.00        675.00       52.31         727.31
    5           675.00      3,375.00      261.56       3,636.56
    3           675.00      2,025.00      156.94       2,181.94
--------                                              -----------
    9                                                   6,545.81

Product Code   A-101

Qty Sold    Unit Price      Subtotal        Tax     Total Price
--------    ----------    ----------    --------    -----------
    1           562.50        562.50       43.59         606.09
    1           562.50        562.50       43.59         606.09
    1           562.50        562.50       43.59         606.09
--------                                              -----------
    3                                                   1,818.28

Product Code   A-200

Qty Sold    Unit Price      Subtotal        Tax     Total Price
--------    ----------    ----------    --------    -----------
    1           900.00        900.00       69.75         969.75
    1           900.00        900.00       69.75         969.75
--------                                              -----------
    2                                                   1,939.50
```

If a group of records is split across two or more pages, by default, Paradox will also print the Group Header band at the top of the next page. You can select whether to include or exclude the headings by following these steps:

1. In the Report Design screen, move the cursor into the Group Header band where you want (or don't want) the heading to be repeated after a page break.

2. Choose **Group ➤ Headings**.

3. Choose **P**age if you want to print group headings at the top of each group and also at the start of each page. Choose **G**roup if you want to print the heading only at the top of each group without regard to page breaks.

Your selection won't be apparent in the Report Design screen, but it will take effect the next time you print or view the report.

Starting Each Group on a New Page

If you want each group in your report to start on a new page, type the PAGEBREAK command as the first line in the Group Header band. Make sure PAGEBREAK starts exactly at the left margin, is alone on the line, and is typed in all uppercase and with no spaces.

If you want the pages on each group to restart page numbering, place the command PAGEBREAK *x* in the Group Header band, where *x* is the page number you want to start on each section of the report. For example, PAGEBREAK 1 will start each group with page 1; PAGEBREAK 3 will start the numbering of each group, after the first group, with page number 3.

NOTE Figure 15.23, later in this chapter, shows the use of PAGEBREAK in a Group Header band to start each inoice on a separate page and number each invoice starting with page 1. It also shows the use of BLANK-LINE 15 to force the beginning of the body of the invoice to start printing on line 15 of the report.

If you want the first group to start numbering on a page other than 1, such as page 3, place another PAGEBREAK *x* command as the last line in the Report Header band. You will get one blank page at the beginning of the report, but the first group will start on the page number you specified.

If you want the entire report to number sequentially from a certain page number, place PAGEBREAK *x* as the last line in the Report Header band and omit any other PAGEBREAK *x* commands. However, you can still place regular PAGEBREAK commands in the Group Header or Page Header band.

Remember, for the PAGEBREAK *x* commands to have any effect, there must be a Page field placed somewhere in the Page Header or Page Footer band of your report.

Positioning Items with BLANKLINE

The BLANKLINE command places a BLANKLINE on the report page during output. Like the PAGEBREAK command, BLANKLINE must be at the beginning of a line, with no other text or fields on the line.

You can use the BLANKLINE *x* command, where *x* is a line number on the page, to position items, such as text, groups, and footers, in your reports. For example, placing BLANKLINE 15 at the beginning of the first line after a body of text in the Group Header band will cause the rest of the text in the heading to start printing on line 15 of each page. Keep in mind that a command such as BLANKLINE 15 does not insert 15 blank lines; it causes the next text, groups, or fields in the report to be printed on line 15 of the page.

NOTE If the next line is an actual blank line or the BLANKLINE command without a number argument, that will be printed next. Use Ctrl-v to display the vertical ruler as a help in using this command.

You can use BLANKLINE in Group Header, Group Footer, Page Header, and Page Footer bands. You may need to experiment to get the desired effect, especially when you are using both PAGEBREAK *x* and BLANKLINE *x* in same heading.

Nesting Groups

As you learned in Chapter 8, you can define up to 16 groups for any given report format. The outermost group determines the main sort order, the next group defines the secondary sort order, and so on. In addition, you can place text and field masks in the Group Header and Group Footer bands independently.

For example, take a look at the tabular report format for the Orders table shown in Figure 15.9. The outermost Group band is based on the Product Code field. The Group Header band contains

——————————— Product Code: AAAAA ———————————

FIGURE 15.9

Sample report with three levels of grouping, based on the Product Code, Sold By, and Date Sold fields

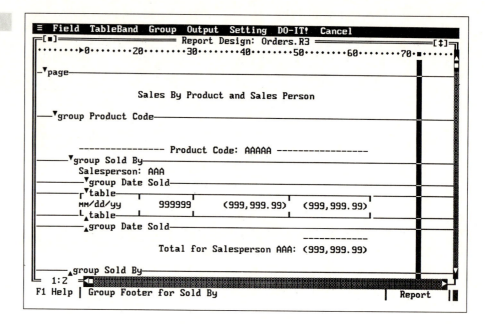

where AAAAA is a field mask for the Product Code field placed with the usual **F**ield ➤ **P**lace ➤ **R**egular.

The Group Footer band (which is scrolled off the screen in Figure 15.9) for the Product Code group contains

   Total Sales for Product AAAAA: (999,999.99)

where AAAAA is once again the mask for the Product Code field, and (999,999.99) is a calculated Sum ➤ PerGroup summary field based on the expression [Qty Sold] * [Selling Price].

Working inward, the next Group band is based on the Sold By field. The Group Header band for that group contains

   Salesperson: AAA

where AAA is the field mask for the Sold By field, placed with **F**ield ➤ **P**lace ➤ **R**egular. The Group Footer band for Sold By, shown at the bottom of Figure 15.9, appears as

   Total for Salesperson AAA: (999,999.99)

where AAA is the mask for the Sold By field, again placed using **Field** ➤ **P**lace ➤ **R**egular. The (999,999.99) field mask was placed using **Field** ➤ **P**lace ➤ **S**ummary ➤ **C**alculated, with the expression [Qty Sold] * [Selling Price]. Again, Sum ➤ PerGroup was used to treat the field as a subtotal.

The next group in is based on the Date Sold field. Both the Group Header and Group Footer bands are empty (that is, they don't even contain blank lines). Thus, all this band does is sort the records within each group by date (from earliest to latest date).

Finally, within the Table band itself, the field names and underlines that Paradox normally places there were removed. The first field masks are from the Date Sold, Qty Sold, and Selling Price fields. A column and field mask for the total sale were added with the expression [Qty Sold] * [Selling Price].

Figure 15.10 shows sample output from the report format, using a larger hypothetical Orders table that contains many records. (So many levels of grouping wouldn't be very useful with our tiny original Orders table.) As you can see, transactions are grouped and subtotaled by product code and salesperson, and dates within each group are listed in earliest-to-latest order.

Omitting the Details

In some situations, you might want to see only the summary data in a report, and not all the details that contributed to the totals. Figure 15.11 is an example of a summary report based on the Orders table, showing the total orders for each item and the date of the most recent order.

Figure 15.12 shows the report format used to print this report. Notice how all the field masks were removed from the Table band. Removing the field masks from the Table band prevents individual records in the table from being printed in the report. The format also includes column headings (Part No, Total Sales, Cumulative Total, and Date of Most Recent Order) and underlines (hyphens) typed into the Table band.

FIGURE 15.10

Output from the report format shown in Figure 15.9, using hypothetical data from a larger Orders table

```
                    Sales by Product and Sales Person


              --------------- Product Code: A-100 -----------------
         Sales Person:   AAA
            10/15/93            1            675.00              675.00
                                                              ------------
                         Total for Sales Person AAA:            675.00
         Sales Person:   BBG
            10/01/93            5            675.00            3,375.00
            10/01/93            5            675.00            3,375.00
            10/01/93            3            675.00            2,025.00
            10/01/93            3            675.00            2,025.00
                                                              ------------
                         Total for Sales Person BBG:          10,800.00
         Sales Person:   JAK
            10/01/93            1            675.00              675.00
            10/01/93            1            675.00              675.00
                                                              ------------
                         Total for Sales Person JAK:           1,350.00
                                                              ============
                     Total Sales for Product A-100:           12,825.00



              --------------- Product Code: A-101 -----------------
         Sales Person:   AAA
            10/15/93            1            562.50              562.50
                                                              ------------
                         Total for Sales Person AAA:            562.50
         Sales Person:   BBG
            10/15/93            1            562.50              562.50
            10/15/93            1            562.50              562.50
            10/15/93            2            562.50            1,125.00
                                                              ------------
                         Total for Sales Person BBG:           2,250.00
         Sales Person:   JAK
            10/04/93            1            562.50              562.50
            10/04/93            1            562.50              562.50
            10/05/93            1            562.50              562.50
            10/05/93            1            562.50              562.50
                                                              ------------
                         Total for Sales Person JAK:           2,250.00
                                                              ============
                     Total Sales for Product A-101:            5,062.50
```

FIGURE 15.11

A summary report based on the Orders table, with the total and most recent order of each product

```
                        Summary Report

                                                   Date of Most
         Part No    Total Sales   Cumulative Total  Recent Order
         -------    -----------   ----------------  ------------
         A-100       6,075.00         6,075.00        10/01/93
         A-101       1,687.50         7,762.50        10/15/93
         A-200       1,800.00         9,562.50        10/15/93
         B-100          37.50         9,600.00        10/15/93
         B-111         240.00         9,840.00        10/15/93
         B-112          22.50         9,862.50        10/15/93
         C-551         337.50        10,200.00        10/15/93
         C-559         135.00        10,335.00        10/15/93
                                    ============
                   Grand Total:   $  10,335.00
```

FIGURE 15.12

Report format for the summary report. This format omits the details by excluding field masks from the Table band, and includes a running total by using an Overall summary calculation within the Group band.

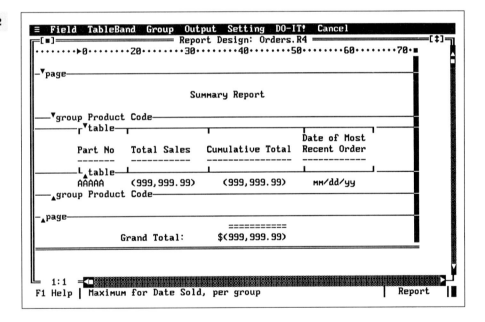

The report format also contains a Group band, based on the Product Code field. The Group Footer band for that group contains

    AAAAA   (999,999.99)   (999,999.99)   mm/dd/yy

The fields are formatted as follows::

- **Part No:** AAAAA is the field mask for the Product Code field, placed with the usual **F**ield ➤ **P**lace ➤ **R**egular options.
- **Total Sales:** (999,999.99) is the field mask for total sales, placed with **F**ield ➤ **P**lace ➤ **S**ummary ➤ **C**alculated, using [Qty Sold] * [Selling Price] as the expression. **S**um ➤ **P**erGroup was used to get a sum of orders for each group of products.
- **Cumulative Total:** The second (999,999.99) field mask is the running total. It's the same as the Total Sales summary field, except that it uses **S**um ➤ **O**verall rather than PerGroup.
- **Date of Most Recent Sale:** mm/dd/yy is the field mask for the most recent date, entered by choosing **F**ield ➤ **P**lace ➤ **S**ummary ➤ **R**egular ➤ **D**ate Sold ➤ **H**igh ➤ **P**erGroup ➤ 1)mm/dd/yy. This displays the highest (latest) date in the Date Sold field for each product.

The Report Footer band contains the following field mask:

Grand Total: $(999,999.99)

as well as a row of equal signs. This field mask was placed with **F**ield ➤ **P**lace ➤ **S**ummary ➤ **C**alculated, again using [Qty Sold] * [Selling Price] as the expression. Then **S**um ➤ **O**verall was chosen, so that this field sums all the records in the table, not individual groups of products.

Displaying Running Totals

You can easily have any report display cumulative totals (also called *running totals*) by placing a summary field calculation within the Table band or a Group band and choosing Overall rather than PerGroup when given those options.

The Cumulative Total column in Figure 15.12 in the preceding section provides an example. The field mask for that column is located within the Group Footer band. We inserted that field mask by choosing **F**ield ➤ **P**lace ➤ **S**ummary ➤ **C**alculated, and entering [Qty Sold] * [Selling Price] as the expression. Then we chose **S**um ➤ **O**verall.

Printing Reports from Multiple Tables

So far, all the advanced report techniques have involved one table. However, if you've divided your data into multiple related tables, you may often want to use data from a combination of these tables to print a single report. You can use either of the following methods to print a report from multiple tables:

- Use Field ➤ Lookup in the Report Design screen to link the common field in the current table to another table.

- Use a query to create an Answer table that contains all the data you need from multiple tables, and design the report from that resulting Answer table.

The Field ➤ Lookup method, though somewhat restrictive, is generally the easiest, so we'll discuss that one first.

Looking Up Data from a Related Table

Field ➤ Lookup lets you link multiple tables by their common fields right in the Report Design screen. You can then create calculated fields that display data from tables other than the table that the report is based on. There are a few guidelines and restrictions involved, as summarized below:

- The table that the report is based on, which we'll refer to as the *master table*, should be the table that's on the "many" side of a one-to-many relationship. We'll refer to other tables that the report borrows data from as *lookup tables*.

- The common field that links the lookup table to the master table must be a key field, and it must be the same field type in both tables.

- Unlike with queries, you can only link data between the master table and the lookup table directly. You cannot create a link from one lookup table to another.

If the tables that you want to use to print the report do not meet these requirements, you need to build the report from an Answer table, as described in the next section.

Figure 15.13 shows an example that meets these criteria. Orders is the master table that the report is built around. Product Code, the field that links Orders and Mastinv, is a key field in the Mastinv table (as indicated by *). Invoice Number, the common field linking the Orders and Invoices tables, is the key field in the Invoices table.

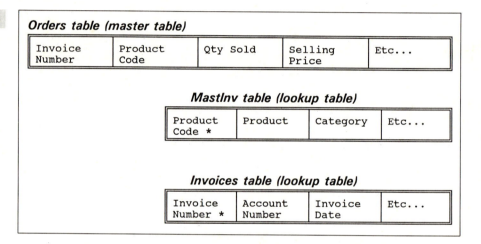

FIGURE 15.13

Using Field ➤ Lookup to link multiple tables via the Report Design screen will work with these tables, because both Mastinv and Invoices link directly to the master table Orders, and the common field is a key field in both lookup tables.

The basic steps to create a report using Field ➤ Lookup, starting at the Paradox desktop, are as follows:

1. Decide which table will act as a master table; that is, the one that contains many records in a one-to-many relationship. Then choose **Report** ➤ **Design** and choose that table as the one to base the report on.

2. From the Report Design screen, choose **Field** ➤ **Lookup** ➤ **Link** to start setting up the link to another table.

3. Choose the table you want to link to the report from the dialog box that appears.

4. From the menu that appears, choose the common field that links the two tables.

5. Repeat steps 2 through 4 to link additional tables as necessary.

You won't notice any immediate change on the Report Design screen. However, you can now place field masks for data from any lookup tables in the report format.

Placing a Field from a Lookup Table

Once you've defined the link between the master table and any lookup tables, you can place data from any lookup table in much the same manner you place regular fields. In fact, you can treat the fields from the multiple tables just as though all the fields were all coming from a single table.

Here are the steps for placing a field from a lookup table in the report format:

1. Choose **F**ield ➤ **P**lace ➤ **R**egular.
2. When the list of field names appears, use the scroll bar or arrow keys to scroll to the bottom of the list. There you'll see *pointers* to the names of any linked lookup tables, which are in brackets followed by a hyphen and greater-than sign, as in the example below:

3. Choose the pointer to the table you want to include data from, and Paradox will then display a menu of field names from that lookup table.
4. Choose the field you want to include in the report, then position and size the field mask in the usual manner, using the mouse or keyboard.

You can also use data from a lookup table in any calculated field. You just need to precede the name of any field that comes from a lookup table with

ADVANCED REPORT AND FORM TECHNIQUES

the name of the lookup table followed by the pointer (->). That is, rather than choosing **Field** ➤ **Place** ➤ **Regular**, you choose **Field** ➤ **Place** ➤ **Calculated** to place the calculated field.

Then, when typing the expression for the calculation, include the pointer to the lookup table with the field name. To enter the -> between the table name and field name, type a hyphen (-) and then a greater-than character (>). For example, to calculate Qty Sold from the master table times Purchase Price from the Mastinv table, enter the calculation expression as

    [Qty Sold] * [Mastinv->Purchase Price]

Figure 15.14 shows a sample report that uses data from both the sample Orders and Mastinv tables. Figure 15.15 shows the report design.

FIGURE 15.14

Sample report that uses data from both the Orders and Mastinv tables

```
                        Cost of Goods Sold


            Product Code:   A-100, Gershwin Bicycle

            Date Sold   Qty Sold  Purchase Price   Cost of Goods
            ---------   --------  --------------   -------------
            10/01/93       1           337.50           337.50
            10/01/93       5           337.50         1,687.50
            10/01/93       3           337.50         1,012.50
                                                    -------------
                                      Subtotal:      3,037.50

            Product Code:   A-101, Nikono Bicycle

            Date Sold   Qty Sold  Purchase Price   Cost of Goods
            ---------   --------  --------------   -------------
            10/05/93       1           281.25           281.25
            10/04/93       1           281.25           281.25
            10/15/93       1           281.25           281.25
                                                    -------------
                                      Subtotal:        843.75

            Product Code:   A-200, Racing Bicycle

            Date Sold   Qty Sold  Purchase Price   Cost of Goods
            ---------   --------  --------------   -------------
            10/06/93       1           450.00           450.00
            10/15/93       1           450.00           450.00
                                                    -------------
                                      Subtotal:        900.00
```

To create this report format, we based the report design on the Orders table. Using **Field** ➤ **Lookup** ➤ **Link**, we then created a link to the Mastinv table. To place the product name in the Group Header band, we chose

FIGURE 15.15

Format used to print the report shown in Figure 15.14

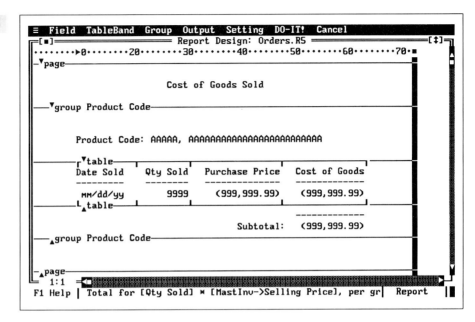

Field ➤ Place ➤ Regular ➤ [Mastinv->] ➤ Product. Then the following procedure was used:

- To place the Purchase Price field mask, we chose Field ➤ Place ➤ Regular ➤ [Mastinv->] ➤ Purchase Price.

- To place the Cost of Goods field, we used Field ➤ Place ➤ Calculated and entered the expression as

  [Qty Sold] * [Mastinv->Purchase Price]

- To enter the group totals in the Group Footer band, we chose Field ➤ Place ➤ Summary ➤ Calculated, and entered

  [Qty Sold] * [Mastinv->Purchase Price]

  as the expression once again, then chose Sum ➤ PerGroup.

NOTE The Product Code field in the Mastinv table structure is a key field, as required when using Field ➤ Lookup for report design.

If you compare the calculated fields in this report to previous examples, you'll see that the calculation expressions are fairly typical. However, because the Purchase Price field comes from the linked Mastinv table rather than the Orders table, we needed to precede the Purchase Price field name with Mastinv-> to indicate that the field comes from that linked table.

Linking Tables in a Many-to-Many Design

Keep in mind that even if your database design involves a many-to-many relationship, you can treat it as really just a combination of one-to-many relationships. For example, in our students and courses database design, there's a one-to-many relationship between Students and Sclink, and a one-to-many relationship between Courses and Sclink.

If you make Sclink the master table (you base the report on that table), you can use **Field ➤ Lookup ➤ Link** to link the Sclink and Students tables on the common Student ID field, and then use **Field ➤ Lookup ➤ Link** a second time to link Sclink and Courses on the common Course ID field. You'll end up with tables with the links illustrated in Figure 15.16.

Creating a report format that groups by Student ID and uses fields from both tables, as in Figure 15.17, lets you print a schedule for each student, as shown in Figure 15.18.

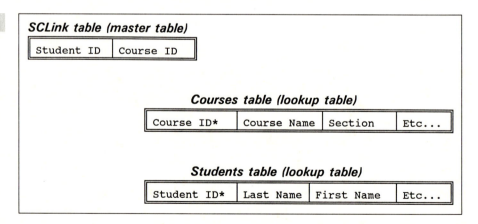

FIGURE 15.16

Links between the Sclink table, defined as the master table for a report, and Students and Courses, defined as lookup tables

PRINTING REPORTS FROM MULTIPLE TABLES

FIGURE 15.17

Courses table. Notice that the Group band is based on the Student ID field.

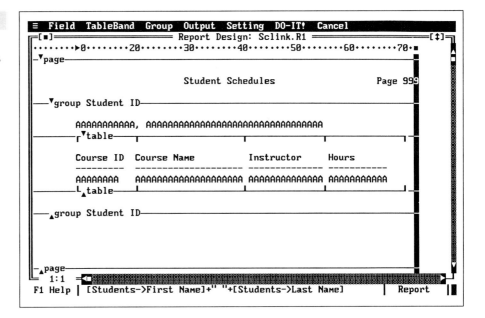

FIGURE 15.18

Sample data printed from the report format shown in Figure 15.17

```
                   Student Schedules                    Page    1

123-45-6789, Annie Adams

Course ID  Course Name           Instructor      Hours
---------  --------------------  --------------  ---------
Alg101-A   Algebra 101           Smith           1:00-1:50
Bio101-B   Biology 101           Ramirez         2:00-2:50
Chm101-A   Chemistry 101         Gomez           3:00-3:50


234-56-7890, Bobbie Baker

Course ID  Course Name           Instructor      Hours
---------  --------------------  --------------  ---------
Alg101-A   Algebra 101           Smith           1:00-1:50
Bio101-B   Biology 101           Ramirez         2:00-2:50
Chm101-A   Chemistry 101         Gomez           3:00-3:50


543-54-3418, Edie Edwards

Course ID  Course Name           Instructor      Hours
---------  --------------------  --------------  ---------
Alg101-A   Algebra 101           Smith           1:00-1:50
Chm101-A   Chemistry 101         Gomez           3:00-3:50
```

On the other hand, using the same links but basing the grouping on Course ID rather than Student ID lets you print a roll sheet of students enrolled in each course, as illustrated in Figures 15.19 and 15.20.

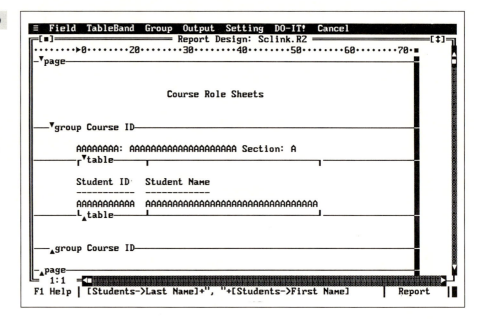

FIGURE 15.19

Report format designed with Sclink as the master table, with links to the Students and Courses table. Notice that the Group band is based on the Course ID field.

NOTE The status bars in Figures 15.17 and 15.19 show the calculated fields used to print student names in the two reports.

About the Linking Options

When you choose Field ➤ Lookup from the Report Design screen's menu bar, you're actually presented with three options, as shown below:

FIGURE 15.20

Sample data printed from the report format shown in Figure 15.19

```
                    Course Role Sheets


   Alg101-A: Algebra 101              Section: A

   Student ID     Student Name
   -----------    ------------
   123-45-6789    Adams, Annie
   234-56-7890    Baker, Bobbie
   543-54-3418    Edwards, Edie



   Bio101-B: Biology 101              Section: B

   Student ID     Student Name
   -----------    ------------
   123-45-6789    Adams, Annie
   234-56-7890    Baker, Bobbie
   555-75-4343    Davis, David



   Chm101-A: Chemistry 101            Section: A

   Student ID     Student Name
   -----------    ------------
   123-45-6789    Adams, Annie
   234-56-7890    Baker, Bobbie
   543-54-3418    Edwards, Edie
   555-75-4343    Davis, David
```

The Link option lets you define the link between the master table and a lookup table based on the common field. When you print the report after defining the link, Paradox will print every record in the master table. As it does so, it will attempt to find an exact match between the common field in the master and lookup tables before extracting any data from the lookup table. If Paradox cannot find an exact match in the lookup table, it still prints the data from the master table, but does not display any data from the lookup table.

Keep in mind that the common field in the lookup table must be a key field. Otherwise, Paradox will not allow you to set up the link. If multiple fields are key fields in the lookup table, Paradox will prompt you to match all the keys from the lookup table to fields in the master table.

The Unlink option lets you end a link between a master and lookup table. When you choose **Field** ➤ **Lookup** ➤ **Unlink**, you'll see a menu of pointers to linked tables, as in the example below:

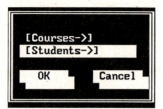

When you choose a table to unlink, Paradox terminates the link between the tables, and also deletes any field masks from the linked table in the current report. So in general, you should use this option to unlink a table only after you've decided not to use a particular lookup table.

The Relink option lets you change the common field used to link two tables without deleting any field masks from the lookup table. Use this option when you simply want to correct a previous mistake—where you used the wrong field or fields—to link two tables, without losing any field masks in the report design.

When you choose Relink, you're presented with a menu of existing links. Choose the table that you want to relink, and you'll see a list of field names in that table. Choose the field or fields that correctly link the lookup table to the master table, then choose OK.

Using Queries to Print Reports from Multiple Tables

In some situations, it isn't possible to directly link data from every lookup table to the master table in a report. For example, take a look at the relationships between the Orders, Mastinv, Invoices, and Accounts tables, as illustrated in Figure 15.21.

To print data from these tables, you need to use a query to join the tables. Then create a report format that prints the data in the format you want.

FIGURE 15.21

There is no direct relationship between the Orders table and Accounts table in this example. Hence, you cannot use Field ➤ Lookup in the Report Design to print data from all four of these tables.

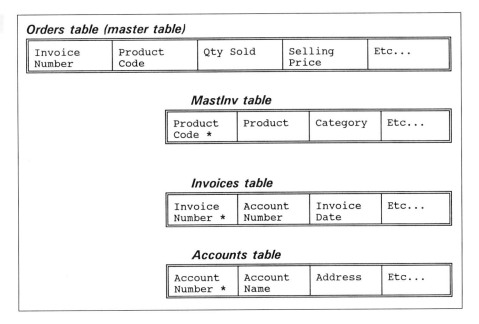

Creating the Report Format from Multiple Tables

To create a report format based on the Answer table results of a query, follow these steps:

1. Create a query that links the tables as required and generates an Answer table that contains all the fields you need to print in the report. (You might want to use **Scripts** ➤ **QuerySave** to save the query, so you don't have to recreate it in the future.)
2. Use **Tools** ➤ **Rename** to rename the Answer table.
3. Use **Report** ➤ **Design** to design the report format based on the renamed Answer table you created in the preceding step.
4. Save the report format with F2.

Once you create and save the report format, you use a different series of steps to actually use that format, as discussed in the next section.

TIP On large tables, creating a single table from which to generate a report is often a good idea, even when you could link the tables in a report format. This is especially true if you are working on a network. Queries execute much faster than report output, and accessing the various linked tables during report output also slows Paradox down. A report based on an Answer table containing only the data fields and the data you need for your report will usually process much faster than a report based on linked tables.

Using the Report Format from Multiple Tables

After you've created your multiple table report format, you can use it at any time to print data from a current Answer table. Here are the steps:

1. Use **S**cripts ➤ **P**lay to bring the query that links the tables to the desktop, then press F2 to perform the query.
2. Use **T**ools ➤ **C**opy ➤ **R**eport ➤ **D**ifferentTable to copy the report format that you created earlier from its source table to the current Answer table.
3. Use **R**eport ➤ **O**utput to print the report from the Answer table.

CAUTION Don't rename or copy the Answer table at this stage, or you may delete the report format you created earlier.

Printing Invoices from Four Tables

Let's work through an example of how you could print invoices from the tables illustrated earlier in Figure 15.21. First, you need to create a query that links the tables. You want to be sure to check all the fields you want to print in the final report. Also, if you need to isolate specific records, enter the appropriate query criteria. For example, in Figure 15.22, we've set up a query to link the Orders, Invoices, Mastinv, and Accounts tables. The

PRINTING REPORTS FROM MULTIPLE TABLES

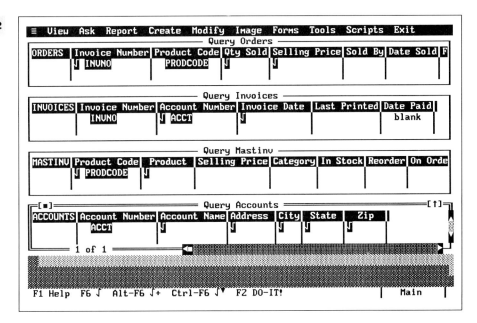

FIGURE 15.22

A query to combine data from the Orders, Invoices, Mastinv, and Accounts tables

query criterion BLANK in the Date Paid field isolates records that have no date in the Date Paid field (unpaid invoices).

When you perform the query, the resulting Answer table contains all the data you need to print the report. Choose **T**ools ➤ **R**ename ➤ **T**able to rename the Answer table to some other name, such as Printinv.

Next, close the Printinv table, then use **S**cripts ➤ **Q**uerySave to save the query on your screen. For this example, let's say you name the query Invoices.

Next, clear the screen, choose **R**eport ➤ **D**esign, and choose the Printinv table as the one to base the report on. Let's say you give this report the description Current Invoices, and make it a tabular report.

In the Report Design screen, use all the usual techniques to design the report. In Figure 15.23, we've used a Group band, based on Invoice Number, to group records with identical invoice numbers.

Note that the report format includes some regular fields (placed with **F**ield ➤ **P**lace ➤ **R**egular), calculated fields (**F**ield ➤ **P**lace ➤ **C**alculated), and summary fields (**F**ield ➤ **P**lace ➤ **S**ummary). Here's a description

FIGURE 15.23

Report format based on the Printinv table, for printing invoices

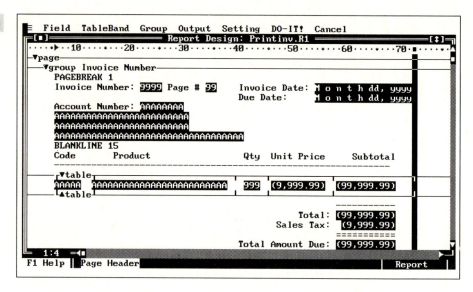

of each of the field masks in the sample report format, numbered here for your reference:

1. Regular, Invoice Number
2. Regular, Invoice Date
3. Calculated, with the expression [Invoice Date] + 30
4. Regular, Account Number
5. Regular, Account Name
6. Regular, Address
7. Calculated, with the expression
   [City] + "," + [State] + " " + [Zip]
8. Regular, Product Code
9. Regular, Product
10. Regular, Qty Sold
11. Regular, Selling Price
12. Calculated, with the expression [Qty Sold] * [Selling Price]

13. Summary, calculated as [Qty Sold] * [Selling Price], **S**um ➤ **P**erGroup

14. Calculated, with the expression
SUM([Qty Sold] * [Selling Price],group) * 0.0775

15. Calculated, with the expression
SUM([Qty Sold] * [Selling Price],group) * 1.0775

After choosing **DO-IT!** to save the report format, you're returned to the desktop. Press Alt-F8 at this point to clear the desktop if necessary.

Now when you want to print current invoices, first choose **S**cripts ➤ **P**lay ➤ **I**nvoices to bring the Query forms to the screen for printing invoices. Then press F2 to display an Answer table containing current data from all four tables.

At this point, it's important that you *do not* copy or rename the Answer table to Printinv, because doing so would delete the report format you created earlier. Instead, choose **T**ools ➤ **C**opy ➤ **R**eport ➤ **D**ifferentTable to copy the Current Invoices report from the Printinv table to the Answer table. Then use **R**eport ➤ **O**utput to print the Current Invoices table from the Answer (not the Printinv) table.

TIP If you have created several reports in the Printinv table to be used with the Answer table, you can copy all of them at once by using Tools ➤ Copy ➤ JustFamily and choosing the Printinv table as the source table and the Answer table as the target table.

Recovering Lost Report Formats

The most common problem that arises when building a report from a renamed Answer table is the possibility of losing that report format in the future. For example, if you were to rename or copy the Answer table to the Printinv table after creating your Current Invoices report format, Paradox would delete that Current Invoices report.

All is not lost, however, if you realize your mistake early on, and have DOS 5 or a third-party utility that can recover deleted files. Recall that all reports have the extension .R followed by a number. If you inadvertently renamed or copied Answer to Printinv, you could recover your Current Invoices report by exiting Paradox, going to the directory where the report was stored, and entering the appropriate command (such as UNDELETE Printinv.R1) to bring back the report format you accidentally deleted.

Sprucing Up Reports with Special Printer Attributes

Unlike Windows products and fancier DOS word processing packages, Paradox does not directly support fonts and other printer features, such as boldface, italics, underline, and fonts. But if you can find the appropriate codes in your printer manual, you can place those codes in calculated fields of a report format to activate the printer feature as the report is being printed.

Because all printers use different codes for different features, the only place that you'll be likely to find any information about the appropriate printer codes is in your printer documentation.

Here are some guidelines to keep in mind when using special printer codes:

- Control characters (Ctrl-A to Ctrl-Z) should be represented as \001 for Ctrl-A, \002 for Ctrl-B, and so on up to \026 for Ctrl-Z.
- The Escape character is represented as \027.
- When using any other characters, be sure to use the correct case and character. For example, if the printer code requires the letter *b*, don't use *B* in your printer code. Also, be sure not to confuse the number *1* (one) with the letter *l*, or 0 (zero) with the letter *O*.
- When typing multiple codes, do not insert blank spaces between the codes.

- When combining actual printed text and a setup code in a calculated field, use **+** to join them.
- Remember that if you enter a code to turn on a print attribute, such as boldface, that code remains in effect for the entire current session (until you turn off the printer). You should include codes in the report that turn the print attribute off, or reset the printer when the report is finished.

Inserting a Printer Code in a Report Format

To insert a printer attribute code into a report format, follow these steps:

1. In the Report Design screen, position the cursor where you want the special printer attribute to begin.
2. Choose **F**ield ➤ **P**lace ➤ **C**alculated.
3. Type the entire setup string, enclosed in quotation marks, following the guidelines listed below.

NOTE Setup strings that affect the entire report, such as paper size, orientation, and overall print size, can be entered via Setting ➤ Setup in the Report Design, as discussed in Chapter 8.

4. Press ↵ or choose OK.
5. When given the opportunity to size the field mask, you can just press ↵ to use the default width. Later, you may need to experiment with **F**ield ➤ **R**eformat to widen or narrow the field mask to prevent extra blank spaces, and to ensure that the code works correctly.

Be aware that if you enter a code that changes the print size, spacing on the Report Design screen won't accurately reflect spacing on the final printed report. For example, if you want to print a report title in very large size, and also want it centered, you'll probably find that you need to shift the title to the left in the Report Design screen to make it appear centered on the printed report. You may also need to place some blank lines above the large title, since Paradox will not automatically adjust the line height to accommodate the tall character size.

Using Compressed Print

As an example of using some fairly simple printer codes, suppose that your printer offers the following attributes:

ATTRIBUTE	CODE
Begin expanded print	Escape-A
End expanded print	Escape-B
Begin compressed print	^15
End compressed print	^29

If you placed your report title in the report format using the calculated field

"\027A" + "Monthly Sales Summary" + "\027B"

the title would appear on the report in expanded print.

If you placed a calculated field containing just

"\015"

in a Table band, and a calculated field containing just the code

"\029"

at the bottom of the Table band, just the text within the Table band would be compressed. Text outside the Table band would be in regular size.

Choosing a Font and Print Size

You can also choose a font and print size, again assuming that you know the codes to use. As an example, Table 15.1 lists some example codes for the HP LaserJet III, already translated for immediate use in a calculated field. The codes in Table 15.1 will work with many laser printers that offer an HP emulation mode. You can get a list of codes for fonts from many laser printers by printing the font test or font list. See your printer manual for instructions.

SPRUCING UP REPORTS WITH SPECIAL PRINTER ATTRIBUTES

TABLE 15.1: Sample Codes for Fonts and Special Printer Attributes with the HP LaserJet III Printer (and Compatible Printers)

PRINT ATTRIBUTE	CODES USED IN CALCULATED FIELD
Boldface On	"\027(s3B"
Boldface Off	"\027(s0B"
Italics On	"\027(s1S"
Italics Off	"\027(s0S"
Underline On	"\027&d3D"
Underline Off	"\027&d@"
Courier 10 cpi	"\027(10U\027(s0p10.00h12.0v0s0b3T"
Courier 12 cpi	"\027(10U\027(s0p12.00h10.0v0s0b3T"
CG Times (Scalable)	"\027(10U\027(s1p____v0s0b4101T"
Univers Bold Italic (Scalable)	"\027(10U\027(s1p____v1s3b4148T"

When reading Table 15.1 be aware that all 0 characters are zeros (not the letter *O*) and all 1 characters are the number 1 (not the letter *l*). Also note that with scalable fonts, you must replace the underscored space with the point size of the font you want. For example, the code for Univers Bold Italic 48pt is

" \027(10U\027(s1p48.0v1s3b4148T"

As an alternative to bothering with all these complicated printer codes, you can just print the report to a file, then spruce up the report with a word processing program, as described in Chapter 12.

NOTE Another alternative, though a bit more expensive, is to add Windows 3 or later to your system, and switch from Paradox for DOS to Paradox for Windows, which greatly simplifies access to printer capabilities.

Figure 15.24 shows the Page Header band for a Current Invoices report, similar to the one described earlier, with a couple of HP LaserJet printer codes added. The field mask above the word *Invoice* contains the expression for printing in 48-point Univers Bold Italic. You can see the expression in the status bar. The field mask below the word Invoice contains the expression for printing in Courier 10 point. (The portion of the report that's scrolled off the bottom of the screen is the same as in Figure 15.23 shown earlier.)

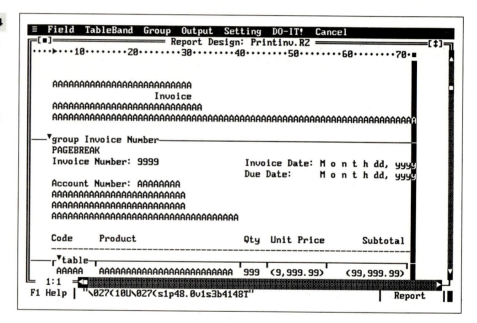

FIGURE 15.24

Page Header band for a Current Invoices report format, containing printer codes to print the title Invoice in Univers Bold Italic 48pt on the HP LaserJet III, similar to Figure 15.23, but without blank lines or page numbering.

The large field mask, with A's spreading the full width of the report, uses the PAL FILL function to print a wide underline, as discussed next.

Using PAL Functions in Calculated Fields

You can also use PAL (Paradox Application Language) functions in your report formats. Chapter 21 presents an introduction to PAL. Any of the

USING PAL FUNCTIONS IN CALCULATED FIELDS

expressions used in that chapter can be used to create calculated fields in your reports. Table 15.2 lists a number of functions that are available for use in your reports. See Chapter 21 for a description of their uses in calculations.

TABLE 15.2: PAL Functions that Can Be Used in Calculated Fields in a Report

PAL FUNCTION	ACTION	PAL FUNCTION	ACTION
ABS	Absolute value	LOG	Base 10 log
ACOS	Arc cosine	LOWER	Lowercase
ASC	ASCII value	MAX	Higher value
ASIN	Arc sine	MIN	Lower value
ATAN	Arc tangent	MOD	Modulo (remainder)
ATAN2	Four-quadrant arc tangent	MONTH	Month number
CAVERAGE	Column average	MOY	Month abbreviation
CCOUNT	Column count	NRECORDS	Record count
CHR	ASCII character	NUMVAL	String to number
CMAX	Column highest value	PI	Pi (π = 3.14…)
CMIN	Column lowest value	PMT	Payment on loan
CNPV	Column net present value	POW	Raise to power
COS	Cosine	PV	Present value
CSTD	Colun standard deviation	RAND	Random number
CSUM	Column total	ROUND	Round number
CVAR	Column variance	SEARCH	Position of small string in larger
DATEVAL	String to date	SIN	Sine

TABLE 15.2: PAL Functions that Can Be Used in Calculated Fields in a Report (continued)

PAL FUNCTION	ACTION	PAL FUNCTION	ACTION
DAY	Day of month	SQRT	Square root
DOW	Day of week	STRVAL	Value to string
EXP	Exponent (base e)	SUBSTR	Substring
FILL	Repeat character	TAN	Tangent
FORMAT	Define format	TIME	System time
FV	Future value	TODAY	System date
INT	Integer portion	UPPER	Uppercase
LEN	Length of string	USERNAME	User name
LN	Natural logarithm	YEAR	Year of date
BLANKNUM	Blank number value	BLANKDATE	Blank date value
FAMILYSIZE	Size of table and family members	FULLFILENAME	Full path and file name
ISONWORKSPACE	True if table is on the workspace	ISSPACE	True if text is only spaces and tabs
KEYNAME	PAL name of the specified keycode	LTRIM	Trims leading spaces and tabs
QUOTESTRING	Returns the string resulting from an expression	RELATIVEFILENAME	File name and path to relative file name
RTRIM	Trims trailing spaces and tabs	STRIM	Removes all spaces and tabs
XTRIM	Removes specified characters		

USING PAL FUNCTIONS IN CALCULATED FIELDS

If you use a PAL function in creating a calculated field in a report, the field placed in the report will be alphanumeric and not numeric, even though the values used to calculate the field are all numeric.

The alphanumeric field mask created when you use a PAL function is also different in that its length is variable; that is, it will expand to fill the space available on the line on which it is placed. Paradox assumes that calculated fields created by your PAL function calculation could be of any length. You must size the field to a length that will be sufficient to handle the results of your calculation.

As an example of using a PAL function in a report, the wide field mask with A's spreading all the way across the page in Figure 15.24 is for a calculated field containing the expression

FILL(CHR(223),68)

where FILL is the name of a PAL function, CHR(223) is the PAL function syntax for a thick horizontal bar (DOS extended character 223), and 68 is the number of times to repeat the character.

As another example, if you placed the PAL Day of Week function (DOW) in the Table band for a Custlist report, as in:

DOW([Start Date])

it would print the day of the week, as a three-letter abbreviation (Mon, Tue, Wed, and so on) for each record's Start Date.

Figure 15.25 shows a sample printed invoice. Notice that the word Invoice appears in different places in the report format (Figure 15.24) and in the printed report. That's because each character, including blank spaces to the left of the title, is much larger than it is represented in the Report Design screen.

CAUTION If you move large print too far to the right in the Report Design screen, it might not appear at all on the printed report. To verify your printer codes, first print the report with any large text aligned at the left margin to see how it is placed.

FIGURE 15.25

Sample printed invoice printed from the report format shown in Figure 15.24, including the printer codes and title

```
                                              Invoice
          ────────────────────────────────────────────────
          Invoice Number: 1001 Page #  1   Invoice Date:   October  1, 1993
                                           Due Date:       October 31, 1993
          Account Number: 555-1212
          Rigoberto Martinez
          4343 Meadowlark Lane
          Escondido, CA 92056




          Code      Product                 Qty  Unit Price     Subtotal
          ────────────────────────────────────────────────────────────────
          B-100     Nikono Safety Helmet      1       30.00        30.00
          A-200     Racing Bicycle            1      900.00       900.00
          C-551     Hobie Skateboard          2       67.50       135.00
          C-559     Flexie Skateboard         5       22.50       112.50
                                                               ──────────
                                                      Total:    1,177.50
                                                  Sales Tax:       91.26
                                                               ==========
                                           Total Amount Due:    1,268.76
```

The wide underline was printed by the FILL function. The rest of the report uses the same field masks as the report format shown in Figure 15.23, earlier in this chapter.

Using a PAL Function to Calculate a Percentage

Although many of the PAL functions operate on, and normally return, a numeric value when used in a script, this doesn't hold true in reports. Nonetheless, the numeric PAL functions can be useful in reports. As an example of using these functions, take a look at the report in Figure 15.26, which includes each salesperson's contribution to total sales. The report format used to print this report is shown in Figure 15.27.

USING PAL FUNCTIONS IN CALCULATED FIELDS

FIGURE 15.26

Sample report that calculates the percent contribution of each record to total sales

```
                Total Sales by SalesPerson


        Sales Person              Sales         Percent
        --------------------   -----------      --------
        Archie Artunian         10,500.00         4.87 %
        Belinda Berp            15,500.00         7.19 %
        Candace Cane            26,550.00        12.32 %
        Dorothy Dweeb           31,354.00        14.55 %
        Eddie Tide               9,324.00         4.33 %
        Fanny Fakir             16,765.00         7.78 %
        Grace Goode             43,234.00        20.06 %
        Horace Hannibal          9,435.00         4.38 %
        Irene Reft              20,495.00         9.51 %
        Julie Jergweid          32,343.00        15.01 %
                               ============
                       Total:  215,500.00
```

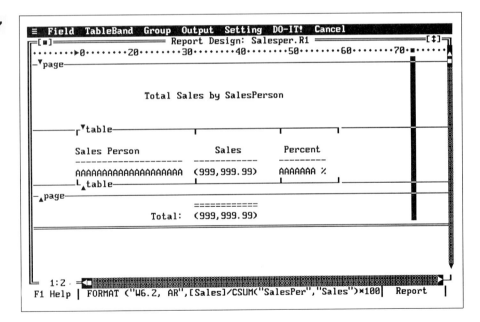

FIGURE 15.27

Report format used to print the report in Figure 15.26. The status bar shows a portion of the calculated field that uses CSUM to help calculate each record's percentage contribution to the whole.

The Sales Person and Sales columns are actual fields from a table named Salespers. The Percent column is a calculated field, which uses the PAL CSUM function to calculate a percentage based on the column sum.

ADVANCED REPORT AND FORM TECHNIQUES

The syntax of the CSUM function is

CSUM ("*table name*","*field name*")

where *table name* is the name of the table, and *field name* is the name of the field you want to sum.

To format the Percent column in the sample report, we used the PAL FORMAT function, which formats text and numbers. The expression in the wide calculated field under the column heading Percent, partially visible in the status bar, is

FORMAT("W6.2, AR",[Sales] / CSUM("SalesPers","Sales") * 100)

W6.2 specifies that the calculation in this expression should be displayed as a five-digit number (plus a decimal point to get the 6 in W6.2) with two decimal places. AR is part of the FORMAT function, and it specifies right alignment. [Sales] is the name of the field that contains each salesperson's total sales, and "Salespers" is the name of the table that the report is generated from.

If you need to calculate percentage contributions based on multiple fields, such as [Qty Sold] * [Selling Price], you'll need to use a query to perform that calculation first, using the AS operator to create a new field in the Answer table. Then you'll need to design the report around the resulting Answer table. The reason for this restriction is that the CSUM function cannot accept an expression, such as [Qty Sold] * [Selling Price], where it expects a single field name.

You can use **T**ools ➤ **R**ename ➤ **T**able to rename the Answer table before creating a report based on that temporary table so the report isn't deleted with the table. Then use **T**ools ➤ **C**opy ➤ **R**eport ➤ **D**ifferentTable to copy the report back to new Answer tables as necessary.

> **NOTE**
>
> In a report, a PAL function's value is always returned as an alphanumeric variety, and its field mask is therefore always of the AAAAA variety. This means that you can't use the SUM or AVERAGE operators to calculate a Per-Group or Overall sum or average for a report column that contains a PAL function.

Now that we've covered advanced techniques for report design, we're ready to move on to techniques for designing forms.

Creating Multipage Forms

On a single table with many fields, it may not be possible to enter and edit data with a one-page custom form. For example, Figure 15.28 shows a portion of the structure of a sample table named Taxes, which might include well over 100 fields to store data for a single income tax form.

FIGURE 15.28

Portion of a sample table named Taxes, which includes many fields to store income tax data

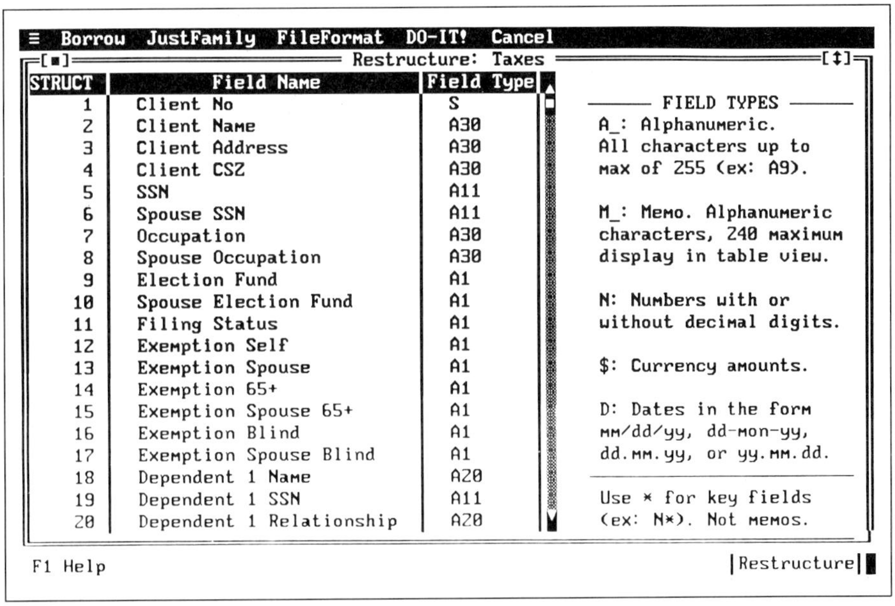

```
≡ Borrow  JustFamily  FileFormat  DO-IT!  Cancel
┌[■]═══════════════════ Restructure: Taxes ═══════════════════[‡]┐
│STRUCT │     Field Name         │ Field Type │                    │
│   1   │ Client No              │ S          │ ───── FIELD TYPES ─────
│   2   │ Client Name            │ A30        │ A_: Alphanumeric.
│   3   │ Client Address         │ A30        │ All characters up to
│   4   │ Client CSZ             │ A30        │ max of 255 (ex: A9).
│   5   │ SSN                    │ A11        │
│   6   │ Spouse SSN             │ A11        │ M_: Memo. Alphanumeric
│   7   │ Occupation             │ A30        │ characters, 240 maximum
│   8   │ Spouse Occupation      │ A30        │ display in table view.
│   9   │ Election Fund          │ A1         │
│  10   │ Spouse Election Fund   │ A1         │ N: Numbers with or
│  11   │ Filing Status          │ A1         │ without decimal digits.
│  12   │ Exemption Self         │ A1         │
│  13   │ Exemption Spouse       │ A1         │ $: Currency amounts.
│  14   │ Exemption 65+          │ A1         │
│  15   │ Exemption Spouse 65+   │ A1         │ D: Dates in the form
│  16   │ Exemption Blind        │ A1         │ mm/dd/yy, dd-mon-yy,
│  17   │ Exemption Spouse Blind │ A1         │ dd.mm.yy, or yy.mm.dd.
│  18   │ Dependent 1 Name       │ A20        │
│  19   │ Dependent 1 SSN        │ A11        │ Use * for key fields
│  20   │ Dependent 1 Relationship│ A20       │ (ex: N*). Not memos.
│ F1 Help                                                │Restructure│
```

If you have a table with so many fields, it probably needs to be normalized, as discussed in Chapter 14. However, sometimes you do need to deal with many fields in a table. When developing a form for a table with a lot of fields, you'll need to divide the form into several pages, where each page is a screenful of text and fields. A single Paradox form can consist of up to 15 pages.

600 CHAPTER 15

ADVANCED REPORT AND FORM TECHNIQUES

> **NOTE** Remember, a single table can contain up to 255 fields. However, each record is restricted to 4000 characters (1350 characters per record in indexed tables). Only the part of a memo field stored with Paradox (the size specified in the Create dialog box) counts toward these totals.

To create a multipage form, choose Forms ➤ Design, specify the table you want to create the form for, and select an unused form number in the usual manner. You can use the Standard Form as the starting point for a new custom form by first using Tools ➤ Copy ➤ Form ➤ SameTable to copy the Standard Form to some unused form, then using Forms ➤ Change to change the copied form.

In the Form Design screen, use the standard techniques described in Chapter 9 to design the first page (screen) of the form, placing whatever fields will fit, in whatever order you wish. For example, Figure 15.29 shows the first page of a sample form for the Taxes table. The indicator in the lower-

FIGURE 15.29

First page of a custom form for the sample Taxes table

left shows that you are currently viewing page 1 of a one-page form.

When you've finished designing the first page of the form, you can add another page. Choose **P**age ➤ **I**nsert. You'll see the options After and Before. If you want to insert a new page below the current page, choose **A**fter. If you want to insert a page above the current page, choose **B**efore.

The indicator at the bottom of the screen will change to indicate the total number of pages in the form. For example, if you inserted a new page after page 1, the indicator will display 2:2, indicating that you are on the second page of the form. You can now place fields and text on the new page with the usual techniques. While designing the display of the form, you can use the PgUp and PgDn keys to scroll from one page to the next.

Using Display-Only Fields to Identify the Current Record

One thought to keep in mind when designing a multipage form is that it can be difficult to remember which record you're currently editing if there is not some field on each page of the form that identifies the current record. For example, in a custom form for the Taxes table, you might want to display the client number or name in the current record on each page of the form. That way, you can see whose data you're working on at a glance, regardless of which page of the form you're on at the moment.

However, you also need to keep in mind that once you use **F**ield ➤ **P**lace ➤ **R**egular to display a field on any given page of a form, you can only use **F**ield ➤ **P**lace ➤ **D**isplayOnly to display that field on additional pages of the form.

Often, some pages of a multipage form are used to display mostly DisplayOnly fields, for informational purposes. Keep in mind that each page of a multipage form must contain at least one regular field.

Figure 15.30 shows a sample second page for the Taxes form (note the indicator, which shows that this is page 2 of 2 on a two-page form). To display the client number and name at the top of this page of the form, we used **F**ield ➤ **P**lace ➤ **D**isplayOnly to insert those fields within the box at the top of the page (we drew the box itself with the usual **B**order ➤ **P**lace commands).

FIGURE 15.30

Second page of custom form for the Taxes table. The client number and name from the first page of the form were placed within the box near the top of the page using Field ➤ Place ➤ DisplayOnly.

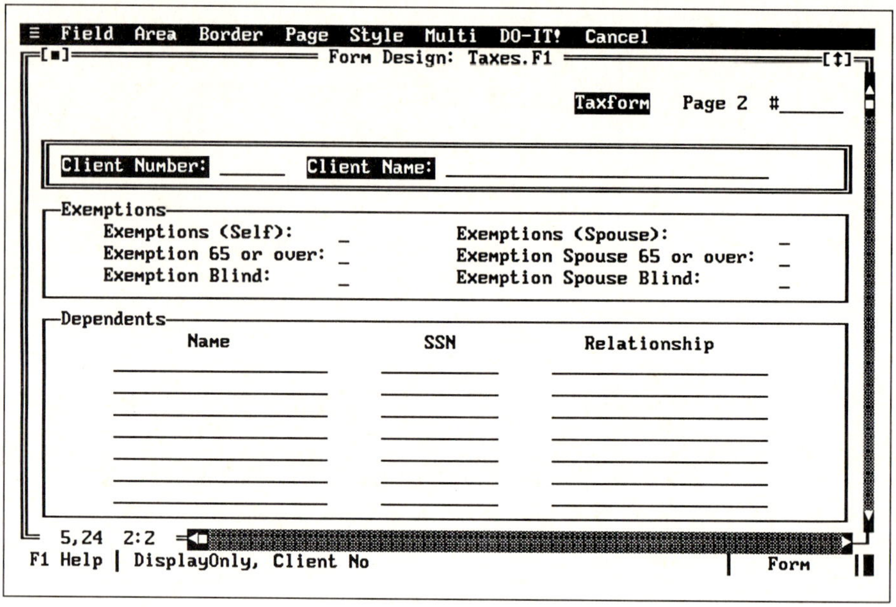

```
≡ Field  Area  Border  Page  Style  Multi  DO-IT!  Cancel
┌[■]═══════════════════ Form Design: Taxes.F1 ═══════════════[↕]┐
│                                              Taxform  Page 2  #_____ │
│                                                                │
│  ┌Client Number:_____    Client Name:_____┐│
│  │ ┌Exemptions─────────────────────────────────────────────┐ ││
│  │ │   Exemptions (Self):   _    Exemptions (Spouse):     _│ ││
│  │ │   Exemption 65 or over:_    Exemption Spouse 65 or over:_│││
│  │ │   Exemption Blind:     _    Exemption Spouse Blind:  _│ ││
│  │ └───────────────────────────────────────────────────────┘ ││
│  │ ┌Dependents─────────────────────────────────────────────┐ ││
│  │ │        Name              SSN          Relationship    │ ││
│  │ │      _____         _____         _____          │ ││
│  │ │      _____         _____         _____          │ ││
│  │ │      _____         _____         _____          │ ││
│  │ │      _____         _____         _____          │ ││
│  │ │      _____         _____         _____          │ ││
│  │ └───────────────────────────────────────────────────────┘ ││
│  └───────────────────────────────────────────────────────────┘│
│  5,24  2:2  ═◁▓▓▓▓▓▓▓▓▓▓▓▓▓▓▓▓▓▓▓▓▓▓▓▓▓▓▓▓▓▓▓▓▓▓▓▓▓▓▷         │
│ F1 Help │ DisplayOnly, Client No                    │ Form  │▊│
└───────────────────────────────────────────────────────────────┘
```

Using a Multipage Form

Once you've designed your multipage form, you can use it as you would any other custom form. That is, open the table, then choose **I**mage ➤ **P**ickForm and the name of the table you want to use. You can then scroll through pages with the PgUp and PgDn keys, just as you did when creating the form.

If you find you need to delete a page from a form, just use the PgUp and PgDn keys to move to the page on the Form Design screen. Then choose **P**age ➤ **D**elete ➤ OK to delete the current page.

Using Calculated Fields in Forms

You've seen how to perform calculations on data in tables using the Ask and Report options, but you can also perform immediate calculations on a custom form in a similar manner.

USING CALCULATED FIELDS IN FORMS

To place a calculated field in a Form Design screen, choose **Field ➤ Place ➤ Calculated**, and enter an expression in the usual manner: enclose field names in square brackets, and use the operators **+** (addition), **−** (subtraction), ***** (multiplication), **/** (division), and parentheses (for grouping). You can also use PAL functions in your calculated fields. After you place a calculated field, you can position it as desired.

The field appears as underscores, just like any other field in the Form Design screen. When the cursor is on the field, the expression appears in the status bar. Figure 15.31 shows an example of a custom form for the Orders table with a calculated field that contains the expression [Qty Sold] * [Selling Price].

FIGURE 15.31

Custom form for the Orders table in the Form Design screen, with a calculated field containing the expression [Qty Sold] * [Selling Price]

```
≡  Field  Area  Border  Page  Style  Multi  DO-IT!  Cancel
┌─[■]══════════════════ Form Design: Orders.F1 ══════════════════[↕]┐
│                                                                    │
│    ┌──────────────────────────────────────────────────────────┐   │
│    │  ENTER AN ORDER                                          │   │
│    └──────────────────────────────────────────────────────────┘   │
│                                                                    │
│       Date:  _____          Sold By:  ___                    │
│                                                                    │
│       Part Number:  _____                                         │
│                                                                    │
│       Quantity:     _____                                      │
│                                                                    │
│       Unit Price:   _____                                    │
│                                                                    │
│       Total:        ████████                                      │
│                                                                    │
│    ┌──────────────────────────────────────────────────────────┐   │
│    │              Remarks:  _____          │   │
│    └──────────────────────────────────────────────────────────┘   │
│                                                                    │
└────────────────────────────────────────────────────────────────────┘
  14,31  1:1
  F1 Help │ Formula, [Qty Sold] * [Selling Price]        │  Form
```

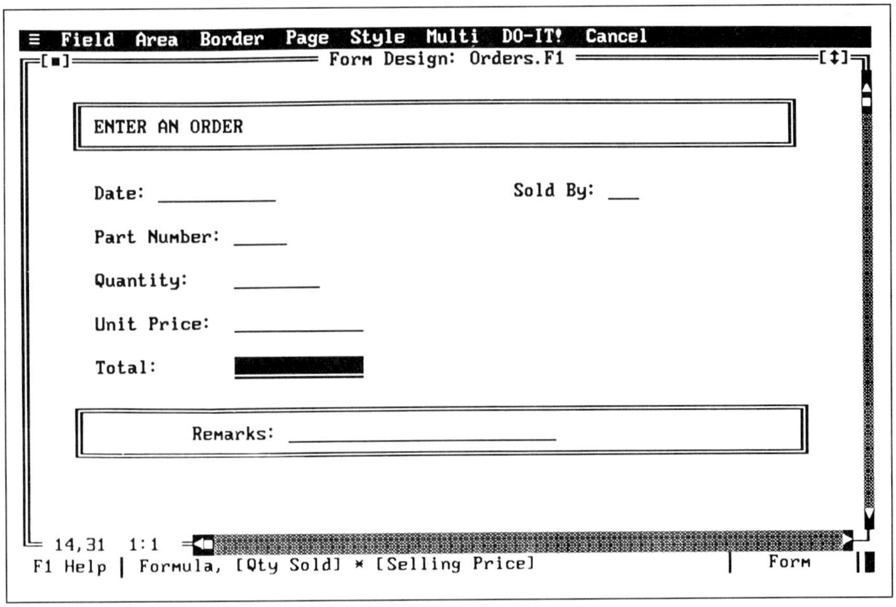

Save the form with the new calculated field with the usual **DO-IT!** option or F2 key. When you're using the form to view or edit data, the calculated field will show the results of the calculation. If you're using the form for data entry, the calculated results will appear as soon as you've filled in all the fields involved in the calculation. Figure 15.32 shows an example in which the calculated field contains the results of the quantity times the unit price.

FIGURE 15.32

Custom form for the Orders table in use on the desktop. The field next to Total displays the quantity times the unit price.

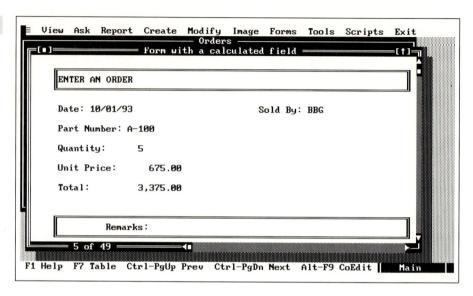

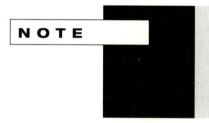

Remember that if you have used the Custom Configuration Program to set Blanks=Zero to No, or if you are using a summary operator in your calculation, any blank value in a field used in your calculation will show a blank field.

Multiple Table Validation and Automatic Fill-in

When your database design involves multiple tables, there are a number of techniques you can use to establish links between tables to validate data in one table based on the contents of another table. For example, you can define multiple table validity checks that perform the following tasks:

- Reject an entry in one table that does not match values in another table (for example, refuses to accept a product code while entering an order if the product code does not exist in the Mastinv table).

- Look up data in another table to find an acceptable entry for the current table (for example, look up a product code in the Mastinv table when entering data into the Orders table).

- Automatically fill in one or more fields in the current table based on values in another table (for example, automatically fill in the Selling Price field in the Orders table based on the current selling price listed in the Mastinv table).

You can define all of these validity checks even without using custom forms. This means you can use them when you're entering and editing data in Table view. But once you define these validity checks, they will automatically carry over to any custom forms.

As when using the Lookup feature in the Report Design screen to combine data from multiple tables for printing, there are a few points to keep in mind when defining multiple table validity checks:

- The table on the "many" side of a one-to-many relationship is the table that should be open when you're defining the relationships. We'll refer to this as the *edited table*, since it's the one that you'll be using to enter or edit data.

- The table that you want to validate entries against is the table on the "one" side of the one-to-many relationship, and it is called the *lookup table*.

- The field you want to search in the lookup table must be the first field in the lookup table's structure, and it must be the same field type and size as the corresponding field in the table being edited (it cannot be a memo or binary field).

- Although the first field in the lookup table need not be a key field, validation will go more quickly if it is.

Defining Validity Checks

Our Mastinv table provides a prime example of a lookup table for the Orders table. You might want to validate or look up a product code while entering an order, and Product Code is indeed the first field in the Mastinv table structure (and is also a key field), so it's already properly structured for the task. (The structures of Mastinv, Orders, and other sample tables are described in Chapter 14.) Here are the steps for defining a multiple table validity check with the sample Orders and Mastinv tables:

1. Open the edited table (the one you'll be entering or editing data in) with the usual **V**iew option from the desktop. (In our example, open the Orders table).

2. Switch to Edit mode (press F9).

3. Choose **V**alCheck ➤ **D**efine, then move the cursor to the field that you want to validate (the Product Code field in this example), then press ↵.

4. Choose **T**ableLookup, then specify the table that contains the data that you want to validate entries against (Mastinv in this example). Then choose OK or press ↵. You'll see this menu:

5. Select the type of validity check you want to define. The options are described in the following sections.

Your selections are saved in a .VAL file (as discussed in Chapter 5) and are active whenever you enter or edit data in the table in the future. If necessary, you can disable the validity check using **V**alCheck ➤ **C**lear (also discussed in Chapter 5).

JustCurrentField

The JustCurrentField option says that you want only the common field that links the edited table with the lookup table to be involved in the validation process. If you select JustCurrentField, you'll be given the options PrivateLookup and HelpAndFill.

Choosing PrivateLookup tells Paradox to just check the entry in the current table against the first field in the lookup table. Any invalid entries into the edited table will simply be rejected, and no further help is offered.

If you choose HelpAndFill, Paradox will validate the current entry against the lookup table, as always. But in addition, you'll have the option of looking up data in the lookup table yourself. Furthermore, Paradox will automatically copy the data from the common field of the lookup table to the current record of the edited table after you've found whatever you're looking for.

AllCorrespondingFields

Choosing AllCorrespondingFields as the type of validity check tells Paradox that you want to validate the entry in the common field against the lookup table and also automatically copy any fields with matching names from the lookup table into the current table. When you choose AllCorrespondingFields, you're given the options FillNoHelp and HelpAndFill.

Choosing FillNoHelp tells Paradox to validate the entry in the common field, as usual. But in addition, when a valid entry has been placed in the field, it copies values from any fields with the same name from the lookup table into the edited table. However, like the PrivateLookup choice for the JustCurrentEntry option, FillNoHelp will not give you the option to actually view and browse through the lookup table.

In our example with the Order and Mastinv tables, both tables contain a field named Selling Price. With AllCorrespondingFields and FillNoHelp activated, entering a valid code into the Product Code field would automatically copy the current Selling Price value from the Mastinv table into the Selling Price field of the Orders table.

Choosing HelpAndFill provides the normal validity check, and also lets you browse through the lookup table to find whatever information you're looking for. Once you choose a record from the lookup table, the contents of the common field, and all fields with the same names, are copied to the table being edited. With the Orders and Mastinv tables example, you would be able to look up and choose a valid product code from the Mastinv table while entering orders, and also copy the product code and the selling price from whatever record you chose in the Mastinv table to the Orders table.

Table 15.3 summarizes the various multiple table validation options. Note that all these options validate data. That is, every option requires that the entry in the current table match some value in the lookup table. The differences between the options are basically whether they do or do not let you view the lookup table, and whether they copy data to the current field only or to all matching fields in the table being edited.

TABLE 15.3: Multi-table Data Entry and Editing Validation Options

OPTION	VALIDATE ENTRY?	VIEW LOOKUP TABLE?	COPY CURRENT FIELD?	COPY ALL MATCHING FIELDS?
JustCurrent ➤ PrivateLookup	Yes	No	No	No
JustCurrent ➤ HelpAndFill	Yes	Yes	Yes	No
AllCorrespond ➤ FillNoHelp	Yes	No	No	Yes
AllCorrespond ➤ HelpAndFill	Yes	Yes	Yes	Yes

Using a Table with Multiple Table Validity Checks

Let's suppose that you've defined Mastinv as the lookup table for Orders, using some combination of the options just described. Now you are entering (or editing) data in the Orders table, either in Table view or Form view. Regardless of which option you chose, if you enter an invalid product code, you'll see this error message

   Not one of the possible values for this field

If you chose one of the options that does not allow you to view the lookup table (PrivateLookUp or FillNoHelp), your only recourse would be to either correct the entry, or to leave it blank.

If you defined the validity check using AllCorrespondingFields ➤ FillNoHelp, and you enter a valid part number into the Product Code field, Paradox will automatically copy the Selling Price for that product from the Mastinv table into the Selling Price field of the current record in the Orders table. But still, you do not have the option of browsing through the Mastinv table.

If you chose one of the HelpAndFill options while defining the validity checks, you'll notice that when the cursor is on the Product Code field,

MULTIPLE TABLE VALIDATION AND AUTOMATIC FILL-IN

the prompt F1 Lookup appears in the Speedbar. When you press F1 (or choose it from the Speedbar), a copy of the Mastinv table pops up onto the screen. It may cover the Orders table, but you can size and move it, as in the example shown in Figure 15.33.

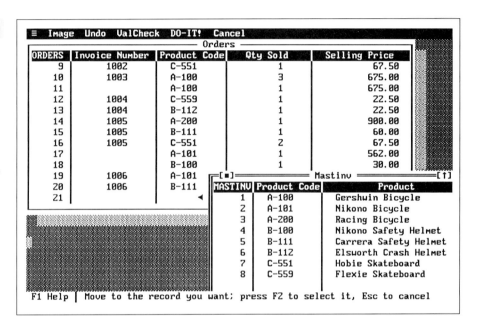

FIGURE 15.33

The Mastinv table pops up on the screen after pressing F1 with the cursor in the Product Code field of the Orders table. In this example, the Mastinv table has been moved and sized.

While the Mastinv table is on your screen, you can do any of the following:

- Scroll through records as usual with PgUp, PgDn, and the arrow keys to move the cursor to whatever value you're looking for.
- Use Zoom (Ctrl-z) and Zoom Next (Alt-z) to look up a value in any field of the Mastinv table.
- Press the Do-It! key, F2, when the cursor is on the record you want to copy data from to the current record in the Orders table, and close the Mastinv table.
- Press Esc to close the Mastinv table without making any selection.

When you press F2, data from the Product Code field of the current record in Mastinv is automatically copied to the Product Code field of the current record in Orders. If you chose AllCorrespondingFields ➤ Help-AndFill when defining the validity check, the selling price for the current product will also be copied from the Mastinv table to the current record in the Orders table.

Looking Up State Abbreviations

A simpler, and the most common, use of a multiple table validity check is to find those two-letter state abbreviations that are almost impossible to memorize. For example, if you want to add this capability to the Custlist table, you need to go to the directory that Custlist is in (using **T**ools ➤ **M**ore ➤ **D**irectory), then use **C**reate to create a table named States with the simple structure:

	NAME	FIELD TYPE
1	State	A2*
2	Spelled Out	A15

You could then fill in all the two-letter abbreviations and State names.

CAUTION You wouldn't want to add this capability to a table that includes addresses outside the United States, since only valid two-letter abbreviations would be accepted once you created the validity check.

Then, using **M**odify ➤ **E**dit, you open the Custlist table, move the cursor to the State field, and choose **V**alCheck ➤ **D**efine ➤ **T**ableLookUp. Specify States as the table to look up values in. Then choose **J**ustCurrentField ➤ **H**elpAndFill.

Later, when entering or editing Custlist table records, you could move the cursor to the State field, then press F1 to pop up the States table, as shown in Figure 15.34. To choose a two-letter state abbreviation, simply browse through the records in the States table until the cursor is on the state you want, then press F2.

DISPLAYING MULTIPLE RECORDS ON A CUSTOM FORM

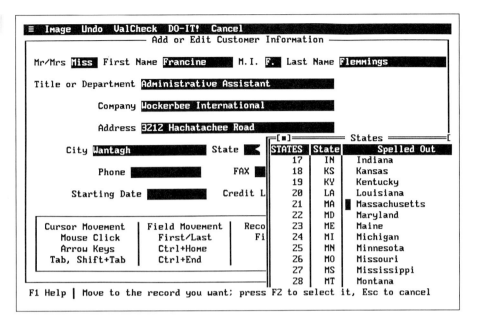

FIGURE 15.34

The States table pops up when the cursor is in the State field in the Custlist table and you press F1. In this example, the table window has been resized and moved.

Displaying Multiple Records on a Custom Form

Normally, a form displays only a single record from a table. If you want to view multiple records, you just use Table view rather than Form view. You can, however, have the best of both worlds by creating multi-record forms. A multi-record form is one that displays multiple records for a single table.

Multi-record forms are particularly useful in situations where you want to display a lookup table on the screen at all times, or when you want to show several records from a table on the "many" side of a one-to-many relationship while showing the record on the "one" side of the relationship.

Creating a Multi-record Form

Here are the basic steps for creating a multi-record form:

1. Starting at the desktop, choose **F**orms ➤ **D**esign, specify the name of the table you want to design the form for, and then select any unused form number.

2. Enter a form description, as usual, and choose OK or press ↵.

3. In the Form Design screen, use **F**ield ➤ **P**lace ➤ **R**egular to place fields on the form in the usual manner.

4. To copy the fields to create a multi-record form, choose **M**ulti ➤ **R**ecords ➤ **D**efine.

5. Use the mouse to drag from one corner of an area or one end of a line to the opposite corner or end. The multi-record area selected will be highlighted. When you have defined the area, release the mouse button.

6. With the mouse, drag the area down the screen. As you drag, repeating areas will appear on the form. When you have the number of repeating areas that you want, release the mouse button.

7. Optionally, draw a border around the screen area, particularly if you'll be using this form as a subform (as described a little later in this chapter).

8. Choose **D**O-IT! or press F2 to save the form.

Figure 15.35 shows a sample multi-record form based on the States table. Here's a summary of how to create this form:

- Move the cursor to row 2 column 2 and place the State field.
- Move the cursor to row 2 column 5 and place the Spelled Out field.
- Use **M**ulti ➤ **R**ecords ➤ **D**efine to make three extra rows of these fields.
- Use **B**order ➤ **P**lace ➤ **D**ouble-Line to draw a border around all the fields.

DISPLAYING MULTIPLE RECORDS ON A CUSTOM FORM   613

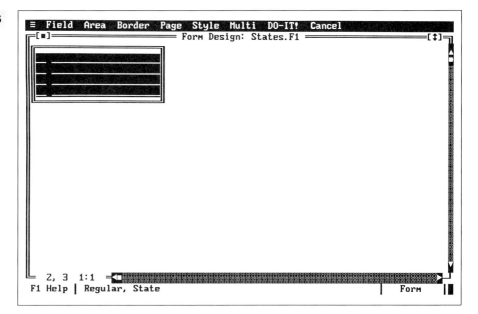

FIGURE 15.35

Sample form with the State and Spelled Out fields placed near the upper-left corner of the screen. Those fields were then duplicated using Multi ➤ Records ➤ Define, and a border was drawn around all the fields.

You could now use this form as you would any other form. But, as you'll see in a moment, the real advantages of a multi-record form become more obvious when you create multi-table forms, as described later in this chapter.

Modifying a Multi-record Form

If you create a multi-record form, then decide you need to change it, you can use **F**orms ➤ **C**hange in the usual manner to modify the form. In the Form Design screen, you can use all the usual techniques to make changes.

If you need to add or delete some of the duplicate records on the form, choose **M**ulti ➤ **R**ecords ➤ **A**djust. Then, as instructed on the screen, use the arrow keys to adjust the size of the original and the duplicate record regions, and press ↵.

If you want to delete all the duplicate records, choose **M**ulti ➤ **R**ecords ➤ **R**emove. The original fields and any text and borders remain on the screen; only the duplicated fields are removed.

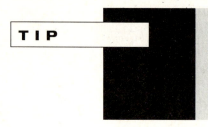

TIP The highlighting used to display the multi-record area of the form during form design is sometimes distracting. You can use Multi ➤ Records ➤ Remove to remove the multi-record area, do your form editing, and then use Multi ➤ Records ➤ Define to recreate the multi-record area.

Editing Multiple Tables with a Single Form

For the remainder of this chapter, we'll discuss how to create forms for entering, viewing, and editing data from multiple related tables. These forms, called *multi-table forms*, let you view data from several related tables simultaneously, which makes it easier to work with several tables at once.

A multi-table form is actually a collection of two or more forms. The *master form* is the main form, which contains fields from the table that's open while you're designing the form. Additional forms, call *subforms* (or *detail forms*) are forms that you've created for other tables and then embedded in the master form.

The first and most important consideration in designing a multi-table form is whether or not the tables in the form should be linked. If the tables are unlinked, the various subforms on the screen are totally independent. Moving through records in one subform has no effect on the record position in a separate form.

There are a few limitations to keep in mind when planning your master form and subforms:

- The master form of a linked table can contain multiple pages but cannot be a multi-record form.
- Any subform can be a multi-record form, but it must fit on a single page.
- You cannot nest subforms, which means that a subform you place on the master form cannot contain another table's subform.

Creating Multi-table Forms with Unlinked Tables

Placing multiple unlinked tables on a form is handy when you want to keep a small lookup table on the screen during data entry and editing, and you don't want to force the entry in one table to contain a value that's listed in the other table.

For example, suppose that you have a table similar to Custlist, but modified slightly to allow for international addresses. That is, rather than a two-letter State field, the table includes a fifteen-character State/Province field. It also has a Zip/Postal Code field (not just Zip) and another field for storing the country name.

For convenience, you want to be able to look up two-letter state abbreviations for U.S. addresses, but don't want to force any record in the Custlist table to contain one of those abbreviations. The sections that follow describe the general steps for creating multi-table forms, using this modified Custlist table and the States table in the example.

Designing the Subform

A *subform* is one that ends up being a part of a larger multi-table form. To create a subform, choose **F**orms ➤ **D**esign and set up the form as usual. When you're finished designing a subform, save your work and return to the desktop with the usual **DO-IT!** option or F2 key. While you're designing that form, however, keep in mind the following:

- Since the form will eventually be used as part of another form, remember to leave empty room on the screen for the other form or forms.
- Regardless of where you plan on positioning the subform on the master form later, you should start the subform near the upper-left corner of the Form Design screen.

Place the first field in a subform at row 2 column 2 so you can later draw a border around the form starting at row 1 column 1.

616 CHAPTER 15

ADVANCED REPORT AND FORM TECHNIQUES

- If you want the subform to stand out on the master form later, you can use the **B**order ➤ **P**lace options to draw a border around the entire subform.

The sample States multi-record form (see Figure 15.35 earlier in the chapter) could easily be used as an unlinked subform, since it was designed with all these guidelines in mind. You can create as many subforms as you wish, following the same guidelines for each one.

Designing the Master Form

After you've created your subforms, you can create the master form. Again, use the standard techniques for creating a custom form. While designing your master form, keep in mind that you need to leave some space for the subform or subforms. For example, Figure 15.36 shows a sample form designed for the modified Custlist table, with some blank space reserved near the lower-left corner for the States subform.

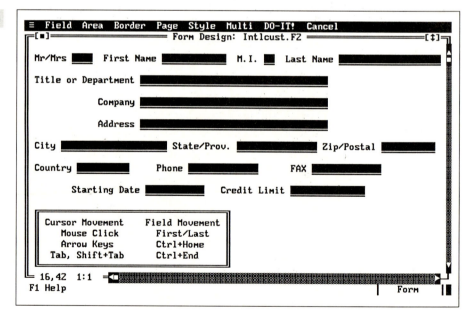

FIGURE 15.36

Sample master form, with some space reserved in the lower-right corner of the screen for a subform

Embedding Subforms

After you've placed whatever fields you want on the master form, you can embed subforms. Follow these steps:

1. From the Form Design screen, choose **Multi** ➤ **T**ables ➤ **P**lace. (If you've left the Form Design screen, just use **F**orms ➤ **C**hange to bring it back with the master form design.)

2. Choose **U**nlinked (the tables in this example are not linked).

3. Choose the name of the table that contains the subform you want to embed (the States table in this example), then choose OK or press ↵.

4. Choose the subform from the list of form names that appears (the State subform in this example). A "ghost image" of the subform appears at the lower-right corner of the screen.

5. Use the arrow keys to move the ghost image of the subform to wherever you want it to appear in the master form. Figure 15.37 shows an example, where the ghost image is positioned below the Credit Limit field.

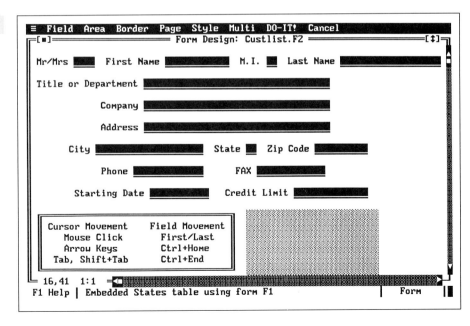

FIGURE 15.37

Ghost image for States subform positioned near the lower-right corner of the master form

618 CHAPTER 15

ADVANCED REPORT AND FORM TECHNIQUES

6. Press ↵ after positioning the subform.

7. Choose **DO-IT!** or press F2 to save the completed form.

Using a Multi-table Form

After you create a multi-table form, you can use the form as you would use any other form. When you use **I**mage ➤ **P**ickForm and choose the name of the master form, the form will appear with its subforms. Figure 15.38 shows the sample master form created in the previous section.

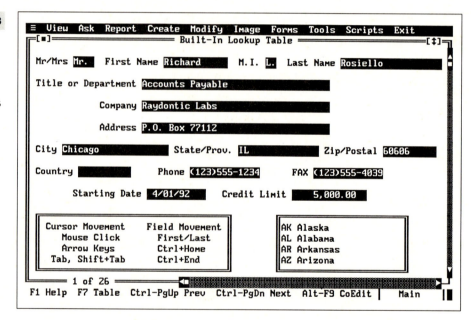

FIGURE 15.38

Sample master form with unlinked embedded form listing two-letter abbreviations for states

While the multi-table form is on your screen, you can use any of the following techniques:

- To switch from one form to the other, click on either form or press the Next Image key, F4, or the Previous Image key, F3.

- You can use the regular scrolling keys (PgUp, PgDn, Ctrl-PgUp, Ctrl-PgDn, and the arrow keys), to scroll through records in the current form independently (assuming the forms are unlinked).

Unlike with the HelpAndFill option described earlier, you cannot copy data from the subform to the larger master form using F2. Thus, after looking up the state abbreviation you want in the subform, you need to click on the State/Prov field in the master form (or press F3), then type in that abbreviation. Because there is no validity checking involved with unlinked tables, you can enter any value in the State/Prov field, not just a two-letter abbreviation from the States table.

To ensure that the State/Prov field can contain any data, remove any validity checks from that field while in Edit mode (using ValCheck ➤ Clear ➤ Field).

Managing Subforms

You can change a multi-table form just as you would modify any other form. Choose **Forms** ➤ **Change**, specify the name of the table that you designed the master form from, and select the master form. The multi-table form appears on the Form Design screen.

In addition to all the usual form editing techniques, you can choose **Multi** ➤ **Tables** to access the options shown below for managing the subforms on your screen:

Use **R**emove to erase a subform or **M**ove to move a subform.

If you want to make all the fields in a subform or the master form display-only fields, so they can be viewed but not edited while the form is being used, choose **Multi** ➤ **Tables** ➤ **DisplayOnly**. You'll see two options. If you want to change the status of the master form's fields, choose **M**aster. If you want to change the status of a subform's fields, choose **O**ther. Then choose **Y**es. To remove any previous DisplayOnly settings, so that data in the fields can be changed, added, or deleted, repeat this procedure, but choose **N**o instead of Yes.

CHAPTER 15
ADVANCED REPORT AND FORM TECHNIQUES

Using Multi-table Forms with Linked Tables

The techniques for creating a multi-table form with multiple linked tables is almost the same for linked tables as it is for unlinked tables, but there are some additional restrictions:

- The common field that links records in a subform's table must be a key field.

- Common fields that link the tables can only be placed in the master form, not in any subforms.

- Any key fields from a subform's table that are not part of the link to the master table must be placed on the subform as a regular field.

Given these restrictions, suppose you want to create a fancy multi-table form, like the one shown in Figure 15.39, for entering and editing invoices. If you want to use the sample Invoices, Accounts, and Orders tables (described in Chapter 14) to create this form, you'll be faced with one problem right off the bat: the Orders table does not have any key fields (so its records don't need to be unique).

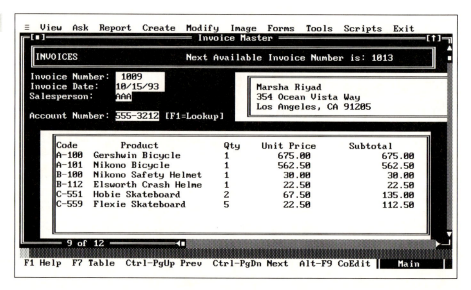

FIGURE 15.39

Multi-table form that lets you enter invoice transactions and stores the data in three different tables

EDITING MULTIPLE TABLES WITH A SINGLE FORM

A fairly easy solution to this problem is to create a temporary table with key fields for storing new invoiced transactions. Then, with some automatic updating (described in the next chapter), you can copy the invoiced transactions from that table to the more generic Orders table so all the orders are in one table for easier processing. Here's how you could create this form:

1. Use **T**ools ➤ **C**opy ➤ **T**able to copy the Orders table to a new table, perhaps named Invdtail (for Invoice Detail).

2. Use **M**odify ➤ **R**estructure and make the first two fields in the Invdtail table key fields.

3. Add a field for storing the product name (which will allow you to display the product name on the screen while entering invoices).

4. Add a field named Invoice Date, which will copy the invoice date from the Invoices table to each record in the Invdtail table.

5. Add a field named Date Posted. You can use this field to keep track of when each record from Invdtail was posted to the more general Orders table.

Figure 15.40 shows the Invdtail table with this structure.

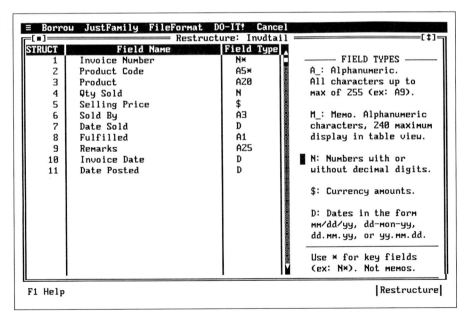

FIGURE 15.40

A table named Invdtail, used for entering invoices through a multi-table form

Because the first two fields in the Invdtail table are key fields, the only records that will be rejected as duplicates are those with identical invoice numbers and product codes. But, since no two line items on a single invoice are likely to have the same product code, this shouldn't pose any problems.

Another thing to think about is data that could be entered once on the master form, rather than being entered for each record in a subform. For example, in the structure of the Invdtail table, each record includes a Date Sold field and a Sold By field (which includes the salesperson's initials). But there's really no reason to include this information on each line item of the Invdtail table when you're entering an invoice, because the Date Sold field will be the same as the Invoice Date, and the salesperson's initials would be the same for each transaction. Therefore, if you just add a Sold By field to the Invoices table, as shown in Figure 15.41, you can have Paradox automatically fill in those fields for you, as you'll see in the next chapter.

Now let's look at how you could use the many form techniques you've learned so far, and our same tables, to create a very powerful and fancy form for entering invoices.

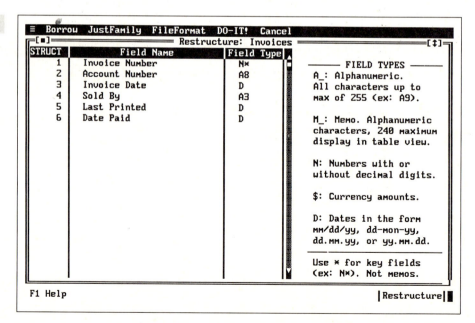

FIGURE 15.41

The Invoices table with a Sold By field added, which will be used to automatically fill in the Sold By field in each record of the Invdtail table

Subform for the Invdtail Table

Figure 15.42 shows a sample multi-record form for the Invdtail table. The field masks starting at row 3, column 3 (from left to right) are as follows:

- **Product Code:** Placed with Field ➤ Place ➤ Regular
- **Product:** Placed with Field ➤ Place ➤ DisplayOnly (since you don't need to change product names while entering an invoice)
- **Qty Sold:** Placed with Field ➤ Place ➤ Regular, and narrowed to 7 characters
- **Selling Price:** Placed with Field ➤ Place ➤ Regular, and narrowed to 12 characters
- **Subtotal:** A calculated field placed using Field ➤ Place ➤ Calculated, with the expression [Qty Sold] * [Selling Price]

FIGURE 15.42

Subform using multiple records from the Invdtail table

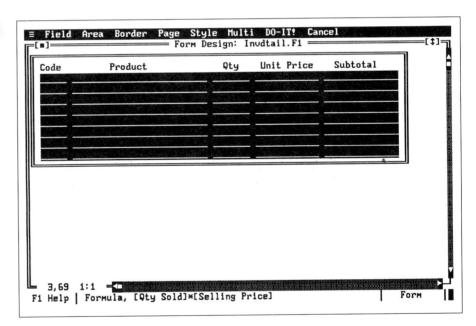

ADVANCED REPORT AND FORM TECHNIQUES

NOTE You can't include the Invoice Number field from the Invdtail table in the subform, because that field is the common field that links this table to the Invoices table.

After placing the field masks across row 3, we used **M**ulti ➤ **R**ecords ➤ **D**efine to copy those field masks down seven rows. Then we typed in the column titles and drew a border around the whole thing using **B**order ➤ **P**lace ➤ **D**ouble-line.

Choosing **DO-IT!** after creating the subform takes you back to the desktop.

Subform for the Accounts Table

Information about accounts (customers) comes from the Accounts table. The subform for the Account table is shown in Figure 15.43. The first two fields, Account Name and Address, were placed using **F**ield ➤ **P**lace ➤ **R**egular. The last field is a calculated field, entered by using **F**ield ➤ **P**lace ➤ **C**alculated, with the expression

[City] + ", " + [State] + " " +[Zip]

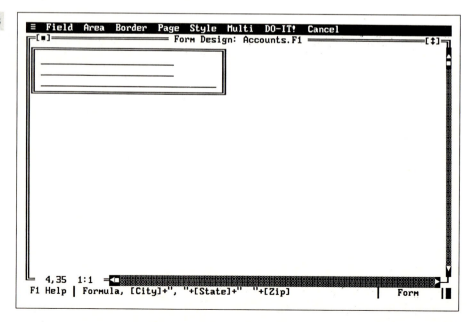

FIGURE 15.43

Accounts subform, designed from the Accounts table, for use on the Invoices multi-table form

EDITING MULTIPLE TABLES WITH A SINGLE FORM

As usual, choose **DO-IT!** after designing the Accounts subform to return to the desktop.

The Invoices Master Form

Figure 15.44 shows the Invoices master form on the Form Design screen. The field masks are as follows:

- **Next Available Invoice Number:** A calculated field, placed with Field ➤ Place ➤ Calculated, with the expression CMAX("Invoices","Invoice Number") + 1, which displays the largest current invoice number in the Invoices table with 1 added to it

- **Invoice Number:** The Invoice Number field from the Invoices table, placed with Field ➤ Place ➤ Regular

- **Invoice Date:** The Invoice Date field from the Invoices table, placed with Field ➤ Place ➤ Regular

- **SalesPerson:** The Sold By field from the Invoices table, placed with Field ➤ Place ➤ Regular

- **Account Number:** The Account Number field from the Invoices table, placed with Field ➤ Place ➤ Regular

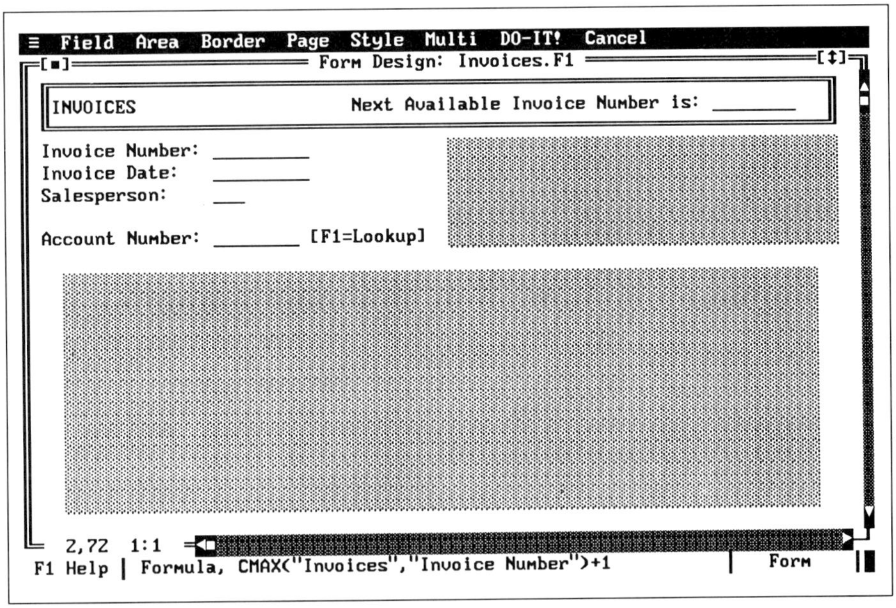

FIGURE 15.44

The Invoices master form

The smaller shaded ghost image is the subform from the Accounts table; the larger ghost image is the subform from the Invdtail table. Both were placed with **Multi ➤ Tables ➤ Place ➤ Linked**.

After saving the master form, there are some nice finishing touches you can add, as described next, to make it especially easy to use.

Finishing Touches for the Invoices Master Form

You can add some lookup validity checks to the Invoices master form that will really make it powerful. As usual, you need to add these in Edit mode, not in the Form Design screen. So, after saving the master form and returning to the desktop, clear the desktop, then choose **Modify ➤ Edit** and specify the Invoices table. Then select **Image ➤ PickForm** and choose your Invoices master form to view it on the screen. Here are some suggested refinements you can make to the various fields:

- **Invoice Date:** Choose **ValCheck ➤ Define ➤ Default**, and set the default date to TODAY so you don't need to fill in the invoice date for every invoice.

- **Account Number:** Choose **Valcheck ➤ Define ➤ TableLookup**, and define Accounts as the lookup table. Then choose **JustCurrentField** and **HelpAndFill** to make it easy to look up account numbers when entering an invoice.

- **Product Code:** In the first Product Code field (under the Code heading), use **ValCheck ➤ Define ➤ TableLookup** and choose Mastinv as the lookup table. Then choose **AllCorrespondingFields** and **HelpAndFill** to make it easy to look up product codes while entering invoices. For this same field, choose **ValCheck ➤ Define ➤ Auto ➤ Filled ➤ Yes** to have the cursor automatically move to the next field when the field is filled.

As usual, choose **DO-IT!** after defining the validity checks for the form.

Using the Invoices Master Form

You can use the Invoices master form for entering and editing data (using **Modify ➤ DataEntry**, **Edit**, or **CoEdit**). If you defined the validity checks described in the previous section, you can use the form as follows:

- When entering the invoice date, you can just skip the field by pressing ⏎ to insert the current date.

- When entering an account number, you can press F1 to look up a customer name and account number. After positioning the cursor on the customer you want, press F2 to return to the Invoices form. You may need to press the Next Image key, F4, or the Re-sync Links key, Ctrl-l, to display the customer name and address, depending on which mode you're in.

- When entering a part code, you can press F1 to look up a part code. Then position the cursor on the code you want and press F2 to copy the part code, product name, and selling price into the current line item.

As usual, when you've finished entering or editing records, choose **DO-IT!** to save your work.

Taking Advantage of Referential Integrity

As you gain experience using multi-table forms, you may find that Paradox occasionally refuses to let you delete or change certain information once it has been entered. That's because Paradox uses a built-in scheme, called *referential integrity*, to protect the relationships among data in the related tables. Paradox applies four basic rules to editing on multi-table forms:

- You cannot delete a record in the master table while linked records in the detail tables depend on it. For example, if a customer in the Custdata table has outstanding orders in the Invoices table, you cannot delete that customer's record until you've deleted his or her outstanding orders.

- If you change a linking field in the master record, Paradox automatically changes the values in the detail tables. For example, if you change a customer's ID number in the Custdata table, all outstanding orders for that customer on a separate Orders table are automatically changed to that new number.

- Once you begin editing a table using a multi-table form, you cannot switch to Table view using the usual toggle key (F7). You must press F2, or press F10 and select Cancel, to end the current multi-table editing session.

- On a network, a multi-table form places a full lock on all the tables accessed on the form. Other users on the network will be able to access the locked data *only* if they use the same multi-table form.

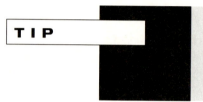

TIP When a multi-table form forbids you from changing or deleting information, you can still access any single table represented on the form, in the usual Table view or Form view, and make changes.

Summary

This chapter covered some advanced topics concerning forms and reports. Here's a quick recap of the more important concepts and techniques:

- Use **F**ield ➤ **P**lace ➤ **C**alculated in the Report Design screen to insert a calculated field in a report.

- Use **F**ield ➤ **P**lace ➤ **S**ummary in the Report Design screen to insert a summary field into a report.

- Use **F**ield ➤ **L**ookUp ➤ **L**ink in the Report Design screen to link to a keyed, related table, then use **F**ield ➤ **P**lace ➤ **R**egular to place fields from that table into the current report.

- To include a field from a linked table in a report calculation, choose **F**ield ➤ **P**lace ➤ **C**alculated as usual. But when entering the calculation expression, precede the field name from the linked table with that table's name followed by a hyphen and greater-than sign, as in [Accounts->Account Name].

- To embed printer codes in a report format for boldface, fonts, or other printer attributes, choose **F**ield ➤ **P**lace ➤ **C**alculated in the Report Design screen, and enter the printer code in quotation marks.

SUMMARY

- To add a new, blank page to a custom form for placing additional fields, choose **P**age ➤ **I**nsert in the Form Design screen.
- You can use the PgUp and PgDn keys to scroll from page to page in multipage forms.
- Use **F**ield ➤ **P**lace ➤ **C**alculated in the Form Design screen to place calculated fields in a custom form.
- To verify, and optionally look up, data in a table based on the contents of another table, use **V**alCheck ➤ **D**efine ➤ **T**ableLookup to define a validity check based on a lookup table.
- To create a multi-record custom form, choose **M**ulti ➤ **R**ecords ➤ **D**efine and follow the instructions on the screen for duplicating fields on the form.
- To create a multi-table custom form, you must first decide which table will be the master table. Then, create a subform for each of the other tables, and use **M**ulti ➤ **T**ables ➤ **P**lace to place the subforms on the master form.

CHAPTER 16

Automatic Updating with Multiple Tables

fast TRACK

- **In an automatic updating procedure**   **635**

    data from one table is used to change data stored in a separate, related table.

- **To ensure proper and consistent updating**   **636**

    you should record the entire updating procedure in a script, and use the script to perform future updates.

- **When you use the contents of one table to change the contents of another**   **638**

    you need to devise some scheme to prevent posted records from being updated again. You can do so by flagging posted records, and devising the update scheme so that it only uses unflagged records. Or you can move all posted records from their original table to a separate history table.

- **To update tables with incompatible formats**   **639**

    use the reserved word INSERT in the query. With INSERT queries, you can add records containing some fields from one table to another table, perform calculations on specific fields before updating, and copy some fields but not others to a table (leaving the other fields in each record blank).

- **When filling in the Query forms for an automatic update**   **640**

    be sure to identify the common field that links the two tables with matching example elements, entered with the Example Element key, F5.

- **To make a saved query auto-executing**   **642**

    so that it actually performs the query, edit the saved query and type a Do_It! command at the bottom of the file, on a line placed after the Endquery statement.

- **In the table that contains the data you want to copy**   **644**

    or the data you want to use in a calculation, identify fields to be copied or used with example elements.

- **In the table that will be receiving data from the other table**   **648**

    use the CHANGETO reserved word with example elements to indicate which data you want to use from the source table.

- **If you want to move posted records from their original table to history tables**   **649**

    use Tools ➤ More ➤ Add to add records to the history table, then use Tools ➤ More ➤ Empty to empty the original table. Be sure to include these steps in any script that performs the update.

- **To correct an error after automatically updating records**   **657**

    enter an adjustment transaction, which leaves an audit trail that permanently records the correction on disk.

IN this chapter, we'll look at techniques for automatically updating information from one table using information from another table. Here we'll pull together many techniques from previous chapters, particularly the methods for querying multiple tables to change data and perform calculations. We'll also be using a few options from the Tools menu.

To be honest, with the exception of the INSERT query, there's really nothing new at all in this chapter, in the sense that all the techniques have been covered previously. But the possibilities that those techniques present are endless. The trick, of course, is knowing how and when to use these various techniques productively to get some real work done. And that's what this chapter is really all about.

At this stage of the game, all we can really do is present some examples as "food for thought" in creating your own databases and applications. While we can take you step by step through the procedures, you need to keep in mind that what we're demonstrating here are just examples. They are intended to demonstrate the fact that there is virtually no limit to the ways in which you can mix and match data from multiple tables.

We'll also discuss the important concept of keeping track of which records have or have not already been used during an automatic updating procedure. Since Paradox has no built-in way of knowing whether a given record in a table has already been posted during an update, it's up to you to devise some scheme for preventing records from being posted more than once. We'll illustrate two commonly used techniques in this chapter: flagging posted records in their original table, and moving posted records from their original table to another table (often called a *history table*).

Copying Fields from One Table to Another

In the preceding chapter, we created two tables for storing invoice information: Invoices and Invdtail. Both tables were structured to allow us to create a multi-table form for entering and editing invoices.

As you may recall, the Invdtail table included a Date Sold field and a Sold By field. However, we didn't include these fields on the multi-record subform for entering invoices, because it would have been redundant to enter that information on every line item on every invoice. Thus, after you enter invoices via the multi-table form, the Date Sold and Sold By fields in the Invdtail table will be empty. For example, Figure 16.1 shows some sample data in these two tables after entering two invoices numbered 1008 and 1009. (We've rotated fields in the Invdtail table so you could see the blank Date Sold and Sold By fields.)

You can easily create a query that quickly copies the Invoice Date and Sold By fields from each record in the Invoices table to the Date Sold and Sold By fields in corresponding records in the Invdtail table. This beats typing that repetitive information over and over again on each invoice. Filling the Sold By and Date Sold records in Invdtail automatically

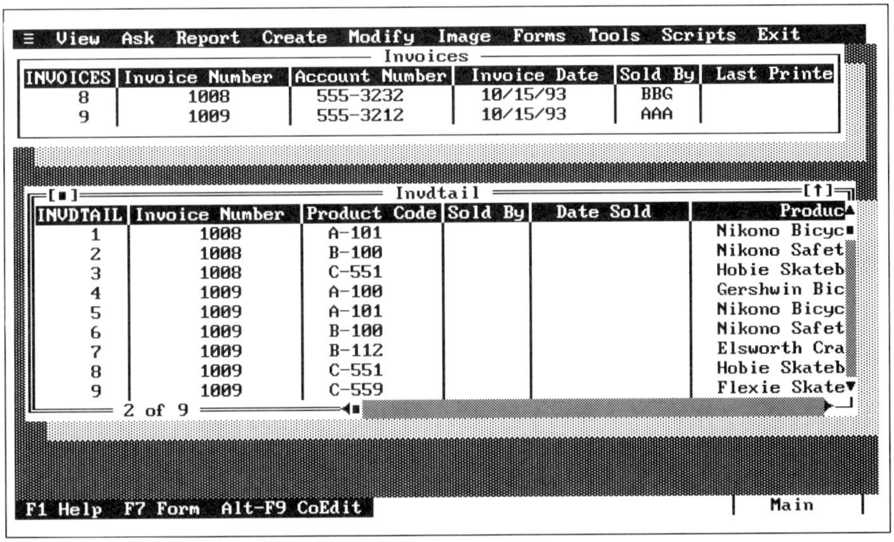

FIGURE 16.1

Sample data on the Invoices and Invdtail tables, entered via the multi-table form described in the previous chapter. The Date Sold and Sold By fields in Invdtail are empty.

```
≡ View  Ask  Report  Create  Modify  Image  Forms  Tools  Scripts  Exit
                              Invoices
 INVOICES | Invoice Number | Account Number | Invoice Date | Sold By | Last Printe
    8     |     1008       |    555-3232    |   10/15/93   |   BBG   |
    9     |     1009       |    555-3212    |   10/15/93   |   AAA   |

                              Invdtail                                        [↑]
 INVDTAIL | Invoice Number | Product Code | Sold By | Date Sold |     Produc▲
    1     |     1008       |    A-101     |         |           | Nikono Bicyc■
    2     |     1008       |    B-100     |         |           | Nikono Safet
    3     |     1008       |    C-551     |         |           | Hobie Skateb
    4     |     1009       |    A-100     |         |           | Gershwin Bic
    5     |     1009       |    A-101     |         |           | Nikono Bicyc
    6     |     1009       |    B-100     |         |           | Nikono Safet
    7     |     1009       |    B-112     |         |           | Elsworth Cra
    8     |     1009       |    C-551     |         |           | Hobie Skateb
    9     |     1009       |    C-559     |         |           | Flexie Skate▼
  2 of 9

 F1 Help  F7 Form  Alt-F9 CoEdit                                        Main
```

flags those records as already being updated. This query only updates records with blanks in both the Sold By and Date Sold fields. Here's the procedure:

1. Use **A**sk to create a query for the table that contains values you want to copy (Invoices in this example).

2. Move the cursor to the field that links this table to the table you'll be copying records to (Invoice Number in this example), and type in an example element using the Example Element key, F5. We used INVNO as the example element.

3. Put an example element in each field that you want to copy. (We placed the example elements IDATE and ISOLD in the Invoice Date and Sold By fields, respectively, as these are the values we want to copy.)

4. Choose **A**sk and create a query for the table you want to copy these values to (Invdtail in this case).

5. Put the appropriate example element in the common field of this Query form. (We put INVNO in the Invoice Number field, since Invoice Number is the common field that links the Invoices and Invdtail tables.)

6. Insert your query criteria, if any, and use CHANGETO commands with example elements from the first table to indicate which fields you want to copy into the current table.

7. If this is a query you might want to repeat often in the future, use **S**cripts ➤ **Q**uerySave to save it.

Figure 16.2 shows the completed Query forms. (We've rotated and narrowed some of the columns in the Invoices and Invdtail table Query forms so you could see the Sold By and Date Sold columns.) The form uses example elements as follows:

- INVNO is the example element linking the common Invoice Number field of the two tables.
- IDATE is the example element representing the Invoice Date in the Invoices table.
- ISOLD is the example element representing the Sold By field in the Invoices table.

- BLANK, CHANGETO ISOLD tells Paradox that if the Sold By field in the current record is blank, fill it with the Sold By value from the Invoices table.
- BLANK, CHANGETO IDATE tells Paradox that if the Date Sold field in the current record is blank, fill it with the Invoice Date field value from the Invoices table.

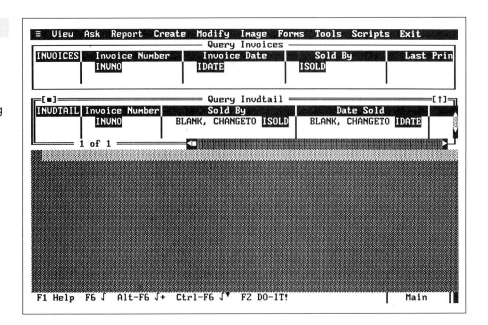

FIGURE 16.2

A query to copy the contents of the Invoice Date and Sold By fields in the Invoices table to corresponding records in the Invdtail table

After you perform the query (using F2), the usual Changed table will appear. If you close that table then open the Invoices and Invdtail tables, you'll see that Paradox has indeed copied the appropriate data from Invoices to Invdtail, as Figure 16.3 shows.

When you've created and tested this query, you might want to save it for future use, so you need not bother to re-create it from scratch each time. Remember, use **S**cripts ➤ **Q**uerySave to save your queries. In the next chapter, where you'll learn to further automate the overall updating procedure, we'll refer to the query presented here by the name Update1.

CHAPTER 16

AUTOMATIC UPDATING WITH MULTIPLE TABLES

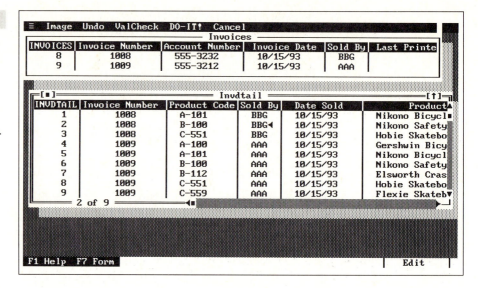

FIGURE 16.3

After performing the query in Figure 16.2, the Date Sold and Sold By fields in the Invdtail table have appropriate values from the Invoices table.

Copying Incompatible Records from One Table to Another

As explained in the previous chapter, you can't create a multi-table form from the sample Orders table because of the rules concerning key fields with multi-table forms. As a solution, we created the Invdtail table, with key fields. That table also includes a Product field (so the form can display product names), an Invoice Date field, and a Date Posted field. Now you'll learn how to put those new fields to use.

The previous chapter also discussed some of the advantages of placing all orders (both cash and credit) in a single table. So, can you have your cake and eat it, too? That is, can you have the luxury of the multi-table form, and still have an unkeyed Orders table of all order transactions? The answer is a qualified Yes. You can if you copy all records from Invdtail to Orders..., and if you then find some way to flag records from Invdtail once they've been copied to the Orders table, so no record is ever copied twice.

Using INSERT and Multiple Queries on a Single Form

The first problem you'll encounter is that, if you try to use **T**ools ➤ **M**ore ➤ **A**dd to add records from Invdtail directly to the Orders table, Paradox will complain that the tables have incompatible structures. That's because we added the Product, Invoice Date, and Date Posted fields to the Invdtail table. For example, Figure 16.4 shows some records in the sample Orders and Invdtail tables. As you can see, the Invdtail table includes a Product field, and the Orders table does not.

FIGURE 16.4

The Orders and Invdtail tables do not have identical structures (Invdtail includes a field named Product).

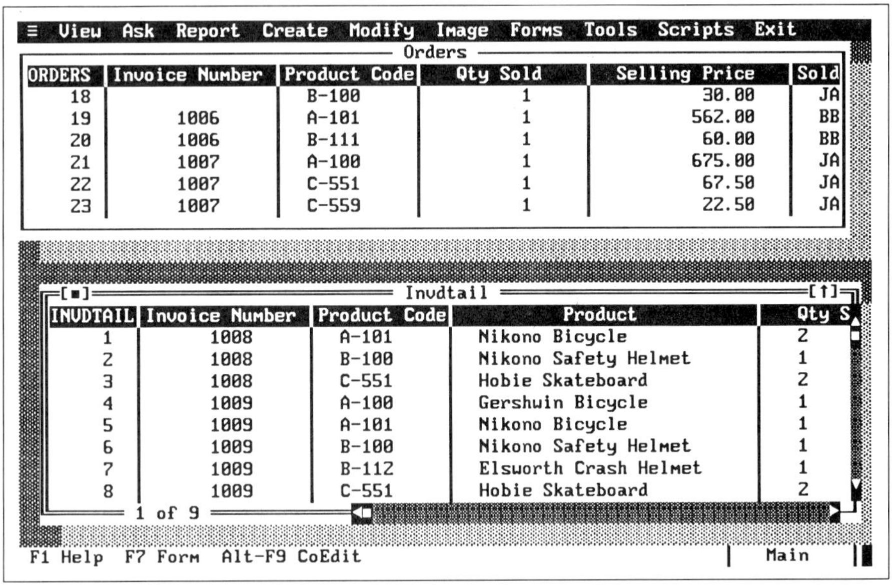

The reserved word INSERT offers a way to bypass this problem. INSERT lets you add new records to a table, based on a query. INSERT, like the DELETE and FIND reserved words (discussed in Chapter 8), must be placed in the leftmost field of a query form.

You can use INSERT to combine fields from several source tables into a single record in the target table The *source* table contains the fields you want to insert. The *target* table receives the data in these fields and places them in a new record. Here's the procedure for setting up a query that uses INSERT:

1. Open the Query form for the source table or tables.

2. Place an example element in all of the fields that you want to insert from the source table or tables. You can also place query criteria in the Query form for each source table to specify which records should be inserted.

3. Open a Query form for the target table.

4. Enter the word INSERT in the leftmost column of the target table's Query form.

5. In the target table's Query form, place an example element in each field that you want inserted in the target table. Each example element should match an example element in a corresponding field in the source table or tables.

You can perform multiple queries at the same time in a Paradox Query form, by using the OR operator, as described in Chapter 8. Normally, when a query creates an Answer table, the results of both lines of the OR criteria are placed together in the Answer table. In special queries such as INSERT, CHANGETO, and DELETE, which don't create an Answer table, the second query is performed independently, after the query placed on the first line of the Query form.

NOTE When more than one of the special reserved words are specified on the same line, they execute in the following order: DELETE, then CHANGETO, then INSERT.

The following example uses INSERT and the ability to perform multiple special queries with one Query form to solve the problem of updating the sample Orders table. Here are the steps:

1. Close all open windows (press Alt-F8).

2. Choose **A**sk, then specify Invdtail as the table to query.

3. Place an example element, using the F5 key, in every field *except* Product, Invoice Date, and Date Posted (because these three fields are not included in the Orders table).

4. Type **BLANK** in the Date Posted field (the last column of the Query form), as shown in Figure 16.5, to limit the inserted records to those with no date in the Date Posted field.

5. Press ↓ and type **BLANK, CHANGETO TODAY** on the second line of the Date Posted field, as shown in Figure 16.5. This will cause Paradox to perform a CHANGETO query on the Invdtail table, after the INSERT query is completed.

6. Press F10 and choose **A**sk, then specify Orders as the table to query.

7. In the left column of the Order table Query form, enter **INSERT**, as shown in Figure 16.5.

8. In the fields of the Orders table's Query form, place example elements that match those you placed in corresponding fields in the Invdtail table's Query form, as shown in Figure 16.5.

9. Choose **S**cripts ➤ QuerySave and specify Update2 as the name of the script file in which to save the Query forms.

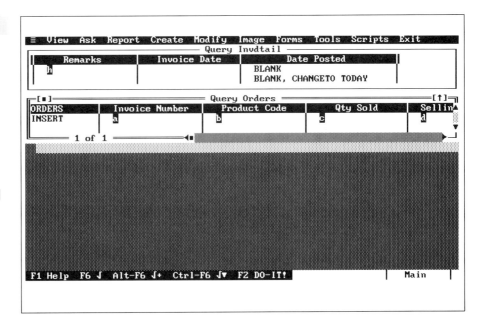

FIGURE 16.5

Combining INSERT and CHANGETO in one query. This query will copy fields from Invdtail table records, which have a blank Date Posted field, to new Orders table records and will then change the value in any blank Date Posted field in the Invdtail table to today's date.

AUTOMATIC UPDATING WITH MULTIPLE TABLES

10. Perform the query (press F2). You won't see an Answer table or the updated Orders and Invdtail tables. Instead, two temporary tables, named Changed and Inserted, will appear on the desktop.

From the Changed and Inserted tables, you can tell that all the Invdtail table records that had blank Date Posted fields have been changed. You can also see that the specified fields from those records have been inserted in the Orders table. Figure 16.6 shows the updated Orders and Invdtail tables.

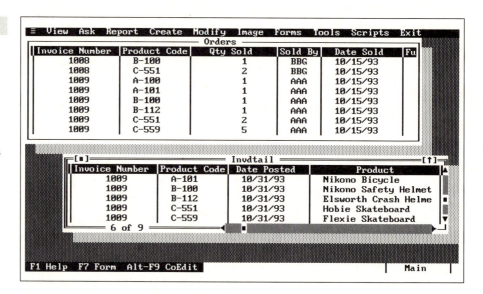

FIGURE 16.6

The Orders table now contains copies of records from the Invdtail table. Also, the Date Posted field of the Invdtail table records that were posted by this query is filled with the current date.

In the future, you can play back the Update2 script to bring up the Query form, and then press F2 to run the update procedure. If there are no new records to post, empty Changed and Inserted tables will be created when you run the query, but no records will be added to the Orders table.

Creating an Auto-Execute Query

When you recall a saved query, its Query form appears on your screen so that you can make changes before executing it. However, any saved query can be made auto-execute by following these steps:

1. Choose **Scripts** ➤ **Edit** ➤ **Open**.

2. Specify the name of the saved query script you want to make auto-executing.

3. Move your cursor to the end of the last line in the saved query, after the command Endquery.

4. Enter the PAL command **Do_It!**. Figure 16.7 shows the saved Update2 script with the PAL Do_It! command inserted at the end.

FIGURE 16.7

The saved Update2 script with the PAL Do_It! command inserted at the end to make the query auto-executing when the script is played back.

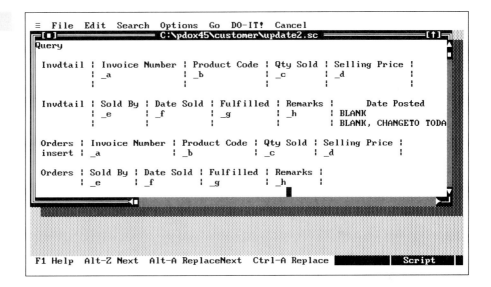

The PAL command requires an underline character (_) between *Do* and *It!*, not a hyphen as displayed in the Paradox menu choice.

5. Press F2 or choose **DO-IT!**.

From now on, when you use **S**cripts ➤ **P**lay to recall the saved query, its Query form will appear on the screen and the query will be performed automatically.

However, there's one potential hazard to this approach: If you were now to edit existing invoices with the multi-table form, the changes would be made in the Invdtail table, and never be posted to the Orders table. To guard against such "unpostable" edits, you could copy posted invoices, which would include records from both the Invoices and Invdtail tables, to history tables. Then you could create a multi-table form that allows you to view data in these history tables, but not to make any changes to those tables. Any changes to posted invoices would then need to be made through adjustment transactions. History tables and adjustment transactions are described later in this chapter.

Calculating with INSERT Queries

INSERT queries can also be used to insert calculation results in the target table. You place calculation fields with example elements in the source table's Query form, along with the reserved word INSERT in the leftmost column. When you execute the query, the fields with matching example elements or the results of calculations based on those example elements will be inserted from records in the source table (or tables) into new records in the target table.

Unlike other types of queries, the values you type in the target table's Query forms are all treated as expressions. In effect, all the criteria in the target table's Query form are calculations. These criteria don't select records; instead, they pick up the values of a field or fields from the source table, perform any calculation you specified, and then insert the value in the new record in the target table. If you've only specified the example element (without a calculation), the field containing the example element is calculated as itself, and the source table's field value is simply copied to the target table.

Another advantage of using INSERT is that you don't need to fill in all the fields in the target table. Only those target table fields that have example elements or calculations based on example elements will be used in the creation of the new records in the target table. You can design a new table with fields for data from an existing table, or even create an identical structure as a single source table. You can then choose which fields to fill in the new table, by choosing example elements from the source table for only those elements.

Changing the Values in One Table Based on Another Table

Perhaps the most common use of automatic updating is to change the contents of one table based on the contents of another. For example, you might want to subtract all the Qty Sold values in the Orders table from In Stock quantities in the MastInv table. That way, your In Stock quantities would be accurate and up to date.

Once again, however, you're faced with the matter of finding some means of ensuring that each record in the Orders table is used only once when subtracting quantities sold from In Stock quantities.

In the previous example, we accomplished this by flagging the Date Posted field in each record of Invdtail with the current date. And we designed the queries that do the updating in such a way that only unflagged records (those with blank Date Posted fields) were used in updating.

Another way to ensure that records are never posted more than once is to move all posted records from the original table to a history table. There are advantages and disadvantages to each approach. The advantage of flagging posted records is that all the records remain in one table, which in some ways makes overall management easier. But the disadvantage is that the table (the Orders table in our example) grows indefinitely, and could be quite huge by the end of the year. This could slow down general processing.

By keeping "live" orders in one table and moving posted orders to a separate table, you gain the advantage of being able to keep the table of live orders fairly small. This can make day-to-day processing of orders go a little faster.

The following sections describe how to use the history table method. For your own applications, you can decide on which approach is best on a case-by-case basis.

Creating an Order History File

First, you need to create a history table to store the posted records. Since this table needs to have exactly the same structure as the original table

(Orders in this example), you can quickly create an empty history table by following these steps:

1. Use **T**ools ➤ **M**ore ➤ **D**irectory to switch to the directory that contains the Orders table.

2. Choose **C**reate and enter a name for the history table (we'll use Ordhist as the table name in this example), then choose OK.

3. In the table's Create screen, choose **B**orrow, specify the name of the table whose structure you want to borrow (Orders in this example), and then choose OK or press ↵.

4. Choose **D**O-IT! to save the table structure.

Now the Orders and Ordhist tables have exactly the same structures. If you like, you can use **T**ools ➤ **C**opy ➤ **J**ustFamily to copy forms and reports from the Orders table to the Ordhist table.

Subtracting Quantities Sold from In Stock Quantities

Subtracting quantities sold from In Stock quantities requires three tasks:

- Calculate the quantity of each item sold in the Orders table.
- Subtract the quantity of each item sold from the In Stock quantity in the Mastinv table.
- Move all records from the Orders table to the Ordhist table so that those same records are not used in future updates.

To make it easy to test and verify the updating procedure, you might want to start with some "dummy" values in the Mastinv table. For example, in Figure 16.8, we've set the In Stock quantity to 100 and the On Order quantity to 10. (We'll use the On Order field in a later update.)

Since several steps are involved in this automatic updating procedure, you might want to record all the necessary steps in a script. Remember that you need to use the keyboard rather than the mouse when you're recording

CHANGING THE VALUES IN ONE TABLE BASED ON ANOTHER TABLE

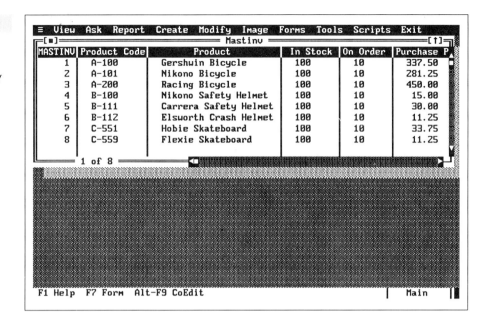

FIGURE 16.8

Some dummy values in the Mastinv table, used to test and verify the automatic updating procedure

a script. Here's the procedure for creating a script to subtract the quantities sold:

1. Start with a clear desktop (press Alt-F8).
2. Choose **S**cripts ➤ **B**eginRecord.
3. Give the script a name (Update3 in this example) and choose OK.
4. Choose **A**sk and specify Orders as the table to query.
5. Check the Product Code field.
6. Type **CALC SUM AS Sold** in the Qty Sold field, as shown at the top of Figure 16.9.
7. Press F2 to perform the query. The resulting Answer table contains the quantity of each item sold, as in the Answer table in Figure 16.9.

NOTE You're still recording the script, so remember that you need to use the keyboard rather than the mouse.

Automatic Updating with Multiple Tables

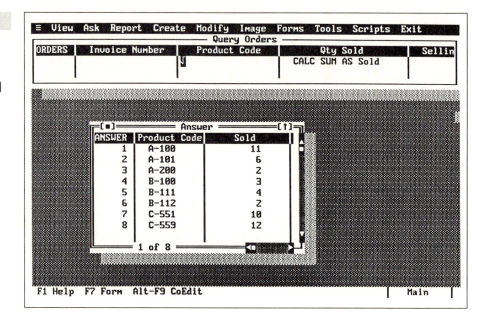

FIGURE 16.9

A CALC query that shows the total quantity of each product sold in a field named Sold in the Answer table

8. Clear the desktop (press Alt-F8).

9. Choose **A**sk, specify Answer as the table to query, and press ↵ to choose OK.

10. Press → then use the F5 key to place an example element (PROD-CODE in this example) in the Product Code field. Also place an example element (SOLDQTY in this example) in the Sold field.

11. Press F10, choose **A**sk, and specify Mastinv as the next table to query.

12. Press →, then use F5 to place an example element (PRODCODE in this example) in the Product Code field of the Mastinv table's Query form, to link the two tables by this common field.

13. Press → and use Ctrl-r to rotate the In Stock field into view. Then, enter an example element (CURRENT in this example) for the In Stock quantity, followed by a comma and a CHANGETO calculation that subtracts the Sold value from the In Stock quantity, again using example elements. In Figure 16.10, CURRENT is the example element for the current In Stock quantity, and SOLDQTY is the example element for the Sold value.

CHANGING THE VALUES IN ONE TABLE BASED ON ANOTHER TABLE

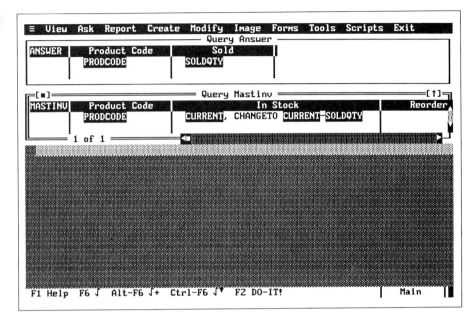

FIGURE 16.10

A query to subtract the quantity of each product sold from the In Stock quantities

14. Press F2 to perform the query.

The Changed table appears, indicating which records have been changed (you don't need to save that table).

Moving Posted Orders to the History Table

Now, while you're still recording the script, you want to make sure to move all the records from the Orders table to the Ordhist table, so those records are not posted again in the future. Here are the steps:

1. Press Alt-F8 to clear the desktop.

2. Choose **T**ools ➤ **M**ore ➤ **A**dd, specify Orders as the source table, and press ↵ to choose OK.

3. Specify Ordhist as the target table, and press ↵ to choose OK.

4. Press F10 and choose **T**ools ➤ **M**ore ➤ **E**mpty.

5. Specify Orders as the table to empty, then press ↵ to choose OK.

AUTOMATIC UPDATING WITH MULTIPLE TABLES

6. Choose **OK** from the pop-up menu (by typing **O** or pressing ↓ then pressing ↵).

7. Clear the desktop (press Alt-F8).

8. Choose **S**cripts ➤ **End-Record**.

If you were to peruse the Mastinv, Orders, and Ordhist tables now, you would find that the In Stock quantities in Mastinv have indeed decreased by the amounts in the calculated Answer table shown back in Figure 16.9. The Ordhist table now contains all the records that were in the Orders table, and the Orders table is empty. Figure 16.11 shows a portion of each of these tables after the updating procedure.

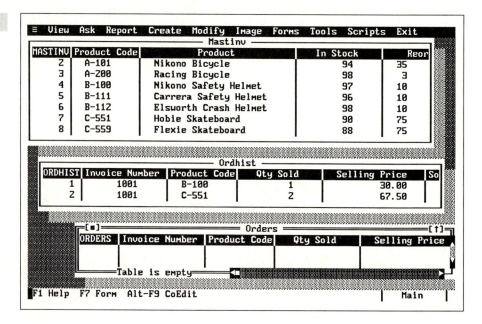

FIGURE 16.11

The Mastinv table In Stock quantities have been decreased. All records from the Orders table have been moved into the Ordhist table.

Because you recorded all the steps involved in performing the query, you need only play back that script when you want to repeat the automatic update in the future. We'll talk about that in a bit more detail in the next chapter. But first, let's look at how you could update the Mastinv table from records in the Purchase table.

Adding Items Received to In Stock Quantities

As you may recall from Chapter 14, the Purchase table (shown in a moment) stores information about products received from vendors. To automatically update Mastinv from the Purchase table, you could follow this procedure:

- Add the quantities of products received to the In Stock quantities in the Mastinv table.
- Subtract the quantities of products received from the On Order quantities in the Mastinv table.
- Change the Purchase Price field in the Mastinv table to the highest Purchase Price in the Purchase table.
- And finally, move all posted purchase transactions from the Purchase table to a history table named Purhist.

The procedure is basically the same as updating the Mastinv table from the Orders table, but we've added some new twists here to demonstrate more updating techniques.

NOTE Although the schemes for updating purchase prices for inventory can get very complex, we have chosen the relatively simple method of updating the Mastinv table's Purchase Price field with the maximum purchase price calculated for each corresponding product code in the Purchase table. This basic example is intended to demonstrate how you can set up your own updating processes.

Creating a History Table for Posted Purchases

First, you'll need to create a history table for storing posted purchase transactions. Use the same basic steps you used to create the Ordhist table:

1. Make sure you're in the correct directory (using **T**ools ➤ **M**ore ➤ **D**irectory).

AUTOMATIC UPDATING WITH MULTIPLE TABLES

2. Choose **C**reate, enter a table name (Purhist in this example), and choose OK.

3. Choose **B**orrow, specify Purchase as the table you want to borrow the structure from, and choose OK.

4. Choose **DO-IT!** to save the new table structure.

Now, as a starting point, let's just assume that the Mastinv, Purchase, and Purhist tables contain the data shown in Figure 16.12 (the Purhist table is empty). That way, you can then go back and verify that the update procedure went as expected.

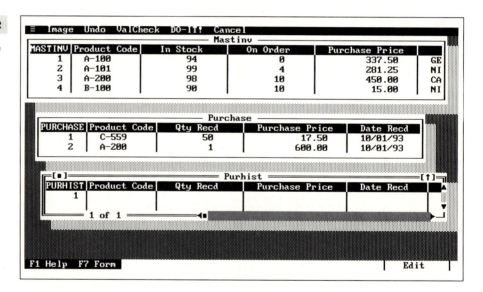

FIGURE 16.12

Sample contents of the Mastinv, Purchase, and (currently empty) Purhist tables

Creating the Updating Script

Once again, we'll record the steps necessary to perform the update in a script. This time we'll name the script Update4. Follow these steps:

1. Clear the desktop (press Alt-F8).

2. Choose **S**cripts ➤ **B**eginRecord.

3. Enter a script name (Update4 in this example) and choose OK.

CHANGING THE VALUES IN ONE TABLE BASED ON ANOTHER TABLE

4. To calculate the sum of all the quantities of product received, choose **A**sk, specify Purchase as the table to query, and press ↵ to choose OK.

5. Set up the query as shown at the top of Figure 16.13, where the Product Code field is checked, CALC SUM AS sums the Qty Recd in a new field named Qty, and CALC MAX AS calculates the highest Purchase Price value in a new field named Cost.

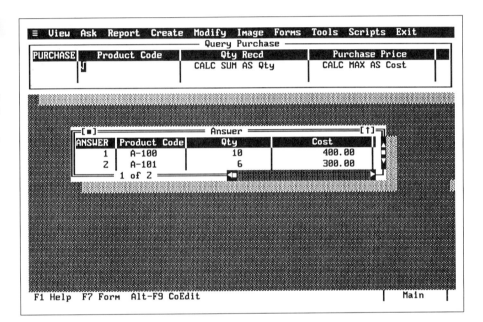

FIGURE 16.13

A query to calculate the total quantity of each item received in the Purchase table, the highest purchase price of each product, and resulting Answer table

6. Press F2 to perform the query, which results in an Answer table like the one shown in Figure 16.13.

7. Clear the desktop (press Alt-F8).

8. Choose **A**sk, and specify Answer as the table to query.

9. Use F5 to define the example elements PRODCODE, QTY, and COST in this Query form, as shown in the Query form for the Answer table at the top of Figure 16.14.

10. Press F10, choose **A**sk, specify Mastinv as the table, and press ↵ to choose OK.

654 CHAPTER 16 — AUTOMATIC UPDATING WITH MULTIPLE TABLES

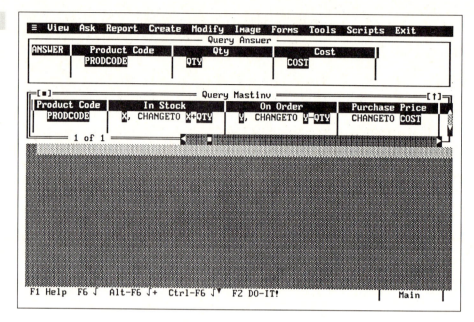

FIGURE 16.14

Query to add quantities from the Purchase table to In Stock quantities, subtract those same quantities from the On Order quantities, and change the Purchase Price to the largest current purchase price

11. Use F5 again to enter the linking example element, PRODCODE, in the Query form for the Mastinv table.

12. Press →, use Ctrl-r to rotate the In Stock field into view, and enter the example elements X and QTY and the CHANGETO formula shown in Figure 16.14.

We rotated and narrowed Query form columns in Figure 16.14 to fit everything on the screen. But all you need to do is make sure to get everything into the correct column.

13. Press →, use Ctrl-r to rotate the On Order field into view, and enter the CHANGETO calculations shown in the On Order column, where Y and QTY are example elements.

14. Press →, rotate the Purchase Price column into view, and enter the CHANGETO calculation shown in the Purchase Price column of the Mastinv table's Query form, where COST is an example element.

15. Press F2 to perform the query. Once again the Changed table appears. Although you don't need to do anything with the Changed table, you do need to move all the updated records from the Purchase table to the Purhist table, so they won't be reposted in future updates.

NOTE Remember, you're still recording a script, so use the keyboard rather than the mouse.

16. Clear the desktop (press Alt-F8).
17. Choose **T**ools ➤ **M**ore ➤ **A**dd, specify Purchase as the source table, and press ↵ to choose OK.
18. Specify Purhist as the target table and press ↵ to choose OK.
19. Press F10 and choose **T**ools ➤ **M**ore ➤ **E**mpty.
20. Specify Purchase as the table to empty, and press ↵ to choose OK.
21. When the Cancel/OK choices appear, type **O** or press ↓ then ↵ to choose OK.
22. Clear the desktop (press Alt-F8).
23. Choose **S**cripts ➤ End-Record.

If you were to peruse the Mastinv, Purhist, and Purchase tables now, you would see the following:

- The In Stock, On Order, and Purchase Price fields in the Mastinv table have been updated according to values in the original Purchase table.
- The Purhist table now contains the posted records from the Purchase table.
- The Purchase table is empty.

Figure 16.15 shows a portion of each of these tables on the desktop.

FIGURE 16.15

Portions of the Mastinv, Purhist, and Purchase tables on the desktop after performing the update

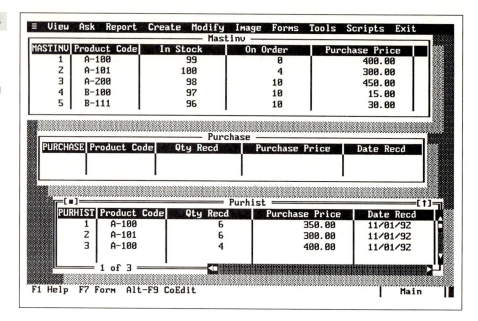

Using the Recorded Scripts

Because you've created scripts to handle all the various updates, your job will be much simpler. All you need to do is play back the scripts to perform the update procedure with current orders and purchases.

You could use **S**cripts ➤ **S**howPlay to play the Update3 or Update4 scripts right now, if you wish, to see them do their jobs. However, since each of these scripts emptied the original Orders and Purchase tables, each of them would update the Mastinv table from blank tables, which has the net result of doing nothing. In actual practice, you would run these scripts periodically, perhaps at the end of each day, to update the Mastinv table with the orders and purchases for that particular day.

In fact, in the next chapter we'll look at ways of combining all the scripts you created in this chapter so that you can do the whole shebang by simply playing one script. But first, let's talk about some issues that these history tables bring up.

NOTE Because Update1 is a saved query rather than a recorded script, it just displays the Query form when you play it back. You must press F2 to actually perform the query, or edit it to make it auto-executing, as described earlier in this chapter.

Correcting Updated Transactions

One question that may have occurred to you is, "If I discover an error in one of the transactions *after* the update, how do I fix it?" For example, suppose you discover an error in an order after performing an update procedure. If you correct the problem in the Ordhist table directly, there's no way for Paradox to know you've made this change. Hence, the correction would never be reflected in the Mastinv table.

If you went in and also manually changed the Mastinv table to make a correction, that would be okay. However, there would be no audit trail indicating that the changes were made to either table.

The best way to correct an error after updating records is to add an *adjustment transaction* to the Orders (or Purchase) table. For example, you may recall that the Orders table contained the record shown in Figure 16.16.

During automatic updating, this adjustment record would be processed just like any other; that is, its Qty Sold field would be subtracted from the Mastinv table's In Stock field. But, given that it's a negative number, the net result is that the value of 1 is actually added to the In Stock quantity. Furthermore, the record will be copied to the Ordhist table, just like any other record; thus, there's a permanent record of the transaction on disk.

FIGURE 16.16

An adjustment transaction on a custom form. The −1 indicates an item was returned, and the Remarks field contains a brief note explaining the negative Qty Sold value.

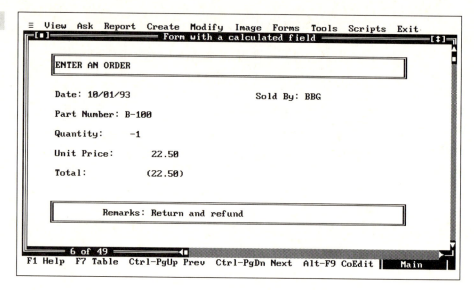

Printing a Reorder Report

After all this automatic updating, it might be nice to know which items need to be reordered. A simple query that isolates records with In Stock plus On Order quantities below the reorder point, as shown below, would do the trick. Notice that IQTY and OQTY are example elements.

The reorder query will produce an empty Answer table until some products have actually fallen below the reorder point.

Of course, you could design a reorder report and store it with the Mastinv table. Then you could record a script that performs the query above, copies the reorder report from the Mastinv table to the Answer table, and prints the report.

Again, as mentioned, the possibilities are endless. As you begin to design and develop sophisticated database applications of your own, you'll find that you can use the general techniques presented in this chapter to combine and update data among multiple related tables in any manner you wish, and a script can always reduce the whole procedure to a few simple menu selections.

Summary

In the next chapter, we'll look at some more advanced script techniques. Here's a quick recap of some of the techniques used in this chapter to perform automatic updates:

- When you'll be using data in one table to update data in another, be sure to devise some scheme for preventing records from being used in more than one update procedure.
- If you want to copy records from one table to another, and the two tables don't have identical structures, use an INSERT query to copy matching fields from a source table or to perform calculations with fields to make the source table fields match the fields in a target table.
- To change a saved query to a script that actually performs the query, edit the saved query and add a Do_It! (with an underline instead of a hyphen) command to the end of the file.
- When creating Query forms to update one table from another, be sure to use example elements to identify the common field that links the tables.
- In the table that contains the data you want to use in an update, identify fields to use with example elements.
- In the table that will be receiving values, or using values from the other table in a calculation, use CHANGETO with example elements defined in the first table.

- To move posted records from their original table to a history table, use **T**ools ➤ **M**ore ➤ **A**dd to copy records to the history table, then use **T**ools ➤ **M**ore ➤ **E**mpty to remove the records from the original table.

- If you discover an error after automatically updating a table, you should enter an adjustment transaction rather than just making the changes manually. The adjustment transaction gives you an audit trail that shows exactly what change was made and why.

CHAPTER 17

Using Advanced Script Techniques

fast TRACK

- **To access the Editor to edit a memo field** — **665**

    double-click on the memo field, or move the cursor to the memo field, then press the Field view key, Alt-F5, or Ctrl-f. Switch to Edit (F9) or CoEdit (Alt-F9) mode if you want to add or change text.

- **To use the Editor to edit a script** — **666**

    choose **S**cripts ➤ **E**ditor ➤ **O**pen, then type the name of the script to edit, or choose OK and choose a script from the list of file names that appears.

- **To use the Editor to create or edit an ASCII text file** — **667**

    choose ≡ ➤ **E**ditor ➤ **O**pen (to open an existing text file) or **N**ew (to create a new file).

- **To select text to move, copy, or delete in the Editor** — **673**

    drag the mouse pointer through the text you want to select, or hold down the Shift key while moving the cursor with any of the standard cursor-movement keys.

- **To save the contents of the editing window without closing the window** — **681**

    choose **F**ile ➤ **S**ave from the Editor menu.

To add programmer comments to a script   694

    start the comment with a semicolon (;) and type the text of the comment. All text from the semicolon to the end of the line will be ignored when you play back the script, so make sure any subsequent commands you want the script to play back start on the next line after the comment.

To use the abbreviated menu command Edit in a script   695

    open a new script, insert the command Edit "*table*", where *table* is the name of an existing Paradox table in the current directory, enclosed in quotation marks, as in "Custlist". Then save the script and play it back.

To have a script display a custom message   696

    insert a PAL Message command, followed by the message you want to display enclosed in quotation marks.

To have a script make an audible sound to get the user's attention   697

    insert a PAL Beep or Sound command at the point where you want the script to make the sound.

To have a script wait for the user to press some key   699

    insert a PAL Wait command into the script using the general syntax Wait Workspace Prompt "*message*" Until "*keypress*", where *message* is the message you want to display enclosed in quotation marks, and *keypress* is the key to press, enclosed in quotation marks.

IN this chapter, we'll discuss techniques that you can use to embellish and improve your recorded scripts. We'll also introduce you to PAL, the Paradox Application Language.

But before we get into the details of editing scripts, we need to talk about the Paradox Editor, since this is the tool you'll use to edit scripts. This is the same Editor that you use to edit memo fields. In fact, you can even use it to edit general-purpose text files, such as DOS text files. So even if you don't plan on getting into more advanced PAL programming and scripts, you'll probably find the general information on using the Editor useful in your work with Paradox.

Getting to the Editor

The Paradox Editor is accessible from just about anywhere in the program, and you can have several editing sessions going at once. This section explains how to open the Paradox Editor to edit a memo field, script, or any text file.

Keep in mind that you cannot use the Paradox Editor to change word processing files, spreadsheets, compiled programs, Windows text files, or any other file that contains strange-looking graphic characters. Editing such a file in the Paradox Editor can damage the file and make it unusable. If you accidentally open up a file that contains anything other than plain text, you should immediately choose the **C**ancel option from the Editor menu bar and then choose **Y**es.

Using the Editor with Memo Fields

The Editor is called into play whenever you edit a memo field. Let's review the techniques for editing a memo field:

1. Double-click on the memo field. With the keyboard, move the cursor to the memo field, then press Alt-F5 or Ctrl-f to enter Field view. The contents of the memo field appear in a window, and the menu bar changes to show the Editor options, as shown in Figure 17.1.

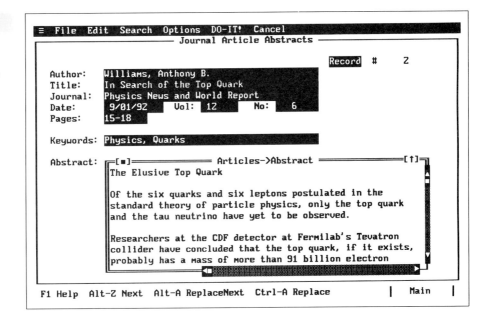

FIGURE 17.1

In Field view, a memo field appears in an editing window that you can move and size.

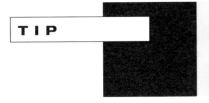

When an editing window is open, you can switch from one open window to another on the desktop by clicking on the window you want to switch to, by choosing ≡ ➤ Next from the menu bar, or by pressing Ctrl-F4.

2. If you're not already in an editing mode, but want to add or change text, press F9 to switch to Edit mode or Alt-F9 to switch to CoEdit mode. All the Editor techniques described in this chapter are now available. When typing paragraphs into a memo field, remember that you press ↵ only to end paragraphs, not to end each line within a paragraph.

3. After making changes to the memo, you can save your changes by choosing **DO-IT!** or by pressing F2. To cancel your changes, choose **C**ancel ➤ **Y**es, or click the Close button on the editing window, then choose **Y**es.

Using the Editor with Scripts

To open the Paradox Editor to create a new script or change an existing script, follow these steps:

1. Choose **S**cripts ➤ **E**ditor from the desktop. You'll see the options New and Open.

2. Choose the appropriate option:

    - To create a new script, choose **N**ew, then type a valid file name (no extension) for the new script. You can include a path if you want to store the script in some directory other than the current directory (for example, C:\PDOX45\Myscript to store the Myscript script in C:\PDOX45).

    - To open an existing script, choose **O**pen. Then you can choose OK (or press ↵) to view a list of scripts in the current directory. Choose the script you want to edit by double-clicking its name, or by highlighting its name and pressing ↵.

3. As with memo fields, you'll be taken to an editing window, with all the Paradox Editor options described in this chapter readily available. Figure 17.2 shows a sample script in an editing window.

4. When you've finished editing, you can save your changes with the usual **DO-IT!** or F2 key, or cancel your changes by choosing **C**ancel ➤ **Y**es or by clicking on the window's Close button.

The Go option on the Editor menu bar appears only when you're editing a script, not when you're editing a memo field or text file. The Go option

GETTING TO THE EDITOR

FIGURE 17.2

When you choose to create or edit a script file, an editing window appears.

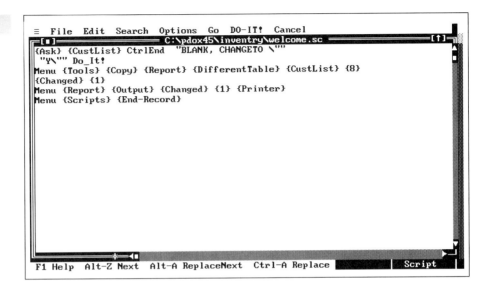

is simply a shortcut for saving the edited script, then playing it back. In other words, choosing **G**o is the same as choosing **DO-IT!** to save the script, then choosing **S**cripts ➤ **P**lay to play back the script.

Using the Editor for ASCII Text Files

You can also use the Paradox Editor as a general-purpose editor for creating and editing ASCII (DOS) text files, including DOS batch files, README files, C:\AUTOEXEC.BAT files, and C:\CONFIG.SYS files.

Never attempt to edit an executable file (any file with the extension .EXE or .COM). And don't edit CONFIG.SYS or AUTOEXEC.BAT files unless you're familiar with the various DOS commands they require.

To use the Editor in this general-purpose context, follow these steps:

1. Starting at any place in Paradox where the System menu (≡) is available on the menu bar, choose ≡ ➤ **E**ditor, or press Alt-e. You'll see the options New and Open.

2. Choose **N**ew to create a new file, or **O**pen to change an existing file.

3. Type in a file name and extension (and path if the file is not in the current directory). As usual, if you chose Open, you can press ↵ instead of typing in a file name, and then select the file name from the list of file names, subdirectory names, and DOS directory indicator (.\ or ..\).

4. After editing the file, you can save or cancel your changes using the same techniques described for memo fields and scripts in the preceding sections.

When you use Alt-e or the ≡ ➤ **E**ditor option to edit a file, Paradox does not automatically add the file name extension; you must specify it yourself. If you want to create or edit a Paradox script file, you must include the .SC extension. For example, type Myapp.SC to edit a script named Myapp. Note that Paradox will not allow you to create or edit a file with an extension of .VAL, .SET, .F??, .R??, .DB, .PX, .X??, or .Y?? (where ?? represents any one or two numbers or blanks).

Each time you choose Alt-e or ≡ ➤ **E**ditor, Paradox starts a new editing session that's independent of any session currently in progress. Hence, you can have several editing sessions going on at once. Use Ctrl-F4 to switch from window to window, and ≡ ➤ **D**esktop ➤ **T**ile or **C**ascade to arrange the various windows. Be sure to end each editing session, by choosing **DO-IT!** or canceling your changes, before leaving Paradox.

> **TIP**
>
> Regardless of how you get into the Editor, you can size and move its window using any of the standard techniques described in Chapter 3.

Working in Editor Windows

Once you're in the Editor, regardless of whether you're editing a memo, script, or text file, you can use any of the keys listed in Table 17.1 to move the cursor through existing text, select text, delete it, and so on.

TABLE 17.1: Keys Used in the Paradox Editor

CURSOR POSITIONING	KEY
Next character	→
Previous character	←
Left one word	Ctrl-←
Right one word	Ctrl-→
Beginning of line	Home
End of line	End
Down one line	↓
Up one line	↑
Down one window screen	PgDn
Up one window screen	PgUp
Beginning of memo field or file	Ctrl-PgUp
End of memo field or file	Ctrl-PgDn
DELETE, INSERT, OVERWRITE TEXT	**KEY**
Delete character at cursor (or selected text)	Delete (Del)
Delete character at left (or selected text)	Backspace
Delete from cursor to end of word	Alt-d
Delete entire line	Ctrl-y
Toggle Insert/Typeover mode	Ins (Insert)
Indent (insert up to eight spaces)	Tab
SELECT, CUT, PASTE	**KEY**
Select next character	Shift-→
Select previous character	Shift-←
Select next word	Shift-Ctrl-→
Select previous word	Shift-Ctrl-←
Select to beginning of line	Shift-Home

USING ADVANCED SCRIPT TECHNIQUES

TABLE 17.1: Keys Used in the Paradox Editor (continued)

SELECT, CUT, PASTE	KEY
Select to end of line	Shift-End
Select one line up	Shift-↑
Select one line down	Shift-↓
Select one windowful up	Shift-PgUp
Select one windowful down	Shift-PgDn
Select to top of memo or file	Shift-Ctrl-PgUp
Select to end of memo or file	Shift-Ctrl-PgDn
Copy selected text to Clipboard	Ctrl-Ins
Cut (move) selected text to Clipboard	Shift-Delete
Paste Clipboard contents at cursor	Shift-Ins
MISCELLANEOUS	**KEY**
Replace text with new text	Ctrl-a
Replace next text with new text (Replace Next)	Alt-a
Find text (Zoom)	Ctrl-a
Repeat last find (Zoom Next)	Alt-a
Show current cursor position	Ctrl-v

Most of the keys listed in Table 17.1 assume that you're editing existing text. You can't move the cursor around in an empty editing window, or past the end of existing text with the arrow keys or mouse. If there is no text beyond the cursor, press ↵ to move down a line, or press the spacebar to move right one character.

To position the cursor with the mouse, just move the mouse pointer to wherever you want to place the cursor, then click the mouse button. If the area you want to move to isn't currently visible, first use the scroll bars to scroll the text you want into view. Then click on the place you want to move the cursor.

Moving to a Specific Row/Column Position

To determine the current line number and column position of the cursor, choose **E**dit ➤ **L**ocation from the Editor menu bar. The current position appears near the bottom-left corner of the window. For example, the message 13:10 means that the cursor is in line 13, column 10 of the editing window. Moving the cursor or resizing the window erases the message.

If you want to move the cursor to a specific line in the editing window, choose **E**dit ➤ **G**oto from the Editor menu bar. You'll see the following dialog box:

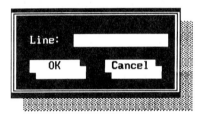

Type the line number you want to go to within the editing window and choose OK (or press ↵). The cursor jumps to that line in the editing window, retaining the same column position if possible. Keep in mind that the line number you enter refers to the position within the file or field. If the specified line number exceeds the number of lines in the field or file, the cursor jumps to the end of the memo field or file.

Inserting and Deleting Text

Once you position the cursor where you want to start typing, just start typing. If there's already text at the cursor position, you can insert newly typed text or replace existing text by switching to either Insert mode or Typeover mode.

Press the Ins (Insert) key to switch between the two modes. In Insert mode, the cursor appears as a small blinking underline, and new text pushes existing text over to the right and down. When you first open an editing window, the Editor is in Insert mode. When you switch to Typeover mode, the cursor appears as a blinking box, and new text overwrites existing text.

Inserting, Deleting, and Joining Lines

To insert a new (blank) line, position the cursor at the end of the existing line (using the End key) above where you want to insert a new line. Then press ↵ once for each blank line you want to insert.

If you inadvertently break an existing line when pressing ↵ and want to rejoin the broken lines, move the cursor to the beginning of the lower line (using the Home key), then press Backspace. Or move the cursor to the end of the top line (using the End key) and press Delete.

To delete an entire line, move the cursor to the line you want to delete and press Ctrl-y.

Selecting Text

The Editor offers a variety of methods for *selecting* (or *highlighting*) a block of text, then working with that block as a whole. The block can be any size—from as small as a single character to as large as the entire file being edited, and any size in between. For example, Figure 17.3 shows a sample memo field with the first paragraph of text selected.

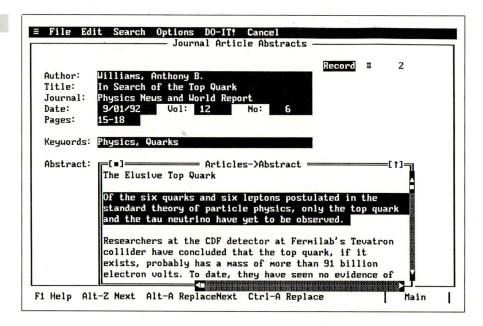

FIGURE 17.3

The first paragraph of text is selected (highlighted) in this sample memo.

As you select text, highlighting appears on the screen to indicate which text is selected. After you've selected a block of text, you can delete, copy, or move it using techniques described in a moment.

Selecting Text with the Mouse

To select text with your mouse, move the mouse pointer to where you want to begin the selection. Then hold down the mouse button and drag the mouse until you reach the end of the text that you want to highlight. Release the mouse button when you're finished highlighting the text. As a shortcut, you can double-click the mouse anywhere on a line to select the entire line.

If you want to select more text than is visible within the window, you could just drag the mouse pointer off the edge of the window. Text will scroll into view and be highlighted.

For large blocks of text it is often easier to use the Shift-click selection method. To use the Shift-click method, place the cursor at one end of the block you want to select, then hold down the Shift key and click at the other end of the block. If the other end of the block is not on the screen, use the scroll bar to scroll down to it, and then Shift-click where you want the selection to end.

Once a block has been selected by any method, Shift-clicking beyond the block will extend the block to the new terminating position, and clicking within the block will shorten the block.

Selecting Text with the Keyboard

To select text using the keyboard, move the cursor to where you want to start selecting text. Then hold down the Shift key while using the PgUp, PgDn, the arrow keys, or any other cursor-movement keys (see Table 17.1). Remember to keep the Shift key depressed as you move the cursor; otherwise, the text will immediately be deselected.

If some of the text you want to select is scrolled out of view, just keep the Shift key depressed and keep moving the cursor in the direction you want to go. Additional text will scroll into view and be highlighted.

Deselecting Text

If you select some text, then change your mind or want to start all over, just press any cursor-movement key (such as →) without holding down the Shift key. *Do not* press a character key, the Delete key, or the Backspace key (unless you want to delete the highlighted text).

Typing a character while text is selected instantly deletes the entire block of selected text and replaces it with the character you type. If you do this by accident, choose **Edit ➤ P**aste or press Shift-Ins to paste the deleted text back into place.

Cutting, Copying, and Pasting Text in an Editing Window

When you delete selected text from the editing window, it's copied to a temporary holding place in the computer's memory, called the Clipboard. The process of deleting selected text and copying it to the Clipboard is known as *cutting* the text.

To cut text in an editing window, first select the text using any of the techniques described in the previous section. Then choose **Edit ➤ X**Cut from the Editor menu bar, or press Shift-Del. Alternatively, you can press a character key to cut the selected text to the Clipboard and replace it with the character you pressed. The selected text will disappear from the editing window and will be copied to the Clipboard.

If you want to copy the selected text to the Clipboard, without removing it from the current editing window, select the text and choose **Edit ➤ C**opy from the Editor menu bar, or press Ctrl-Ins. The text will be copied to the Clipboard and will remain highlighted in the editing window.

Normally, the text you cut or copy to the Clipboard replaces all existing text in the Clipboard. Exceptions are discussed later in this chapter.

After cutting or copying text to the Clipboard, you can paste that text back from the Clipboard into the current editing window. (Pasting does not change the text in the Clipboard itself.) To paste text from the Clipboard, position the cursor where you want to paste (copy) that text and choose **Edit ➤ P**aste from the Editor menu bar, or press Shift-Ins. Any text in the Clipboard is copied into the editing window at the cursor position.

Deleting Selected Text

You can also delete selected text from the editing window without copying it to the Clipboard, but you should be very careful when doing so because, once deleted, the text can't easily be restored.

To delete selected text, select the text you want to remove and choose **Edit ➤ E**rase from the Editor menu bar, or press Delete. The highlighted text disappears from the editing window, without being copied to the Clipboard. If you accidentally delete text using this method, the only way to restore it is by canceling the current editing sessions (by choosing **C**ancel ➤ **Y**es).

Cutting and Pasting between Windows

Paradox uses one Clipboard for all the editing sessions that are taking place on the desktop. Therefore, you can easily transfer text from one editing window to another. To do this, start an editing session in the editing window containing the text you want to copy (the *source* window), and another editing session in the editing window where you want to copy that text (the *target* window). Then switch to the source editing window and copy or cut the text. Now, switch to the target editing window, position the cursor, and then paste in the text as usual.

NOTE To switch to a different editing window, click on the window you want to edit, or press Ctrl-F4, or choose ≡ ➤ Next from the Editor menu bar until you activate the window you want to edit.

It's not even necessary to have all the editing windows open at the same time. For example, let's suppose that you want to copy some text from the memo field in Record 1 of a table to Record 10 in the same table. Here's how:

1. Starting in Table or Form view, double-click on the memo field that contains the text you want to copy (or move the cursor to that memo field and press Alt-F5).

2. Select the text you want to copy, then choose **Edit ➤ C**opy or press Ctrl-Ins.

3. Go back to Table or Form view by clicking on its window, or by pressing the Do-It! key (F2).

4. Scroll to the memo field of the record that you want to copy the text to.

5. Double-click on the memo field, or press Alt-F5, to open that memo field.

6. If you're not already in an editing mode, press F9 (Edit) or Alt-F9 (CoEdit).

7. If the memo field already contains text, move the cursor to where you want to insert the copied text.

8. Choose **E**dit ➤ **P**aste or press Shift-Ins.

The selected text is copied from the Clipboard to the current cursor position.

Viewing the Clipboard

As mentioned earlier, the Clipboard is a temporary area in memory that contains text that you cut or copy from the editing window, and Paradox uses the same Clipboard for all the editing sessions. If you want to see what's currently stored in the Clipboard, choose **E**dit ➤ **S**howClipboard from the Editor menu bar.

To view your memo field or file at the same time as the Clipboard, choose ≡ ➤ **D**esktop ➤ **T**ile from the Editor menu bar. You can then switch between the editing window and the Clipboard window in the usual manner (by clicking on the window you want to change, pressing Ctrl-F4, or choosing ≡ ➤ **N**ext). Figure 17.4 shows an example in which the last paragraph of a memo was copied to the Clipboard, and then the windows were tiled on the screen.

When you're ready to close the Clipboard window, choose DO-IT! or press F2 to save any changes (described in the next section) or choose **C**ancel to discard any changes you made. You can also click on the Clipboard's Close button, press Ctrl-F8, or choose ≡ ➤ **C**lose from the Editor menu bar.

Making Changes in the Clipboard

Once the Clipboard window is open (after you choose **E**dit ➤ **S**howClipboard from the Editor menu bar), you can insert, change, and delete text in the Clipboard, and select options from the Editor menu bar. However,

WORKING IN EDITOR WINDOWS

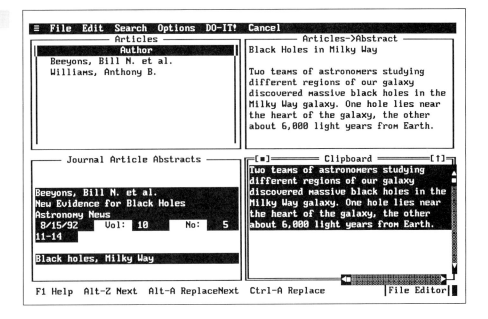

FIGURE 17.4

The text in the Clipboard window is highlighted, showing the last text that was copied or cut to the Clipboard. Choose ≡ ➤ Desktop ➤ Tile from the Editor menu bar to display all the windows in a tiled format.

while you're in the Clipboard window, the XCut, Copy, and Paste options are not available in the editing window.

Cutting or copying normally replaces all the existing contents of the Clipboard with selected text from the editing window, and pasting normally pastes the entire contents of the Clipboard back into the editing window, unless you make changes described in this section.

In most cases, you won't want to change the Clipboard at all, since the normal behavior of cut, copy, and paste is just fine for most people. Before making changes to the Clipboard, you should understand the following rules about Copy, Cut, and Paste:

- After every Copy or XCut operation, *all* text in the Clipboard window is automatically selected again, regardless of any previous changes you made to the Clipboard.

- If you deselect text in the Clipboard (by clicking the mouse or pressing a cursor-movement key in that window), and then return to the editing window and cut or copy text, the selected text from the editing window is inserted at the cursor position on the Clipboard; it does not replace any text in the Clipboard.

- If you deselect text in the Clipboard and then return to the editing window, pasting from the Clipboard has no effect on the editing window, because only *highlighted* text can be pasted from the Clipboard to the editing window.

- If you select just some text in the Clipboard, subsequent cutting or copying in the editing window replaces just that selected text in the Clipboard. Similarly, pasting copies only that selected text from the Clipboard back into the editing window.

Using Word-Wrap in the Editor

The Editor can operate in word-wrap or non-word-wrap mode. In word-wrap mode, lines of text automatically break at a blank space and wrap to the next line when the text reaches the boundary of the window. Word-wrapping for a particular paragraph continues until the end of the paragraph (the spot where you pressed ↵). When word-wrap is on, as is normally the case for memo fields, resizing the window automatically adjusts the text to wrap within the new window boundaries. Thus, when you're typing a paragraph in a memo field, you only want to press ↵ at the end of each paragraph, not at the end of each line. This way, the text will automatically wrap within the current window, no matter what its size.

In non-word-wrap mode, a line of text continues past the window boundary and doesn't return to the left edge of the window until you press ↵. Thus, when word-wrapping is off, parts of the text might disappear off the right edge of the window. You can either scroll the text or widen the window to see more of the file, or you can temporarily turn word-wrapping on.

If you look back at Figure 17.1, you can see that the memo field in the Articles table is word-wrapped. We pressed the ↵ key twice after the first line, and twice after each paragraph of the abstract. Each time we pressed the ↵ key, word-wrapping stopped for the line or paragraph we were typing. The script example in Figure 17.2 contains six lines, each of which is ended by the ↵ character.

Word-wrap is automatically turned *on* when you edit a memo field or a non-script file (a file that doesn't have a .SC extension). Word-wrap is automatically *off* when you edit a script file. To temporarily change the default word-wrapping for the editing window, follow these steps:

1. Choose **O**ptions from the Editor menu bar. You'll see the following submenu:

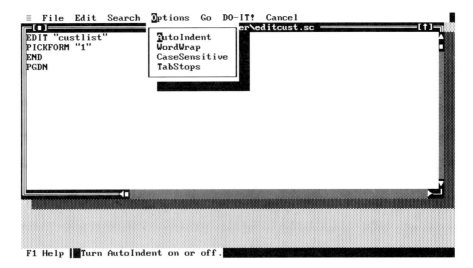

2. Choose **W**ordWrap. You'll see the options Set and Clear.

3. Choose **S**et to turn word-wrap on, or **C**lear to turn it off.

As with all the Editor options, changing the default word-wrap setting lasts only for the current Editor session, and only in the current window, or until you change the word-wrap again. This means that word-wrap can be on in one editing window and off in another. Furthermore, even if you've set word-wrapping for a script file, the next time you edit that file, it will appear without word-wrapping. Likewise, if you turn word-wrapping off for a memo field, that field will be word-wrapped the next time you edit it.

By default, word-wrap is on in memo fields and text files and off when you are editing scripts (any file with an .SC extension). You can change the word-wrap default for memo fields and text files in the Custom Configuration Program, described in Appendix D, but you can't change the script file word-wrap default.

Specifying Tab Stop Distance

You can adjust distance between tab stops, measured in characters, by choosing **O**ptions ➤ **T**abStops from the Editor menu bar. A smaller number in the tab stop setting will give you more tabs per document line length. The default tab stop setting for script files, memo windows, and text files is 8.

You can change the default tab stop distance in the Custom Configuration Program, as follows:

- Change the tab stop distance setting for script files by choosing **PAL** ➤ **T**abStops in the Custom Configuration Program.
- Change the tab stop distance default setting in memo fields and text files by choosing **Format Data** ➤ **E**ditor Tab Stops in the Custom Configuration Program.

Auto-Indenting Text

The Editor can automatically indent a new line by the same amount as the previous line. This feature works best when word-wrap is off. To control automatic indenting, choose **O**ptions ➤ **A**utoIndent from the Editor menu bar. You'll see the options Set and Clear. Choose **S**et to turn auto-indenting on, or **C**lear to turn it off.

To indent a line when entering text, press the Tab key to indent the equivalent of eight spaces, or press the spacebar once for each space that you want to indent. Then type the text of the line and press ↵. If auto-indent is on, the Editor automatically starts the next line with the same number of tabs or spaces that you typed for the previous line. (If you don't want to indent this new line, you need to press Backspace until the cursor is wherever you want to start typing this new line.)

Auto-indenting is best reserved for writing advanced PAL scripts, where you might want to indent several lines in succession. You can change the auto-indent default setting for memo fields, text files, and scripts using the Custom Configuration Program, as described in Appendix D.

Working with Files in the Editor

Whenever you're in an editing window, you can choose **F**ile from the menu bar to view the menu shown below. These options let you save, open, copy, and print Editor documents, as described in the sections that follow.

"Quick-Saving" Your Changes

When editing text in the Editor, you may want to save your current changes from time to time rather than waiting until you've made all your changes. That way, if you inadvertently delete a large chunk of text, then close the current editing window, you'll only lose the work you've done since the last "quick-save."

To quick-save your work, choose **F**ile ➤ **S**ave from the Editor menu bar. Your changes are saved immediately, and you'll still be able to make additional changes to the text.

Copying the Current Editing Window to a File

You can save the file or memo field currently in memory to a new DOS text file by following these steps:

1. Choose **F**ile ➤ **C**opyToFile from the Editor menu bar.

2. Type the file name and extension for the new file. (If you don't want to store the file in the current directory, precede the file name with the path to the directory you want.)

3. Choose OK or press ↵.

4. If the file name you entered already exists, you'll be prompted with the usual Cancel and Replace options.

    - Choose **C**ancel to return to step 2, where you can enter a different file name.
    - Choose **R**eplace to replace the contents of the existing file.

The Editor copies all the text in the current editing window into the file you specified and returns to the current editing session.

Reading an External File into Current Text

You can insert an existing file into the current file or memo field by following these steps:

1. Position the cursor where you want to insert the text file. (The text will be inserted to the right of the cursor.)

2. Choose **F**ile ➤ **I**nsertFile from the Editor menu bar. You'll see the usual dialog box for selecting a file name.

3. Type the file name and choose OK. If the file you want to insert is not in the current directory, precede the file name with the appropriate path. Optionally, you can choose OK or press ↵ to view a list of files, subdirectory names, and DOS directory indicators (.\ or ..\) in the current directory, then choose a file by double-clicking or highlighting and pressing ↵.

The Editor inserts a copy of the file at the cursor position.

CAUTION: Paradox won't let you insert executable files (.COM and .EXE) or table files (.DB), but it will let you insert word processing file non-ASCII or graphics characters and binary files with extensions other than .EXE and .COM. These files can't be edited in the Editor, and if you accidentally open one under its DOS name, and then save it, you will probably make the file unusable. Choose Cancel (not Close or DO-IT!) from the Editor menu bar if you accidentally insert such a file.

Copying Selected Text to a File

You can copy selected text from the current editing window to a new file by following these steps:

1. Select the text you want to copy, as described earlier.
2. Choose **File** ➤ **WriteBlock** from the Editor menu bar.
3. Type a file name and extension for the copied text. Include the path if you don't want to store the file in the current directory.
4. Choose OK.
5. As usual, if you typed the name of an existing file, you'll be asked to choose **C**ancel if you want to enter a different file name, or **R**eplace to replace the existing file.

After copying the selected text to the new file, Paradox returns to the current editing session.

Transferring Text between Programs

The contents of the Paradox Clipboard are erased as soon as you exit Paradox. So you can't use the Clipboard to transfer text to and from other programs. But you can use the various options on the File menu to transfer text between programs.

For example, suppose you wanted to copy the contents of a memo field to another file for use with a word processor. You first need to bring the contents of the memo field into an editing window (by switching to Field view). Then you can use **File ➤ CopyToFile** to copy the entire file, or **File ➤ WriteBlock** to copy selected text to an external file, such as C:\WP51\Memo.TXT.

After you leave Paradox and run your word processor, you can then use whatever techniques that program requires to read in the text file. For example, in WordPerfect 5.1 for DOS, you choose **File ➤ Text In ➤ DOS Text (CR/LF to SRt)** and specify the file name (for example, C:\WP51\Memo.TXT).

Reversing the process, suppose you wanted to copy a word processing document into a memo field. You start by bringing the document to the screen in your word processor in the usual manner. Then you need to save a copy in ASCII (DOS) text format. For example, in WordPerfect 5.1 for DOS, you choose **File ➤ Text Out ➤ Generic** and provide a path and file name, such as C:\PDOX45\Customer\Fromwp.TXT.

After exiting your word processor and starting Paradox, you then open the table that contains the memo field you want to copy text to. Open the memo field and enter Field view to get to the Paradox Editor. Switch to Edit mode (F9) or CoEdit mode (Alt-F9), choose **File ➤ InsertFile**, and specify the file name, such as C:\PDOX45\Customer\Fromwp.TXT.

Keep in mind that you can only transfer plain text in this manner. If your word processing document includes codes for fonts, graphics, or other unique capabilities, those codes will be lost in the transfer.

If you do want to retain all the fancy formatting codes from your word processor in a Paradox table, you need to store the word processed documents in a binary field (BLOB) rather than a memo field. Then you need to define your word processor as the external BLOB Editor using the Custom Configuration Program, as discussed in Appendix D. The downside to this approach, however, is that you cannot use Paradox to print the contents of a binary field, or even to search its contents.

Printing the Current File

If you would like a printed copy of the file or memo field in the current editing window, make sure your printer is on-line and ready to go, then choose **File ➤ Print** from the Editor menu bar. Note that if you're using a laser printer, you may need to manually eject the last page of the printout.

When used with memo fields, File ➤ Print prints only the current memo. To print multiple memo fields, use the reporting techniques described in Chapter 8.

Opening an Existing File while Editing

If you are currently editing one file and want to open a new window to view or edit another existing file, follow these steps:

1. Choose **File** ➤ **O**pen from the Editor menu bar.

2. Type the name of the file you want to open, including the path if the file is not in the current directory. Optionally, just choose OK or press ↵ to view a list of files in the current directory, subdirectory names, and DOS directory indicators (..\), and move the highlight to the file you want to open.

3. Choose OK or press ↵.

The file appears in a new editing window. If you inadvertently chose a non-ASCII file (such as a word processor file), be sure to choose **C**ancel ➤ **Y**es to end the editing session without saving the file.

Starting a New File while Editing

If you are currently editing text and want to open a new editing window to create another text file, choose **File** ➤ **N**ew. Type a name for the new file, including a path if you don't want to create it in the current directory. Then choose OK.

As usual, if you enter a name of a file that exists, you'll be given the options Cancel or Replace. If you choose Replace, the existing file will be replaced by this new, blank file you're about to create. If you choose Cancel, you'll be given the opportunity to enter a different file name.

Finding and Replacing Text

You can search for text in the editing window, and also replace text with other text. Searching can be a handy way to quickly move the cursor to a specific word or phrase in the file. Replacing text can help you make consistent changes with a minimum amount of typing. All the search and replace options are available when you choose **S**earch from the Editor menu bar, as shown below:

   (Search menu)

Searching for Text

To search for specific text in the current editing window:

1. Move the cursor to where you want the search to begin.

2. If you wish, select the text that you want to use as the value to search for.

3. Choose **S**earch ➤ **F**ind from the Editor menu bar or press Ctrl-z (Zoom). The Find dialog box shown below appears:

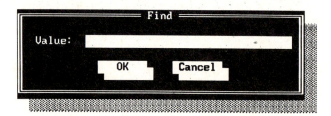

4. Type in the text or pattern you want to search for or use the highlighted text if any appears in the box. As with table searches (Zoom) and queries, you can use @ to stand for any single character, and .. to stand for any combination of characters. You can also specify whether searches should be case sensitive, as described in the next section.

5. Press ↵ to begin the search. The Editor starts the search at the cursor position and continues to the end of the file or memo field. If it finds the text you're searching for, the Editor highlights that text. If it doesn't find the text, the cursor stays put and Paradox displays the message

Search value not found

 Paradox uses the terms *search value* and *find value* synonymously.

If the Editor finds the text you're looking for, but you want to find the next occurrence of that text, choose Search ➤ Next or press Alt-z.

If you selected text before choosing Find, that text will automatically appear in the Find dialog box. If you've already searched for text during the editing session, and didn't select any text in step 2 above, the Editor initially suggests the previous search text.

To edit the search value, press the arrow keys or click the mouse to position the cursor, then press Delete or Backspace to delete characters, and type text as needed. To delete all the text in the Find dialog box, you can press Ctrl-Backspace if the text isn't highlighted. If the text is highlighted, you can delete it by simply pressing Delete or Backspace, or typing a character (which deletes the text and inserts that character).

Controlling Case Sensitivity in Editor Searches

By default, Editor searches are not case sensitive. Choose Options ➤ CaseSensitive to control how the Editor matches uppercase and lowercase letters during a Find operation. As usual, you can Set or Clear this feature. Choose Set to turn case sensitivity on. With this option set, text in the window must exactly match the letters you typed for the search value. Choose Clear to have the Editor match the search value without regard to capitalization. (Clear is the default setting.)

Remember that using wildcard characters (.. or @) in the search value temporarily turns off case sensitivity for a search, even if the CaseSensitive option is set.

Replacing Text

The **Search ➤ Replace** option lets you automatically make changes throughout all the text in the Editor window. The Editor offers two types of replacement: replace-and-confirm, and replace-without-confirm. The replace-and-confirm method lets you double-check each match before replacing it. The replace-without-confirm method lets you make global changes, without confirming each change before it takes place.

Using Replace-and-Confirm

To use the replace-and-confirm technique, follow these steps:

1. Move the cursor to where you want the operation to begin.

2. Optionally, select the text that you want to use as the value to search for.

3. Choose **Search ➤ Replace** from the Editor menu bar. You'll see the Find dialog box (shown earlier).

4. Type in the text or pattern you want to search for, or use (or edit) the highlighted text if any appears in the box, and then press ↵. You can use the usual wildcards in the Find dialog box. Case sensitivity follows the rules described in the previous section. You'll see the Replace dialog box, as shown below:

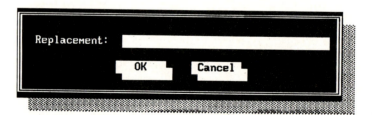

5. Type the replacement text, exactly as you want it to appear. Or use the highlighted text if any appears in the box (the Editor remembers the replacement text from the most recent Replace operation). Then press ↵. If the search value is found, the Editor highlights it and displays the message:

   To continue, use Alt-A ReplaceNext or Alt-Z Next

6. At this point, you actually have four options:

- Press Ctrl-a (Replace) to replace the search text with the replacement text. After replacing the text, the Editor leaves the cursor to the right of the replaced text.
- Press Alt-a (Replace Next) to replace the search text with the replacement text. After replacing the text, the Editor moves the cursor to the next occurrence of the search text and highlights it.
- Press Alt-z (Zoom Next) to leave the highlighted text unchanged. The Editor moves the cursor to the next occurrence of the search text and highlights it.
- Edit selected text by typing; this cuts the highlighted text to the Clipboard and replaces it with text you typed. (But remember, if you press Delete, no text is copied to the Clipboard.)

If the search text isn't found, the cursor stays put and you'll see a message indicating that the Editor couldn't find the search value you entered.

Using Replace-without-Confirm

The steps for replacing text without confirmation are almost the same as for the **S**earch ➤ **R**eplace option, and all the usual rules for typing search and replacement text and matching case apply here as well. Briefly, here are the steps for performing a global replacement:

1. Move the cursor to where you want the operation to begin.
2. Optionally, select the text for the search value.
3. Choose **S**earch ➤ **C**hangeToEnd from the Editor menu bar.
4. Type the search text, or use the highlighted text (if any), and press ↵.
5. Type the replacement text, or use the highlighted text (if any), and press ↵.
6. You'll see a menu with the options No and Yes.

- Choosing **N**o returns you to step 5. (You can cancel the replacement operation entirely by pressing Esc until all the dialog boxes are cleared from the screen.)

- If you're certain that you want to replace all the matching search text with the replacement text, choose **Yes**.

If you chose Yes, the Editor replaces all occurrences of the search text with the replacement text, from the current cursor position to the end of the memo field or file, without prompting you for confirmation. As usual, if your editing session has gone haywire, you can choose **Cancel** from the Editor menu bar to exit the session without making the changes permanent.

Leaving the Editor

To save your work and close the editing window, choose **DO-IT!** from the Editor menu bar, or press the Do-It! key (F2).

Memo fields behave somewhat differently than files. For example, if you're changing a memo field in Edit or CoEdit mode, pressing F2 or choosing **DO-IT!** saves the changes to the current memo field only. It does not update other changes made to the table. Also, keep in mind that moving to another field or record in the same table while you're editing a memo field automatically posts the changes to that field. Once changes are posted automatically, you can't cancel or undo them.

The Cancel option on the Editor menu bar lets you exit the Editor without saving any changes since the last save. To use this option, choose **Cancel** from the menu, then choose **Yes** from the submenu that appears (choose **No** if you prefer to stay in the Editor).

You can also cancel changes in any of the following ways:

- Click the Close button on the editing window.
- Choose ≡ ➤ **Close** from the Editor menu bar.
- Press the Close key, Ctrl-F8.
- Press Ctrl-Break.

If you've made any changes to the file or memo field, the first three methods listed above will require you to answer **Yes** to cancel the editing session and discard your changes, or **No** to remain in the Editor.

Editing an Existing Script

Now that you know a bit about the Editor, and know how to create a script by recording keystrokes, let's take a look at how you might use the Editor to change an existing script. First, you need to open the script in an editing window by choosing **S**cripts ➤ **E**ditor ➤ **O**pen, as described at the beginning of this chapter.

The script appears in an editing window. Figure 17.5 shows an example, in which the Update3 script recorded in the previous chapter is being edited.

Elements of a Recorded Script

A recorded script that you see in an editing window contains three basic elements:

- Menu equivalent commands and selections you make from lists that you make while recording a script, which are enclosed in curly braces. For example, {Ask} {Orders} is the recorded equivalent of selecting Ask from the desktop menu and Orders from the list of table names.

FIGURE 17.5

Sample recorded script in an editing window

```
  File   Edit   Search   Options   Go   DO-IT!   Cancel
================ C:\pdox45\inventry\update3.sc ================
{Ask} {Orders} Right Right Check Right  "CALC SUM AS Sold" Do_It!
ClearAll {Ask} {Answer} Right Example   "PRODCODE" Right Example
 "SOLDQTY"
Menu {Ask} {MastInv} Right Example   "PRODCODE" Right Rotate
Rotate Rotate Example  "CURRENT, CHANGETO " Example   "CURREN"
 "T-" Example   "SOLDQTY" Do_It! ClearAll
{Tools} {More} {Add} {Orders} {OrdHist}
Menu {Tools} {More} {Empty} {Orders} {OK} ClearAll {Scripts}
{End-Record}
```

F1 Help   Alt-Z Next   Alt-A ReplaceNext   Ctrl-A Replace   Script

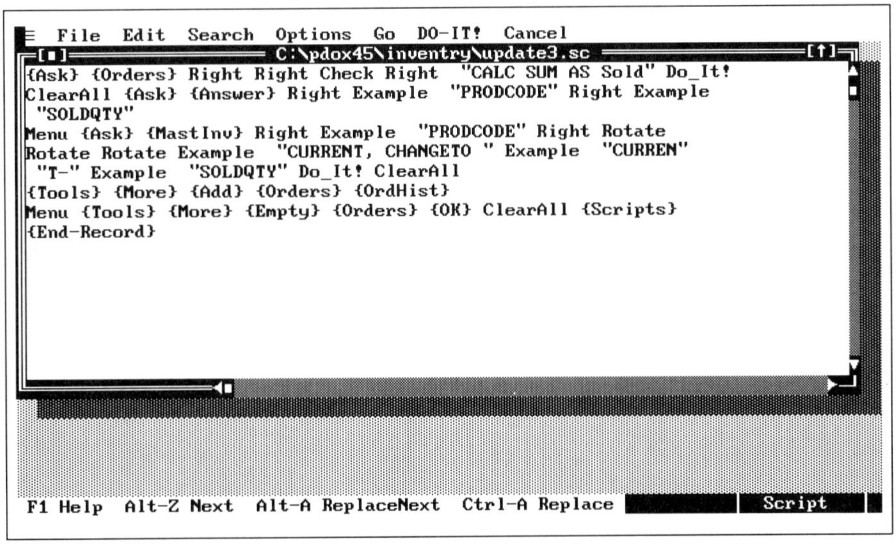

- Recorded keypresses appear as the key name, without braces around them. For example, in Figure 17.5 Right is the recorded → keypress, Check is the recorded F6 keypress, Do_It! is the recorded F2 keypress, Example is the recorded F5 keypress, and so on.

- Any literal text (text and numbers that you actually typed while recording the script) is enclosed in quotation marks. For example, "CALC SUM AS Sold" is the actual text you typed into the Query form while recording the script.

Notice that each action in the script is separated by a blank space. When you play a script, Paradox reads and executes each of these separate items in left-to-right, top-to-bottom order.

NOTE All the commands recorded in the script belong to a general type of PAL commands called keypress interaction commands.

Now let's take a look at how a saved query (a query you saved with the **S**cripts ➤ **Q**uerySave options) appears when edited. (If you're currently editing a script, just press F2 for now to close its editing window without saving any changes.)

Editing a Saved Query

When you save a query using **S**cripts ➤ **Q**uerySave, Paradox records the query as a script. Thus, you can use the same steps as above to open any saved query. However, a saved query looks a little different than a recorded script. For example, Figure 17.6 shows the sample Update1 query (created in Chapter 16) in an editing window after choosing **S**cripts ➤ **O**pen.

A saved query is always surrounded by the two statements of the PAL Query command: Query and Endquery. A sort of "textual image" of the query appears inside the Query and Endquery statements, where the vertical bars (¦) represent columns, and an underscore (_) represents the start of an example element.

USING PAL COMMANDS IN SCRIPTS

FIGURE 17.6

The sample query, saved as Update1 in Chapter 16, in an editing window

```
≡   File   Edit   Search   Options   Go   DO-IT!   Cancel
┌─[■]─────────────── C:\pdox45\inventry\update1.sc ═══════════════[↑]─┐
│Query                                                                │
│                                                                     │
│   Invoices │ Invoice Number │ Invoice Date │ Sold By │              │
│            │ _invno         │ _idate       │ _isold  │              │
│                                                                     │
│   Invdtail │ Invoice Number │       Sold By                │        │
│            │ _invno         │ BLANK, CHANGETO _isold       │        │
│                                                                     │
│   Invdtail │       Date Sold              │                         │
│            │ BLANK, CHANGETO _idate       │                         │
│                                                                     │
│Endquery                                                             │
│                                                                     │
└─────────────────────────────────────────────────────────────────────┘
   F1 Help   Alt-Z Next   Alt-A ReplaceNext   Ctrl-A Replace    Script
```

Using PAL Commands in Scripts

In addition to the various elements described so far, a script can also contain PAL commands and functions. There are literally hundreds of such commands and functions, all documented in the PAL reference manual that came with your Paradox package. The following sections describe some particularly useful commands that you can use to spruce up your recorded scripts. In Chapter 21, you'll learn how to use PAL commands more extensively to create scripts from scratch.

NOTE A saved query is just a script, which like all scripts, contains PAL commands. A saved query has the same file name extension, .SC, as any other query.

Adding Programmer Comments

A *comment*, often used by programmers, is any text preceded by a semicolon (;). The semicolon tells PAL to ignore the comment when executing the script. The purpose of using comments is simply to write notes to yourself within a script as reminders about what the various commands, keystrokes, and so on are for. Comments are also useful for anyone else who needs to understand or modify the contents of the script.

To insert a comment in a script, simply type a semicolon (;) followed by the comment. All text from the semicolon to the end of the line is ignored when you play back the script. Therefore, you should make sure that any commands or keystrokes that you don't want to be ignored are placed before any semicolon on a line.

If you like, you might want to follow the semicolon with some asterisks (***). This is a common practice used by programmers to make the comment stand out from the rest of the text in the script. It's also somewhat customary to put the name of the script and a brief description of what it does near the top of the script. For example, Figure 17.7 shows some comments typed in at the top of the Update1 script. Notice that the first actual command in the script, Query, starts on a new line after the last comment.

Placing Objects on the Desktop

Like many PAL commands, the Query command in a saved query simply places a Paradox object on the desktop. In the last chapter, you saw how

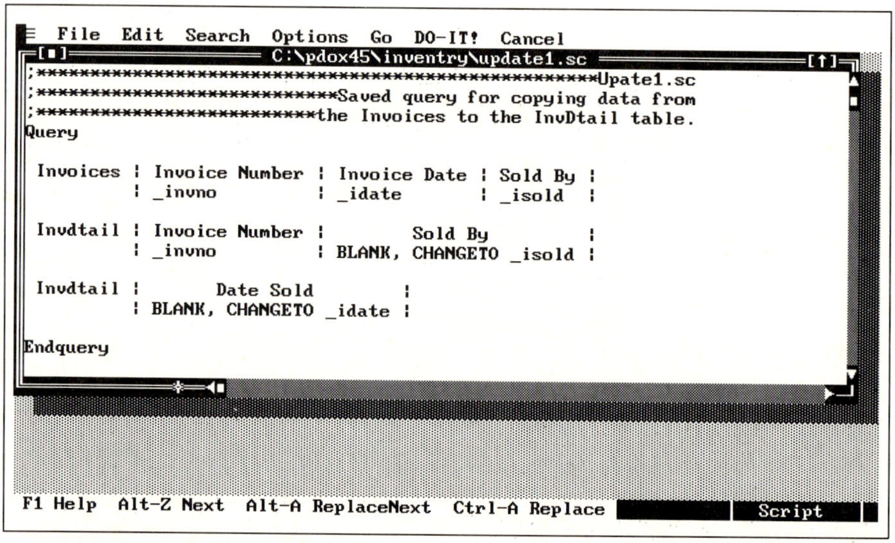

FIGURE 17.7

Some programmer comments added to the top of a script. The first actual script command, Query, starts on a new line after the last comment.

USING PAL COMMANDS IN SCRIPTS

to edit a saved query script by adding the PAL command Do_It!, which causes the query to be executed once it is placed on the desktop.

You can place any Paradox object on the desktop by using PAL in a script. For example, the following one-line scripts place the objects described:

- View "Custlist" places the Custlist table on the desktop.
- Edit "Custlist" places the Custlist table on the desktop in Edit mode.
- Edit "Custlist" PickForm "1" places the Custlist table on the desktop and displays form number 1.

All of these scripts use a general type of PAL command called an abbreviated menu command to perform the same functions you could perform by making menu selections. You could exactly duplicate the execution of these commands by recording a script while selecting the equivalent menu commands. For example, Edit "Custlist" is the same as choosing **M**odify ➤ **E**dit, then the Custlist table.

The advantage of the abbreviated menu command is that it is shorter to type and easier to read than the menu equivalent commands. Scripts using abbreviated menu commands also execute a bit faster. Figure 17.8 shows a slightly more complicated PAL script that places the Custlist table on the desktop in Edit mode, opens custom form 1, and moves to a new record at the end of the table, ready for data entry. You'll learn more about creating scripts like this from scratch later in this chapter.

CAUTION

Remember that you can only successfully play back a script if Paradox is in a state in which you could manually choose the options carried out by the script commands. Part of learning to create successful PAL scripts is learning to make sure that your scripts start and finish with Paradox in an appropriate state. Otherwise, you'll get the disconcerting Cancel/Debug dialog box (discussed in Chapter 11 and later in this chapter).

696 CHAPTER 17 USING ADVANCED SCRIPT TECHNIQUES

FIGURE 17.8

This script uses abbreviated menu and keypress commands to perform the same functions as recorded menu equivalent commands in a shorter, easier to read, faster executing script.

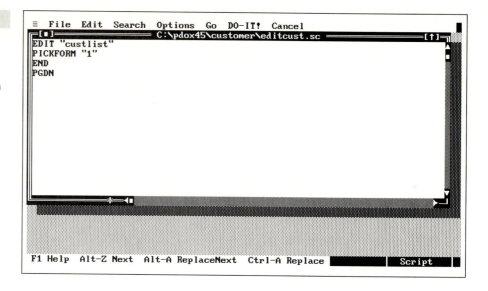

Displaying a Custom Message

Many PAL commands allow you to perform operations that you cannot choose from Paradox menus. For example, you can have a script display a custom message on the screen, by adding the PAL command Message to the script. The basic syntax for this command is

Message *"text"*

where *text* is the text of the message that you want to display, enclosed in quotation marks. When the script plays the command, the message appears near the lower-right corner of the screen, in reverse video or a contrasting color. The message stays on the screen until one of the following events:

- Another Message command is executed, replacing the previous message.

- A blank message command (Message "") removes the message from the screen.

- A regular Paradox message that appears while the script is playing back replaces the message.

- The user presses some key (if the script is paused with a Wait command, described a little later).
- The script ends.

If the Message command is the last command in the script, the message will flash on and off the screen so quickly that you probably won't even see it. If you want the message to appear for a specific amount of time, follow it with a Sleep command. The syntax of the Sleep command is

Sleep *milliseconds*

where *milliseconds* is the duration (in thousandths of a second) for which you want to pause the script. For example, the command Sleep 3000 pauses the script (and any message on the screen) for 3 seconds.

Using Sound to Get Attention

Another useful embellishment for a script is sound, which you can use to get the user's attention. You have a choice of two different sound-making commands: Beep, which simply sounds the computer's normal beep, and Sound, for a more custom tone.

The Sound command requires the syntax

Sound *frequency duration*

where *frequency* is a value between 1 and 50,000 Hertz, and *duration* is a number, expressed in milliseconds, that the tone should last.

In practice, the frequency range is dependent on your equipment, so you will probably need to experiment to find a suitable number for the frequency (pitch). For example, the command Sound 500 5000 sounds a 500 Hertz tone for 5 seconds. Don't include commas in any of the numbers.

In the next section, you'll learn to actually use these commands in a sample script.

Creating a Script from Scratch

As you saw earlier in Figure 17.8, it's not necessary to record keystrokes to create a script (although that's certainly the easiest way to create one). But suppose that you want to create a script that's composed entirely of PAL commands. To do so, you use **S**cripts ▶ **E**ditor ▶ **N**ew (rather than **O**pen) to create the script from scratch.

USING ADVANCED SCRIPT TECHNIQUES

Let's go through the exact steps required to create a script, named Hello, that demonstrates the commands just described:

1. Start with a clear desktop by saving any work in progress with the Do-It! key (F2) and pressing Alt-F8 to close all open windows.

2. Choose **Scripts** ➤ **Editor** ➤ **New**.

3. Type **Hello** as the name of the new script, and choose OK (or press ↵).

4. Now type in the script exactly as shown in Figure 17.9, keeping the following points in mind:

   - The first two lines are comments, and each starts with a semicolon (;).
   - The number of asterisks after the semicolon is unimportant. In fact, you can omit them altogether if you want.
   - After typing each line, press ↵ to go to the next line.
   - Although the number of spaces between each command and the comment that follows it is unimportant, the semicolon that starts each comment is required.

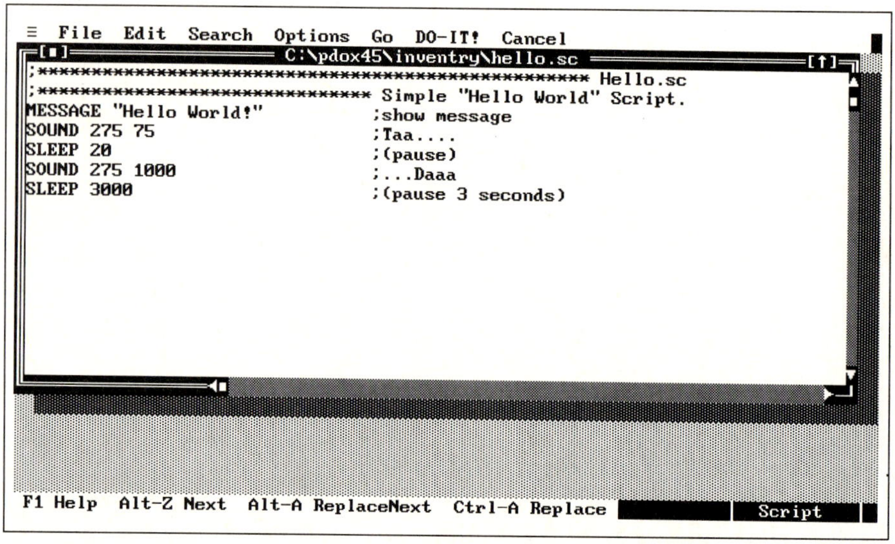

FIGURE 17.9

Sample script typed in entirely from scratch (none of the actions were recorded). The script consists entirely of PAL comments and commands.

```
≡ File  Edit  Search  Options  Go  DO-IT!  Cancel
                    C:\pdox45\inventry\hello.sc
;*********************************************** Hello.sc
;*********************************** Simple "Hello World" Script.
MESSAGE "Hello World!"           ;show message
SOUND 275 75                     ;Taa....
SLEEP 20                         ;(pause)
SOUND 275 1000                   ;...Daaa
SLEEP 3000                       ;(pause 3 seconds)




F1 Help   Alt-Z Next   Alt-A ReplaceNext   Ctrl-A Replace        Script
```

5. When you're finished typing in the script, you can take the shortcut to saving and playing it by choosing **G**o from the Editor menu bar.

If you typed the script correctly, it should display the message

Hello World!

and make a sound roughly resembling "Ta Dah!" (If you missed the message on the screen, just play the script again by choosing **S**cripts ➤ **P**lay and then typing or choosing the script name, Hello.)

If you made a mistake in the script, you'll most likely see the Cancel and Debug options. You can choose **D**ebug to view the faulty line at the bottom of the screen. Then, as a quick shortcut back to the editing window, press Alt-F10 and choose Editor, or press Ctrl-e. After making your corrections, you can then save and play the executed script by choosing **G**o from the Editor menu bar again.

About {Scripts} and {End-Record} in Scripts

When you record a script, then stop recording keystrokes using the regular desktop menu (rather than the PAL menu), Paradox records those menu selections at the bottom of the script as either

{Scripts} {End-Record}

or

Menu {Scripts} {End-Record}

When you play back the script, these commands basically do nothing (although you'll see the menu activity if you play back the script using **S**how-Play). Because these commands have no real value, you can delete them from the bottom of the script whenever you happen to be editing the script.

Pausing for User Input

In some cases, you might want a script to pause, allow the user to do something at his or her leisure (such as fill in a Query form, make a change to a table, or change the paper in the printer), then resume executing when the user presses some key. For this type of a pause, you use the Wait command.

For simply pausing a script, displaying a message, and waiting for some keypress, the basic syntax of the Wait command is

>   Wait Workspace
>   Prompt "*message*"
>   Until "*keypress*"

where *message* is text that appears on the status line during the pause, and *keypress* is the key you want to wait for, such as F2 or Enter (for ↵). Note that both the message and the keypress must be enclosed in quotation marks.

The Wait Workspace and Until commands in this example display a prompt on the status line while the user works with objects on the desktop. The status line is restored to its usual appearance as soon as the user presses the specified key. (Before playing back a script containing these commands, be sure to place some object, such as a table or a Query form, on the desktop.)

The Message command displays a message at the lower-right corner of the desktop, but does not change the Paradox status line. However, the Prompt command replaces the Paradox status line with a custom prompt that you specify.

Combining and Embellishing Scripts

Now let's take a look at how you could combine some of the techniques and PAL commands described so far to embellish your recorded scripts. In Chapter 11, we used a script named Welcome to print welcome letters for new customers in the sample Custlist table. We also recorded a script named Welclab (or Welcenv) to print labels or envelopes to go with the form letters.

Suppose now that you want to combine these into a single script that prints the letters, pauses to allow the user to load the labels or envelopes into the printer and then press a key, then prints the labels or envelopes.

Assuming you've already recorded the Welcome and Welclab or Welcenv scripts, you can proceed as follows:

1. First clear the desktop (Alt-F8) and, if you have not done so already, use **T**ools ➤ **M**ore ➤ **D**irectory to get to the directory that the Custlist table and the recorded scripts are in.

2. Choose **S**cripts ➤ **E**ditor ➤ **O**pen and type or choose the name of the first script (Welcome in this example). Then choose OK. The script appears in an editing window, similar to Figure 17.10.

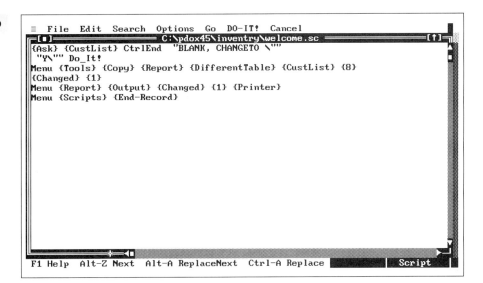

FIGURE 17.10

The Welcome script in an editing window

Your recorded scripts might not look exactly like the ones shown, because you may have used different keystrokes when you recorded the sample scripts.

3. For starters, you might want to add some comments, the ClearAll command (to clear the desktop), and a Message command to the top of the script, as shown at the top of Figure 17.11.

FIGURE 17.11

Welcome script embellished with some programmer comments and Message and Wait commands

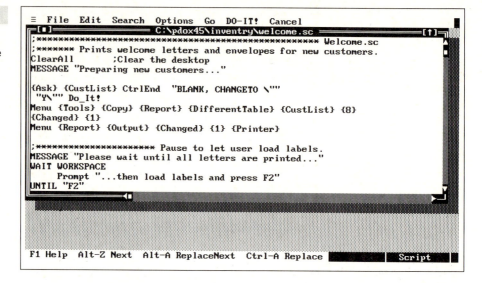

4. You can also delete the Menu {Scripts} {End-Record} from the bottom of the script. (They serve no purpose.)

5. Now you can add the following comment and commands to the bottom of the script to make it pause (see Figure 17.11):

   ;*********************** Pause to let user load labels.
   Message "Please wait until all letters are printed..."
   Wait Workspace
        Prompt "...then load labels and press F2"
   Until "F2"

6. Make sure you're at the bottom of the script (press Ctrl-PgDn) and start on a new line (press ↵).

7. Type whatever comments you wish. (In our example, we typed Recorded Welclab script follows, to print labels).

8. Press ↵ after typing the last comment, then choose File ➤ Insert-File, and type or choose the name of the script to read in (either Welclab.SC or Welcenv.SC in this example), then choose OK. Remember, when using File ➤ InsertFile to read in a file, you need to include the file name extension .SC with the script name.

9. Once again, you can delete Menu {Scripts} {End-Record} from the bottom of this script. Figure 17.12 shows the completed script.

FIGURE 17.12

A separately recorded script added to the bottom of the Welcome script

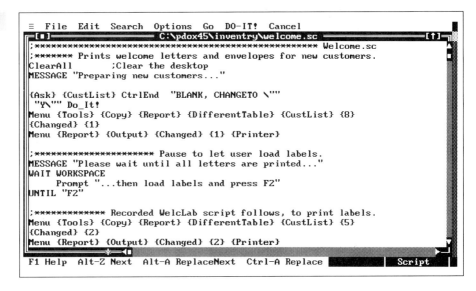

10. Press F2 to save the script.

Now to print Welcome letters and labels or envelopes for new customers, you need only run the Welcome script. It will pause to give you time to load labels or envelopes in the printer after printing the letters.

This script will only work if the original Welcome and Welclab scripts you recorded did their jobs properly after you first recorded them, and you previously defined valid report formats for the form letter and labels or envelopes.

Combining the Automatic Update Scripts

In Chapter 16, we developed several scripts to update the sample Mastinv table from the Invdtail, Orders, and Purchase tables. We named these scripts Update1, Update2, and so on.

Using **File ➤ InsertFile**, you could combine all these smaller scripts into a single script named Update that does the whole job of updating, in the correct order, in one fell swoop.

> **TIP** Another way to combine scripts is to record a new script that uses **Scripts ➤ Play** to play each of the smaller scripts.

To combine the scripts, first use **Scripts ➤ Editor ➤ New** to create a new script named Update. Perhaps start off with some comments, a Message command, and then use **File ➤ InsertFile** to read in the Update1 script.

Because Update1 and Update2 were saved as queries, you want to insert a Do_It! command at the bottom, as well as a ClearAll command to clear the desktop after the query finishes its job, as shown in Figure 17.13.

Next, you might want to add some comments to the bottom of the script, then use **File ➤ InsertFile** again to read in the Update2 script. Repeat the same basic procedure to add comments to and read in the Update3 and Update4 scripts, and then perhaps add Message, Sound, and Sleep commands to the end to signal the user when the script has completed its job.

FIGURE 17.13

A sample script named Update, with comments, commands, and a copy of the Update1 script read in

Figure 17.14 shows the lower portion of the completed Update script, where you can see the inserted Update3 and Update4 scripts, as well as the closing PAL commands (on the last line).

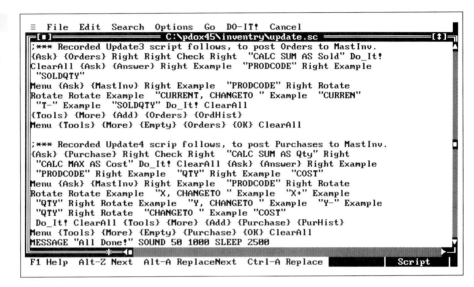

FIGURE 17.14

The Update3 and Update4 scripts visible at the bottom of the larger Update script

Because the user doesn't need to do anything between the Update1, Update2, and other scripts, this large script doesn't require a pause.

After saving the new Update script, you only need to choose **S**cripts ➤ **P**lay ➤ **U**pdate to play all four automatic updating scripts (assuming, of course, that each of the recorded scripts—Update1, Update2, and so on—works correctly on its own).

Tips on Scripts

Even though we've covered quite a bit of ground on scripts here, we've really barely scratched the proverbial surface. You'll learn more advanced uses of PAL in Chapter 21. For now, just keep the following points in mind:

- When creating scripts, it might be easiest to record small scripts that both start at a clear desktop and end at a clear desktop. That way, if you combine the scripts later, you won't need to clean up the screen between scripts.

- You can also insert a ClearAll command into the script, either by pressing Alt-F8 while recording the script or by inserting a ClearAll command while editing the script, if you want the script itself to clear the desktop.

- Always test a recorded script to be sure that it works before inserting it into a larger script.

- A single misplaced Do_It! or ClearAll command, or even a missing blank space or semicolon, can cause a script to crash. To correct the script, you might first want to run it with **S**cripts ➤ **S**howPlay ➤ **S**low so you can see it played back in slow motion. Then, when the Cancel/Debug options appear, pay close attention to the actual line and command that caused the error for clues as to what went wrong and where.

- Remember, just running the script in the wrong context can also cause a script to crash. For example, if the script contains {Ask} to perform a query, but there's already a Query form on the screen when you run the script, the script might crash. (Running the script from a cleared desktop would take care of this problem.)

- Workshop, an ancillary Borland program described in the next chapter, provides an excellent alternative to writing scripts from scratch when developing an application.

- You can password-protect your scripts so that other users can play them back but cannot view or change their contents. See Chapter 12 for information about password protection.

About the .SC2 File

When you create a script, Paradox always saves it with the .SC extension. The first time you run the script, Paradox creates a *parsed* (streamlined) version of the script for its own use, and stores that version of the script in a file with the same file name, but the .SC2 extension.

In the future (at least, up until the time you change the original .SC file), Paradox will run the .SC2 copy of the script rather than the .SC version, which makes the script run faster.

NOTE Paradox handles all aspects of the .SC2 file automatically behind the scenes. You need not (and cannot) edit the .SC2 file yourself.

Cautions on Using Go from the Editor

As mentioned earlier in the chapter, the Go option appears on the Editor menu bar only when you're editing scripts. This option saves the changes to your script, exits the Editor, and then plays back the script—all in one step.

Go is handy, but it can cause problems in some situations. You can get unpredictable results and even lose data if you play a script while multiple editing sessions are in progress (you have several editing windows open at the same time) or when you're not in the Main mode at the desktop. Therefore, you should reserve your use of the Go option for times when you're at the Paradox desktop and no other editing sessions are taking place.

Summary

In this chapter, we've covered the Paradox Editor and techniques you can use with the Editor to embellish your recorded scripts. The next chapter begins Part Three of this book, where you'll learn about developing Paradox applications with Workshop. Here's a quick recap of the topics covered in this chapter:

- To get to the Editor to edit a memo field, double-click on the memo field, or move the cursor to it and press Alt-F5 (or Ctrl-f).

- To use the Editor to edit a script, choose **S**cripts ➤ Editor ➤ **O**pen and type or choose the name of the script you want to edit.

- To use the Editor to edit an ASCII (DOS) text file, choose ≡ ➤ **Editor** ➤ **O**pen and type the location and name of the text file you want to edit.

- To position the cursor within an editing window, click on the character you want to move the cursor to, or use any of the standard cursor-movement keys.

- To select text to move, copy, or delete in the Editor, drag the mouse pointer through the text you want to select, or hold down the Shift key while moving the cursor with the cursor-movement keys.

- To transfer text between the current editing window and external ASCII files, use the **C**opyToFile, **I**nsertFile, and WriteBlock options on the Editor's **F**ile menu.

- To display a table on the desktop in Edit mode, use the PAL abbreviated menu command Edit.

- To have a script display a custom message, add a PAL Message command to the script.

- To have a script sound an audible tone, insert a PAL Beep or Sound command.

- To have a script pause for a keypress, insert a PAL Wait…Until command wherever you want the script to pause.

- To save your work and leave the Editor window, choose **DO-IT!** from the Editor menu bar, or press F2.

PART THREE

Developing Paradox Applications

CHAPTER 18

Designing an Application

fast TRACK

- **An application is** — 714

    an automated collection of database management system (DBMS) objects and functions, usually controlled through a menu system. Paradox applications include objects such as tables, forms, reports, queries, graphs, and scripts designed to automate a specialized task, such as managing accounts payable for a business.

- **Workshop is** — 716

    a powerful tool that helps you develop, test, and refine your applications, all without programming. (However, programmers can use Workshop to link in their own PAL code and extend the application's capabilities.)

- **To design an application** — 717

    follow these six general steps: (1) Define the goals of the application, (2) Design the menu structure on paper, (3) Using Paradox, design and create the database, (4) Create the application with Workshop, (5) Test and refine as needed, (6) Document the application and distribute it to your end-users.

- **To define the goals of the application** — 718

    analyze the existing system (if any); get copies of forms and reports being used; note what information is already stored in electronic or paper form; and interview potential users of the application to determine their needs. Then jot down a broad definition of what the system must do, and refine it into specific goals and features.

To design the menu structure on paper   **719**

> place desktop menu options across the top row of the design, and pull-down menus (or submenus) beneath the desktop menu in a hierarchical manner.

To design and create the database   **721**

> first create a directory to hold all the database objects. Then switch to that directory and use Paradox to design and test tables, reports, forms, queries, and scripts for the application.

To test and refine the application   **724**

> see how each separate piece works. Once you're satisfied that each piece of the application works correctly, test the entire application thoroughly. Make any needed adjustments in Workshop, changing menu options, actions, tables, reports, scripts, forms, queries, and prompts.

To complete the application   **724**

> use Workshop to generate all the application scripts and create some preliminary documentation. Finally, finish documenting the application in your word processor and distribute the application and documentation to the end-users.

THIS chapter introduces Paradox applications and Workshop, a Paradox ancillary program you can use to create and refine applications. First we'll discuss applications in general, then techniques for designing and developing larger applications, and finally we'll review the components of a sample membership and subscription management application. In Chapters 19 and 20, you learn how to use Workshop to develop, test, and modify your own applications.

What Is an Application?

An application is an automated collection of database management system (DBMS) objects and actions, often controlled by a menu system. Paradox applications include objects such as tables, forms, reports, queries, graphs, and scripts and can provide control for whatever complex set of objects and actions you need to manage your data.

It may take many Paradox objects and actions to manage your data. Figure 18.1 shows some of the objects you might develop, in a single directory, to manage a subscription membership database. Manually maintaining the relationships among many such files would become tedious, even for the person who created them, in this case you. For a novice, the task can be impossible. A custom, menu-driven application makes it easier and more efficient to use your system. Your application can display a personalized splash screen (discussed in Chapter 19) and present the user with menus designed to provide specific options for managing memberships and subscriptions. The menu bar shown in Figure 18.2 is from the sample Membership application.

WHAT IS AN APPLICATION?

FIGURE 18.1

A sample inventory of files for managing a membership database

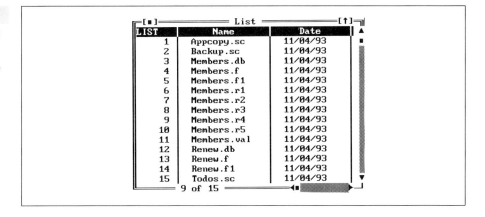

FIGURE 18.2

Custom menus for maintaining the Members table

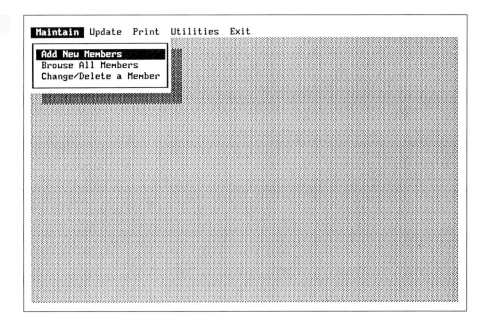

This application menu system defines specific tasks involved in maintaining the Members table. Each choice opens a pull-down menu of related tasks:

- The Maintain menu (shown in Figure 18.2) provides choices for adding new members, browsing the membership roster, and changing or deleting a member record.

- The Update menu controls updating this month's renewals and deleting expired memberships.
- The Print menu controls output of membership rosters, mailing labels, and letters.
- The Utilities menu provides facilities for temporary escape to DOS and backing up files.
- The Exit menu allows the user to exit the application to return to Paradox or DOS.

A Workshop application requires no knowledge of the underlying Paradox objects. Although application menus operate just like the Paradox menus, the user need not even know that Paradox is involved, or that such things as Paradox and Paradox objects exist. Users deal only with the Membership application itself.

Applications often have long-range potential for use and profit. For example, a well-designed application that is convenient and easy to use can be copied and marketed to others who have similar data management needs.

> **TIP** You can order Paradox Runtime, from Borland, which allows an application to be distributed to people who don't even own Paradox.

What Is Workshop?

Workshop is a powerful tool for developing, testing, and refining applications—all without programming. Workshop leads you step by step through the development process and automatically generates PAL programs and scripts for you. You don't need to know anything about PAL programming, even when creating or changing sophisticated applications. Programmers can use Workshop to link in PAL code, extending an application's capabilities even further.

Through Workshop, you can accomplish the following:

- Create Paradox-style menu bars and pull-down menus.
- Define actions for every menu option.
- Create all needed tables, forms, reports, and scripts.
- Create custom table-editing sessions.
- Create context-sensitive, cross-referenced Help screens.
- Test your application at any stage of development.
- Modify the application until it works perfectly.

An Overview of Designing an Application

Before you start pounding the keyboard to bring your great application idea to fruition, take some time to design the end product. Approach the application development process as several separate tasks:

1. Define the goals of the application on paper.
2. Define the menu structure on paper.
3. Use Paradox to design and create the objects (tables, forms, reports, scripts, and so on) for the application.
4. Start Workshop and build your application.
5. Test and refine the finished application as necessary.
6. Document the application and distribute it to your end users.

The following sections describe these steps in more detail. Think of these steps as a series of refinements. As you refine, you can backtrack and make changes along the way.

> **NOTE** The steps above present a simplified version of program design. Building the application actually consists of many smaller steps, which are discussed in Chapter 19.

Defining the Goals of the Application

First, simply jot down some notes about what the application must do. If you are automating an existing manual system, analyze it and get copies of currently used forms and reports. Make note of the information currently stored in manual files, such as Rolodexes, index cards, and forms. Use these to help you design the tables.

If the application is for a client, find out, in as much detail as possible, what the client wants. Use your knowledge of the capabilities of Paradox to offer suggestions to make the client's work easier. As you make notes, create a broad definition, such as:

> Automate tasks for the membership committee of a computer user's group.

Then refine this definition into specific goals and features, focusing on the fundamental aspects of database management: table structure, sorting and searching requirements, types of reports needed, and specific types of updating or other processes that are required. For example, the broad definition above can be refined as:

> Automate tasks for the membership committee of a computer user's group, as follows:

- Store members' names, addresses, starting and expiration dates, and other useful information.
- At any time during the month:
  - Add, change, and delete members as necessary.
  - Print an alphabetized membership roster.
  - Print mailing labels sorted by zip code.
  - Update renewed memberships.

- Perform, at any time, these basic housekeeping tasks:
    - Temporarily exit to DOS, for example, to change the system date.
    - Back up the Members table.
    - Copy the entire application to a floppy disk.
- Automate printing of these monthly form letters:
    - Welcome letters and mailing labels for new members
    - Renewal reminders and labels for expiring memberships
    - Overdue notices and labels for expired memberships

At this point, you can start refining each feature by making rough drafts (on paper) of table, report and form designs, as well as form letters and mailing labels.

As you refine the written definition, try to break the overall goal of the application into smaller, more manageable tasks. That way, each task becomes a more easily achievable goal.

Designing the Menu Structure on Paper

Although you can easily change your application's menu structure in Workshop at any time, it's best to design the application's menus on paper first. Place desktop menu options across the top row of the design, and pull-down menus (or submenus) beneath the desktop menu in a hierarchical manner.

Design from general to more specific, as in the structure for the Membership application shown in Figure 18.3. Under the Maintain option are several specific options for managing the membership information. The Print option is divided into an overall membership roster and two additional submenus for printing letters and mailing labels.

You should also keep notes about the tables, objects, and actions associated with each menu option. Later, while you're developing the application, these notes will help you keep track of the details. Figure 18.4 shows an example of notes with the menu and submenu under the Maintain option.

CHAPTER 18 — DESIGNING AN APPLICATION

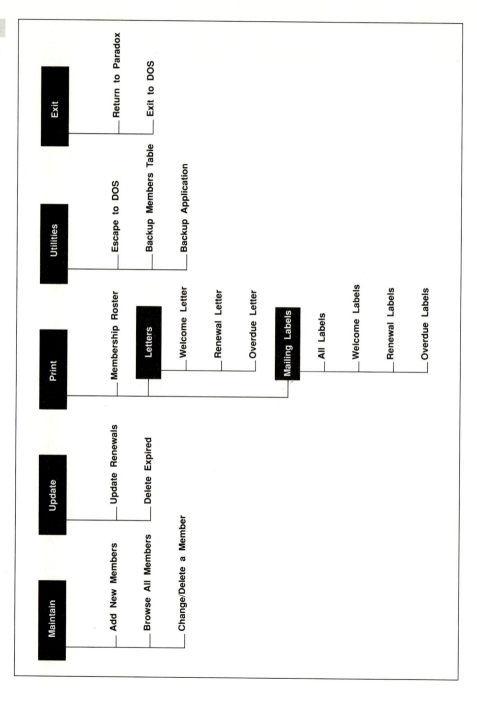

FIGURE 18.3

Sample menu structure

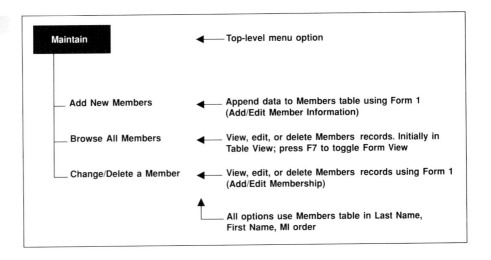

FIGURE 18.4

Notes about objects used for each menu option

In the example, the Maintain menu has three options:

- Add New Members, to let the user append new records to the Members table using a custom form (Form 1 - Add/Edit Member Information)
- Browse All Members, to let the user see and (optionally) edit any record in the table using either Table view or Form view
- Change/Delete a Member, to let the user use the Add/Edit Member Information custom form to change any record in the table

Designing and Testing the Database Objects

The next step is to design and test the tables, reports, forms, queries, and any custom scripts you wish to use. Although you can design and change objects in Workshop, the initial design and creation is best done in Paradox, which provides more flexibility. If your application will use queries, you can either create the queries in Workshop (as described in the next chapter) or develop the queries in Paradox using the methods described later in this chapter.

Creating a Directory for the Application

To avoid confusion, you should create each new application in a separate directory. This subdirectory should not be \PDOX45 itself, or the

\PDOX45\Workshop subdirectory, which contains Workshop programs. In the examples that follow, we assume the sample Membership application is stored in a directory named C:\PDOX45\Members.

Use these steps to create and switch to a new directory:

1. If you are currently running Paradox, save any work in progress, then choose ≡ ➤ **U**tilities ➤ **R**un Workshop from the desktop menu.

2. From the Workshop main menu bar, choose **A**pplication ➤ **D**irectory. The Change directory dialog box will appear, with the current directory name in its text box.

3. If the current directory name is C:\PDOX45, press the → key and type in **\Members** into the text box, or press Ctrl-Backspace to clear the text box and enter **C:\PDOX45\Members** (or whatever the full DOS path of your desired new directory might be). Then press ↵. You'll see the Create Directory dialog box, displaying the message

   Directory C:\PDOX45\MEMBERS does not exist. Create?

   and the choices OK or Cancel.

4. Choose OK to create the new directory.

The new directory will be created and will automatically become your current working directory. In the future, remember to switch to the Membership application directory when you want to use the application. For example, to switch to the C:\PDOX45\Members directory, type the command

   CD \PDOX45\Members

and press ↵ at the DOS prompt (before you run Paradox). If Paradox is already running, you can use **T**ools ➤ **M**ore ➤ **D**irectory to switch directories, as described in Chapter 12. You can also change the default directory in the Custom Configuration Program, as discussed in Appendix D.

Designing the Tables

When designing your tables, you must first determine the fields required to store the information needed in the application. For efficiency, you may need to use several related table files, as discussed in Chapter 13. Use the techniques discussed in that chapter to design table structures for your own applications.

After you have decided on your table structures, create each table in Paradox in the usual manner. Index any common fields that relate two or more tables. Sorts, queries, and quick lookups can be speeded up by indexing fields that will be used regularly for these operations. You can also design your tables with key fields to prevent users from entering duplicate records. For example, to prevent entry of duplicate member records, the Members table in the sample Membership application is defined with Last Name, First Name, and Middle Initial as key fields.

After creating each table file, enter some sample data so that you can test other components of the application as you build them.

Designing the Queries

Design appropriate queries if any forms or reports in your applications will require calculated or summarized data, multiple tables, or special sorting. Test the queries to ensure proper performance. Query techniques are discussed in Chapters 7 and 14.

You can create queries either in Paradox or Workshop. Try each method to determine which works best for you. If you create the query in Paradox, you can save it as a script file by using **S**cripts ➤ **Q**uerySave. Then add the PAL Do_It! command at the end of the script to execute the query when the script is played back, as described in Chapter 17.

You can also record a query script by using **S**cripts ➤ **B**eginRecord. Perform the query, rename the temporary table or tables if you desire, and then choose **S**cript ➤ **E**nd-Record to finish recording the script. See Chapter 11 for more information about recording scripts.

In Workshop, the Done menu choice has the same effect as choosing Scripts ➤ QuerySave in Paradox. In the next chapter, you'll learn how to use query scripts in your applications.

Designing the Forms, Reports, and Scripts

The next step is to create the custom forms for your application. When you are designing an application that includes data entry from two or more tables, use the multi-table form techniques described in Chapter 15.

DESIGNING AN APPLICATION

Make life easier for your end-users by setting up the field order in your forms to match the order on corresponding manual forms. Also, place similar information on different forms in the same order on each form.

If you need a form with several screens of information per record, repeat some identifying information on each screen, such as an ID number or name. Use validity checks to trap faulty entries before they are stored on the table and to simplify data entry. Use boxes, lines, and graphic characters (but sparingly!) to enhance the form. Keep in mind that a form with open space is easier to comprehend than an overcrowded form. Test the form by entering sample data.

Next, create the report and mailing label formats for your application, as described in Chapter 8. Print sample data to test the report format.

Then record the scripts your application needs and create any special PAL programs required. Test them thoroughly on some sample data before placing them in your application.

Testing and Refining the Application

After you've designed the menu structure and created all the objects, begin developing the application. Use Workshop to define menu options and attach one or more actions to each, as described in the next chapter.

Test your application piece by piece as you develop it. You can test at almost any point, so test small pieces as you go. After you're satisfied with all the pieces, you should test every step of the entire application. Use Workshop to change menu options, actions, objects, and prompts as needed. When you're satisfied with the basic application, add your extras, such as custom Help screens.

Remember that developing an application is an iterative process. First you design, then you develop and use the application. Use Workshop to make improvements and changes, repeating the process of testing and refining until you're satisfied with the application.

Documenting and Distributing the Application

When you're finished, use Workshop to generate the application scripts and to create the preliminary documentation. Finally, complete the application documentation in your word processor and distribute the application and documentation to your end-users.

Now let's take a closer look at the sample Membership application to see how it was designed.

The Design of the Membership Application Database

You already know a lot about the sample Membership application's goals and menu structure. After reviewing the operations of the sample application in the following sections and reading Chapters 19 and 20, you might want to try designing this application yourself. To obtain a finished, ready-to-run copy of the application, you can send for the companion disk, using the coupon at the back of the book.

For the Membership application, the Members table holds information about each member. Figure 18.5 shows the structure of this table. The Last Name, First Name, and MI fields are marked with an * to define them as key fields and create a primary index. Thus, all records must have a unique combination of Last Name, First Name, and MI entries. Any duplicates create a violation of the key and are rejected during data entry. The Members table also has a secondary index named Zip Code to speed up printing mailing labels, created using **M**odify ➤ **I**ndex, as described in Chapter 13.

NOTE To display the structure of an existing table, choose Tools ➤ Info ➤ Structure from the Paradox desktop menu and enter the table name when prompted. See Chapter 12 for more information about the Tools ➤ Info submenu options.

FIGURE 18.5

Structure of the Members table

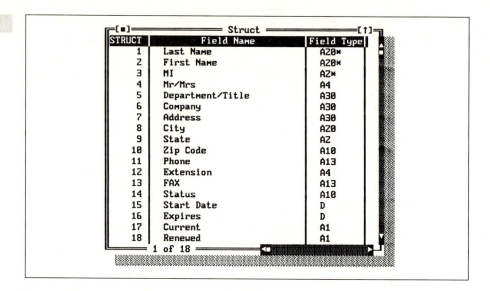

We also added validity checks to several fields of the Members table, as follows:

FIELD NAME	VALIDITY CHECK
MI	Picture format is &., to automatically convert the middle initial to uppercase and insert a period after the initial. A validity check of **Auto** ➤ **Picture** ➤ **Y**es advances the cursor as soon as the Picture format is satisfied.
State	Picture format is &&, to automatically convert the State to uppercase. A validity check of **Auto** ➤ **Picture** ➤ **Y**es advances the cursor as soon as the Picture format is satisfied.
Phone	Picture format is (###)###-####.
Extension	Picture format is *#.
FAX	Picture format is (###)###-####.
Status	Picture format is {R}EGULAR, {O}FFICER for REGULAR or OFFICER. REGULAR is the default.

THE DESIGN OF THE MEMBERSHIP APPLICATION DATABASE

FIELD NAME	VALIDITY CHECK
Start Date	Required field. TODAY (today's date) is the default.
Current	Required field. Picture format is Y,N for Yes or No. Y is the default.
Renewed	Required field. Picture format is N,Y for No or Yes. N is the default.

The validity checks speed up data entry and improve accuracy. The most important validity checks are for the essential membership status fields: Start Date, Current, and Renewed. See Chapter 5 for more information about setting up validity checks.

Since Paradox does not allow a validity check of TODAY + 365, we used a query to fill in this value for blank Expires fields. After data entry, the Expires field is filled in by a query that replaces any blank Expires fields with Start Date + 365. The same query runs before membership renewals are updated and expired memberships are deleted.

The Renew table is used to temporarily hold renewal records when the application user chooses **Update ➤ Update**. Its structure is identical to that of Members, and it uses the same key fields. Renew is never sorted by zip code and needs no secondary index. The Renew table is updated using a custom form displaying only the member's renewal status, name, start date, and expiration date, and the form allows changes to only the renewal status. Therefore, the only validity check is in the Renewed field, and this check is identical to the one in the Renewed field in the Members table (N,Y; N is the default).

Custom Forms for the Membership Application

The Membership application uses one custom form for entering and editing membership data, and another for updating the renewal status. Form 1 of the Members table, named Add/Edit Member Information, is used for entering and editing data. Its field arrangement is shown in Figure 18.6.

Designing an Application

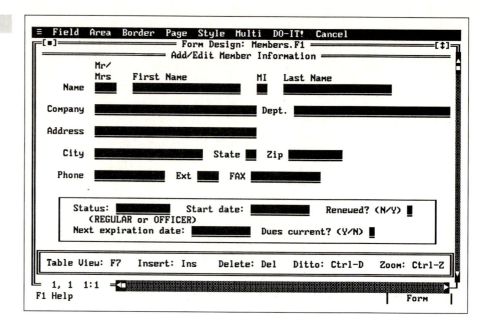

FIGURE 18.6

The custom form for adding or editing records for the Membership application

The user can toggle between Form view and Table view while adding new members.

Form 1 of the Renew table, Renew Membership, is shown in Figure 18.7. It is used to flag (identify) members with renewed memberships. This form displays multiple records, an advanced feature discussed in Chapter 15. Only the Renewed field can be updated through this form; the form's other fields are display-only.

Membership Application Reports

The Membership application uses four report formats, three of which are form letters. The first report format, named Membership Roster,

THE DESIGN OF THE MEMBERSHIP APPLICATION DATABASE

FIGURE 18.7

Form for renewing memberships

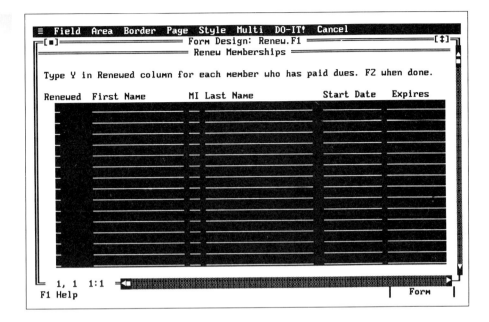

displays a list of all members, with fields arranged as below:

```
Last Name    Mr/Mrs     First Name    MI
Company
Department/Title
Address
City     State    Zip Code
Phone    Extension    FAX
Status   Current    Renewed
Start Date    Expires
```

Figure 18.8 shows the report format. A single blank line is included in the Form band to separate printed records.

The other three reports are form letters, each of which uses the following identical name and address format near the top of the letter.

```
Mr/Mrs    First Name    MI    Last Name
Company
Department/Title
Address
City     State    Zip
First Name (after Dear)
```

730 CHAPTER 18 DESIGNING AN APPLICATION

FIGURE 18.8

Format of the Membership Roster report (report 1 of the Members table)

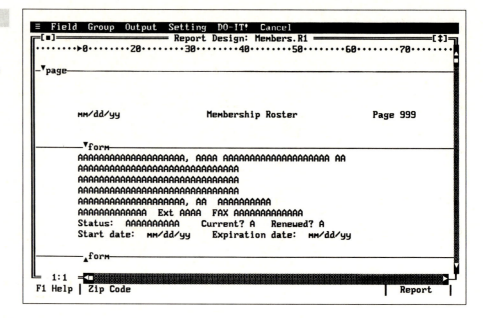

Because these letters are designed for bulk mailing, they are grouped by zip code, to print in zip code order. Figure 18.9 shows the report format for a form letter.

The renewal letter and overdue letter (reports 3 and 4 of the Members table) have the same design. The body text of the renewal letter is shown below:

> Our records indicate that your membership expires on *Month dd yyyy*. If you wish to continue being a member of the Paradox 4.5 User's Group in San Diego, please send your payment right away.

The body text of the overdue letter is as follows:

> If you have already renewed your membership to the San Diego Paradox 4.5 User's Group (PUG-45), please excuse this intrusion. However, our records indicate that your membership expired on *Month dd yyyy*. To continue your monthly PUG-45 newsletters, please remit your renewal membership dues at your earliest convenience.

Notice that the Expires field is embedded in the body of each letter. It will print the appropriate expiration date in *Month dd yyyy* format.

FIGURE 18.9

Format for the Welcome letter (report 2 of the Members table)

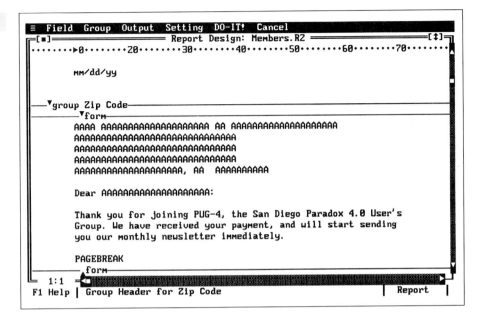

Membership Application Mailing Label Format

The application's mailing labels are arranged like this:

Mr/Mrs   First Name   MI   Last Name
Company
Department/Title
Address
City   State   Zip Code

The labels, like the letters, are grouped in zip code order, as shown in Figure 18.10. If the user first prints Welcome letters, then prints the Welcome labels, it will be an easy task to match the correct mailing label with its letter.

FIGURE 18.10

Format for the mailing labels (report 5 of the Members table)

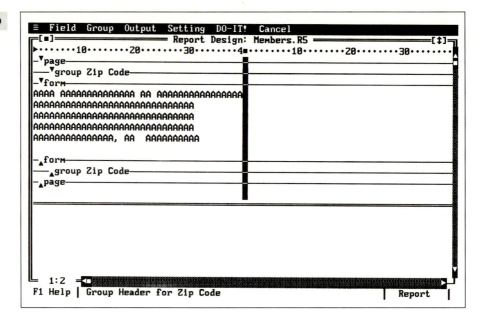

Membership Application Menu Structure

Figure 18.3, earlier in this chapter, shows the menu structure for the Membership application, with all the pull-down menus. Here's a summary of each menu option action:

- **Maintain ➤ Add New Members:** Using DataEntry mode, lets the user insert, delete, and edit records in the Entry table. After the user presses F2, the records are moved to the Members table. Blank Status, Start Date, Current, and Renewed fields are replaced with default values. Blank Expires fields are replaced with Start Date + 365.

- **Maintain ➤ Browse All Members:** Using CoEdit mode, lets the user insert, delete, and edit records in the Members table, which initially appears in Table view. After the user presses F2, the blank Status, Start Date, Current, and Renewed fields are replaced (as with the Add New Members option).

THE DESIGN OF THE MEMBERSHIP APPLICATION DATABASE

- **Maintain ➤ Change/Delete a Member:** Using CoEdit mode, lets the user insert, delete, and edit records, which initially appear in Form view. After the user presses F2, the blank fields are replaced (as with the other editing options).

- **Update ➤ Update Renewals:** Lets the user update the Renew field in the Renew table. It updates the Members table with records from the Renew table and, using a query, adds 365 days to the expiration dates for newly renewed memberships, changes Current to Y, and resets Renewed to N for those records. (The next section describes the process for updating renewals.)

- **Update ➤ Delete Expired:** Replaces blank Status, Start Date, Current, or Renewed fields with default values and replaces blank Expires fields with Start Date + 365. Then queries the Members table for memberships that expired more than 60 days ago (Expires < TODAY – 60 and Current NOT "Y"). Then displays the number of records that expired, asks for permission to delete expired members and, if the user says OK, deletes members with expired membership.

- **Print ➤ Membership Roster:** Lets the user choose to print to the screen or printer, then prints the Members table using report 1.

- **Print ➤ Letters ➤ Welcome Letter:** Queries the Members table to select new members (Start Date > TODAY – 30 and <= TODAY). Then stores the results in an Answer table. Lets the user choose to print to the screen or printer, then prints Welcome letters using data from the Answer table and report 2 from the Members table.

- **Print ➤ Letters ➤ Renewal Letter:** Queries the Members table to select members whose memberships will expire within 30 days (Expires >= TODAY and <= TODAY + 30). Stores the result in an Answer table and lets the user choose to print to the screen or printer. Then prints Renewal letters using data from the Answer table and report 3 from the Members table.

- **Print ➤ Letters ➤ Overdue Letter:** Queries the Members table to select memberships that expired within the last 60 days (Expires < TODAY and >= TODAY – 60). Stores the result in an Answer table and lets the user choose to print to the screen or printer. Then prints Overdue letters using data from the Answer table and report 4 from the Members table.

- **Print ▶ Mailing Labels ▶ All Labels:** Lets the user choose to print to the screen or printer, then prints report 5 (mailing labels) from the Members table.

- **Print ▶ Mailing Labels ▶ Welcome Labels, Renewal Labels, Overdue Labels:** These three options work like their corresponding letter options, but use report 5 (mailing labels) from the Members table.

- **Utilities ▶ Escape to DOS:** Plays a recorded script named ToDOS, which uses Tools ▶ More ▶ ToDOS to temporarily escape to DOS (or to Windows).

- **Utilities ▶ Backup Members Table:** Prompts the user to insert a disk in drive A, then plays a script named Backup, which uses Tools ▶ Copy ▶ Table to copy the Members table and family files to corresponding backup files on the disk in drive A.

- **Utilities ▶ Backup Application:** Prompts the user to insert a disk in drive A, then plays a PAL script named Appcopy, which runs the DOS XCOPY *.* A: /S command to back up the application directory and subdirectories to drive A.

- **Exit ▶ Return to Paradox:** Exits to Paradox.

- **Exit ▶ Exit to DOS:** Exits to the DOS prompt (or to Windows).

Understanding the Update Renewals Process

To demonstrate what each operation in the Update Renewals process does, assume that the current date is February 28, 1994, and the Members table contains the following four records (only relevant fields are used in this example). Note that because Andy Adams' membership expired last month his Current field is already marked as N:

LAST NAME	FIRST NAME	START DATE	EXPIRES	CURRENT	RENEWED
Adams	Andy	01/01/93	01/01/94	N	N
Baker	Bob	02/01/93	02/01/94	Y	N
Carlson	Cara	02/28/93	02/28/94	Y	N
Davis	Deedra	03/31/93	03/31/94	Y	N

The Update Renewals option performs these operations:

1. Runs a query to replace any blank Status, Start Date, Current, or Renewed fields with default values. Then runs a second query to replace any blank Expires fields with Start Date + 365.

2. Runs a query to find expired memberships (Expires <= TODAY) and change their Current field to N.

3. Runs a query to find all records with expired memberships (Current = N), storing the result in an Answer table. Then empties Renew and copies the Answer table records to Renew.

4. Displays the Renewal form for expired memberships and lets the user change the Renewed field in the Renew table from N to Y for those members who have renewed.

5. Plays a script (named Renewals), which updates the Members table with data from the Renew table.

6. Runs a query that finds all Members table records where Renewed = Y. In those records only, the query changes Current to Y, adds 365 days to the date in Expires, and changes Renewed back to N.

The Start Date, Expires, Current, and Renewed fields are crucial to many parts of this application, especially the options for updating renewals and deleting expired memberships. For this reason, we must prevent blank entries in these fields. The validity checks described earlier in this chapter force entry if the user visits a field before pressing F2. However, if a field isn't visited, it remains blank. Furthermore, there's the problem of not being able to automatically insert a default expiration date of one year in the future. Therefore, we must fill in some of the blank fields outside the data entry procedures.

Operation 1 performs two separate queries to take care of this automatic fill-in job. The first changes blank Status, Start Date, Current, and Renewed fields to the same default values that appear when the user visits the field. By setting up the query form with each condition on a separate line (OR conditions), we can take care of all four fields at once. Here are the conditions used for each relevant field in the Query form:

Status	BLANK, CHANGETO "REGULAR"
Start Date	BLANK, CHANGETO TODAY
Current	BLANK, CHANGETO Y
Renewed	BLANK, CHANGETO N

In plain English, this query reads, "If Status is blank, change it to REGULAR. Or if Start Date is blank, change it to today's date. Or if Current is blank, change it to Y. Or if Renewed is blank, change it to N."

NOTE While not crucial to any calculations, blank Status fields are less than desirable. Therefore, the query also fills in a default value if the user leaves the Status field blank.

The next query in operation 1 replaces any blank Expires fields (expiration date) with Start Date plus 365 (one year later). Shown here is the relevant portion of the Query form.

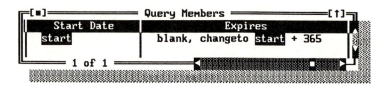

In fact, just to be safe, we run these queries as the last two steps of each option on the Maintain menu and as the first two steps of each option on the Update menu. On a large table with hundreds of records, these queries can slow down the application. If this becomes a problem on your computer, delete the query steps from the options on the Maintain and Update menus, then create a new option on the same or another menu that does nothing but run these two queries. For example, create a Utilities ➤ **F**ix Blank Fields option to do the job, then you can use the option only when you need it, taking special care to do so before updating renewals or deleting expired memberships.

TIP Workshop lets you take several actions from a single menu option. See Chapter 19 for more information.

With our queries completed, we're ready for the next operation. Assuming that the current date is 02/28/94, operation 2 will modify two of the four records, bringing the Current field up to date in all records, as shown below:

LAST NAME	FIRST NAME	START DATE	EXPIRES	CURRENT	RENEWED
Adams	Andy	01/01/93	01/01/94	N	N
Baker	Bob	02/01/93	02/01/94	N	N
Carlson	Cara	02/28/93	02/28/94	N	N
Davis	Deedra	03/31/93	03/31/94	Y	N

Operation 3 copies all the expired memberships to the Renew table. Operation 4 then displays expired memberships (only) on a browse screen. The user, who presumably has payments from all renewed members, can then change the Renewed field from N to Y for members who have renewed. As you know, fields on the Renewal form are display-only, except for Renewed, and the cursor is locked into the Renewed field.

NOTE Figure 18.11, later in this chapter, shows the browse screen with some sample data.

As an example, let's say that the user updates memberships for Adams and Baker by changing N to Y in the Renewed field, because those members have paid for a new subscription. After the fifth operation updates the Members table with the records in Renewed, Members contains the following data:

LAST NAME	FIRST NAME	START DATE	EXPIRES	CUR-RENT	RE-NEWED
Adams	Andy	01/01/93	01/01/94	N	Y
Baker	Bob	02/01/93	02/01/94	N	Y
Carlson	Cara	02/28/93	02/28/94	N	N
Davis	Deedra	03/31/93	03/31/94	Y	N

The final operation automatically changes the Current fields for records that have just been renewed to Y, extends the expiration dates by one year, and changes Renewed back to N to prevent the system from accidentally extending expirations another year. The final results are as below:

LAST NAME	FIRST NAME	START DATE	EXPIRES	CUR-RENT	RE-NEWED
Adams	Andy	01/01/93	01/01/95	Y	N
Baker	Bob	02/01/93	02/01/95	Y	N
Carlson	Cara	02/28/93	02/28/94	N	N
Davis	Deedra	03/31/93	03/31/94	Y	N

Now the Members table is accurate for the current month and ready for next month's updates. Adams and Baker need not be renewed again until next year. When March 31 rolls around, the user repeats the renewal operation, and Carlson and Davis will appear on the browse screen for possible renewal. The user will identify those members that have renewed (if any) by placing Y in the Renewed field, and all appropriate memberships for the month of March will be updated.

Testing the Completed Membership Application

Before you give a completed application to the user (or before you yourself use the application for serious work), test it thoroughly. Using sample data, try out each menu option. The following sections describe using the Membership application, and show examples for testing the application.

Running the Membership Application

Use any method described in the next chapter to run the application (the sample application is named MemMgr). The splash screen will appear, and the cursor will highlight the first option on the desktop menu, which is Maintain. Scroll through menu options in the usual manner.

Let's look at procedures for testing each option to make sure the application works as expected. You should develop similar testing procedures for any application you create to make sure that it works properly and that you've tested all circumstances that your application must handle.

Adding New Members

To test adding new members, select **Maintain** ➤ **Add** New Members. You'll be taken to a blank form for entering new records. Enter the records below, with the dates specified:

Mr. Andy A. Adams
ABC Technology
Engineering Dept.
13307 Artesia Avenue
Los Angeles, CA 90165
(818)555-0101   Ext: 123   Fax: (818)555-1212
Status: REGULAR   Start Date: 01/01/94   Renewed? N
Expiration date: 01/01/95   Dues Current? Y

Mr. Bob B. Baker
Boeing International
Ballistics Dept.
2744 Bering St.
El Monte, CA 91704
(818)555-1232   Ext: 999   Fax: (818)555-1222
Status: REGULAR   Start date: 02/01/94   Renewed? N
Expiration date: 02/01/95   Dues Current? Y

Miss Cara C. Carlson
Cookie Haven
Purchasing Dept. 3211 Cantamar
Cucamonga, CA 91655
(818)555-9988

740 CHAPTER 18

DESIGNING AN APPLICATION

       Status: OFFICER   Start date: 03/15/94   Renewed? N
       Expiration date: 03/15/95   Dues Current? Y

Dr. Deedra D. Davis
Doctor's Hospital 15th Floor
8843 Donga Dr.
Duarte, CA 91555
(818)555-9910   Ext: 8851   Fax: (818)555-9921
Status: REGULAR   Start date: 04/30/94   Renewed? N
Expiration date: 04/30/95   Dues Current? Y

NOTE   Pressing ↵ in the Status, Start Date, Renewed, or Current fields automatically enters the default values of REGULAR, the computer's system date, N, and Y, respectively.

After entering the sample records, press F2 to save the changes and return to the application menu.

Changing Members' Data

The Maintain menu offers two options for editing membership data: Browse All Members and Change/Delete a Member. Test each method, but don't change any starting or expiration dates. Note that records should be displayed in alphabetical order by last name.

NOTE   Be sure to try using these options in both Table view and Form view.

You can delete any record using the Delete key as usual. (For now, if you delete a record, immediately choose **U**ndo ➤ **Y**es to restore the record.)

After testing each option, save the changes and return to the application menu.

Updating the Membership Roster

Here are the steps to test updating renewed members and deleting expired memberships in the Members table:

1. To set up a test date, choose **U**tilities ➤ Escape to **DOS** from the application's desktop menu. At the DOS prompt, type **DATE** and press ↵. You'll see a prompt similar to

   Current date is Tue 01-04-1994
   Enter new date (mm-dd-yy): _

   Type in the test date **3-31-95** and press ↵. Then type **EXIT** and press ↵ to return to the application menu.

2. Choose **U**pdate ➤ **U**pdate Renewals. You'll see a brief message as the application replaces the Current field of expired memberships with N; then the application reports the number of records found (3). Choose OK or press ↵ to continue to the browse screen showing the expired memberships.

3. Mark the record for Carlson with a Y (which assumes this is the only renewed membership). Note that the cursor stays locked into the Renewed field, even if you press ← or → or click the mouse elsewhere.

4. After updating the one member, press F2. You'll see brief messages as the application updates the renewed membership and then be returned to the application's menu.

5. To verify an accurate update, open the **M**aintain menu and choose **B**rowse All Members or **C**hange/Delete a Member. You should see that Carlson's membership has been extended to 1996, and the Current field for the record is marked Y.

6. Press F2 to return to the application's desktop menu.

Deleting Expired Memberships

To delete memberships that expired more than 60 days ago and were never renewed, choose **U**pdate ➤ **D**elete Expired. You'll see a message as the application marks one record for deletion (Andy Adams) and indicates the number of records marked for deletion (1). Choose OK to continue. You'll see the dialog box below. To delete the membership record, choose OK. Choose Cancel to cancel the deletion.

Choose **M**aintain ➤ **B**rowse All Members to check that Andy Adams' record has been permanently deleted.

To recover the deleted record, choose Exit ➤ Return to Paradox. Then choose Tools ➤ More ➤ Add. Specify Deleted as the source table and Members as the target table, then choose NewEntries from the submenu that appears.

Printing the Membership Roster

You can print an alphabetical list of all members currently in the Members table by choosing **P**rint ➤ **M**embership Roster. This option opens a dialog box giving you the options to preview the roster on the **S**creen, send the roster to the **P**rinter, or **E**xit to the application menu without printing. Make a selection and choose OK.

If you choose **P**rinter, the application displays the Ready Printer dialog box, which prompts you to prepare the printer. Press ↵ or click on Print to print the membership roster (in alphabetical order), and then return to the Screen/Printer/Exit dialog box. Choose Exit or Cancel to return to the application menu.

Printing All Mailing Labels

To print mailing labels for all members, choose **P**rint ➤ **M**ailing Labels ➤ **A**ll Labels. For the membership roster report, you can choose options from the Screen/Printer/Exit dialog box as described earlier. Mailing labels are printed in zip code order, as specified by the report format.

Renewal Letters and Labels

Each month, you can print letters, reminding members whose memberships expire next month that it's time to renew. Choose **P**rint ➤ **L**etters ➤ **R**enewal Letter to print a letter for Deedra Davis, whose membership expires next month (April 1995). The application displays the number of records found. Press ↵ or click on OK to continue, then choose options from the Screen/Printer/Exit dialog box.

After printing the letters, choose **P**rint ➤ **M**ailing Labels ➤ **R**enewal Labels to print a label for this member.

Overdue Letters and Labels

You can print monthly overdue letters, reminding late payers that their memberships expired within the past 60 days and have not been renewed. Bob Baker's membership is the only one that meets this description; it expired in February 1995, and has not been renewed.

Choose **P**rint ➤ **L**etters ➤ **O**verdue Letter to print the reminder letters. Then choose **P**rint ➤ **M**ailing Labels ➤ Overdue Labels to print corresponding mailing labels.

Welcome Letter and Labels

Each month, you can print welcome letters and matching mailing labels for all new members (those who joined in the current month and year). Currently, no records in the test table meet this description, so you need to fake the current date to print at least one letter. Choose **U**tilities ➤ **E**scape to **DOS**, then enter **DATE** as just described and change the current date to **3-31-94**. Type **EXIT** and press ↵ to return to the application menu.

NOTE Changing the system date in this chapter is only for testing with a small table. In actual use with real data, you would rarely need to change the date to print a particular type of letter or mailing label.

Now choose **P**rint ➤ **L**etters ➤ **W**elcome Letter. The application will report the number of records found (1) and allow you to print to the screen or printer. You should see a letter printed for Cara Carlson. To print a mailing label for the letter, choose **P**rint ➤ **M**ailing Labels ➤ **W**elcome Labels.

You may want to reset the current date back to 3-31-95 now, or to the actual current date.

If you have the companion disk you can use F1 to try out the Help facility. You'll learn how to create Help screens in Chapter 19.

Testing the Utilities

You've already had a chance to test the Escape to DOS option from the Utilities menu. You should also test the other options on that menu. Place a blank, formatted disk in drive A of your computer and choose **U**tilities ➤ **B**ackup Members Table. The disk drive light should come on as the application backs up the Members table and its family to corresponding Membak files on drive A.

Next, choose **U**tilities ➤ **B**ackup Application. Once again, you should see the drive light and see the names of all files being copied on the screen, as the application copies the entire \PDOX45\Members directory and the directories below it to the disk in drive A.

If your Membership application tables become quite large, the entire application and its subdirectories may not fit on a single floppy disk. In this case, you should modify the Appcopy script by replacing the XCOPY command with the BACKUP command, which will prompt you for each backup disk as needed. The following command line will do the trick:

BACKUP *.* A:\ /S /L

In English, this command translates to "Back up all the files (*.*) in the current directory and all subdirectories (/S) to drive A, and create a log file (/L)."

If you decide to use the BACKUP command, do not be concerned by the

*** Not able to backup file ***

messages that appear when BACKUP tries to back up certain temporary files that are currently tied up by Paradox (such as files ending in .T00 and the $PALMEM$ file). These files are created "on the fly" and are usually removed when you exit Paradox; they are not a necessary part of your application.

NOTE The XCOPY command was introduced in DOS 3.2. If you're using DOS 3.0 or 3.1, you should replace the XCOPY command with BACKUP as described. (Keep in mind that Paradox itself requires DOS 3.0 or higher.)

If you use the BACKUP command (as opposed to XCOPY), you must use the DOS RESTORE command if you later need to copy the contents of the floppy disk back to your hard disk, or to another user's hard disk. For example, the following RESTORE command restores the application directory and subdirectories drive A diskette to the hard disk (drive C):

RESTORE A: C:*.* /S

NOTE See your DOS documentation for more information about using the XCOPY, BACKUP, and RESTORE commands.

Exiting the Application

If you choose Exit ➤ **R**eturn to Paradox, you'll be returned to Paradox. Choosing Exit ➤ Exit to DOS will return you all the way to the DOS prompt.

Tips on Using the Membership Application

If you have actual data to store in the membership table, delete the dummy test records by choosing **M**aintain ➤ **B**rowse All Members. Press Delete to delete each record, then press F2 to save your changes. Next,

DESIGNING AN APPLICATION

type in at least some portion of your real data. When you use the Membership application with real data, remember these points:

- When you first run the application, choose Utilities ➤ Escape to DOS and verify the current system date.

- Make a habit of always printing monthly letters on the same day each month (preferably the last day of the month).

- If you miss a month and want to print the previous month's letters in the current month, change the system date to the month that you are printing for. For example, if you don't get around to printing February's letters until March 2, change the system date to February 28 (or February 29 if it's a leap year), so that the application behaves as though it were still February.

- Before printing any monthly letters, always perform the options on the Update menu in the order they are presented: update the renewals, then delete the expired memberships. This will ensure that your mailing is based on current, accurate data.

- Make a habit of backing up the table to the disk in drive A at least once a month, using Utilities ➤ Backup Members Table. The best time to make this backup is after printing monthly letters, when the table is thoroughly up to date.

- You can renew memberships by placing Y in the Renewed field when using the Maintain ➤ Browse All Members option. However, don't change the expiration date if you do so. The next time you choose Update ➤ Update Renewals, the expiration date will be extended by one year (as long as the Renewed field still contains Y).

If you previously used a manual technique to manage your membership system, you may want to use both the manual technique and the Membership application for a couple of months to make sure the application is operating correctly. This is called running the application *in parallel* with the existing system, and it is one of the most common techniques used to test all types of applications.

Summary

This chapter discussed the application design process and took an in-depth look at a sample Membership application. Before moving on to the next chapter, which explains how to use Workshop to build an application, let's look at the highlights of application design presented here:

- An application is an automated collection of database management system (DBMS) objects and functions, often controlled by a menu system. Paradox applications include objects such as tables, forms, reports, queries, graphs, and scripts and can provide control for whatever complex set of objects and functions you need to manage your data.
- To design an application, follow these general steps:
    1. Define the goals of the application.
    2. Design the menu structure on paper.
    3. Use Paradox to design and create tables, forms, and reports, queries, and scripts.
    4. Create the application with Workshop.
    5. Test and refine it as needed.
    6. Document and distribute the application to your end-users.

# CHAPTER 19

Creating an Application

fast TRACK

- **To start Workshop** — 754

    start Paradox and choose **T**ools ➤ **M**ore ➤ **D**irectory to switch to the directory you want to use for the application. Then choose ≡ ➤ **U**tilities ➤ **W**orkshop from the Paradox desktop menu.

- **To create a new application** — 759

    choose **A**pplication ➤ **N**ew from the Workshop desktop menu and define the application attributes.

- **To create a new menu option on the desktop menu or on a submenu** — 765

    move the cursor to where you want the new option to appear, then choose the Add button on the mouse palette, or press Ins, or double-click on the <New> option. Then choose **A**ction to create an action menu option, or Sub**M**enu to add a submenu.

- **To change an existing menu option** — 767

    highlight it and choose the Edit button on the mouse palette, or press F9, or double-click on that option.

- **To attach a utility action object to an action menu option** — 773

    choose the Select button in the Action area, then choose an object type from the Object Type dialog box. If you chose **E**xit Paradox or **Q**uit to Paradox, you're finished. If you chose **P**lay a Script or **P**roc (ExecProc), enter the script or procedure name.

CHAPTER 19   **751**

To attach a non-utility action object to an action menu option   **773**

    choose the Select button in the Action area near the left side of the Menu Definition dialog box, then choose an object type from the Object Type dialog box. Highlight the action object you want, and choose OK or press ↵. Alternatively, you can just double-click on that object.

To change an existing action object   **775**

    choose ActionEdit from the Workshop desktop menu, and select an object type. Highlight the action you want to change, then choose the Edit button, or press F9, or press ↵. As a shortcut, you can just double-click on the object.

To change an existing action object while editing a menu option   **775**

    choose the Edit button in the Action area.

To attach a Help text object   **797**

    create or edit the menu or submenu option, then choose the Select button in the Help Screen (or Help ID) area near the right side of the Menu Definition dialog box. Choose an existing Help text object by double-clicking it, or use the New or Borrow buttons to create one.

To edit a Help text object while editing an action menu option   **798**

    choose the Edit button in the Help Screen area.

CHAPTER 18 introduced you to applications and covered the six basic steps involved in the design and testing process. In this chapter, we'll expand on these basic steps for creating an application with Workshop. You'll learn how to use Workshop to assemble all of your Paradox objects into an easy-to-use system of menus and scripts. In the next chapter, you'll learn how to test, refine, run, and document your application.

An Overview of Application Creation

Like application design, application creation involves several steps, listed below. Neither application design nor application development is a linear process. Once you complete the first two steps below, the remaining steps can be performed in almost any order. However, the order described represents a logical approach requiring the least backtracking.

1. Create or select a separate directory to hold all Paradox objects that you developed earlier. If necessary, copy those objects to the new directory. Workshop provides tools for this purpose, as described in Chapter 20.

2. Create an application. Identify the name of the application script (the Application ID) and provide other information needed by Workshop to generate the application and its objects.

3. Optionally, create a splash screen or sign-on banner to introduce your application.

4. Create the menu structure using the guidelines you developed earlier on paper.

5. Define the actions you want to perform and attach them to each menu command. Steps 4 and 5 are the meat and potatoes of application development.

6. Test all or part of the application as needed.

7. Adjust the application, as needed.

8. Finish the application, to generate all the application scripts.

9. Return to Paradox, DOS, or Windows, and perform a step-by-step test of the entire application.

10. Document the application and distribute it to your users.

As you test, you may need to repeat some of these steps. In this chapter, we'll focus on the first six steps. Chapter 20 covers the remaining steps.

As mentioned in Chapter 18, it's best to create most or all of your application's objects (tables, reports, forms, queries, scripts, and PAL programs) in Paradox instead of in Workshop, primarily because Paradox offers more flexibility and features for doing so. In this chapter, we'll assume these objects already exist and that you've either copied them to the directory where you plan to develop your application or, even better, that you created them in that directory to start with. We'll also assume that you are familiar with all the concepts presented so far in this book for creating and working with Paradox objects. (Chapter 20 covers menu options for creating, editing, and copying tables, forms, reports, scripts, and action objects from Workshop itself.)

An *action object* is an action that you attach to a menu option. Examples of action objects include table editing sessions, report printing, queries, help screens, scripts, OK/Cancel buttons, and combinations of these.

Starting Workshop

You must first have installed Paradox and Workshop. Workshop is included on your Paradox installation disks, and is automatically installed if you elect to perform the Optional Software Installation. Appendix A explains in detail how to install Paradox and the optional software.

To start Workshop, start Paradox as usual. Then follow these steps:

1. Switch to the directory you have created for your application, using **T**ools ➤ **M**ore ➤ **D**irectory from the Paradox desktop menu.

NOTE You can also switch to a new directory by choosing **A**pplication ➤ **D**irectory from Workshop's desktop menu, as described later. Or, you can change the default working directory using the Custom Configuration Program (see Appendix D).

2. To copy needed Paradox objects to the application directory, use **T**ools ➤ **C**opy from the Paradox desktop menu as described in Chapter 12. You can usually get by with using just the Table, Script, and Graph options from the **T**ools ➤ **C**opy menu.

3. Choose ≡ ➤ **U**tilities ➤ **W**orkshop from the Paradox desktop menu.

If you aren't currently working on an application, you'll see an opening screen like the one shown in Figure 19.1. If you're working on an application (such as the sample Membership application described in Chapter 18), the screen will resemble Figure 19.2 instead.

Selecting Options in Workshop

Here's a brief overview of the options on Workshop's desktop menu, described in detail in this and the next chapter:

- **Application:** Used to open, create, edit, close, delete, test, and finish an application, or switch to and create new directories.
- **ActionEdit:** Used to create and edit action objects.

SELECTING OPTIONS IN WORKSHOP

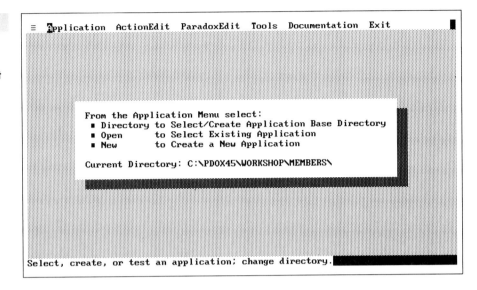

FIGURE 19.1

Workshop's opening screen and desktop menu when you're not currently working on an application

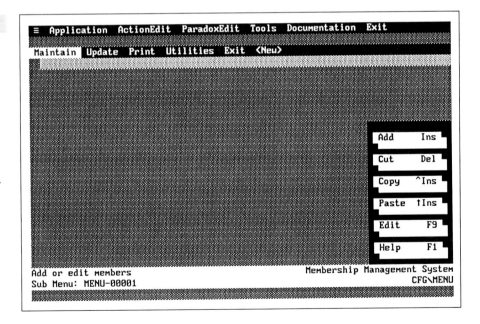

FIGURE 19.2

When you are working on an application, Workshop's opening screen and desktop menu also include the desktop menu for the application. This example shows the Membership application's desktop menu.

Creating an Application

- **ParadoxEdit:** Used to create and edit Paradox tables, forms, reports, or scripts.

- **Tools:** Used to copy, rename, and delete action objects, tables, forms, reports, and scripts.

- **Documentation:** Used to create documentation for your application.

- **Exit:** Used to return to Paradox or to DOS.

Dialog boxes in Workshop work like dialog boxes in the Custom Configuration Program (see Appendix D). Many Workshop dialog boxes feature text boxes that you fill in and buttons that you select to open additional dialog boxes or perform certain actions. In Workshop dialog boxes, when presented with a list of choices, you can quickly move the highlight bar to the item you want by typing in the first few letters. After highlighting the item, choose OK or press ↵ to complete the selection. For example, in the Object Type dialog box shown in Figure 19.3, typing **Q** automatically moves the highlight to the QUERY selection, while typing **QUI** moves the highlight to the QUIT TO PARADOX choice.

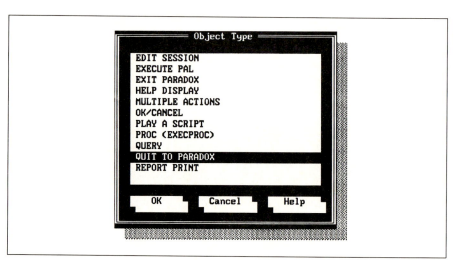

FIGURE 19.3

The Object Type dialog box after we typed QUI to move the highlight

NOTE You'll learn about the specific options in the Object Type dialog box later on. For now, we're just describing the shortcut for quickly moving to a selection in a list of choices.

Table 19.1 provides a summary of the most common Workshop buttons and their keystroke equivalents.

TABLE 19.1: Common Buttons in Workshop Dialog Boxes

BUTTON	KEYBOARD EQUIVALENT	PURPOSE
Add	Ins	Adds a menu option or action object.
Borrow	Ctrl-Ins	Creates a new item from the highlighted item (similar to Copy).
Cancel	Esc	Closes the dialog box without saving your changes.
Copy	Ctrl-Ins	Copies a menu option to the paste buffer.
Cut or Remove/Cut	Delete	Deletes the highlighted menu option or action object from its current position and copies it to the paste buffer.
Edit	F9	Edits the highlighted menu option or action object.
Help	F1	Displays on-line help for the dialog box.
Modify	F9	Same as Edit.
New	Ins	Same as Add.
OK	F2	Exits the dialog box and saves your changes.
Paste	Shift-Ins	Pastes the contents of the paste buffer at the cursor position.
Test		Saves changes made so far and tests an action object or menu option.

Help screens in Workshop work similarly to those in Paradox itself. However, unlike Paradox, Workshop has no Help index. To exit Help screens, choose **R**eturn from the Help menu or press Esc.

Creating or Selecting the Application Directory

Use a separate directory for each application that you develop. Before creating, changing, or using an application, you need to switch to whatever directory contains (or will contain) the application. You can create or switch to the application directory from Paradox (or from DOS or the Custom Configuration Program), or from Workshop using these steps:

1. Choose **A**pplication from the Workshop desktop menu. The Application menu opens, as shown below.

2. Choose **D**irectory. The Change Directory dialog box appears.

3. Type the complete path name of the directory, then choose OK or press ↵. Type in a new directory or an existing directory (such as C:\PDOX45\Members) to switch directories.

Workshop will make the selected existing directory the working directory, returning you to the Workshop desktop. (Open applications in other directories will be automatically closed.) If the selected directory doesn't exist, the Create Directory dialog box opens. Choose OK or press ↵ to create the directory making it the current directory; choose Cancel to enter a different directory.

Workshop displays a new current directory (as in Figure 19.1).

Creating a New Application

With the objects for the application in the current directory, you're ready to create the new application. Here are the steps:

1. Choose **Application** ➤ **New** from the Workshop desktop menu.

2. For the first application in a directory, you're prompted for the creation of a new application table. Choose OK.

CAUTION

The application table, named Applic.DB and stored in the Cfg subdirectory, keeps track of all the applications that you create in the current directory. If you're creating an application in the C:\PDOX45\Members directory, the application table is named C:\PDOX45\Members\Cfg\Applic.DB. *Never* change or delete any of the objects in the Cfg or Workshop directories below the current directory. These directories are required by Workshop, and changing them in any way could damage your application.

3. Complete the New Application dialog box as described in the following sections. Use this dialog box to define attributes for your application such as the application's startup script, splash screen, and system tables location.

4. Define the attributes and choose OK to save your changes.

CREATING AN APPLICATION

An empty menu bar, a mouse palette, and the application name will appear on the desktop. The only option on the menu bar is <New>. After you create the menu choices discussed in the following sections, this screen will look like the one shown earlier in Figure 19.2.

Defining Application Attributes

For a new application, you must specify the Application ID. All the other dialog box selections are optional. Here's a summary of the options in the New Application dialog box:

- **Application ID:** Provides the file name of the startup script that will run your finished application. Enter any valid DOS file name, Workshop automatically adds a .SC extension when the startup script is generated. For example, Memmgr creates a startup script named Memmgr.SC.

- **Application Name:** Provides the name displayed on the lower-right side of the Workshop desktop during application design (as in Figure 19.2, shown earlier).

- **Menu Table:** Stores all the menus created for the new application. The default menu table, Menu, is stored in the Cfg subdirectory, below the current directory.

> **NOTE**
> It's best to use the default settings for the menu table, object table, and top-level menu object ID. These tables must always reside in the Cfg subdirectory, just below the current directory.

- **Object Table:** Contains all the action objects for your application. The default object table, Objects, is stored in the Cfg subdirectory, below the current directory.

- **Top-Level Menu Object ID:** Defines the name for the application's desktop menu. Like all menu objects, it is stored as a record in the Menu table. The application desktop menu's default name is Main.

- **Startup Procedure:** Defines the name of a procedure to call before starting the application. If used, the startup procedure must be compiled into a library, and the name of that library must appear in the Autolib text box.
- **Autolib:** Defines the path name of the library containing procedures that you will call from your application.

NOTE Startup Procedure and Autolib are primarily of interest to PAL programmers. For information about creating libraries and defining procedures, refer to the *PAL Reference* manual and *PAL Programmer's Guide*, which come with Paradox. Figure 19.18, later in this chapter, displays a script that creates a library named Paradox for the sample Membership application.

- **Change Description:** Opens a Paradox Editor window for entering or changing a detailed description of your application, its limitations, objects, and so forth. (When the **A**pplication ➤ **O**pen option is chosen, the first few lines of this description appear in the Application Selection dialog box.) Save your description and return to the dialog box or choose **C**ancel ➤ **Y**es to discard your description changes.
- **Splash Screen:** Opens a Paradox Editor window for creating or editing a splash screen (sign-on banner) that appears when you start your application. Figure 19.4 shows the splash-screen editing window for the Membership application. Chapter 4 describes creating graphics characters like the thick rules shown in Figure 19.4. See Table 4.1 in Chapter 4 for a list of special graphics characters from the IBM PC Extended Character Set. The three-digit code used is 223 (Alt-223). Save the splash screen changes and return to the dialog box or choose **C**ancel ➤ **Y**es to discard your changes.

762 CHAPTER 19 CREATING AN APPLICATION

FIGURE 19.4

The splash screen editing window for the sample Membership application

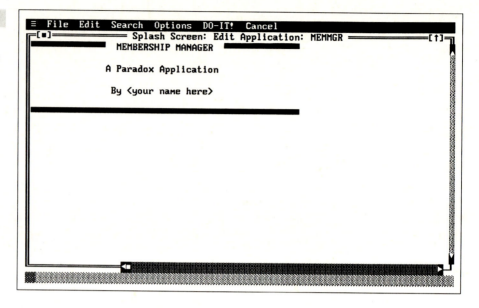

Figure 19.5 shows a completed New Application dialog box for the Membership application discussed in Chapter 18. Assuming that the current directory is C:\PDOX45\Members, the information entered into the dialog box in Figure 19.5 directs Workshop as follows:

- Startup application script: Memmgr.SC.
- Application name: Membership Management Application.
- Menus table: C:\PDOX45\Members\Cfg\Menu.DB.
- Action objects table: C:\PDOX45\Members\Cfg\Objects.DB.
- Top-level menu object ID (desktop menu): Main.
- Startup procedure: (none defined).
- Membership application's procedure library: C:\PDOX45\Paradox.LIB. This library contains a procedure named Keyviol (described later in this chapter), which prints an error message if the user tries to enter duplicate member names.

CREATING A NEW APPLICATION

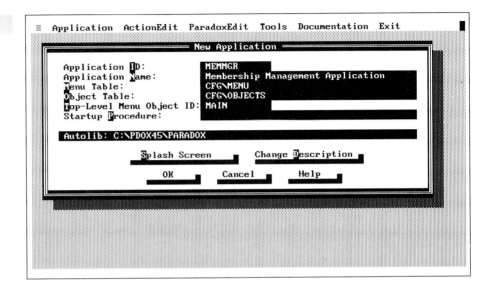

FIGURE 19.5

The completed New Application dialog box for the sample Membership application.

Creating the Menu Structure

After filling in the New Application dialog box, you're ready to define the application menus and actions. You can create up to 16 levels of menus, each with up to 50 options. For each application action, create a menu command.

Applications created in Workshop use the same hierarchical menu structure used by Paradox. Figure 19.2 (shown earlier in this chapter) illustrates a completed desktop menu for the sample Membership application, which includes Maintain, Update, Print, Utilities, and Exit choices. The <New> option on the menu bar lets you add more options to the menu. This is a Workshop option, and it does not appear in your finished application. Initially, <New> is the only option on a new application's desktop menu.

Figure 19.6 shows the Membership application's Print menu. This menu consists of an action menu option named Membership Roster and two submenus named Letters and Mailing Labels. The figure includes the Mailing Labels submenu, which lists options for printing various types of mailing labels. Notice the ➤ symbols to the right of the Letters and Mailing Labels options. Workshop automatically adds a ➤ symbol to options that display submenus as a visual cue to the user.

764 CHAPTER **19**   CREATING AN APPLICATION

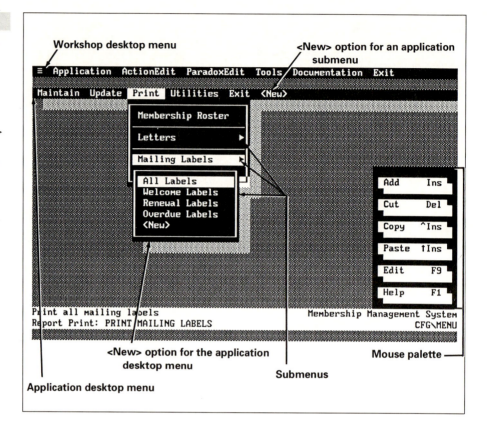

FIGURE 19.6

The Print menu of the sample Membership application consists of one action menu option and two submenus: Letters and Mailing Labels. The ▶ symbol to the right of an option indicates a submenu.

The Print menu also includes optional separator lines. These lines simply serve to divide the menu into logical sections, making it easier for the user to find and select the desired option.

Note the <New> option at the bottom of the Mailing Labels menu. This option on a submenu is similar to the <New> option on the desktop menu. It lets you add more options to that submenu. These <New> options do not appear when you run the finished application.

Begin with a written plan for the menus, as described in Chapter 18, and keep in mind that you can change your menu structure at any time. The next sections explain desktop menu options and submenu creation and editing. Later, you'll learn how to create actions and assign them to menu options.

Note the two desktop menu bars in Figure 19.6. The top desktop menu is used to access Workshop commands. To move to the Workshop desktop menu, press the F10 key. The lower desktop menu is for the application you're designing, and always has <New> as its last option. To make changes to the application menus, you must select the application's desktop menu by pressing the Esc key (one or more times). You can select either menu by clicking on it with your mouse. Select options from the menus as usual.

Adding New Menu and Submenu Options

To add a new desktop menu or a submenu option, you can begin by using one of these techniques:

- Double-click on <New> with your mouse.
- Highlight <New> with the arrow keys, or type < (less-than sign) as a shortcut. Then press ↵.
- Position the cursor wherever you want to add the option and press the Ins key or click on the Add button.

If you're adding an option to a submenu, the pop-up menu below appears. When you're adding to the menu bar, you'll see the same pop-up menu, but without a Separator option.

Choose an option from the pop-up menu, as follows:

- **Action:** Use this option for menu options that perform actions, such as the Print ➤ Membership Roster option in Figure 19.6. After choosing Action, you'll see the dialog box in Figure 19.7.
- **SubMenu:** Use this option for menu options leading to a submenu, such as the Print ➤ Letters option in Figure 19.6. After choosing SubMenu, you'll see the dialog box in Figure 19.8.
- **Separator:** Use this option to add a separator line to submenus. The separator line will immediately appear at the cursor location, pushing down the entries at and below the cursor.

FIGURE 19.7

This Menu Definition dialog box appears if you choose Action from the pop-up menu.

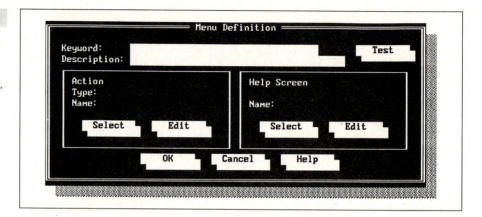

FIGURE 19.8

This Menu Definition dialog box appears if you choose SubMenu from the pop-up menu.

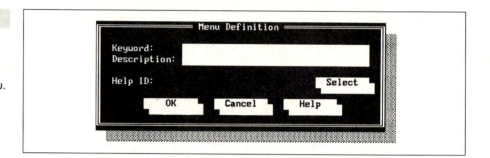

After choosing the Action or SubMenu option, enter the name of the menu option in the Keyword text box. This keyword is automatically capitalized and the first letter is highlighted on the menu, to be used as a shortcut for selecting the option, either while designing the application or while running it. To choose a different letter to highlight type a tilde (~) before and after it, as in U~t~ilities.

The cursor always moves to the first option having a given highlighted letter when you press the shortcut key. Therefore, make sure all highlighted letters on the desktop menu and on any given submenu are unique.

Next, fill in the Description text box. If you leave it blank for an action option, Workshop places an appropriate description for you. The description appears in the lower-left corner of the screen when you move the cursor to the associated option on the completed menu.

Keywords and description lines can contain any printable character from the IBM PC Extended Character Set. For example, Alt + 156 inserts the pound currency symbol (£) into a keyword or description. Refer to Chapter 4 and Table 4.1 for other character codes.

Once you define the keyword and description, you can define additional attributes for the menu option, such as an action to perform or on-line help, as described later in this chapter. You'll need to assign an action or submenu to every menu option. But, it's often easier to define the entire menu structure before assigning actions and help.

Here's a summary of the buttons in the Menu Definition dialog box. Note that a SubMenu option only has the Select button for the Help ID. An Action menu option has all the buttons listed below (see Figures 19.7 and 19.8):

- **Select (Action area):** Selects an action to perform.
- **Edit (Action area):** Edits the currently selected action.
- **Select (Help Screen or Help ID):** Selects the Help text to display.
- **Edit (Help Screen area):** Edits the currently selected Help text.
- **Test:** Saves changes and lets you test this menu option.

When you're finished, choose OK to save your changes and add the option to the menu at the cursor position. Choose Cancel or press Esc to abandon any changes.

Deleting Menu Options

To delete an option or submenu and save it in a paste buffer, first highlight the option or submenu. If you clicked on a submenu with your mouse, next press Esc to close the submenu; otherwise, you'll end up deleting the option at the beginning of the submenu instead of the submenu itself. Then press the Delete key or click on the Cut button.

You can delete a separator line by pressing Delete or choosing the Cut button, but it won't be copied to the paste buffer.

Copying Menu Options

To copy an existing menu option to the paste buffer, highlight or click on the option, then press Ctrl-Ins or click on the Copy button.

You cannot copy submenus this way. Instead, cut the submenu and then paste it elsewhere.

To place the most recently cut or copied submenu or menu option, position the highlight as if you were inserting a new option or submenu, then press Shift-Ins or click on the Paste button.

Renaming a Menu Option

To rename (or edit) an existing menu option or submenu, follow these steps:

1. Highlight or click on the menu option or submenu.

2. If you clicked on a submenu with your mouse, press Esc to close the submenu.

3. Press F9 or click on Edit to display the Menu Definition dialog box.

Double-click on a menu option or submenu to quickly reach the Menu Definition dialog box.

4. Change the Keyword to rename the menu option or submenu. You can also change the Description, Action, or Help Screen options.

5. Choose OK to save your changes. Select Cancel if you want to abandon the changes.

Creating Action Objects

Most of application's work is done by action objects assigned to menu options. You can define action objects in the following ways (mix and match methods as you wish):

- Define action objects first, then attach them to menu options.
- Define and attach an action object at the same time you define the associated menu option.
- Attach special utility action objects at the same time you define the associated menu option.

Each of these methods is described in the following sections.

Creating Actions before Attaching Them to Menus

To create new actions without assigning them to a specific menu option, follow these general steps:

1. Choose ActionEdit to open the menu shown below:

2. Choose an action type from the menu. You'll see a dialog box listing all the currently defined actions of the selected type. For example, if you chose **M**ulti Action from the ActionEdit submenu, you might see a dialog box like the one in Figure 19.9, which shows multi-action objects defined for the sample Membership application. (Of course, the first time you run Workshop to create a new application, the Edit Multiple Actions dialog box is empty.)

FIGURE 19.9

The Edit: Multiple Actions dialog box for the sample Membership application

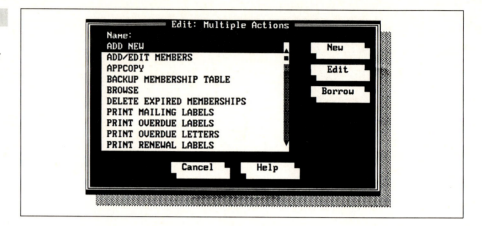

3. Choose the **New** button to define a new action. You'll see the New Multiple Actions Name dialog box.

4. Type a name for the new action object. The name can be up to 32 characters and can contain letters, numbers, and blanks. The name must be unique for the object type, but different object types can have the same names. For example, two query actions can't be named Members, but, a query, a multi-action, and a Help text action object can all be named Members.

 Workshop converts action object names to uppercase.

5. Choose OK to accept the name and open the dialog box for defining the new action.

6. Complete the dialog box or dialog boxes for defining the new action object. Each type of action object has a different set of dialog boxes, as described later in this chapter.

7. Save your changes by choosing OK or pressing F2.

After defining and saving the new action object, you're returned to the Workshop desktop. You can then attach the new action object to one or more action menu options as described shortly. You must eventually assign an action object to each action menu option in your application. Chapter 20 explains how to copy, rename, and delete action objects.

Creating and Attaching Action Items to Menu Options

As mentioned earlier, you can define a new action object and attach it to an action menu option at the same time. You can attach action objects to menu options defined as actions.

TIP: To change a submenu option to an action, delete the incorrectly defined option and re-create it.

Here are the general steps for defining a new *non-utility* action object and attaching it to an action menu option at the same time (the next section covers utility actions):

1. Create or edit an action menu option as described earlier. The Menu Definition dialog box will appear.

2. Choose the Select button in the Action area. The Object Type dialog box will appear (see Figure 19.3 shown earlier), displaying action types available on the ActionEdit submenu, plus the four utility options. The EXECUTE PAL, MULTIPLE ACTIONS, and HELP DISPLAY action types in the Object Type dialog box are named Execute, MultiAction, and Help Text, respectively, on the ActionEdit submenu.

3. Highlight the desired action type and choose OK, or double-click on the action. A dialog box listing currently defined actions of the type you selected will appear. Figure 19.10 shows an example for the multi-action objects in the Membership application.

NOTE The dialog boxes in Figure 19.10 and Figure 19.9 are identical, except for *Select* instead of *Edit* in the title, showing that you're selecting an action to attach to a menu.

FIGURE 19.10

The Select: Multiple Actions dialog box for the Membership application

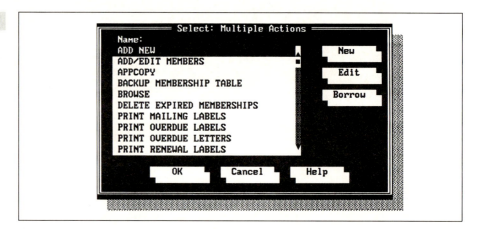

4. Choose the New button and type a name for the new action object. Choose OK or press ↵.

5. Fill in the dialog boxes for the type of action object you're defining, as described later in this chapter.

6. Save your changes by choosing OK or pressing F2 to return to the Menu Definition dialog box. The action type and name will appear in the framed Action area at the left side of the dialog box. Figure 19.11 shows a completed Menu Definition dialog box for the Maintain ➤ Add New Members option of the sample Membership application.

7. To save the menu definition, choose OK or press F2.

FIGURE 19.11

The completed Menu Definition dialog box for the Maintain ➤ Add New Members option of the Membership application. This option has a multi-action object named ADD NEW and a Help Screen named ADD NEW assigned to it.

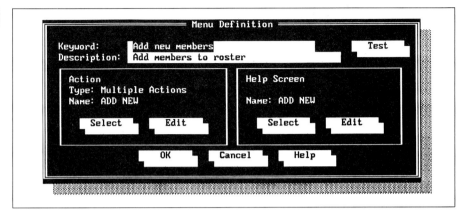

Attaching Utility Objects to Menu Options

As mentioned earlier, you can attach the following utility commands to menus: Exit Paradox, Quit to Paradox, Play a Script, and Proc (ExecProc). Here are the steps:

1. Create or edit an action menu option as usual.
2. Choose the Select button in the Action area of the Menu Definition dialog box.
3. Choose one of the four utility commands.
4. Choose OK or press ↵ to return to the Menu Definition dialog box.
5. Choose OK or press F2 to save the menu definition.

Attaching an Existing Action Object to a Menu Option

You can easily attach an existing non-utility action object to a menu option by following the first three steps for creating and attaching action items to menu options. You'll be returned to the Menu Definition dialog box.

The action type and name you selected will appear in the dialog box. Choose OK or press F2 to save the menu definition.

Creating an Action Object by Borrowing

Notice the Borrow button in Figures 19.9 and 19.10. Use this button to create a new action object identical to an existing object of the same type. After borrowing the definition to create the new object, you can edit the new object as needed, as described later in this chapter.

Changes made to the borrowed object definition have no effect on the object you borrowed from.

To create an action object definition from an existing object, use any method already described to reach the Edit: <*action type*> or Select: <*action type*> dialog box, where <*action type*> stands for the type of action you want to borrow. When the list of existing objects appears, follow these steps:

1. Highlight the object you want to borrow from.

2. Choose the **B**orrow button. A dialog box like the one below will appear, depending on the type of object being borrowed.

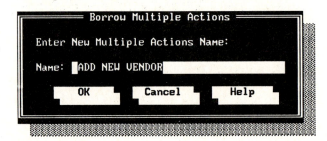

3. Type the name of the new object.

4. Choose OK or press ↵. If you entered an existing object name, Workshop will ask if you want to overwrite that object. Choose OK, or select Cancel, then enter a new name.

A completed dialog box for whatever object you borrowed appears, ready for you to make any necessary changes. The contents of the dialog box are the same as the original object definition you borrowed from, but the dialog box title will display the new object's name.

Changing an Existing Action Object

You can easily edit an action object at any time using the same methods used for creating action objects.

The following steps are perhaps the easiest:

1. Choose ActionEdit from the Workshop desktop menu.
2. Choose the type of object you want to change.
3. Highlight the action object you want to change in the Edit: <*action object*> dialog box (see Figure 19.9) and choose the Edit button (or press F9 or ↵). Alternatively, double-click on the object to change. An editing dialog box for the selected action type will appear.
4. Make changes, as described in the following sections.
5. Save your changes. You'll be returned to the Workshop desktop.

If you want to make changes to an action object while editing a menu option, highlight the menu option you've attached the action object to, then choose the Edit button or press F9. Or double-click on the menu option to change. Next, choose the Edit button in the Action area in the Menu Definition dialog box or press F9.

The following sections describe steps for filling in the dialog boxes for each type of action object that you can create or edit in Workshop.

Defining Edit Session Objects

Create a well-controlled edit session for updating of your application's tables. You can let the end-user view, add, or edit the records in one or more tables. You can display records in Form view, Table view, or both.

CHAPTER 19
CREATING AN APPLICATION

Use any method described in the section about creating action objects to reach the Edit Session dialog box. Figure 19.12 shows the Edit Session dialog box for a new edit session named ADD NEW MEMBERS.

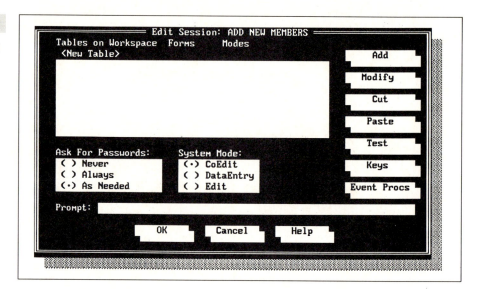

FIGURE 19.12

An Edit Session dialog box for a new edit session. The name of the edit session (ADD NEW MEMBERS) appears in the dialog box title.

Choose the Add button to add tables to the Tables on Workspace List, then use the Edit Session dialog box to further define or change the edit session. When you're finished, choose OK to save your changes and return to the Workshop desktop, Menu Definition dialog box, or Multiple Action dialog box; or choose Cancel to discard the changes.

Choices available in the Edit Session dialog box are as follows:

- **Add:** Add one or more tables (for your end user to work with) to the Tables on Workspace list at the cursor position. Choosing Add (or pressing the Ins key) leads to the Edit Session–Table Information dialog box, described later in this chapter.

NOTE Adding or modifying a table with a multi-table form adds or modifies all of the detail tables as well.

DEFINING EDIT SESSION OBJECTS

- **Modify:** Modify the information for a table in the Tables on Workspace list. Highlight the table and select the Modify button to open The Edit Session–Table Information dialog box.

- **Cut:** Remove a table from the Tables on Workspace list. Highlight the table you want to cut from the edit session, then choose the Cut button (or press the Delete key). The information is removed from the list but remains in the paste buffer until you take the next action. This allows you to paste the table back in if you removed it accidentally. Note that cutting a table from the Tables on Workspace list has no effect on the actual table.

- **Paste:** Paste the most recently cut table into the Tables on Workspace list at the cursor position. Use Paste to position an accidentally deleted table or to reorder the tables in the list. Move the cursor to where you want the table name placed, then choose the Paste button or press Shift-Ins.

- **Test:** Save the changes made so far and test the edit session from the dialog box. If the table has a password, you'll be prompted to enter it when you test the edit session. Return to the Edit Session dialog box after testing by saving your changes to the table (with F2 or DO-IT!) to end the edit session.

- **Keys:** Define the effects of various keys during an edit session, or assign your own procedures to keys, as described later in this chapter.

- **Event Procs:** Define the name of procedures that run when a certain action occurs. See the section about assigning event procedures to the edit session, later in this chapter.

The word *proc* is short for *procedure*, a specially structured set of PAL commands that you store in a library.

- **Ask For Passwords:** Workshop honors Paradox table password protection. This option's radio button options determine how your application handles attempts to edit password-protected tables, as follows:
    - Never cancels the edit session if access is attempted.

- Always prompts for a password every time a user attempts to access the table.
- As Needed (the default) prompts the user for a password the first time an edit session is run. If an application is left and restarted, the password is requested again.

NOTE Select radio button options by clicking with your mouse. Or highlight the option group you want (for example, press Alt-f to highlight Ask For Passwords), then use ↑ or ↓ to move the selector.

- **System Mode:** Set the system mode for an edit session. Choose one of the following radio button options:
    - CoEdit (the default) posts each record as soon as the user finishes entering it (makes record available to others on a network). Records with duplicate key fields cannot be posted.
    - DataEntry has the user edit records in a separate Entry table, as described in Chapter 4. Note that records with duplicate key fields cannot be posted. When using DataEntry mode for keyed tables, specify a procedure to handle key violations during the edit session. See the section about assigning event procedures to the edit session, later in this chapter.
    - Edit lets the user edit new and old entries in the table. On a network, other users must wait until the edit session is finished before they can access the table.
- **Prompt:** Display a prompt at the bottom of the screen during the edit session. Note that any prompt defined in the Edit Session–Table Information dialog box overrides the prompt you define here.

Adding Tables to the Edit Session

Choose Add (or press Ins) in the Edit Session dialog box to display the Edit Session–Table Information dialog box, shown in Figure 19.13. You can add a table to the Tables on Workspace list and control end-user

FIGURE 19.13

The Edit Session–Table Information dialog box with its default settings

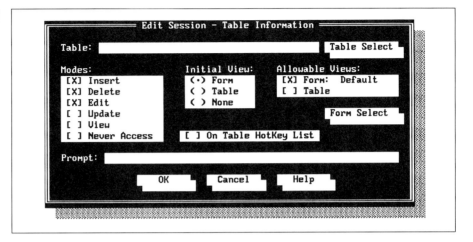

changes to tables. Return to the Edit Session dialog box by choosing OK to save changes or Cancel to discard your changes.

The following options and buttons are available in the dialog box (you are only required to specify a table with the Table text box or Table Select option):

- **Table:** Enter the name of the table you want to work with, or use the Table Select button to list the available tables.

- **Table Select:** List available tables, as in Figure 19.14. After selecting a table, you'll be returned to the Edit Session–Table Information dialog box with the table name filled in.

- **Modes:** Define the level of editing allowed for the table. These modes override any modes set in the System Mode option of the Edit Session dialog box (see Figure 19.12). Choose one or more checkbox options, as listed below:

    - Insert allows the user to insert records into the table.
    - Delete lets the user delete records from the table.
    - Edit lets the user edit old and current entries and change key fields.
    - Update lets the user edit old and current entries, but not change key fields. You can't select both Edit and Update.

FIGURE 19.14

The Select Table dialog box lists the available tables.

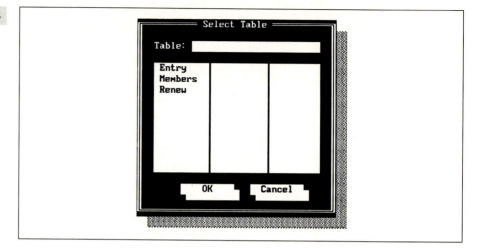

- View allows the user to view data but not to make changes. If you select View and Update or Edit, the user must press F9 before making changes.
- Never Access prevents the user from accessing the table or image control.

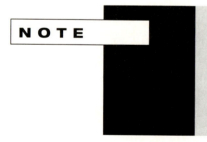

Click on a checkbox option to select or deselect it. Or highlight the option, use ↑ or ↓ to move to the checkbox, then press the spacebar. Clicking on the checkbox or pressing the spacebar will either insert an X (selecting the option) or remove an X (deselecting the option).

- **Initial View:** Choose Form (the default) or Table. None is available only if you set the Mode to Never Access.
- **Allowable Views:** Determines views allowed during data entry or display. Choose either Form (the default), Table, or both. Choose both Form and Table view to allow user to press F7 to switch between the views. To change the default form used in Form view, highlight the Allowable Views option and press Tab (or click to the right of the Form check box), then type the form number you want to use, or use the Form Select button described next.

- **Form Select:** Select the form used in Form view. Make sure a table is selected, then you'll see the Form Selection dialog box, as shown in Figure 19.15. Highlight the form you want to use and choose OK to return to the Edit Session–Table Information dialog box with the form number filled in.

FIGURE 19.15

A sample Form Selection dialog box

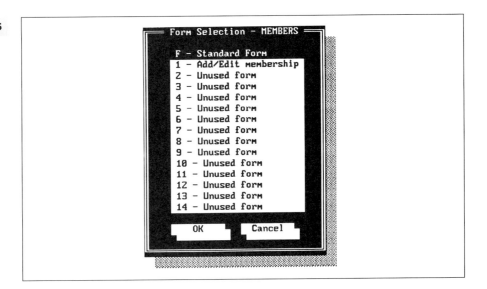

- **On Table HotKey List:** A check places the current table in a pick list. Use Alt-0 (zero) to display a HotKey pick list when running or testing the application, as shown in the example below. Highlight the desired table name (or type the table's list number) and choose OK, or double-click on the table name. Whether or not a HotKey pick list is defined, the F3 and F4 keys still work for switching active table images.

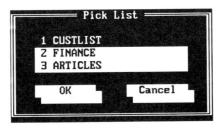

- **Prompt:** Display a message at the lower-left corner of the screen during table viewing or editing. This prompt overrides a prompt defined in the Edit Session dialog box.

Assigning Key Actions to the Edit Session

Choosing the Keys button in the Edit Session dialog box displays the Session Key Procs dialog box shown in Figure 19.16. Use it to define actions for any key in an edit session. You can assign any of the predefined actions (these begin with a $ sign), or assign your own procedures.

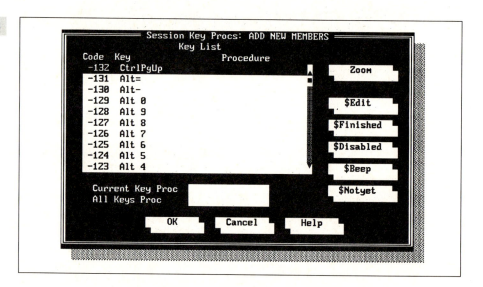

FIGURE 19.16

The Session Key Procs dialog box for defining special keys used during an edit session

To assign an action to a key, highlight the key you want to define, or choose the **Z**oom button and press the key you want to zoom to. Then type the name of the procedure to assign to this key, or choose a $ button to assign a predefined action.

Keys not assigned a procedure retain their normal function.

DEFINING EDIT SESSION OBJECTS

To globally assign an action to all keys, type the procedure name into the All Keys Proc text box. You can then override this action by assigning actions to individual keys.

Choose OK to save your changes and return to the Edit Session dialog box. Choosing Cancel discards your changes.

The effects of predefined action buttons that you can assign to keys are listed below:

- **$Edit:** Emulates the usual effect of pressing F9, if you've assigned Edit and View modes to the table.
- **$Finished:** Emulates the usual effect of pressing F2.
- **$Disabled:** Disables any key action or display.
- **$Beep:** The key beeps when pressed.
- **$Notyet:** Displays the message

    This procedure is not yet defined

    when the key is pressed. $Notyet is useful as a temporary function while you're developing the application.

If you attach your own procedure to a key, the procedure must be compiled into the procedure library listed in the Autolib text box of the New Application or Edit Application dialog box. Refer to the *PAL Reference* manual and *PAL Programmer's Guide* for information about procedures and procedure libraries.

Assigning Event Procedures to the Edit Session

Choosing the EventProcs button in the Edit Session dialog box displays the Session Event Procs dialog box, as in Figure 19.17. All procedures must be compiled into the procedure library listed in the Autolib text box of the New Application or Edit Application dialog box.

To specify a procedure to run, enter the name of the procedure into the appropriate text box and choose OK to save your changes. The following list shows each type of event that you can intercept with a procedure and when the procedure will run. Items are in order from left to right and top to bottom of the dialog box shown in Figure 19.17.

FIGURE 19.17

The Session Event Procs dialog box for defining procedures that run when certain conditions occur during an edit session. Here the procedure named Keyviol runs if the user enters a record that has a duplicate key while in DataEntry mode.

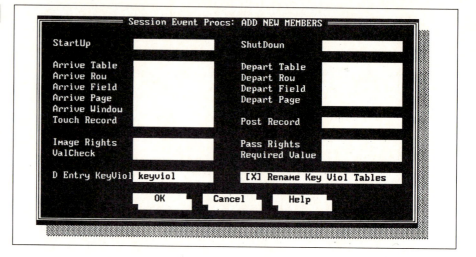

- **Startup:** Runs before the tables are loaded.
- **ShutDown:** Runs just before the user leaves the edit session. If the procedure returns a 1 or 2, the edit session won't shut down.
- **Arrive Table:** Runs when the cursor arrives on the table (or on a new table, if there is more than one table in the edit session).
- **Depart Table:** Runs just before the cursor departs the table.
- **Arrive Row:** Runs when the cursor arrives in a new record.
- **Depart Row:** Runs just before the cursor departs a record.
- **Arrive Field:** Runs when the cursor arrives in a new field.
- **Depart Field:** Runs just before the cursor departs a field.
- **Arrive Page:** Runs when the cursor moves to a new page of a multipage form (Form view only).
- **Depart Page:** Runs when the cursor leaves a page of a multipage form (Form view only).
- **Arrive Window:** Runs the first time the user clicks on a different window.
- **Touch Record:** Runs the first time the user tries to make a change in a record, but before the change is actually made.
- **Post Record:** Runs just before a changed record is posted.

- **Image Rights:** Runs if the user attempts to change a field without having modify rights on the table.
- **Pass Rights:** Runs if the user attempts an action in a password-protected field without having sufficient rights to do so. See Chapter 12 for information about using an auxiliary password to control access rights to table fields.
- **ValCheck:** Runs if a ValCheck error occurs.
- **Required Value:** Runs if a field requires a value and no value is entered.
- **D Entry KeyViol:** Runs when the user tries to post a record with a duplicate key in DataEntry mode.
- **Rename KeyViol Tables:** If you mark this option with an X and a key violation occurs during data entry, the Keyviol table is renamed to Kv1, Kv2, Kv3, and so forth (in numeric sequence) and stored in the user's private directory. Then any procedure named in the D Entry KeyViol option is run.

As mentioned earlier, the sample Membership application uses a simple procedure named Keyviol to display an error message when the user enters a membership record with a duplicate key. After the user presses a key (as instructed by the procedure), the edit session ends and the user is returned to the desktop. The top portion of Figure 19.18 shows the error message displayed when a key violation occurs. The bottom portion shows a script named Addlib, which creates a library named Paradox.LIB. This script defines the Keyviol procedure and writes that procedure to the library.

After running the Addlib script to create the library, we returned to Workshop and typed Paradox into the Autolib test box of the New Application dialog box. Later, we typed Keyviol into the D Entry KeyViol text box shown in Figure 19.17.

The Addlib script shown in Figure 19.18 is included with the optional companion disk.

FIGURE 19.18

Top: The window that appears if the user enters a record with the same Last Name, First Name, and Middle Initial as a record that already exists in the Members table. Bottom: The Addlib script (Addlib.SC), which creates a library named Paradox (Paradox.LIB), defines the Keyviol procedure, then writes the procedure to the library.

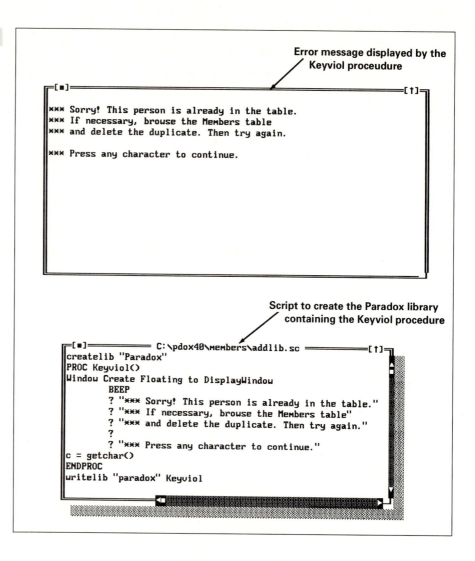

Defining Report Print Objects

You can define a report print object to control end-user report printing, determine which table to report on, and control the printer settings. First, use any method described earlier in the section about creating action objects to reach the Report Print dialog box. Figure 19.19 shows the Report

DEFINING REPORT PRINT OBJECTS

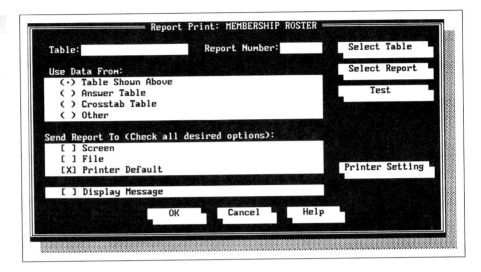

FIGURE 19.19

A Report Print dialog box for a new report print object. The name of the report print object (e.g., MEMBERSHIP ROSTER) appears in the dialog box title.

Print dialog box for a new report print object named MEMBERSHIP ROSTER.

To define a report print object, specify the table containing the report, the report number you want to use, and where you want to send the report output. Then choose OK to save your changes and return to the desktop or previous dialog box. Choose Cancel to discard the changes.

The Report Print dialog has these options:

- **Table:** Enter the name of the table providing a report format. Choose the Select Table button to list available tables.

- **Select Table:** Select this button to list available tables. To choose a table from the list, type the table name and choose OK, or double-click on the name you want. You'll return to the Report Print dialog box, with the table name filled in.

- **Report Number:** Enter the report number you want to use. Choose the Select Report button for a list of report numbers.

- **Select Report:** Select this button to list the table's available report numbers, as shown in Figure 19.20. If you have not chosen a table, the Select Table dialog box appears. Choose a table, then select a report. To choose a report, highlight the report you want and choose OK. You'll return to the Report Print dialog box, with the report number filled in.

FIGURE 19.20

A sample list of reports

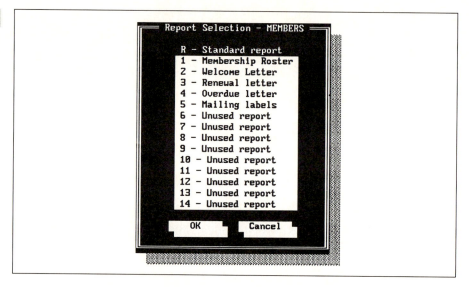

- **Test:** This button saves the changes made so far and lets you test the report print object without leaving the dialog box.

- **Use Data From:** Choose this option to print the report from a table other than the one that defines the report format. The table you specify must have the same fields, in the same order, as the table that holds the report format. Select one of the radio button options listed below:

    - Table Shown Above (the default) uses data from the table listed in the Table text box.
    - Answer Table copies the report to the Answer table before printing. Use after querying.
    - Crosstab Table copies the report to the Crosstab table before printing. Use after using CrossTabs.
    - Other copies the report to an existing table named in the Other option.

- **Send Report To:** Choose this button to specify the report destination. If you specify more than one, Workshop creates an end-user choice dialog box. Choose one or more of these options:

    - Screen sends the report to the screen.

- File sends the report to a file. You can specify a file name or leave the file name blank and let the user specify the file name.
- Printer sends the report to the printer. To change the default printer setting, choose the Printer Setting button.
- **Printer Setting:** Displays the Printer Setting dialog box. This dialog box and the procedure for defining the printer settings are described in the next section.
- **Display Message:** Displays a message during report output. After checking this option, press Tab (or click to the right of the Display Message option) and type the message you want to display.

Defining the Printer Settings

Workshop uses the default settings from the Paradox Custom Configuration Program. For finer printer control, choose the Report Print dialog box's Printer Setting button. You'll see the Printer Setting dialog box, shown in Figure 19.21.

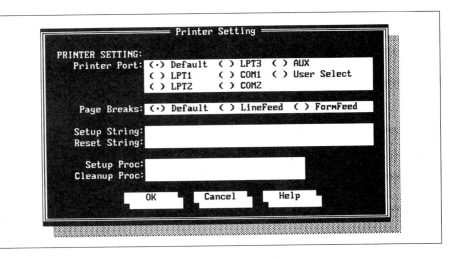

FIGURE 19.21

The Printer Setting dialog box lets you exercise finer control over the printer. Choose the Printer Setting button from the Report Print dialog box to define the printer settings for a report.

You can change printer settings by choosing the options described below. When you're finished, choose OK to save the settings and return to the Report Print dialog box.

- **Printer Port:** Defines the port to which the printer is connected. To use the Paradox default setting, choose the Default option. Choose User Select to prompt the end-user for a port address.
- **Page Breaks:** Specifies the method used to print page breaks. Choose Default to use the Paradox default setting. Choose Line-Feed to print without form feeds (for continuous paper). Choose FormFeed to send a form feed character to the printer to align the next page. (For more information about printing page breaks, refer to Chapter 8.)
- **Setup String:** Enter a setup string if you wish to send special commands to the printer before the report prints.

See the documentation for your end-user's printer for information about relevant setup strings and reset strings.

- **Reset String:** Enter a reset string if you wish to send special commands to the printer after the report prints.
- **Setup Proc:** Specify a procedure to run before the report prints. As explained earlier, procedures must be compiled in the procedure library listed in the Autolib text box of the New Application or Edit Application dialog box.
- **Cleanup Proc:** Specify a procedure to run after the report prints.

Defining Query Objects

From Paradox, set up your query forms and use **Scripts ➤ QuerySave**. Chapters 7 and 14 cover simple and advanced query techniques, respectively. Add a Do_It! command to the saved script. Alternatively, you can define a query from Workshop. To do so, use the method described earlier

DEFINING QUERY OBJECTS

in the section about creating action objects, to reach the Query By Example dialog box. Figure 19.22 shows the Query By Example dialog box for a new query object named RESET RENEWED.

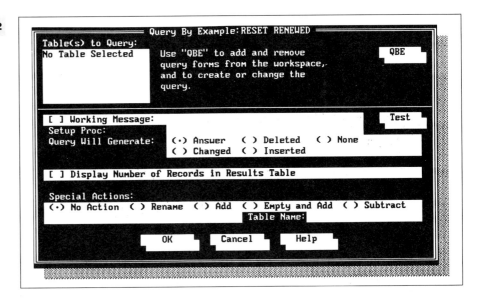

FIGURE 19.22

The Query By Example dialog box for a new query object. The name of the query object (RESET RENEWED in this example) appears in the dialog box title.

After using the QBE button to define and save the query and set desired options (as described in a moment), choose OK to save your changes and return to the Workshop desktop or previous dialog box. Choose Cancel to discard changes.

Choosing the QBE button opens the Query By Example dialog box for choosing these buttons and options:

- **QBE:** Specify queried tables and details of the query. See the next section for more information.
- **Working Message:** Specify the message displayed during the query. Type the message you want to display. If you omit the message, "Working..." appears while the query runs.
- **Setup Proc:** Specify a procedure to run before the query.
- **Query Will Generate:** Defines the type of temporary table you want generated. Choose the appropriate option:
    - Answer (the default) generates an Answer table.

- Deleted runs a DELETE query, generating a Deleted table.
- None runs a CHANGETO, DELETE, or INSERT query, but no Changed, Deleted, or Inserted tables are generated.
- Changed runs a CHANGETO query, generating a Changed table.
- Inserted runs an INSERT query, generating an Inserted table.

- **Display Number of Records in Results Table:** Specifies display of a Records Found dialog box telling the user how many records were matched by the query. The Records Found dialog box provides the user with OK and Cancel options.

- **Special Actions:** Defines any special actions taken after the query runs. (Multi-action objects are described later in this chapter.) You can choose from the following options:

  - No Action (the default) deletes temporary tables, such as Answer, when the query (or multi-action) completes.
  - Rename renames the temporary table to the name specified in the Table Name text box. If an existing table is named, Rename will overwrite it.
  - Add adds the temporary table data to the named table.
  - Empty and Add empties the table named, then adds temporary table data to it.
  - Subtract deletes matching records in the temporary table from the table named in the Table Name text box.

CAUTION The Add, Empty and Add, and Subtract options require identical structures for the temporary table and the table named in the Table Name text box.

- **Table Name:** Specify the named table affected by the Rename, Add, Empty and Add, or Subtract special action. Choose the Table Name option and type in the name of the table.
- **Test:** Saves the changes made so far and tests the query without leaving the dialog box.

Defining the Query

Choosing the QBE button displays a new desktop and a menu that lets you add, change, and remove Query forms. If no tables are specified for the query, the desktop is blank; otherwise, selected Query forms are shown, as in Figure 19.23.

Use the options described below to add or remove Query forms, then complete the forms as you would in Paradox. When you're finished, save your query and return to the Query By Example dialog box. Choose **Cancel ➤ Y**es to cancel changes.

The menu options are as follows:

- **Add:** Add a new Query form to the desktop. Type the name of the table you want to add to the desktop and choose OK, or double-click on the table name.

- **Remove:** Remove a Query form from the desktop. Choose **Remove ➤ C**urrent to remove the active Query form. Choose **R**emove ➤ **A**ll to remove all Query forms from the desktop.

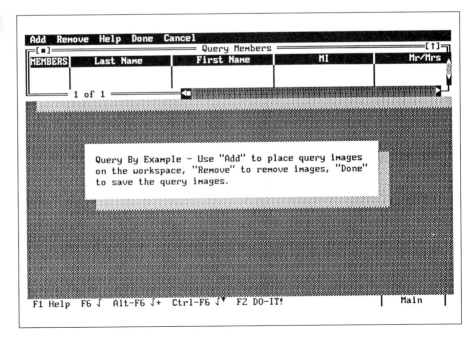

FIGURE 19.23

The desktop for defining Query forms. Initially, the desktop is blank. Choose Add to add Query forms to the desktop.

794 CHAPTER 19 CREATING AN APPLICATION

NOTE Add, Remove ➤ Current, and Remove ➤ All are equivalent to Ask, F8, and Alt-F8, respectively, in Paradox.

- **Help:** Displays help on query design and menu options.
- **Done:** Choose **D**one ➤ **S**ave (or press F2) to save the Query forms and return to the Query by Example dialog box.
- **Cancel:** Choose **C**ancel ➤ **Y**es to return to the Query By Example dialog box, abandoning any Query form changes.

Defining Multi-Action Objects

Multi-action objects perform multiple actions, one after the other, from a single menu option. See Chapter 18 for a summary of steps performed by the **U**pdate ➤ **U**pdate Renewals option and of the multi-action objects used in the sample Membership application.

To create or edit a multi-action object, open the Multi-Action dialog box. Figure 19.24 shows a completed dialog box for the multi-action object named UPDATE RENEWALS, which performs the actions summarized in Chapter 18.

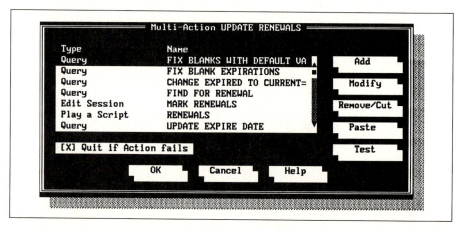

FIGURE 19.24

A completed Multi-Action dialog box for a multi-action object. The name of the multi-action object (UPDATE RENEWALS in this example) appears in the dialog box title.

The actions in the Multi-Action dialog box are performed in the order they appear. Use the Add, Modify, Remove/Cut, and Paste buttons to define and rearrange actions. You can add any type of action object, except another multi-action object, to the list. Then choose OK to save your selections.

Use these options and buttons to define multi-action objects:

- **Add:** Adds an action to the list. Place the cursor to insert a new action. When you choose the Add button (or press Ins), the Object Type dialog box opens. Choose an object type and select, create, or change the object. You'll return to the Multi-Action dialog box, with the object's name in the list.

- **Modify:** Changes an action in the list. Highlight the action, then choose Modify or press F9. Change the object and save it. You'll be returned to the Multi-Action dialog box.

- **Remove/Cut:** Cuts an action from the list to the paste buffer. Highlight the object and choose the Remove/Cut button or press Delete. The cut object is copied to the paste buffer, where it remains until you save (or discard) your changes or cut another action object. Deleting the object from the list does not delete the object itself (see Chapter 20 for information about deleting action objects).

- **Paste (or Shift-Ins):** Pastes an action into the list at the cursor position. Move the cursor to the desired insert location, then choose the Paste button or press Shift-Ins.

- **Test:** Saves the changes made and tests the multi-action object.

- **Quit if Action fails:** Stops execution of the entire set of multi-actions if any one fails (the default).

Defining Help Text Objects

In Workshop, you can create a detailed system of on-line help, which closely resembles its own Help system. Figure 19.25 shows an example.

FIGURE 19.25

The Maintain ➤ Change/Delete a Member Help screen from the Membership application. The menu options provide access to additional, related Help screens called cross-references. The Return option (added automatically) returns the user to the application menus.

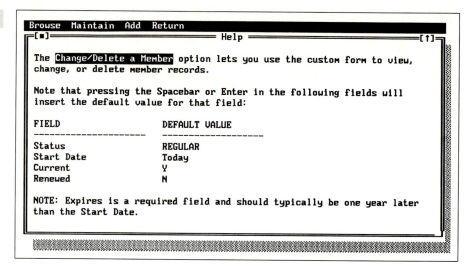

A Help screen is essentially a special kind of action object that you can assign to a menu option. You can create a Help screen before attaching it to a menu, or develop it while attaching it to a menu. It is easiest to choose ActionEdit ➤ Help Text from Workshop's desktop menu.

Adding Help Text Objects to Menu Options

You can attach help to application menus in two ways:

- Commonly you attach help to a menu option that performs some other (non-help) action or displays a submenu. The primary job of the menu option is to display another submenu or perform an action. To use this type of attached help, the user must highlight the option and press F1.

- You can have help be the only action attached to an action menu option. For example, you can add a Help option to the desktop menu or to a submenu. Then the end-user can simply choose that Help option to get help.

To attach Help text to a submenu or action menu option, create or edit a submenu or action menu option as usual. Then take one of these actions:

- For a submenu option, choose Select in the Help ID area of the Menu Definition dialog box (see Figure 19.8).
- For an action menu option, choose Select in the Help Screen area in the Menu Definition dialog box (see Figure 19.7). (To edit Help text, choose the Edit button on the right side of the dialog box.)

Then choose the help display object from the Select: Help Display dialog box, or use the **N**ew or **B**orrow button to create a new object. (When choosing New or Borrow, type the new help display object name and choose OK or press ↵.)

Define Help as a menu option action with these steps:

1. Create or edit the action menu option as usual.
2. Choose the **S**elect button in the Action area of the Menu Definition dialog box.
3. Choose HELP DISPLAY as the object type.
4. Choose the help display object from the Help Display dialog box, or create a new object as described earlier.

Completing a Help Text Object

Figure 19.26 shows a completed Help screen dialog box. Note that it includes Help text and several cross-references.

To create the Help text, choose the Edit Text button or press F9. Add cross-references by using the buttons in the Cross-References area of the dialog box. (Cross-references appear as menu options when you test or run help.) Choose OK to save your changes and return to the Workshop desktop or the previous dialog box. Choose Cancel to discard changes.

Use these buttons to create and edit Help text objects:

- **Edit Text (or F9 key):** Create or edit the Help text.
- **Add (or Ins key):** Add a cross-reference.
- **Delete (or Delete key):** Delete the highlighted cross-reference from the list. This has no effect on the actual Help text object. (Chapter 20 describes deleting objects.)

CREATING AN APPLICATION

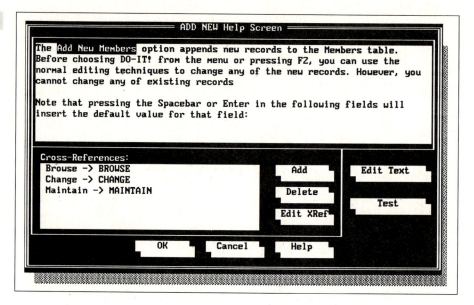

FIGURE 19.26

The completed Help Screen dialog box for the ADD NEW Help text object with Help text and cross-references

- **Edit XRef:** Save the changes you've made so far, then switch to editing the highlighted cross-reference.
- **Test:** Save the changes made so far and test on-line help.

Editing a Help Screen

Choosing the Edit Text button or pressing F9 in the Help Screen dialog box opens a Paradox Editor window. While editing the Help text, you can enter the usual letters, numbers, blank spaces, international characters, and printable symbols. You can also use some special style indicators to display text with intense, reverse, blinking, and normal styles, as listed below:

STYLE	SPECIAL CHARACTER
Intense (bold) on	<I>
Reverse on	<R>
Blink on	<B>
Normal on (turns off all special styles)	<N>

The following example displays *Add New Members* in reverse video style. The rest of the text is in normal style.

The <R>Add New Members<N> option appends new records to ...

Adding a Cross-Reference

The Cross-References area of the Help Screen dialog box lists cross-references defined for the current Help text object. You can create as many cross-references as needed. To prevent endless loops, Workshop adds a Return option at the far right of every Help menu.

Linking more cross-references than will fit across the menu bar creates a More option to the left of the Return option. Choosing More opens a dialog box that displays the remaining cross-references.

Add a new cross-reference by using the Add button (or press Ins) in the Help Screen dialog box to open the Adding Cross-References dialog box, then follow these steps:

1. Specify a cross-reference title to appear on the Help menu.
2. In the Help Screen Name text box, specify the Help text object you're cross-referencing. Choose the Select button to display a list of existing Help text objects. Select from the list to place a name in the Help Screen Name text box, then choose OK.

The Cross-Reference Title and Help Screen Name options can be the same, but neither can be blank.

The new cross-reference will appear in the Cross-References area in the form. For example, for a cross-reference title of Add and a Help Screen Name of ADD NEW, the new entry appears as

Add -> ADD NEW

Editing a Cross-Reference

As you develop your application, create a "skeleton" Help system and then flesh it out with cross-references later. Here's how:

1. Highlight the Help cross-reference you want to edit in the Cross-References area of the Help Screen dialog box.

2. Choose the Edit XRef button. Workshop saves changes before switching to a cross-referenced object's Help screen if you choose OK or press ↵. Choose Cancel or press Esc to cancel the process.

3. For a new cross-referenced object, another dialog box, with New and Cancel buttons, will appear. Choose New to create the Help text object.

You can also create or edit cross-referenced Help text objects using the methods described previously, such as ActionEdit ➤ Help Text.

This handy shortcut makes it much easier to develop an entire system of related Help text objects.

Testing On-Line Help

You can try out your Help system by choosing the Test button in the Help Screen dialog box. When you're finished testing the Help text, choose the Return option from the menu to return to the Help Screen dialog box.

If you choose an option that doesn't yet exist, you'll see the error message

    Not Found HELP: <name>

where <name> is the name of the nonexistent Help text object. Choose OK or press ↵ to return to the Help Screen dialog box.

Defining Execute Objects

Execute (or Execute PAL) objects let you attach small amounts of PAL code to menu options.

Execute objects are sometimes called *miniscripts*.

You can use the methods described earlier for creating action objects to open the Execute PAL dialog box. Saved PAL code is stored as a memo field in the Object table.

Defining OK/Cancel Objects

The OK/Cancel object lets you create a message dialog box that displays OK and Cancel buttons. Use this object as part of a multi-action sequence to let the user decide whether or not to continue with the remaining actions.

To create an OK/Cancel object, use the normal method for creating or changing an action object. Figure 19.27 shows a completed OK/Cancel Object dialog box for the OK/Cancel example shown earlier.

Choose one or more options from the dialog box. Choosing OK saves your changes and returns to the Workshop desktop or the previous dialog box.

The options and buttons are as follows:

- **Title:** Enter a title up of up to 50 characters.
- **Text to display:** Enter up to four lines of 50 characters each for additional text.

FIGURE 19.27

A completed OK/Cancel dialog box that asks the user for permission to delete expired memberships

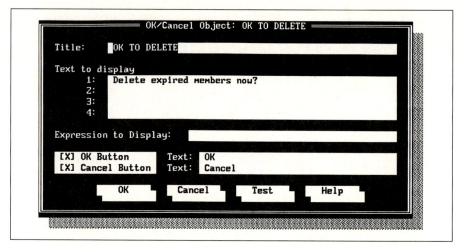

- **Expression to Display:** To display the value returned by a PAL function in the dialog box, enter the function here. Entering the expression Directory( ) displays the current directory in the dialog box. Entering Drivespace("A") displays the free space on the floppy disk in drive A.

See the *PAL Reference* manual for a list of PAL functions.

- **OK Button and Text:** This option places an OK button in the dialog box. Enter a new button name by entering up to 30 characters in the box to the right of this option. Define a shortcut key by enclosing the letter between tildes. For example, ~G~o makes Alt-G a hot key for an OK button renamed to **G**o.

- **Cancel Button and Text:** This option places a Cancel button in the dialog box. You can enter a new button name to the right of the option. Identify any shortcut letter as above.

- **Test:** Saves your changes and lets you test the action.

Summary

In Chapter 20, you'll learn how to test, change, finish, and document your application, and how to use Workshop tools to manage Paradox objects and action objects. Here's a review of key points covered in this chapter:

- To create a new application, choose **A**pplication ➤ **N**ew from the Workshop desktop menu and define attributes.

- To create a new application menu or submenu option, move the cursor to the desired location and choose the Add button on the mouse palette, or press Ins, or double-click on the <New> option. Then choose **A**ction or Sub**M**enu.

- Choose OK or press F2 to save Workshop dialog box changes. Discard changes with Cancel or press Esc.

- To change an existing menu option, double-click on it.

- To attach a Help text object, create or edit the menu option, then choose the Se**l**ect button in the Help Screen (or Help ID) area near the right side of the Menu Definition dialog box.

- To return to Paradox or to DOS (or Windows), choose E**x**it from the Workshop desktop menu.

CHAPTER 20

Testing and Fine-Tuning Your Application

fast TRACK

- **To test an action object** — 808

  use the Test button in the action object dialog box.

- **To test the entire application** — 809

  open the application if necessary. Then choose Application ➤ Test from the Workshop desktop menu.

- **To change the application attributes for an open application** — 810

  choose Application ➤ Edit.

- **To close an application** — 811

  and clear it from the desktop, choose Application ➤ Close.

- **To remove an application** — 811

  from the application table in the current directory, choose Application ➤ Remove, highlight the application you want to remove, then choose OK.

- **To finish an application** — 815

  choose Application ➤ Finish from the Workshop desktop menu.

- **To generate documentation about the application** — 815

  open the application, and choose Documentation from Workshop's desktop menu. Then choose Menu Tree, Action Detail, or Cross Reference, and specify a destination for the documentation (Screen, File, or Printer). Choose OK to begin generating the documentation.

To copy an application and its subdirectories   823

use the XCOPY (or BACKUP) command from the DOS prompt.

To start an application from Paradox   824

switch to the correct subdirectory (**T**ools ➤ **M**ore ➤ **D**irectory) if necessary. Then choose **S**cripts ➤ **P**lay and enter the name of the application's startup script.

To start an application from DOS   824

first make sure you will be in your application's directory when you run the startup script. Return to DOS, switch to the drive containing your application, and switch to the directory that contains the application's startup script. Then type PARADOX *script* and press ↵ (where *script* is the name of the application's startup script).

To install an application as an icon in Windows   826

start Windows, use the PIF Editor to create a program information file, then choose **F**ile ➤ **N**ew in the Program Manager and create a program item icon for the application.

IN Chapter 19, you learned how to create and test application menus and action objects. In this chapter, you'll learn how to test, fine-tune, document, and start your application. You'll also discover many handy tools included with Workshop to help you manage Paradox and application objects more conveniently, and you'll learn how to package your applications for distribution to end-users.

Testing an Application

The Test button, included in many action object dialog boxes, should be used as soon as you feel an action object is fully defined, to quickly uncover flaws or deficiencies in the application's design. Exercise all the paths your application must take, and enter test data that tests both normal cases and odd situations that could lead to problems if not handled correctly. To enter additional records into your application's tables, either return to Paradox or use the ParadoxEdit option from Workshop's desktop menu, described later in this chapter.

Make your tests with small tables with only a few sample records. Don't using large tables of important data that would take considerable time to reenter if something went wrong.

To test the entire application, place your desktop menu on the screen, as described in Chapter 18. You'll see the Workshop screen for editing your application (similar to the one shown in Figure 19.2 at the beginning of Chapter 19). Then choose **A**pplication ➤ **T**est from the Workshop desktop menu.

A brief message appears, followed by a splash screen (if you defined one), then the application's desktop menu, as in Figure 20.1. Note the message near the bottom of the screen:

> Press the F9 key to go back to editing your application.

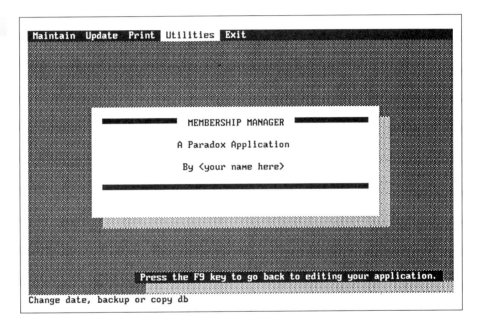

FIGURE 20.1

After you choose Application ➤ Test from Workshop's desktop menu, there's a brief delay. Then the desktop menu and splash screen of your application appear. To return to Workshop and make more changes to the application, press F9.

Now test every menu option thoroughly, using the testing procedures discussed in Chapter 18. Press F9 when you want to return to the application and make corrections.

Modifying an Application

You can change virtually anything in an existing application—from its splash screen and desktop menu options to the smallest details of its action objects. Once the application's menu appears on the Workshop desktop, you can make changes to your menu options and action objects, as described in the previous chapter.

You can also change the attributes you defined for an application (in the New Application dialog box, reached by choosing **Application ➤ New**), such as the Application ID, Application Name, Menu Table, and other options. To change this information for an existing application, open the application and choose **Application ➤ Edit**.

Figure 20.2 shows the Edit Application dialog box for the sample Membership application. The options in this dialog box are the same as those in the New Application dialog box (described in Chapter 19). Change the options as needed, then choose OK when you are finished (or choose Cancel to discard your changes).

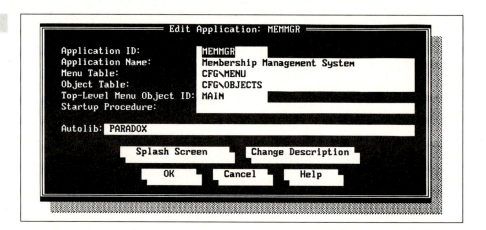

FIGURE 20.2

The Edit Application dialog box for the sample Membership application

Although Workshop allows you to change any of the settings in the Edit Application dialog box, it's best to reserve your changes to the settings listed below:

- Application Name
- Startup Procedure
- Autolib
- Splash Screen
- Description

Closing an Application

If you wish to close an application and remove it from the Workshop desktop, you can choose Application ➤ Close from Workshop's desktop menu. Closing an application doesn't delete anything; it simply clears the application from the Workshop desktop.

The Application ➤ Close option is something of a vestigial option. You don't really need to use it, because Workshop automatically closes any currently open application whenever you switch to another directory or open an application (even the same one).

Removing an Application

If you no longer need an application, you can remove it from the list of applications by following these steps:

1. Choose Application ➤ Remove. You'll see a dialog box similar to Figure 20.3.

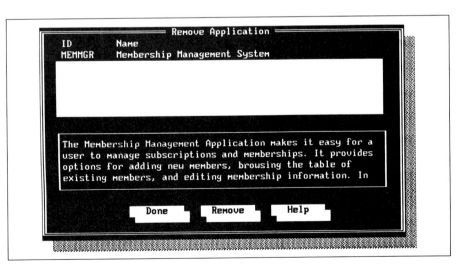

FIGURE 20.3

The Remove Application dialog box appears when you choose Application ➤ Remove.

2. Highlight the application you want to remove and choose **R**emove. You'll see a dialog box with the choices OK and Cancel.

3. If you're sure you want to remove the application from the list, choose OK. Otherwise choose Cancel.

4. Choose **D**one (or press F2 or Esc) to return to the Workshop desktop.

NOTE: If you accidentally remove an application, you must add it back to the Application table. Use Application ➤ New and specify the same application ID you used before, then redefine the splash screen and description. When you're finished, choose OK until you reach the Workshop desktop.

When you remove an application, the application *name* is removed from the list of applications, but none of the action objects or tables is affected. To delete action objects and tables, you'll need to use Tools menu options, as described later in this chapter.

Editing Paradox Objects

Since Paradox offers so much flexibility for defining and changing the objects used in your application, it's usually best to develop these objects within Paradox itself. You can, however, define or change them within Workshop, using the ParadoxEdit desktop option. Using this option can save you time when you need to change a Paradox object while developing your application. You can perform the following tasks:

- Create, restructure, edit, and add validity checks to tables
- Create and change reports and forms
- Create, change, and play back scripts

Choose ParadoxEdit from the Workshop desktop. You'll see the submenu below:

Choose one of the options listed. After you make your selection, you can create, restructure, or change Paradox objects as you would in Paradox itself. Although the dialog boxes are slightly different than those in Paradox itself, the choices will be familiar.

Managing Paradox and Application Objects

Like ParadoxEdit, Workshop's Tools menu, shown below, can save you time, making it easier to manage your application's objects without switching back to Paradox.

The Tables, Forms, Reports, and Scripts options open dialog boxes that are somewhat different than those in Paradox itself, but the tools work like their Paradox counterparts. The ActionObjects choice allows you to copy, rename, or delete action objects.

NOTE Tables, reports, forms, and scripts can be copied, renamed, or deleted from Paradox or Workshop. Action objects, however, are accessible only from Workshop.

To work with an action object, choose **T**ools ➤ **A**ctionObjects. You'll see the Action Object Tools dialog box, as shown in Figure 20.4.

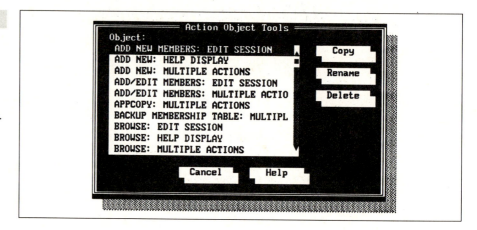

FIGURE 20.4

The Action Object Tools dialog box appears when you choose Tools ➤ ActionObjects from the Workshop desktop.

Highlight the object you want to copy, rename, or delete. Then choose one of the following buttons:

- **Copy:** Copies the selected object to a new object. When prompted, type the name for the new object and choose OK.

- **Rename:** Changes the name of the selected object. When prompted, type the new name for the object and choose OK.

- **Delete:** Deletes the selected object. Choose OK from the dialog box that appears to confirm the deletion (choose Cancel if you change your mind).

As usual, choosing Cancel or pressing Esc cancels the operation.

Finishing the Application

After thoroughly testing your application, the next step is to *finish* it. Finishing the application makes the application directory self-contained. This operation places everything you need to run the application (except Paradox itself) into the application directory and its Cfg and Workshop subdirectories. Always finish an application before distributing it to your end-users.

To finish the application, open it and choose **A**pplication ➤ Finish from the Workshop desktop. If you make additional changes to the application after finishing it, be sure to choose **A**pplication ➤ Finish again. After the first time you choose the Finish option, you'll be asked if you want to replace the previously copied items. Choose OK to continue, or choose Cancel to cancel.

Documenting the Application

You can generate documentation to the screen, a file, or to the printer. You can use this documentation for reference as you develop and fine-tune your application. To generate documentation on the current menu structure (the *menu tree*), all the actions that you've defined so far, and which objects are referenced by which action objects, follow these steps:

1. Choose **D**ocumentation from Workshop's desktop to see this menu:

2. Choose an option, as follows:

   - **Menu Tree:** Lists your application menu structure in a tree format.

- **Action Detail:** Lists all actions currently defined in the Object table.
- **Cross Reference:** Lists which objects are referenced by which action objects.

You'll see a Documentation Destination Selection dialog box, similar to the one shown below:

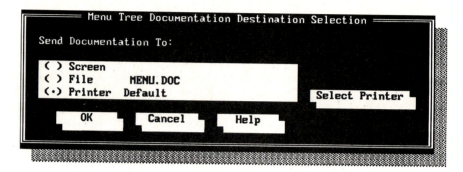

3. Choose one of the following destinations:

- **Screen:** Sends output to the screen.
- **File:** Sends output to a file. The default file names are Menu.DOC for menu tree documentation, Action.DOC for action detail documentation, and Crossref.DOC for cross reference documentation.
- **Printer:** Sends output to the printer assigned by the Select Printer button.
- **Select Printer:** Directs output to a different printer or changes the graphics characters used for box and line drawing, regardless of destination. This option is described in the next section.

4. After you select an output destination, choose OK. If the destination is an existing file, Workshop will ask if you want to overwrite the file or cancel the operation.

Selecting a Printer for Documentation

When you choose the Select Printer button from the Documentation Destination Selection dialog box, you'll see the dialog box shown in

DOCUMENTING THE APPLICATION

Figure 20.5. This dialog box contains the following options:

- **Printer Port:** Sends printed output to the specified port.
- **Lines Per Page:** Defines the number of lines per page.
- **Setup String:** Defines the string sent to the printer before printing starts.
- **Reset String:** Defines the string sent to the printer after printing is complete.
- **Styles:** Allows you to control the appearance of boxes and lines used in the documentation report, as described in the next section.

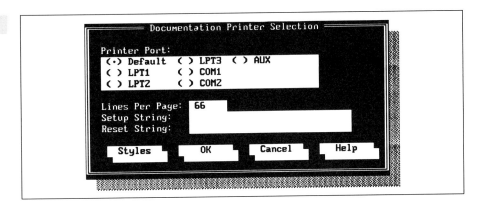

FIGURE 20.5

The Documentation Printer Selection dialog box

After you've finished with your printer selections, choose OK to return to the Documentation Destination Selection dialog box.

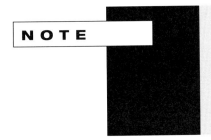

With the exception of the Styles button, the options in the dialog box are similar to those in the Reports option of the Custom Configuration Program. Workshop uses the default settings from the Custom Configuration Program unless you change them here. See Appendix D for details.

Changing the Style of Boxes and Lines in the Documentation

When you choose Styles in the Documentation Printer Selection dialog box, you'll see the dialog box shown in Figure 20.6. If your printer cannot print the extended graphic characters shown in the dialog box, choose the Non IBM button to get to the dialog box shown in Figure 20.7.

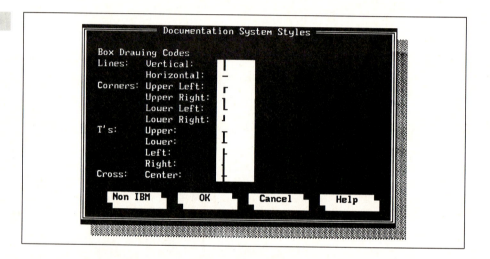

FIGURE 20.6

The Documentation Systems Styles—IBM dialog box

FIGURE 20.7

The Documentation System Styles—Non IBM dialog box

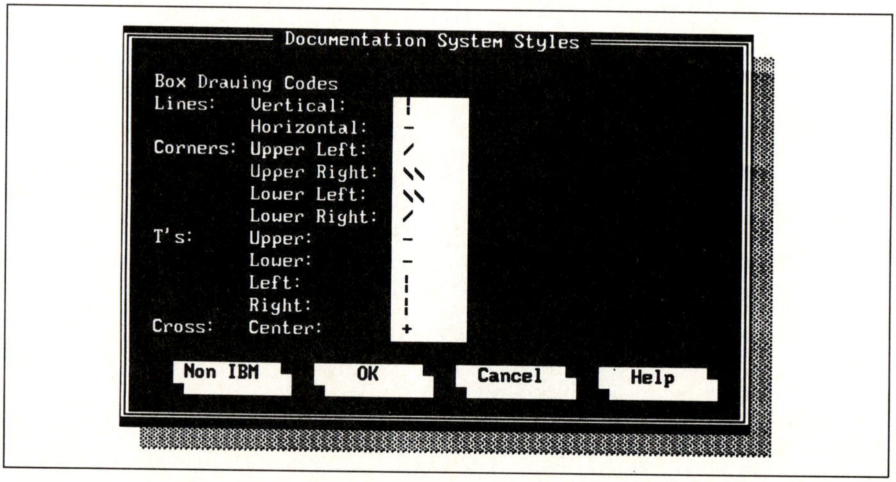

NOTE: To print the extended ASCII characters on an HP LaserJet III printer, choose the PC-8 symbol set. See your printer documentation for information about printer settings.

You can replace any box or line drawing characters. Erasing a character prevents *any* character from being printed for that box drawing code. Choose OK to return to the Documentation Printer Selection dialog box.

Using a Word Processor to Embellish Your Documentation

As mentioned, Workshop's documentation can help you refine your application or help others who will be called upon to enhance your application later. However, this developer-friendly documentation might not benefit your end-users much, because it doesn't take a how-to approach to the application. (The book you are reading now takes a how-to approach to Paradox and Workshop.) Users must rely on Help screens you've developed in Workshop, or on instruction manuals you've written with a word processor.

The documentation generated by Workshop can provide a useful starting point for reader documentation. Save it to a disk file (by choosing File as the document destination), then read the saved file into your word processor. Workshop documentation is saved to an ASCII text file, which you can read with any text editor (such as Edit or Edlin) or word processor that can accept ASCII files. Most word processors accept ASCII files.

When you're ready to work on the documentation with your word processor, choose Exit ➤ To DOS from the Workshop desktop menu. Then use the normal methods to run your word processor and retrieve the file. In your word processor, you can embellish, expand, or edit your documentation. You may need to make some of the following changes:

- Reduce the margins (especially the left and right margins).
- Reduce the font size.
- Change the paper orientation from portrait ($8\frac{1}{2}$ by 11 inches) to landscape (11 by $8\frac{1}{2}$ inches).

TIP Switching to a landscape (wide) page orientation can be helpful when working with the menu tree documentation in Menu.DOC.

- Delete the Workshop's page-heading text and replace it with your own heading.

Packaging the Application

After finishing your application, as described above, you must package it. *Packaging* means to copy all the necessary files to the end-user's computer. To help you better understand how to package your application, let's take a quick look at the structure of an application and at what actually happens when you choose **Application ➤ Finish**.

Anatomy of an Application

To distribute your Workshop applications, with no required royalty to Borland, include only these files:

- Workshop's library code (usually Workshop\Wsrun.LIB)
- Workshop's Master table of action objects (usually Workshop\Mstrobj.DB and Workshop\Mstrobj.PX)
- Your Application table (usually Cfg\Applic.DB and Cfg\Applic.PX)
- Generated scripts for your application, including the startup script
- Your Object table (typically Cfg\Objects.DB and related memo and index files)
- Your Menu table (typically Cfg\Menu.DB and Cfg\Menu.PX)
- Any Paradox objects that you created for your application

NOTE: The application ID (startup script name), Menu table, Object table, and top-level menu object ID (main menu) locations are set via Application ➤ New or Application ➤ Edit.

Your Application table (Applic.DB) stores information about your application, including the name of the Object table and the application Menu table.

The application Menu table (Menu.DB) stores the menu structure for your application. It also stores the Quit to Paradox, Exit Paradox, and Play a Script utility actions. You can create one Menu table for each application, or several applications can share the same table.

Note that if you use the same Menu table for several applications, you should use a different top-level menu object ID (main menu name) when defining each new application, unless you want the applications to have the same menu. For best results, you should stick with one application per directory and one Menu table for each application, especially when you're first learning Workshop.

The application Object table stores the definition of complex actions, including edit sessions, report prints, queries, Help text, multi-actions, executes, and OK/Cancel choices.

Putting Applications Together for the End-User

After running the Application ➤ Finish procedure, you can use the DOS XCOPY command, with the /S switch, to copy all of your application files to another disk (assuming that you've created only one application in the subdirectory and have no other files stored there). XCOPY, which is available in DOS version 3.2 and later, can be useful for creating a backup, or when you're ready to give the application to an end-user.

CAUTION: In the unlikely event that your application references Paradox objects or scripts that are outside the application directory, be sure to copy them as well.

Copying an Application to a Floppy

For example, to copy an application (including its Cfg and Workshop subdirectories) that is stored in the Member subdirectory of C:\PDOX 45 to the floppy disk in drive A, return to the DOS prompt and type these commands (pressing ↵ after each one):

```
C:
CD C:\PDOX45\Members
XCOPY C:*.* A: /S
```

If you're using drive B, substitute that drive letter:

```
XCOPY C:*.* B: /S
```

The *.* option copies all files, and the /S option copies all subdirectories below the current directory (creating the subdirectories on the destination disk if necessary).

Copying an Application from a Floppy to a Hard Disk

To copy the application onto another computer that has either Paradox or Paradox Runtime already installed, insert the floppy disk containing the application into drive A (or drive B) of the user's computer. If the subdirectory doesn't already exist on the user's computer, use the DOS MD command to create it. For example, to create the Members subdirectory on the user's hard disk (where Paradox is installed on C:\PDOX45), type the command

```
MD C:\PDOX45\Members
```

at the DOS prompt and press ↵.

Then change to the subdirectory and use the XCOPY command to copy the files. For example to copy the Members application on a disk in drive A to the user's hard disk, type these two commands (pressing ⏎ after each one):

C:
CD C:\PDOX45\Members
XCOPY A:*.* C: /S

If you're using drive B, substitute that drive letter:

XCOPY B:*.* C: /S

NOTE A network may require different installation steps. Consult your network documentation for details.

Using BACKUP and RESTORE for Large Applications

If your application is too large to fit onto a single floppy disk, you'll need to substitute the BACKUP command for XCOPY when you copy the application from your hard disk. Unlike XCOPY, the BACKUP command prompts you to insert a new disk when the current backup disk is full. If you use the BACKUP command, you must use its companion command, RESTORE, to copy the files from the floppy disk to another computer's hard disk.

When you're copying the application to floppy disks, use BACKUP in place of the XCOPY command, as in:

BACKUP C:*.* A: /S

To restore the application files from the backup disks created with the BACKUP command (to copy them to the user's hard disk), use the RESTORE command, as in :

RESTORE A: C:*.* /S

See your DOS manual for more information about using the BACKUP, RESTORE, and XCOPY commands.

Starting a Completed Application

A completely finished application can be started in one of several ways. In the following sections, we'll explain how to start an application from Paradox, DOS, and Windows.

If you've purchased the optional companion disk, you can use the methods described here to try out the sample Membership application.

Starting an Application from Paradox

If you're still in Workshop, return to Paradox, Then follow these steps:

1. Make the directory containing the application the current directory and then choose **Scripts ➤ P**lay.

2. Type the name of the startup script for the application and press ↵. For example, type **Memmgr** to play the script for the sample Membership application. The application will open, displaying its splash screen, if any.

Starting an Application from the DOS Command Line

You can start an application from the DOS command line as long as *both* of these conditions are true:

- The working directory in the Custom Configuration Program must either be blank or be set to the directory containing your application. (See Appendix D for information about this setting.)

- Any Init.SC script must not switch you to a directory other than your application directory. (See Chapter 11 for a description of the Init.SC script.)

If the above conditions are true, you can exit to DOS and follow these steps to run your application from the DOS command line:

1. If necessary, switch to the disk drive and directory containing your application.

2. Type **Paradox**, press the spacebar, type the name of the application startup script, and press ↵. For example, to start the Membership application script named Memmgr, type the command **Paradox Memmgr** and press ↵.

To automate starting the application from DOS, put these commands in a batch file or add them to the end of your Autoexec.BAT file.

If you get the message

Bad command or file name

and you're sure you typed the command correctly, use the PATH command to make certain that \PDOX45 is in your path. This directory will automatically be in the path if you followed the normal installation procedure for Paradox. If necessary, you can run Paradox by including the path in the command. For example, if Paradox is stored on the \PDOX45 directory on drive C, you can enter the command

C:\PDOX45\Paradox Memmgr

Starting an Application from Windows

If you are running Paradox from Windows 3.x, you can run your application from Windows as well. First, you must add the application's program item icon to one of the group windows, if it hasn't already been added for you. Once the icon is in place, you (or the end-user) can simply double-click on that icon to start the application. The conditions listed in the previous section for starting the application from the DOS prompt also apply when starting an application from Windows.

NOTE

The dialog boxes shown in this section are for Windows 3.1; however, the essential steps are the same in both Windows 3.0 and Windows 3.1. See your Windows documentation for more detailed information about using the PIF Editor and adding icons to Windows.

Follow these general steps to add an icon for your application:

1. Double-click on the PIF Editor (typically found in the Main or Accessories group window) and create a Program Information File (PIF) for the application. Figure 20.8 shows an example of a PIF for the Membership application.

FIGURE 20.8

The PIF Editor screen for the sample Membership application. Notice the Program Filename, Window Title, Optional Parameters, and Startup Directory settings.

2. After filling in the PIF Editor dialog box, choose File ➤ Save from the PIF Editor menu and specify a file name. (We saved the sample PIF with the name C:\Windows\Members.PIF.)

3. Choose **File** ➤ **Exit** to exit the PIF Editor.
4. Open a group to hold the application icon.
5. Choose **File** ➤ **N**ew from the Program Manager menu.
6. Choose Program **I**tem, then choose OK.
7. Fill in the Program Item Properties dialog box, as in Figure 20.9. Then choose OK to save the icon.

Now you can use the new application icon like any other Windows icon.

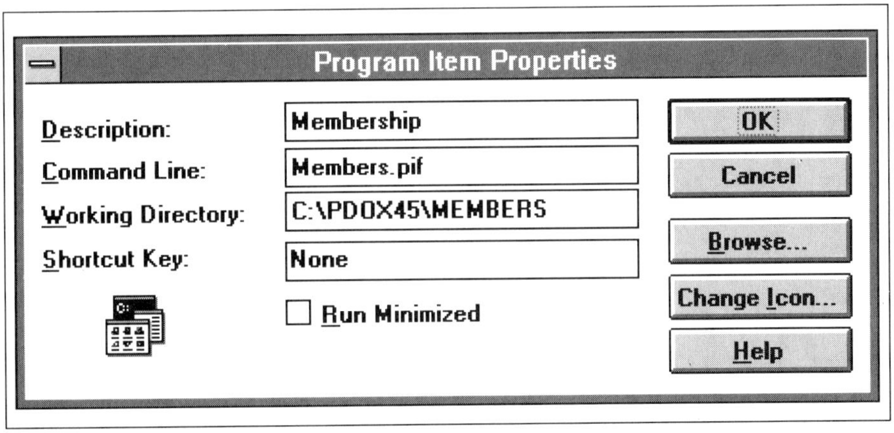

FIGURE 20.9

The Program Item Properties for a sample Membership application program item. After the icon is created, an end-user can double-click on the icon in the appropriate Windows group to start the application.

Program Item Properties	
Description:	Membership
Command Line:	Members.pif
Working Directory:	C:\PDOX45\MEMBERS
Shortcut Key:	None
☐ Run Minimized	

Buttons: OK, Cancel, Browse..., Change Icon..., Help

Creating Closed Applications

If you want to create a closed application that cannot access Paradox, make sure the menus include only an EXIT PARADOX object type, and not a QUIT TO PARADOX object type. Note that applications that run with Paradox Runtime always exit to DOS.

You can also password-protect the startup script to prevent Ctrl-Break from interrupting actions and switching the user to Debug mode while the application is running. This does not require the user to enter a password to run the application. It simply prevents the user from entering Debug mode by pressing Ctrl-Break, as well as from editing the startup script without knowing the password.

> **CAUTION**
>
> Do not use the same password for scripts that you use for any table, because Paradox can't discriminate between a password entered for a table and one entered for the startup script. If you don't heed this warning and the user enters a table password that's the same as the startup script password, the user *will* be able to enter Debug mode by pressing Ctrl-Break.

Summary

Here's a quick summary of this chapter's main topics:

- To open an application to make changes, switch to its directory (if necessary) by choosing **A**pplication ➤ **D**irectory and specifying the directory, then choose **A**pplication ➤ **O**pen and specify the application to open.

- To change the application attributes for an existing application, choose **A**pplication ➤ **E**dit.

- To test an application action, use the **T**est button in the action object dialog box.

- To test or start the entire application from Workshop, choose **A**pplication ➤ **T**est from the Workshop desktop menu.

- To finish an application, choose **A**pplication ➤ **F**inish.

- To copy an application and its subdirectories, use the XCOPY (or BACKUP) command from the DOS prompt.

- To generate documentation about the application, open the application and choose **D**ocumentation from the Workshop desktop. Then choose **M**enu Tree, **A**ction Detail, or **C**ross Reference, and specify a destination for the documentation.

SUMMARY

- To start an application from Paradox, switch to the correct subdirectory by choosing **T**ools ➤ **M**ore ➤ **D**irectory and entering a directory name. Then choose **S**cripts ➤ **P**lay and enter the name of the startup script.

- To start an application from DOS, switch to the drive and subdirectory containing the startup script and type Paradox *script*, where *script* is the name of the startup script.

- To start an application from Windows, install it as a program item icon by using the PIF Editor and Program Manager's **F**ile ➤ **N**ew option, then use the icon to start the application.

CHAPTER 21

Learning to Use PAL

fast TRACK

- **To use the Miniscript window** — 837

    press Alt-F10 and choose **M**iniScript. Then enter up to a 175-character PAL script, without carriage returns (one line only). Press ↵ to play the script.

- **To use a PAL function or other expression in the Value dialog box** — 838

    press Alt-F10 and choose **V**alue. Enter the function and its arguments or another expression, as in 3 * 9. When you press ↵ or choose OK, the value of the expression appears in a message window on the desktop.

- **To use variables** — 848

    assign them with an equation. The variable name goes on the left, and the value or expression goes on the right, as in x = 64. Reference the variable name to retrieve the value. For example, if x = 64, then SQRT(x) evaluates to 8.

- **To change a variable's data type** — 849

    use the PAL function STRVAL() to convert the value to alphanumeric data type. Place the value or expression to be converted inside the STRVAL() function's parentheses, as in STRVAL(x) or STRVAL(Pi()).

- **To use arrays** — 850

    use the commands CopyToArray and CopyFromArray. For example, CopyToArray a sends the values in the current record to the variable array a. The command CopyFromArray a retrieves the values in the array a, in order.

- **To branch in a PAL script** — 851

    use the If..Then commands, with the syntax If *Condition* Then *Command* [Else *Command*] EndIf.

- **To loop in a PAL script** — 854

    use the While..EndWhile commands, with the syntax While *Condition* [*Commands*] EndWhile. The most common condition to set for While is (True).

- **To create new key definitions with PAL** — 863

    use the SetKey command, with the syntax SetKey *KeyCode*, where *KeyCode* is one of the PAL keyboard extended codes listed in the *PAL Reference* manual.

- **To create new Paradox menu choices with Paradox.ADD** — 881

    in the directory containing Paradox.EXE, press Alt-e and choose **O**pen to open the Mini-editor. Then type Paradox.ADD as the name of the file. Move to the end of the file. On a single line by itself, type the new menu entry in the proper format. Copy the script you designated to the directory with Paradox.EXE. Exit and then reload Paradox.

IN the preceding chapters, you learned a lot about automating Paradox sessions using the built-in functions of Paradox Workshop. Your ability to manage and control your data in Paradox and in Workshop itself is greatly enhanced when you use scripts created in the Paradox Application Language (PAL). Many functions can be easily automated or enhanced using relatively simple PAL scripts. PAL is designed to be easy to learn in small steps. It uses many commands that are Paradox menu equivalents and others that are English language words (such as Do_It!, Message, Beep, and Wait).

This chapter presents an introduction to PAL and shows many relatively simple techniques that provide access to much of PAL's power. First, you'll learn about some basic PAL concepts and the PAL Menu. Then you will learn how to apply PAL concepts to create flexible utility objects that can be used in your interactive Paradox sessions or Workshop applications.

You will also see examples of how to use PAL commands to customize Paradox from the Init script (discussed in Chapter 11). Later in this chapter, you will learn how to use PAL to create new Paradox ≡ ▶ Utility, Report, and Form menu choices using the powerful Paradox.ADD file, new to version 4.5. All the PAL commands, functions, and techniques you learn about in this chapter can be used to create utility objects for use with Workshop, as well as to build full-fledged, stand-alone applications.

Some Basic PAL Concepts

PAL is a high-level, structured database programming language. PAL programs are called *scripts*. PAL can be used to automate Paradox tasks that you would normally perform manually and to create application menus that look and work like Paradox's own menu system. PAL supports such programming concepts as variables, arrays, and procedures. It includes built-in mathematical, statistical, financial, string, and system functions to aid in the management and manipulation of Paradox objects, such as tables, forms, reports, queries, and graphs.

So far in this book, you have been introduced to PAL mainly as a means of enhancing the flexibility and power of your existing recorded scripts. In this section, you will learn the basic concepts behind the use of PAL in these recorded scripts and in written scripts.

Interactive Paradox versus PAL-Controlled Paradox

The menu-driven Paradox desktop and the keyboard and mouse commands available when you work in a Paradox session are known as *interactive Paradox*, as opposed to *PAL program-controlled Paradox*. In interactive Paradox, you perform each step manually by issuing specific keyboard or mouse instructions through the use of menus and dialog boxes.

In PAL scripts, your commands are automated. Your scripts may include PAL language commands that have no direct menu or dialog box choice equivalents. The PAL commands allow you to exercise greater control over your data and to perform many tasks that are difficult (or even impossible) to perform in interactive Paradox sessions.

PAL Script Types and Creation

Recorded scripts are really a type of PAL program, one which is initially generated in response to your keystrokes. Every character in a recorded script can be keyed in manually, and will work as PAL programming code. As you saw in Chapters 11 and 17, this code can be modified by typing in changes or by adding PAL commands using the Paradox Editor.

PAL scripts consist of recorded keystrokes, saved Query forms, manually typed PAL code, or a combination of the three. Figure 21.1 shows an example of a script in an editing window.

You can create PAL scripts in one of six ways, as described in the following sections.

CHAPTER 21

LEARNING TO USE PAL

FIGURE 21.1

A PAL script in an editing window

```
  ≡  File   Edit   Search   Options   Go   DO-IT!   Cancel
┌─[■]──────────────── C:\pdox45\customer\payments.sc ────────────[↕]─┐
│IF                                                                   │
│  SYSMODE()="Main" or SYSMODE()="Edit" or SYSMODE()="Report"         │
│THEN                                                                 │
│  While (True)                                                       │
│    CLEAR                                                            │
│    @10,10                                                           │
│    ?? "Enter a the loan amount(no dollar signs or commas): "        │
│    ACCEPT "N"                                                       │
│    PICTURE "#[#][#][#]{[.][#][#]}"                                  │
│    TO x                                                             │
│    CLEAR                                                            │
│    @09,10                                                           │
│    ?? "Enter the rate PER PAYMENT PERIOD- enter the decimal"        │
│    @10,10                                                           │
│    ?? "(Example: .01 rate for monthly payment on 12% a year: "      │
│    ACCEPT "N"                                                       │
│    PICTURE ".[#][#][#][#]]"                                         │
│    TO y                                                             │
│    CLEAR                                                            │
│    @10,10                                                           │
│    ?? "Enter a number of payment periods: "                         │
└─────────────────────────────────────────────────────────────────────┘
  F1 Help   Alt-Z Next   Alt-A ReplaceNext   Ctrl-A Replace      Script
```

BeginRecord/EndRecord

As you've learned already, you can record scripts by using the **B**eginRecord and **E**ndRecord options on the **S**cripts menu or on the PAL Menu, which is accessed by pressing Alt-F10. Remember that Paradox mouse support is suspended when **B**eginRecord is selected and reactivated when **E**ndRecord is selected. You cannot record mouse clicks.

QuerySave

Another method of script creation that you've been introduced to in this book is saved queries. When you use **S**cripts ➤ **Q**uerySave, any Query forms that are currently on the Paradox desktop are saved and stored in a script file.

Paradox Editor

A third way to create scripts, covered in Chapter 17, is by typing the appropriate PAL command, function, or expression into a new script using the Paradox Editor. The Editor is available as a menu choice in the **S**cripts menu. You can create a new script file by choosing **S**cripts ➤ **E**ditor ➤ **N**ew, or edit an existing script file by choosing **S**cripts ➤ **E**ditor ➤ **O**pen.

SOME BASIC PAL CONCEPTS

You can also get to the Editor from a script Debug/Cancel prompt. If you see this error message while playing back a script, choose **D**ebug, then press Ctrl-e to open the script in an editing window. The PAL Debugger is discussed later in this chapter.

Miniscripts

A *miniscript* is a temporary one-line script of up to 175 characters. The Miniscript window provides a PAL command line, so you can write and execute PAL code without going through the Editor. The Miniscript window is opened from the PAL Menu by pressing Alt-F10 and choosing **M**iniScript.

Miniscripts are retained and can be replayed during a session. The Miniscript window displays all miniscripts that have been run during the current session. Figure 21.2 shows an example of the Miniscript window with several miniscripts. You can edit a previous miniscript or enter a new one. Miniscripts are deleted at the end of the Paradox session.

You can save your miniscripts in the current directory by pressing Alt-F3 when the Miniscript window is open. Paradox creates a script named Minihist.SC. If you want to keep it as a permanent script, rename it. Otherwise, the saved miniscript will be overwritten the next time you press Alt-F3 in the Miniscript window when you are in the same directory.

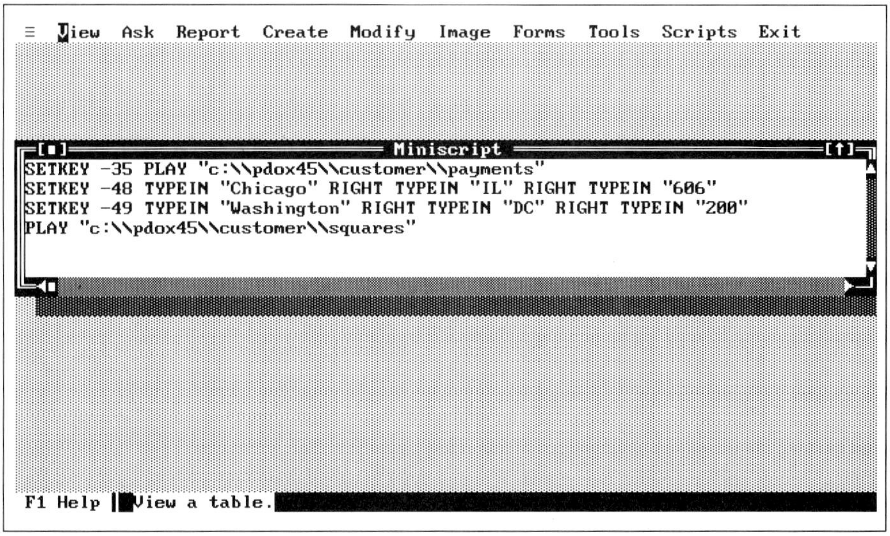

FIGURE 21.2

The Miniscript window, introduced in Paradox 4.5, showing several miniscripts. Miniscripts are restricted to one line but can execute up to 175 characters of PAL code.

Value

The Value option on the PAL menu creates a temporary script that will return the value of any PAL expression as a message on the desktop. To use this option, press Alt-F10 to display the PAL menu and choose **V**alue. You'll see the Value dialog box, as shown in Figure 21.3.

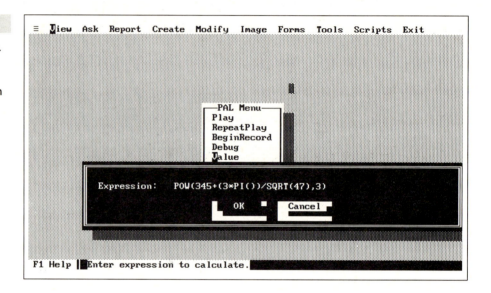

FIGURE 21.3

The Value dialog box. To access this dialog box, press Alt-F10 and choose Value from the PAL menu. The answer to this calculation, by the way, is 41556470.79673.

You can recall the most recent Value script run in a session by pressing Ctrl-e in the Value dialog box. Value scripts are erased at the end of a session.

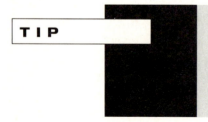

TIP

Since Value displays its answer in a message on the desktop, you can use it as a pop-up calculator, with access to any PAL mathematical, statistical, scientific, or financial function. This and other uses of Value are described later in this chapter.

Instant Scripts

As you learned in Chapter 11, an Instant Script is recorded and saved "on-the-fly." You simply press Alt-F3 to turn Instant Script recording on and off. Then your Instant Script can be replayed by pressing Alt-F4.

Each time you use Alt-F3 to create a new Instant.SC script file, the existing Instant.SC is deleted. Instant scripts can be edited, copied, and renamed, like any other script file.

Remember, any script can be played with the Alt-F4 key. Just use **T**ools ➤ **C**opy ➤ **S**cripts to make a copy of an existing script and name the copy Instant. You can have a different Instant Script in each working directory.

TIP Keep a copy of your Instant Script, with a different name. Then, if you accidentally overwrite it by recording a new Instant Script with Alt-F3, you'll still have a copy.

Other Temporary Scripts

Paradox automatically creates two special temporary scripts, Execute and Savevars, during certain PAL operations. The Init.SC script is another special type of script file, as described later in this chapter.

Just as you should not name a table with any name that Paradox uses for its temporary tables, you should not name any of your scripts to the special names Mini, Minihist, Value, Savevars, or Execute. You may want to use scripts with the names Init and Instant, as long as you are aware of the special treatment these script names receive from Paradox.

PAL Script Format and Structure

PAL scripts are stored in a file format known as ASCII or DOS text. These files are normally edited in the Paradox Editor. In Chapter 17, you learned how to use the Editor to change a PAL script or create a PAL script from scratch. However, any DOS text or programming editor that reads and writes unformatted DOS text (ASCII) files can be used to edit or write a PAL script.

Learning to Use PAL

The steps for using an external script editor for script files in Paradox are described in Appendix D. However, you do not even need to be in Paradox to edit or create a script file. You can load an ASCII editor in DOS and create and edit script files.

No matter how a script file was created, all script files execute in the same manner. The code in a PAL script is executed one command at a time, from left to right and from top to bottom (unless you place some branching statements into the PAL file, as described later in this chapter).

As mentioned in Chapter 17, placing a semicolon (;) on a line in a PAL script causes PAL to ignore all text after the semicolon when the script executes. Semicolons are normally used to place comments in a PAL script.

PAL scripts are freeform. Blank lines, extra spaces, and line breaks (with a few exceptions) in a script are ignored when the script executes. You can place each command, even each word, on a separate line, or place all commands on the same line. Thus, you can create a useful 175-character script on one line in the Miniscript window or Value dialog box. A line in a regular PAL script can be up to 132 characters long.

Formatting a script with indentations, line breaks, and blank lines makes it easier to read, without affecting how the script executes. However, one restriction is that you can't break a PAL command or function name across lines.

Using Scripts Together

A series of scripts can be used to create a complete application. In Chapters 18 and 19, you learned how to use Workshop to automatically generate the scripts to create a Paradox application. Each time you defined a menu or routine in Workshop, Paradox automatically wrote the script needed to create the menu or perform the desired function. In this chapter, you will learn to write scripts that work individually and together, using the Play command, to allow you to control your Paradox environment.

All the PAL scripts described in this chapter can be used as utility objects attached to Workshop menus and included in Workshop applications.

An Overview of PAL Commands and Functions

In Chapter 17, you learned how to use some basic PAL commands. In Chapter 15, you were introduced to the use of PAL functions in calculated report fields. Several hundred PAL commands and functions are available to control the operation of Paradox from a PAL script. In this chapter, you will learn how to use a number of the basic PAL commands and functions. The following sections describe general characteristics of PAL commands and functions.

Types of PAL Commands

PAL commands are used to specify actions for Paradox to perform and to control the conditions in which Paradox will perform those actions. There are three major types of PAL commands: programming commands, keypress interactions, and abbreviated menu and keystroke commands.

Programming Commands

Programming commands allow you to perform tasks that you cannot perform directly in Paradox. These include PAL's branching and looping commands, as well as user, window, mouse, and screen control commands. The Message and Beep commands described in Chapter 17 are examples of simple programming commands.

Keypress Interaction Commands

Keypress interaction commands are the commands that are generated when you record a script in Paradox. You can also type these commands directly into a PAL script. Keypress interaction commands include cursor-movement and Paradox special key commands. Keypress interaction commands can also include the responses required in dialog boxes. Text in quotation marks, sometimes referred to as *quoted strings*, which you can type into a Query form or a field in a table, as well as the saved Query form itself, are special types of keypress interaction commands. For example, the command

Menu{Tools}{More}{Directory}{C:\\PDOX45\\Sample}

is a typical recorded keypress interaction command sequence.

NOTE: The backslash is used as a code that means to take the next text literally. Therefore, you must type two backslashes (\\) when you want to place a backslash in a PAL script.

Abbreviated Menu Commands

Abbreviated menu commands provide an alternative way to represent certain PAL commands generated when you record a script. For example, the abbreviated command for the keypress interaction command shown in the preceding section is

SetDir "C:\\PDOX45\\Sample"

Note that the syntax of the SetDir command requires quotation marks around the directory path name.

As another example, the command

Report "Custlist" 1

is the abbreviated menu command equivalent of the keystroke interaction commands

Menu {Report}{Output}{Custlist}{1}{Printer}

As you can see, abbreviated commands make typing PAL code easier. However, they have the following limitations:

- Some menu and special keystroke selections do not have abbreviated equivalents.

- Some of the abbreviated commands automatically select only one choice when there are several available menu choices. For example, in the case of the Report command, the printer is assumed as the output device. If you want to output to the screen or to a file, you must use the keypress interaction commands for equivalents to the {Screen} or {File} menu choices.

- Abbreviated menu and keystroke commands sometimes have built-in responses to dialog box choices that are not always the ones you want. For example, the abbreviated menu command Copy is equivalent to Menu{Tools} {Copy} {Replace}, which assumes that you want to overwrite the specified file. The keypress interaction commands Menu{Tools} {Copy} will generate an overwrite query dialog box, giving you a chance to cancel.

You must decide on a case-by-case basis whether the abbreviated command or the keypress interaction commands are the most appropriate for your needs.

Special Key Commands

Special key commands in scripts are the equivalent of pressing one of the keys that has a special meaning in Paradox. These include such commands as the following:

- Menu is equivalent to pressing F10.
- Do_It! is equivalent to pressing F2.
- ClearImage is equivalent to pressing F8.

Each of these commands, as well as the ones in the previously discussed categories, requires that you be in the correct mode. If you issue any command in an inappropriate context, your script may crash and take you to the Debugger, discussed later in this chapter.

Using Arguments and Parameters in PAL Commands

Commands in PAL often consist of *keywords* (the command itself) and one or more arguments. An *argument* is a set of characters that modifies the action of the command. The abbreviated menu command Report, for example, takes two arguments: a table name and a report number. To use the Report command in a script to print report number 1 of the Custlist.DB table, the complete command is

　　Report "Custlist" 1

A command's arguments are usually separated from the command, and from each other, by a space. If two or more arguments are used with a command, they must be placed in the correct order. In most cases, an argument must be presented in a specific form. For example, with the Report command, the table name must precede the report number, and the report number must be surrounded by quotation marks.

As another example, the command TypeIn allows you to use PAL as an automated typist to fill in data in tables, forms, Query forms, and so on. TypeIn takes one argument, as in

TypeIn TODAY() –30

This command types in the value of a date 30 days prior to the current date, placing the value at the current cursor position, as an alphanumeric string, in the current date entry format.

In most cases, the TypeIn command automatically converts date, currency, and numeric expressions to an alphanumeric string, so you do not need to use the STRVAL( ) function, described shortly, with it.

Arguments are generally values used by the command or function in performing its task. Some commands and functions also take *parameters*, which are generally limitations or conditions set on a command or function to help define its task.

The rules that govern the format of a command—the spaces around arguments, the order of the arguments, the form that each argument must take—is called the command's *syntax*. In order for a PAL command to work correctly in a script, you must follow the correct PAL syntax for that command. The *PAL Reference* manual lists all PAL commands and describes their functions, as well as the syntax required for each.

Types of PAL Functions

PAL functions are used to retrieve or calculate values during the course of the operation of your script. PAL functions always end in a set of open and closed parentheses, as in DOW( ). PAL functions often execute predefined formulas or check on the condition of Paradox system settings, specific Paradox objects, or data in Paradox files.

Reporting Functions

Reporting functions are used to return the value of a given DOS or Paradox system setting or to report on the existence of or condition of a Paradox object. Some of these functions report on data from your computer system. For example, TIME() and DAY() return the current value of your system clock.

Other reporting functions report on the condition, existence, or value of Paradox objects, data, and settings. For example, DIRECTORY() reports the name of the current Paradox working directory, and SYSMODE() returns the current Paradox mode.

Many reporting functions, such as the examples shown in this section, don't take any arguments inside the parentheses at the end of the function name. Other reporting functions require that you specify the object or data to be reported upon. For example ISTABLE( ), which returns a logical value of True or False, requires one argument (also called an *expression*), which is the name of the table. The syntax of the ISTABLE( ) function is

ISTABLE(*TableName*)

The arguments that a given function requires must be entered in the correct order and are usually separated by commas. The *PAL Reference* manual lists all functions, the arguments they require, and the correct syntax.

Calculating Functions

Many PAL functions return the value of a calculation. Almost all of these functions require one or more arguments within their parentheses.

NOTE One calculating function that doesn't require an argument is PI( ), which always returns the same value, based on a built-in constant.

Other calculating functions execute formulas that can accept variable values. The values the function uses in its calculations are passed to the function by placing them in parentheses as arguments. For example, the mathematical function POW( ) raises a number to its exponential value. It requires two numeric expressions as arguments. The syntax of POW( ) is

>POW(*Base,Exponent*)

For example, POW(5,2) returns 25, and POW(5,3) returns 625. POW( ), and a number of other calculation functions, can take either literal expressions or variables, discussed below, as arguments.

Other calculation functions accept arguments that are references to Paradox data. These functions access the data and use its value as the basis for their calculations. For example the function CAVERAGE( ) has the syntax

>CAVERAGE(*TableName,FieldName*)

CAVERAGE( ) averages all the nonblank values in the *FieldName* field of the *TableName* table and returns the average as its output.

The PAL function DOW( ) has the syntax

>DOW(*Date*)

The DOW( ) function calculates the day of the week of any date given as an argument. It returns a three-letter string, such as Sat or Mon, representing the day of the week of the date expression specified as an argument.

Using Arguments and Parameters in PAL Functions

As you've seen, the arguments and parameters passed to functions are placed in the parentheses following the function name, separated by commas, in the form

>Function(*Argument,Argument,...*)

For example, the financial function PMT( ), which returns the amortized payment on a loan, requires three arguments: *Amount*, *Rate* (as a decimal number representing a percentage and adjusted to match the payment period), and *Term* (number of payment periods), as in

>PMT(10000,.01,36)

This example returns the payments for an amortized loan of $10,000 at 12 percent per year over 36 months.

NOTE The PMT( ) function is used later in this chapter in creating a pop-up calculator.

Remember, not all functions take arguments, but all functions require the parentheses.

Using Values and Expressions

A *value* is data which is expressed as a valid example of one of the PAL data types: alphanumeric, numeric, currency, short number, date, or logical. In the PMT function example in the previous section, the arguments 10000, 01, and 36 are all values.

NOTE Although interactive Paradox does not support a logical type field, PAL returns a logical True/False data type in many operations.

An *expression* is a single value or set of one or more elements that results in a single value. All values, such as the ones shown in the PMT() example, are expressions. However, many expressions are not single values themselves. Instead, they *evaluate* to a single value. For example, the formula 3 * 3 is an expression that evaluates to the value 9.

In the example

    TypeIn TODAY() –30

shown earlier, TODAY() –30 is an expression that evaluates to a date value, such as 12/5/94. The TypeIn command evaluates the date value 12/5/94 to an alphanumeric value 12/5/94, which looks the same on the screen but is stored as a different data type by Paradox.

NOTE Date values are displayed alphanumerically with formatting, but they are stored as numbers—specifically, the number of days since January 1, 100 A.D. Although you can add and subtract dates, they must still be evaluated to a numeric data type before they can be used by some commands and functions.

PAL expressions evaluate to one of seven data types. These include four data types used in interactive Paradox: alphanumeric, number, currency, and short number. The other three types—logical, array (fixed and dynamic), and procedure (a set of PAL statements designed to perform a task)—are available only in PAL scripts.

PAL expressions can contain constants, variables, fixed and dynamic arrays, operators (*,+,/,-,<,>, and so on), field specifiers, and functions (built-in or user-defined procedures). Here are some examples of common types of expressions:

EXPRESSION	EVALUATES TO
33 * 10	330
DOW(12/7/41)	Sun (DOW returns the day of the week)
POW(25,2)	625 (POW raises a number to a power)
SQRT(625)	25 (SQRT returns the number's square root)

NOTE PAL automatically converts an alphanumeric string of more than 255 characters to the memo data type.

Using Variables

The term *variable* refers to a named location (usually a memory location) that can hold a value. The value at the location can be referred to in formulas, commands, and function arguments by using the name given to the location. You can have the value at the location change by entering an equation that has the name of the location on the left side and the new value on the right side.

Assigning Variables in PAL Scripts

In a PAL script you can assign a variable by simply typing an equation such as $x = 3$. Paradox places the value 3 in a memory location, which is assigned the name x. To change the value of x, you simply type in a new equation, such as $x = 10$. Paradox keeps track of the named variable location and the value assigned to it for the duration of a Paradox session, or until you use PAL to clear the variable.

Assigning Variables in PAL Functions

One common use of a variable is to hold the value returned by a PAL function so that the value can be used by subsequent PAL commands or functions. For example, the equation x = DIRECTORY() in a PAL script assigns the current directory name to the variable x. Note that the value assigned to the variable x is not the name of the DIRECTORY() function, but the value returned when DIRECTORY() is executed.

Once the current directory name has been assigned to the variable x, PAL code can refer to that variable to retrieve the value. For example, if the current working directory is C:\PDOX45\Sample, the PAL code

```
x = DIRECTORY()
Message " The current working directory is " + x
```

will place the message

```
The current working directory is C:\PDOX45\Sample
```

on the desktop. Later in this chapter, you will learn how to use PAL to assign this code to a hotkey, so that you can see the current working directory name with a single keystroke.

Changing a Variable's Data Type

Paradox stores values in variables in their original data type and format. If a variable is assigned using a function that returns a date or numeric value, the value is stored in the variable as a date or numeric value.

For example, if you assigned a value to the variable x using the PAL code x = TODAY(), today's date would be stored at the location x as a value of the date data type. If you tried to place a message on the desktop, using the same syntax as the previous example, you would get a PAL error, because the PAL Message command displays only alphanumeric values.

To get around this problem, you need to use the PAL function STRVAL(), which converts data to alphanumeric type. STRVAL(x) returns the value of the variable *x* as an alphanumeric string, even though the value is stored as a date.

If executed on 3/31/94, the PAL code

```
x = TODAY()
Message " Today's date is " + STRVAL(x)
```

will display the message

Today's date is 3/31/94

Later in this chapter, you will learn how to assign and call PAL variables to perform many useful functions in Paradox.

Using Arrays

An *array* is a set of related named memory locations (variables) used for the temporary storage of values. Each memory location or each variable in an array is called an *element*. An array is, in effect, a set of variables, the values of which can be addressed either singly or as a group. Paradox supports two types of arrays: fixed and dynamic.

Paradox offers two commands that greatly simplify dealing with arrays: CopyToArray and CopyFromArray. The CopyToArray command places a copy of the current record in an array in memory. It takes one argument, an array name. The array created by CopyToArray contains one more element than the number of fields in the current record. The extra element, the first one in the array, stores the name of the table from which the record was copied. The remaining elements in the array contain the fields in the record, in the order of the table structure. The order of the image (such as with rotated fields) has no effect on the order of the elements in the array.

The CopyFromArray command, which takes the same argument as CopyToArray, copies the elements from an array into the current record in a table.

Once a CopyToArray command has been executed, each element in the array can also be referred to as a separate variable. The name of the elements in the array is the name of the array followed by the number of the element in square brackets. For example, if your script executes the PAL command

CopyToArray a

while the cursor is located in the first record in the Custlist table, the array element holding the name of the Custlist table would be named a[1], the last name of the customer in the first record of the table would be stored in the element a[2], and so on, across the table. If, after executing this command, your script executes the command

TypeIn a[3] + " " + a[4] + " " + a[2]

PAL will type in, at the current cursor location, the value in the Mr./Mrs. field, the First Name field, and then the Last Name field (the second, third, and first fields in the record). If your script executes the command

TypeIn a[1]

PAL types in the table name Custlist at the current cursor location.

Later in this chapter, you will see how to use these commands to create GetRecord and PasteRecord keys, to copy or move complete records in your Paradox tables.

Controlling PAL Script Execution

Like all advanced programming languages, PAL contains commands which are used to control when and if other commands within a program (script) execute, as well as commands to control movement through the script, based on criteria determined by the programmer (script writer). In the following sections, you will learn about some of the most powerful of these control commands.

Branching in a PAL Script

When you write a PAL script, you often need to have your script do one of two or more things, depending on the condition of the desktop, the

LEARNING TO USE PAL

existence of Paradox objects, or the value of some expression. This is called *branching*.

A common use of branching is to check for the existence of a file that you want to work on. For example, if you issue the command

View "Custlist"

and there is no table named Custlist.DB, your script will fail. To avoid this, you need to be able to check if Custlist.DB exists and cancel your View command if Custlist does not exist.

The If..Then..EndIf Branch

PAL provides a simple means for making such a test with the If command. The If command has three required keywords, If, Then, and EndIf, and the optional keyword Else. The syntax for the If command is

If *Condition* Then *Command* [Else *Command*] EndIf

The command after the Then statement executes if the condition in the If statement evaluates to True. If the condition in the If statement is False, the Then command is not executed, and the script passes by the EndIf statement to the next statement in the script.

In the syntax examples in this chapter, optional commands and arguments are shown in brackets.

The optional Else statement is used when you want the script to execute a specific command if the If condition is False. For example, the following PAL script, which you could name Viewcust, uses the ISTABLE() function to test for the existence of a table:

If ISTABLE("Custlist") = True Then View "Custlist" Else
Message "The Custlist table not found!" Sleep 3000 EndIf

This script will only find the Custlist table if it is in the current directory.

The script above will work, but it is hard to read, especially if you write an entire page in this format. For purposes of clarity, you should indent and comment your script. Below is the same script, indented two spaces inside the If statement, and indented two spaces each time there is a line with a condition or command. The script in indented style looks like this:

```
If
  ISTABLE("Custlist") = True
  Then
    View "Custlist"
  Else
    Message "The Custlist table not found!"
    Sleep 3000
Endif
```

If you are going to write scripts, you should get into the habit of documenting the scripts. As discussed in Chapter 11, you document a script by placing comments in the script explaining what each line is doing. Below is an example of the same script indented, and documented.

```
If      ;this line begins the If command
  ISTABLE("Custlist") = True
          ;the line above tests for Custlist.DB
  Then    ;lines from here to the Else statement execute
          ;if the If condition is true
    View "Custlist"
          ;this line opens Custlist.DB
  Else    ;lines from here to the Endif statement execute
          ;if the If condition is false
    Message "The Custlist table not found!"
    Sleep 3000
          ;The two lines above place a message
          ;on the screen
          ;telling the user that the Custlist.DB
          ;table was not found and pause operation for
          ;two seconds to allow the user time to
          ;read the message.
Endif     ; This is the end of the If command.
```

There are many possible formats for indenting and documenting scripts. If you do much work in PAL, you should acquaint yourself with the various methods used by programmers and choose one that makes sense to you. In the rest of this chapter, multiple line scripts will be indented for clarity, but will not be commented.

There are several other ways to branch a script in PAL, notably the Switch command, which is very useful when constructing menus; however, we'll stick with the If command in the examples in this chapter.

Looping in a PAL Script

It is often desirable to repeat the execution of a portion of PAL code a specified number of times. The following sections describe the While..EndWhile commands and the related Loop, QuitLoop, Quit, and Exit commands.

The While..EndWhile Loop

The While command has the syntax

> While *Condition* [*Commands*] EndWhile

The most common condition to set for While is (True). This is a special logical condition that is always true. The effect of setting this condition is to loop your script within the While and EndWhile commands indefinitely, until some command within the loop executes to move the script out of the Loop.

Getting Out of the Loop

When your script creates a loop, it is very important that it also create a way to get out of the loop.

The following are the most common commands for breaking out of a loop:

- The QuitLoop command leaves the current loop and takes you to the next highest level in the script, outside the loop.

- The Quit command leaves the current script and takes you back to Paradox or to a higher level script, if one exists. Quit takes an optional expression as an argument. The expression is evaluated as a message after Quit executes.

- The Exit command is the equivalent of choosing Exit from the desktop. Exit leaves the script and shuts Paradox down in the normal manner.

Later in this chapter, you will see how to create a pop-up calculator to find the square of a number by using While and Quit and an If..EndIf statement.

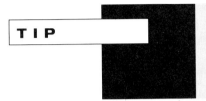

TIP Holding down the Ctrl and Shift key and then pressing the Break key will break out of many script loops, as long as Disable Break is set to No (the default) in the Custom Configuration Program (see Appendix D).

Using the PAL Menu

You were introduced to the PAL menu, accessed by pressing Alt-F10, in Chapter 11. The most common use of the PAL menu is to allow you to record and play back scripts in modes in which these choices are not available from the desktop menu.

However, the PAL menu, shown below, offers much more than the ability to record and play scripts. The following sections describe the options on the PAL menu. Since the PAL menu is available from almost everywhere in Paradox, these features are usually available during your Paradox sessions.

```
┌─PAL Menu──┐
│ Play      │
│ RepeatPlay│
│ BeginRecord│
│ Debug     │
│ Value     │
│ MiniScript│
└───────────┘
```

Playing Back Scripts

The Play choice in the PAL menu operates like the Play option on the Scripts menu. As mentioned in Chapter 11, when you choose to play back a script, you must be sure that you are in the mode expected by the script. This consideration becomes especially important when you use Play from the PAL menu, because the PAL menu allows you to start the script from almost any Paradox mode. The script Squares, described later in this chapter, contains an example of a simple error-checking statement that you can build into your scripts so that they will only try to run in an appropriate Paradox mode.

In addition to being a menu choice, Play is also a PAL command, which can be placed in a script or a miniscript. Uses of the Play command are discussed later in this chapter.

Repeating Script Playback

The RepeatPlay choice in the PAL menu is used exactly like the Script ➤ RepeatPlay choice described in Chapter 11. RepeatPlay allows you to play back a script a specified number of times, or continuously.

Note that when you use the Quit command, described earlier, to terminate a script, RepeatPlay will not operate. This is because the Quit command escapes the loop that Paradox sets up when you choose RepeatPlay.

Beginnning and Ending Script Recording

The BeginRecord and EndRecord commands also operate in the same manner when chosen from the PAL menu as they do when chosen from the Scripts menu, as described in Chapter 11. Choose BeginRecord when you're ready to record your keystrokes; select EndRecord when you want to stop recording.

Remember that even if you start a script from the desktop using Scripts ➤ BeginRecord, you can press Alt-F10 to access the PAL menu from almost anywhere in Paradox and choose EndRecord to end the script.

Debugging Scripts

The Debug choice in the PAL menu gives you access to the PAL Debugger. The Debugger allows you to test and correct a script by stepping through it one instruction at a time. You can also get to the Debugger when something goes wrong with an executing script. If you make an error in PAL command syntax, or if your script finds Paradox or a Paradox object in an unexpected condition, the script will stop executing and you will see the Debugger dialog box with the choices, Cancel and Debug, as shown below.

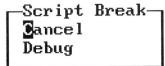

Choosing **C**ancel will end script playback and return you to Paradox. The Paradox desktop will be in the state it was in after the last executed command of the script. Choosing **D**ebug opens the Debugger.

Whether you choose **D**ebug from the PAL menu or the script-error dialog box, you'll see the PAL Debugger window, as shown in Figure 21.4.

FIGURE 21.4

The PAL Debugger window consists of three panes: Script, Watch, and MiniScript.

LEARNING TO USE PAL

The Debugger window, introduced in Paradox 4.5, consists of three panes:

- **Script:** This pane displays multiple lines of the script being debugged. The Debugger window also displays a pointer (the ➤ symbol), showing you the script command that is about to run.
- **Watch:** This pane allows you to see the value of expressions or to track variables defined in the script.
- **MiniScript:** This pane lets you run PAL commands before running the next command in the script. It is the same as the MiniScript option in the PAL menu, described shortly.

> **TIP** Each of the Debugger panes can be resized.

If you write a script and it bombs, chances are that it is because of a syntax error, often a simple typo. The Debugger window is useful because it shows you where the error occurs in the script. In many cases, you can see the typo or syntax error immediately. In addition, Paradox will display an error message, often telling you exactly what the problem is. In Figure 21.4, you can see the message

Missing right quote

In other cases, the error will be caused by a logical inconsistency or by the fact that you are trying to perform an action when Paradox is in the wrong mode or when the required Paradox object (such as a window, table, or form) is not available.

Once you have determined as much as possible from viewing the Debugger window, you have two simple choices:

- Press Ctrl-q from the Debugger window to end script execution and return to Paradox. Paradox will be in the state that it was put in by the last command actually executed by your script.
- Press Ctrl-e from the Debugger window to cancel your script playback and go to the Paradox Editor, with the script that was executing in the editing window. You are taken to the exact point in the script at which it stopped executing.

Pressing Ctrl-q from the Debugger window is useful when you need to look at what your script has done so far, or when you want to perform some operations in Paradox that you have determined are necessary for your script to run properly. For example, if your script stopped because it needed a table that was not in the current directory, you may want to copy that table into the directory.

Pressing Ctrl-e is useful when you have identified the script problem by looking at the Debugger window and want to edit the script. Once you have entered the Paradox Editor, you can edit your script as you would in any editing session. When you save your work and leave the Editor, you are taken back to Paradox, again, in the state it was in when your script stopped executing.

NOTE The Debugger window includes numerous tools for stepping through script execution, setting breakpoints, and performing other debugging. These functions are described in the *PAL Programmer's Guide*. See Appendix B for a description of the new features in the Debugger.

Evaluating Expressions

The Value choice in the PAL menu provides you with a means of quickly determining the value of (evaluating) any valid PAL expression. Value can be used to evaluate mathematical formulas, including those using PAL mathematical, statistical, and financial functions. You enter the expression in the Value dialog box, shown in Figure 21.3, earlier in this chapter. It will return the current value of any PAL function or any assigned variable.

Value can be used as an on-line calculator or in conjunction with PAL functions, at almost anytime during a Paradox session. It displays the results of its calculations in a message area in the lower-right corner of the screen. See the examples of valid PAL expressions presented earlier in this chapter.

Value is also available as a choice in the PAL Debugger, where it is often used to interrogate the current values of variable, array elements, or other PAL expressions.

Creating Miniscripts

The MiniScript choice in the PAL menu accesses the Miniscript window, in which you can write one-line scripts of up to 175 characters, as explained earlier in the chapter. A miniscript is executed when you press ↵ while the cursor is on the miniscript line.

Miniscripts created during a Paradox session are stored in the Miniscript window for the duration of the session. Each time you open the Miniscript window during a session, all miniscripts written during the current session are displayed.

NOTE Use the Esc key, not the F8 key, to close the Miniscript window.

When you open the Miniscript window, your cursor is always positioned on a new line, after any previously executed miniscripts, ready for you to write a new script. At this point, you can do any of the following:

- Double-click on any existing miniscript line or move to a line using the cursor key and press ↵ to execute the miniscript.

- Edit an existing miniscript by moving to any line and pressing the spacebar. As soon as you begin editing, the miniscript is copied to the last line of the window, where you can complete editing and execute the script.

- Use the mouse or press Alt-F10 to close the Miniscript window and return to the PAL menu. Pressing Esc closes the Miniscript window and the Pal menu.

Miniscripts give you command line access to PAL from within Paradox and can be used to produce useful temporary scripts that are available for the duration of a PAL session. As mentioned earlier, miniscripts recorded in a session can be saved to the Minihist script by pressing Alt-F3 when the MiniScript window is open. Miniscripts are also available in the PAL Debugger.

Using PAL Functions for Instant Field Summaries

The following functions return summaries of values in a specified column (field) in a specified table:

CCOUNT()	Count
CSUM()	Sum
CAVERAGE()	Average
CMAX()	Maximum value
CMIN()	Minimum value
CSTD()	Standard deviation
CVAR()	Population variance

The syntax for all these summary functions is the same. For example, the syntax of CAVERAGE() is

CAVERAGE(*TableName,FieldName*)

The *TableName* and *FieldName* arguments must be in quotation marks, as in "Custlist" or "Credit Limit". The field designated must have a numeric, short number, or currency data type. A summary function used on a field with all blank entries returns an error.

You do not need to have the table displayed on the desktop to use PAL summary functions. In fact, you can include the path in the file name and return a summary value from a table in any directory. If you do not include a path, the current directory is assumed.

NOTE The summary functions operate slightly differently than the summary operators used with the reserved word CALC in Query forms. For example, CCOUNT( ) is the equivalent of CALC COUNT ALL in a Query form.

Instant Field Summaries Using Value

You can use the Value option on the PAL menu for field summaries. For example, to display the average credit limit of the customers in the sample Custlist table, press Alt-F10 and choose **Value**. Then enter this expression in the Value dialog box:

The value of the average of customer credit limits will appear as a message in the bottom-right corner of the desktop. This same format can be used with all the summary functions listed above on any numeric field in any table.

Although Value is useful, each time you want to see the summary value, or another one like it, you must type the entire expression again. Value does not save your expression. If you want to use the same expression again, or one like it, use a miniscript instead, as described in the next section.

Instant Field Summaries Using Miniscripts

To get the same results from a miniscript that you get from the Value dialog box, you must place the command Message in front of your summary function expression. To do so, press Alt-F10 and choose **MiniScript**. In the Miniscript window, enter

    Message CAVERAGE("Custlist","Credit Limit")

Then press ↵. The value will be displayed on the desktop.

Two miniscripts are shown in Figure 21.5:

    Message CAVERAGE("Custlist","Credit Limit"
    Message CAVERAGE("c:\\PDOX45\\Customer\\Custlist","Credit Limit")

FIGURE 21.5

Both of these miniscripts accomplish the same task. But the bottom miniscript can be executed from any directory. Note that double backslashes are required in any DOS path included in a PAL statement.

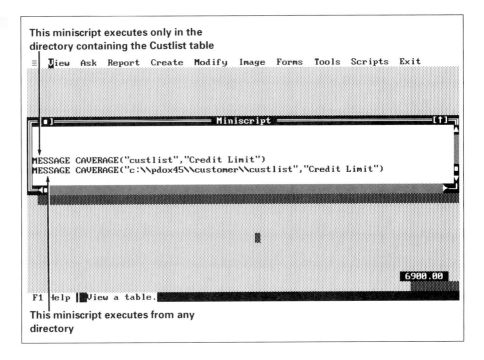

These perform the same average calculation, but the second miniscript can be executed from any directory.

The miniscript remains in the window after execution. You can use it any time during your session, and you can edit it to make similar miniscripts. Figure 21.6 shows several miniscripts based on the original. All of these can be used throughout your session.

Defining Hotkeys

If you write a miniscript that you will want to use often during your session, you can use PAL to assign it to a hotkey. PAL allows you to redefine all the keys on the Paradox keyboard. Each key on the Paradox keyboard has a PAL extended code, which can be used with the SetKey command to redefine the keys. You can use a SetKey command to play back a complicated PAL script, or place all the commands in the miniscript.

FIGURE 21.6

A Query form and Answer table and the miniscript used to return the average value of the credit limits in the Answer table. Each miniscript was created by editing a previous one, and they are all available throughout the session.

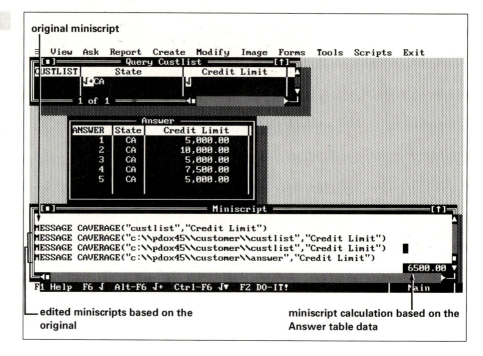

The SetKey command is a natural for the one-line miniscript, since SetKey definitions must be on one line in any script. Although the Instant Script key, Alt-F3, allows you to record keystrokes to create a hotkey, using the PAL command SetKey is much more flexible.

The syntax of SetKey is

   SetKey *KeyCode Commands*

All of the PAL extended key codes are listed in the back of the *PAL Reference* manual.

As an example, the following steps define Alt-h as a hotkey to return the value of a summary function expression:

1. Press Alt-F10 and choose **M**iniScript.

2. Enter the following miniscript (all on one line):

   SetKey –35 Message CAVERAGE("Custlist","Credit Limit") Sleep 3000

NOTE If you already have a similar miniscript, like the ones discussed earlier, move to the similar line and press the spacebar. Then edit it to match this script. The edited miniscript will be placed on the last line in the Miniscript window.

3. Press ↵.
4. Press the Esc key to close the Miniscript window.

Note the Sleep command at the end of this miniscript. As discussed in Chapter 11, this PAL command suspends Paradox for a length of time measured in thousandths of seconds. Without the Sleep command, the hotkey would be defined, but you would never see the value, because it would be cleared from the screen immediately. This Sleep command holds the message on the screen for 3 seconds, which is long enough to read it.

Now pressing the Alt-h key will show you the current average credit of customers in the Custlist table. Note that the hotkey will work only when you are in the directory which contains the Custlist table. If you accidentally use it in any other directory, you'll see the Cancel/Debug choices.

If you want this hotkey to work from any directory, you must include the complete DOS path of the file name in the function argument. In this case, it would be something like

CAVERAGE("C:\\PDOX45\\Customer\\Custlist","Credit Limit")

NOTE Be careful using hotkeys. You can redefine Paradox keys such as F10 or F2 and cause yourself big trouble. To be safe, restrict yourself to the Alt key extended key codes that aren't assigned a function by Paradox.

Creating Multiple Hotkey Macros

You can edit a SetKey miniscript so that the key performs a different task, depending on your needs. Suppose you will be entering a lot of customers into the Custlist table and many of them are from the same city. You can use SetKey and the PAL commands TypeIn and Tab to create miniscripts to make data entry easier.

The TypeIn command simulates typing in text from the keyboard. The TypeIn command uses the syntax

> TypeIn *Expression*

where *Expression* is an alphanumeric string (in quotation marks), the name of a variable holding an alphanumeric string, or an expression converted to alphanumeric type by the STRVAL() function.

The Tab command is the equivalent of pressing the Tab key. It does not take any arguments.

For example, to create multiple data-entry hotkeys for the Custlist table, open a Miniscript window (press Alt-F10 and choose **MiniScript**), then enter the following three miniscripts, pressing ↵ after each one:

```
SetKey -47 TypeIn "Indianapolis" Tab TypeIn "IN" Tab TypeIn "462"
SetKey -48 TypeIn "Chicago" Tab TypeIn "IL" Tab TypeIn "606"
SetKey -49 TypeIn "Washington" Tab TypeIn "DC" TypeIn "200"
```

TIP After you type in the first miniscript, edit it, changing the key code and the city, state, and partial zip code, instead of typing in each entire line.

Press the Esc key to close the Miniscript window. The Alt-v, Alt-b, and Alt-n keys are now hotkeys that will fill in the city, state, and first part of the zip code in *any* table, as long as those fields are in the correct order.

To change the text assigned to one of the hotkeys, just open the Miniscript window and edit the alphanumeric strings (city, state, and zip code) assigned to the key you want to redefine. Then press ↵ to run the edited miniscript.

To cancel a SetKey definition, run a miniscript with just the SetKey command and the key code. For example, the miniscript

   SetKey -47

cancels the hotkey definition in the first miniscript shown above. Use this technique to cancel the redefinition of any key when you have made an error.

Creating GetRecord and PasteRecord Keys

Assigning the CAVERAGE() or another summary function to a hotkey gives you new capabilities in your Paradox sessions, but those capabilities are restricted to the file and fields you use as the function's arguments. You can use other PAL functions to create new Paradox capabilities that you can use with any existing table.

As mentioned earlier in the chapter, the PAL commands CopyToArray and CopyFromArray place the contents of a record in a variable array and retrieve the contents from the array, respectively. The syntax of these commands is

   CopyToArray *ArrayName*
   CopyFromArray *ArrayName*

where *ArrayName* is any valid Paradox variable name.

You don't need to understand anything more about arrays to create a powerful set of new Paradox capabilities. For example, suppose you need to place data in a table with many fields and many of the records have the same data in most of the fields. Or suppose you have a record in one table and you need to place it in another table with the same structure. To accomplish these tasks, you need GetRecord and PasteRecord keys, which Paradox does not have. However, you can use the PAL commands SetKey, CopyToArray, and CopyFromArray to create them.

To make Alt-g a GetRecord key and Alt-p a PasteRecord key, enter the following miniscripts in the Miniscript window, pressing ↵ after each one:

   SetKey –34 CopyToArray a Message "Got it!" Sleep 1000
   SetKey –25 CopyFromArray a

Then press Esc to close the Miniscript window.

Now, in View, Edit, or CoEdit mode, with any table or form on your screen, move to a record and press Alt-g. You'll see the message "Got it!" flash on the screen. You can then move to any other record in the same table or another table with the same structure and, in Edit or CoEdit mode) press Alt-p. The last record that you got will be pasted into the current record.

Your new GetRecord and PasteRecord keys have the following features and restrictions:

- The GetRecord key (Alt-g) must be used on a table, form, or Query form, or you'll be thrown into the Debugger. A table can be in View, Edit, or CoEdit mode.

- The PasteRecord key (Alt-p) must be used on a table, form, or Query form. If a Table view or Form view window is on your screen, it must be in Edit or CoEdit mode, or you'll be placed in the Debugger.

- If you use the PasteRecord key when the cursor is in a record with data, the data will be replaced with data placed in the array the last time you used the GetRecord key.

- Once you have placed the contents of a record in the array using the GetRecord key, you can use the PasteRecord key to place it as many times as you want. The record in the array will remain until you use Alt-g again or end your session.

You can modify the GetRecord and PasteRecord key miniscripts to create other hotkey functions. For example, if you change the Alt-g miniscript to read

SetKey –34 CopyToArray a Del Message "Got it!" Sleep 1000

pressing Alt-g will now get and delete a record in Edit or CoEdit mode. Then you can use Alt-g and Alt-p to automatically move records—getting and deleting with Alt-g and placing with Alt-p.

Changing the Alt-p miniscript to read

SetKey –25 Ins CopyFromArray a

causes the Alt-p key to insert a blank record in which to place the contents of the array. This keeps Alt-p from automatically writing over the contents of the current record.

Loading Hotkeys and Scripts Automatically

So far, all the hotkeys described are temporary, since the contents of the Miniscript window are removed when you end your Paradox session. You can create regular scripts containing the same commands as any of these miniscripts, but you still need to play back the script to use the hotkeys.

As you learned in Chapter 11, the Init script is a script that Paradox automatically looks for and executes upon startup. You can rename any script to Init, and Paradox will execute that script when you open your session. You can use the Play command in the Init script to play other scripts on startup, and you can place SetKey and other commands in the Init script to permanently define key assignments so that they will be in effect whenever you work in Paradox. You can also use the Init script to execute PAL commands, change the way in which Paradox operates, and give you messages about your files and system.

Creating Key Assignment Scripts

By using the PAL branching command If and the SYSMODE() function, you can create more sophisticated versions of the GetRecord and PasteRecord keys described in the previous section. You can then use the Init script to make these keys permanently available in all your Paradox sessions.

The instructions here assume that Paradox starts in the directory containing Paradox.EXE. If you have specified another directory as the startup directory (in the Custom utility), you should perform all the steps in that directory.

Follow these steps to create the scripts for the GetRecord and PasteRecord keys:

1. Choose **T**ools ➤ **M**ore ➤ **D**irectory and change to your Paradox directory containing Paradox.EXE (often C:\PDOX45).

2. Choose **S**cripts ➤ **E**ditor ➤ **N**ew and enter **Getpaste** as the name of the script.

3. Enter the following commands into the editing window (each SetKey command must be on a single line):

   SetKey –34 If SYSMODE() = "Edit" Then CopyToArray a Message "Got It" Sleep 1000 Else Beep EndIf
   SetKey –25 If SYSMODE() = "Edit" Then Ins CopyFromArray a Else Beep EndIf

4. Press F2 or choose **D**O-IT!.

5. Choose **S**cripts ➤ **P**lay and specify Getpaste as the name of the script to play back.

If the Cancel/Debug dialog box appears, press Ctrl-e. In the editing window, fix any typos. When you are finished, save the edited script and play it back again.

The version of the GetRecord and PasteRecord keys created by the Getpaste script works only in Edit mode and does not delete a record if it is copied with Alt-g, because of the If branching and the SYSMODE() check. If you normally work in CoEdit mode, you can change that specification in the SYSMODE() checking part of the script. This version also inserts a new blank record before it pastes the contents of the array.

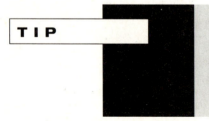

TIP The more you learn about placing error-checking controls in your scripts, the more powerful you can make those scripts. The SYSMODE( ) function goes a long way toward making the hotkeys defined in the sample script behave correctly.

Playing a Script Automatically on Startup

When the Getpaste script is working correctly, you can set up the Init script to automatically play that script on startup. Follow these steps:

1. If you have not done so already, choose **Tools ➤ More ➤ D**irectory and change to your Paradox directory containing Paradox.EXE (usually C:\PDOX45).

2. If you don't have an Init script yet, choose **Scripts ➤ E**ditor ➤ New, then enter Init as the name of the script. If an Init script already exists in your startup directory, choose **Scripts ➤ E**ditor ➤ **O**pen, then enter Init as the name of the script.

3. If you opened an existing Init script, move to the bottom of the script, unless it already contains a SetDir command. If the script contains a SetDir command to set a startup directory, move to the beginning of that line and press ↵ to insert a blank line above the line with the SetDir command, then place the cursor at the beginning of the new blank line.

4. Enter the following commands into the editing window:

    Play "Getpaste"

5. Press F2 or choose **DO-IT!**.

6. Choose **S**cripts ➤ **P**lay and enter Init as the name of the script to play back.

If the Cancel/Debug dialog box appears, press Ctrl-e and edit the script as necessary to fix errors. Then save and play back the script again.

The Getpaste script will now be played every time Paradox is started, and the GetRecord and PasteRecord keys will become, in effect, permanent Paradox features.

Creating Pop-Up Calculators

This section describes the steps for creating on-line calculators using PAL commands and functions. The techniques described work using any

Paradox financial, statistical, and mathematical functions.

Controlling the PAL Canvas

The @, ??, and Accept commands, used in the calculator scripts, let you place text and accept input from the PAL canvas. You may not be aware of the PAL canvas, but you see it often when working with Paradox. Paradox performs many actions behind the scenes, showing you only the results. While the operation is being performed, Paradox hides it from you by taking a picture of the screen and placing it in the foreground. This picture is called the *canvas*. Screen changes during the operation are hidden behind the canvas. When the operation is complete, Paradox removes the canvas and lets you see the results.

Whenever you run a PAL script, the canvas is placed on the screen. You can use PAL to control what is displayed on the canvas.

There are actually three different canvases available in PAL. You can use PAL commands to turn the canvases off and on again, to show or hide operations. The canvas used in this chapter is called the full-screen canvas.

If you run the scripts described in this and the following sections, it will sometimes seem as though text is being written over whatever windows are open on the desktop. When you use the PAL command Clear command, all the open windows disappear from the screen. Don't worry; what you are seeing is not the real desktop or open windows, only the PAL canvas. When the script finishes execution, the canvas will be cleared, and the real desktop will reappear, unchanged. See the chapter on controlling screen display in the *PAL Programmers Guide* for more information about PAL canvases.

> **TIP**
>
> Interactive Paradox hides the desktop from you and shows you a canvas during many operations, especially long queries. You can tell when Paradox is playing this trick on you by the fact that a blinking cursor appears in the upper-left corner of the screen. This is an indication that you are looking at a canvas, not the real Paradox desktop.

Creating the Squares Calculator

First let's start with a basic calculator to figure the square of a number. The script uses the PAL function POW( ) and the PAL commands @, ??, and Accept. The syntax of the POW( ) function is described earlier in the chapter.

The @ command, requires the syntax

    @ *Row, Column*

where *Row* is a row on your PAL canvas and *Column* is a column. The @ command places the cursor at a particular position on the PAL canvas.

The ?? command requires the syntax

    ?? [*ExpressionList*]

where *ExpressionList* is the values of a PAL expression. This command is most often used to put alphanumeric text strings on the PAL canvas.

The Accept command requires the syntax

    Accept *DataType*
    To *VarName*

where *DataType* is the type of data to accept from the user. You specify data types as you do when you're creating or modifying a table structure. If an alphanumeric data type is specified, it must include a length, as in A10.

The *VarName* part of the Accept command places the accepted input in a memory variable location and assigns the name *VarName* to that location. You can then retrieve the input by specifying, or *calling*, the variable name in your script.

The Accept command can include optional value-checking commands, which are equivalent to the first six validity check options available in the ValCheck ► Define menu in Edit mode. See Chapter 5 for more information about the validity checks. The optional value-checking commands are placed immediately after the Accept command's *DataType* argument.

The Picture value-checking command has the syntax

    Picture *Picture*

where *Picture* is a valid Picture format. In the sample calculator scripts, Picture is used as an optional command with Accept.

The Min, Max, and Default value-checking commands have the syntax

> Min *Value*
> Max *Value*
> Default *Value*

where *Value* is a valid value for the designated data type.

The Required value-checking command takes no arguments. It requires an entry (a nonblank value).

Finally, the value-checking command Lookup has the syntax

> Lookup *TableName*

where *TableName* is a valid lookup table.

> **NOTE** See the discussion of special network considerations in the *PAL Reference* manual before using Lookup on a network.

To create a calculator that will calculate the square of a number, follow these steps:

1. If you have not done so already, choose **T**ools ➤ **M**ore ➤ **D**irectory and change to your Paradox directory containing Paradox.EXE.

2. If you don't have an Init script yet, choose **S**cripts ➤ **E**ditor ➤ **N**ew and enter **Squares** as the name of the script.

3. Enter the following commands into the editing window:

   ```
   @10,10
   ?? "Enter a number to be squared: "
   Accept "N"
   Picture "#[#][#][#]{[.][#][#]}"
   To x
   Message "The square of "+STRVAL(x)+" is "+STRVAL(POW(x,2))
   Sleep 5000
   ```

4. Press F2 or choose **DO-IT!**.

5. Choose **S**cripts ➤ **P**lay and specify Squares as the name of the script to play back.

As with the other script examples, if your script won't run, choose **D**ebug when you see the Cancel/Debug dialog box, press Ctrl-e, and make the necessary corrections.

Note that the POW( ) function, which actually performs the calculation, is in the Message expression list. POW( ) is passed the value of the variable x, which was assigned based on the value placed in response to the Accept command.

This script is fine, but if you want to do multiple calculations, you must play back the script for each one. For multiple calculations, you need to add a While..EndWhile loop, as described earlier, to the script. You could (but shouldn't) edit the script so that it looks like this:

```
While (True)
  @10,10
  ?? "Enter a number to be squared: "
  Accept "N"
  Picture "@[@][@][@]{[.][#][#]}"
  To x
  Message "The square of "+STRVAL(x)+" is "+STRVAL(POW(x,2))
EndWhile
```

Note that the Sleep line has been deleted. Since the script does not end after the message is executed, the canvas is not cleared, and the message automatically stays on the screen.

This script will loop back to the beginning and let you do another calculation. But this script has a major problem: it never stops looping. When you create a loop, you must always create a way out of the loop. To end the loop, use the If and Quit commands, described earlier in this chapter. You can edit the script to read:

```
While (True)
  @10,10
  ?? "Enter a number to be squared: "
  Accept "N"
  Picture "@[@][@][@]{[.][#][#]}"
  To x
  Message "The square of "+STRVAL(x)+" is "+STRVAL(POW(x,2))
    If
    x=0
```

```
        Then
            Quit "So long -- Stay Square!"
        Else
        EndIf
    EndWhile
```

The If command after the message checks to see if you entered a zero. If you did, the Quit command is executed and the script ends. If you used any other number but zero, the script continues to the EndWhile command and loops back to the beginning so that you can do another calculation.

As noted earlier, If commands can be *nested*, which means that one can go inside another. In the following version of Squares script, the entire script is inside the Then clause of an If command. The If command checks to see what mode Paradox is in. If the mode is not one specified in the If command, the Then part of the command—the rest of the script—is not executed. Instead, the script issues a Beep and ends. This is the Squares script with a nested If statement:

```
If SYSMODE()="Main" or SYSMODE()="Edit"
Then
   While (True)
     @10,10
     ?? "Enter a number to be squared: "
     Accept "N"
     Picture "@[@][@][@]{[.][#][#]}"
     To x
     Message "The square of "+STRVAL(x)+" is "+STRVAL(POW(x,2))
        If
          x=0
        Then
           Quit "So long -- Stay Square!"
        Else
        EndIf
   EndWhile
Else
   Beep
EndIf
```

This final version of the Squares script does not need the Sleep command, because the While loop keeps the script active. The message remains on the screen until you press a key.

To make the Squares script always available, you can assign it to the Alt-m key by placing a command similar to

SetKey –50 Play "C:\\PDOX45\\Squares"

in your Init script.

Figure 21.7 shows the result of using the Squares script. The result of the calculation appears in the lower-right corner of the desktop. Remember, what you see in the figure is the canvas, not the actual desktop. PAL has taken a picture of the desktop, and displayed the picture of the desktop on the canvas. Then the Squares script has written the calculator input line on the canvas. The desktop is hidden under the canvas, and will be exposed when the script terminates.

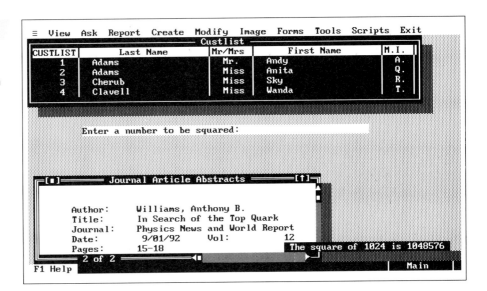

FIGURE 21.7

The Squares script canvas displays an entry line created with the Accept command.

Creating the Loan Payments Calculator

Suppose that you work for a mortgage company and frequently need to figure the payments for an amortized loan. A pop-up calculator that can calculate loan payments would make your work much easier.

A variation of the steps used to create the Squares script can be used to create a loan payment calculator. The script for this calculator uses the Clear command to clear the canvas and the function PMT( ) to do the

LEARNING TO USE PAL

actual calculation. The syntax of the PMT( ) function is described earlier in this chapter.

The syntax of Clear is

   Clear [EOL] [EOS]

Clear will normally clear the entire canvas. The optional parameter EOL causes Clear to clear the canvas from the position of the cursor to the end of the line. The optional parameter EOS causes Clear to clear a rectangle of the canvas across and down from the cursor position to the end of the screen.

NOTE Remember, it is the canvas that is being cleared; any images on the desktop are unaffected and will reappear when you exit the script.

The major difference between the Payments script for loan payments calculator and the final version of the Squares script (in the previous section) is that Payments executes three Accept statements to get the values needed for the three PMT( ) function arguments. These values are then sent to three variable locations: x, y, and z. The script sends the responses to three different variables. The values at the variable locations are then passed to the PMT( ) function, which calculates and returns the value of the payment. The result is displayed in the message sent to the canvas.

Use the following steps to create the Payments script for the loan payment calculator:

1. Choose **T**ools ➤ **M**ore ➤ **D**irectory and change to your Paradox directory containing Paradox.EXE.

2. Choose **S**cripts ➤ **E**ditor ➤ **N**ew and enter Payments as the name of the script.

3. Enter the commands shown in Figure 21.8 into the editing window.

4. Press F2 or choose **DO-IT!**.

5. Choose **S**cripts ➤ **P**lay and enter Payments as the name of the script to play back.

FIGURE 21.8

The Payments script for the loan payment calculator

```
        If
~MSSYSMODE()="Main" or SYSMODE()="Edit" or
SYSMODE()="Report"
        Then
          While (True)
            Clear
            @10,10
            ?? "Enter the loan amount(no dollar signs or
punctuation): "
            Accept "N"
            Picture "[#][#][#][#][#][#][#]"
            To x
            Clear
            @09,10
            ?? "Enter the rate PER PAYMENT PERIOD - enter the
decimal"
            @10,10
            ?? "(Example: .01 rate for monthly payment on 12% a
year: "
            Accept "N"
            Picture ".[#][#][#][#]"
            To y
            Clear
            @10,10
            ?? "Enter a number of payment periods: "
            Accept "N"
            Picture "[#][#][#][#]"
            To z
            Message "The amortized loan payment per period is:
"+STRVAL(PMT(x,y,z))
              If
                x=0
              Then
                 Quit "Tell them about our new low interest car
loans!"
              Else
              EndIf
          EndWhile
        Else
          Beep
        EndIf
```

If the script doesn't run, choose **D**ebug, press Ctrl-e, and make corrections as necessary.

Figure 21.9 shows how the loan payments calculator appears on the screen. PAL placed the same canvas over the desktop as it did with the Squares script, but the Payments script used the Clear command to clear the picture of the desktop and wrote the input line on a blank canvas. The desktop is hidden under the canvas, just as in Figure 21.9, and will be exposed when the script terminates. Figure 21.10 shows the restored desktop after the Payments script finishes. Note the Payments script Quit message displayed at the bottom of the desktop.

FIGURE 21.9

The PAL canvas of the hidden desktop has been cleared by the Payments script. It displays the loan payment calculator entry line (created with the Accept command) on a blank PAL canvas.

```
Enter a the loan amount(no dollar signs or commas):




                          The amortized loan payment per period is: 2224.444768490
```

FIGURE 21.10

The restored Paradox desktop after the Payments script has terminated. The Payments script's Quit command has written an exit message to the desktop.

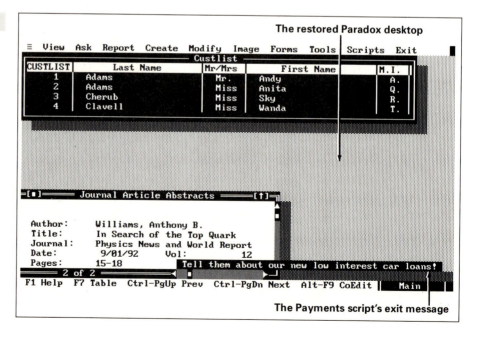

The restored Paradox desktop

The Payments script's exit message

Note that the PMT( ) function and its arguments in the message line are placed inside the STRVAL( ) function. This is because the PMT( ) function returns a numeric value and the Message command requires alphanumeric values. The STRVAL( ) function converts the numeric value returned by PMT( ).

Nested functions are evaluated by PAL from the inside out. The function STRVAL(PMT(x,y,z)) is evaluated as follows:

1. The values at the memory locations assigned to the variable names x, y, and z are substituted in the PMT( ) function for the variable names.

2. The PMT( ) function is executed, returning the loan payment value as a number.

3. The numeric value is passed to the STRVAL( ) function, which converts it to alphanumeric data type.

To make the Payments calculator a permanent feature of your Paradox sessions, assigned to the Alt-h hey, enter a line similar to the following one in the Init script in your startup directory:

SetKey –35 Play "C:\\PDOX45\\Payments"

You do not need to keep all the scripts called by Init in the directory containing Paradox.EXE. You can place them in other directories, as long as the Play command argument includes the path to the called script.

Creating New Paradox Menu Choices

The previous sections describe various ways to create and call PAL scripts. In version 4.5, Paradox adds a built-in facility called Paradox.ADD, which allows you to add menu choices based on PAL scripts.

About Paradox.ADD

Paradox.ADD is a semihidden text file, which is accessed through the Mini-editor available via the System menu (≡) or by pressing Alt-e. By "semihidden," we mean that it doesn't show up in the Mini-editor file list, even though it is a regular text file. However, it does appear in a DOS directory listing. If you are in the Paradox directory containing Paradox.EXE and type Paradox.ADD as the file name in the Mini-editor dialog box, the Paradox.ADD file will open.

Paradox.ADD works differently than any other file that you can use with Paradox. The first part of the file is a short tutorial on how to use Paradox.ADD. At the end are two predefined definitions of Paradox add-ins. These definitions create the menu choices **C**ustom and **W**orkshop in the ≡ ▶ **U**tilities menu.

With Paradox.ADD you can do the following:

- Add up to 14 menu choices to the ≡ ▶ **U**tilities menu. If you delete the **C**ustom and **W**orkshop definitions, you can have 16 user-defined menu choices available under the ≡ ▶ **U**tilities menu.

- Place lines in the ≡ ▶ **U**tilities menu to separate menu choices (be aware, however, that each line takes up an available menu choice).

- Add one menu choice each to the **F**orm and **R**eport menus available on the main desktop menu bar.

NOTE If the Paradox add-in SQL Link is installed, Paradox reserves the first two ≡ ▶ Utilities menu choices for SQLSetup and UseSQL. In addition, if you specify any custom menu items, and SQL Link is installed, Paradox reserves one more menu choice for a separator line. See Appendix C for more information about SQL Link.

The add-ins that are defined in the Paradox.ADD file are specified using four specifiers, referred to as *tokens*:

- The location of the add-in in the menu system: UTILITY, FORM, or REPORT

- The menu choice
- The menu prompt
- The name of the script to execute when the user selects this menu choice

Any script can be designated as an add-in in Paradox.ADD. When designating the script name, you cannot include the script file DOS extension or a path. Paradox will search for any script designated as an extension in Paradox.ADD by searching four ways, in this order:

1. The current directory
2. The Paradox directory containing Paradox.EXE
3. The Paradox startup directory
4. Any directories specified in your DOS PATH command (usually located in your Autoexec.BAT file)

The Paradox.ADD file acts like a script file in that blank lines and any text on a line preceded by a semicolon (;) are ignored. However, the four tokens in Paradox.ADD follow unique rules:

- The script name designated as an add-in does not require (or accept) the PAL Play command and should not be surrounded by quotation marks.
- Tokens are delimited by the vertical line character (|). On most keyboards, | is entered by pressing Shift-backslash.
- Lines with errors or extra lines are simply ignored. For example, if you specify two Report or two Form menu add-ins, the second one will be ignored.
- Each menu add-in must be specified on one line.

Many third-party companies make add-in products for Paradox. You can purchase enhanced report and form designers, statistical products, programming tools, and so on. Paradox.ADD allows you to specify the script that loads such a third-party add-in, so that it becomes a Paradox menu choice. But, you are not restricted to that use. You can add your own scripts, as described in the following section.

Adding Options to Menus

As an example, suppose that your day-to-day work requires the following tasks:

- You run a phone list update report every morning using custom report 1 from the Custlist table.
- You update the customer list information several times a day using custom form 1 in the Custlist table.
- You often need to stop working on your Paradox table and type a letter, or do other work in WordPerfect 5.1.
- Several times a day, you answer questions about how much a mortgage payment would be for a given size loan, at a given percentage, over a given payment period.

Paradox.ADD can come to your rescue.

First, use **Scripts** ➤ **Editor** ➤ **New** to create three short scripts in the directory containing the Paradox.EXE file (the working directory you set with the SetDir command might differ).

Name the first script **Custlst1** and enter the commands

```
SetDir "C:\\PDOX45\\Customer"
Edit "Custlist"
Pickform 1
```

Name the next script **Custlst2** and enter the commands

```
SetDir "C:\\PDOX45\\Customer"
Report "Custlist" 1
```

Finally, name the third script **Wordperf** and type the command

```
Run "C:\\WP51\\Wp.EXE"
```

After creating and saving each of these scripts, and assuming you had already created the Payments script described earlier in this chapter, you can automate all your work by following these steps:

1. If you are not already in the directory containing your Paradox.EXE file, use **Tools** ➤ **More** ➤ **Directory** to change the working directory to that directory.

CREATING NEW PARADOX MENU CHOICES

2. Open the Paradox Mini-editor dialog box by choosing ≡ ➤ **Editor** ➤ **O**pen or by pressing Alt-e and choosing **O**pen.

3. Enter the file name Paradox.ADD.

4. Move down in the Paradox.ADD file until you see the two lines below:

   UTILITY ¦ Custom ¦ Customize Paradox configuration. ¦ CUSTOM
   UTILITY ¦ Workshop ¦ Run the Paradox Application Workshop. ¦ WSSTART

5. Edit the file to add the four new lines shown below above the two lines shown in step 4. The last six lines of your file should look like this (they are six separate lines in the file):

   FORM ¦ Edit Custlist ¦ Edit the Custlist with custom form ¦ CUSTLST1
   REPORT ¦ Phone Report ¦ Customer list phone update ¦ CUSTLST2
   UTILITY ¦ WordPerfect ¦ Run WordPerfect 5.1 ¦ WORDPERF
   UTILITY ¦ Payments ¦ Runs the amortized payments calculator ¦ PAYMENTS
   UTILITY ¦ Custom ¦ Customize Paradox configuration. ¦ CUSTOM
   UTILITY ¦ Run Workshop ¦ Run the Paradox Application Work shop. ¦ WSSTART

6. When the last six lines look like the ones above, save Paradox.ADD using the F2 key or by choosing **DO-IT!** from the Mini-editor menu.

7. In order for your changes to Paradox.ADD to take effect, you must end you Paradox session by choosing **Exit** ➤ **Y**es from the desktop main menu.

When you open Paradox again you will have four new menu commands:

- Form ➤ Edit Custlist, as shown below, which will open the Custlist table in editing mode, using custom form 1.

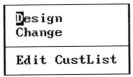

- **R**eport ▶ **P**hone Report, as shown below, which will print the Custlist report 1 custom report.

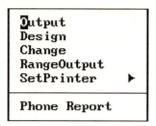

- ≡ ▶ **U**tilities ▶ **W**ordPerfect, which will run WordPerfect 5.1 and take you back to Paradox when you finish your WordPerfect editing session.

- ≡ ▶ **U**tilities ▶ **P**ayments, which will run the loan payment calculator created by the Payments script. The two new commands on the System menu are shown below.

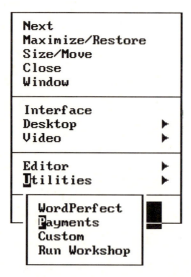

Each of these new menu choices will be available in any working directory because you placed the scripts called by Paradox.ADD in the directory with the Paradox.EXE file, and you set the working directory to the directory in which the required tables, reports, and forms reside. There are other ways to ensure that the scripts called by a Paradox.ADD add-in menu selection will work, but this is the most reliable method.

Summary

The PAL commands and functions covered in this chapter, used in conjunction with the PAL menu options (such as Value and MiniScript), the Init script, the Paradox.ADD file, and the utility object facilities of Workshop, offer many ways to enhance the value of Paradox in your system. Here's a review of the important points covered:

- You can write PAL scripts using PAL commands, functions, variables, arrays, branching, and looping.
- You can use miniscripts to redefine the Paradox keyboard and to assign hotkeys to run PAL scripts.
- You can use the Init script as a launching pad for hotkey assignment and script playing.
- You can write to, receive messages from, and clear the PAL full-screen canvas.
- You can use Paradox.ADD to create new Paradox menu options in the ≡ ➤ Utilities, Form, and Report menus.

Installing Paradox

YOU need only install Paradox once, not each time you wish to use it. If Paradox is already installed on your computer, you can skip this appendix and go right to Chapter 1. See Appendix C for information about network and SQL installation.

Single-User Hardware Requirements

Your hardware must meet or exceed the following minimum requirements to install Paradox on a single-user system:

- An IBM-compatible computer with an 80286, 80386, or 80486 microprocessor

Unlike Paradox 3.5, which could run in real or protected mode, Paradox 4.x and above runs *only* in protected mode. Versions above 3.5 do not run on 8086 or 8088 computers such as IBM XTs.

- A hard disk with at least 5Mb storage space available, 10Mb if you want to install the optional software
- At least one floppy drive
- DOS 3.0 or higher

- 2Mb RAM (640K conventional memory plus extended memory); 4Mb is recommended (you need 4Mb RAM to run Paradox for DOS under Windows)
- Compatible MDA, MCGA, CGA, EGA, or VGA monitor, with adapter (for displaying graphs, you need a compatible MCGA, CGA, EGA, VGA, 8514, 3270, ATT, Tandy T1000, or Hercules monitor with adapter)
- Free disk space at least three times the size of your largest table to process complex queries

You may also use any of the following pointing devices (or any other pointing devices that are 100 percent compatible):

- Microsoft bus or serial mouse
- Logitech bus or serial mouse
- IBM PS/2 mouse

Installing Paradox

To install Paradox on a single-user computer, start at the DOS command prompt (usually C:\>) and follow these steps:

1. At the DOS command prompt, switch to the hard drive that you want to install Paradox on. For example, to install Paradox onto drive C, type **C:** and press ↵.

In earlier versions of Paradox, you were asked to enter your serial number. Paradox 4.5 does not ask for a serial number during the installation process.

2. Place Paradox Installation Disk 1 into a floppy drive and close the drive door.

INSTALLING PARADOX

3. If you inserted the disk into your A drive, type **A:INSTALL** and press ↵. If you inserted the disk into drive B, type **B:INSTALL** and press ↵. You'll see an opening screen that briefly summarizes the installation procedure.

4. Press ↵ to continue the installation.

5. When prompted, type in the letter of the source drive that you'll be installing from: **A** for drive A, or **B** for drive B. Then press ↵ to continue.

6. If Standalone Installation isn't already highlighted, press the ↑ or ↓ key to highlight it.

7. Press the Do-It! key, F2, to proceed. You'll see a dialog box requesting signature information. Here's how to fill in the dialog box:

    - Press ↵, type your name, then press ↵ again.
    - Press Tab to move the highlight to the Company name field. Press ↵ and type your company name, then press ↵ again. If you try to leave this field blank, Paradox will insist that you enter a company name. If you don't have a company name, a period will do.
    - Press ↓ to move to the Country Group option. If you want to use date and number formats for a country other than the United States, press ↵, move the highlight to the country of your choice, then press ↵ again.
    - Press ↓ to move to the Sort Order option. This option affects how information in tables will be alphabetized later. The ASCII order sorts capital letters before lowercase letters. The Dictionary order sorts without regard to capitalization. Dictionary is the more common sorting technique. Pressing ↵ toggles you between ASCII and Dictionary sort order.
    - Check to make sure all your entries are correct. To change any entry, use the arrow keys to move the highlight to the option you want to change, press ↵, type or select your new entry, then press ↵.

8. When you're satisfied with your entries, press the Do-It! key, F2.

9. If your current CONFIG.SYS file does not provide for adequate file handles and buffers, you'll see a message telling you so. Press ↵ to proceed, then press F2 to choose Modify config.sys.

NOTE The CONFIG.SYS file is read when you start up or reboot your computer. It tells DOS how to configure your hardware.

10. The next dialog box asks where you want to install Paradox, and whether or not to install various optional files. By default, the dialog box suggests a directory named C:\PDOX45 on drive C. If you want to change that entry, press ↵, type the drive and directory where you want to install Paradox, then press ↵ again.

11. If you don't want to install sample tables and applications, use the ↑ and ↓ keys to highlight whatever options describe the files you *don't* want to install. Then press ↵ to toggle Yes to No.

12. When you've filled in the dialog box to your satisfaction, press F2 to begin copying the Paradox files to your hard disk.

13. As installation progresses, watch for instructions on the screen telling you when to insert a different disk. When instructed, replace the disk that's currently in drive A or B with the disk indicated in the instructions, then press ↵ (or any letter key) to proceed.

NOTE If you accidentally put in the wrong disk, the installation program will display an error message informing you of the problem. To continue, press Esc to clear the message from the screen, insert the correct disk, and then press any key.

When the installation is complete, you'll see a message telling you that Paradox has been successfully installed. If Install needed to modify your CONFIG.SYS file, you'll see some additional instructions asking you to reboot your computer. Be sure to remove any disks from the floppy drives before you press Ctrl-Alt-Del (or turn the computer off, then back on) to reboot.

If Paradox was not successfully installed, you'll see a message telling you why the installation failed and what to do to correct the problem.

INSTALLING PARADOX

After you install Paradox, you'll need to switch to the Paradox directory (using the DOS CD command) prior to starting Paradox. If you want to be able to start Paradox from any drive and directory, you need to add its directory name to the PATH statement in your AUTOEXEC.BAT file. (If you add the Paradox directory to the path, you don't need to add the Workshop directory.) For information about the AUTOEXEC.BAT file and the PATH command, refer to your DOS documentation.

TIP Additional information about configuring Paradox 4.5 to run on your computer is included in the documentation that comes with the Paradox 4.5 package. Also, for late-breaking news on this topic, and current compatibility with other products such as DESQView and Windows 3.x, see the README file in your Paradox directory.

Installing Workshop and Sample Files

Like Paradox itself, Workshop and any sample applications provided with Paradox must be installed on your computer before you can use them. Normally, these components are installed automatically when you install Paradox for the first time. If you opted not to install these optional files, you can do so at any time by following these steps:

1. Follow steps 1 through 5 in the previous section to run the Paradox installation program.
2. Select Optional Software Installation when the menu with that option appears.
3. Highlight whichever option describes the files that you want to install, If the word No is displayed, press ↵ to toggle from No to Yes.
4. When the options are as you wish, press F2.

As during the initial installation, you'll be prompted to switch disks when necessary.

NOTE Workshop was named the Paradox Personal Programmer in previous versions of Paradox.

Running Paradox 4.5 under Windows 3 or 3.1

You can run Paradox 4.5 as a non-Windows application under Windows 3 or 3.1, provided you have at least 4Mb of RAM. First you need to install Paradox, as described previously. Then you need to install a program icon for starting Paradox from the Windows Program Manager. Here are the basic steps for doing so, assuming you're using Windows 3.1:

1. Run Windows in the usual manner on your computer (usually by typing **WIN** and pressing ↵).

2. If you installed Paradox in C:\PDOX45, skip to step 7. Otherwise, open the Main group (or Accessories group in Windows 3.0), and double-click the PIF Editor icon.

3. Choose **F**ile ➤ **O**pen and work your way to the drive and directory that you stored Paradox in. When you get to that directory, double-click on the PDOXDOS.PIF file name.

4. In the Program Filename and Start-up Directory boxes of the PIF Editor dialog box, change C:\PDOX45 to the drive and directory in which you stored Paradox. Be sure to make the same change to both text boxes.

INSTALLING PARADOX

NOTE As an alternative to these steps, you can "drag and drop" PDOXDOS.PIF from the Paradox directory into any program group. See your Windows 3.1 documentation for more information about PIF files.

5. Choose File ➤ Exit, then Yes, when asked about saving your changes.

6. Close the Main group, either by double-clicking its Control box, or by pressing Ctrl-F4.

7. If you want to add the icon for starting Paradox for DOS to an existing program group, such as the Non-Windows Applications group, double-click that group icon to open it. Then skip to step 11.

8. If you want to create a new group for Paradox for DOS, choose File ➤ New.

9. Choose Program Group, then choose OK.

10. Type a Description, such as **Paradox for DOS**, then choose OK.

11. Choose File ➤ New.

12. Choose Program Item, then choose OK.

13. Enter a description in the Description box, such as **Paradox for DOS**, then press Tab.

14. In the Command Line box, type the path to your Paradox program, followed by the file name PDOXDOS.PIF. For example, if you stored Paradox in C:\PDOX45, type

    C:\PDOX45\PDOXDOS.PIF

15. You can specify a shortcut key if you wish.

16. If you want to change the icon, choose Change Icon. (If you see a message indicating that no icon is available, just choose OK.)

17. Choose any of the available icons from the Change Icon dialog box. Or, in the File Name box, type the path to your Paradox program followed by the icon file name PDOXDOS.ICO (such as **C:\PDOX45\PDOXDOS.ICO**).

18. Choose OK until you get back to the Program Manager.

You can run Paradox for DOS from the Windows Program Manager at any time by double-clicking its icon. Keep in mind, however, that Paradox for DOS is a *DOS* application. You can use Ctrl-Esc to switch between applications, as well as the cut-and-paste techniques for non-Windows applications. However, you won't have access to all the Windows capabilities, such as OLE (Object Linking and Embedding), DDE (Dynamic Data Exchange), and other features that only Windows applications can provide.

NOTE For more information about running DOS applications with Windows, see your Windows documentation.

How Paradox 4.5 Manages Memory

For those of you who are more technically inclined and concerned with such matters, we should point out that unlike version 3.5 of Paradox, Paradox versions 4.0 and above *require* extended memory. So you cannot run Paradox 4.5 on an 8088 or 8086 machine, and there is no Tune option as there was in earlier versions to choose between real and protected modes of operation.

Paradox 4.5 uses the DOS Protected Mode Interface (DPMI) memory protocol used by Windows 3. Thus, it uses extended memory in the same way that Windows applications do in 386 enhanced mode.

Compatibility Issues

Paradox 4.5 is compatible with any extended memory driver that is compatible with Windows 3, including HIMEM, QEMM version 7.01 and higher, and 386MAX versions 5.1 and higher. The following conditions, however, might cause memory conflicts that prevent Paradox from running:

- If your system is using shadow RAM, you need at least 1.5Mb of RAM to run Paradox in protected mode. Consult the documentation for your computer to find out if it's using shadow RAM.

- An incompatible memory manager may be in use. For example, if you have used a device driver to convert all extended memory to expanded memory, Paradox won't have any extended memory to work with.

- If you have an 80286 computer with expanded memory only, you can't run in protected mode and, therefore, can't run Paradox. Check the documentation for your memory board to see if you can reconfigure the expanded memory to extended memory.

- Paradox won't run under Windows 3 if you use the File ➤ Run options from the Program Manager menu, or you fail to use the correct \PDOX45\PDOXDOS.PIF file when installing the Paradox program icon. Be sure to follow the instructions given earlier in the section about running Paradox under Windows 3 or 3.1 to avoid such problems.

- If you are using version 7.01 of QEMM with the QDPMI.SYS to manage DPMI memory, the default installation value of the QEMM device driver may cause problems loading Paradox. Paradox will load correctly if you remove the QEMM QDPMI.SYS. Or you can consult the QEMM documentation to reset the driver defaults.

Paradox Command-Line Configuration

You can type in certain settings at the DOS command prompt to override the defaults for the current session only. These options are sometimes used by advanced programmers to gain more control over how Paradox behaves in a given situation.

Command-line options always begin with a space and hyphen, followed by a command, and they are always placed to the right of the command

PARADOX COMMAND-LINE CONFIGURATION

used to start Paradox from the DOS command prompt. You can type them in uppercase or lowercase (or any combination). For example, entering the command

PARADOX -SPACE

at the DOS command prompt starts Paradox and displays an informational message about memory allocation in the lower-right portion of the screen.

NOTE If you mistype a command-line option, you'll see a message that the option is not a valid command-line argument, and Paradox will not start. Simply retype the command line correctly.

You can combine these options as well. For example, the command

PARADOX -B&W -SPACE

starts Paradox, sets the colors to black and white, and displays the informational memory message.

Some command-line options, such as -MOUSE and most of the options that allocate memory, require you to type a space followed by a *parameter* after the option. For example, to tell Paradox that you are using a left-handed mouse (which reverses the operation of the left and right mouse buttons), use this command to start the program:

PARADOX -MOUSE REVERSE

Keep in mind that the command-line options are in effect for the current Paradox session only. You can use the Custom Configuration Program (CCP) within Paradox to permanently change many of the settings discussed in the following sections. Note, however, that typing a command-line option will override the corresponding setting in the CCP. For example, even if you've changed the CCP settings to tell Paradox that your computer has a color monitor, you can temporarily change the screen display to black-and-white by typing PARADOX -B&W at the DOS command line.

INSTALLING PARADOX

See Appendix D for information about the Custom Configuration Program.

Video Options

Four video options are available for informing Paradox about your monitor and adapter. These are useful, for example, if you're temporarily using a different monitor, you have two different monitors, or you want to change the appearance of Paradox on the monitor you normally use. The options are:

-B&W Tells Paradox that you're using a monochrome or black-and-white monitor with a color graphics adapter (CGA, EGA, or VGA), or that you want to run Paradox in black and white.

-COLOR Notifies Paradox that you're using a color adapter and monitor (CGA, EGA, or VGA).

-MONO Tells Paradox that you're using a monochrome monitor with a monochrome adapter.

-SNOW If you're using an IBM CGA adapter and see snow (random white dots that appear in bursts) on the screen when its contents are altered, use this option to clear the snow. You can combine -SNOW with another video option if you wish (as in PARADOX -COLOR -SNOW).

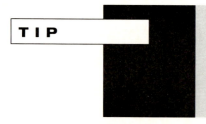

If you're using a DOS-compatible machine (as opposed to an actual DOS machine) and the text cursor appears to be tracking improperly or otherwise misbehaving, try using the -BIOS option, described later, to correct the problem.

Memory Options

The memory options give you finer control over how Paradox allocates memory for a variety of tasks. But keep in mind that Paradox normally chooses the optimal memory allocation settings for your computer, whether you're using DOS or Windows, so you'll seldom need to change them. Programmers sometimes adjust these settings when working with extensive queries or sorts, very large tables, or huge PAL applications. If you're not an experienced programmer, or are not familiar with protected mode memory and such, you really need not be concerned about any of these command-line switches. Paradox will run just fine on your computer without any of them.

CAUTION: Changing memory options is best left to someone with an in-depth understanding of Paradox and DOS memory management, because incorrect settings can do more harm than good. You can, however, use the -SPACE option at any time without causing problems.

With the exception of the -SPACE option, all the memory command-line options require a parameter that specifies the amount of memory to allocate, in kilobytes. For example, to set the cache to 64K, type the command

    PARADOX -CACHEK 64

If you are using a hard disk cache program, such as SMARTDRV.SYS or PC-KWIK, you will get the best performance if you set the Paradox cache to zero, with the command

    PARADOX -CACHEK 0

To set expanded memory to 1Mb, type the command

    PARADOX -EMK 1024

INSTALLING PARADOX

Here are the memory allocation options:

-SPACE — Typing the command line PARADOX -SPACE displays a memory allocation report at the lower-right portion of the Paradox desktop. The report includes total memory before allocating space for table buffers, size of the table buffers, maximum swap memory available for queries and sorts, remaining memory for table buffers, and the total codepool. (All amounts are in kilobytes.) The report disappears when you press a key or click the mouse button.

-CACHEK — Overrides the size of the cache for PAL scripts, PAL libraries, forms, and reports (not tables or memo fields). The maximum cache amount is 200K.

-CODEPOOL — Overrides the default codepool memory allocation for user-interface commands and other commands that don't access data.

-EMK — Restricts the amount of expanded memory that Paradox can use. Normally Paradox uses all of the available expanded memory, unless it's running under a DPMI server, such as Microsoft Windows 3.x, that virtualizes memory. In a DPMI environment, Paradox uses no expanded memory, unless you have a physically separate expanded card and driver, such as AST Rampage.

-EXTK — Restricts the amount of extended memory that Paradox can use. Normally, Paradox uses all of the available extended memory, unless it's running under a DPMI server (see -EMK above). In a DPMI environment, Paradox uses the maximum amount of extended memory available.

PARADOX COMMAND-LINE CONFIGURATION

-NOREALHEAP — Paradox uses very little of the conventional memory in the first 640K RAM, since it runs in protected mode. However, if you have lots of extended memory, and need to reserve all of the 640K RAM for DOS programs such as large TSRs (terminate-and-stay-resident programs), type PARADOX -NOREALHEAP at the command line.

-STACK — If you ever get a resource error indicating a lack of stack space, you can increase the default stack allocation of 12K with this option. For example, type PARADOX -STACK 32 to increase the stack to 32K. The stack setting can be between 8 (8K) and 64 (64K).

-TABLEK — A buffer is temporary storage that Paradox allocates and maintains dynamically to speed up input and output from tables and indexes. Normally the table's block size determines the table buffer size. The default minimum buffer size is 24K, but you can use the -TABLEK option to increase this. The smallest allowable allocation is 24K; the largest depends on the amount of memory in the machine. In Paradox 4.x (unlike Paradox 3.5), you use -TABLEK, not -CACHEK, to speed up table data access.

NOTE In general, larger buffer sizes improve performance for operations involving multiple table images. Smaller buffer sizes can speed up applications that do little table access, but allocate many PAL variables and sometimes get resource errors. Once a buffer is allocated, Paradox cannot reuse this memory. Thus, a smaller minimum size can tie up less memory. Remember, Paradox can always allocate a larger buffer than the minimum, but never a smaller one.

Mouse Option

The -MOUSE option lets you tell Paradox how to interact with your mouse. This option has three parameters: ON, OFF, and REVERSE, which are described below:

-MOUSE OFF	Tells Paradox that you're not using a mouse.
-MOUSE ON	Tells Paradox that you're using the normal right-handed mouse, where pressing the left mouse button makes a selection.
-MOUSE REVERSE	Tells Paradox that you're using a left-handed mouse, where pressing the right mouse button makes a selection.

Share Option

The -SHARE option tells Paradox to emulate network operation on a single machine, so you can take advantage of some network features, such as table protection, or use multitasking to emulate a network. For example, you should use this option if you plan to run more than one application to access the same Paradox tables under Windows.

NOTE You can actually run more than one instance of Paradox under Windows.

Query Options

Paradox's two query options let you control the order of fields in the Answer table following a query, as follows:

-TABLEORDER	Displays fields in the Answer table in the same order that they appear in the tables on which the query is based. (This is the initial default setting.)

-IMAGEORDER   Displays fields in the Answer table in the same order that they appear in Query forms.

BIOS Option

The -BIOS option tells Paradox that you're using a DOS- compatible machine, as opposed to an actual DOS machine. Try this option if your cursor doesn't seem to be tracking properly.

Compatibility Mode Options

The compatibility mode options are:

-COMPFILE   Tells Paradox to create and restructure tables in compatible (Paradox 3.5) file format, instead of the normal Paradox 4.5 format.

-COMPMODE   Starts Paradox in Full Screen mode instead of standard Paradox 4.5 mode (see Appendix B for a description of the new Full Screen User Interface).

Using Command-Line Options in a Batch File

If you discover that you're using a particular set of command-line options frequently, but don't want to (or can't) change the settings in Paradox's CCP, you can use a batch file to save some typing. For example, let's assume you've added C:\PDOX45 to your PATH statement (as described earlier) and that you're tired of typing PARADOX -B&W - SPACE every time you want to start Paradox with the monochrome monitor and memory message options. A batch file offers the perfect solution.

Using an ASCII (DOS) text editor, you could create the following batch file, named PDOX.BAT, in any directory that's included in your current

DOS PATH statement:

    PARADOX -B&W - SPACE

After saving the batch file, you can simply type PDOX and press ⏎ to start Paradox with the appropriate options.

Of course, your batch file can contain other commands as well. For example, adding a command line such as

    CD \PDOX45\SAMPLES

to the beginning of the batch file would change the working directory before starting Paradox. But this would only work if (1) the Paradox directory is included in the current DOS PATH statement, and (2) you did not set a different working directory in the CCP.

> **NOTE** See your DOS manual for more information about the PATH statement and creating batch files.

Using Command-Line Options in Windows 3 or 3.1

If you want to use command-line parameters when running Paradox under Windows, you must use the Windows PIF Editor to modify the \PDOX45\PDOXDOS.PIF file. While the details of using the PIF editor are best left to your Windows manual, the general steps are listed here:

1. From Windows, start the PIF Editor by double-clicking it.
2. Choose **F**ile ➤ **O**pen from the PIF Editor menu.
3. Work your way to the drive and directory that Paradox is installed in.
4. Double-click PDOXDOS.PIF in the File name list box.
5. Type the appropriate command-line options into the Optional Parameters text box. For example, type -B&W -SPACE to add the monochrome and memory allocation message options.

NOTE When entering command-line options into the Optional Parameters box, do not type the word *Paradox*. Just start with the hyphen that precedes the first option.

   6. Choose **File** ➤ **Exit** from the PIF Editor menu, then choose **Yes** when asked if you want to save the current changes.

The next time you start Paradox from Windows, your command-line options will take effect.

You may want to periodically make changes in the Display Usage setting in the PDOXDOS.PIF. The default setting is to open Paradox 4.5 in a DOS window. If you want Paradox to open full screen in Microsoft Windows, select the Full Screen radio button.

Autoexecuting Scripts at Startup

You can also pass a script name to Paradox from the command line or the Optional Parameters text box in the Windows PIF Editor, to autoexecute a script when Paradox first starts. At the command line, follow the command PARADOX with a blank space, then the path and name of the script.

NOTE Unlike the command-line configuration commands, the name of the script to autoexecute should not be preceded with a hyphen.

For example, if you create a script named STARTAPP.SC in a directory named C:\MYAPP, starting Paradox with the command:

   PARADOX C:\MYAPP\STARTAPP

will start Paradox, then immediately run the STARTAPP script.

APPENDIX B

What's New in Paradox 4.5

EXPERIENCED users of Paradox 4.0 will be pleased by the exciting new features introduced in Paradox 4.5. Essentially, these features fall into three main categories: visible end-user changes, speed improvements and other behind-the-scenes changes, and enhancements for application developers. This appendix highlights some of the most impressive and useful new features.

Changes for End-Users

Most of the improvements in Paradox 4.5 will not be immediately visible to end-users, but cumulatively they will increase the productivity of all those who use Paradox. These new improvements include a new Full Screen User Interface, the ability to create custom user-defined menu choices, expanded mouse support in form and report design, improved file and directory navigation, and improved speed in desktop operations such as View, Edit, and PickForm. Let's take a closer look at some of the most important of these changes.

User Interface

When you first use the ≡ ➤ **I**nterface menu choice in Paradox 4.5, you'll instantly notice the biggest visible enhancement to the product: a full-screen, character-oriented window interface. This interface is a cross between the standard interface and the compatibility mode available in Paradox 4.0, and replaces the latter. All commands that worked in 4.0's compatibility mode are still available.

When you choose the Full Screen User Interface, you are presented with the following features:

- The workspace is cleared and all Paradox table locks are released.
- Form and form designer windows; editing windows; and sort, index, graph, and password definition windows all open full-screen, with no frames. These windows do not respond to window-resizing commands, such as Shift-F5 (Maximize/Restore), Ctrl-F8 (Window Close), or Ctrl-F5 (Size/Move).
- Report design, preview, creation, and restructuring windows come up full-screen, but retain their frames and scroll bars.
- Tables are displayed in windows with scroll bars, but in a manner similar to that used in Paradox 3.5 (full-screen width and with a window height determined by the number of rows in the table). Tables with more than 20 rows are opened maximized.
- The Full Screen User Interface uses the modern Paradox 4.5 pull-down menus, buttons, dialog boxes, and Speedbar of the Standard Interface. It does not support the old-style ring menus and prompts of version 3.5 and earlier.

Expanded Mouse Support

Paradox 4.5 adds extensive enhancements to mouse support in several areas. These enhancements are described in the following sections.

The Image Menu

Paradox now allows you to choose fields with a mouse click when you are asked to specify field while using the Image submenu's Format, Move, OrderTable, and Graph ➤ CrossTab field choices.

The Mouse in the Report Design Screen

Paradox 4.5's expanded mouse support in the Report Design screen allows you to:

- Click a field name or mask when asked for a field to affect in most operations, such as Delete and Place.
- Use the mouse to place and size fields.

- Use the mouse with **Field ➤ R**eformat and **TableBand ➤ R**esize.

Use of the mouse in the Report Design screen is described in detail in Chapter 8.

The Mouse in the Form Design Screen

In Paradox 4.5, you can use the mouse in the Form Design screen whenever Paradox prompts you for a field, a location, or an area. Specifically, you can:

- Specify a field to affect by pointing and clicking.
- Place a field by pointing and clicking.
- Resize a field by dragging with the mouse.
- Define an area by dragging with the mouse.
- Use the mouse to place, resize, or delete a border.

Use of the mouse in the Form Design screen is described in Chapter 9.

Other New Report Designer Enhancements

In addition to enhanced mouse support, there are a number of new report design capabilities offered in Paradox 4.5, such as the ones described in the following sections.

Setting Page Numbers in Reports with PAGEBREAK

The PAGEBREAK command now accepts a numeric argument. This form of the command allows you to specify new page numbering, with a specified beginning page number, for each group, or even for each page, during report output.

Positioning Text in Reports with BLANKLINE

The BLANKLINE command now accepts a numeric argument. This form of the command places blank lines on the page until the specified page line number. You can use this feature to control the vertical positioning of text in your reports.

Using RangeOutput for Continuous Paper Reports

In Paradox 4.5, the RangeOutput choice starts printing on the line specified, as opposed to the next line, as was the case in previous versions of Paradox. This allows you to use RangeOutput effectively with continuous reports.

File Management and Directory Support Enhancement

Many Paradox 4.5 dialog boxes now supply directory names and directory indicators (..\), which allow you to browse through the directories on your hard disk to find the file you want to retrieve.

File prompts now support the DOS wild cards * and ? which let you restrict the file listing shown in a file list box. For instance, if you specify CUST*.DB, only those tables with names beginning with CUST will be displayed in the file list box.

Paradox 4.5 can now display a directory tree or an available drive list in the **Tools** ➤ **More** ➤ **Directory**, **Tools** ➤ **Net** ➤ **Lock**, and **Tools** ➤ **Net** ➤ **S**et**Private** dialog boxes. You can specify a directory or even change logged drives using the displayed tree. Chapter 2 describes the use of this new feature.

Enhancements in the Paradox Editor

You can now customize the tab stop settings in the Paradox 4.5 Editor. The Editor supports two independent default tab stop settings: one for use in memo fields and while editing DOS text files in the Editor, and one for use during script file creation or editing. The Paradox 4.5 default for both settings is 8 characters. Appendix D describes the procedure for using the Custom Configuration Program (CCP) to change the default tab stop settings. Chapter 17 contains instructions on overriding the default tab stop settings for a file or memo field.

Enhancements and Changes to the Custom Configuration Program (CCP)

The following sections describe the enhancement and changes to the Paradox CCP.

Video

Here's a summary of the Video changes:

- References to the compatible mode have been removed from the Video ➤ Color Settings dialog box. In Paradox 4.5, the Standard Interface and Full Screen User Interface share the same video color settings.

- The Compatible User Interface color settings options have been removed from the ScreenObjects submenu.

- A Form command has been added to the ScreenObjects submenu so that you can adjust the default colors displayed in the Form Design screen.

- The PAL color settings option has been removed. The PAL Debugger now uses system colors.

Standard Settings

A new option in the CCP Standard Settings dialog box, Maximum Table Size, lets you set the maximum table size for a Paradox table. You will probably never need to adjust this setting but, if you do, keep these facts about the Maximum Table Size setting in mind:

- Maximum Table Size works by adjusting the size of block (1K, 2K, 4K) that Paradox uses when storing records. The larger the block, the more inefficiently small tables are stored, but the larger the possible maximum table size.

- You can change the Maximum Table Size setting to a larger or smaller setting at any time, using the CCP.

- Changing the Maximum Table Size setting does not affect existing tables. Tables keep the settings that are in effect when they are created or restructured. Any table restructured or created while a given Maximum Table Size setting is in effect will retain that setting until it is restructured.
- If a table reaches the Maximum Table Size set when it was created, you may receive the error message "Table is full—no more blocks may be added." If this happens, change the Maximum Table Size setting to a larger size and then restructure the table.

Format Data

Paradox 4.5 displays three new options in the Format Data dialog box. These choices allow you to set defaults for the Paradox Editor treatment of word-wrap, tab stops, and auto-indent. These settings control the default in effect for these features during memo field and DOS text file editing; they do not affect the Editor during script editing.

PAL

Paradox 4.5 displays three new options in the PAL dialog box: Auto Indent, Tab Stops, and Blob Editor Screen Swap. The first two of these options set the defaults for the tab stop and auto-indent functions in the Paradox Editor during script file editing. These settings have no effect on the Editor during memo field or DOS text file editing.

The Blob Editor Screen Swap setting default is Yes. You will generally not need to change this setting. The Yes choice clears the Paradox screen before displaying your BLOB Editor. The No choice sets the BLOB Editor's screen to be displayed over the existing Paradox screen.

See Appendix D for a more detailed discussion of the settings choices in the Custom Configuration Program, including those new in Paradox 4.5.

Other End-User Features

Here are some of the other features new to Paradox 4.5 that end-users will notice:

- Paradox 4.5 increases the number of images you can have on the screen from Paradox 4.0's 24 to a new maximum of 60.

- The number of tables that can be linked together in a query is similarly increased in Paradox 4.5, to 60, minus the number of desktop images generated by the query; that is temporary tables, such as Answer, Changed, and Deleted.

- The new Paradox 4.5 TableAdd choice in the CoEdit menu allows you to open additional tables while working in CoEdit mode. You can't add an image in a non-shared directory if it is already on the desktop.

- Paradox 4.5 supports a new, easier way of displaying special characters in borders: using the backslash key and a three-digit code (see Chapter 9).

- Several new PAL functions are available for use in calculations in forms and reports (see Chapter 16).

- The NETWORK.TXT file, which is copied to the Paradox system directory during installation contains the information from the former *Network Installation Guide*. This file is also on Paradox 4.5's Program Disk 1 (see Appendix C).

- Paradox 4.0 users will notice improvements in the speed of application loading in Paradox 4.5, notably the performance of the View, CoEdit, and PickForm commands.

Improvements for Advanced Users and Application Developers

Paradox 4.5 contains many new features designed to aid advanced uers and application developers. These features are summarized in the following sections.

Adding User Defined-Choices to Paradox Menus

Paradox 4.5 has a new feature called Paradox.ADD, which lets you attach up to 18 menu selections to the Paradox 4.5 menus. You can add up to 16 user-defined menu selections to the ≡ ➤ Utilities menu and one menu selection each to the Form and Report menus.

Paradox.ADD is a special file, intalled by Paradox 4.5 in your Paradox system directory. You can open Paradox.ADD with the Paradox Mini-editor, using the methods described in Chapter 21. Any Paradox script, whether a recorded macro or a complete Workshop or PAL application, can be attached to a user-defined menu choice.

The Miniscript Window

Miniscripts (a PAL menu option) are now displayed in a window, which keeps all miniscripts played during the session available for replay or editing. The contents of the Paradox 4.5 Miniscript window can be saved to a script file. See Chapter 21 for details.

NOTE If you want to use Paradox 4.5 to play back scripts created with the Data Entry Toolkit in Paradox 3.5, you will need to disable the new Paradox 4.5 key codes. See the Paradox documentation for the codes you need to use.

Just for Developers

There are more than 40 new commands available in Paradox 4.5, and 26 of the previous version's commands now have enhanced functions. Paradox 4.5 also recognizes more than 40 new extended key codes. In addition to these PAL language enhancements, PAL now has powerful new Wait

What's New in Paradox 4.5

triggers. It also offers a full-screen, full-featured debugger, with support for breakpoints and for watching variables, expressions, and system functions. The debugger has a built-in Miniscript window and file-browsing facilities.

There is a brief description of the Debugger window in Chapter 21. For more information about the new commands and capabilities in PAL, see the PAL manuals that come with Paradox 4.5.

APPENDIX C

Networks, SQL Link, and Interoperability

IF you are using Paradox in an office environment where several people share the same data on separate networked computers, or on a computer connected to a mainframe or minicomputer through Paradox's separate SQL Link package, Paradox will behave slightly differently than described in the main chapters of this book. This appendix covers some of the most important differences between single-user and multiuser applications of Paradox and directs you to more detailed sources of information about using networking and SQL Link. We'll also introduce you to *interoperability*, which allows Paradox to share files with other Borland products.

About Network Installation

A local area network (LAN, often called simply a network) is a collection of interconnected computers on which several users can share files. Installing Paradox on the network is generally the responsibility of the network manager or network administrator (the person in charge of the network). Network installation is beyond the scope and available space for this book; however, you can find complete coverage of the subject in the NETWORK.TXT file that is copied to the Paradox system directory during installation.

The NETWORK.TXT file is also on the Paradox 4.5 Program Disk 1. NETWORK.TXT is an ASCII text file. You can print the ASCII file directly from the DOS command line on dot-matrix or Hewlett Packard LaserJet compatible printers (but not on PostScript laser printers). To print the file, place the Paradox 4.5 Program Disk 1 in drive A, and type

```
PRINT A:NETWORK.TXT
```

Then press ↵. (You must have the DOS program PRINT.EXE in your DOS path.)

You can import NETWORK.TXT into most word processors to view it or print it. You can also view and print NETWORK.TXT from the Paradox 4.5 Editor. Another alternative is to log on to drive A (or whatever floppy disk drive you have placed the Program Disk 1 in), and type:

    REAMDE NETWORK.TXT

NOTE You cannot share tables or work in the same directory as a user running Paradox 3.5 or earlier.

After you install Paradox, the exact procedures for starting Paradox vary from one network to the next. See your network administrator for information about starting Paradox on your system.

Network Hardware Requirements

The requirements for running a network workstation are listed below:

- An 80286, 80386, or 80486 microprocessor capable of running in protected mode
- Any combination of hard and floppy disk drives, or no drives at all if you have access to a network drive (a workstation hard disk will improve Paradox's performance)
- 2Mb or more of RAM; 4Mb recommended
- DOS 3.1 or higher
- Compatible MDA, MCGA, CGA, EGA, or VGA monitor, with adapter (for displaying graphs, MCGA, CGA, EGA, VGA, 8514, 3270, ATT, Tandy T1000, or Hercules monitor and adapter required)

NETWORKS, SQL LINK, AND INTEROPERABILITY

For the network server, you'll need one of the following networks (or any other network that is 100 percent compatible with DOS 3.1 and these networks):

- 3Com 3+, version 1.5.1 or higher
- AT&T StarGROUP DOS software, version 3.1 or higher
- Banyan VINES, version 2.10 or higher
- DEC Pathworks, version 1.0 or higher
- IBM Token Ring or PC Network with IBM PC LAN program, version 1.12 or higher
- Microsoft LANMAN, version 2.0 or higher
- Novell Advanced NetWare, version 2.0A or higher

Locking

One of the key concepts in using Paradox on a network is *locking*. Paradox automatically locks tables and other objects, such as reports and forms, on an as-needed basis only. When a particular user no longer needs to have a lock on an object, Paradox automatically clears the lock.

> **NOTE** If your workstation crashes, the network operating system may lock tables or records you were using until you reboot and log back into the network. See the *Network Installation Guide* for troubleshooting information.

Paradox's automatic locking and unlocking is designed to minimize locking, which in turn maximizes all users' access to all files. However, locking is required from time to time. In some situations, you may not be able to gain access to a file because another user on the network already has that object locked. When this happens, you'll see a message on your screen indicating which user on the network currently has the object locked. You'll need to wait for that user to finish his or her work before you can gain access to the file.

It's important to understand that placing a lock on an object does not place any restrictions on what you can do with that object. Rather, it restricts what everyone else on the network can do with that object while you have it locked. In consideration of other network users, you should avoid locking records or tables for long periods of time.

Basically, five types of locks can be placed on Paradox objects. These locks are listed below, in order from most restrictive to least restrictive.

- **Directory Lock:** A directory lock, or "Dir lock," provides read-only access to all of a directory's files and tables for all users. Hence, no one (not even the person who placed the lock) can modify the directory's objects. This is equivalent to placing full locks on all tables in the locked directory. Only the person who places a directory lock can remove it, so you should be very conservative about placing this type of lock.

NOTE Directory locks can speed up performance considerably since Paradox doesn't need to write any objects to disk. However, these locks are only useful for objects that you don't need to modify, and they apply to all objects in the directory.

- **Full Lock:** The person with a full lock has exclusive use of the object. No other user can access (read or change) that object until the lock is released. You cannot full lock an object if that object is already locked in any way.

- **Write Lock:** The person who has a write lock is the only one who can change the object. Other users may still use and view the object. You cannot write lock an object if it already has a directory lock, full lock, or a prevent write lock on it.

- **Prevent Write Lock:** This lock doesn't actually lock an object, but it does prevent other users from placing a directory lock, full lock, or a write lock on the object. All users can view and change the object, but no individual user can place a write lock on the table. You cannot add a prevent write lock to an object if it already has a directory lock, full lock, or write lock on it.
- **Prevent Full Lock:** This lock allows all users to view and change data concurrently. However, no single user can place a directory lock or full lock on the object.

As mentioned, Paradox automatically places and removes the above locks on an as-needed basis to maintain data integrity and maximize access to all users. You can also explicitly set or remove locks using options on the Tools ➤ Net menu, as described later in this chapter.

In addition to the five locks mentioned above, Paradox uses four more special types of automatic locks: family locks, record locks, group locks, and write-record locks. Only Paradox can place family, group locks, or write-record locks, and it does so only under certain circumstances.

Family Locks

A family lock is automatically placed on all the objects in a family during a Tools ➤ Copy ➤ Table or Tools ➤ Copy ➤ JustFamily operation. During the operation, other users can still view the contents of the locked objects, but cannot make changes to those objects (like a write lock). The family lock is automatically removed as soon as the copy operation is complete.

Record Locks

The Paradox CoEdit mode lets multiple users make simultaneous changes to the same record. However, whenever you start editing a record, Paradox automatically places a write lock on that single record, preventing others from changing that record at the same time. Similarly, if you try to edit a record that is currently locked by another user, you'll see a message indicating the name of the user who has the record locked, and you'll need to wait for that user to finish before you can edit the record.

You can also explicitly lock a single record by pressing Alt-l (Lock Toggle) while the cursor is in the record. The triangular field indicator is highlighted when the current record is locked. The record will be unlocked automatically as soon as you move the cursor to a different record. You can also press Alt-l to explicitly unlock the record.

Group Locks and Write-Record Locks

Paradox automatically applies group locks and write-record locks only when you press Alt-F9 to coedit multi-table forms. These locks, which are at the record level (not the table level), ensure that the one-to-many, many-to-one relationships are properly maintained during coediting.

Paradox places a *group lock* on the detail records owned by a master record when you coedit the primary key of a master record in a multi-table form. This prevents other users from changing the detail records, whether they're coediting in Table view or any Form view that uses those records. When you press F2 to save the record, Paradox automatically makes the same changes to the linked fields of the detailed records, and then removes the group lock.

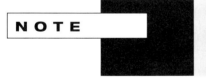

NOTE You cannot edit the primary key of a master record if Paradox can't obtain a group lock on all the linked detail records.

Write-record locks are the inverse of group locks. Paradox places a write-record lock on the associated master record whenever you open or coedit an existing detail record in a multi-table form. This prevents other users from deleting or changing the associated master record, whether they're coediting it in Table view or any Form view that uses that record. The write-record lock is released when you press F2 or move the cursor to the next master record (the lock is *not* released after posting changes to detail records).

NOTE You cannot edit the detail record if Paradox can't obtain a write-record lock on the associated master record.

NETWORKS, SQL LINK, AND INTEROPERABILITY

Table C.1 summarizes Paradox's automatic locking schemes by operations selected from the Paradox desktop or the Edit or CoEdit menus.

TABLE C.1: Paradox's Automatic Locking Schemes

MENU	OPTION	PURPOSE
View	Table or Form view	Prevent full lock
Ask	Regular, Find, or Set	Prevent full lock; snapshot at Do-It! *
	Insert, Delete, or Changeto	Prevent full lock; full lock at Do-It!
Report **	Output or RangeOutput	Prevent full lock; snapshot at Do-It! *
	Design or Change	Prevent full lock on table; full lock on report design or change
Create	Create	Full lock
	Borrow	Full lock on table; prevent full lock on table being borrowed
Modify	Sort ➤ New	Write lock on table; full lock on new table
	Sort ➤ Same	Full lock
	Edit **	Full lock
	CoEdit **	Prevent full lock; prevent write lock while any record is locked
	DataEntry **	Prevent full lock on source; prevent write lock on source at Do-It!
	MultiEntry	Write lock on source; write lock on map; prevent write lock on all targets at Do-It!
	Restructure	Full lock
	ValCheck ➤ Define or Clear	Full lock
	TableLookup	Prevent full lock on lookup table

TABLE C.1: Paradox's Automatic Locking Schemes (continued)

MENU	OPTION	PURPOSE
Image	KeepSet	Full lock
	Graph ➤ CrossTab	Prevent full lock; snapshot at Do-It! *
	Graph ➤ ViewGraph	Prevent full lock
Forms **	Design or Change	Prevent full lock on table; full lock on form
Tools	Rename	Full lock on source and target
	QuerySpeed	Same as Ask at Do-It!
	ExportImport ➤ Export	Write lock on source
	ExportImport ➤ Import	Full lock on target
	Copy ➤ Table	Family lock on source; full lock on target
	Copy ➤ (object other than table)	Write lock on source object; full lock on target; prevent full lock on associated table
	JustFamily	Prevent full lock on source table; family lock on objects; full lock on target table and objects
	Delete ➤ Table	Full lock on table
	Delete ➤ Form or Report	Full lock on object; prevent full lock on table
	Delete ➤ KeepSet or ValCheck	Full lock on object; full lock on table
	Info ➤ Structure	Prevent full lock
	Info ➤ Family	Family lock
	More ➤ Add	Write lock on source; prevent write lock on target

TABLE C.1: Paradox's Automatic Locking Schemes (continued)

MENU	OPTION	PURPOSE
	More ➤ MultiAdd	Write locks on source and map; prevent write lock on targets
	More ➤ Form-Add **	Prevent full lock on all targets and sources; for update, write lock on all targets and sources at Do-It!; for new entries, write lock on all sources and prevent write lock on all targets at Do-It!
	More ➤ Subtract	Full lock on source and target
	More ➤ Empty	Full lock
	More ➤ Protect	Full lock

* Automatically restarts if other users make changes while the snapshot is in progress. However, if you choose Tools ➤ Net ➤ Changes ➤ Continue (or use the corresponding option in the Custom Configuration Program), processing continues without restarting, regardless of other activity on the table or tables.

** For multi-table operations, the specified locks are applied to all tables involved in the operation.

Explicit Locks

Although Paradox's automatic locks normally take care of all required locking behind the scenes, you might want to explicitly place a lock to guarantee that a table will be available when you need it, or to create a read-only directory. You should be very careful when placing explicit locks, since they can needlessly prevent other network users from accessing Paradox objects. Always be sure to release an explicit lock when you no longer need it.

> **NOTE** Explicit locks are most often used by Paradox application developers in multiuser situations.

LOCKING

To set or remove explicit table or directory locks, start with this step:

- Choose **T**ools ➤ **N**et from the Paradox desktop. You'll see the submenu shown earlier.

Now, if you want to set or remove a full, write, or directory lock, follow these steps:

1. Choose **L**ock.
2. Choose **F**ullLock or **W**riteLock to set or clear a full or write lock on a table. Or choose **D**irLock to set or clear a directory lock.

    - If you chose FullLock or WriteLock, Paradox will display the usual dialog box requesting the name of the table. Type in the table name and press ↵, or press ↵ and select the table from the list that appears.
    - If you chose DirLock, Paradox will prompt for a directory name. Type in the name of the directory you want to lock and press ↵.

NOTE You cannot lock your current working directory, your private directory, or a nonexistent directory.

3. After you define the type of lock you want, you'll see the options Set and Clear.
4. Choose **S**et to set the lock, or **C**lear to remove the lock.

If you want to set or remove a prevent full lock or prevent write lock, choose **T**ools ➤ **N**et from the Paradox desktop, then follow these steps:

1. Choose **P**reventLock to display the options FullLock and WriteLock.
2. Choose **F**ullLock to set or remove a prevent full lock on a table, or choose **W**riteLock to set or remove a prevent write lock.

3. When the familiar table dialog box appears, type the name of the table and press ↵, or press ↵ and select the table name from the list. You'll see the Set and Clear options again.

4. Choose **S**et to place the prevent lock, or **C**lear to remove the prevent lock.

It's important to remember that if you place an explicit lock on a table, the table remains locked until you explicitly remove the lock (by following the same general steps you used to lock it, but selecting Clear rather then Set in the last step). You'll want to keep your explicit locks to a minimum so that other users can have access to the data.

Of course, if another user has already locked a table, or has already placed a prevent lock on a table, you cannot override that lock. For example, if another user has placed a prevent write lock on a table to make sure he or she can keep changing data in a table, you cannot place a write lock on that table.

Again, individual users rarely need to place explicit locks on objects, since Paradox automatically sets and clears locks on an efficient, as-needed basis.

Avoiding Waits for Busy Tables

When multiple users have access to the same files, there is always the possibility that one user will change data while another user is performing a lengthy operation with that table, such as printing a report or performing a query. To maximize data integrity, Paradox takes a "snapshot" of the current data and uses that snapshot to perform the lengthy operation.

Normally, if another user changes data while Paradox is taking the snapshot, Paradox automatically tries to take the snapshot again. You'll see a message each time this happens. If you change your mind and don't want Paradox to continue trying to take the snapshot, press Ctrl-Break.

Alternatively, you can just base your query or report on the most recent version of the table or tables involved, without waiting for other users to finish working with those tables. To avoid long waits for busy tables, follow these steps before starting your query or report:

1. Choose **T**ools ➤ **N**et. You'll see the submenu shown below:

2. Choose **C**hanges. Paradox displays the options Restart and Continue.

3. Choose **C**ontinue to continue the query or report even if data changes. Or, if you prefer to restart the query or report whenever data changes (the default setting), choose **R**estart instead.

Keep in mind that your query or report may not reflect the most recent version of the table or tables if you choose Tools ➤ Net ➤ Changes ➤ Continue.

Setting the Changes option to Continue affects only the current Paradox session. When you exit Paradox and return later, the setting automatically reverts to Restart, unless you change the default setting in the Custom Configuration Program (CCP), as described later in this appendix.

Using Paradox on a Network

The sections that follow describe specific differences between single-user Paradox, which is the main emphasis throughout the chapters of this book, and Paradox on a network.

Private Directories

Each user on a network must have his or her own private directory, in which Paradox stores temporary objects, such as the Answer table generated by queries. The private directory prevents another user's temporary objects from overwriting yours. It will seem as though these objects are stored in your current network directory, because the table names from both the network working directory and the private directory appear in lists of table names (as when you press ↵ in response to the request for a table name). However, if you were to list all table names using Tools ➤ Info ➤ Inventory, you would see only the files on the network directory, not the ones from your private directory.

In most cases, the network administrator is responsible for setting up the private directory at each workstation, so chances are that you don't need to do anything to declare a private directory when you use Paradox.

To choose a private directory, which will be in effect for the current Paradox session only, follow these steps:

1. Choose **T**ools ➤ **N**et from the Paradox desktop. You'll see the submenu shown earlier in the appendix.
2. Choose **S**etPrivate. A dialog box will prompt for the private directory name.
3. Type in a valid drive and directory (such as C:\MYDATA) and press ↵.

You must specify a directory that already exists, preferably on your own workstation rather than on the network. (If you declare a network directory as private, other users will lose access to that directory.)

If you try to declare a directory that other people are currently using as private, or if you try to declare somebody else's private directory as your own, Paradox will reject your request.

In addition to setting the private directory for the current session only, you (or the network administrator) can use the CCP to change your default private directory, as described later in this appendix.

NOTE If you do not establish a private directory, Paradox will use the current directory on drive C:.

Network User Names

Each workstation in a network has a name, commonly referred to as *user name*. This name appears when you try to use an object that's currently locked by another user (for example, you may get the message "Names table has been locked by Martha").

You can enter user names in any of four ways:

- Through the network operating system, if it has the capability. Paradox will use this as the user name if it's available.

- From Paradox at each workstation, using the CCP and specifying a user name in the Network Settings dialog box. This name will be the default for the workstation, and will override the name defined in the network operating system.

- By starting Paradox with the -USER command-line option (assuming this is allowed on your network). For example, to start Paradox with a user name of *Keith*, type the following at the DOS command prompt (C:\>).

    PARADOX -USER Keith ↵

- By selecting **T**ools ➤ **N**et ➤ **U**serName, typing in a name, and pressing ↵. This name will override any of the above for the remainder of the session, or until you enter a different user name.

For example, you might want to change the default user name using Tools ➤ Net ➤ UserName when you are working at another person's workstation and want to identify yourself as the user at that workstation.

Refreshing the Screen

If several people are working on the same table at once, the data on the various screens may become out of sync from time to time. You can bring your own screen up to date with other user's screens at any time simply by pressing the Refresh key, Alt-r.

NETWORKS, SQL LINK, AND INTEROPERABILITY

You can also determine how frequently your screen is automatically refreshed by following these steps:

1. Choose **T**ools ➤ **N**et from the Paradox desktop.

2. Choose **A**utoRefresh from the submenu shown earlier in the appendix, or from the CoEdit menu bar if available.

3. Type in a refresh interval (in seconds, between 1 and 3600—one hour). If you want to disable the Autorefresh feature, leave the interval blank.

As described next, you can also use the CCP to change the default refresh rate for your workstation.

Changing Default Network Settings with CCP

The Custom Configuration Program, or CCP, lets you control many of Paradox's default settings, including several network defaults. If you change network settings in the CCP, your changes will become the new defaults for your workstation and will override network operating system settings, as well as Paradox's original default settings. Of course, you can always change the defaults again, or you can override the settings for the current session only by choosing options from the Tools ➤ Net submenu.

Appendix D provides a full discussion of the network settings options in the CCP, so we'll just summarize the steps here.

1. Starting at the Paradox desktop, choose ≡ ➤ **U**tilities ➤ **C**ustom ➤ **N**etwork. You'll see the Network Settings dialog box, as shown in Figure C.1.

2. Change any of the following settings:

    - **User name:** Your default user name.
    - **Private directory:** The directory for storing your temporary files.

FIGURE C.1

The Network Settings dialog box lets you change the default network settings for your workstation.

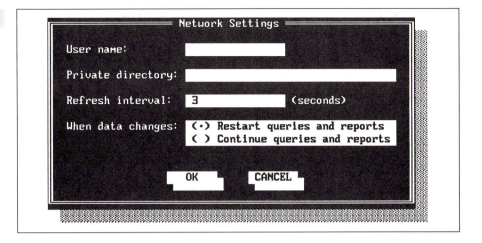

- **Refresh interval:** The time, in seconds, before Paradox looks again to see if other users have updated a table you are using and refreshes your screen with those changes.
- **When data changes:** Determines whether or not Paradox automatically restarts a query or report when other users are changing the tables used by that query or report.

3. Press ↵ or choose OK when you're finished making your changes. You'll be returned to the CCP desktop menu.

4. Press the Do-It! key, F2, or choose **DO-IT!** from the menu bar to save your changes.

5. Choose **N**etwork from the Save Changes submenu that appears. You'll see the Network Save dialog box.

6. Type in the complete path to the private directory where you want to store the PARADOX.CFG configuration file, then press ↵. (If you supplied the name of a private directory in the Network Settings dialog box, that name will already be filled in and you can just press ↵.)

If your workstation has a hard disk, you should store PARADOX.CFG there. If your workstation doesn't have a hard disk, you should store the PARADOX.CFG file on your network home directory. (If you're not sure of the name or location of your Paradox private directory, you should contact your network administrator.)

936 APPENDIX C

NETWORKS, SQL LINK, AND INTEROPERABILITY

NOTE See the *Network Installation Guide* for information about setting up the PARADOX.CFG file for all network users.

Getting Network Information

The Tools ➤ Info options from the Paradox desktop display information about the Paradox environment. Most of the information options are described in Chapter 12, but those pertaining to networks are mentioned here.

To get a list of all the users currently on the network, choose **T**ools ➤ **I**nfo ➤ **W**ho from the Paradox desktop. Paradox lists the names of current network users in a temporary table named List, as shown below. You can rename this table with **T**ools ➤ **R**ename ➤ **T**able if you wish to save it.

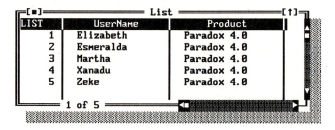

To see a list of all the locks on a table, follow these steps:

1. Choose **T**ools ➤ **I**nfo ➤ **L**ock from the Paradox desktop.
2. Type in a table name and press ↵, or press ↵ and select a table from the usual table dialog box.

NOTE If the requested table isn't in a shared directory, you'll see the message "File is not shared." If someone has a full lock on the table, you can't display its lock information.

Paradox again uses the List table to display the file or object name that is locked, the name of the user who placed the lock, and the type of lock, as shown below. As usual, you can rename the List table to save the information. The Lock option is particularly handy in a situation where you get a message like "Table is in use by Martha and 2 others" and you want to find out who the "others" are.

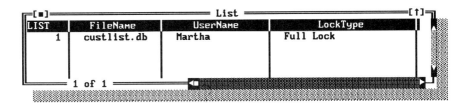

Creating a Table on a Network

While you are creating a table on a network, Paradox places a full lock on it to prevent other users from creating a table with the same name.

If you want to borrow the structure of an existing table, you will be allowed to do so only if another user has not placed a full lock on that file. While you are borrowing another table's structure, that table will (briefly) have a prevent full lock placed on it while its structure is copied to the new table.

Data Entry on a Network

In a multiuser environment, the network administrator has the power to decide which users have access to which fields. The restrictions placed on you for adding new records are the same as described in the section about editing on a network, later in this appendix.

If you do have the right to add new records to a table, you should be aware that when adding new records with the Modify ➤ DataEntry options, Paradox places a prevent full lock on the table (or tables) so that other users can still access the data currently in the table. However, none of these other users can place a full lock on the table while you are adding records. This means that they cannot perform any operations that require exclusive use of the table, such as deleting all its records or changing the table's structure.

If somebody on the network already has exclusive use of a table when you select Modify ➤ DataEntry, you won't be able to start adding data until that other user releases the lock.

Keep in mind that when you add new data to a Paradox table through Modify ➤ DataEntry, the records are actually added to temporary entry tables; your new records do not become part of the target table until you press F2 or choose DO-IT! from the menu. Paradox then places a prevent write lock on the target table so that data from the Entry tables can be sent to the target tables.

However, if another user already had the table locked, you cannot move records from the Entry table to the target table. In that situation, you can use the KeepEntry option on the DataEntry menu to save the newly added records without passing them to the target table, by following these steps:

1. Choose KeepEntry from the DataEntry menu. The table is saved with the name Entry.
2. Choose Tools ➤ Rename ➤ Table.
3. Type Entry as the name of the table to rename, then press ↵.
4. Enter a unique, valid name for the new name (such as Newrecs), then press ↵.

Later, when the target table is available, you can choose Tools ➤ More ➤ Add from the Paradox desktop to copy data from the source table (Newrecs in this example) to the target table. (For more information about the Tools menu options, see Chapter 12.)

Viewing Data on a Network

The steps for viewing table data on a network are identical to those for viewing table data on a single-user system. While you have the table in view, Paradox places a prevent full lock on the table to allow other users access to the same table for all operations excluding those that require a full lock.

When you try to view a table on a network, your request might be denied for any of the following reasons:

- Another user has a full lock on the table.

- You are trying to view the table via a custom form, but another user has a full lock on that form.
- You do not have full access rights to that table because of the protection scheme designed by the network administrator.

If either of the first two items prevents your access, you can just wait a few minutes and try to view the table again later. If the network administrator has limited your access to the table (or certain fields in the table), you won't be able to view the protected data unless you know the password. (When viewing protected fields without access to those fields, they appear as blanks on your screen.)

Editing on a Network

When you select the Modify ➤ Edit options or press F9 to edit a table on a network, Paradox places a full lock on the table, thereby preventing other users from viewing or accessing the table in any way.

In most situations it's preferable to select Modify ➤ CoEdit or press Alt-F9 to edit a table on a network. This allows other users to view and edit the same table that you are editing.

When you are editing tables, remember that your company's network administrator may have implemented a protection scheme that limits your access to certain tables and certain fields within those tables. If you are not sure which data you are allowed to access, or don't know the necessary passwords, ask your network administrator.

Sorting on a Network

Using the Modify ➤ Sort options to sort to the same table on a network requires that you have a write lock on that table. If another user has a full lock or prevent write lock on the table, you cannot begin your sort operation until the other user releases the lock. Once you do successfully begin your sort operation, your full lock stays in effect for the duration of the sort, preventing other users from accessing that table.

If you are sorting the contents of your table to another, separate table, Paradox places a full lock on the target table and a write lock on the source table for the duration of the sorting operation.

Querying on a Network

When you access a Query form for a particular table on a network, Paradox places a prevent full lock on that table. If another user already has a full lock on the table you want to query, you'll need to wait until that user releases the lock to access the Query form.

If other users are editing the table that you are querying, Paradox takes a "snapshot" of the current data as soon as you press F2 to activate the query. Thus you can perform a query even while other users are modifying data in the table.

If another user happens to change the table data in the small period of time required to take the snapshot, Paradox will try taking the snapshot again. If so many changes are taking place that you can no longer wait for Paradox to take the snapshot to complete the query, you can press Ctrl-Break to prevent additional tries. If you choose Tools ➤ Net ➤ Changes ➤ Continue (or change the default in the CCP) before starting a query, Paradox will complete the query without waiting for users to stop changing the table.

Reports on a Network

Paradox places a prevent full lock on a table while you are designing, modifying, or printing from a report format. This means that other users can still access the data in the table, but cannot change its structure or delete all its records. If another user already has a full lock on the table before you begin your report operation, your request will be denied, and you'll need to try again later.

Also, while you are designing or changing a report format, the format itself is locked so that other users cannot view, change, or print from that format.

The network administrator can assign passwords to reports, so you may need to enter a password in order to print or view those reports.

Paradox will take a snapshot of the table before printing a report, and will retry the snapshot if other users are changing the table while the snapshot is being taken. Again, you can press Ctrl-Break if you no longer want to retry the snapshot, and you can use Tools ➤ Net ➤ Changes ➤ Continue (or change the default in the CCP) to print the report without waiting for users to finish changing the table.

If your network offers several printers, you can use Report ➤ SetPrinter to select a network printer for your report.

Forms on a Network

While you are designing or modifying a form, Paradox places a prevent full lock on that form's table, and a full lock on the form itself (as with reports, described in the preceding section). This allows other users to continue editing data in the table (without the form), but prevents them from accessing the form you are working with at the moment.

If you try to edit a form while another user has a full lock on its associated table, Paradox will reject your request, and you'll need to try again later after the lock has been released by the other user. Similarly, if another user is already modifying the form that you want to modify, your request will be denied until the other user is finished with the form.

If the network administrator has placed access limitations on a form, you can only access that form if you know the password.

If one user on a network is coediting a table with a particular form, other users who want to edit that same table must also use the same form.

Graphs on a Network

The only restriction to viewing graphs on a network is the obvious fact that in order to view a graph for a table, you must first be able to view the table. The only situation that would prevent this is when another user has exclusive use of the table, such as when that user is changing the table's structure or emptying all the records from that table.

Once you gain access to the table to view your graph, Paradox places a prevent full lock on that table to ensure that others can still view and edit the table, but cannot take the table away from you by fully locking it. Similarly, if you graph data based on the results of a query or crosstab, the Answer or Crosstab table is private and cannot be locked by another user.

Scripts on a Network

Multiple users on a network can simultaneously play back the same script, provided that another user isn't editing the script. A script that is currently being played back by any user cannot be edited. A script that is being edited cannot be played back by any user.

Note that Paradox does not tell you which user is currently editing a script. Instead, it simply displays the message "Can't access script."

Update Queries on a Network

When you perform an INSERT, DELETE, or CHANGETO query on a network by pressing F2, Paradox automatically places a full lock on all the tables involved in the query. If other users are already using any table involved in the query, you will not be able to perform the query until those users have finished their operations and the locks have been released.

Tools on a Network

Most Tools menu operations, such as copying and renaming objects, involve full locks and write locks on the objects being manipulated (see the Tools section near the bottom of Table C.1 presented earlier in this appendix). As usual, when you have these locks in place, other users will have little or no access to the files. When you finish the operation, Paradox will release the lock automatically.

If another user already has a lock or a prevent lock on an object you want to manipulate with a Tools operation, you'll need to wait until that other user releases the lock.

Security and Protection

One potential problem with networks results from the simple fact that everyone on the network has access to all the data. Some of that data, such as employee salaries, might be confidential. Paradox provides Tools ➤ More ➤ Protect as a means of protecting data. This tool gives the network administrator specific control over every item of data that users have access to. You (or the network administrator) can use the Tools ➤ More ➤ Protect ➤ Password options to create *owner-level* passwords (that is, passwords for each individual table) and *auxiliary* passwords to define different access rights to different users of the same table.

SECURITY AND PROTECTION

NOTE Security and protection are generally the responsibility of the network administrator rather than individual users on the network.

For instance, as the "owner" of a table, you have full access to the table (no restrictions), and even have complete access to all the auxiliary passwords that you define for the table.

Now let's say you want some users to also have complete rights to the table. You could define an auxiliary password that offers full access, and then tell the appropriate users that password. Those users, in turn, would have unlimited access to the table (but could not change any other passwords).

Now suppose you also want to give some other users the right to view but not to change data in this same table. You could then define another auxiliary password that only allows users to view data, and tell only *that* password to the appropriate users.

In other words, you can delegate access to any given table by defining multiple auxiliary passwords for a given table. Deciding how much freedom a given user has in accessing the table becomes a simple matter of deciding which password to give that user.

Creating Owner and Auxiliary Passwords

To define the passwords for any given table, start at the Paradox desktop, then follow these steps:

1. Choose **T**ools ➤ **M**ore ➤ **P**rotect ➤ **P**assword.

NOTE Don't forget to use Tools ➤ More ➤ Directory to get to the table's directory before assigning passwords.

2. Choose **T**able (or **S**cript, if you want to protect a script).

3. Specify the table you want to protect, either by typing its name and pressing ↵, or by pressing ↵ and selecting the name from the list that appears. If this is the first time you are assigning passwords to this table, you'll see a dialog box and prompt to type an owner password. This password provides unlimited access to the table, and even access to the passwords themselves.

4. Carefully type in the owner password (up to 15 characters in length) and press ↵. Be aware that passwords are case-sensitive—for example, *HONCHO*, *Honcho*, and *honcho* are three different passwords.

5. Type the password a second time for verification and press ↵.

> **TIP** To remove the owner password, enter a blank password.

One thing you definitely don't want to do is forget the owner password. It's a good idea to write it down (be sure to use the same uppercase and lowercase letters) and store it somewhere safe, where you can easily find it but other network users cannot.

After entering the owner password, you'll see the screen for defining auxiliary passwords, as shown in Figure C.2. An auxiliary password partially unlocks a table and confers certain table, family, and field rights to anyone opening the table with that auxiliary password. You can define as many auxiliary passwords as you wish for the table, each providing its own level of access.

The auxiliary password screen is actually a form for the Password table of auxiliary passwords. You can switch between Form view and Table view by pressing F7. And because your passwords are being stored in a Paradox table, you can scroll through fields and records in the usual manner, with PgUp, PgDn, ↵, and the arrow keys, or your mouse. If the table you are assigning passwords to has more than 16 fields, the auxiliary passwords form will contain multiple pages of field names, which you can scroll through with the usual PgUp and PgDn keys.

To add another auxiliary password to the table, press Ctrl-PgDn while in Form view, or ↓ while in Table view. To delete the currently displayed auxiliary password, press Delete, as for any Paradox table or form.

SECURITY AND PROTECTION

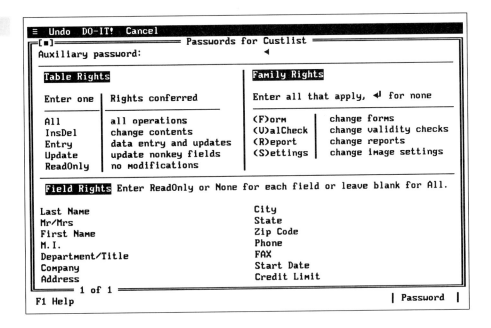

FIGURE C.2

Screen for defining auxiliary passwords

You can use the following menu options while defining auxiliary passwords:

OPTION	PURPOSE
≡	Provides access to the System menu
Undo	"Undoes" the most recent change to the auxiliary password (same as pressing Ctrl-u)
DO-IT!	Saves all the password changes (same as pressing F2) and returns to the desktop
Cancel	Cancels all recent changes and returns to the desktop

Here are the general steps for defining an auxiliary password:

1. Type the auxiliary password.
2. Specify the Table Rights, as described below.
3. Specify one or more Family Rights, as described below.
4. Specify Field Rights for each field, as described below.

If you want to add another auxiliary password, press Ctrl-PgDn in Form view (or ↓ in Table view) and repeat the four steps above. When you're finished, choose **DO-IT!** from the menu, or press F2.

For each auxiliary password you create, you can define table rights, family rights, and field rights, as summarized in the following sections.

Table Rights

Specify the level of access to the overall table. To change the table rights, type the first letter of the option below:

- **All:** User can do anything the table owner can do: insert and delete records, view the contents of any field, empty the table, restructure or delete the entire table, and change the table's passwords. If you specify this level of access, you cannot restrict the field rights.

- **InsDel:** User can insert records, delete records, view the contents of any field, and empty the table, but cannot restructure or delete the table.

- **Entry:** User can edit non-key fields, view the table, and add new records using the Modify ➤ DataEntry and Tools ➤ More ➤ Add options, but cannot delete records or empty the table.

- **Update:** User can view data and make changes to non-key fields, but cannot insert or delete records or change key fields.

- **ReadOnly:** User can view the contents of the table, but cannot make any changes.

Family Rights

Family rights determine whether or not the user can modify the table's objects (forms, validity checks, reports, and image settings). You can specify one or more family rights, in any order, by typing the first letter of the option. For example, FR (or RF) gives the user rights to change forms and reports. If you omit the family right (or leave all rights blank), the user can use the omitted object but cannot modify it. The family rights are:

- **F:** User can design, change, and delete any form associated with the table.

- **V:** User can create, change, or delete validity checks for the table.

SECURITY AND PROTECTION

- **R:** User can modify any report associated with the table.
- **S:** User can create, change, or delete image settings for the table.

Field Rights

The bottom of the form shows the names of each field in the table. Here, you can assign any of three levels of access to each field by leaving the field blank, or typing the first letter of the access you want to grant:

- *(blank)*: User can view the field and change its contents.
- **R**eadOnly: User can view the contents of the field, but cannot change the contents.
- **N**one: User can neither view the field nor change its contents. The field will appear blank when the user views the table or form.

NOTE Paradox won't let you assign table rights that aren't compatible with the field rights, and vice-versa.

As an example, suppose you have a table named Payroll that includes employee salaries. Its owner password is YENOM, and only you know this password. While you could set up any number of auxiliary passwords, you might want to set up at least three:

- FULLSALARY, which provides complete access to the salaries
- VIEWSALARY, which allows a user to view the salary but not change it
- HIDESALARY, which does not allow the user to view or change the salary, but provides some access to other fields

When any user first opens the Payroll table, Paradox will prompt for a password. Depending on which password the user enters (FULLSALARY, VIEWSALARY, HIDESALARY, or YENOM), the user will be granted the appropriate rights.

See Chapter 12 for more information about using passwords and changing existing passwords.

Paradox SQL Link

SQL stands for Structured Query Language, a standardized technique for accessing data stored in a database, particularly on mainframes and minicomputers. SQL Link is a package offered by Borland that translates your Paradox Query-By-Example (QBE) queries to SQL format so that you can access these databases via Paradox.

> **NOTE** SQL is often pronounced "sequel."

Typically, you would use SQL Link to query or add records to a remote table—that is, one that is not on your computer. The remote database might be on a mainframe or minicomputer, or on a dedicated microcomputer commonly referred to as the database server. What's nice about SQL Link is that you only need to know how to use Paradox; you don't need to know how to type SQL commands (which can be quite arcane) in order to access or update the remote database.

SQL Link is based on client-server architecture. The computer that the database is stored on is the server, and acts as an intelligent back-end by taking care of security restraints, data integrity, and other database management jobs that normally require substantial computing resources.

Paradox is the client, or front-end to the server, and is your interface for querying the remote database. You can query the remote database through your normal Paradox Query form. SQL Link translates that query to SQL and sends the query to the remote database. The remote database performs the query, and sends back only the results. Because the remote database performs all the actions required to complete the query, only data is sent back to the client. This minimizes network traffic and keeps the overall system running more quickly.

Installing SQL Link on the company computers is the responsibility of the person in charge of the overall database (often referred to as the database administrator), and is a topic that goes beyond the scope of this book. If you happen to be the person responsible for installing SQL Link, you should note that a SQL server must already be installed before you can install Paradox SQL Link. The user's guide that comes with the SQL

Link package documents the installation procedures.

NOTE Supported SQL servers include Microsoft SQL Server, Oracle Server, IBM OS/2 Extended Edition DBMS, all Sybase platforms, and DEC RDB.

Once it is properly installed, you can start the Paradox SQL Link, a process that is generally the same as starting single-user Paradox, and then connect to the server using either an automatic method set up by your database administrator or a manual method.

From this point on, you can perform operations either on local tables (those on your own workstation), or remote tables (those stored on the database server). While many operations are the same as for the single-user version of Paradox described in this book, some procedures will differ slightly or have certain minor restrictions.

When you're using Paradox SQL Link, the Tools menu offers an additional SQL option with its own submenu. This submenu offers more advanced SQL options, such as transaction processing support. Most likely, if you are a user of Paradox SQL Link, your database administrator will have already automated many of the SQL operations. For more information, you should see the database administrator or consult the user's guide that comes with the Paradox SQL Link package.

Interoperability

Borland provides connections between Paradox and the company's other major product offerings using concepts and techniques referred to as *interoperability*. As the name implies, interoperability makes it possible for Borland products to operate together and connect with one another. Practically speaking, interoperability means that Borland's products—Paradox, dBASE, Quattro Pro, SideKick, and Object Vision to name a few—can share the same files without you needing to worry about what's going on behind the scenes. In a Windows environment, interoperability lets multiple sessions work on the same sets of data at the same time.

NOTE: Contact Borland International for more information about interoperability or other Borland products.

Interoperability in DOS

The heart of Paradox interoperability in DOS is the Paradox Engine, which handles all the input and output to the database files and lets the Borland family of languages and application products work together. This engine has been extracted from Paradox and is available as a separate product known as the Paradox Engine, Version 3.0 (PXE 3.0). The Paradox Engine supports DOS, Windows, and networked applications by providing a set of C and Pascal libraries, plus a Windows Dynamic Link Library (DLL), that lets programmers tap into Paradox's internal resources.

The Paradox Engine is completely compatible with Paradox 4.5. For example, tables created within a PXE 3.0 application are accessible from Paradox or PAL applications in the usual way. A Paradox Engine application can access tables created by Paradox or PAL applications. As you might expect, the Paradox Engine can also handle all the requisite file and record locking in a shared network environment, and all the popular networks are supported.

In addition to providing all the support for standard Paradox data types, PXE 3.0 exceeds Paradox 4.5's capabilities for handling BLOB (Binary Large OBject) data. Whereas Paradox 4.5 is limited to dealing with BLOB data as either a text memo or "undefined" type, the Engine recognizes and can update rich text, bitmapped graphics, video or sound data, or OLE objects.

Interoperability in Windows

In addition to the routines supplied in the Windows DLL mentioned above, Borland is developing additional capabilities and products for Windows. The company's master plan to ensure Windows interoperability is called the Borland Object-Component Architecture, or BOCA. Central to this architecture is a new database engine called the Interbase Engine, which is used in Borland's newest Windows-based products including Paradox for Windows and dBASE for Windows. The Interbase Engine consists of special driver programs that support a wide variety of file formats, including Paradox files, dBASE files, and SQL databases.

Customizing Paradox

WHEN you install Paradox, the default settings for various options are automatically determined. These settings include, among other things, screen colors, date and number formats, and printed report settings. Paradox defaults reflect the most commonly used settings, but are not necessarily best for everyone.

You can change the default settings at any time using the Paradox Custom Configuration Program, abbreviated CCP. However, any settings that you make while using the CCP take effect only after you save the changes and return to Paradox. Once you change a CCP setting, that new setting becomes the default for all future Paradox sessions (or until you change the defaults again). Changing default settings is entirely optional. If you are satisfied with the way Paradox is running on your computer, leave the defaults the way they are.

> **NOTE** See Appendix A for ways to temporarily override some default settings when you start Paradox from the DOS command line.

Running the Custom Configuration Program

Either of these methods run the Custom Configuration Program:

- Select ≡ ➤ **Utilities** ➤ **Custom**.

- From the directory containing Paradox.EXE, choose **S**cripts ➤ **P**lay. In the dialog box requesting the name of the script to play. Choose or type Custom, then choose OK or press ↵.

To run the CCP from another directory, you must include its full path name in the second step above, for example, if the CCP is in C:\PDOX45, you need to type

C:\PDOX45\Custom

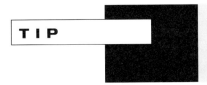

TIP To run the CCP from the DOS prompt, switch to the Paradox program directory (usually \PDOX45) and enter the DOS command PARADOX CUSTOM.

If you're using a color monitor, you may see the small menu below:

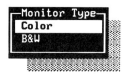

Choose either Color or B&W (black and white) to proceed. You'll see the CCP desktop and menu, shown in Figure D.1. If your screen is difficult to read, choose the B&W option rather than Color.

Before we talk about the specific options on the CCP menu, let's cover some of the basic techniques that you need to learn in order to use the various dialog boxes the CCP will present.

Basic Skills for Using CCP Dialog Boxes

When you use the CCP, you'll find that most of the options it offers are presented in dialog boxes, like the one shown in Figure D.2. Some options in these dialog boxes are *radio buttons*. These are mutually exclusive options, meaning that you can choose only one of the options in the group

CUSTOMIZING PARADOX

FIGURE D.1

The Custom Configuration Program's desktop menu

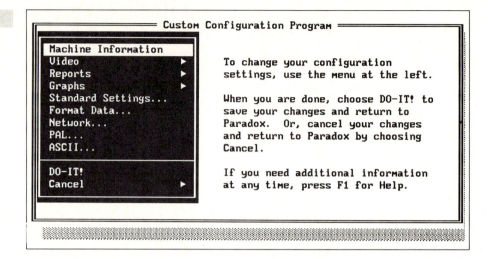

FIGURE D.2

The Video Settings dialog box lets you change default screen settings for Paradox.

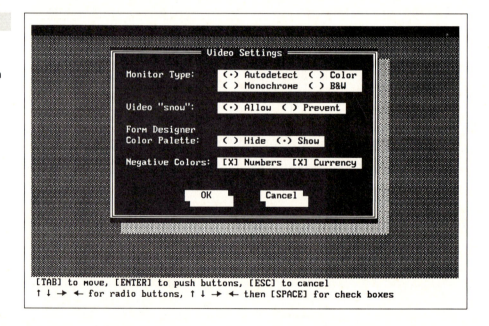

(for example, either Hide or Show, but not both). To choose a radio button, click the option you want, or use Tab or Shift-Tab to get to the group of options, then use the arrow keys to move the highlight to the option you want. The selected radio button option has a dot within the parentheses: (•).

BASIC SKILLS FOR USING CCP DIALOG BOXES

NOTE The CCP usually displays instructions at the bottom of the screen to remind you about keyboard techniques for choosing dialog box options. (To conserve space and focus your attention on the dialog boxes themselves, the remaining figures in this chapter just show the dialog boxes and omit these instructions.)

Some of the options (such as Numbers and Currency in Figure D.2) are *check boxes*, which are not mutually exclusive. You can activate or deactivate any or all of these options either by clicking the option with your mouse or by pressing Tab or Shift-Tab to highlight the option, then the spacebar to mark or unmark the option. When there's an X in the brackets, [X], the option is selected. When the brackets are empty, the option is not selected.

Many options and buttons also include a bold or colored letter that you can type in combination with the Alt key, as a shortcut method for moving to an option or selecting a button. For example, you can press Alt-v to choose the Video Snow option in the Video Settings dialog box. Similarly, you can press Alt-p as a shortcut for selecting the SetPrinterType button in the Graph Printer Settings dialog box.

Some CCP dialog boxes, such as the Color Settings dialog box shown in Figure D.3, present lists. The first step when choosing an item is to highlight it by moving the cursor to that item. If the cursor isn't already in the list you want to choose from, select the list by pressing Tab, typing the shortcut key for this list, or clicking the mouse. For example, typing Alt-s, the shortcut key for the Settings Available list in Figure D.3, moves the cursor to the first item in the list. To move the cursor to the appropriate item in the list, press PgUp, PgDn, or the arrow keys to scroll through the list; use the scroll bar and scroll arrows (if available); or type the first few letters of the item you want.

To save your choices in a dialog box, choose OK or press ↵. To abandon your current settings, choose Cancel or press Esc.

CUSTOMIZING PARADOX

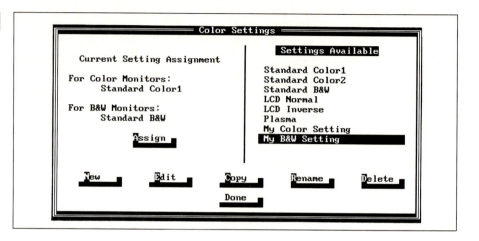

FIGURE D.3

A sample Color Settings dialog box displaying the six predefined settings. The Paradox default settings Standard Color 1 and Standard B&W are currently assigned to the color and black-and-white monitors, respectively.

Getting Information about Your Computer

The Machine Information option provides information about your computer system, which might be particularly useful when you're calling Borland's technical support hotline, or when you're refining the default settings to maximize Paradox's performance on your computer.

After choosing the Machine Information option from the CCP main menu, there will be a short delay while your machine's configuration is analyzed. Then you'll see a detailed report on the screen. You can scroll through the information using the scroll bars, PgUp, PgDn, and the arrow keys, as usual.

The report provides the following information about your computer:

- DOS Version and BIOS (Basic Input/Output System) used by your computer, if available
- CPU (central processing unit) type (such as 80386)
- Coprocessor (if any)
- Mode used by Paradox
- Amount of conventional (main) memory

- Amount of extended and expanded memory available (if any)
- Display adapter and monitor being used
- Mouse driver version (if any)
- Configuration signature (if any)
- System boot drive
- Floppy disk drive information
- Hard disk drive information
- Contents of CONFIG.SYS
- Contents of AUTOEXEC.BAT

CONFIG.SYS and AUTOEXEC.BAT are DOS files that are executed automatically to configure your system whenever you start up or reboot the computer. Both of these files are stored on the root directory of the startup drive. For more information about these files and the commands within them, see your DOS documentation.

Machine Information Menu Options

In addition to scrolling through the information on the machine information report, you can also get machine information via the following menu options:

- **File ➤ CopyToFile** lets you save a copy of the report that's currently on your screen to a text file.
- **File ➤ Print** prints a copy of the report.

You may need to eject the page from the printer to see the report, using the printer's Form Feed or FF button, per instructions in your printer manual.

- **Search ➤ Find** lets you find matching text in the machine information file, like the Zoom feature discussed in Chapter 5.
- **Search ➤ Next** lets you find the next match, if any, like the Zoom Next feature described in Chapter 5.

Customizing Paradox

When you're finished viewing the machine information report, choose **C**ancel from the menu, click the close button in the upper-left corner of the window, or press Ctrl-F8.

Changing the Screen Display

To change the screen settings, choose Video from the CCP desktop menu. You'll see the options shown below, which are described in the following sections.

Video Settings

Choosing Video Settings displays the Video Settings dialog box shown earlier in Figure D.2. The options in this dialog box are described in the sections that follow.

Choosing a Monitor Type

You can choose any one of four display types from the Monitor Type options:

- **Autodetect:** Lets Paradox automatically determine the type of monitor you have, based on the type of display card installed. Choose this option if you're not sure what type of monitor you have.

- **Color:** If you have a color display adapter and color monitor, including CGA, EGA, VGA, and Super VGA, choose this option.

- **Monochrome:** If you have a monochrome adapter and monochrome monitor, choose this option.

CHANGING THE SCREEN DISPLAY

- **B&W:** If you have a CGA or EGA display card, but have a monochrome or black-and-white monitor attached to it, choose B&W. You can also choose this option if you have a color display adapter and color monitor, but want to run Paradox in black and white.

Eliminating "Snow"

If you see "snow" (irritating dots that appear in bursts) on the screen, and you are using a CGA monitor, you can eliminate it by selecting the Video "snow" option and choosing Prevent. Turning on snow prevention will cause some monitors to slow down, so don't do so unless you really need to.

Hiding or Displaying the Color Palette

When you are designing a custom form (Chapter 9) and choose Style ➤ Color from the Form Design screen to color a portion of the screen, the color palette appears automatically. The Color Palette setting in the Video Settings dialog box offers the options Show and Hide for choosing whether or not the color palette is automatically displayed after you choose Style ➤ Color to color a part of the form. (You can also press Alt-c to turn the color palette on and off as necessary to see what's behind the palette in the Form Design screen.)

Coloring Negative Numbers

Normally, Paradox displays negative numbers and negative currency values in unique colors, or in reverse video on a monochrome monitor. If you don't want Paradox to display the negative values differently from positive ones, deselect (remove the X from the check box) the appropriate option next to Negative Colors.

As mentioned, you can use either your mouse or the spacebar to select [X] or deselect [ ] check box options.

- **Numbers:** When selected, negative numeric and short numeric numbers (but not negative currency numbers) appear in a different color or in reverse video. When deselected, negative values appear in the same color as positive values.

CUSTOMIZING PARADOX

- **Currency:** When selected, negative currency amounts (the $ field type) appear in a different color. When deselected, negative currency values appear in the same color as positive ones.

Keep in mind that these options are only used to determine whether or not negative numbers and currency values are colored at all. If you want to change the actual colors, use the color settings, as described in the next section.

CAUTION: Keep in mind that although you usually have an OK or DO-IT! and Cancel option in each CCP dialog box, if you don't choose DO-IT! as you leave the CCP program and return to the desktop, any settings you have changed will not be saved or activated, no matter how many times you chose OK or DO-IT! to exit various dialog boxes within the CCP program.

Saving/Canceling Video Settings Selections

When you've finished making choices from the Video Settings dialog box, choose OK or press ↵ to accept those settings. Optionally, you can choose Cancel or press Esc to abandon your changes.

Changing the Color Settings

You can change the colors used for a variety of Paradox screen elements, such as the Paradox desktop, tables, report design screen, menu bars, help windows, and so forth. The color definition for a set of screen elements is called a *color setting*. You can create up to nine different color settings and then link a setting to a specific video mode (Color or B&W).

NOTE: Color settings are shared between the Standard and Full Screen User Interface modes. See the section about customizing the standard settings, later in this appendix, for details on setting the default user-interface mode.

CHANGING THE SCREEN DISPLAY

To define or change a color setting, or link a color setting to a video mode, choose Video ➤ Color Settings from the CCP desktop menu. You'll see a Color Settings dialog box like the one in Figure D.3, shown earlier. The Current Setting Assignment area of the dialog box shows which setting is currently assigned to the Color Monitor and B&W Monitor video modes. The example in Figure D.3 uses Paradox's default settings for both modes. The Settings Available area of the dialog box lists all the currently defined color settings. The example shows the six predefined color settings and two user-defined color settings: My Color Setting and My B&W Setting.

Here is a brief description of the buttons in the Color Settings screen. The following sections explain how to use each one in more detail.

- **Assign:** Lets you assign the currently highlighted setting to a specified video mode.
- **New:** Lets you create a new color setting The new color setting will be based on the default color setting for the specified video mode: Standard Color1 for color monitors and Standard B&W for monitors.
- **Edit:** Lets you change an existing color setting.
- **Copy:** Lets you copy the currently highlighted color setting settings to a new color setting.
- **Rename:** Lets you change the name of the currently highlighted color setting.
- **Delete:** Lets you delete the currently highlighted color setting.
- **Done:** Choosing the Done button or pressing F2 accepts the changes you made in the Color Settings dialog box and returns you to the CCP desktop menu. If you wish to cancel your changes, you must exit the CCP without saving any changes made while in the CCP program.

The Predefined and Default Color Settings

Paradox comes with these predefined color settings which can be assigned to either video mode:

- Standard Color1 (Default for Color mode)
- Standard Color2

Customizing Paradox

- Standard B&W (Default for B&W mode)
- LCD Normal
- LCD Inverse
- Plasma

These original default settings for Standard Color1 and Standard B&W will always be used when you specify a New setting, even if you have modified the settings with these names listed in the dialog box. Therefore, you always have access to the original default settings.

Creating a New Color Setting

To create a new setting, follow these steps:

1. Choose the **N**ew button from the Color Settings dialog box. You'll see the New Color Setting dialog box, shown in Figure D.4.

FIGURE D.4

The New Color Setting dialog box lets you name a new setting and choose which default setting (Color or B&W) to use.

2. Type the name for the new setting in the New Setting Name text box. Setting names can be up to 25 characters in length and can contain spaces.

3. If you typed the name of an existing setting, a pop-up menu will ask you to decide whether to overwrite it. If you're sure you want to overwrite it, choose **O**K; otherwise, choose **C**ancel and enter a different setting name.

4. Choose Color or B&W from the **S**tart With Default For radio buttons.

5. Choose OK or press ↵.

CHANGING THE SCREEN DISPLAY

After naming the color setting, you'll see the screen in Figure D.5. This screen lets you assign colors to all the areas of Paradox objects (tables, Query forms, and Report Design screens). To assign colors for other types of objects, choose options from the ScreenObjects submenu.

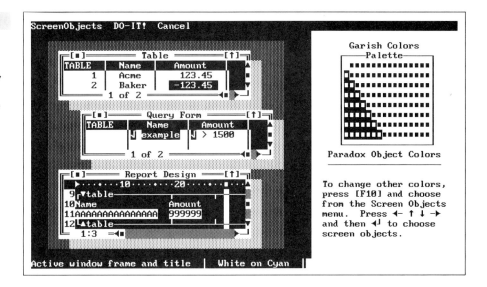

FIGURE D.5

This dialog box lets you assign colors to all the areas of tables, query tables, and report design screens. To change the colors of elements of forms, PAL objects, the desktop, the Help system, and dialog boxes, make selections from the ScreenObjects menu.

If you save the newly created color setting without changing its colors, it will have the colors (or black, white, and grays) of the default color setting.

Here are the basic steps for changing the colors of a specific image area:

1. Move the cursor to the area of the displayed image that you want to change. To do so, click your mouse on that area, press Tab, Shift-Tab, or the arrow keys until the cursor lands on the area you want to change. As you move the cursor, the status line at the bottom of the screen displays the following information about the currently selected area:

    - Currently selected screen element (for example, active window frame and title)

- Current color assignments for the selected area (for example, white on cyan)

2. To activate the Palette box, double-click the mouse on the area you want to select, or press ↵ or the spacebar. The cursor will place an outline highlight on whatever color is currently assigned to the selected area.

> **NOTE** Always check the status line very carefully before changing the colors. In Figure D.5, the cursor is on the active window frame and title of the table object.

3. Use the arrow keys or click your mouse to select the desired color in the Palette box. The screen will change to reflect your selection as you move the cursor to different colors.

4. To choose the current color definition for the selected area, double-click the mouse on that color in the Palette box, or press ↵ or the spacebar. To discard the current color definition and return the selected area to its previous color, press Esc instead.

After you complete step 4, the cursor will return to the image area. Repeat the above steps for all the areas you want to change.

To change the colors of other objects that don't appear on the current image, choose **S**creenObjects from the menu bar. You'll see the following submenu:

Choose an option from the submenu, then use the four steps above to select and change the colors for areas of the displayed image. Here is a brief description of each option on the ScreenObjects menu:

- **Paradox Objects:** Displays the image for defining colors of Paradox tables, Query forms, and Report Design screens, as in Figure D.5.
- **Form:** Displays the image for defining default form colors and form design area colors.
- **Desktop:** Displays the image for defining colors of menu bars; pull-down menus; inactive, dragging, and active windows; and function-key bars on the Speedbar.
- **Help:** Displays the image for defining colors of Help screens.
- **Dialog Box:** Displays the image for defining colors of dialog box frames, contents, radio buttons, check boxes, and command buttons.

When you're finished making changes to the new color setting, choose **DO-IT!** from the menu or press F2 to save the new color setting and return to the Color Settings dialog box. The new setting will appear highlighted in the Settings Available list. If you want to return to the Color Settings dialog box without saving your changes, choose **C**ancel ➤ **Y**es from the menu instead.

Editing a Color Setting

If you later decide that the colors defined for a color setting aren't quite right, you can change them:

1. Move the cursor to the color setting you want to change (or click on that setting with your mouse) in the **S**ettings Available list.
2. Choose the **E**dit button. You'll see the screen shown earlier in Figure D.5.
3. Follow the steps described in the previous section for changing the color of various image areas and objects.
4. When you're finished making changes, choose **DO-IT!** from the menu or press the Do-It! key, F2, to accept the revised colors and return to the Color Settings dialog box. If you want to return to the Color Settings dialog box without saving your changes, choose **C**ancel ➤ **Y**es from the menu instead.

Assigning a Color Setting

To assign or link an available color setting to a video mode, follow these steps:

1. Move the cursor to the color setting you want to assign (or click on that setting with your mouse) in the **S**ettings Available list.

2. Choose the **A**ssign button. You'll see the Assign Color Setting dialog box, shown in Figure D.6.

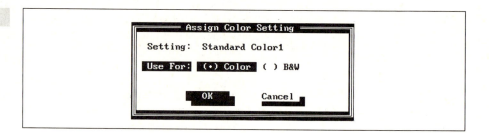

FIGURE D.6

The Assign Color Setting dialog box appears after your choose the Assign button.

3. Choose the **U**se For area of the dialog box and choose either the Color or B&W radio button.

You'll be returned to the Color Settings dialog box, and the name of the color setting you chose will appear below the name of the appropriate video mode in the Current Setting Assignment area of the dialog box.

Copying, Renaming, or Deleting a Color Setting

The **C**opy button lets you copy an existing color setting to a new color setting. This is handy when you want to create a new color setting using colors that are similar to an existing color setting. After copying to the new color setting, you can use the Edit button to adjust its colors. To copy a color setting, follow these steps:

1. Move the cursor to the color setting you want to copy (or click on that color setting with your mouse) in the **S**ettings Available list.

2. Choose the **C**opy button.

3. Type the name for the new color setting. This name cannot be the same as the current colors setting.

4. If you typed the name of an existing color setting, a pop-up menu will ask you to decide whether to overwrite it. If you're sure you want to overwrite it, choose **O**K; otherwise, choose **C**ancel and enter a different color setting name.

5. Choose OK or press ↵ to complete the copy (or choose Cancel to cancel the copy operation).

You'll be returned to the Color Settings dialog box. The new color setting name will appear in the **S**ettings Available list and will be highlighted. You can now choose the **E**dit button to begin editing the new color setting, if you wish.

Renaming a Color Setting

Here are the steps for changing the name of an existing color setting:

1. Move the cursor to the color setting you want to rename (or click on that color setting with your mouse) in the **S**ettings Available list.

2. Choose the **R**ename button.

3. Type the new name for the color setting. Again, if you typed the name of an existing color setting, a pop-up menu will ask if you want to overwrite it. If you're sure you want to overwrite it, choose **O**K; otherwise, choose **C**ancel and enter a different color setting name.

4. Choose OK or press ↵ to complete the operation (or choose Cancel to cancel the operation).

You'll be returned to the Color Settings dialog box. The revised color setting name will appear in the **S**ettings Available list and will be highlighted. If you renamed a color setting that is currently assigned to a video mode, the new name will appear in place of the old name in the Current Setting Assignment area.

Deleting a Color Setting

If you no longer need an existing color setting, you can delete it as follows:

1. Move the cursor to the color setting you want to delete (or click on that color setting with your mouse) in the **S**ettings Available list.

CUSTOMIZING PARADOX

2. Choose the **D**elete button.

3. If you're sure you want to delete the color setting, choose OK from the pop-up menu that appears. (If you do not want to delete the color setting, choose Cancel instead.)

The color setting will be deleted from the list. As usual, your changes are not permanently saved until you choose **DO-IT!** from the CCP desktop menu (or press F2 while at that menu) to save all changes and return to the Paradox desktop.

NOTE If a color setting is assigned to a video mode when you attempt to delete it, Paradox will prompt you to change the assignment before deleting the color setting.

Saving/Canceling the Color Settings

When you've finished making choices from the Color Settings dialog box, choose the **D**one button or press Do-It! (F2) to accept those settings. Optionally, you can press Esc to abandon your changes (this dialog box doesn't have a Cancel button).

Changing the Report Defaults

The Reports option on the CCP desktop menu lets you choose default settings for any new formatted reports you create, as discussed in Chapters 8 and 15. (Existing formatted and Instant Reports are not affected by any changes you make in the CCP.)

When you are designing a specific report, you can override many of the default settings for just that report using options on the Settings menu in the Report Design screen or by using the **R**eport ➤ **S**etPrinter options from the Paradox desktop, as discussed in Chapter 8.

CHANGING THE REPORT DEFAULTS

When you first choose Reports from the CCP desktop menu, you'll see a submenu with these options, discussed in detail in the sections that follow.

Changing the Report Settings

Choosing Report Settings takes you to the Report Settings dialog box shown in Figure D.7. Each option of the dialog box is summarized below:

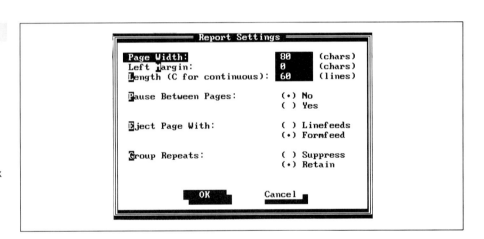

FIGURE D.7

The Report Settings dialog box lets you change the default settings for future Instant Reports and formatted reports. As discussed in Chapter 8, you can adjust these settings to get Paradox and your printer in sync.

- **Page Width:** Use this to set the default for the number of character columns across the page. The original default is 80 (10 characters to the inch across an 8-inch page). Reduce this number to allow a wider right margin (e.g., to about 72 or 75 for a 1-inch right margin).

The suggested settings in this section work well with many laser printers.

Customizing Paradox

- **Left Margin:** Use this to set the default width of the left margin in characters. The original default is 0, meaning that Paradox will start printing at the left edge of that page (that is, as far to the left edge of the page as the printer can reach). To create a 1-inch margin at the left edge of the page, change this option to about 8 or 10.

- **Length:** This option specifies the number of lines to print per page. Typically, this is either 60 or 66 when printing on $8\frac{1}{2}$-×-11-inch paper, and you should set it to match the number of lines your printer currently prints per page. You can enter a new length in the range of 2 to 2000, or you can enter C (for continuous) to treat the paper as one long page, as when printing on tractor-fed mailing labels.

- **Pause Between Pages:** If you want Paradox to pause between printed pages to give you time to insert a new page, select Yes; otherwise, leave this option at the default setting of No. If you choose Yes, you'll be prompted to insert a new page into the printer and press any key when you print the report.

- **Eject Page With:** Determines whether Paradox ejects the current page from the printer using a linefeeds or a formfeed code. For Hewlett-Packard (HP) and similar laser printers, you might want to choose the form feed method. As discussed in Chapter 8, the form feed method can be easier to work with because it ensures that the completed page is ejected from the printer and printing starts at the top of the next page.

- **Group Repeats:** Paradox lets you decide whether to print repetitive group values in reports that use Group bands. Your options are Retain (to print repeated values), the default, and Suppress (to prevent printing of repeated values).

Remember that you can override report settings made in the CCP by using options on the Setting menu in the Report Design screen.

> **NOTE** See Chapter 8 for more information on getting Paradox and your printer in sync, and testing your new report settings. See Chapter 15 for more information on grouping and group repeats.

Saving or Canceling Report Settings

When you're finished choosing options from the Report Settings dialog box, choose OK or press ↵ to accept your changes. Or, choose Cancel or press Esc to abandon your changes. Either selection will return you to the CCP desktop menu.

Remember, only new reports that you create will be affected by any changes you make here. Existing reports will remain unchanged. This includes the Standard Reports that are already created for existing tables. Standard Reports are automatically created when you press the Instant Report key (Alt-F7). If you want an Instant Report to use your new settings, first use **T**ools ➤ **D**elete ➤ **R**eport to delete the existing Standard Report, then press Alt-F7 to print a new Instant Report.

Defining Printer Setup Strings

When you choose Reports ➤ Printer Setup from the CCP desktop menu, you'll see the Paradox Printer Setup table, shown in Figure D.8. The table already includes some sample setup strings for IBM, HP, Epson, Okidata, and PostScript printers. You can change this table to define printer setup strings that are relevant to your particular printer.

FIGURE D.8

Predefined printer setup strings in the Paradox Printer Setup table

DO-IT! Cancel

Printer Setup

PRINTER	Name	Port	Setup String	Reset String
1	StandardPrinter*	LPT1		
2	Small-IBMgraphics	LPT1	\027W\000\015	
3	Reg-IBMgraphics	LPT1	\027W\000\018	
4	Small-Epson-MX/FX	LPT1	\015	\027@
5	Small-Oki-92/93	LPT1	\015	
6	Small-Oki-82/83	LPT1	\029	
7	Small-Oki-192	LPT1	\029	
8	HPLaserJet	LPT1	\027E\027&l0o6d3e60	\027E
9	HP-Portrait-66lines	LPT1	\027E\027&l0o7.27c3	\027E
10	HP-Landscape-Normal	LPT1	\027E\027&l1o6d3e45	\027E
11	HP-Compressed	LPT1	\027E\027&l0o6d3e60	\027E
12	HP-LandscpCompressed	LPT1	\027E\027&l1o6d3e45	\027E
13	Intl-IBMcompatible	LPT1	\027\054	
14	Intl-IBMcondensed	LPT1	\027\054\015	
15	Postscript-Portrait	LPT1	FILE=PDOXPORT.PS	\004
16	Postscript-Landscape	LPT1	FILE=PDOXLAND.PS	\004

1 of 16

Editing printer setup table. [F1]: Help, [F2]: DO-IT!, [F10]: Menu

Customizing Paradox

This table lets you define printer setup strings for use in the Report Design screen to change the paper size or print size for the entire report. You need to provide the following for each setup string you create:

- **Name:** You can provide a descriptive name of your own choosing, up to 25 characters (but no blank spaces).

- **Port:** Specify the port to which the printer is attached. This must be a valid DOS printer port name, such as LPT1 (parallel port 1), COM1 (serial port 1), PRN, or AUX.

- **Setup String:** Specify the setup string you want to send to the printer *before* the report is printed. For information about setup strings that are unique to your printer, consult your printer's documentation. As discussed in Chapter 15, the setup string must be defined in Paradox format, with control characters identified by a backslash and a three-digit number. For example, Ctrl-A is \001, Ctrl-B is \002, and so forth up to Ctrl-Z, which is \026. The Escape character is \027. The maximum length of the setup string is 50 characters.

- **Reset String:** Specify a reset string to send to the printer *after* the report is printed. If you don't specify a reset string, the printer stays in whatever mode the setup string put it in before you printed the report. Thus, any additional text you print will be printed in the mode defined by the setup string (unless you turn the printer off and then on again).

> **TIP**
> To define printer strings for portions of text within the report—for example, for boldface or italic—use calculated fields, as described in Chapter 15.

The Printer Setup table is like any other Paradox table, and it is already in Edit mode when it appears on the screen. You can insert records by pressing Ins, delete records by pressing Delete, switch to Field view by pressing Alt-F5 or Ctrl-f (or double-clicking the mouse), and so on.

Figure D.9 shows an example in which new printer setup strings in records 17 and 18 switch the HP LaserJet to print legal-size $8\frac{1}{2}$-×-14-inch paper at 16.66 characters per inch (cpi) using a legal-size paper tray.

CHANGING THE REPORT DEFAULTS

FIGURE D.9

Records 17 and 18 are new entries to the Printer Setup table: one to print on legal-size paper in portrait mode, and the other to print on legal-size paper in landscape mode (sideways).

```
 DO-IT! Cancel
================================ Printer Setup ================================[↕]
 PRINTER │       Name          │ Port │    Setup String      │ Reset String
    1    │ StandardPrinter*    │ LPT1 │                      │
    2    │ Small-IBMgraphics   │ LPT1 │ \027W\000\015        │
    3    │ Reg-IBMgraphics     │ LPT1 │ \027W\000\018        │
    4    │ Small-Epson-MX/FX   │ LPT1 │ \015                 │ \027@
    5    │ Small-Oki-92/93     │ LPT1 │ \015                 │
    6    │ Small-Oki-82/83     │ LPT1 │ \029                 │
    7    │ Small-Oki-192       │ LPT1 │ \029                 │
    8    │ HPLaserJet          │ LPT1 │ \027E\027&l0o6d3e60  │ \027E
    9    │ HP-Portrait-66lines │ LPT1 │ \027E\027&l0o7.27c3  │ \027E
   10    │ HP-Landscape-Normal │ LPT1 │ \027E\027&l1o6d3e45  │ \027E
   11    │ HP-Compressed       │ LPT1 │ \027E\027&l0o6d3e60  │ \027E
   12    │ HP-LandscpCompressed│ LPT1 │ \027E\027&l1o6d3e45  │ \027E
   13    │ Intl-IBMcompatible  │ LPT1 │ \027\054             │
   14    │ Intl-IBMcondensed   │ LPT1 │ \027\054\015         │
   15    │ Postscript-Portrait │ LPT1 │ FILE=PDOXPORT.PS     │ \004
   16    │ Postscript-Landscape│ LPT1 │ FILE=PDOXLAND.PS     │ \004
   17    │ HP-Legal-Port-Small │ LPT1 │ \027E\027(s16.66H    │ \027E
   18    │ HP-Legal-Land-Small │ LPT1 │ \027E\&l1O\027(s16.  │ \027E

======== 18 of 18 ========
Editing printer setup table. [F1]: Help, [F2]: DO-IT!, [F10]: Menu
```

These are named HP-Legal-Port-Small (portrait orientation) and HP-Legal-Land-Small (landscape orientation), respectively. The setup strings are defined per the documentation for that printer. The \027E at the start of each string ensures that the printer is reset first. The reset string is Esc-e (\027E), so that the printer will return to standard $8\tfrac{1}{2}$-×-11-inch paper after the report is printed.

NOTE The setup strings for the HP printers (records 8 through 12) are truncated in Figure D.9. To see the full strings, you would need to switch to Field view.

StandardPrinter* is usually the default setup string, and sends no codes to the printer, this works well with many dot-matrix printers. To define one of the setup strings as the default for all future printed reports, just type an asterisk at the end of its name. (Be sure to also remove any other asterisks, since only one setup string can be designated as the default.)

CUSTOMIZING PARADOX

After defining your setup string(s), choose **DO-IT!** or press F2 to accept your changes. As usual, your changes are saved when you exit the CCP and return to the Paradox desktop.

Next time you're in the Report Design screen, the names of your new setup strings will be available in the submenu that appears when you choose **S**etting ➤ **S**etup ➤ **P**redefined to define the setup string for the current report. You can choose the new settings at that point. Don't forget that when you choose a new paper size, you'll also want to change the page length and width to take advantage of that size. Use the **S**etting ➤ **P**age-Layout options in the Report Design screen to do so. For example, to print on legal portrait paper at 16.66 cpi, change the page length to about 78 and the right margin to about 120. To print on legal landscape paper at 16.66 cpi, set the page length to about 45 and the width to about 220.

> **NOTE** See Chapter 8 for more information about using setup strings to change the print size or page size of the current report.

Now when you print the report, Paradox will send the printer the setup string you specified. Then, when Paradox has finished printing the report, it will send the reset string, if any.

Changing the Graph Defaults

The CCP lets you change default settings for various aspects of displaying and printing graphs. When you select Graphs from the CCP desktop menu, you'll see the submenu below:

These submenu options are described in the sections that follow.

Choosing the Instant Graph Defaults

The Graph Settings option lets you change the settings that Paradox automatically uses to display a graph when you press the Instant Graph key (Ctrl-F7).

When you choose **Graphs ➤ Graph Settings** from the CCP desktop menu, you're taken to a screen and set of menu options that are virtually identical to those that appear when you choose **Image ➤ Graph ➤ Modify** in Paradox. From there you can change just about any graph settings, as discussed in Chapter 10. However, unlike **Image ➤ Graph ➤ Modify** in Paradox, the selections you make here in the CCP affect all future Instant Graphs—not just the graph you happen to be viewing at the moment.

For instance, suppose you use **Overall ➤ Titles** to change the main title to your company name. After you choose DO-IT! and leave the CCP, your company name becomes the standard main title for future graphs. So, when you get back to Paradox and press Ctrl-F7 to view a graph, your company name, rather than the table name, appears at the top of the graph. Of course, you can still use **Image ➤ Graph ➤ Modify** while viewing that graph to change the settings for the current graph only.

Choosing a Printer for Graphs

As mentioned in Chapter 10, you need to define a graphics printer before you can print graphs. Choosing **Graphs ➤ Printers** from the CCP desktop menu allows you to do so. It displays the dialog box shown in Figure D.10.

Once you get to the Graph Printer Settings dialog box, you can follow these steps to define one or more printers for printing graphs:

1. In the **C**hoose Printer group of options, choose one of the printers by using your mouse or the arrow keys. If you're defining your first graphic printer, choose Printer 1.

2. Choose the Set**P**rinterType button. You'll see a list of supported graphic printer manufacturers, as in Figure D.11.

3. Move the cursor to your printer manufacturer and then press ↵, or simply double-click on the manufacturer name for your printer. The printer models for that manufacturer will appear in the Model list.

Customizing Paradox

FIGURE D.10

The Graph Printer Settings dialog box, accessed by choosing Graphs ➤ Printers from the CCP desktop menu, lets you define printers for printing graphs.

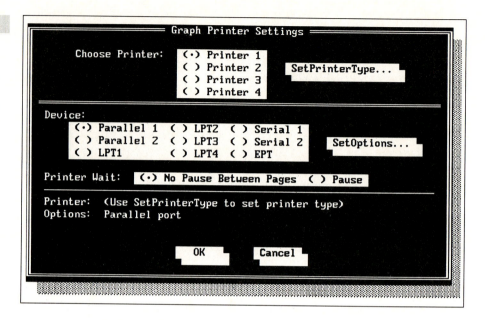

FIGURE D.11

List of supported printer manufacturers

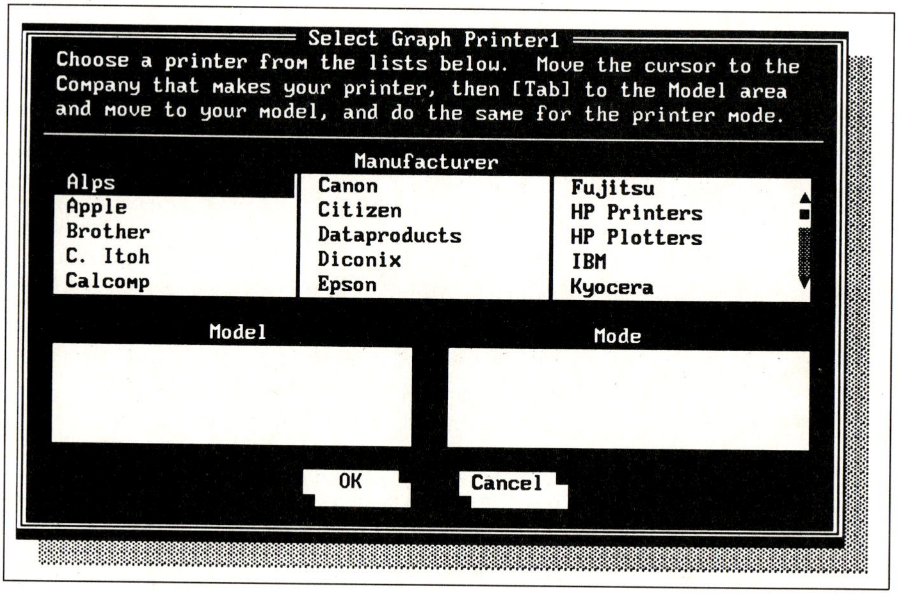

4. Move the cursor to the model name for your printer in the Model list and then press ↵, or double-click on that model name.

5. Depending on the printer manufacturer and model you chose, a list of available modes for that printer may appear in the Mode list. For example, for a laser printer, you might see Medium quality (150×150 dpi) and High Quality (300×300 dpi) options, as well as paper size options. Choose a mode by moving the cursor to it and pressing ↵ or by double-clicking on that mode.

NOTE The abbreviation dpi stands for dots per inch. The more dots per inch, the better the print quality of the graphic, but the longer it takes to print it.

6. Choose OK or press ↵ to accept the settings. You'll be returned to the Graph Printer Settings dialog box. The name and manufacturer of the printer you chose appear next to the printer title, near the bottom of the dialog box.

7. Choose the port to which the printer is connected by selecting a radio button in the Device group, either by clicking the appropriate option, or by pressing Tab until the highlight is within that group, then using the arrow keys. (If you're defining a parallel printer, skip to step 10.)

8. If the printer is attached to a serial port, and you chose a Serial option in the preceding step, choose the SetOptions button: press Alt-o, or click on the button, or press Tab until that button is highlighted and then press ↵.

9. Define the Baud Rate, Parity, and Stop Bits for the serial port. (If you're not sure what these settings are, try leaving each option set to Leave As Is.) Choose OK or press ↵ to leave the Serial Printer dialog box.

10. If you want the printer to wait for you to manually feed a page before printing each graph, choose Pause next to the Printer Wait option. Otherwise, leave this option set to No Pause Between Pages to feed paper normally.

11. Choose OK or press ↵ after defining the printer settings.

Customizing Paradox

If you want to define multiple graphics printers, or change existing settings, you can choose Graphs ➤ Printers again, then repeat the steps above, choosing a different printer in step 1. When you've finished defining graphics printers, you can save your CCP changes.

Choosing a Screen Mode for Graphs

By default, Paradox automatically displays graphs on the screen in the highest resolution available for your monitor. If your graphics display card supports a variety of graphics, such as CGA, EGA, and VGA, and you specifically want to use one of those options, follow these steps:

1. Choose **G**raphs ➤ **S**creen from the CCP desktop menu. You'll see the screen shown in Figure D.12.

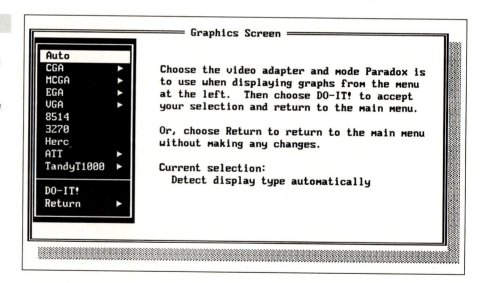

FIGURE D.12

Display card adapter options for displaying graphs on the screen. The first option, Auto, displays graphs in the highest resolution available for your monitor.

2. Choose the display adapter type and, if available, a resolution option from the submenu that appears. If in doubt, choose **A**uto.

CAUTION Do not choose an option that is not supported by your display adapter.

3. Choose **DO-IT!** from the menu (or press F2) to accept the changes and return to the CCP desktop menu. (To abandon your changes and return, choose **R**eturn ➤ **Y**es instead.)

Customizing the Standard Settings

The Standard Settings option on the CCP desktop menu lets you customize a number of Paradox's standard settings. When you choose Standard Settings, the Standard Settings dialog box, shown in Figure D.13, appears. Options in this dialog box are described in the following sections.

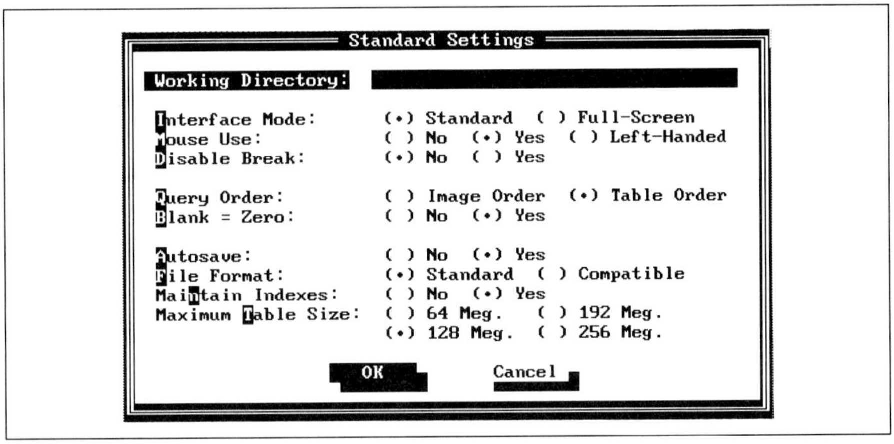

FIGURE D.13

The Standard Settings dialog box lets you change default settings for the general Paradox interface.

```
======================= Standard Settings =======================
Working Directory:

Interface Mode:       (•) Standard    ( ) Full-Screen
Mouse Use:            ( ) No  (•) Yes  ( ) Left-Handed
Disable Break:        (•) No  ( ) Yes

Query Order:          ( ) Image Order  (•) Table Order
Blank = Zero:         ( ) No  (•) Yes

Autosave:             ( ) No  (•) Yes
File Format:          (•) Standard    ( ) Compatible
Maintain Indexes:     ( ) No  (•) Yes
Maximum Table Size:   ( ) 64 Meg.   ( ) 192 Meg.
                      (•) 128 Meg.  ( ) 256 Meg.

          OK               Cancel
```

When you're finished with the Standard Settings dialog box, choose OK to accept your changes, or Cancel to abandon them. Either selection will return you to the CCP desktop menu.

Working Directory

Use the Working Directory option to designate the default working directory where Paradox stores and searches for tables, report formats, custom forms, and other files that you create. Be sure to specify the name of an existing directory. Within Paradox, you can override this default by using **Tools ➤ More ➤ Directory** from the desktop, or by placing a SetDir command in the Init script.

Changing the working directory for the current session is described in Chapter 2. Using SetDir in the Init script to set the working directory is described in Chapter 21.

Interface Mode

Use the Interface Mode option to specify Standard or Full Screen mode as the default startup mode for Paradox. Standard mode is Paradox 4.5's default user interface. Full Screen mode automatically opens tables, forms, and some Paradox objects in full-screen windows (see Appendix B for more information about the new Full Screen User Interface).

Mouse Use

Paradox automatically senses whether a mouse is part of your configuration; therefore, you only need to use the Mouse Use option for the following reasons:

- If you want to tell Paradox that you're using a left-handed mouse (choose Left-Handed)
- To switch back to the default right-handed mouse setting (choose Yes)
- To disable your mouse for some reason (choose No).

Disable Break

Normally, you can press Ctrl-Break to interrupt and cancel any operation in Paradox that takes a long time, such as sorting a large table or printing a report. If you want to disable this interrupt capability, set Disable Break to Yes. Disabling the Break key might improve processing speed slightly.

Query Order

As discussed in Chapter 7, the Query Order option lets you specify whether the order of fields in the Answer table after a query is the same as the original table (Table Order), or the same as the Query form order (Image Order).

NOTE Remember that you can also use the Rotate key, Ctrl-r, or Image ➤ Move to rearrange the fields in the Answer table.

Blank = Zero

Set Blank = Zero to No to treat blank fields used in calculations as though they contain no value. Set the option to Yes to treat blank fields used in calculations as though they contain a numeric value of zero.

If Blank = Zero is set to No, any calculation that attempts to use a blank field value will end up with a blank result. This setting assumes that if a field is empty, its contents are probably either intentionally or accidentally omitted. So rather than assume the blank field means zero, Paradox just refuses to perform the calculation so you don't end up with an incorrect result in the calculation.

If Blank = Zero is set to Yes, any field that's blank is treated as though it contains a value of zero in a calculation.

Let's look at an example. Suppose a table contains fields named Qty, Unit Price, and Tax Rate, where Tax Rate is usually some number like 7.75 to indicate a sales tax rate of 7.75%. Then in the calculated field of a query, report, or form, you include an expression like

[Qty] * [Unit Price] * (1 + ([Tax Rate]/100))

to calculate the extended price, including sales tax, in each record. If the Blank = Zero option is No, Paradox will not display a result in the calculated field for any record that has an empty Qty, Unit Price, or Tax Rate field. However, if the Blank = Zero option is set to Yes, Paradox will perform a calculation in every record of the table. When calculating records that have a blank in the Qty, Unit Price, or Tax Rate fields, Paradox would just treat these blank fields as though they contain a value of zero.

CAUTION Keep in mind that the probability of getting incorrect results in a calculation is higher if you treat blank fields as zeros. Because a blank result in a calculated field is readily noticeable, it might alert you to the fact that one or more fields in the record were accidentally omitted.

Autosave

The Autosave option determines whether Paradox automatically saves your new data from time to time. If Autosave is set to Yes (the preset default), Paradox automatically saves your work during entry or edit operations, even if you don't press the Do-It! key (F2).

Setting Autosave to Yes can minimize data loss in the event of a power failure or other mishap. You can still use Cancel to cancel your changes or Undo to undo them incrementally. Furthermore, you should notice no performance difference with Autosave set to Yes. Therefore, it's best to leave this option set to Yes.

If Autosave is set to No, Paradox saves your work only when you explicitly ask it to (for example, by pressing F2, choosing **DO-IT!** from a menu, or moving to another record in CoEdit mode).

File Format

You can change the File Format settings to determine the default file format used to save your tables when you first create them. Choose Standard to use the Paradox 4.5 and 4.0 format, or Compatible to use the older Paradox 3.5 format. Standard is the default setting and is preferred unless you need to create tables that are accessible by versions of Paradox earlier than 4.0.

CUSTOMIZING THE STANDARD SETTINGS

If you choose Compatible as the file format, you will not be able to create or use memo or binary fields.

Maintain Indexes

The Maintain Indexes option controls whether Paradox automatically maintains secondary indexes for keyed tables created with Tools ➤ QuerySpeed. This option affects only tables that have a primary index and one or more secondary indexes.

When Maintain Indexes is set to Yes, secondary indexes in keyed tables are updated incrementally, on a record-by-record basis. This approach can slow down data entry and editing for very large tables. With the option set to No (the preset default), the secondary indexes are updated in groups or batches, and only when they are about to be used; you might notice some delays when performing operations (such as queries) that require updated indexes.

Be aware that changing this setting affects only new tables and indexes you will create in the future; it has no effect on existing tables or indexes. If you do want an existing secondary index to use the new settings, you must first use **T**ools ➤ **D**elete ➤ **I**ndex from the Paradox desktop to delete the existing secondary indexes for the table that contains them. Next you must set up a query that will regenerate the desired secondary indexes, then use **T**ools ➤ **Q**uerySpeed to recreate the secondary indexes you just deleted.

For more information about indexes and keyed tables, see Chapter 13. See Chapter 12 for more information about the Tools menu options.

Maximum Table Size

The Maximum Table Size setting allows you to set the maximum number of bytes that Paradox can handle in a single table. The default setting of 128 megabytes is probably best for most situations.

Customizing Paradox

Paradox will run slightly less efficiently, but offer a savings in disk storage of small to medium sized tables if you choose the lowest setting of 64 megabytes. If you will be creating tables of 20 megabytes or more, you may want to select one of the higher maximums.

Paradox sets the maximum table size at the time of table creation. If you want to change the maximum table size of an existing table with a lot of data in it, the safest method is to follow these steps:

1. Change the Maximum Table Size Setting in the CCP.
2. Create a new table structure, with the same structure as your existing table, using the **C**reate choice on the Paradox desktop main menu bar.
3. Use **T**ools ➤ **M**ore ➤ **A**dd to add the records from your old table to the new table.

Formatting Data

Choosing the Format Data option on the CCP desktop menu takes you to the Format Data dialog box shown in Figure D.14. In this dialog box, you can set defaults for operation of the Paradox Editor in non-script text files and memo fields. This dialog box also contains settings for changing the default number and date formats.

FIGURE D.14

The Format Data dialog box lets you set formatting options in the Paradox Editor and set the format of dates and numbers in all Paradox tables.

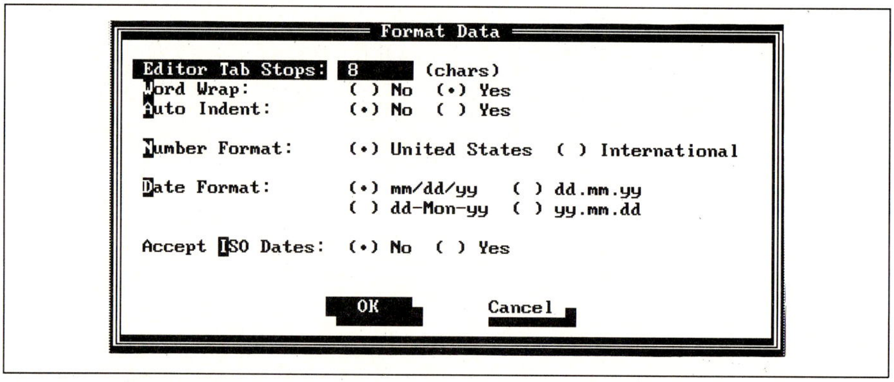

```
================= Format Data =================
Editor Tab Stops:  8        (chars)
Word Wrap:        ( ) No  (•) Yes
Auto Indent:      (•) No  ( ) Yes

Number Format:    (•) United States  ( ) International
Date Format:      (•) mm/dd/yy     ( ) dd.mm.yy
                  ( ) dd-Mon-yy    ( ) yy.mm.dd

Accept ISO Dates: (•) No  ( ) Yes

          OK              Cancel
```

Setting Editor Defaults in Text Files and Memo Fields

The first three options in the Format Data dialog box allow you to choose tab stop settings, change the default word-wrap setting, and specify whether the Editor will auto-indent paragraphs.

The following settings affect the Editor's settings in text files (other than script files) and in memo fields. They do not affect the Editor's operation when editing script files. See the section about setting PAL defaults, later in this chapter, for information about setting defaults for script editing.

- **Editor Tab Stops:** This setting determines the number of spaces between tab stops in text files and in memo fields. Enter a number for the default number of spaces the Tab key moves the cursor. The default is 8 spaces.

- **Word Wrap**: This setting determines whether the Editor will automatically wrap lines between carriage returns in non-script text files and in memo fields. The default is Yes, which enables the word-wrap feature.

- **Auto Indent:** This setting turns on the auto-indenting of paragraphs in the Editor in non-script text files and in memo fields. The auto-indent is equal to the indent of the previous line. The default for the setting is No.

Changing the Default Format of Numbers and Dates

The Format Data dialog box also lets you define the format of dates and numbers in all your Paradox tables. The options are described below:

- **Number Format:** Lets you choose a format for displaying numbers and currency values in either United States format (comma for separator, period for decimal point, e.g., 123,456.78) or International format (decimal for separator, comma for decimal point, e.g., 123.456,78).

- **Date Format:** Lets you choose a format for displaying Paradox dates: mm/dd/yy (e.g., 12/31/93), dd-Mon-yy (e.g., 31-Dec-93), dd.mm.yy (31.12.93), or yy.mm.dd (e.g., 93.12.31).

CUSTOMIZING PARADOX

- **Accept ISO Dates:** Set this option to Yes if you want Paradox to accept dates expressed in ISO format (e.g., 19931231 for 12/31/93). Otherwise, leave the option set to No.

When you're finished, choose OK to accept your changes, or Cancel to abandon them, and return to the CCP desktop menu.

If you want to override the default date format settings for a specific table, you can use the **Image ➤ Format** options from the Paradox desktop while viewing or editing that table.

Changing the Network Defaults

The Network option on the CCP desktop menu lets you change default settings at the current workstation in a network. When you select Network, the Network Settings dialog box, shown in Figure D.15, appears. Options in this dialog box are described in the following sections.

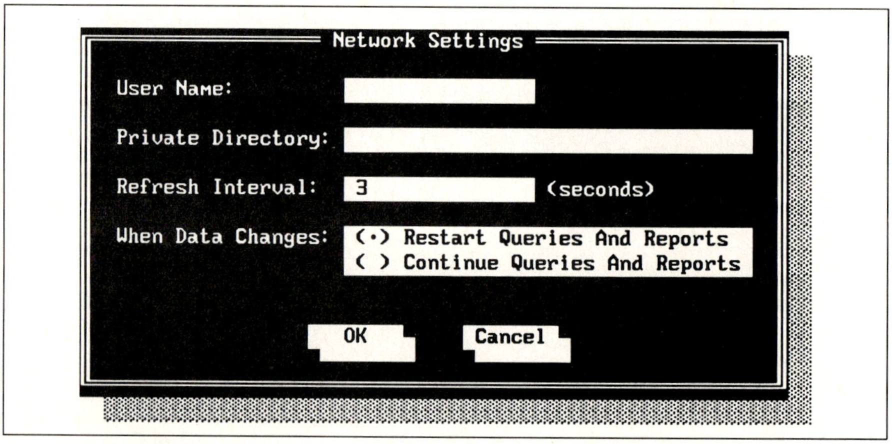

FIGURE D.15

The Network Settings dialog box lets you change the default settings used by the current network workstation. To get to this dialog box, choose Network from the CCP desktop menu.

NOTE See Appendix C for more information about using Paradox on a network.

User Name

The User Name option sets the default network user name for the current workstation. Other users will see this name if they try to gain access to an object that you've locked.

Paradox will use the name set in your network's operating system if you do not specify a user name in the CCP or through the **T**ools ➤ **N**et ➤ **U**ser Name options from the Paradox desktop.

Private Directory

The Private Directory option lets you choose a private directory for the current workstation. Each workstation must have its own private directory for storing temporary tables such as Answer and Keyviol. Typically, this is the \PDOX45 directory on the local hard disk. When specifying a private directory, be sure to include both the drive and directory name—for example, C:\PDOX45—and be sure that the specified directory exists.

NOTE To temporarily change the default private directory, choose Tools ➤ Net ➤ SetPrivate from the Paradox desktop.

Refresh Interval

The Refresh Interval option designates the interval between the screen refreshes (screen refreshes let network users see one another's changes to shared table data). The default setting for this refresh interval is every 3 seconds. You can change this to any value from 1 second to 3600 seconds (one hour), or you can leave it blank, which disables the automatic refreshing.

To change the refresh interval from the Paradox desktop, choose **T**ools ➤ **N**et ➤ **A**utoRefresh or select the AutoRefresh option from the CoEdit menu when editing a table.

When Data Changes

The When Data Changes option lets you decide how Paradox handles your queries or reports when other users on the network are making changes. Your options are:

- **Restart Queries and Reports:** With this option set, Paradox restarts your query or report as soon as it notices that another user has changed the data in a table that you're querying or printing from.

- **Continue Queries and Reports:** With this option set, Paradox ignores changes made by other users to the table you're querying or printing from; it simply proceeds with the operation as though other users hadn't even made changes to the table involved.

If you frequently perform queries or output reports from a large table on a network, you may want to change the When Data Changes setting to Continue Queries and Reports. Reports from a large database on an active network can cause your reports and queries to "hiccup," repeatedly starting over as users change data in the reporting or queried table. To temporarily change the default during a query or report output, choose **Tools ➤ Net ➤ Changes** from the Paradox desktop, then choose Restart or Continue.

When you're finished with the Network Settings dialog box, choose OK to accept your changes, or Cancel to abandon them. You'll then be returned to the CCP desktop menu.

Setting the PAL Defaults

The PAL option in the CCP desktop menu lets you change general defaults that pertain primarily to PAL, the Paradox Application Language. When you choose PAL, you're taken to the PAL dialog box shown in Figure D.16, which contains the options described in the following sections.

> **NOTE** See Chapters 17 and 21 for more information about using PAL in scripts.

FIGURE D.16

The PAL dialog box, accessed by choosing PAL from the CCP desktop menu, lets you change the defaults for options that pertain to the Paradox Application Language.

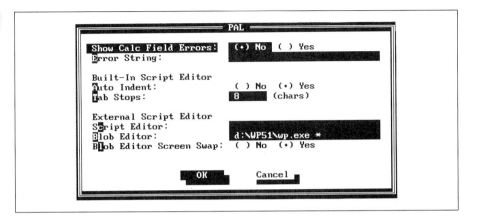

Showing or Hiding Calculation Field Errors

The Show Calc Field Errors option in the PAL dialog box lets you determine whether PAL displays an error message in response to an error in a calculated field. Normally, no error message is displayed.

To have PAL display an error message in a faulty calculated field, follow these steps:

1. Set **S**how Calc Field Error to Yes.
2. Choose **E**rror String, then type the message that you want the faulty calculation to display (such as *Bad calc field*).

Setting Editor Defaults in Script Files

The choices under Built-in Script Editor set default tab stop settings and specify whether the Editor will auto-indent paragraphs. The following settings affect the Editor's settings when working in script files. (See the Format Data dialog box description, earlier in this chapter, for information about changing the Editor's defaults for these settings when working in text file, other than scripts, and in memo fields).

- **Auto Indent:** This setting turns on the auto-indenting of paragraphs in the Editor in script files. The auto-indent is equal to indent of the previous line. The default for the setting is Yes. Disable auto-indent by choosing No.

CUSTOMIZING PARADOX

- **Tab Stops:** This setting determines the number of spaces between tab stops in script files. Enter a number to set the default number of spaces the Tab key moves the cursor. The default is 8 spaces.

The Paradox script-editing facilities do not support the word-wrap feature available when editing other text files and memo fields

Using an External Script Editor

If you prefer to use a word processor or other outside editor instead of the Paradox Editor to create and edit PAL scripts, choose Script Editor and then specify the location and program file name of the editor. For example, if you wanted to use WordPerfect 5.1 as your script editor, and WordPerfect is stored in C:\WP51, specify C:\WP51\WP.EXE as your script editor. In the future, whenever you create or modify a script, Paradox will automatically start WordPerfect instead of its own built-in editor.

Memo fields are always edited with Paradox's built-in editor, regardless of the settings for either the script editor or BLOB editor (described in the next section).

Keep the following important points in mind when using an external editor to create and modify PAL scripts:

- Your external editor is called automatically whenever you create or modify a script. However, the standard Paradox editor is still used to fill in or edit memo fields, and whenever you choose ≡ ➤ Editor or press Alt-e.

- While the external editor is in control of the screen, Paradox is suspended. If you forget to exit the external editor and return to Paradox before turning off your computer, you will likely lose data and/or corrupt your Paradox table.

- Suspending the external editor after you've accessed it from Paradox might also cause data loss.
- If you use a word processor, such as WordPerfect as the external editor, you *must* remember to save the script in ASCII (DOS) text format, *not* the word processor's default format. Failure to do so will insert hidden codes into the script, which will make it impossible for Paradox to run the script. For more information about saving word processing files in ASCII text format, see your word processing program documentation.
- If you ever want to use the standard Paradox script editor after specifying an external script editor, you must return to the CCP and delete the entry in the Script Editor option of the PAL dialog box.
- If you're running Paradox under Windows, do not use a Windows-based editor, such as Write, as the external editor.

If you specify only the path and file name of the external editor, Paradox allots the same amount of memory for running that program as it allots when you shell out to DOS using Ctrl-o. You can increase the amount of memory allocated to the external program by preceding its path and file name with an exclamation point, as in this example:

!C:\WP51\WP.EXE

Using ! in this manner allots the same amount of memory that pressing the DOS Big key (Alt-o) does.

Chapter 12 explains how to use the Tools ➤ More ➤ ToDOS option, Ctrl-o, and Alt-o to temporarily exit to the DOS operating system prompt.

If the external editor can accept a file name on the command line (as most editor and word processing programs can), you can save some steps by having Paradox pass the name of the script to edit to that program. Just follow the program name with a blank space and an asterisk (*), as in this example:

!C:\WP51\WP.EXE *

If the external editor can also accept a line number (which is generally only true of editors specifically designed for programmers), follow the single asterisk with a space and two asterisks, as in the example below:

!C:\UTILS\ED.EXE * **

This option is particularly handy for editing scripts right after an error occurs (by pressing Ctrl-e from the Debugger window, as described in Chapter 21), because it places the cursor at the offending line automatically. (In our example, ED.EXE is a hypothetical text editor stored in C:\UTILS.)

Specifying a BLOB Editor

The BLOB Editor option lets you specify an outside (external) editor for creating and editing data stored in a binary field of a table. The BLOB editor can be just about any DOS program—a word processor, graphics program, or spreadsheet. The only requirement is that the program be able to accept the name of the file to edit at the DOS command prompt.

> **NOTE** BLOB is an acronym for Binary Large OBject.

As when using a script editor, you can specify ! in front of the path and file name to allot extra memory to the BLOB editor. However, with a BLOB editor, the asterisk following the editor name is not optional, because Paradox must be able to pass data to and from the BLOB editor. Therefore, you *must* specify a blank space and asterisk following the path and name of the program. Thus, if you want to use DrawPerfect (DR.EXE) as your BLOB editor, and that program is stored in the directory C:\DR11, specify the BLOB editor in the PAL dialog box as follows:

!C:\DR11\DR.EXE *

After saving your changes and exiting the CCP, you can use the BLOB editor to edit any table that contains a binary field of a type supported by the BLOB editor. To enter or edit data in the binary field, move the cursor to it, then switch to Field view (press Alt-F5 or Ctrl-f or double-click the mouse). Paradox will run the external editor, DrawPerfect in this example, and you can make your changes while in that program.

TIP To determine whether or not a particular program can accept a file name at the DOS command prompt, just try it out with an existing file.

After editing your graphic image (or whatever) in the external editor, just exit that program normally. When asked about saving the current file, be sure to do so, using whatever response the external program expects. Paradox uses the temporary file name $ZMEMZ$.ZZ as the name of the file you're saving. Don't change that name; just press ↵ (or whatever) to use the suggested file name. After you've fully exited the external editor, you'll be returned to Paradox and your Paradox table.

CAUTION Do not use the reserved file name $ZMEMZ$.ZZ for any other purpose, because Paradox automatically deletes that file after you exit the BLOB editor.

Only the word *BLOB* appears in a binary field that contains data. To view or change that information in the future, you must again move the cursor to that field and switch to Field view by pressing Alt-F5 or Ctrl-f, or double-clicking the mouse. Paradox will again run the external editor and display whatever you previously stored in that field.

NOTE You cannot place a BLOB field into a Paradox report.

The same warnings given in the previous section about using an external script editor apply to the BLOB editor as well. Most important, be sure to exit the BLOB editor (and also exit Paradox) before turning off your computer, to ensure that you don't lose any data.

In case you have problems with your BLOB editor, or are just curious about how it all works, here are the basic facts in a nutshell:

- The data for the BLOB is stored in the same file as memo data (the .MB file). The size and starting location of the data for each BLOB field are also stored in each record.

- When you switch to Field view to edit a BLOB, Paradox copies the existing BLOB data (if any) from the .MB file to a temporary file named $ZMEMZ$.ZZ. Then Paradox runs the BLOB editor program, passing that temporary file name to it as the name of the file to edit. You can then use the external program to edit or print the data.

- When you exit the BLOB editor and save your work, your changes are saved to the temporary $ZMEMZ$.ZZ file, and control returns to Paradox.

- When Paradox regains control, it copies the temporary $ZMEMZ$.ZZ file back into the .MB file, adjusts the size and starting location of the BLOB field accordingly, then deletes the temporary $ZMEMZ$.ZZ file.

One potentially interesting application of a binary field might be to use WordPerfect or some other word processor as the BLOB editor. That way, you could enter a large body of text into a binary field rather than into a memo field, using the fonts and graphics capabilities of your word processor. For instance, you could type up a nicely formatted resume for each record in a table of personnel data.

Of course, the disadvantage to this approach is that you couldn't print the fancy resumes directly from Paradox. But if you only needed to print a resume occasionally, the benefits of using a high-powered word processor and binary field might outweigh the limitations of using a memo field and the Paradox memo field editor.

Changing the BLOB Editor Screen Swap Default

Some BLOB editors, such as DOS applications, will work better when the screen is swapped when you run them and when you leave them and return to Paradox. The preset default is not to swap screens. If you are having problems accessing your desired BLOB editor, you can change the BLOB Editor Screen Swap option to No.

Setting ASCII File Defaults

When you import or export Paradox tables in ASCII format, you typically use a delimiter and separator to differentiate the fields. The default separator is the comma, placed between fields. The delimiter enclosing strings (textual fields) is the quotation mark ("). The ASCII option on the CCP desktop menu lets you change these defaults for both imported and exported ASCII files. When you choose ASCII, the ASCII Export/Import Settings dialog box, shown in Figure D.17, appears.

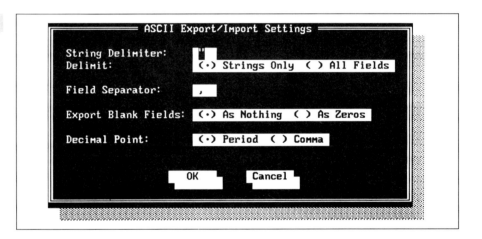

FIGURE D.17

The ASCII Export/Import Settings dialog box, which appears after you choose ASCII from the CCP desktop menu, lets you change the default format of imported and exported ASCII text files.

See Chapter 12 for information about importing and exporting ASCII text files.

The options in this dialog box are as follows:

- **String Delimiter:** Designates the string delimiter. The default setting uses double quotation marks ("). When you import an ASCII file, Paradox also recognizes an apostrophe or single quotation mark (') as the delimiter by default. If the delimiter is any other character, you must make that character the default by placing it in the String Delimiter field. The field cannot be left blank.

CUSTOMIZING PARADOX

- **Delimit:** Lets you decide whether only strings (textual data) are delimited, or if all fields are delimited. The most common setting is Strings Only, but when exporting to certain programs, you may want to delimit all the fields, by selecting All Fields. For example, if you're exporting to a WordPerfect secondary merge file, enclosing all the fields in quotation marks makes it easier for WordPerfect to find and strip out those quotation marks when performing an ASCII merge.

- **Field Separator:** Designates the character used to separate fields in the ASCII file. The default, a comma, is the most common. But you can use any keyboard character you wish, except a Tab.

- **Export Blank Fields:** Lets you determine how to export blank numeric and currency fields. Choose the As Nothing (an empty field) or As Zeros (the number 0) option according to the requirements of the program that will later operate on the ASCII file. Essentially, you want to ensure that the field is treated as a numeric, rather than text, field.

- **Decimal Point:** Lets you specify whether imported and exported numeric and currency fields use a period or a comma as a decimal point in numbers. The United States convention is to use a period, but when importing and exporting numbers in International format, you must choose the Comma option so that Paradox knows what role the comma plays in numeric fields. If you do opt to use the comma as a decimal point, you should also choose All Fields in the Delimit option, to ensure that the commas used as decimal points are not confused with the commas used to separate fields. (As an alternative to switching the Delimit option to All Fields, you could also change the Field Separator to some character other than a comma.)

When you're finished with the ASCII Export/Import Settings dialog box, choose OK or press ↵ to accept those changes. Or press Esc or choose Cancel to abandon them. You'll be returned to the CCP desktop menu.

Saving or Canceling CCP Changes

After making your selections and accepting them in the CCP, choose **DO-IT!** from the CCP desktop menu, or press the Do-It! key (F2), to save those changes. (Optionally, you can choose Cancel ➤ Yes to leave the CCP without saving any changes made in the CCP.) Assuming you did save your changes, you'll see these options:

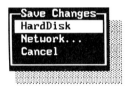

If you're using Paradox on a single-user machine, choose **HardDisk**. The CCP restarts Paradox in order to activate the new defaults. You'll be returned to the Paradox desktop, and your CCP changes will be in effect.

Any changes you make in the CCP are stored in a file named PARADOX.CFG (for Paradox configuration), which Paradox reads at startup to determine how to configure itself to your liking.

Saving CCP Changes on a Network

If you're using Paradox on a network, choose **N**etwork from the popup menu shown above. You'll see the Network Save dialog box. Fill in the complete path to your Paradox private directory. If your workstation has a hard disk, this will be a local drive and directory.

Customizing Paradox

NOTE: If you've already defined your private directory in the CCP, that directory automatically appears in the Network Save dialog box.

If your workstation has no hard disk, your private directory will be your network home directory. If you're not sure where your private directory is located, ask your network administrator.

After filling in the dialog box, choose OK or press ↵.

APPENDIX E

Sample Table Structures

THIS appendix lists the sample tables presented in this book, the chapter in which these tables were introduced, and number of the page on which the table structure is presented.

TABLE NAME	CHAPTER INTRODUCED	STRUCTURE PRESENTED
Articles.DB	3	51
Custlist.DB	3	54
Custlist.DB (Welcomed field added)	11	377
Custlist.DB (Restructured- 2 key fields)	13	478
Custlist.DB (Restructured- 4 key fields)	13	479
Custlist.DB (Restructured- 10 key fields)	13	480
Finsum.DB	10	310
Salesreg.DB	10	356
Charges.DB	12	407
Customer.DB	13	462
Inventory.DB	13	465
Sales.DB	13	465
Courses.DB	13	467
Students.DB	13	468
Sclink.DB	13	468

TABLE NAME	CHAPTER INTRODUCED	STRUCTURE PRESENTED
Products.DB	13	469
Componen.DB	13	470
Linker.DB	13	471
Mastinv.DB	14	495
Invoices.DB	14	495
Accounts.DB	14	496
Orders.DB	14	497
Purchase.DB	14	498
Yearend.DB	14	538
Taxes.DB	15	599
States.DB	15	611
Intlcust.DB (Modified Custlist table)	15	616
Invdtail.DB	15	621
Invoices.DB (Restructured)	15	622
Purhist.DB (Borrowed from Purchases.DB)	16	652
Members.DB	18	726
Renewed.DB	18	729

INDEX

Note to the Reader: **Boldfaced** numbers indicate pages where you will find the principal discussion of a topic or the definition of a term. *Italic* numbers indicate pages where a topic is illustrated in a figure.

Numbers and Symbols

3-D bar graphs, 317–318, *318*
& (ampersand), in Picture formats, 111, 114
➤ (arrow symbol), in menus, 27
* (asterisk)
  in comments in scripts, 693–694
  for defining primary key fields, 457, 476, 490
  as multiplication operator, 516–517, 552–553
  in Picture formats, 111
  as wildcard character, 399
@ (at sign)
  in Find dialog box, 686, 687
  in Picture formats, 111
  in query criteria, 156, 161, 164
  in Zoom dialog box, 32, 96, 97
\ (backslash)
  for creating form borders, 294–295
  in PAL scripts, 842
  in query criteria, 176–177
| (bar symbol), in saved queries, 692, *693*
{ } (braces), in Picture formats, 112, 113–114
[ ] (brackets)
  in expressions, 553
  in field masks, 219
  in Picture formats, 112
√ (check marks)
  check-descending check marks (√▼), **145**, *147*, 148–149
  check-plus check marks (√+), **145**, *146*, 148–149, 156
  plain check marks (√), **145–146**, *145*, *147*, 148–149, 156

in set queries, 540
in summary calculations with queries, 526–527
, (comma)
  in data entry, 72
  in Picture formats, 112
  in query criteria, 158–159, 166, 171–172, 520
.. (double-dot)
  in Find dialog box, 686, 687
  in query criteria, 156, 161–164, 165, 178
  in Zoom dialog box, 32, 96, 97
= (equal to), in query criteria, 156, **166–168**
! (exclamation point)
  as inclusion operator, 515–516
  in Picture formats, 111
> (greater than), in query criteria, 156, **166–168**
>= (greater than or equal to), in query criteria, 156, **166–168**
- (hyphen)
  for negative numbers, 68
  as subtraction operator, 516–517, 552–553
< (less than), in query criteria, 156, **166–168**
<= (less than or equal to), in query criteria, 156, **166–168**
– (minus sign)
  for negative numbers, 68
  as subtraction operator, 516–517, 552–553
(number sign), in Picture formats, 111
() (parentheses)
  as grouping operator, 516–517, 552–553

for negative numbers, 68, 73
+ (plus sign)
  as addition operator, 516–517, 552–553
  in field masks, 219
? (question mark), in Picture formats, 111, 114
" " (quotation marks)
  as ASCII file delimiter, 995
  in field masks, 219
  in query criteria, 155
; (semicolon)
  for commenting in scripts, 693–694, 840
  in Picture formats, 112
/ (slash), as division operator, 516–517, 552–553
~(tilde), for menu option shortcut keys, 766
_ (underscore), in saved queries, 692, *693*

A

"A border can't intersect a field or multi-record region" message, 295
"A field has already been placed here" message, 285
abbreviated menu commands, in PAL, 842–843
access rights. *See* passwords; protecting
Action Object Tools dialog box, Workshop program, *814*
action objects, **769–775**. *See also* applications
attaching
  existing actions to menu options, 773

INDEX

utility commands to menus, 750, **773**
changing, 751, **775**
creating
   and attaching to menu options, 751, **771–772**, *772*, *773*
   before attaching to menus, 769–771, *770*
   by borrowing, 774–775
   managing, **814**
   testing, **808**
ActionEdit menu, Workshop program, 775
   Help Text option, 796
   Multi Action option, 769
activating
   menu bar, 36–37
   System menu, 90
   windows, 86, **89–90**, 118
active window, **88**, *89*. *See also* windows
Add option
   Tools/More submenu, 401, 405, 409, 481, 482
   Workshop Edit Session dialog box, 776, 778
adding
   calculated fields to reports, 552–555, *554*, *556*
   cross-references to application Help, 799
   Help text to application menu options, 751, **795–797**, *796*
   passwords to tables and scripts, 411–413, *413*
   records, **67**, 83
   summary fields to reports, 557–558
   tables to edit session, 778–782, *779*, *780*, *781*
addition operator (+), 516–517, 552–553
adjustment transactions, 633, **657**, *658*, 660
aligning
   field masks, 224
   pages for reports, 197
   zip codes, 224

All option, ValCheck/Clear submenu, 117
ALL qualifier, 526, 527, 531
AllCorrespondingFields option, ValCheck/Define/TableLookup submenu, 607–608
allotting space
   for alphanumeric fields, 48
   for memo fields, 48, **49–50**, *51*
alphanumeric fields. *See also* fields
   allotting space for, 48
   defined, **47**
   field masks for, 218, 221, 222–224
   grouping reports on, 240–241
   word-wrapping on forms, 274, **287–289**, *288*, 291, 293, **301**, 303
   for zip codes and phone numbers, 49
Alt key
   + F3 (Record Instant Script), 382, 384, 839
   + F4 (Play Instant Script), 382, 384, 839
   + F5 (Field view), 50
   + F6 (check-plus check marks), 148
   + F7 (Instant Report), 190
   + F8 (Close All Windows), 82, 91
   + F9 (CoEdit mode), 64
   + F10 (PAL menu), 370, 371, 855
   + K (Keyviol key), 483
   + spacebar (System menu), 90
   in Editor, 669–670
ampersand (&), in Picture formats, 111, 114
AND queries, 141, **170–172**, **509–511**. *See also* queries
   across several fields, 171
   for multiple tables, 509–511, *512*
   versus OR queries, 175
   in a single field, 171–172
Answer tables, **150–155**, **519–521**, **583–584**. *See also* queries

closing, 151
creating multiple table report formats from, **583–584**
displaying calculated results in, **517–518**
field order in, 140, **151–155**, *152*, *154*, 508, 981
making changes in, 150
moving, 150
moving fields in, 151
printing, 151
printing formatted reports from, 151
renaming, 150, **394**
renaming calculated fields in, **519–521**, *520*
saving, 150
sizing, 150
sorting, **150–151**, *152*
Application menu, Workshop program
   Close option, 811
   Directory submenu, 34, 53, 722, 758–759
   Edit option, 810
   Finish option, 815
   New option, 759
   Remove option, 811
   Test option, 809
applications, **712–747**, **750–803**, **806–829**. *See also* Workshop program
   action objects, **769–775**, **808**, **814**
   attaching existing actions to menu options, 773
   attaching utility commands to menus, 750, **773**
   changing actions, 751, **775**
   creating and attaching to menu options, 751, **771–772**, *772*, *773*
   creating before attaching to menus, 769–771, *770*
   creating by borrowing, 774–775
   managing, **814**
   testing, **808**
   closing, 806, **811**
   copying, **820–823**, 828
      files to include, 820–821

to floppy disks, 821–822
from floppy disks to hard
  disk, 822–823
large applications, 823
creating, 750, **752–753**,
  759–768, 803
 closed applications, **827–828**
 defining application
  attributes, 760–762, *762*,
  763
 directories for, 721–722,
  758–759
 overview of, **752–753**
defined, **712**, **714**, 747
deleting from application
  table, 806, **811–812**, *811*
designing, 712, **717–725**, 747
 creating directory for
  application, 721–722
 defining goals of application,
  712, **718–719**
 designing menu structure on
  paper, 713, **719–721**, *720*,
  721
 distributing, 716, **724–725**
 documentation, **724–725**
 forms, reports, and scripts,
  723–724
 overview of, **717–718**
 queries, 723
 tables, 722–723
 and testing database objects,
  721–724
 testing and refining
  application, 713, **724**
developing with Tools menu,
  409–410
directories for
 creating, 721–722, 758–759
 switching to, 806, 828
distributing, 716, **724–725**,
  820–823, 828
 copying files to floppy disks,
  821–822
 copying from floppy disks to
  hard disk, 822–823
 copying large applications,
  823
 files to include, 820–821
documentation, **724–725**,
  815–820, 828

box and line styles in,
  818–819, *818*
 embellishing with word
  processor, 819–820
 selecting printers for,
  816–817, *817*
edit session objects, **775–785**
 adding tables to edit session,
  778–782, *779*, *780*, *781*
 assigning event procedures
  to edit session, 783–785,
  784, *786*
 assigning key actions to edit
  session, 782–783, *782*
 defining, 775–778, *776*
editing Paradox objects,
  812–813
execute objects, **801**
finishing, 807, **815**, 828
Help text objects, **795–800**,
  803
 adding cross-references, 799
 adding to menu options,
  751, **795–797**, *796*
 completing, **797–800**, *798*
 editing cross-references, 800
 editing Help screens, 751,
  798–799
 testing on-line help, 800
managing objects, **813–814**,
  814
Membership application
  example, 714–716, *715*,
  725–746
 adding new members,
  739–740
 changing members' data,
  740
 custom forms, **727–728**, *728*,
  729
 deleting expired members,
  741–742
 exiting, 745
 letters (reports), **728–730**,
  730, *731*
 mailing label format, **731**,
  732
 menu structure, **732–734**
 overview of, 714–716, *715*,
  725–727, *726*

printing letters and mailing
  labels, 742–744
 printing roster, 742
 running, 739
 testing, **738–745**
 testing utilities, 744–745
 tips, **745–746**
 Update Renewals process,
  734–738
 updating roster, 741
 validity checks, **726–727**
menu structures, 751,
  763–768, **795–797**
 adding Help text to menu
  options, 751, **795–797**, *796*
 copying menu options, 768
 creating menu and submenu
  options, 750, **765–767**,
  766, 803
 defining menu option
  shortcut keys, 766
 deleting menu options, 767
 overview of creating,
  763–765, *764*
 renaming or editing menu
  options, 750, **768**, 803
modifying, 806, **809–810**,
  810, 828
multi-action objects, **794–795**,
  794
objects
 editing, **812–813**
 managing, **813–814**, *814*
OK/Cancel objects, **801–802**,
  802
overview of, 17–18, **714–716**
password-protecting, **827–828**
query objects, **790–794**
 defining queries, 793–794,
  793
 Query By Example dialog
  box, 791–792, *791*
report print objects, **786–790**
 defining, 786–789, *787*, *788*
 defining printer settings,
  789–790, *789*
starting, 807, **824–827**, 828
 from DOS, 824–825
 from Paradox, 824
 from Windows, 825–827,
  826, *827*

INDEX

testing, 713, **724**, 806, **808–809**, *809*, 828
"The area designated for the word wrap must be clear" message, 289
area graphs, **323–324**, *325*
Area menu. *See also* Form Design screen
  Erase option, 292–293
  Move option, 281, 286, **290–291**
arguments
  in PAL commands, **843–844**
  in PAL functions, **846–847**
arithmetic operators, in query criteria, 156, 169–170, 516–517
arrays, in PAL, 833, **850–851**
arrow keys
  in Editor, 669–670
  in Field view, 77
  in Form Design screen, 282
  navigating with, 74, 76
  in Query form window, 144
  in Report Design screen, 204
arrow symbol (➤), in menus, 27
AS operator, 493, 518, **519–521**, *520*, 548
ascending sorts, 122, **127**, 129, 137
ASCII character set, for form borders, 294–295
ASCII Export/Import Settings dialog box, Custom Configuration Program (CCP), 438, **995–996**, *995*
ASCII files
  delimited files
    delimiter character for, 438, **995–996**
    exporting, **436–439**, *437*, 440–442
    importing, **436–439**, 451
  text files
    editing, 662, **667–668**, 708
    Editor defaults in, 680, 985
    exporting and importing, 439, 683–684
    word-wrap feature and, 679

ASCII option, Custom Configuration Program, 438
ASCII.SOR file, 136
ASCII sort order, 123, **135–137**
Ask option and dialog box, 142–143, 249
Assign Color Setting dialog box, Custom Configuration Program, 966
assigning
  color settings, 966
  event procedures to application edit sessions, 783–785, *784*, *786*
  key actions to application edit sessions, 782–783, *782*
  miniscripts to hotkeys, 863–865, *864*
  variables in functions, 849
asterisk (*)
  in comments in scripts, 693–694
  for defining primary key fields, 457, 476, 490
  as multiplication operator, 516–517, 552–553
  in Picture formats, 111
  as wildcard character, 399
at sign (@)
  in Find dialog box, 686, 687
  in Picture formats, 111
  in query criteria, 156, 161, 164
  in Zoom dialog box, 32, 96, 97
attaching
  existing actions to menu options, 773
  utility commands to menus, 750, **773**
audit trails, **465**
Auto submenu, ValCheck/Define submenu, **115–117**
  Filled option, 116
  overview of, 115–116
  Picture option, 116–117
AUTOEXEC.BAT file, 894, 957
auto-indenting text, in Editor, 680, 985, 989

automatic fill-in, on forms, **607–608**
automatic locking schemes, 923–924, 926–928
AutoRefresh option, Tools/Net submenu, 934
Autosave option, CCP Standard Settings dialog box, 982
auxiliary passwords, 943–947, *945*
AVERAGE operator, 523–524, 526, 555
avoiding waits on networks, **930–931**
axes
  customizing graph, 328, **333–338**
  modifying axes labels, 341–343
  scaling, 328, 334–335
Axes option, Overall menu, 333

B

backing up tables, **179–180**, **399–402**
  with DOS BACKUP command, 400–401
  with queries, 401–402
backslash (\)
  for creating form borders, 294–295
  in PAL scripts, 842
  in query criteria, 176–177
Backspace key
  editing with, 74–75, 76
  in Editor, 669
  in Field view, 77
  in Form Design screen, 282
  in Query form window, 144
  in Report Design screen, 204
BACKUP command, DOS, 400–401, 823
bands, report, **206–209**. *See also* Group bands
  Form band, *206*, 208–209
  Page Footer band, *206*, 209
  Page Header band, *206*, 207, *592*, 592

Report Footer band, *206*, 209, 572
Report Header band, 206–207, *206*
Table band, 189, *206*, **207–208**, **209–214**, 271
 copying columns, 213–214
 deleting columns, 211
 inserting columns, 211
 mouse versus keyboard operations in, 210
 moving columns, 213
 overview of, **207–208**
 placing field masks in, 214
 sizing columns, 211–213
bar graphs, **316–319**. *See also* graphs
 3-D, 317–318, *318*
 regular, 316, *317*
 rotated, 318–319, *319*
 stacked, 316
bar symbol (|), in saved queries, 692, *693*
batch files, configuring Paradox with, **905–906**
BeginRecord option
 PAL menu, 370, 856
 Scripts menu, 370, 836
binary fields. *See also* fields
 defined, **47**
 entering data in, **68–70**, *69*
 importing text into, 684
 in previous versions, 57
 selecting BLOB editor, 48, 70, 684, **992–994**
Binary Large Objects (BLOBs). *See also* binary fields
 defined, **48**
 selecting editor for, 48, 70, 684, **992–994**
BIOS configuration option, 905
Blank = Zero option, CCP Standard Settings dialog box, 981–982
blank fields
 calculations on, **518–519**, 604, **981–982**
 export setting, 996
 query criteria for, 157, **168–169**

blank lines
 deleting, in free-form reports, 232–233
 inserting
  in Editor, 672
  in reports, 188, **203–205**, **244–245**
BLANK operator, in query criteria, 157, 168–169
blank spaces, in free-form reports, 231–232, *232*
BLANKLINE command, Report Design screen, 244–245, 567, 912–913
blinking screen style, on forms, 298
BLOB editors, 48, 70, 684, **992–994**
book's sample tables listed, **1000–1001**
"A border can't intersect a field or multi-record region" message, 295
Border menu. *See also* Form Design screen
 Erase option, 296
 Place submenu, 294
borders and lines
 in application documentation, 818–819, *818*
 on forms, 275, **293–296**, 303
 deleting borders and lines, 296
 drawing borders, 294–295
 drawing lines, 295
borrowing
 creating action objects by, 774–775
 table structures, 56
boxes. *See* borders and lines
braces ({ }), in Picture formats, 112, 113–114
brackets ([ ])
 in expressions, 553
 in field masks, 219
 in Picture formats, 112
branching, in PAL scripts, 833, **851–854**. *See also* looping
Break key, 980–981
buttons, in Workshop program, 757

C

CALC expressions, 492, **517–518**, *519*, 520, 548
CalcEdit option, Field menu, 220
calculated fields
 displaying error messages for, **989**
 field masks for, 215, 219–220
 in forms, 551, **602–604**, *603*, *604*, 629
 renaming in Answer tables, 493, 518, **519–521**, *520*, 548
 in reports, 550, **552–561**, **592–599**, 628
  adding calculated fields, 552–555, *554*, *556*
  adding summary fields, 557–558
  calculating percentages with PAL functions, 596–599, *597*
  PAL functions in, **592–599**, *596*
  running totals, 557
  for totals and subtotals, **555–561**, *559*, *560*, 628
calculating functions, in PAL, 845–846
calculating with queries, 492, **516–533**, **543–546**. *See also* queries
 arithmetic operators in, **516–517**
 blank fields and, **518–519**, 604, **981–982**
 calculating percentages, **543–546**, *544*, *546*
 complex calculations with multiple tables, **531–533**, *532*, *533*
 displaying calculation results with CALC reserved word, 492, **517–518**, *519*, 548
 expressions for, 516–517
 with fields from multiple tables, 492, **521–522**, *521*, 548

to increase or decrease values, **522–523**
with INSERT queries, **644**
multiple CALC expressions, 520
renaming calculated fields with AS operator, 493, 518, **519–521**, *520*, 548
summary calculations, 493, **523–531**, 542–543
  comparing records to with set queries, 542–543, *542*
  default grouping for, 524
  frequency distributions, 527, *528*
  on groups of records, 526–527, *527*, *528*
  selecting records based on summary calculations, 529–531, *529*, *530*
  summarizing all records, 525–526, *525*
  summary operators, 523–524
Cancel option
  Editor, 690
  PAL menu, 371
canceling
  CCP report settings, 971
  CCP Video settings, 960
  changes to data, 61, **81–82**
  color settings, 968
  Custom Configuration Program settings, **997**
  menu options, 22, **28**, 38
  script play back, 374
"Cannot split field during column resize" message, 212
canvas, in PAL, 872, 887
cascading, windows, 86, **91**, 119
case sensitivity
  in Editor searches, 687
  in query criteria, 164–165
  of reserved words and operators, 518
  secondary indexes and, 487
  in sorts, 123, **135–137**
CaseSensitive option, Editor Options menu, 687

CAVERAGE() PAL function, 861–863
CCOUNT() PAL function, 861–863
CCP. *See* Custom Configuration Program
Change option
  Forms menu, 302
  Report menu, 252–253
CHANGETO queries
  globally changing values with, **179–182**, *181*, 378–379
  increasing or decreasing values with, **522–523**
  in update queries, **640–642**
ChangeToEnd option, Editor Search menu, 689–690
changing. *See also* editing; modifying
  action objects, 751, **775**
  Answer tables, 150
  column width in Table view, 99–101, *100*
  data type of PAL variables, 832, **849–850**
  default form, 275, **300–301**, 303
  directories, 33–34, 41, 53
  field masks for calculated fields, 220
  field types, **423–424**
  fields in table structures, 422–423
  forms, 275, **302**, 303
  page and print size for reports, 227–228
  passwords, 414–415
  printer ports, 229–230
  sort methods, 135–137
  table size in Table view, 98–99
  table structures, 391, **420–428**, 451
    changing field types, **423–424**
    confirming deleted fields, 424
    confirming shortened fields, 424–425
    converting between older and newer versions of Paradox, **426–427**

fixing corrupted objects, **427–428**
imported tables, **430**
inserting, deleting, and moving fields, 422–423
modifying table structure, **420–423**, *422*
saving new structures, **424–425**
using Problems or Keyviol tables, 425–426, *425*
character sets, for form borders, 294–295
characters
  query criteria for matching single characters, 164
  query criteria for ranges of letters, 167
charts. *See* graphs
check marks (√)
  check-descending check marks (√▼), **145**, *147*, 148–149
  check-plus check marks (√+), **145**, *146*, 148–149, 156
  plain check marks (√), **145–146**, *145*, *147*, 148–149, 156
  in set queries, 540
  in summary calculations with queries, 526–527
choosing. *See* selecting
Clear option, Tools/More/Protect submenu, 414, 416
Clear submenu, ValCheck menu, 117
clearing. *See also* deleting
  passwords, 414
Clipboard. *See also* Editor
  making changes in, 676–678
  viewing, 676, *677*
Close option
  System menu, 91
  Workshop Application menu, 811
closing
  Answer tables, 151
  applications, 806, **811**
  Query forms, 151
  sorted tables, 123, 132

tables, 61, **82**, 83
windows, 86, **91–92**, *92*, 119
CMAX() PAL function, 861–863
CMIN() PAL function, 861–863
CoEdit mode
  closing windows in, 92
  editing tables in, 60, 81
  entering data in, 67
  key violations in, 482–483
  on networks, 924, **925–928**
  opening tables in, **81**
  switching to, 60, **64–65**, 83
  TableAdd option, 916
  Undo feature in, 78–79, 81
Color Palette, hiding and displaying, 959
Color Settings dialog box, Custom Configuration Program, 955, *956*, **960–968**
  Assign Color Setting dialog box, *966*
  assigning settings, 966
  copying settings, 966–967
  creating new settings, 962–965
  deleting settings, 967–968
  editing settings, 965
  New Color Setting dialog box, *962*
  overview of, 960–961
  Paradox Object Colors dialog box, 963–965, *963*
  predefined and default settings, 961–962
  renaming settings, 967
  saving and canceling settings, 968
coloring
  forms, 275, **296–299**, 303
    blinking screen style, 298
    changing form colors, **296–297**
    monochrome video attributes, **297–298**
    reverse screen style, 297–298
    tips, 298–299
  negative numbers, 959–960
  objects, **962–968**, *962*, *963*

colors
  customizing graph, 332–333, *332*
  matching screen colors to printer colors, 333
  Colors submenu, Overall menu, 332, 333
columns. *See also* fields
  changing width of in Table view, 99–101, *100*
  deleting all in spillover pages, 211
  heading display in Group bands, **561–562**, *562*
  moving, in Table view, 104–105
  multicolumn labels and reports, 233–236, *235*, *237*
  in reports
    copying, 213–214
    deleting, 211
    inserting, 211
    moving, 213
    sizing, 211–213
  ColumnSize option, Image menu, 99–101
.COM files, 667, 683
combined graphs, **321**, *322*, **324–325**, *326*
combining data from multiple tables, 16–17, *17*, 492, **499–508**. *See also* multiple table queries; multiple tables
  entering example elements in a Query form, 492, **500**, 548
  example elements explained, **499–503**
  linking more than two tables, **503–508**, *504*, *505*
  linking tables with example elements, **500–503**, *502*, *503*, 548
  scheduling database example, 506–508, *506*
combining scripts, **700–705**, *701*, *702*, *703*
comma (,)
  in data entry, 72
  in Picture formats, 112
  in query criteria, 158–159, 166, 171–172, 520
Comma option, Image/Format submenu, 101–103
command-line configuration options, **898–907**
  in batch files, **905–906**
  BIOS option, 905
  compatibility mode options, 905
  memory options, 901–903
  in Microsoft Windows, **906–907**
  mouse options, 904
  network emulation, 904
  overview of, 898–899
  query options, 904–905
  SHARE option, 904
  video options, 900
commands. *See also* PAL commands
  book's notation for, 27
  canceling, 22, **28**, 38
  selecting from menus, **27**, 38
Commas submenu, Field/Reformat submenu, 222
commenting, in scripts, 663, **693–694**, *694*, 840
comparison operators, in query criteria, 156, **166–168**, 529
compatibility
  configuration options for version, 905
  of tables from previous versions, **57**
COMPATIBLE command, 37
Compatible option, Create screen, 57
composite keys, **476**. *See also* key fields
compressed print, 590
computers
  getting information about, **956–958**
  required by Paradox, 890–891, 921–922
conditional branching, in PAL scripts, 833, **851–854**. *See also* looping

INDEX

CONFIG.SYS file, 892–893, 957
configuration options, **898–907**. *See also* customizing
  in batch files, **905–906**
  BIOS option, 905
  compatibility mode options, 905
  memory options, 901–903
  in Microsoft Windows, **906–907**
  mouse options, 904
  network emulation, 904
  overview of, 898–899
  query options, 904–905
  SHARE option, 904
  video options, 900
context-sensitive Help, 29, *30*
converting tables from previous versions, 57, 426–427, **982–983**
COPY command, DOS, 399, 401, 427
Copy option
  Editor Edit menu, 674, 675, 677
  TableBand menu, 213–214
  Tools/More submenu, 401
Copy submenu, Tools menu, **395–399**
  Form option, 398
  Graph option, 351, 398–399
  JustFamily option, 396, 398–399, 401, 924
  Report option, 398
  Script option, 398–399
  Table option, 179–180, 395, 398–399, 924
copying. *See also* update queries
  application menu options, 768
  applications, **820–823**, 828
    files to include, 820–821
    to floppy disks, 821–822
    from floppy disks to hard disk, 822–823
    large applications, 823
  color settings, 966–967
  columns in reports, 213–214
  current editing window to a file, 681–682
  fields from previous record, 72
  forms, 398
  graphs, 398–399

JustFamily objects, 398–399
objects, 390, **395–402**, 450
  backing up large tables, **399–402**
    with DOS BACKUP command, 400–401
    with DOS COPY command, 399, 401
    to floppy disks, 399, 401–402
  forms and reports, 398
  overview of, **395–396**
  specifying source and target files, 396–397
  tables, scripts, graphs, and JustFamily objects, 398–399
  tables to floppy disks with queries, 401–402
  and pasting in Editor, 669–670, 674
reports, 398
scripts, 398–399
selected text to a file, 683
tables, 398–399
CopyToFile option, Editor File menu, 681–682, 683–684
correcting, updated transactions, 633, **657**, *658*, 660
corrupted objects, fixing, **427–428**
COUNT operator, 523–524, 526, 527, 531, 555
Create screen
  Borrow option, 56
  defining tables, 54–56, *54*, *56*, 58
FileFormat menu, Compatible option, 57
creating. *See also* defining
  action objects, **769–775**
    attaching existing actions to menu options, 773
    and attaching to menu options, 751, **771–772**, *772*, *773*
    attaching utility commands to menus, 750, **773**
    before attaching to menus, 769–771, *770*

by borrowing, 774–775
changing actions, 751, **775**
application menu and submenu options, 750, **763–767**, *764*, *766*, 803
applications, 750, **752–753**, **759–768**, 803
  defining application attributes, 760–762, *762*, *763*
  directories for, 721–722, 758–759
  overview of, **752–753**
auto-execute queries, 632, **642–644**, *643*
color settings, 962–965
Crosstab tables, 358–359, *359*
directories, 34, 41, **52–53**, 57
  for applications, 721–722, 758–759
  files while editing, 685
form letter script, 377–379, *378*
GetRecord and PasteRecord keys, 867–868
graphs from custom graph settings, 307, **348–349**, 350–351, 364
history tables, **645–646**, 651–652, *652*
hotkeys, **863–865**, *864*, 866–867
label or envelope script, 380
menu structures, **763–768**
  copying menu options, 768
  creating menu and submenu options, 750, **765–767**, *766*, 803
  defining menu option shortcut keys, 766
  deleting menu options, 767
  overview of, **763–765**, *764*
  renaming or editing menu options, 750, **768**, 803
miniscripts, 837, 860, 887
multipage forms, 551, **599–601**, *599*, *600*, 629
multiple table reports
  from lookup tables, 550, **574–575**
  using queries, 583–584

multi-record forms, 612–613, *613*
multi-table forms
  with linked tables, **620–627**, *620*, *621*, *622*
  with unlinked tables, **615–618**
PAL scripts, **835–840**
  with Editor, 836–837
  Execute scripts, 839
  Init script, 839, 887
  Instant Scripts, 839
  miniscripts, **837**, **860**, 887
  Savevars scripts, 839
  with Scripts/BeginRecord and Scripts/EndRecord options, 836
  with Scripts/QuerySave option, 836
  with Value dialog box, *838*
passwords on networks, 943–947
scripts, 366, **370–371**, 386, 856
  Instant Scripts, 366, **382**, 387
  preparing for, **368–370**
  from scratch, 697–699, *698*
secondary indexes, **428–429**, **484–488**
  with Image/OrderTable option, 484–485
  with Modify/Index option, 484, 486–488, *486*, *488*
  with Tools/QuerySpeed option, 428–429, 484, 485
tables, 41, **53–56**, *54*, 58
  from existing table structures, 56
  on networks, 52, **937**
updating scripts, 632, **636**, **637**, 647–649, *649*, 652–655, *653*, *654*, *656*, 659
cross tabulations, **355–364**. *See also* summary calculations
  arranging fields for Crosstab tables, 360–362, *362*
  explained, **355–357**, *356*
  generating Crosstab tables, 358–359, *359*
  graphing Crosstab tables, 307, **359–360**, *360*
  shortcut for, 362–363, *363*
cross-references, in application Help, 799, 800
CrossTab submenu, Image/Graph submenu, 355–358, 361
CSTD() PAL function, 861–863
CSUM() PAL function, 861–863
Ctrl key
  + Backspace (deleting field contents), 76
  + Break, 980–981
  + D (copying data from previous record), 72
  + F4 (cycling through windows on desktop), 90, 665
  + F5 (sizing/moving windows), 90
  + F6 (check-descending check marks), 148
  + F7 (Instant Graph), 312
  + F (Field view), 50
  + R (moving fields), 105, 213
  + U (Undo), 75, 78–79
  + Z (Zoom dialog box), 96
  in Editor, 669–670
  in Field view, 77
  in Form Design screen, 282
  navigating with, 74–75
  in Query form window, 144
  in Report Design screen, 204, 205
cumulative totals. *See* running totals
curly braces. *See* braces ({ })
currency fields. *See also* fields
  data entry shortcuts in, **73**
  defined, **47**, 49
  field masks for, 202, 218
  grouping reports on, 242
  placing on forms, 285
  query criteria for, 158–160, *160*
current directory. *See* working directory
cursor, positioning in Editor, 669, 671, 708
cursor movement keys. *See* arrow keys
custom applications. *See* applications
Custom Configuration Program (CCP), **952–998**. *See also* defaults
  ASCII Export/Import Settings dialog box, 438, **995–996**, *995*
  canceling new settings, **997**
  Color Settings dialog box, 955, *956*, **960–968**
    Assign Color Setting dialog box, *966*
    assigning settings, 966
    copying settings, 966–967
    creating new settings, 962–965
    deleting settings, 967–968
    editing settings, 965
    New Color Setting dialog box, *962*
    overview of, 960–961
    Paradox Object Colors dialog box, 963–965, *963*
    predefined and default settings, 961–962
    renaming settings, 967
    saving and canceling settings, 968
  dialog boxes in, **953–955**, *954*, *956*
  Format Data dialog box, 915, **984–986**, *984*
    default format for numbers and dates, 985–986
    Editor defaults in text files and memo fields, 680, 985
    new features, 915
    tab stop settings, 680, 985
  Graph settings, 314, **974–979**
    Graph Printer Settings dialog box, 975–978, *976*
    Graphics Screen dialog box, 978–979, *978*
    Instant Graph defaults, 975
    Select Graph Printer dialog box, 975–977, *976*

INDEX

selecting printer for graphs, 975–978
selecting screen mode for graphs, 978–979
Machine Information options, **956–958**
menu options, 953, *954*
Network Settings dialog box, **934–936**, *935*, **986–988**, *986*
Private Directory option, 934, 987
Refresh Interval option, 935, 987
User Name option, 934, 987
When Data Changes option, 935, 988
new features, **914–915**
PAL dialog box, 429, 915, **988–994**, *989*
BLOB Editor option, 48, 70, 684, 992–994
BLOB Editor Screen Swap option, 994
Built-in Script Editor options, 989–990
External Script Editor options, 990–992
new features, 915
Show Calc Field Errors option, 989
Printer Setup table, 195–197, *196*, **971–974**, *971*, *973*
Report Settings dialog box, 195, *196*, **968–971**, *969*
Group band repeats setting, 563, 970
options, **969–970**
saving or canceling settings, 971
running, **952–953**, *954*
saving settings, **997–998**
Standard Settings dialog box, 153, 914–915, **979–984**, *979*
Autosave option, 982
Blank = Zero option, 981–982
Disable Break option, 980–981
File Format option, 982–983
Interface Mode option, 980

Maintain Indexes option, 983
Maximum Table Size option, 983–984
Mouse Use option, 980
new features, 914–915
Query Order option, 140, **151–155**, *152*, *154*, 508, 981
Working Directory option, 980
Video Settings dialog box, 914, *954*, **958–960**
canceling and saving settings, 960
Color Palette option, 959
Color Settings option, 960–961
Monitor Type options, 958–959
Negative Colors option, 959–960
Video "snow" option, 959
custom graph settings, 309, 327, **347–351**. *See also* graphs
creating graphs from, 307, **348–349**, 350–351, 364
modifying existing, 307, **350**
saving, 306, **347–348**, 364
Custom option
Setting/Setup submenu, 228–229
System/Utilities submenu, 153, 934–935, 952
Customize Fills and Markers screen, 343–344, *343*
Customize Graph Axes screen, 333–338, *334*, *337*
Customize Graph Colors screen, 332–333, *332*
Customize Graph Layout for Printing screen, 352–353, *353*
Customize Graph Titles screen, 329–330, *329*
Customize Graph Type screen, 315–316, *315*, 324–325
Customize Grids and Frames screen, 339–340, *339*
Customize Pie Graph screen, 345–346, *345*

Customize Series Legends and Labels screen, 340–342, *341*
customizing. *See also* configuration options
graph series, 328, **340–344**
modifying labels, 341–343
modifying legends, 328, 340–341
modifying markers and fill patterns, 343–344
graphs, 306, 309, **327–340**, 364
colors, 332–333, *332*
graph axes, 328, **333–338**
graph frames, *339*, 340
grid lines, 339–340, *339*
matching screen colors to printer colors, 333
printed graph layout, 352–353, *353*, 364
sample custom axes, 336–338, *337*
scaling of axes, 328, 334–335
tick mark formats, 328, 335–336
tick mark labels, 328, 336
titles, 328, 329–330, *329*, *331*
working in Customize Graph screens, 328–329
X-axis labels for keyed table graphs, 338
Table view, 87, **97–107**, 119
changing column width, 99–101, *100*
changing table size, 98–99
formatting date fields, 103
formatting numeric fields, 101–103
moving columns, 104–105
moving fields, 105
saving and restoring Image menu settings, **105–107**
when data does not fit, 107
cutting and pasting, 669–670, 674
Clipboard and, 677–678
between windows, 675–676
CVAR() PAL function, 861–863
cycling through windows, 90

D

data entry. *See also* forms; validity checks
  adding and saving records, 67
  in binary and memo fields, 60, **68–70**, *69*
  copying data from previous record, 72
  DataEntry feature, **73**
  dates, 67–68, 72
  key violations, **481–483**
    in CoEdit mode, 482–483
    in Edit mode, 483
    using Modify/DataEntry option, 482
  locks and, **937–938**
  negative numbers, 68, 73
  on networks, **937–938**
  numbers, 72–73
  shortcuts for, **70–73**
  special characters, 70, *71*
  in temporary tables, **73**
Data Interchange Format (.DIF)
  exporting to, 436, 438, 440
  importing from, 436, 439, 446–447
data types. *See also* fields
  changing PAL variable, 832, **849–850**
  defining, 40, **47–49**
  PAL functions and, 847
database management systems
  overview of, 4
  versus spreadsheet programs, 14
  versus word processors, 14
database normalization. *See* normalizing databases
databases. *See* multiple tables; tables
DataEntry option, Modify menu, 73, 481, 482, 483, 937–938
date fields. *See also* fields
  defined, **47**
  field masks for, 202, 216, 217, 218
  formats for, 67, 985–986
  formatting in Table view, 103
  grouping reports on, 242–243
  query criteria for, 158–160, *160*
  shortcuts for data entry in, **72**
dates
  default formats for, 985–986
  entering, 67–68, 72
  query criteria
    for ranges of dates, 167–168
    for relative dates, 141, **169–170**
.DB file name extension, 54, 399
dBASE
  exporting and importing from, 434–435
  Paradox and, 949–950
.DBF file name extension, 435
DBMS. *See* database management systems
debugging, scripts, **375–376**, *375*, **856–859**, *857*
decimal places, in numeric formats, 101–103, 996
Default option, ValCheck/Define submenu, 110
defaults. *See also* Custom Configuration Program
  changing default form, 275, **300–301**, 303
  default color settings, 961–962
  default grouping for summary calculations, 524
  formats for numbers and dates, 985–986
  for Group band repeats, 563
  selecting default printer, 195–197, *196*
Define submenu, ValCheck menu
  Auto submenu, 115–117
  Default option, 110
  HighValue option, 109–110
  LowValue option, 109–110
  overview of, 107–109
  Picture option, 110–114
  Required option, 114–115
  TableLookup submenu, 109, 605–608
defining. *See also* creating
  application attributes, 760–762, *762*, *763*
  application menu shortcut keys, 766
  data types, 40, **47–49**
  edit session objects, 775–778, *776*
  fields, 54–55
  goals of application, 712, **718–719**
  key fields, 55
  memo fields, 49–50, *51*
  multiple table validity checks, 605–608
  primary key fields
    in multiple-table designs, **477**
    for primary indexes, 476
    in single-table design, **478–480**, *478*, *479*, *480*
  printer settings, in applications, 789–790, *789*
  queries in applications, 793–794, *793*
  report print objects in applications, 786–789, *787*, *788*
  sets, 535–540, *536*, *538*
Delete key
  in Editor, 669–670
  in Field view, 77
  in Form Design screen, 282
  in Report Design screen, 204
Delete option, Setting/PageLayout submenu, 205, 211, 235
DELETE queries, **182–184**, *183*, 410, 640
Delete submenu, Group menu, 239
Delete submenu, Tools menu, **402–403**
  Form option, 403
  Graph option, 402
  Index option, 403, 429, 489
  KeepSet option, 106, 301, 403
  Report option, 403
  Script option, 402
  Table option, 402
  ValCheck option, 118, 403

INDEX

deleting
  all columns in spillover pages, 211
  application menu options, 767
  applications from application table, 806, **811–812**, *811*
  areas from forms, 274, **292–293**, 303
  blank lines
    in free-form reports, 232–233
    in reports, 188, **203–205**, **244–245**
  blank spaces, in free-form reports, 231–232, *232*
  borders and lines on forms, 296
  color settings, 967–968
  columns in reports, 211
  field masks, 220
  fields
    from forms, 274, **292–293**, 303
    from table structures, 422–423
    from tables, 55
  forms, 403
  graphs, 402
  Group bands, 239
  Image menu settings, 107
  indexes, **403**, 429
  lines of text, 672
  objects, 390, **402–403**, 450
  passwords, 414–415
  records, 61, **80–81**, 83
    all records from a table, 390, **410–411**, 451
    with DELETE queries, **182–184**, *183*
    and recovering disk space, **410**
    that match records in another table, 390, **406–409**, *407*, *408*, *409*, 451
  reports, 403
  scripts, 402
  secondary indexes, 489
  spillover pages, 205
  tables, 402
  text, 669, 671, 674–675
  validity checks, **117–118**, 403

delimited ASCII files. *See also* text files
  delimiter character for, 438, **995–996**
  exporting, **436–439**, *437*, 440–442
  importing, **436–439**, 451
dependencies. *See also* normalizing databases
  partial dependencies, 472–473
  transitive dependencies, 473–474
descending sorts, 122, **127**, 129, 137
Design option, Report menu, 199, 225
designing
  applications, 712, **717–725**, 747. *See also* Membership application example
    creating directory for application, 721–722
    defining goals of application, 712, **718–719**
    designing menu structure on paper, 713, **719–721**, *720*, *721*
    distributing, 716, **724–725**
    documenting, **724–725**
    forms, reports, and scripts, 723–724
    overview of, **717–718**
    queries, 723
    tables, 722–723
    and testing database objects, **721–724**
    testing and refining application, 713, **724**
  forms, 274, **277–293**, *278*, **299–300**, 302–303
    for applications, 723–724
    deleting fields and areas, 274, **292–293**, 303
    displaying field names during, 275, **299–300**, *299*
    moving items on forms, 274, **290–291**, *291*, *292*, 303
    opening Form Design screen, **279–281**, *281*
    overview of, 277–278

placing DisplayOnly fields, 286
placing fields, 274, **283–286**, *285*, 302
placing record numbers, 286
placing regular fields, 283–286
placing text, 274, 283, 286
sizing fields, **289**
word-wrapping alphanumeric and memo fields, 274, **287–289**, *288*, 291, 293, **301**, 303
working in Form Design screen, **281–283**
  master forms, 614, *616*
  menu structure for applications, 713, **719–721**, *720*, *721*
  queries for applications, 723
  reports, 188, **198–209**, 271, **723–724**. *See also* field masks; Report Design screen; Table band
    for applications, **723–724**
    changing page layout, 189, **224–225**, 272
    free-form reports, 199–201, *201*
    inserting and deleting blank lines, 188, **203–205**, **244–245**
    inserting and deleting spillover pages, 205
    inserting literal text, 188, **203–205**
    inserting page breaks, **244–245**
    moving text and field masks, 205
    new features, **912–913**
    saving report formats, 201
    selecting a report format, 199–201, *200*, *201*
    tabular reports, 199–201, *200*
  scripts for applications, 723–724
  subforms, 614, 615–616

tables, 40, **42–51**, *43*, *44*,
 722–723. *See also* indexes;
 multiple tables; table
 structures
 for applications, 722–723
 defining data types, 40,
 47–49
 defining memo fields,
 49–50, *51*
 limitations of tables, 50–51
 naming fields, 40, **46–47**
 overview of, 42–44
 planning fields, **44–46**, 57
desktop. *See also* dialog boxes;
 windows
 defined, **25**
 placing objects on in scripts,
 663, **694–695**, *696*, 708
 printing reports from, 246
Desktop submenu, System
 menu
 Redraw option, 92
 Surface-Queries option, 151
detail forms. *See* subforms
detail table/master table
 relationship
 defined, **458**
 in one-to-many database
 design, 464–465, *465*
details, omitting in Group
 bands, **569–572**, *571*
developers, new features for,
 916–918
developing applications, with
 Tools menu, **409–410**
Device submenu, Overall
 menu, 352, 354
dialog boxes, 86, **93**, **94**
 in Custom Configuration
 Program, **953–955**, *954*,
 956
 in Workshop program, 756
.DIF (Data Interchange
 Format)
 exporting to, 436, 438, 440
 importing from, 436, 439,
 446–447
Digits option, Field/Reformat
 submenu, 221
directories
 changing, 33–34, 41, 53

creating, 34, 41, **52–53**, 57
 for applications, 721–722,
 758–759
 exporting and importing and,
 430
 on networks, **932–933**, 934
 new directory support
 features, **913**
 script play back and,
 368–369, 371–372
 selecting a working directory,
 23, **32–34**, 38, 980
directory listing report,
 260–262, *261*
directory locks, **923**
Directory submenu, Workshop
 Application menu, 34, 53,
 722, 758–759
Disable Break option, CCP
 Standard Settings dialog
 box, 980–981
displaying. *See also* hiding
 calculation results with
 CALC reserved word, 492,
 517–518, *519*, 548
 Color Palette, 959
 column headings in Group
 bands, **561–562**, *562*
 error messages for calculated
 fields, **989**
 field names during form
 design, 299–300
 graphs in scripts, 327
 messages in scripts, 663,
 696–697
 nonmatching records with
 multiple table queries,
 514–516, *515*
 repetitive data in Group
 bands, **562–563**, *563*, 970
DisplayOnly fields, Form
 Design screen, 286, **601**,
 602
distributing applications, 716,
 724–725, **820–823**, 828
 copying files to floppy disks,
 821–822
 copying from floppy disks to
 hard disk, 822–823
 copying large applications, 823
 files to include, 820–821

division operator (/), 516–517,
 552–553
documentation
 for applications, **724–725**,
 815–820, 828
 box and line styles in,
 818–819, *818*
 embellishing with word
 processor, 819–820
 selecting a printer for,
 816–817, *817*
 commenting in scripts, 663,
 693–694, *694*, 840
Documentation menu,
 Workshop program,
 815–816
DO-IT! option, 35, 37, 57
DOS
 BACKUP command,
 400–401, 823
 Borland applications and
 Paradox in, **950**
 COPY command, 399, 401,
 427
 creating directories in, 52–53
 EXIT command, 450
 interoperability in, **950**
 printing graph files from,
 354–355
 RESTORE command, 401,
 823
 running Custom
 Configuration Program
 from, 953
 shelling out to, 52, 53, 391,
 449–450, 451
 starting applications from,
 824–825
 UNDELETE command, 403
 version required by Paradox,
 890
 XCOPY command, 821–823
double quotation marks. *See*
 quotation marks (″ ″)
double-dot operator (..)
 in Find dialog box, 686, 687
 in query criteria, 156,
 161–164, 165, 178
 in Zoom dialog box, 32, 96, 97
drawing, borders and lines on
 forms, 294–295

INDEX

duration of graph display, 306, **326–327**

E

Edit: Multiple Actions dialog box, Workshop program, 770–771, *770*
Edit Application dialog box, Workshop program, *810*
Edit command, PAL, 832
Edit menu, Editor
   Copy option, 674, 675, 677
   Erase option, 675
   Goto option, 671
   Location option, 671
   Paste option, 674, 676, 677
   ShowClipboard option, 676
   XCut option, 674, 677
Edit mode
   closing windows in, 92
   editing tables in, 60, 81
   entering data in, 67
   key violations in, 483
   on networks, **925–928**
   opening tables in, **81**
   switching to, 60, **64–65**, *65*, 83
   Undo feature in, 78
Edit option, Workshop Application menu, 810
Edit Session dialog box, Workshop program, **776–785**, *776*
   Add option, 776, 778
   EventProcs option, 777, 783
   Keys option, 777, 782
   System Mode option, 778, 779
edit session objects, **775–785**. *See also* applications
   adding tables to edit session, 778–782, *779*, *780*, *781*
   assigning event procedures to edit session, 783–785, *784*, *786*
   assigning key actions to edit session, 782–783, *782*
   defining, 775–778, *776*
Edit Session-Table Information dialog box, Workshop program, 778–782, *779*

Edit Text option, Workshop Help Screen dialog box, 798–799
Edit XRef option, Workshop Help Screen dialog box, 800
editing. *See also* changing; data entry; Editor; modifying
   application menu options, 750, **768**, 803
   ASCII text files, 662, **667–668**, 708
   color settings, 965
   cross-references in application Help, 800
   with Editor, **665–668**
   fields, 55, **76–78**, 83
   Help screens in application, 751, **798–799**
   memo fields, 50, **79**, 83, 662, **665–666**, *665*
   on multi-table forms, 627–628
   on networks, **939**
   objects in applications, **812–813**
   PAL scripts, 839–840, 990–992
   with queries, 141, **177–184**
      finding information, 177–179, *178*
      global deletions, 141, **182–184**
      global edits, 141, **179–182**, *181*
   queries saved as scripts, 692, *693*
   referential integrity and, **627–628**
   scripts, 662, **666–667**, *667*, **691–692**, *691*, 707
   selecting editor for, **990–992**
   tables, 60, 61, **64–65**, **74–82**
      contents of fields, 76–78
      deleting records, 61, **80–81**, 83, **182–184**
      in Edit or CoEdit mode, 60, 81
      inserting records, 61, **79–80**, *80*, 83
   memo fields, 79

saving or canceling changes, 61, **81–82**, 83
switching to Edit or CoEdit mode, 60, **64–65**, *65*
undoing changes to records, 61, 75, **78–79**, 83
Editor, **664–690**
   auto-indenting text, 680, 985, 989
   Cancel option, 690
   Clipboard
      cutting, copying, and pasting and, 677–678
      making changes in, 676–678
      viewing, 676, *677*
   copying
      current editing window to a file, 681–682
      selected text to a file, 683
   creating PAL scripts with, 836–837
   cutting, copying, and pasting operations, 669–670, 674
   Clipboard and, 677–678
   cutting and pasting between windows, 675–676
   defaults for text files and memo fields, 680, 985
   deleting
      lines of text, 672
      selected text, 674–675
      text, 669, 671
   Edit menu
      Copy option, 674, 675, 677
      Erase option, 675
      Goto option, 671
      Location option, 671
      Paste option, 674, 676, 677
      ShowClipboard option, 676
      XCut option, 674, 677
   editing, **665–668**
      ASCII text files, 662, **667–668**, 708
      memo fields, 662, **665–666**, *665*
      queries saved as scripts, 692, *693*
      scripts, 662, **666–667**, *667*, **691–692**, *691*, 707
   exiting, **690**
   File menu, **681–685**

CopyToFile option,
  681–682, 683–684
InsertFile option, 682–683,
  684, 702, 704
New option, 685
Open option, 685
Print option, 684–685
Save option, 681
WriteBlock option, 683–684
file operations
  copying current editing
    window to a file, 681–682
  copying selected text to a
    file, 683
  creating files while editing,
    685
  inserting external files into
    text, 682–683
  opening existing files while
    editing, 685
  printing current file,
    684–685
  saving changes, 662, **681**
  transferring text between
    programs, **683–684**, 708
Go option, 666–667, 707
inserting
  blank lines, 672
  external files into text,
    682–683
  text, 669, 671
joining lines of text, 672
keyboard operations in,
  668–670
moving Editor window, 668
new features, **913**
opening, **664**, 707
opening multiple windows,
  685
Options menu
  AutoIndent submenu, 680
  CaseSensitive option, 687
  TabStops option, 680
  WordWrap submenu, 679
Overwrite mode, 669, 671
positioning cursor, 669, 671,
  708
printing current file, 684–685
saving
  changes, 662, **681**, 690

scripts and playing back,
  666–667, 707
Search menu
  ChangeToEnd option,
    689–690
  Find option, 686–687
  Next option, 687
  Replace option, 688–689
searching and replacing text,
  670, **685–690**
case sensitivity in searches,
  687
replacing text with confirm
  feature, 688–689
replacing text without
  confirm feature, 689–690
searching for text, 686–687
selecting external editor for
  scripts, **990–992**
selecting text, 662, **672–674**,
  672, 708
and copying to a file, 683
and deleting, 674–675
deselecting text, 673–674
with keyboard, 669–670, 673
with mouse, 673
sizing Editor window, 668
switching between editing
  windows, 675
tab stop settings, 680, 985,
  990
transferring text between
  programs, **683–684**, 708
word-wrap feature, **678–679**,
  679, 985
Editor submenu
  Scripts menu
    New option, 697–698
    Open option, 413–414, 666
  System menu, 667–668
elements
  of graphs, **328**
  of scripts, **691–692**
embedded text, query criteria
  for, 161–163, *162*
emptying, tables, 406, **410–411**
End key
  in Editor, 669–670
  in Field view, 77
  in Form Design screen, 282
  navigating with, 74

in Query form window, 144
in Report Design screen, 204
sizing tables in Table view, 99
EndRecord option
  PAL menu, 856
  Scripts menu, 371, 384, 836
ensuring uniqueness, in
  one-to-many database
  design, 463–464
"Enter directory or leave blank
  for working directory"
  message, 417
"Enter DOS pattern, e.g.,
  *.TXT" message, 418
Enter key, in Report Design
  screen, 204
"Enter password for table"
  message, 413
"Enter table with records to
  add or press ↵ for a list"
  message, 405
entering data. *See* data entry
envelopes
  printing, 267–269, *268*, *269*
  script for, 380
equal to (=), in query criteria,
  156, **166–168**
Erase option
  Editor Edit menu, 675
  Field menu, 220, 235
  Form Design Area menu,
    292–293
  Form Design Border menu,
    296
  Form Design Field menu, 292
  TableBand menu, 211
"Erase text and delete fields in
  page width 2 and higher"
  message, 234
erasing. *See* deleting
error messages. *See* messages
error-checking controls, in PAL
  scripts, 870
Esc key, canceling with, 28, 93,
  100
event procedures, in
  applications, 783–785,
  784, *786*
EventProcs option, Workshop
  Edit Session dialog box,
  777, 783

INDEX

EVERY operator, **535**, *536*, 537–538, *538*
exact values, query criteria for, 140, **158–160**, *159*
EXACTLY operator, **535**, *536*, 540
example elements, **499–503**. *See also* Query forms
  entering, 500
  explained, 499–500
  linking tables with, 500–503, *502*, *503*
  in update queries, 633, **636–637**, *637*
examples. *See* sample
exclamation point (!)
  as inclusion operator, 515–516
  in Picture formats, 111
.EXE files, 667, 683
execute objects, **801**. *See also* applications
Execute PAL dialog box, Workshop program, 801
Execute scripts, **839**
EXIT command, DOS, 450
Exit command, PAL, 854
exiting
  Editor, 690
  Field view, 77, **78**
  Help, 23, **32**
  loops in PAL scripts, 854–855
  Paradox, 23, **37**, **38**
  shelling out to DOS, 52, 53, 391, **449–450**, 451
explicit locks, **928–930**
exploded inventory database example, 469–471, *469*, *470*, *471*
ExportImport submenu, Tools menu, **429–449**. *See also* exporting; importing
  ASCII options, 436–442, 481
  dBASE options, 435
  overview of, 431–432
  PFS options, 435
  Reflex options, 435
  VisiCalc options, 436
exporting, 391, **429–449**, 451. *See also* importing
  ASCII delimited files, **436–439**, *437*, 440–442, **995-996**
  ASCII text files, 439, 683–684
  blank fields, **996**
  to Data Interchange Format (.DIF), 436, 438, 440
  to dBASE, 434–435
  directories and, 430
  file name extensions for, **432**
  to IBM Filing Assistant format (.PFS), 435
  to Lotus 1-2-3, 432–433
  overview of, **429–432**
  .PFS files, 435
  to Quattro Pro, 433
  to Reflex, 435
  reports to word processors, 448–449
  to spreadsheets, 432–433
  text to word processors, 683–684
  to VisiCalc, 436
  to WordPerfect merge files, **439–445**
    printing structure of Paradox table, 440
    defining format of ASCII file, 440–441
    exporting Paradox data, 442
    preparing WordPerfect for imported file, 442–443
    creating primary merge file, 443–444, *444*
    performing the merge, 445
expressions
  for calculating with queries, 516–517
  in PAL, **847–848**, 859
extended character set, for form borders, 294–295
extensions. *See* file name extensions

F

.F file name extension, 281
F1 key, for Help, 29–30
F2 key, Do-It! key, 35, 37, 57
F3 key
  Alt + F3 (Record Instant Script), 382, 384, 839
  cycling backward through windows, 90
F4 key
  Alt + F4 (Play Instant Script), 382, 384, 839
  Ctrl + F4 (cycling through windows on desktop), 90, 665
  cycling forward through windows, 90
F5 key
  Alt + F5 (Field view), 50
  Ctrl + F5 (sizing/moving windows), 90
  Shift + F5 (maximizing/restoring windows), 91
F6 key
  plain check marks, 148
  Alt + F6 (check-plus check marks), 148
  Ctrl + F6 (check-descending check marks), 148
F7 key
  Table/Form view toggle, 66, 276
  Alt + F7 (Instant Report), 190
  Ctrl + F7 (Instant Graph), 312
F8 key
  Close Active Window, 82, 91
  Alt + F8 (Close All Windows), 82, 91
F9 key
  Edit mode, 64
  Alt + F9 (CoEdit mode), 64
F10 key
  activating menu bar, 36–37
  Alt + F10 (PAL menu), 370, 371, 855
families
  family locks, **924**
  family rights, **946–947**
  viewing tables', *419*, 488
fax lists, 255–257, *256*
"A field has already been placed here" message, 285
field masks, 189, **201–202**, **214–224**, 272. *See also* reports
  for alphanumeric fields, 218, 221, 222–224

for calculated fields, 215,
   219–220
for currency fields, 202, 218
for date fields, 202, 216, 217,
   218
deleting, **220**
explained, **201–202**
justifying (aligning), **224**
for memo fields, 218, 221,
   222–224
moving, 205
for numbering records, 216
for numeric fields, 202, 218
for page numbers, 216
placing, **214–217**
#Record field mask, 216
reformatting, **220–222**
Regular field mask, 215
sizing, 218
for time fields, 202, 216
for totals and subtotals, 215
word-wrapping in, **222–224**
Field menu, Form Design
   screen
   Erase option, 292
   Place submenu
      DisplayOnly option, 286
      #Record option, 286
      Regular option, 283–286
   Reformat option, 289
   WordWrap option, 287–289
Field menu, Report Design
   screen, **214–224**
   CalcEdit option, 220
   Erase option, 220, 235
   Justify submenu, 224
   Lookup submenu, 574, 576,
      578, 580–582
   Place submenu, 214–220
      Calculated option, 219–220,
         553, 555
      Reformat submenu, 212,
         220–222, 235
         Commas submenu, 222
         Digits option, 221
         International submenu, 222
         Sign-Convention option, 222
         WordWrap option, 222–224
Field option
   GroupInsert submenu,
      239–240

Image/Zoom submenu, 94–95
ValCheck/Clear submenu, 117
field rights, **947**
field separator, in ASCII files,
   438, **995–996**
field summaries, **861–863**
   with miniscripts, 862–863, *863*
   with PAL/Value option, 862
"Field of type Memo, Blob, or
   Unknown not supported"
   message, 436
field types, **47–49**
   summary operators and,
      523–524
Field view
   exiting, 77, 78
   switching to, 77
   Undo feature and, 78
   viewing and editing binary
      and memo fields, 50,
      68–70, *69*
fields. *See also* columns; records;
   tables; update queries
   alphanumeric fields
      allotting space for, 48
      defined, **47**
      for zip codes and phone
         numbers, 49
   arranging for Crosstab tables,
      360–362, *362*
   binary fields
      defined, **47**
      entering data in, **68–70**, *69*
      importing text into, 684
      in previous versions, 57
      selecting BLOB editor, 48,
         70, 684, **992–994**
   Binary Large Object (BLOB)
      fields
      defined, **48**
      selecting editor for, 48, 70,
         684, **992–994**
   blank fields
      calculations on, **518–519**,
         604, **981–982**
      export setting, 996
      query criteria for, 157,
         168–169
   changing field types, **423–424**
   copying from previous record,
      72

currency fields, defined, **47**, 49
date fields, defined, **47**
defined, **40**, 42
defining, **54–55**
defining data types, 40, **47–49**
deleting, 55
   from table structures,
      422–423
editing, 55, **76–78**, 83
inserting, 55
in table structures, 422–423
key fields
   defining, 55
   sorting with, 135
memo fields
   allotting space for, 48,
      49–50, *51*
   defined, **47**
   defining, 48, **49–50**, *51*
   editing, 50, 79, 83, 662,
      665–666, *665*
   Editor defaults for, 680, 985
   entering data in, **68–70**, *69*,
      83
   field masks for, 218, 221,
      222–224
   placing on forms, 285
   in previous versions, 57
   printing reports with,
      270–271, *270*
   query criteria for text in, 164
   searching for text in, 97
   sorting on, 130
   viewing, 50
   word-wrap feature and, 679
   word-wrapping on forms,
      274, **287–289**, *288*, 291,
      293, **301**, 303
moving
   in Answer tables, 151
   for Crosstab tables,
      360–362, *362*
   to see sort order, 123,
      132–133, *132*, *133*, *134*, 137
   in table structures, 422–423
   in Table view, 105
naming, 40, **46–47**
navigating, **67**, **74–76**, *76*
numeric fields, defined, **47**, 49

order of in Answer tables, 140, **151–155**, *152*, *154*, 508, 981
planning, **44–46**, 57
searching for, 87, **94–95**, 119
short numeric fields, defined, 47, 49
types of, **47–49**
viewing field names for secondary indexes, 419–420
FieldSqueeze option, Setting/RemoveBlanks submenu, 232, 236
File Format option, CCP Standard Settings dialog box, 982–983
file formats, for previous versions, 57, 426–427, **982–983**. *See also* exporting; file name extensions; importing
File menu, Editor, **681–685**
  CopyToFile option, 681–682, 683–684
  InsertFile option, 682–683, 684, 702, 704
  New option, 685
  Open option, 685
  Print option, 684–685
  Save option, 681
  WriteBlock option, 683–684
file name extensions
  .COM, 667, 683
  .DB, 54, 399
  .DBF, 435
  .DIF (Data Interchange Format)
    exporting to, 436, 438, 440
    importing from, 436, 439, 446–447
  .EXE, 667, 683
  for exporting and importing, **432**
  .F, 281
  .MB, 49, 399
  for objects, 399, **400**
  .R, 252
  .SC, 371, 668, 693
  .SC2, 706–707

for secondary indexes, 399, 487
  .SET, 107
  .TXT, 438
  .VAL, 108, 118
  .XG, 399, 487
  .YG, 399, 487
File option, Report/Output submenu, 448
FileFormat menu
  Create screen, 57
  Restructure screen, 426–427
files. *See also* objects; tables
  copying
    current editing window to a file, 681–682
    selected text to a file, 683
  creating files while editing, 685
  file formats, 57, **982–983**
  inserting external files into text, 682–683
  new file management features, **913**
  opening existing files while editing, 685
  Paradox.ADD file, **882–883**, 887, 917
  printing
    current file, 684–685
    graph files, 354–355
    graphs to files, 307, **353–354**
  saving Editor changes to, 662, **681**
  sharing with other Borland applications, **949–950**
  viewing information about, 391, **416–420**, 451
    field names for secondary indexes, 419–420
    file inventory, 417–418, *418*
    table structures, 416–417, *417*
    a table's family, *419*, 488
fill patterns, modifying graph, 343–344
Filled option, ValCheck/Auto submenu, 116
Find dialog box, 686–687
Find option, Editor Search menu, 686–687

FIND queries, **177–179**, *178*
finding. *See* searching; searching and replacing
Finish option, Workshop Application menu, 815
finishing, applications, 807, **815**, 828
Fixed option, Image/Format submenu, 101–103
fixing, corrupted objects, **427–428**
flagging, records in update queries, 632, **635–636**, 642, 645
floppy disks, copying objects to, 399, 401–402
fonts
  for graph titles, 330, *331*
  printer codes for, 590–592, *592*
foreign key fields, **462**
Form band, Report Design screen, *206*, 208–209
Form Design screen. *See also* forms
  Area menu
    Erase option, 292–293
    Move option, 281, 286, **290–291**
  Border menu
    Erase option, 296
    Place submenu, 294
  Field menu
    Erase option, 292
    Place submenu, 283–286
    Reformat option, 289
    WordWrap option, 287–289
  keyboard operations in, **281–282**
  moving items on forms, 274, **290–291**, *291*, *292*, 303
  Multi menu, 613–614, 619
  new features, **912**
  opening, **279–281**, *281*
  placing fields, **283–286**
    DisplayOnly fields, 286
    #Record fields, 286
    Regular fields, 283–286
  versus Report Design screen, 280, 281
  sizing fields, 289

Style menu, **296–300**
　Color submenu, 296–297
　Fieldnames submenu, 299–300
　Monochrome submenu, 297–298
　word-wrapping alphanumeric and memo fields, 274, **287–289**, *288*, 291, 293, **301**, 303
form letters, 262–264, *263*
　script for, **376–381**, *377*
　　adding Welcomed field for, 376
　　creating form letter script, 377–379, *378*
　　creating label or envelope script, 380
　　using scripts, 380–381
Form option
　Tools/Copy submenu, 398
　Tools/Delete submenu, 403
　Tools/Rename submenu, 393–394
Form Selection dialog box, Workshop program, *781*
Form view
　adding records, 67
　navigating in, **74–76**, *76*
　switching to, 60, **66**, *66*, 83, 276
　versus Table view, **277–278**
Format Data dialog box, Custom Configuration Program, 915, **984–986**, *984*
　default format for numbers and dates, 985–986
　Editor defaults in text files and memo fields, 680, 985
　new features, 915
　tab stop settings, 680, 985
Format submenu
　Image menu
　　Comma option, 101–103
　　Fixed option, 101–103
　　formatting date fields, 103
　　formatting numeric fields, 101–103
　　General option, 101–103
　　Scientific option, 102–103

Report Design Setting menu, 561–562, *562*
formats. *See also* formatting; Picture formats; report formats
　application mailing label formats, **731**, *732*
　for date fields, 67, 985–986
　file formats. *See also* exporting; file name extensions; importing
　　for previous versions, 57, 426–427, **982–983**
　label formats for pie charts, 345–346
　for numeric fields, 101–103, 985–986, 996
　tick mark formats, 328, 335–336
formatted reports. *See also* free-form reports; reports; tabular reports
　printing, 151, 189, **245–249**, 272
　　from Answer tables, 151
　　previewing reports, 189, **248**
　　printing ranges of pages, 247
　　from Report Design screen, 246
　　searching for values in report previews, 249
　sorting with, 133
formatting
　date fields in Table view, 103
　Group headers, 564–566, *564*, 565
　numbers, 101–103, 985–986, 996
　PAL scripts, 840
　reformatting field masks, **220–222**
　forms, **274–303**, **599–628**. *See also* data entry; Form Design screen; objects; update queries
　automatic fill-in on, **607–608**
　borders and lines, 275, **293–296**, 303
　　deleting borders and lines, 296
　　drawing borders, 294–295

　　drawing lines, 295
　calculated fields in, 551, **602–604**, *603*, *604*, 629
　changing, 275, **302**, 303
　changing default form, 275, **300–301**, 303
　coloring and highlighting, 275, **296–299**, 303
　　blinking screen style, 298
　　changing form colors, **296–297**
　　monochrome video attributes, **297–298**
　　reverse screen style, 297–298
　　tips, 298–299
　copying, **398**
　defined, **7**
　deleting, **403**
　designing, 274, **277–293**, *278*, **299–300**, 302–303, **723–724**
　　for applications, **723–724**
　　deleting fields and areas, 274, **292–293**, 303
　　displaying field names during, 275, **299–300**, *299*
　　moving items on forms, 274, **290–291**, *291*, *292*, 303
　　opening Form Design screen, **279–281**, *281*
　　overview of, 277–278
　　placing DisplayOnly fields, 286
　　placing fields, 274, **283–286**, *285*, 302
　　placing record numbers, 286
　　placing regular fields, 283–286
　　placing text, 274, 283, 286
　　sizing fields, **289**
　　word-wrapping alphanumeric and memo fields, 274, **287–289**, *288*, 291, 293, **301**, 303
　　working in Form Design screen, **281–283**
　Help boxes in, *278*, **294**
　locks and, **941**
　in Membership application example, **727–728**, *728*, *729*
　multipage forms, **599–602**, 629

INDEX

creating, 551, **599–601**, *599*, *600*, 629
identifying current record with DisplayOnly fields, 601, *602*
using, 602
multiple table validity checks, 551, **604–610**, 629
  AllCorrespondingFields option, 607–608
  defining, **605–608**
  JustCurrentField option, 606–607, 608
  overview of, **604–605**
  state abbreviations example, 610, *611*
  using tables with, 608–610, *609*
multi-record forms, 551, **611–614**, 629
  creating, 612–613, *613*
  modifying, 613–614
multi-table forms, 551, **614–628**, 629
  creating with linked tables, **620–627**, *620*, *621*, *622*
  creating with unlinked tables, **615–618**
  designing master forms, 614, *616*
  designing subforms, 614, 615–616
  editing on, **627–628**
  embedding subforms, 617–618, *617*
  managing subforms, 619
  master form for Invoices table, 625–627, *625*
  on networks, **628**
  overview of, 614
  referential integrity and, **627–628**
  subform for Accounts table, 624–625, *624*
  subform for Invdtail table, 623–624, *623*
  using, 618–619, *618*
on networks, 628, **941**
overview of, 6, *7*

recovering deleted, **403**
renaming, **393–394**
saving, **280–281**, 289, 293, 302, 303
Standard Form screen, **276–277**, *277*, 278
versus Table view, **277–278**
using, 275, **300**, 303
using word-wrapped fields, **301**
Forms menu, Change option, 302
forward slash (/), as division operator, 516–517, 552–553
frames, customizing graph, *339*, 340
free-form reports, **230–236**, 272. *See also* reports
  defined, **198**
  deleting
    blank lines in, 232–233
    blank spaces in, 231–232, *232*
  designing, 199–201, *201*
  examples, **260–271**
    directory listing, 260–262, *261*
    envelopes, 267–269, *268*, *269*
    form letter, 262–264, *263*
    laser printer labels, 264–267, *265*
    reports with memo fields, 270–271, *270*
  Form band and, 208–209
  printing multicolumn labels and reports, 233–236, *235*, *237*
frequency distributions, 527, *528*
full locks, **923**
Full Screen User Interface
  new features, **910–911**
  selecting as default, 980
  switching to, 23, **35–37**, *36*
  windows in, 89
fully normalized databases, **474**
function keys. *See* F keys
functions. *See* PAL functions

G

General option, Image/Format submenu, 101–103
generating, Crosstab tables, 358–359, *359*
GetRecord key, 870
getting information
  about computers, **956–958**
  about files, 391, **416–420**, 451
    field names for secondary indexes, 419–420
    file inventory, 417–418, *418*
    table structures, 416–417, *417*
  a table's family, *419*, 488
  about network users and locks, **936–937**
global deletions, 141, **182–184**
global edits, 141, **179–182**, *181*
Go option, Editor, 666–667, 707
Goto menu, Report Preview screen, 248
Goto option, Editor Edit menu, 671
Graph option
  Tools/Copy submenu, 351, 398–399
  Tools/Delete submenu, 402
  Tools/Rename submenu, 394
Graph settings, Custom Configuration Program, 314, **974–979**
  Graph Printer Settings dialog box, 975–978, *976*
  Graphics Screen dialog box, 978–979, *978*
  Instant Graph defaults, 975
  Select Graph Printer dialog box, 975–977, *976*
  selecting printer for graphs, 975–978
  selecting screen mode for graphs, 978–979
Graph submenu, Image menu
  CrossTab submenu, 355–358, 361
  Load option, 309, 349

Modify option, 309, 315
Replace option, 350
Reset option, 350
Save option, 309, 350
ViewGraph submenu, 309, 313
graphs, **306–364**
  area graphs, **323–324**, *325*
  bar graphs, **316–319**
    3-D, 317–318, *318*
    regular, 316, *317*
    rotated, 318–319, *319*
    stacked, 316
  combined graphs, **324–325**, *326*
  combined line and markers graphs, **321**, *322*
  copying, **398–399**
  cross tabulations, **355–364**
    arranging fields for Crosstab tables, 360–362, *362*
    explained, **355–357**, *356*
    generating Crosstab tables, 358–359, *359*
    graphing Crosstab tables, 307, **359–360**, *360*
    shortcut for, 362–363, *363*
  custom graph settings, 309, 327, **347–351**
    creating graphs from, 307, **348–349**, 350–351, 364
    modifying existing, 307, **350**
    saving, 306, **347–348**, 364
  Customize Fills and Markers screen, 343–344, *343*
  Customize Graph Axes screen, 333–338, *334*, *337*
  Customize Graph Colors screen, 332–333, *332*
  Customize Graph Layout for Printing screen, 352–353, *353*
  Customize Graph Titles screen, 329–330, *329*
  Customize Graph Type screen, 315–316, *315*, 324–325
  Customize Grids and Frames screen, 339–340, *339*
  Customize Pie Graph screen, 345–346, *345*
  Customize Series Legends and Labels screen, 340–342, *341*
  customizing, 306, 309, **327–340**, 364
    colors, 332–333, *332*
    graph axes, 328, **333–338**
    graph frames, *339*, 340
    grid lines, 339–340, *339*
    matching screen colors to printer colors, 333
    pie charts, **344–346**, *344*, *345*, *347*
    pie chart labels, 345–346
    pie chart slices, 346
    printed graph layout, **352–353**, *353*, 364
    sample custom axes, 336–338, *337*
    scaling of axes, 328, 334–335
    tick mark formats, 328, 335–336
    tick mark labels, 328, 336
    titles, 328, 329–330, *329*, *331*
    working in Customize Graph screens, 328–329
    X-axis labels for keyed table graphs, 338
  customizing graph series, 328, **340–344**
    modifying labels, 341–343
    modifying legends, 328, 340–341
    modifying markers and fill patterns, 343–344
  deleting, **402**
  elements of, **328**
  graphing Crosstab tables, 307, **359–360**, *360*
  how Paradox graphs data, **310–311**
  Instant Graphs, 306, 309, **312–314**, *314*, 364, 975
  line graphs, **319**, *320*
    combined line and markers graphs, **321**, *322*
  locks and, **941**
  markers graphs, **320–321**, *321*, *322*
  on networks, **941**
Overall menu
  Axes option, 333
  Colors submenu, 332, 333
  Device submenu, 352, 354
  PrinterLayout option, 352
  Titles option, 329
  Wait option, 326
overview of, 11, *12–13*, **308–310**
pie charts, **322–323**, *324*
  calculating percentages with, 543–544, *544*
  customizing, **344–346**, *344*, *345*, *347*
  customizing label formats, 345–346
  customizing pie slices, 346
printer settings for, 975–978, *976*
printing, 307, 309, **351–355**, 364
  customizing printed graph layout, 352–353, *353*, 364
  to files, 307, **353–354**
  printing graph files, 354–355
  selecting printer, 351–352
renaming, **394**
selecting
  graph type, 306, **315–316**, *315*, 364
  printers for, 351–352, 975–978
  screen mode for, 978–979
Series menu
  LegendsAndLabels option, 340
  MarkersAndFills option, 343
setting duration of graph display, 306, **326–327**
types of, 312
X-axis labels, 308, 311, 338
X-Y graphs, **321–322**, *323*
greater than (>), in query criteria, 156, **166–168**
greater than or equal to (>=), in query criteria, 156, **166–168**
grid lines, customizing graph, 339–340, *339*
Group bands, 189, **237–244**, *238*, 272. *See also* bands; reports

INDEX

BLANKLINE command in, 567
changing group specifier, 243–244
column heading display, **561–562**, *562*
formatting Group headers, **564–566**, *564*, *565*
Group Header and Group Footer bands, 239, **564–566**, 567–569, 571–572
grouping
  on alphanumeric ranges, 240–241
  on date ranges, 242–243
  on field values, 239–240
  on numeric, currency, or short numeric ranges, 242
  on a record count, 243
  hiding or displaying repetitive data, **562–563**, *563*, 970
  inserting and deleting, 239
  nesting groups, **567–569**, *568*, *570*
  omitting details, **569–572**, *571*
  overview of, 237–238
  PAGEBREAK command in, 566
  positioning items in, 567
  running totals, **572**
  selecting sort direction for groups, 243
  starting groups on a new page, **566**
group locks, **925**
Group menu. *See also* Report Design screen
  Delete submenu, 239
  Headings submenu, 565–566
  Insert submenu, **239–243**
    Field option, 239–240
    NumberRecords option, 243
    Range option, 240–243
  Regroup option, 243–244
  SortDirection submenu, 243
GroupBy operator, 540–542, *541*
grouping operator (), in queries, 516–517, 552–553

GroupRepeats submenu, Setting menu, 562–563, *563*
GroupsOfTables option, Setting/Format submenu, 561–562, *562*

H

hard disk drives, required by Paradox, 890, 891, 921
hardware requirements
  for installing Paradox, 890–891, 897–898
  for networks, 921–922
header and footer bands, Group, 239, 567–569, 571–572
Headings submenu, Group menu, 565–566
Help, 23, **29–32**, 38
  context-sensitive, 29, *30*
  creating in forms, *278*, **294**
  exiting, 23, **32**
  Help Index, 23, 29, **30–32**, *31*
  overview of, **29–30**
  for Query form operators, 523
  searching for topics, 31–32
  in Workshop program, 758
Help Screen dialog box, Workshop program, 797–800, *798*
  Cross-References area, 799
  Edit Text option, 798–799
  Edit XRef option, 800
  Test option, 800
Help text objects, **795–800**, 803. *See also* applications
  adding
    cross-references, 799
    to menu options, 751, **795–797**, *796*
  completing, **797–800**, *798*
  editing cross-references, 800
  editing Help screens, 751, **798–799**
  testing on-line help, 800
Help Text option, Workshop ActionEdit menu, 796
Hewlett-Packard printers
  printer codes for, 590–592

settings for, 196–197, *196*, 227, *228*
hiding. *See also* displaying
  Color Palette, 959
  field names during form design, 300
  repetitive data in Group bands, **562–563**, *563*, 970
highlighting and coloring forms, 275, **296–299**, 303
  blinking screen style, 298
  changing form colors, **296–297**
  monochrome video attributes, **297–298**
  reverse screen style, 297–298
  tips, 298–299
HighValue option, ValCheck/Define submenu, 109–110
history tables. *See also* update queries
  adding items received to In Stock quantities, **651–655**
  creating, **645–646**, 651–652, *652*
  moving posted records to, 633, **649–650**, *650*, 660
  subtracting quantities sold from In Stock quantities, 646–649, *647*, *648*, *649*
  updating scripts and, 652–655, *653*, *654*, *656*
Home key
  in Editor, 669
  in Field view, 77
  in Form Design screen, 282
  navigating with, 74
  in Query form window, 144
  in Report Design screen, 204, 205
  sizing tables in Table view, 99
hotkeys, **863–871**
  creating with miniscripts, **863–865**, *864*
    GetRecord and PasteRecord keys, 867–868
    multiple hotkey macros, 866–867
  creating with PAL scripts, **869–871**
    creating, 869–870

playing automatically at
  startup, 869, 871
hyphen (-)
  for negative numbers, 68
  as subtraction operator,
    516–517, 552–553

I

IBM Filing Assistant format
  (.PFS), exporting and
  importing, 435
If...Then...EndIf branches, in
  PAL scripts, 852–854
Image menu. *See also* Table
  view, customizing
  ColumnSize option, 99–101
  deleting settings, 106–107
  Format submenu
    Comma option, 101–103
    Fixed option, 101–103
    formatting date fields, 103
    formatting numeric fields,
      101–103
    General option, 101–103
    Scientific option, 102–103
  Graph submenu
    CrossTab submenu,
      355–358, 361
    Load option, 309, 349
    Modify option, 309, 315
    Replace option, 350
    Reset option, 350
    Save option, 309, 350
    ViewGraph submenu, 309,
      313
  KeepSet option, 98, **105–107**,
    301
  Move option, 104–105, 316
  new features, **911**
  OrderTable option, 484–485,
    508
  PickForm option, 300, 602,
    618
  saving and restoring settings,
    105–106
  Table Size option, 98–99
  Zoom submenu
    Field option, 94–95
    Record option, 95, 481
    Value option, 95–97

image settings. *See* Image menu;
  Table view, customizing
importing, 391, **429–449**, 451.
  See also exporting
  ASCII delimited files,
    436–439, 451, **995–996**
  ASCII text files, 439
  changing table structure of
    imported tables, **430**
  from Data Interchange
    Format (.DIF), 436, 439,
    446–447
  from dBASE, 434–435
  directories and, 430
  external files into text,
    682–683
  file name extensions for, **432**
  from IBM Filing Assistant
    format (.PFS), 435
  from Lotus 1-2-3, 433–434
  overview of, **429–432**
  .PFS files, 435
  from Reflex, 435
  from spreadsheets, 433–434
  text, 684
  from VisiCalc, 436
  WordPerfect merge files,
    445–448, *447*
inclusion operator (!), 515–516
Index option
  Modify menu, 419, 429, 484,
    486–488, *486*, *488*
  Tools/Delete submenu, 403,
    429, 489
indexes, **475–489**. *See also*
  multiple tables; table
  structures
  deleting, **403**, 429
  key violations, **481–483**
    in CoEdit mode, 482–483
    in Edit mode, 483
    using Modify/DataEntry
      option, 482
  keyed tables
    entering and editing records
      in, 481
    X-axis labels for graphs of,
      338
  limitations of, 428–429
  primary indexes
    defined, **475**

defining primary key fields
  for, 457, **476**, 490
primary key fields, **475–481**
  composite keys, **476**
  defining in multiple-table
    designs, **477**
  defining for primary
    indexes, 476
  defining in single-table
    design, **478–480**, *478*, *479*,
    480
  entering and editing data in
    keyed tables, 481
  many-to-many relationships
    and, 477
  one-to-many relationships
    and, 457, 462–464, **477**,
    490
  rule of uniqueness and, 476
secondary indexes, 457,
  484–489, 490
  creating with
    Image/OrderTable option,
    484–485
  creating with Modify/Index
    option, 484, 486–488, *486*,
    488
  creating with
    Tools/QuerySpeed option,
    428–429, 484, 485
  defined, **475**
  deleting, **489**
  file name extensions for,
    399, 487
  listing, 488
  maintaining automatically,
    983
  Secondary Index screen,
    486–488, *486*, *488*
  speeding up queries with,
    428–429, 484, **485**
  viewing field names for,
    419–420
  sorting and, 126
inexact match operators, in
  query criteria, 140, 156,
  161–165
Info submenu, Tools menu,
  416–420
  Family option, 419, *419*, 488

INDEX

Inventory submenu, 417–418, *418*
Lock option, 936–937
Structure option, 416–417, *417*
TableIndex option, 419–420
Who option, 936
information
  about computers, **956–958**
  about files, 391, **416–420**, 451
    field names for secondary indexes, 419–420
    file inventory, 417–418, *418*
    table structures, 416–417, *417*
    a table's family, *419*, 488
  about network users and locks, **936–937**
Init.SC script, 385–386, 824, 839, **869–871**, 887
Insert key
  in Editor, 669–670
  in Field view, 77
  in Form Design screen, 282
  inserting records with, 74
  in Report Design screen, 204, 205
Insert mode, 205, 286
"Insert next page in printer. Press any key to continue" message, 230
Insert option
  Setting/PageLayout submenu, 205, 213, 235
  TableBand menu, 211, 554
INSERT queries
  calculating with, **644**
  copying incompatible records between tables, 639–642, *639*, *641*, *642*
Insert submenu, Group menu, **239–243**
  Field option, 239–240
  NumberRecords option, 243
  Range option, 240–243
InsertFile option, Editor File menu, 682–683, 684, 702, 704
inserting
  blank lines
    in Editor, 672

in reports, 188, **203–205**, **244–245**
columns in reports, 211
external files into text, 682–683
fields, 55
fields in table structures, 422–423
Group bands, 239
literal text in reports, 188, **203–205**
page breaks in reports, **244–245**, 244–245
printer codes in reports, 550, **589–590**, 628
records, 61, **79–80**, *80*, 83
spillover pages, 205
text with Editor, 669, 671
installing
Paradox, **891–894, 920–921**
  AUTOEXEC.BAT and, 894
  CONFIG.SYS and, 892–893
  hardware requirements for, 890–891, 897–898
  on networks, **920–921**
  Workshop program and sample files, 894–895
instant field summaries, **861–863**
  with miniscripts, 862–863, *863*
  with PAL/Value option, 862
Instant Graphs, 306, 309, **312–314**, *314*, 364, 975
Instant Reports, 188, **190–191**, *191*, *192*, **197–198**, 271
Instant Scripts, **381–384**
  playing back existing scripts as, 367, **383–384**, 387
  recording and playing back, 366–367, **382**, 387
Interface Mode option, CCP Standard Settings dialog box, 980
Interface option, System menu, 35–36
interfaces. *See also* Full Screen User Interface
  choosing, 35, 980
  Common User Access (CUA) and, 25

Standard User Interface, 35, 37
international (NORDAN dictionary) sort order, 123, **135–137**
International submenu, Field/Reformat submenu, 222
interoperability, **949–950**
INTL.SOR file, 137
"Invalid password" message, 414
inventories, file, 417–418, *418*
invoices
  master forms for, 625–627, *625*
  printing from four tables, *583*, 584–587, *585*, *586*

J

joining lines of text, 672
joining tables. *See* combining data from multiple tables
JustCurrentField option, ValCheck/Define/TableLook up submenu, 606–607, 608
JustFamily objects, copying, 398–399
JustFamily option, Tools/Copy submenu, 396, 398–399, 401, 924
justifying
  field masks, 224
  zip codes, 224

K

KeepSet option
  Image menu, 98, **105–107**, 301
  Tools/Delete submenu, 106, 301, 403
key actions, in applications, 782–783, *782*
key assignment scripts. *See* hotkeys
key fields. *See also* indexes
  defining, 55
  entering and editing data in keyed tables, 481
  one-to-many relationships and, 457, 462–464, **477**, 490

primary key fields, **475–481**
  composite keys, **476**
  defining in multiple-table designs, **477**
  defining for primary indexes, 476
  defining in single-table design, **478–480**, *478, 479, 480*
  entering and editing data in keyed tables, 481
  many-to-many relationships and, 477
  rule of uniqueness and, 476
  sorting with, 135
key violations, **481–483**. *See also* data entry; indexes
  in CoEdit mode, 482–483
  in Edit mode, 483
  using Modify/DataEntry option, 482
keyboard operations
  in Editor, 668–670
  in Form Design screen, 281–282
  moving items on forms, 290–291, *291, 292*
  in Query form window, 144
  in Report Design screen, 204–205, 271
  in Speedbar, 29
  in TableBand menu, 210
  in Workshop program, **757**
keyed tables. *See also* indexes
  entering and editing records in, 481
  X-axis labels for graphs of, 338
keypress interaction commands, PAL, 841–842
Keys option, Workshop Edit Session dialog box, 777, 782
Keyviol tables
  and changing table structures, 425–426, *425*
  and copying records in keyed tables, 405, 481
  key violations and, 481–482

L

"Label status has been recorded" message, 233
labels
  axes labels, 341–343
  laser printer labels, 264–267, *265*
  in Membership application example, **731**, *732*, 742–744
  multicolumn labels, 233–236, *235, 237*
  for pie charts, 345–346
  printing, 264–267, *265*
  script for, 380
  tick mark labels, 328, 336
  X-axis labels, 308, 311, 338
Labels option, Setting menu, 233–236
LANs. *See* networks
left margin settings, for reports, 194, 970
legends, modifying graph, 328, 340–341
LegendsAndLabels option, Series menu, 340
Length option, Setting/PageLayout submenu, 225, 236
less than (<), in query criteria, 156, **166–168**
less than or equal to (<=), in query criteria, 156, **166–168**
letterhead, printing on, 11
letters, query criteria for ranges of letters, 167
LIKE operator, in query criteria, 161, 164–165, 178
limitations, of tables, 50–51
line graphs, **319**, *320*, **321**, *322*
lines and borders
  in application documentation, 818–819, *818*
  on forms, 275, **293–296**, 303
    deleting borders and lines, 296
    drawing borders, 294–295
    drawing lines, 295

LineSqueeze submenu, Setting/RemoveBlanks submenu, 233, 236
linking tables. *See* combining data from multiple tables
listing
  Query form operators, 523
  secondary indexes, 488
literal text, in reports, 188, **203–205**
Load option, Image/Graph submenu, 309, 349
loan payments calculator, 877–881, *879, 880*
local area networks. *See* networks
Location option, Editor Edit menu, 671
lock feature, **922–931**, 936–942. *See also* networks
  automatic locking schemes, 923–924, 926–928
  and creating tables, 937
  and data entry, 937–938
  directory locks, **923**
  explicit locks, **928–930**
  family locks, **924**
  forms and, 941
  full locks, **923**
  getting information about locks, 936–937
  graphs and, 941
  group locks, **925**
  overview of, 922–924
  prevent full locks, **924**
  prevent write locks, **924**
  queries and, 940
  record locks, **924–925**
  reports and, 940
  and sorting tables, 939
  Tools menu and, 942
  types of locks, **923–924**
  update queries and, 942
  and viewing data, 938–939
  write locks, **923**
  write-record locks, **925**
Lock option, Tools/Info submenu, 936–937
Lookup submenu, Field menu
  Link option, 574, 576, 578, 580–581

Relink option, 582
Unlink option, 582
lookup tables
  for multiple table reports, **573–582**, *576*, *577*
  creating, 550, **574–575**
  Field/Lookup options, 580–582
  guidelines for, 573–574, *574*
  linking tables in many-to-many design, 578–580, *578*, *579*, *580*, *581*
  placing fields from lookup tables, **575–578**, 628
  for multiple table validity checks, 551, **604–610**, 629
  AllCorrespondingFields option, 607–608
  defining, **605–608**
  JustCurrentField option, 606–607, 608
  overview of, **604–605**
  state abbreviations example, 610, *611*
  using tables with, 608–610, *609*
looping in PAL scripts, 833, **854–855**. *See also* branching
  exiting loops, 854–855
  While…EndWhile loops, 854
Lotus 1-2-3 files, exporting and importing, 432–433
lowercase
  in Editor searches, 687
  in query criteria, 164–165
  reserved words and operators and, 518
  secondary indexes and, 487
  in sorts, 123, **135–137**
LowValue option, ValCheck/Define submenu, 109–110

M

Machine Information options, Custom Configuration Program, **956–958**
macros. *See* scripts
mailing labels. *See* labels

Maintain Indexes option, CCP Standard Settings dialog box, 983
many-to-many database design, 456, **465–470**, 490, 578–580. *See also* multiple tables
  exploded inventory database example, 469–471, *469*, *470*, *471*
  linking tables in, 578–580, *578*, *579*, *580*, *581*
  one-to-many database design and, **465–466**, *466*
  overview of, 465–466, *466*
  scheduling database example, 466–467, *467*, *468*
margin indicator, Report Design screen, 202–203, *203*
Margin option, Setting/PageLayout submenu, 225
margin settings, for reports, 194, 970
markers, modifying graph, 343–344
markers graphs, **320–321**, *321*, *322*
MarkersAndFills option, Series menu, 343
master forms. *See also* multi-table forms
  designing, 614, *616*
  for Invoices table, 625–627, *625*
master table/detail table relationship
  defined, **458**
  in one-to-many database design, 464–465, *465*
matching, screen colors to printer colors, 333
MAX operator, 523–524, 555
maximizing, windows, 86, **91**, 119
Maximum Table Size option, CCP Standard Settings dialog box, 983–984
.MB file name extension, 49, 399

Membership application
  example, 714–716, *715*, **725–746**. *See also* applications, designing
  custom forms, **727–728**, *728*, *729*
  letters (reports), **728–730**, *730*, *731*
  mailing label format, **731**, *732*
  menu structure, **732–734**
  overview of, 714–716, *715*, **725–727**, *726*
  testing, **738–745**
    adding new members, 739–740
    changing members' data, 740
    deleting expired members, 741–742
    exiting, 745
    printing letters and mailing labels, 742–744
    printing roster, 742
    running, 739
    testing utilities, 744–745
    updating roster, 741
  tips, **745–746**
  Update Renewals process, **734–738**
  validity checks, **726–727**
memo fields. *See also* fields
  allotting space for, 48, **49–50**, *51*
  defined, **47**
  defining, 48, **49–50**, *51*
  editing, 50, 79, 83, 662, **665–666**, *665*
  Editor defaults for, 680, 985
  entering data in, **68–70**, *69*, 83
  field masks for, 218, 221, 222–224
  placing on forms, 285
  in previous versions, 57
  printing reports with, 270–271, *270*
  query criteria for text in, 164
  searching for text in, 97
  sorting on, 130
  viewing, 50
  word-wrap feature and, 679

word-wrapping on forms, 274, **287–289**, *288*, 291, 293, **301**, 303
memory (RAM)
  configuration options for, 901–903
  indexes and, 475
  memory conflicts, 897–898
  Paradox use of, 433
  required by Paradox, 891, 897, 921
menu commands (abbreviated), in PAL, 842–843
Menu Definition dialog box, Workshop program
  Borrow button, 774
  creating and attaching actions to menu options, 771–772, *773*
  defining Help text, 797
  defining menu and submenu options, 766–767, *766*
  renaming/editing menu options, 768
Menu Insert menu, Workshop program, 765–766
menu options. *See also* applications
  in applications, 750–751, **763–767**, **795–797**, 803
  adding Help text to, 751, **795–797**, *796*
  copying, 768
  creating, 750, **763–767**, *764*, *766*, 803
  defining shortcut keys for, 766
  deleting, 767
  renaming or editing, 750, **768**, 803
  creating with PAL scripts, 833, **881–886**, 917
  adding options to menus, 884–886
  Paradox.ADD file, **882–883**, 887, 917
  in Custom Configuration Program, 953, *954*
menus
  activating, 26–27
  arrow symbol (➤) in, 27
book's notation for, 27
canceling options, 22, **28**, 38
designing menu structure for applications, 713, **719–721**, *720*, *721*
menu structure in Membership application example, **732–734**
overview of, 22, **26–28**
selecting options from, **27**, 38
submenus in, 27
in Workshop program, **754–758**, *755*, *756*
merge files. *See* WordPerfect
messages
"A border can't intersect a field or multi-record region," 295
"A field has already been placed here," 285
"Cannot split field during column resize," 212
displaying error messages for calculated fields, **989**
displaying in scripts, 663, **696–697**
"Enter directory or leave blank for working directory," 417
"Enter DOS pattern, e.g., *.TXT," 418
"Enter password for table," 413
"Enter table with records to add or press ↵ for a list," 405
"Erase text and delete fields in page width 2 and higher," 234
"Field of type Memo, Blob, or Unknown not supported," 436
"Insert next page in printer. Press any key to continue," 230
"Invalid password," 414
"Label status has been recorded," 233
"Move to column containing crosstab column labels, then press ↵...," 358
"Move to column containing crosstab values, then press ↵...," 359
"Move to a corner of the area to be moved, then press ↵...," 290
"No speedup possible," 485
"Now move to diagonal corner, then press ↵," 295
"Search value not found," 687
"Setup string recorded," 227
"Syntax error in expression," 219–220
"The area designated for the word wrap must be clear," 289
"This procedure is not yet defined," 783
"WARNING! Structure contains non-compatible field types," 427
Microsoft Windows
  Borland applications and Paradox in, **950**
  command-line configuration options in, **906–907**
  interoperability in, **950**
  running Paradox under, **895–897**
  starting applications from, **825–827**, *826*, *827*
MIN operator, 523–524, 555
MiniScript option, PAL menu, 832, **837**, 860, 862–863
Miniscript window, PAL, 832, *837*, 860, 917
miniscripts, **837**, 860, **863–865**, 887. *See also* PAL scripts; scripts
  assigning to hotkeys, **863–865**, *864*
  creating, **837**, 860, 887
  creating GetRecord and PasteRecord keys, 867–868
  creating multiple hotkeys, 866–867
  defined, **801**
minor tick mark labels, 336
minus sign (–)
  for negative numbers, 68

as subtraction operator, 516–517, 552–553
Modify menu
  DataEntry option, 73, 481, 482, 483, 937–938
  Index option, 419, 429, 484, 486–488, *486*, *488*
  Restructure option, 136, 410, 421–423, *422*, 478
  Sort option, 128
Modify option, Image/Graph submenu, 309, 315
modifying. *See also* changing; editing
  applications, 806, **809–810**, *810*, 828
  axes labels, 341–343
  graph legends, 328, 340–341
  graph markers and fill patterns, 343–344
  graph settings, 307, **350**
  multi-record forms, 613–614
monitors. *See also* Video Settings dialog box
  configuration options for, 900
  required by Paradox, 333, 891, 921
  selecting type of, 958–959
monochrome video attributes, for forms, **297–298**
More submenu, Tools menu, **403–416**
  Add option, 401, 405, 409, 481, 482
  Copy option, 401
  Empty option, 406, 410–411
  Protect submenu, 411–416, 942–947
  Subtract option, 406–409, 410
  ToDOS option, 449–450
mouse
  accessing Speedbar items, 29
  configuration options for, 904, 980
  moving items on forms, 290
  moving windows, 90
  new support features, **911–912**
  overview of, **26**
  sizing windows, 90
  in TableBand menu, 210

Mouse Use option, CCP Standard Settings dialog box, 980
Move option
  Form Design Area menu, 281, 286, **290–291**
  Image menu, 104–105
  TableBand menu, 213
"Move to column containing crosstab column labels, then press ↵..." message, 358
"Move to column containing crosstab values, then press ↵..." message, 359
"Move to a corner of the area to be moved, then press ↵..." message, 290
moving
  Answer tables, 150
  columns
    in reports, 213
    in Table view, 104–105
  dialog boxes, 93
  Editor window, 668
  field masks, 205
  fields
    in Answer tables, 151
    for Crosstab tables, 360–362, *362*
    to see sort order, 123, **132–133**, *132*, *133*, *134*, 137
  in table structures, 422–423
  in Table view, 105
  items on forms, 274, **290–291**, *291*, *292*, 303
  text in reports, 205
  windows, **90**, 119
MS-DOS. *See* DOS
Multi Action option, Workshop ActionEdit menu, 769
Multi menu, Form Design screen, 613–614, 619
Multi-Action dialog box, Workshop program, 794–795, *794*
multi-action objects, **794–795**, *794*. *See also* applications
multicolumn labels and reports, printing, 233–236, *235*, *237*

multipage forms, **599–602**, 629. *See also* forms
  creating, 551, **599–601**, *599*, *600*, 629
  identifying current record with DisplayOnly fields, 601, *602*
  using, 602
multiple table queries, **499–516**. *See also* multiple tables; queries; update queries
  AND queries, 509–511, *512*
  combining data with, 16–17, *17*, 492, **499–508**
  displaying nonmatching records, **514–516**, *515*
  entering example elements in a Query form, 492, **500**, 548
  example elements explained, **499–503**
  inclusion operator (!) in, 514–516
  linking more than two tables, **503–508**, *504*, *505*
  linking tables with example elements, **500–503**, *502*, *503*, 548
  OR queries, 509–510, 511–513, *512*, *513*
  query criteria for, 508–509, *509*, *510*
  reports using, **582–588**
    creating report formats from Answer tables, 583–584
    printing invoices from four tables, *583*, 584–587, *585*, *586*
    recovering deleted report formats, 587–588
    using multiple table report formats, 584
  scheduling database example, 506–508, *506*
multiple table validity checks, 551, **604–610**, 629. *See also* forms; validity checks
  AllCorrespondingFields option, 607–608
  defining, **605–608**

JustCurrentField option,
606–607, 608
overview of, **604–605**
state abbreviations example,
610, *611*
using tables with, 608–610,
609
multiple tables, **456–474**, 489.
See also indexes; table
structures; tables
calculating with queries on
fields from, 492, **521–522**,
521, 548
combining data from, 16–17,
17, 492, **499–508**
entering example elements
in a Query form, 492, **500**,
548
example elements explained,
499–503
linking more than two
tables, **503–508**, *504*, *505*
linking tables with example
elements, **500–503**, *502*,
503, 548
scheduling database
example, 506–508, *506*
complex calculations with,
531–533, *532*, *533*
defining primary key fields in,
477
displaying nonmatching
records, **514–516**
many-to-many database
design, 456, **465–470**, 490,
578–580
exploded inventory database
example, 469–471, *469*,
470, *471*
linking tables in, 578–580,
578, *579*, *580*, *581*
one-to-many database
design and, **465–466**, *466*
overview of, 465–466, *466*
scheduling database
example, 466–467, *467*,
468
master table/detail table
relationship
defined, **458**

in one-to-many database
design, 464–465, *465*
normalizing databases,
471–474
defined, **471–472**
fully normalized databases,
474
removing partial
dependencies, 472–473
removing redundant data,
472
removing repetitive groups
of fields, 472
removing transitive
dependencies, 473–474
one-to-many database design,
456, **459–466**, *462*, *463*,
489
audit trails, 465
ensuring uniqueness,
463–464
explained, **459–463**
foreign key fields, **462**
many-to-many relationships
and, **465–466**, *466*
master table/detail table
relationship, 458,
464–465, *465*
primary key fields and, 457,
462–464, **477**, 490
redundant data and,
461–462, *461*
repetitive data and,
460–461, *460*
transaction tables, 464–465
one-to-one database design,
459
overview of, **14–17**
reports on using lookup
tables, **573–582**, *576*, *577*
creating, 550, **574–575**
Field/Lookup options,
580–582
guidelines for, 573–574, *574*
linking tables in
many-to-many design,
578–580, *578*, *579*, *580*,
581
placing fields from lookup
tables, **575–578**, 628

reports on using queries,
582–588
creating report formats from
Answer tables, 583–584
printing invoices from four
tables, *583*, 584–587, *585*,
586
recovering deleted report
formats, 587–588
using multiple table report
formats, 584
sample tables, **494–499**,
1000–1001
Accounts table, *496*
Invoices table, *495*
listed, **1000–1001**
Mastinv table, 494, *495*
Orders table, 496–498, *497*
Purchase table, 498–499,
498
multiplication operator (*),
516–517, 552–553
multi-record forms, 551,
611–614, 629. *See also*
forms
creating, 612–613, *613*
modifying, 613–614
multi-table forms, 551,
614–628, 629. *See also*
forms
creating
with linked tables, **620–627**,
620, *621*, *622*
with unlinked tables,
615–618
editing on, **627–628**
master forms
designing, 614, *616*
for Invoices table, 625–627,
625
on networks, **628**
overview of, 614
referential integrity and,
627–628
subforms
for Accounts table,
624–625, *624*
designing, 614, 615–616
embedding, 617–618, *617*
for Invdtail table, 623–624,
623

managing, 619
using, 618–619, *618*

N

naming. *See also* renaming
  Answer tables, 150
  fields, 40, **46–47**
  report formats, **252**
  tables, **54**
navigating
  in dialog boxes, 93
  fields, 67, **74–76**, *76*
  in Query form window, 144
  in Query forms, 143–144
  Report Design screen, 204
  in tables, **74–76**, *76*
negative numbers
  coloring, 959–960
  entering, 68, 73
nesting groups, in reports, **567–569**, *568*, *570*
Net submenu, Tools menu
  AutoRefresh option, 934
  lock options, 929–931
  UserName option, 933
Network Settings dialog box, Custom Configuration Program, **934–936**, *935*, **986–988**, *986*
  Private Directory option, 934, 987
  Refresh Interval option, 935, 987
  User Name option, 934, 987
  When Data Changes option, 935, 988
NETWORK.TXT file, 916, 920–921
networks, **920–947**
  avoiding waits on, **930–931**
  configuration option for emulating, 904
  creating tables on, 52, **937**
  Custom Configuration Program settings, **934–936**, **997–998**
  data entry on, **937–938**
  directories on, **932–933**, 934, 987
  editing on, **939**

forms on, 628, **941**
getting information about users and locks, **936–937**
graphs on, **941**
hardware requirements for, **921–922**
installing Paradox on, **920–921**
lock feature, **922–931**, 936–942
  automatic locking schemes, 923–924, 926–928
  and creating tables, 937
  and data entry, 937–938
  directory locks, **923**
  explicit locks, **928–930**
  family locks, **924**
  forms and, 941
  full locks, **923**
  getting information about, **936–937**
  graphs and, 941
  group locks, **925**
  overview of, 922–924
  prevent full locks, **924**
  prevent write locks, **924**
  queries and, 940
  record locks, **924–925**
  reports and, 940
  and sorting tables, 939
  Tools menu and, 942
  types of locks, **923–924**
  update queries and, 942
  and viewing data, 938–939
  write locks, **923**
  write-record locks, **925**
multi-table forms on, **628**
private directories, **932–933**, 934, 987
queries on, **940**, 988
refreshing data on, **933–934**, 935, 987
reports on, **940–941**, 988
saving Custom Configuration Program settings on, **997–998**
scripts on, **941–942**
security and protection, **942–947**
  creating owner and auxiliary passwords, **943–946**, *945*

  family rights, 946–947
  field rights, 947
  overview of, 942–943
  table rights, 946
SHARE configuration option, 904
sorting on, **939**
suppressing messages on, 92
Tools menu on, **942**
update queries on, **942**
user names, **933**, 934, 987
viewing data on, **938–939**
New Application dialog box, Workshop program, 759–762, *763*, 783, 785
new features, **910–918**
  BLANKLINE command, 912–913
  in Custom Configuration Program, 914–915
  for developers, 916–918
  in Editor, 913
  file management and directory support, 913
  in Form Design screen, 912
  Full Screen User Interface, 910–911
  in Image menu, 911
  Miniscript window, 917
  mouse support, 911–912
  PAGEBREAK command, 912
  report design capabilities, 912–913
  in Report Design screen, 911–912
  user-defined menu options, 917
New option
  Editor File menu, 685
  Scripts/Editor submenu, 697–698
  Workshop Application menu, 759
Next option
  Editor Search menu, 687
  System menu, 90, 675
NO operator, **535**, *536*, 538, *539*
"No speedup possible" message, 485

NORDAN dictionary sort order, 123, **135–137**
NORDAN.SOR file, 136
normalizing databases, **471–474**. *See also* multiple tables
  defined, **471–472**
  fully normalized databases, 474
  removing partial dependencies, 472–473
  removing redundant data, 472
  removing repetitive groups of fields, 472
  removing transitive dependencies, 473–474
NOT operator, in query criteria, 157, 168, 169
"Now move to diagonal corner, then press ↵." message, 295
number sign (#), in Picture formats, 111
numbering records, field masks for, 216
NumberRecords option, Group/Insert submenu, 243
numbers
  default formats for, 985–986
  entering, 72–73
  formatting, 101–103, 985–986, 996
  negative numbers
    coloring, 959–960
    entering, 68, 73
  query criteria for ranges of numbers, 167
numeric fields. *See also* fields
  CoEdit mode, 64
  defined, **47**, 49
  field masks for, 202, 218
  formatting, **101–103**, 985–986, 996
  grouping reports on, 242
  placing on forms, 285
  query criteria for, 158–160, *160*
  short numeric fields, defined, **47**, 49

O

Object Type dialog box, Workshop program, 771
objects, **392–403**. *See also* applications; files; forms; records; reports; scripts; tables
  Binary Large Objects (BLOBs)
    defined, **48**
    selecting editor for, 48, 70, 684, **992–994**
  color settings for, 962–965, *962, 963*
  copying, 390, **395–402**, 450
    backing up large tables, **399–402**
    with DOS BACKUP command, 400–401
    with DOS COPY command, 399, 401
    to floppy disks, 399, 401–402
    forms and reports, 398
    overview of, **395–396**
    specifying source and target files, 396–397
    tables, scripts, graphs, and JustFamily objects, 398–399
    tables to floppy disks with queries, 401–402
  deleting, 390, **402–403**, 450
  editing in applications, **812–813**
  file name extensions for, 399, **400**
  fixing corrupted, **427–428**
  managing in applications, **813–814**, *814*
  placing on desktop in scripts, 663, **694–695**, *696*, 708
  protecting, 390, **411–416**, 451
    adding passwords, 411–413, *413*
    changing or deleting passwords, 414–415
    reactivating (clearing) passwords, 414
    using password-protected tables and scripts, 413–414
    write-protecting tables, 411, 415–416
  recovering deleted, **403**
  renaming, 390, **393–394**, 450
    Answer tables, 150, **394**
    forms and reports, 393–394
    tables, scripts, and graphs, **394**
OK/Cancel Object dialog box, Workshop program, 801–802, *802*
OK/Cancel objects, **801–802**, *802*. *See also* applications
omitting details, in Group bands, **569–572**, *571*
one-to-many database design, 456, **459–466**, *462, 463*, 489. *See also* multiple tables
  audit trails, 465
  common or key fields, 462–464
  ensuring uniqueness, 463–464
  explained, **459–463**
  foreign key fields, **462**
  many-to-many relationships and, **465–466**, *466*
  master table/detail table relationship, 458, 464–465, *465*
  redundant data and, 461–462, *461*
  repetitive data and, 460–461, *460*
  transaction tables, 464–465
one-to-one database design, **459**. *See also* multiple tables
ONLY operator, **535**, *536*, 538, *539*
Open option
  Editor File menu, 685
  Scripts/Editor submenu, 413–414, 666
opening
  Editor, **664**, 707
  multiple windows in Editor, 685
  Query forms, 143
  Report Design screen, 199–201

System menu, 90
tables, 60, **62–64**, *64*, 81, 82
operators
  arithmetic operators in query criteria, 156, 169–170, 516–517
  AS operator, 493, 518, **519–521**, *520*, 548
  BLANK operator, 157, 168–169
  case sensitivity of, 518
  comparison operators in query criteria, 156, **166–168**, 529
  double-dot operator (..)
    in Find dialog box, 686, 687
    in query criteria, 156, 161–164, 165, 178
    in Zoom dialog box, 32, 96, 97
  EVERY operator, **535**, *536*, 537–538, *538*
  EXACTLY operator, **535**, *536*, *540*
  GroupBy operator, 540–542, *541*
  inclusion operator (!), 515–516
  LIKE operator, 161, 164–165, 178
  listing Query form operators, 523
  NO operator, **535**, *536*, 538, *539*
  NOT operator, 157, 168, 169
  ONLY operator, **535**, *536*, 538, *539*
  in query criteria, 156–158
  searching for with query criteria, 155, **176–177**
  summary operators
    blank fields and, 604
    in query criteria, 157, 523–524
    in reports, 555–561
  TODAY operator, 169–170
Options menu, Editor
  AutoIndent submenu, 680
  CaseSensitive option, 687
  TabStops option, 680
  WordWrap submenu, 679
OR queries, 141, **172–175**, **509–510**, **511–513**. *See also* queries

  across several fields, 172–174
  versus AND queries, 175
  for multiple tables, 509–510, 511–513, *512*, *513*
  in a single field, 174–175
  in update queries, **640**
order of fields, in Answer tables, 140, **151–155**, *152*, *154*, 508, 981
OrderTable option, Image menu, 484–485, 508
outer joins, **515–516**
Output menu. *See also* Report Design screen
  Printer option, 227, 246
  Screen option, 248
Output submenu, Report menu
  File option, 448
  Printer option, 246
  Screen option, 248
Overall menu. *See also* graphs
  Axes option, 333
  Colors submenu, 332, 333
  Device submenu, 352, 354
  PrinterLayout option, 352
  Titles option, 329
  Wait option, 326
Overwrite mode, 77, 205, 286
  .in Editor, 669, 671
owner passwords, 943–947, *945*

P

packaging applications, **820–823**, 828
  copying files to floppy disks, 821–822
  copying from floppy disks to hard disk, 822–823
  copying large applications, 823
  files to include, 820–821
Page Footer band, Report Design screen, *206*, 209
Page Header band, Report Design screen, *206*, 207, 592, *592*
PAGEBREAK command, Report Design screen, 244–245, 566, 912
PageLayout submenu, Setting menu

Delete option, 205, 211, 235
Insert option, 205, 213, 235
Length option, 225, 236
Margin option, 225
Width option, 225
pages in reports
  changing page layout, 189, **224–225**, 272
  changing size of, 227–228
  length and width of, 193–194, *193*, 969, 970
  numbering, 216
  page breaks, **244–245**
  page ejection settings, 190, 195, 970
  printing ranges of, 247
page-width indicator, Report Design screen, 202–203, *203*
PAL, **832–887**
  arrays, 833, **850–851**
  expressions, **847–848**, 859
  interactive Paradox versus PAL-controlled Paradox, 835, 872
  Miniscript window, 832, *837*, **860**, 917
  overview of, **834–835**
  procedures and procedure libraries, 761
  Value dialog box, 832, *838*
  values in, **847**
  variables, 832, **848–850**
    assigning in PAL functions, 849
    assigning in PAL scripts, 849
    changing data type of, 832, **849–850**
PAL commands, 596–599, **693–700**, **841–844**. *See also* PAL scripts; scripts
  arguments and parameters in, **843–844**
  calculating percentages with, 596–599, *597*
  commenting in scripts, 663, **693–694**, *694*, 840
  creating scripts from scratch, 697–699, *698*

displaying custom messages
(Message command), 663,
696–697
Edit command, 832
examples, **700–705**
Exit command, 854
pausing for user input, 663,
699–700
placing objects on desktop,
663, **694–695**, *696*, 708
Prompt command, 700
Quit command, 854
QuitLoop command, 854
SetKey command, 833,
863–868
creating GetRecord and
PasteRecord keys, 867–868
creating hotkeys, 863–865
creating multiple hotkey
macros, 866–867
Sleep command, 697, 865
Sound command, 663, **697**
syntax of, **843–844**
TypeIn command, 844
types of, **841–843**
abbreviated menu
commands, 842–843
keypress interaction
commands, 841–842
programming commands,
841
special key commands, 843
Until command, 700
Wait Workspace command,
700
PAL Debugger window,
375–376, *375*, **856–859**,
857
PAL dialog box, Custom
Configuration Program,
429, 915, **988–994**, *989*
BLOB Editor option, 48, 70,
684, 992–994
BLOB Editor Screen Swap
option, 994
Built-in Script Editor options,
989–990
External Script Editor
options, 990–992
new features, 915

Show Calc Field Errors
option, 989
PAL expressions, **847–848**, 859
PAL functions, **844–847**,
861–863. *See also* PAL
scripts
arguments and parameters in,
846–847
assigning variables in, **849**
calculating functions, 845–846
instant field summaries with,
861–863
with miniscripts, 862–863,
863
with PAL/Value option, 862
reporting functions, 845
in reports, **592–599**, *596*
summary functions, **861**
SYSMODE() function, 870
types of, **844–846**
in update queries, 643, *643*
PAL menu, **855–860**
BeginRecord option, 370, 856
Cancel option, 371
Debug option, 856
EndRecord option, 856
MiniScript option, 832, **837**,
860, 862–863
Play option, 372, 855–856
RepeatPlay option, 856
script recording and, 369
Value option, 832, **838**, 859,
862
PAL option, Custom
Configuration Program,
429
PAL scripts, **835–840**, *836*,
851–855, **869–886**, 887.
See also scripts
backslash (\) in, 842
branching in, 833, **851–854**
If...Then...EndIf branches,
852–854
commenting in, 840
creating, **835–840**
with Editor, 836–837
Execute scripts, 839
Init.SC script, 839, 887
Instant Scripts, 839
miniscripts, **837**, 860, 887
Savevars scripts, 839

with Scripts/BeginRecord
and Scripts/EndRecord
options, 836
with Scripts/QuerySave
option, 836
with Value dialog box, *838*
debugging, **856–859**
editing, **839–840**, **990–992**
error-checking controls in, 870
formatting, **840**
for hotkeys, **869–871**
creating, 869–870
playing automatically at
startup, 869, 871
Init.SC script, 385–386, 824,
839, **869–871**, 887
Instant Scripts and, 839
looping in, 833, **854–855**
exiting loops, 854–855
While...EndWhile loops, 854
miniscripts, **837**, 860,
863–865, 887
assigning to hotkeys,
863–865, *864*
creating, **837**, 860, 887
creating GetRecord and
PasteRecord keys, 867–868
creating multiple hotkeys,
866–867
defined, **801**
for Paradox menu options,
833, **881–886**, 917
adding options to menus,
884–886
Paradox.ADD file, **882–883**,
887, 917
playing back, 855–856
for pop-up calculators,
871–881
controlling PAL canvas, **872**,
887
loan payments calculator,
877–881, *879*, *880*
squares calculator, 873–877,
877
recording, 856
using scripts together, 840
Value scripts, 838
Paradox. *See also* networks; PAL
Borland applications and,
949–950

INDEX

command-line configuration
  options, **898–907**
  in batch files, **905–906**
  BIOS option, 905
  compatibility mode options, 905
  In Microsoft Windows, **906–907**
  memory options, 901–903
  mouse options, 904
  network emulation, 904
  overview of, 898–899
  query options, 904–905
  SHARE option, 904
  video options, 900
exiting, 23, 37, 38
installing, **891–894, 920–921**
  AUTOEXEC.BAT and, 894
  CONFIG.SYS and, 892–893
  hardware requirements for, 890–891, 897–898, 921–922
  on networks, **920–921**
  Workshop program and sample files, 894–895
interactive versus PAL-controlled Paradox, 835, 872
interoperability, **949–950**
memory management and, **897–898**, 901–903
memory usage, **433**
new features, **910–918**
  BLANKLINE command, 912–913
  Custom Configuration Program, 914–915
  for developers, 916–918
  Editor, 913
  file management and directory support, 913
  Form Design screen, 912
  Full Screen User Interface, 910–911
  Image menu, 911
  Miniscript window, 917
  mouse support, 911–912
  PAGEBREAK command, 912
  report design capabilities, 912–913
  Report Design screen, 911–912
  user-defined menu options, 917
overview of, 4–5, 18–19
Paradox Runtime program, 716
previous versions
  binary and memo fields in, 57
  compatibility of, **57**
  configuration options for emulating, 905
  converting tables from, **426–427**
  file format settings for, **982–983**
  script commands from, 37
running under Microsoft Windows, **895–897**
sharing files with other Borland applications, **949–950**
shelling out to DOS, 52, 53, 391, **449–450**, 451
versus spreadsheet programs, 14
starting, 22, **24–25**, 38
  applications from, **824**
  choosing a working directory, **32–34**
  and playing back scripts, 367, **385–386**
  playing scripts at startup, 869, 871, 907
versus word processors, 14
Paradox.ADD file, **882–883**, 887, 917
Paradox Application Language. *See* PAL
PARADOX.CFG file, 935–936
Paradox Editor. *See* Editor
Paradox Engine, 950
Paradox Personal Programmer. *See* Workshop program
PARADOX.SOR file, 136, 137
Paradox Workshop program. *See* Workshop program
ParadoxEdit menu, Workshop program, 812–813

parameters
  in PAL commands, **843–844**
  in PAL functions, **846–847**
parentheses ()
  as grouping operator, 516–517, 552–553
  for negative numbers, 68, 73
partial dependencies, **472–473**
Password option, Tools/More/Protect submenu, 411–413, 414–415
passwords, **411–415**. *See also* write-protecting
  adding to tables and scripts, 411–413, *413*
  for applications, **827–828**
  changing or deleting, 414–415
  on networks, **942–947**
    creating owner and auxiliary passwords, 943–946, *945*
    family rights, 946–947
    field rights, 947
    overview of, 942–943
    table rights, 946, 947
  reactivating (clearing), 414
  using password-protected tables and scripts, 413–414
Paste option, Editor Edit menu, 674, 676, 677
PasteRecord key, 870
pasting. *See* copying, and pasting; cutting and pasting
patterns, modifying graph, 343–344
pausing
  printer for each page, 230, 970
  for user input in scripts, 663, **699–700**
percentages, calculating, **543–546**, *544*, *546*
performance, increasing query, 391, **428–429**, 451
period. *See* double-dot operator (..)
Personal Programmer. *See* Workshop program
.PFS files, exporting and importing, 435

PgUp/PgDn keys
  in Editor, 669–670
  in Form Design screen, 282
  navigating with, 74, 75
  in Report Design screen, 204
phone lists, 253–257, *254*, *256*
PickForm option, Image menu, 300, 602, 618
Picture formats, **110–114**
  advancing cursor when Picture format is complete, 116–117
  defined, **110**
  defining acceptable entries in, 113
  examples of, *112*
  forcing entries in, 113–114
  guidelines for, **114**
  literal characters in, 112
  symbols in, 111–112
Picture option, ValCheck/Auto submenu, 116–117
Picture option and dialog box, ValCheck/Define submenu, **110–114**
pie charts, **322–323**, *324*
  calculating percentages with, 543–544, *544*
  customizing, **344–346**, *344*, *345*, *347*
  label formats, 345–346
  pie slices, 346
Place submenu
  Form Design Border menu, 294
  Form Design Field menu
    DisplayOnly option, 286
    #Record option, 286
    Regular option, 283–286
  Report Design Field menu, 214–220
    Calculated option, 219–220, 553
placing
  field masks, **214–217**
  fields on forms, 274, **283–286**, *285*, 302
    DisplayOnly fields, 286
    record numbers, 286
    regular fields, 283–286

objects on desktop in scripts, 663, **694–695**, *696*, 708
text on forms, 274, 283, 286
plain check marks, **145–146**, *145*, *147*, 148–149
Play option
  PAL menu, 372, 855–856
  Scripts menu, 372, 384, 493, 547, 548
playing back scripts, **371–374**, **384–386**, 855–856. *See also* PAL scripts; scripts
  from another script, 367, **384**
  automatically at Paradox startup, 367, **385–386**
  canceling, 374
  directories and, 368–369, 371–372
  existing scripts as Instant Scripts, 383–384
  Instant Scripts, 367, **382**, 387
  at maximum speed, 366, **372–373**, 386
  preparing for, **371–372**
  repeatedly, 373–374
  and watching keystrokes, 366, **373**, 386
plus sign (+)
  as addition operator, 516–517, 552–553
  in field masks, 219
pop-up calculators, **871–881**
  controlling PAL canvas, **872**, 887
  loan payments calculator, 877–881, *879*, *880*
  squares calculator, 873–877, *877*
positioning
  cursor in Editor, 669, 671, 708
  items in Group bands, 567
pound sign (#), in Picture formats, 111
predefined color settings, 961–962
predefined printer setup strings, 226–227, *228*, **971–974**, *971*, *973*
Predefined submenu, Setting/Setup submenu, 226–227

prevent full locks, **924**
prevent write locks, **924**
previewing reports, 189, **248–249**, *248*
primary indexes. *See also* indexes
  defined, **475**
  defining primary key fields for, 457, **476**, 490
primary key fields, **475–481**. *See also* indexes; key fields
  composite keys, **476**
  defining
    in multiple-table designs, 477
    for primary indexes, 476
    in single-table design, **478–480**, *478*, *479*, *480*
  entering and editing data in keyed tables, 481
  many-to-many relationships and, 477
  one-to-many relationships and, 457, 462–464, **477**, 490
  rule of uniqueness and, 476
Print option, Editor File menu, 684–685
print size
  changing for reports, 227–228
  printer codes for, 590–592, *592*
printer codes in reports, **588–592**
  for compressed print, 590
  for font and print size, 590–592, *592*
  guidelines for, 588–589
  for Hewlett-Packard printers, 590–592
  inserting in report formats, 550, **589–590**, 628
Printer option, Output menu, 227, 246
printer ports, changing, 229–230
Printer Setting dialog box, Workshop program, 789–790, *789*
printer settings
  defining in applications, **789–790**, *789*
  for graphs, 975–978, *976*

INDEX

for reports, 188, **192–198**, *193*, **224–230**, 271
  changing page and print size, 227–228
  changing printer port, 229–230
  for Hewlett-Packard printers, 196–197, *196*, 227, *228*
  left margin settings, 194, 970
  page ejection settings, 190, 195, 970
  page length and width, 193–194, *193*, 969, 970
  pausing printer for each page, 230, 970
  predefined printer setup strings, 226–227, *228*, **971–974**, *971*, *973*
  printer defaults, 195–197, *196*
  selecting printer, 228–229
  for spillover pages, 191, *192*, 194
  testing, 197–198
  vertical alignment, 197
Printer Setup table, Custom Configuration Program, 195–197, *196*, **971–974**, *971*, *973*
PrinterLayout option, Overall menu, 352
printers
  matching screen colors to printer colors, 333
  selecting, **228–229**
    for application documentation, 816–817, *817*
    for graphs, 351–352, 975–978
printing
  Answer tables, 151
  directory listings, 260–262, *261*
  envelopes, 267–269, *268*, *269*
  fax lists, 255–257, *256*
  files from Editor, 684–685
  form letters, 262–264, *263*
  graphs, 307, 309, **351–355**, 364
    customizing printed graph layout, 352–353, *353*, 364
    to files, 307, **353–354**
    printing graph files, 354–355
    selecting printer, 351–352
  invoices from four tables, *583*, 584–587, *585*, *586*
  labels, 264–267, *265*
  on letterhead, 11
  multicolumn labels and reports, 233–236, *235*, *237*
  phone lists, 253–257, *254*, *256*
  reports, 151, 189, **245–249**, 272
    from Answer tables, 151
    from the desktop, 246
    with memo fields, 270–271, *270*
    previewing reports, 189, *248*
    printing ranges of pages, 247
    from queries, **249–250**
    from Report Design screen, 246
    searching for values in report previews, 249
    from sorted tables, **251–252**
    table structures, 416
    wide tabular reports, 257–259, *257*, *258*
private directories, on networks, **932–933**, 934
Problems tables, and changing table structures, 425–426, *425*
"This procedure is not yet defined" message, 783
procedures, in PAL, 761
programming. *See* PAL
programming commands, PAL, 841
Prompt command, PAL, 700
Protect submenu, Tools/More submenu, **411–416**, **942–947**
  Clear option, 414, 416
  Password options, 411–413, 414–415, 942–947
  Write-protect option, 415–416
protecting
  applications, **827–828**
  networks, **942–947**
  creating owner and auxiliary passwords, 943–946, *945*
  family rights, 946–947
  field rights, 947
  overview of, 942–943
  table rights, 946
tables and scripts, 390, **411–416**, 451
  adding passwords, 411–413, *413*
  changing or deleting passwords, 414–415
  reactivating (clearing) passwords, 414
  using password-protected tables and scripts, 413–414
  write-protecting tables, 411, 415–416
punctuation marks, query criteria for, 155, **176–177**

Q

QBE (Query By Example). *See* queries
Quattro Pro
  exporting to, 433
  Paradox and, 949–950
queries, **140–185**. *See also* query criteria; Query forms; query objects; searching; update queries
  AND queries, 141, **170–172**, **509–511**
    across several fields, 171
    for multiple tables, 509–511, *512*
    versus OR queries, 175
    in a single field, 171–172
  Answer tables, **150–155**
    closing, 151
    creating multiple table report formats from, **583–584**
    displaying calculated results in, **517–518**
    field order in, 140, **151–155**, *152*, *154*, 508, 981
    making changes in, 150
    moving, 150
    moving fields in, 151

printing, 151
printing formatted reports from, 151
renaming, 150
renaming calculated fields in, **519–521**, *520*
saving, 150
sizing, 150
sorting, **150–151**, **152**
auto-execute queries, 632, **642–644**, *643*
calculating with, 492, **516–533**, **543–546**
  arithmetic operators in, **516–517**
  blank fields and, **518–519**, 604, **981–982**
  calculating percentages, **543–546**, *544*, *546*
  comparing records to summary calculations with set queries, 542–543, *542*
  complex calculations with multiple tables, **531–533**, *532*, *533*
  default grouping for summary calculations, 524
  displaying calculation results with CALC reserved word, 492, **517–518**, *519*, 548
  expressions for, 516–517
  with fields from multiple tables, 492, **521–522**, *521*, 548
  frequency distributions, 527, *528*
  on groups of records, 526–527, *527*, *528*
  to increase or decrease values, **522–523**
  multiple CALC expressions, 520
  renaming calculated fields with AS operator, 493, 518, **519–521**, *520*, 548
  selecting records based on summary calculations, 529–531, *529*, *530*
  summarizing all records, 525–526, *525*

summary calculations, 493, **523–531**
summary calculations on groups of records, 526–527, *527*, *528*
summary operators, 523–524
CHANGETO queries
  globally changing values with, **179–182**, *181*, 378–379
  increasing or decreasing values with, **522–523**
  in update queries, **640–642**
configuration options for, **904–905**
copying tables to floppy disks with, **401–402**
defined, **11**
defining in applications, **793–794**, *793*
DELETE queries, **182–184**, *183*, 410, 640
designing for applications, 723
editing saved queries, 692, *693*
editing with, 141, **177–184**
  finding information, 177–179, *178*
  global deletions, 141, **182–184**
  global edits, 141, **179–182**, *181*
FIND queries, **177–179**, *178*
INSERT queries
  calculating with, **644**
  copying incompatible records between tables, 639–642, *639*, *641*, *642*
locks and, **940**
multiple table queries, **499–516**
  AND queries, 509–511, *512*
  combining data with, 16–17, *17*, 492, **499–508**
  displaying nonmatching records, **514–516**, *515*
  entering example elements in a Query form, 492, **500**, 548
  example elements explained, **499–503**

inclusion operator (!) in, 514–516
linking more than two tables, **503–508**, *504*, *505*
linking tables with example elements, **500–503**, *502*, *503*, 548
OR queries, 509–510, 511–513, *512*, *513*
query criteria for, 508–509, *509*, *510*
scheduling database example, 506–508, *506*
for multiple table reports, **582–588**
  creating report formats from Answer tables, 583–584
  printing invoices from four tables, **583**, 584–587, *585*, *586*
  recovering deleted report formats, 587–588
  using multiple table report formats, 584
on networks, **940**, 988
OR queries, 141, **172–175**, **509–510**, **511–513**
  across several fields, 172–174
  versus AND queries, 175
  for multiple tables, 509–510, 511–513, *512*, *513*
  in a single field, 174–175
  in update queries, **640**
overview of, 11, 140, **142–143**
performing, 140, **149**
printing reports from, **249–250**
reusing saved queries, 493, **547**, 548
saving, 493, **546–547**, 548
  editing saved queries, 692, *693*
scripts for printing reports from, 250
selecting fields for, 140, **145–149**
  check mark types, 145–148, *145*, *146*, *147*, *148*
  checking multiple fields, 148, *148*
  placing check marks, 148–149, *149*

INDEX

unchecking fields, 149
set queries, 493, **534–543**, 548
  calculating percentages with, 546
  check marks (√) in, 540
  comparing records to summary values, 542–543, *542*
  defining sets, 535–540, *536*, *538*
  EVERY operator, **535**, *536*, 537–538, *538*
  EXACTLY operator, **535**, *536*, 540, *540*
  GroupBy operator, 540–542, *541*
  NO operator, **535**, *536*, 538, *539*
  ONLY operator, **535**, *536*, 538, *539*
  overview of, 534–535, *534*
sorting with, 133, 149
speeding up, 391, **428–429**, 451, 485
summary calculations, 493, **523–531**, 542–543
  comparing records to summary calculations with set queries, 542–543, *542*
  default grouping for, 524
  frequency distributions, 527, *528*
  on groups of records, 526–527, *527*, *528*
  selecting records based on, 529–531, *529*, *530*
  summarizing all records, 525–526, *525*
  summary operators, 523–524
Query By Example dialog box, Workshop program, **791–794**
  defining queries, 793–794, *793*
  overview of, 791–792, *791*
query criteria, **155–177**, 508–509. *See also* queries
  for AND queries, 141, **170–172**
  arithmetic operators in, 156, 169–170, 516–517

backslash (\) in, 176–177
for blank fields, 157, **168–169**
BLANK operator in, 157, 168–169
commas (,) in, 158–159, 166, 171–172
comparison operators in, 156, **166–168**, 529
double-dot operator (..) in, 156, 161–164, 165, 178
for embedded text, 161–163, *162*
for everything except some value, **168**
for exact values, 140, **158–160**, *159*
for inexact spellings, 164–165
for inexact values, 140, 156, **161–165**
LIKE operator in, 161, 164–165, 178
for matching single characters, 164
for multiple table queries, 508–509, *509*, *510*
NOT operator in, 157, 168, 169
operators and reserved words listed, **156–158**
for OR queries, 141, **172–175**
for punctuation marks and symbols, 155, **176–177**
quotation marks (" ") in, 155, 176–177
for ranges of dates, 167–168
for ranges of letters, 167
for ranges of numbers, 167
for ranges of values, 141, **166–168**
for relative dates, 141, **169–170**
for searching numeric, currency, and date fields, 158–160, *160*
for searching operators and reserved words, 155, **176–177**
at sign (@) in, 156, 161, 164
for text in memo fields, 164
TODAY operator in, 169–170

uppercase and lowercase in, 164–165
Query forms, **143–144**, *144*
  bringing to foreground, 151
  closing, 151
  combining data from multiple tables, 16–17, *17*, 492, **499–508**
    linking more than two tables, 503–505, *504*, *505*
    scheduling database example, 506–508, *506*
  example elements, **499–503**
    entering, 500
    explained, 499–500
    linking tables with, 500–503, *502*, *503*
  in update queries, 633, **636–637**, *637*
  listing operators, 523
  navigating in, 143–144
  opening, 143
  for update queries, 633, **636–637**, *637*, 659
query objects, **790–794**. *See also* applications
  defining queries, 793–794, *793*
  Query By Example dialog box, 791–792, *791*
Query Order option, CCP Standard Settings dialog box, 140, **151–155**, *152*, *154*, 508, 981
QuerySave option, Scripts menu, 493, 547, 548, 692, *693*, 836
QuerySpeed option, Tools menu, 419, 428–429, 484, 485, 983
question mark (?), in Picture formats, 111, 114
Quit command, PAL, 854
QuitLoop command, PAL, 854
quitting. *See* exiting
quotation marks (" ")
  as ASCII file delimiter, 995
  in field masks, 219
  in query criteria, 155, 176–177

R

.R file name extension, 252
RAM
  configuration options for, 901–903
  indexes and, 475
  memory conflicts, 897–898
  Paradox use of, 433
  required by Paradox, 891, 897–898, 921
Range option, GroupInsert submenu, 240–243
RangeOutput option, Report menu, 247
reactivating, passwords, 414
#Record field mask, 216
#Record fields, Form Design screen, 286
record locks, **924–925**
Record option, Image/Zoom submenu, 95
recording scripts, 366, **370–371**, 386, 856. *See also* PAL scripts; scripts
  creating scripts from scratch, **697–699**, *698*
  Instant Scripts, 366, **382**, 387
  preparing for, **368–370**
records. *See also* fields; objects; tables; update queries
  adding, **67**, 83
  comparing to summary values, 542–543, *542*
  copying, **403–406**
    in keyed tables, 405–406
    between tables, 390, **404–405**, 450
  copying fields from previous, 72
  defined, **40**, **42**
  deleting, 61, **80–81**, 83
    all records from a table, 390, **410–411**, 451
    with DELETE queries, **182–184**, *183*
    records that match records in another table, 390, **406–409**, *407*, *408*, *409*, 451
    and recovering disk space, **410**
  displaying nonmatching records with multiple table queries, **514–516**, *515*
  editing with CHANGETO queries, **179–182**, *181*, 378–379
  field masks for numbering, 216
  flagging in update queries, 632, **635–636**, 642, 645
  grouping reports on count of, 243
  inserting, 61, **79–80**, *80*, 83
  moving to other tables, **403–404**, 406
  multi-record forms, 551, **611–614**, 629
    creating, 612–613, *613*
    modifying, 613–614
  navigating, **74–76**, *76*
  saving, 67
    changes to, 61, **81–82**, 83
  searching for, 87, **94–95**, 119
    with FIND queries, **177–179**, *178*
    values in, 87, **95–97**, 119
  selecting based on summary calculations, 529–531, *529*, *530*
  size of, **51**
  summary calculations
    on groups of records, 526–527, *527*, *528*
    selecting records based on, 529–531, *529*, *530*
    summarizing all records, 525–526, *525*
  undoing changes to, 61, 75, **78–79**, 83
recovering. *See also* restoring
  deleted objects, **403**
  deleted report formats, 587–588
Redraw option, System/Desktop submenu, 92
redundant data, 461–462, *461*, 472
referential integrity, editing and, **627–628**

Reflex files, exporting and importing, 435
Reformat option, Form Design Field menu, 289
Reformat submenu, Field menu, 212, **220–222**, 235
  Commas submenu, 222
  Digits option, 221
  Sign-Convention option, 222
reformatting field masks, **220–222**
  alphanumeric and memo field masks, 221
  date field masks, 221
  numeric and currency field masks, 221–222
refreshing data, on networks, **933–934**, 935, 987
Regroup option, Group menu, 243–244
regular bar graphs, 316, *317*
Regular field mask, 215
Regular fields, Form Design screen, 283–286
relational database management systems. *See* database management systems
Remove Application dialog box, Workshop program, 811–812
RemoveBlanks submenu, Setting menu
  FieldSqueeze option, 232, 236
  LineSqueeze submenu, 233, 236
removing. *See* deleting
Rename submenu, Tools menu, **393–394**, 409
  Form option, 393–394
  Graph option, 394
  Report option, 393–394
  Script option, 382–383, 394
  Table option, 394
renaming. *See also* naming
  application menu options, 750, **768**, 803
  calculated fields, 493, 518, **519–521**, *520*, 548

color settings, 967
objects, 390, **393–394**, 450
   Answer tables, 150, **394**
   forms and reports, 393–394
   tables, scripts, and graphs, 394
RepeatPlay option
   PAL menu, 856
   Scripts menu, 373–374, 384
repetitive data
   database design and, 460–461, *460*, 472
   in Group bands, **562–563**, *563*, 970
Replace option
   Editor Search menu, 688–689
   Image/Graph submenu, 350
replacing, scripts, 370
Report Design screen, **198–209**. *See also* field masks
   bands, **206–209**, *206*. *See also* Group bands; Table band
     Form band, 208–209
     Page Footer band, 209
     Page Header band, 207, *592*
     Report Footer band, 209, 572
     Report Header band, 206–207
   BLANKLINE command, 244–245, 567, 912–913
   Field menu, **214–224**
     CalcEdit option, 220
     Erase option, 220, 235
     Justify submenu, 224
     Lookup submenu, 574, 576, 578, 580–582
     Place submenu, 214–220, 553
     Reformat submenu, 212, **220–222**, 235
     WordWrap option, 222–224
   versus Form Design screen, 280, 281
   Group menu
     Delete submenu, 239
     Headings submenu, 565–566
     Insert submenu, 239–243
     Regroup option, 243–244
     SortDirection submenu, 243

inserting and deleting blank lines, 188, **203–205**, **244–245**
inserting and deleting spillover pages, 205
inserting and overwriting text, 205
inserting page breaks, **244–245**
keyboard operations in, 204–205, 271
literal text in, 188, **203–205**
moving text and field masks, 205
navigating, **204**
new features, **911–912**
opening, 199–201
Output menu
   Printer option, 227, 246
   Screen option, 248
PAGEBREAK command, 244–245, 566, 912
printing reports from, **246**
ruler, margin, and page-width indicators, 202–203, *203*
saving report formats, **201**
Setting menu
   Format submenu, 561–562, *562*
   GroupRepeats submenu, 562–563, *563*
   Labels option, 233–236
   PageLayout submenu, 205, 211, 213, 225, 227–228, 235
   RemoveBlanks submenu, 232–233
   Setup submenu, 226–227, 228–229
   Wait option, 230
Table band, 189, *206*, **207–208**, 209–214, 271
   copying columns, 213–214
   deleting columns, 211
   inserting columns, 211
   mouse versus keyboard operations in, 210
   moving columns, 213
   overview of, **207–208**
   placing field masks in, 214
   sizing columns, 211–213
TableBand menu, **209–214**

Copy option, 213–214
Erase option, 211
Insert option, 211, 554
mouse versus keyboard operations in, 210
Move option, 213
overview of, 209–210
Resize option, 211–213, 221, 554
Report Footer band, Report Design screen, *206*, 209, 572
report formats
   changing existing, **252–253**, 272
   inserting printer codes in, 550, **589–590**, 628
   for multiple tables, **583–584**
   naming, **252**
   recovering deleted, 587–588
   saving, 189, 201, **252**, 272
   selecting, 199–201, *200*, *201*
Report Header band, Report Design screen, 206–207, *206*
Report menu
   Change option, 252–253
   Design option, 199, 225
   Output submenu
     File option, 448
     Printer option, 246
     Screen option, 248
   RangeOutput option, 247
   SetPrinter submenu, 229–230
Report option
   Tools/Copy submenu, 398
   Tools/Delete submenu, 403
   Tools/Rename submenu, 393–394
Report Preview screen, 248–249
Report Print dialog box, Workshop program, **786–789**, *787*
report print objects, **786–790**. *See also* applications
   defining, 786–789, *787*, *788*
   defining printer settings, 789–790, *789*
Report Selection dialog box, Workshop program, 787, *788*

Report Settings dialog box,
  Custom Configuration
  Program, 195, *196*,
  968–971, *969*
  Group band repeats setting,
    563, 970
  options, **969–970**
  saving or canceling settings,
    971
reporting functions, PAL, 845
reports, **188–272**, **552–599**. *See
  also* objects; report formats
  bands, **206–209**, *206*, 272. *See
    also* Group bands; Table
    band
    Form band, 208–209
    Page Footer band, 209
    Page Header band, 207,
      592, *592*
    Report Footer band, 209, 572
    Report Header band,
      206–207
  calculated fields in, 550,
    552–561, **592–599**, 628
    adding calculated fields,
      552–555, *554*, *556*
    adding summary fields,
      557–558
    calculating percentages with
      PAL functions, 596–599,
      597
    PAL functions in, **592–599**,
      596
    running totals, 557
    for totals and subtotals,
      555–561, *559*, *560*, 628
  copying, **398**
  defined, 7
  deleting, **403**
  designing, 188, **198–209**, 271,
    723–724. *See also* field
    masks; Report Design
    screen; Table band
    for applications, **723–724**
    changing page layout, 189,
      224–225, 272
    free-form reports, 199–201,
      201
    inserting and deleting blank
      lines, 188, **203–205**,
      244–245

inserting and deleting
  spillover pages, 205
inserting literal text, 188,
  203–205
inserting page breaks,
  244–245
moving text and field masks,
  205
new features, **912–913**
saving report formats, 201
selecting a report format,
  199–201, *200*, *201*
tabular reports, 199–201,
  200
exporting to word processors,
  448–449
field masks, 189, **201–202**,
  214–224, 272
  for alphanumeric fields, 218,
    221, 222–224
  for calculated fields, 215,
    219–220
  for currency fields, 202, 218
  for date fields, 202, 216,
    217, 218
  deleting, **220**
  explained, **201–202**
  justifying (aligning), 224
  for memo fields, 218, 221,
    222–224
  moving, 205
  for numbering records, 216
  for numeric fields, 202, 218
  for page numbers, 216
  placing, **214–217**
  #Record field mask, 216
  reformatting, **220–222**
  Regular field mask, 215
  sizing, 218
  for time fields, 202, 216
  for totals and subtotals, 215
  word-wrapping in, **222–224**
formatted reports. *See also*
  free-form reports; tabular
  reports
  printing, 151, 189, **245–249**,
    272
  sorting with, 133
free-form reports, **230–236**,
  272
  defined, **198**

deleting blank lines in,
  232–233
deleting blank spaces in,
  231–232, *232*
designing, 199–201, *201*
directory listing example,
  260–262, *261*
envelopes example,
  267–269, *268*, *269*
examples, **260–271**
Form band and, 208–209
form letter example,
  262–264, *263*
laser printer labels example,
  264–267, *265*
printing multicolumn labels
  and reports, 233–236, *235*,
  237
report example with memo
  fields, 270–271, *270*
Group bands, 189, **237–244**,
  238, 272, **561–572**
  BLANKLINE command in,
    567
  changing group specifier,
    243–244
  column heading display,
    561–562, *562*
  formatting Group headers,
    564–566, *564*, *565*
  Group Header and Group
    Footer bands, 239,
    567–569, 571–572
  grouping on alphanumeric
    ranges, 240–241
  grouping on date ranges,
    242–243
  grouping on field values,
    239–240
  grouping on numeric,
    currency, or short numeric
    ranges, 242
  grouping on a record count,
    243
  hiding or displaying
    repetitive data, **562–563**,
    563, 970
  inserting and deleting, 239
  nesting groups, **567–569**,
    568, *570*

omitting details, **569–572**, *571*
overview of, 237–238
PAGEBREAK command in, 566
positioning items in, 567
running totals, **572**
selecting sort direction for groups, 243
starting groups on a new page, **566**
Instant Reports, 188, **190–191**, *191*, *192*, **197–198**, 271
locks and, **940**
in Membership application example, **728–730**, *730*, *731*
on multiple tables using lookup tables, 550, **573–582**, *576*, *577*
creating, 550, **574–575**
Field/Lookup options, 580–582
guidelines for, 573–574, *574*
linking tables in many-to-many design, 578–580, *578*, *579*, *580*, *581*
placing fields from lookup tables, **575–578**, 628
on multiple tables using queries, **582–588**
creating report formats from Answer tables, 583–584
printing invoices from four tables, *583*, 584–587, *585*, *586*
recovering deleted report formats, 587–588
using the report format, 584
on networks, **940–941**, 988
overview of, 7–11, *8–10*
pages in
changing page layout, 189, **224–225**, 272
changing size of, 227–228
length and width of, 193–194, *193*, 969, 970
numbering, 216
page breaks, **244–245**

page ejection settings, 190, 195, 970
printing ranges of, 247
previewing, 189, **248**, *248*
printer codes in, **588–592**
for compressed print, 590
for font and print size, 590–592, *592*
guidelines for, 588–589
for Hewlett-Packard printers, 590–592
inserting in report formats, 550, **589–590**, 628
printer settings for, 188, **192–198**, *193*, **224–230**, 271
changing page and print size, 227–228
changing printer port, 229–230
for Hewlett-Packard printers, 196–197, *196*, 227, *228*
left margin settings, 194, 970
page ejection settings, 190, 195, 970
page length and width, 193–194, *193*, 969, 970
pausing printer for each page, 230, 970
predefined printer setup strings, 226–227, *228*, **971–974**, *971*, *973*
printer defaults, 195–197, *196*
selecting printer, 228–229
for spillover pages, 191, *192*, 194
testing, 197–198
vertical alignment, 197
printing, 151, 189, **245–249**, 272
from the desktop, 246
with memo fields, 270–271, *270*
previewing reports, 189, **248**, *248*
printing ranges of pages, 247
from queries, **249–250**
from Report Design screen, 246

searching for values in report previews, 249
from sorted tables, **251–252**
recovering deleted, **403**
renaming, **393–394**
spillover pages
deleting all columns in, 211
inserting and deleting, 205
for Instant Reports, 191, *191*, *192*
margin settings and, 194
printer settings for, 191, *192*, 194
summary calculations in, **555–561**
Table band, 189, *206*, **207–208**, *209–214*, 271
copying columns, 213–214
defined, **207–208**
deleting columns, 211
inserting columns, 211
mouse versus keyboard operations in, 210
moving columns, 213
placing field masks in, 214
sizing columns, 211–213
tabular reports. *See also* Table band
defined, **198**
designing, 199–201, *200*
examples, **253–259**
phone and fax list example, 255–257, *256*
phone list example, 253–254, *254*
wide tabular report example, 257–259, *257*, *258*
types of, **198**, 271
Required option, ValCheck/Define submenu, 114–115
reserved names, of temporary tables, 46–47
reserved words
case sensitivity of, 518
in query criteria, 157
searching for with query criteria, 155, **176–177**
using multiple, 640
Resize option, TableBand menu, 211–213, 221, 554

RESTORE command, DOS,
  401, 823
restoring. *See also* recovering
  deleted objects, **403**
  deleted report formats,
    587–588
  Image menu settings, 105–107
  windows, 86, **91**, 119
Restructure option, Modify
  menu, 136, 410, 421–423,
  422, 478
Retain option,
  Setting/GroupRepeats
  submenu, 562–563, *563*
reverse screen style, on forms,
  297–298
Rotate key (Ctrl+R), 105
rotated bar graphs, 318–319,
  319
rule of uniqueness, **476**
ruler indicator, Report Design
  screen, 202–203, *203*
running
  Custom Configuration
    Program, **952–953**, *954*
  Paradox under Microsoft
    Windows, **895–897**
  queries, 140, **149**
  scripts. *See* playing back
    scripts
running totals
  in Group bands, **572**
  in reports, 557
Runtime program, Paradox, 716

S

sample custom axes, 336–338,
  337. *See also* graphs
sample free-form reports,
  260–271. *See also* free-form
  reports; reports
  directory listing, 260–262, *261*
  envelopes, 267–269, *268*, *269*
  form letter, 262–264, *263*
  laser printer labels, 264–267,
    265
  reports with memo fields,
    270–271, *270*
sample tables, **494–499**,
  1000–1001. *See also*

multiple tables
  Accounts table, *496*
  Invoices table, *495*
  listed, **1000–1001**
  Mastinv table, 494, *495*
  Orders table, 496–498, *497*
  Purchase table, 498–499, *498*
sample tabular reports,
  253–259. *See also* reports;
  tabular reports
  phone and fax list, 255–257,
    256
  phone list, 253–254, *254*
  wide tabular report, 257–259,
    257, *258*
Save option
  Editor File menu, 681
  Image/Graph submenu, 309,
    350
Savevars scripts, **839**
saving
  Answer tables, 150
  Autosave option, 982
  CCP report settings, 971
  CCP Video settings, 960
  changes in Editor, 662, **681**,
    690
  changes to data, 61, **81–82**, 83
  changing directories and, 34
  color settings, 968
  Custom Configuration
    Program settings, 997–998
  with DO-IT! option, 35, 37
  forms, **280–281**, 289, 293,
    302, 303
  graph settings, 306, **347–348**,
    364
  Image menu settings, **105–107**
  queries, 493, **546–547**, 548
  records, 67
  report formats, 189, 201, **252**,
    272
  scripts, 371
    Instant Scripts, 383
    and playing back, 666–667,
      707
    and switching to Full Screen
      User Interface, 35
  table structures, 41, **57**, 58,
    424–425

.SC file name extension, 371,
  668, 693
.SC2 file name extension,
  706–707
scaling, graph axes, 328,
  334–335
scheduling database example
  of many-to-many database
    design, 466–467, *467*, *468*
  using multiple table queries,
    506–508, *506*
Scientific option, Image/Format
  submenu, 102–103
Screen option, Output menu,
  248
screens. *See also* Video Settings
  dialog box
  eliminating "snow," 959
  matching screen colors to
    printer colors, 333
  refreshing on networks,
    933–934, *935*, 987
  selecting screen mode for
    graphs, 978–979
Script option
  Tools/Copy submenu,
    398–399
  Tools/Delete submenu, 402
  Tools/Rename submenu,
    382–383, 394
scripts, **366–387**, **691–708**. *See
  also* objects; PAL; update
  queries
  auto-indenting in, **680**
  automated form letter
    example, **376–381**, *377*
    adding Welcomed field for,
      376
    creating form letter script,
      377–379, *378*
    creating label or envelope
      script, 380
    using scripts, 380–381
  combining and embellishing,
    700–705, *701*, *702*, *703*
  combining updating scripts,
    703–705, *704*, *705*
  commands from previous
    versions in, 37
  commenting in, 663, **693–694**,
    694, 840

COMPATIBLE command, 37
copying, **398–399**
creating from scratch, 697–699, *698*
debugging, **375–376**, *375*, **856–859**
deleting, **402**
designing for applications, 723–724
displaying
  graphs in, 327
  messages in, 663, **696–697**
editing, 662, **666–667**, *667*, **691–692**, *691*, 707. *See also* Editor
  queries saved as scripts, 692, *693*
  selecting editor for, **990–992**
Editor Go option and, **707**
elements of, **691–692**
Execute scripts, **839**
guidelines for, **705–706**
Init.SC script, 385–386, 824, 839, **869–871**, 887
Instant Scripts, **381–384**
  playing back existing scripts as, 367, **383–384**, 387
  recording and playing back, 366–367, **382**, 387, 839
  saving, 383
miniscripts, **801**
on networks, **941–942**
PAL commands, **693–700**
  commenting in scripts, 663, **693–694**, *694*
  creating scripts from scratch, 697–699, *698*
  displaying custom messages (Message command), 663, **696–697**
  examples, **700–705**
  pausing for user input, 663, **699–700**
  placing objects on desktop, 663, **694–695**, *696*, 708
  Prompt command, 700
  Sleep command, 697
  Sound command, 663, **697**
  Until command, 700
  Wait Workspace command, 700

password-protecting, **411–415**
  adding passwords, 411–413, *413*
  changing or deleting passwords, 414–415
  reactivating (clearing) passwords, 414
  using password-protected scripts, 413–414
pausing for user input in, 663, **699–700**
placing objects on desktop in, 663, **694–695**, *696*, 708
playing back, **371–374**, **384–386**, 695, **855–856**
  from another script, 367, **384**
  automatically at Paradox startup, 367, **385–386**
  canceling, 374
  directories and, 368–369, 371–372
  existing scripts as Instant Scripts, 383–384
  Instant Scripts, 367, **382**, 387
  at maximum speed, 366, **372–373**, 386
  preparing for, **371–372**, 695
  repeating playback, 373–374, 856
  at startup, 869, 871, 907
  and watching keystrokes, 366, **373**, 386
for printing reports from queries, 250
recording, 366, **370–371**, 386, 697–699, 856
  creating scripts from scratch, 697–699, *698*
  Instant Scripts, 366, **382**, 387
  preparing for, **368–370**
recovering deleted, **403**
renaming, **394**
replacing, 370
replaying queries saved as, 493, **547**, 548
Savevars scripts, **839**
saving, **371**
  Instant Scripts, 383

and playing back, 666–667, 707
queries as, 493, **546–547**, 548
.SC2 files, **706–707**
{Scripts} and {End-Record} commands, 699
scripts within scripts, 367, **384**
SETUIMODE command, 37
for updating
  combining, 703–705, *704*, *705*
  creating, 407, 632, **636**, **637**
  examples, 647–649, *649*, 652–655, *653*, *654*, *656*, 659
  using, **656–657**
viewing inventory of, 417–418
word-wrap feature and, 679
Scripts menu
  BeginRecord option, 370, 836
  Editor submenu
    New option, 697–698
    Open option, 413–414, 666
  EndRecord option, 371, 384, 836
  Play option, 372, 384, 493, 547, 548
  QuerySave option, 493, 547, 548, 692, *693*, 836
  RepeatPlay option, 373–374, 384
  ShowPlay option, 373
scroll bars, 75–76, *76*, 99
Search menu
  Editor
    ChangeToEnd option, 689–690
    Find option, 686–687
    Next option, 687
    Replace option, 688–689
  Report Preview screen, 248–249
"Search value not found" message, 687
searching, **93–97**. *See also* queries
  for fields or records, 87, **94–95**, 119
  for Help topics, 31–32

for operators with query
criteria, 155, **176–177**
for punctuation with query
criteria, 155, **176–177**
for records, 87, **94–95**, 119
with FIND queries,
177–179, *178*
for reserved words with query
criteria, 155, **176–177**
for symbols with query
criteria, 155, **176–177**
for text in memo fields, 97
for values in records, 87,
95–97, 119
for values in report previews,
249
with wildcards, 32, 96, 97
searching and replacing in
Editor, 670, **685–690**
case sensitivity in searches,
687
replacing text with confirm
feature, 688–689
replacing text without confirm
feature, 689–690
searching for text, 686–687
Secondary Index screen,
486–488, *486*, *488*
secondary indexes, 457,
484–489, 490. *See also*
indexes
creating, **428–429**, **484–488**
with Image/OrderTable
option, 484–485
with Modify/Index option,
484, 486–488, *486*, *488*
with Tools/QuerySpeed
option, 428–429, 484, 485
defined, **475**
deleting, **489**
file name extensions for, 399,
487
listing, **488**
maintaining automatically, **983**
speeding up queries with,
428–429, 484, 485
viewing field names for,
419–420
security. *See* passwords;
protecting

Select: Help Display dialog box,
Workshop program, 797
Select: Multiple Actions dialog
box, Workshop program,
771–772, *772*
Select Table dialog box,
Workshop program, 779,
780
selecting
active window, 86, **89–90**, 118
BLOB editor, 48, 70, 684,
992–994
editor for scripts, **990–992**
fields for queries, 140,
145–149
check mark types, 145–148,
145, *146*, *147*, *148*
checking multiple fields,
148, *148*
placing check marks,
148–149, *149*
unchecking fields, 149
graph type, 306, **315–316**,
315, 364
options in dialog boxes, 93
options from menus, **27**, 38
printers, 228–229
for application
documentation, 816–817,
817
for graphs, 351–352,
975–978
records based on summary
calculations, 529–531,
529, *530*
report formats, 199–201, *200*,
201
screen mode for graphs,
978–979
sort direction for groups, 243
text in Editor, 662, **672–674**,
672, 708
and copying to a file, 683
and deleting, 674–675
deselecting text, 673–674
with keyboard, 669–670, 673
with mouse, 673
a working directory, 23,
32–34, 38

semicolon (;)
for commenting in scripts,
693–694, 840
in Picture formats, 112
separator character, for ASCII
files, 438, **995–996**
sequential data files. *See* ASCII
delimited files
Series menu. *See also* graphs
LegendsAndLabels option,
340
MarkersAndFills option, 343
Session Event Procs dialog box,
Workshop program,
783–785, *784*
Session Key Procs dialog box,
Workshop program,
782–783, *782*
set comparison operators, in
query criteria, 157
.SET files, 107
set queries, 493, **534–543**, 548.
See also queries
calculating percentages with,
546
check marks (✓) in, 540
comparing records to
summary values, 542–543,
542
defining sets, 535–540, *536*,
538
EVERY operator, **535**, *536*,
537–538, *538*
EXACTLY operator, **535**,
536, 540
GroupBy operator, 540–542,
541
NO operator, **535**, *536*, 538,
539
ONLY operator, **535**, *536*,
538, *539*
overview of, 534–535, *534*
SetKey command (PAL), 833,
863–868
creating GetRecord and
PasteRecord keys, 867–868
creating hotkeys, 863–865
creating multiple hotkey
macros, 866–867
SetPrinter submenu, Report
menu, 229–230

INDEX

setting
  delimiter character, 438
  duration of graph display, 306, **326–327**
Setting menu. *See also* Report Design screen
  Format submenu, 561–562, *562*
  GroupRepeats submenu, 562–563, *563*
  Labels option, 233–236
  PageLayout submenu
    Delete option, 205, 211, 235
    Insert option, 205, 213, 235
    Length option, 225, 236
    Margin option, 225
    Width option, 225
  RemoveBlanks submenu
    FieldSqueeze option, 232, 236
    LineSqueeze submenu, 233, 236
  Setup submenu
    Custom option, 228–229
    Predefined submenu, 226–227
  Wait option, 230
SETUIMODE command, 37
"Setup string recorded" message, 227
setup strings, printer, 226–227, *228*, **971–974**, *971*, *973*
Setup submenu, Setting menu
  Custom option, 228–229
  Predefined submenu, 226–227
SHARE configuration option, 904
sharing files, with other Borland applications, **949–950**
shelling out to DOS, 52, 53, 391, **449–450**, 451
Shift key
  + F5 (maximizing/restoring windows), 91
  in Editor, 669–670
  navigating with, 74
  in Query form window, 144
short numeric fields. *See also* fields; numeric fields
  defined, **47**, 49
  grouping reports on, 242

shortcuts
  for cross tabulations, 362–363, *363*
  for entering data, **70–73**
ShowClipboard option, Editor Edit menu, 676
ShowPlay option, Scripts menu, 373
Sign-Convention option, Field/Reformat submenu, 222
size
  of records, 51
  of tables, 50–51, **983–984**
Size/Move option, System menu, 90, 150
sizing
  Answer tables, 150
  columns in reports, 211–213
  columns in Table view, 99–101, *100*
  Editor window, 668
  field masks, 218
  fields on forms, **289**
  tables in Table view, 98–99
  windows, 86, **90**, 119
slash (/), as division operator, 516–517, 552–553
Sleep command, PAL, 697, 865
Sort option and screen, **128–132**, *129*, *130*, *131*
SortDirection submenu, Group menu, 243
sorting, **122–138**. *See also* Group bands
  Answer tables, **150–151**, 152
  ascending versus descending sorts, 122, **127**, 129, 137
  in ASCII versus international (NORDAN dictionary) order, 123, **135–137**
  changing sort methods, 135–137
  closing sorted tables, 123, 132
  to current table versus to a separate table, 122, **126**, 128, 137
  with formatted reports, 133
  indexes and, 126
  with key fields, 135
  locks and, **939**

making changes in sorted tables, 131
  on memo fields, 130
  with Modify/Sort option, 122, **128–132**, *129*, *130*, *131*, 137
  on networks, **939**
  other techniques for, **133–135**
  printing reports from sorted tables, **251–252**
  with queries, 133, 149
  rearranging fields to see sort order, 123, **132–133**, *132*, *133*, *134*, 137
  sorts within sorts, **124–126**, 137
  uppercase and lowercase in, 123, **135–137**
Sound command, PAL, 663, **697**
source tables
  and copying records, 404
  in INSERT queries, 639–640, 644
  specifying for copying objects, 396–397
  and Tools/Subtract option, 406
spacebar
  Alt + spacebar (System menu), 90
  for data entry shortcuts, 72
special characters, 70, *71*, 916
special key commands, PAL, 843
Speedbar
  overview of, 22, **28–29**, 38
  switching Table and Form views, 66, 276
speeding up, queries, 391, **428–429**, 451, 485
spillover pages. *See also* reports
  deleting all columns in, 211
  inserting and deleting, 205
  for Instant Reports, 191, *191*, *192*
  margin settings and, 194
  printer settings for, 191, *192*, 194
spreadsheet programs
  exporting to, **432–433**
  versus Paradox, 14
SQL Link program, **948–949**

square brackets. *See* brackets ([ ])
squares calculator, 873–877, *877*
stacked bar graphs, 316
Standard Form screen, **276–277**, *277, 278. See also* forms
Standard Settings dialog box, Custom Configuration Program, 153, 914–915, **979–984**, *979*
  Autosave option, 982
  Blank = Zero option, 981–982
  Disable Break option, 980–981
  File Format option, 982–983
  Interface Mode option, 980
  Maintain Indexes option, 983
  Maximum Table Size option, 983–984
  Mouse Use option, 980
  new features, 914–915
  Query Order option, 140, **151–155**, *152, 154*, 508, 981
  Working Directory option, 980
Standard User Interface, 35, 37, 980
starting
  applications, 807, **824–827**, 828
    from DOS, 824–825
    from Paradox, 824
    from Windows, 825–827, *826, 827*
  Paradox, 22, **24–25**, 38
    choosing a working directory, **32–34**
    and playing back scripts, 367, **385–386**
    playing scripts at startup, 869, 871, 907
    report groups on a new page, **566**
  Workshop program, 722, 750, **753–754**, *755*
status bar, **28–29**, 93
Structured Query Language, SQL Link program, **948–949**

structures. *See* table structures
Style menu, Form Design screen, **296–300**
  Color submenu, 296–297
  Fieldnames submenu
    Hide option, 300
    Show option, 299–300
  Monochrome submenu, 297–298
subforms. *See also* multi-table forms
  for Accounts table, 624–625, *624*
  designing, 614, 615–616
  embedding, 617–618, *617*
  for Invdtail table, 623–624, *623*
  managing, 619
submenus
  creating in applications, 750, **763–767**, *764, 766*, 803
  in menus, 27
subtotals. *See also* summary calculations
  field masks for, 215
  in reports, **555–561**, *559, 560*, 628
Subtract option, Tools/More submenu, 406–409, 410
subtraction operator (–), 516–517, 552–553
SUM operator, 523–524, 530, 555, 557
summary calculations. *See also* cross tabulations; subtotals; totals
  instant field summaries, **861–863**
    with miniscripts, 862–863, *863*
    with PAL/Value option, 862
  in queries, 493, **523–531**, 542–543
    comparing records to with set queries, 542–543, *542*
    default grouping for, 524
    frequency distributions, 527, *528*
    on groups of records, 526–527, *527, 528*

selecting records based on, 529–531, *529, 530*
summarizing all records, 525–526, *525*
in reports, **555–561**
  inserting summary fields in reports, 557–558
  running totals, 557
summary functions, PAL, **861**
summary operators
  blank fields and, 604
  in query criteria, 157, 523–524
  in reports, 555–561
Suppress option, Setting/GroupRepeats submenu, 562–563, *563*
Surface-Queries option, System/Desktop submenu, 151
SWEDFIN.SOR file, 137
switching
  directories, 33–34, 41, 53
  to Edit or CoEdit mode, 60, **64–65**, *65*, 83
  between editing windows, 675
  to Field view, 77
  to Full Screen User Interface, 23, **35–37**, *36*
  to Standard User Interface, 37
  Table and Form views, 60, **66**, 83, 276
symbols. *See also* special characters; *Symbols section of index*
  in Picture formats, 111–112
  query criteria for, 155, **176–177**
syntax, of PAL commands, **843–844**
"Syntax error in expression" message, 219–220
SYSMODE() function, PAL, 870
System menu, *36*, 89
  activating, 90
  Close option, 91
  Desktop submenu
    Cascade option, 91
    Redraw option, 92
    Surface-Queries option, 151

Tile option, 91
Editor submenu, 667–668
Interface option, 35–36
Maximize/Restore option, 91
Next option, 90, 675
Size/Move option, 90, 150
Utilities submenu
  Custom option, 153, 934–935, 952
  Workshop option, 722, 754
Window option, 89
System Mode option, Workshop Edit Session dialog box, 778, 779

T

Tab key
  in dialog boxes, 93
  in Editor, 669
  navigating with, 74
  in Query form window, 144
tab stops, in Editor, 680, 985, 990
Table band, 189, *206*, **207–208**, **209–214**, 271. *See also* Report Design screen; reports
  copying columns, 213–214
  deleting columns, 211
  inserting columns, 211
  mouse versus keyboard operations in, 210
  moving columns, 213
  overview of, **207–208**
  placing field masks in, 214
  sizing columns, 211–213
Table option
  Tools/Copy submenu, 179–180, 395, 398–399, 924
  Tools/Delete submenu, 402
  Tools/Rename submenu, 394
table rights, **946**
Table Size option, Image menu, 98–99
table structures. *See also* indexes; multiple tables; tables
  borrowing, 56
  changing, 391, **420–428**, 451

changing field types, **423–424**
confirming deleted fields, 424
confirming shortened fields, 424–425
converting between older and newer versions of Paradox, **426–427**
fixing corrupted objects, **427–428**
imported tables, **430**
inserting, deleting, and moving fields, 422–423
modifying table structure, **420–423**, *422*
saving new structures, **424–425**
using Problems or Keyviol tables, 425–426, *425*
creating tables from existing, 56
designing, 40, **42–51**, *43*, *44*, **722–723**
  for applications, **722–723**
  defining data types, 40, **47–49**
  defining memo fields, 49–50, *51*
  limitations of tables, 50–51
  naming fields, 40, **46–47**
  overview of, 42–44
  planning fields, **44–46**, 57
printing, 416
saving, 41, *57*, *58*, **424–425**
viewing, 416–417, *417*
Table view
  adding records, 67
  asterisks (*) in fields, 103, 107
  closing windows in, *92*
  customizing, 87, **97–107**, 119
    changing column width, 99–101, *100*
    changing table size, 98–99
    formatting date fields, 103
    formatting numeric fields, 101–103
    moving columns, 104–105
    moving fields, 105
    saving and restoring Image menu settings, **105–107**
    when data does not fit, 107

navigating in, **74–76**, *76*
switching to, 60, **66**, 83
TableAdd option, CoEdit mode, 916
TableBand menu, **209–214**. *See also* Report Design screen
  Copy option, 213–214
  Erase option, 211
  Insert option, 211, 554
  mouse versus keyboard operations in, 210
  Move option, 213
  overview of, 209–210
  Resize option, 211–213, 221, 554
TableIndex option, Tools/Info submenu, 419–420
TableLookup submenu, ValCheck/Define submenu, 109, 605–608
TableOfGroups option, Setting/Format submenu, 561–562
tables, **40–58**, **60–83**. *See also* Answer tables; fields; indexes; multiple tables; multi-table forms; objects; records; table structures
  backing up, **179–180**
  with DOS BACKUP command, 400–401
  with queries, 401–402
  book's sample tables listed, **1000–1001**
  closing, 61, **82**, 83
  compatibility of tables from previous versions, **57**
  copying, **398–399**
  creating, 41, **53–56**, *54*, 58
    from existing table structures, 56
    on networks, 52, **937**
  creating directories for, 34, 41, **52–53**, 57
  defined, **5**
  deleting, **402**
  designing, 40, **42–51**, *43*, *44*, **722–723**. *See also* indexes; multiple tables; table structures
    for applications, **722–723**

defining data types, 40,
47–49
defining memo fields,
49–50, *51*
limitations of tables, 50–51
naming fields, 40, **46–47**
overview of, 42–44
planning fields, **44–46**, 57
editing, 60, 61, **64–65**, **74–82**
contents of fields, 76–78
deleting records, 61, **80–81**,
83
in Edit or CoEdit mode, 60,
81
inserting records, 61, **79–80**,
80, 83
memo fields, 79
saving or canceling changes,
61, **81–82**, 83
switching to Edit or CoEdit
mode, 60, **64–65**, *65*, 83
undoing changes to records,
61, 75, **78–79**, 83
emptying, **410–411**
entering data, 60, **67–73**. *See
also* data entry
adding and saving records,
67, 83
copying data from previous
record, 72
DataEntry feature, **73**
dates, 67–68, 72
in memo and binary fields,
60, **68–70**, 83
negative numbers, 68, 73
numbers, 72–73
shortcuts for, **70–73**
special characters, 70, *71*
limitations of, **50–51**
locks and, **937**
naming, **54**
navigating in, **74–76**, *76*
opening, 60, **62–64**, *64*, 82
in Edit or CoEdit mode, 81
overview of, 5–6, *6*
from previous Paradox
versions, 57
printing reports from sorted
tables, **251–252**
protecting, **411–416**

adding passwords, 411–413,
413
changing or deleting
passwords, 414–415
reactivating (clearing)
passwords, 414
using password-protected
tables, 413–414
write-protecting, 415–416
recovering deleted, **403**
renaming, **394**
restructuring, 391, **420–428**,
451
changing field types, **423–424**
confirming deleted fields,
424
confirming shortened fields,
424–425
converting between older
and newer versions of
Paradox, **426–427**
fixing corrupted objects,
427–428
imported tables, **430**
inserting, deleting, and
moving fields, 422–423
modifying table structure,
420–423, *422*
saving new structures,
424–425
using Problems or Keyviol
tables, 425–426, *425*
sample tables listed,
1000–1001
saving, 41, **57**, 58
size of, 50–51, **983–984**
source and target tables
and copying records, 404
in INSERT queries,
639–640, 644
specifying for copying
objects, 396–397
and Tools/Subtract option,
406
transaction tables, **464–465**
viewing, **66**
inventory of, 417–418
a table's family, *419*
write-protecting, 411, **415–416**
TabStops option, Editor
Options menu, 680

tabular reports. *See also* Table
band
defined, **198**
designing, 199–201, *200*
examples, **253–259**
phone and fax list, 255–257,
256
phone list, 253–254, *254*
wide tabular report,
257–259, *257*, *258*
target tables
and copying records, 404
in INSERT queries, 639–640,
644
specifying for copying objects,
396–397
and Tools/Subtract option, 406
temporary tables. *See also* tables
data entry in, **73**
making changes in, 131
reserved names of, 46–47
Test option
Workshop Application menu,
809
Workshop Help Screen dialog
box, 800
testing
action objects, 808
application Help systems, 800
applications, 713, **724**, 806,
808–809, *809*, 828
database objects, **721–724**
printer settings for reports,
197–198
text. *See also* Editor
auto-indenting, 680
deleting, 669, 671, 674–675
lines of, 672
exporting and importing,
683–684, 708
importing external files into,
682–683
inserting with Editor, 669, 671
literal text in reports, 188,
203–205
moving in reports, 205
overwriting in Editor, 669, 671
query criteria for
embedded text, 161–163,
162
text in memo fields, 164

INDEX

searching for
  in Editor, 686–687
  in memo fields, 97
searching and replacing, 670, **685–690**
  case sensitivity in searches, 687
  replacing text with confirm feature, 688–689
  replacing text without confirm feature, 689–690
  searching for text, 686–687
selecting in Editor, 662, **672–674**, *672*, 708
  and copying to a file, 683
  and deleting, 674–675
  deselecting text, 673–674
  with keyboard, 669–670, 673
  with mouse, 673
text files. *See also* ASCII files
  editing, 662, **667–668**, 708
  Editor defaults for, 680, 985
  exporting and importing, 439, 683–684
  word-wrap feature and, 679
"The area designated for the word wrap must be clear" message, 289
"This procedure is not yet defined" message, 783
three-dimensional bar graphs, 317–318, *318*
tick mark formats, for graphs, 328, 335–336
tick mark labels, for graphs, 328, 336
tilde (~), for menu option shortcut keys, 766
tiling, windows, 86, **91**, 119
time fields, field masks for, 202, 216
titles, for graphs, 328, 329–330, *329*, *331*
Titles option, Overall menu, 329
TODAY operator, in query criteria, 169–170
ToDOS option, Tools/More submenu, 449–450
Tools menu
  Copy submenu, **395–399**

Form option, 398
Graph option, 351, 398–399
JustFamily option, 396, 398–399, 401, 924
Report option, 398
Script option, 398–399
Table option, 179–180, 395, 398–399, 924
Delete submenu, **402–403**
  Form option, 403
  Graph option, 402
  Index option, 403, 429, 489
  KeepSet option, 106, 301, 403
  Report option, 403
  Script option, 402
  Table option, 402
  ValCheck option, 118, 403
developing applications with, **409–410**
ExportImport submenu, **429–449**. *See also* exporting; importing
  ASCII options, 436–442, 481
  dBASE options, 435
  overview of, 431–432
  PFS options, 435
  Reflex options, 435
  VisiCalc options, 436
Info submenu, **416–420**
  Family option, *419*, 488
  Inventory submenu, 417–418, *418*
  Lock option, 936–937
  Structure option, 416–417, *417*
  TableIndex option, 419–420
  Who option, 936
locks and, **942**
More submenu, **403–416**
  Add option, 401, 405, 409, 481, 482
  Copy option, 401
  Empty option, 406, 410–411
  Protect submenu, 411–416, 942–947
  Subtract option, 406–409, 410
  ToDOS option, 449–450

Net submenu
  AutoRefresh option, 934
  lock options, 929–931
  UserName option, 933
on networks, **942**
QuerySpeed option, 419, 428–429, 484, 485, 983
Rename submenu, **393–394**, 409
  Form option, 393–394
  Graph option, 394
  Report option, 393–394
  Script option, 382–383, 394
  Table option, 394
totals. *See also* summary calculations
  field masks for, 215
  in reports, **555–561**, *559*, *560*, 628
  running totals
    in Group bands, **572**
    in reports, 557
transaction tables, **464–465**
transferring data. *See* exporting; importing
transitive dependencies, **473–474**
.TXT file name extension, 438
TypeIn command, PAL, 844
Typeover mode, 77, 205, 286

U

UNDELETE command, DOS, 403
underscore (_), in saved queries, 692, *693*
undoing
  changes to records, 61, 75, **78–79**, 83
  record deletions, 80–81
uniqueness
  ensuring in one-to-many database design, 463–464
  rule of, **476**
Until command, PAL, 700
update queries, **632–660**, 703–705
  adjustment transactions, 633, 657, *658*, 660

changing values in one table based on another table, **645–655**, 659
  adding items received to In Stock quantities, **651–655**
  creating history tables, **645–646**, 651–652, *652*
  creating updating scripts, 652–655, *653, 654*, 656
  moving posted records to history tables, 633, **649–650**, *650*, 660
  subtracting quantities sold from In Stock quantities, 646–649, *647, 648, 649*
  combining updating scripts, 703–705, *704, 705*
  copying fields between tables, **635–637**, *635, 637, 638*, 659
  copying incompatible records between tables, 632, **638–644**, 659
  calculating with INSERT queries, 644
  with CHANGETO queries, 633, **640–642**, 659
  creating auto-execute queries, 632, **642–644**, *643*
  with INSERT and multiple queries, 639–642, *639, 641, 642*
  correcting updated transactions, 633, **657**, *658*, 660
  flagging records, 632, **635–636**, 642, 645
history tables
  adding items received to In Stock quantities, **651–655**
  creating, **645–646**, 651–652, *652*
  moving posted records to, 633, **649–650**, *650*, 660
  subtracting quantities sold from In Stock quantities, 646–649, *647, 648, 649*
  updating scripts and, 652–655, *653, 654*, 656
locks and, **942**
on networks, **942**

printing a reorder report, **658–659**
Query forms for, 633, **636–637**, *637*, 659
update scripts
  combining, 703–705, *704, 705*
  creating, 407, 632, **636**, 637
  examples, 647–649, *649*, 652–655, *653, 654*, 656, 659
  using, **656–657**
uppercase
  in Editor searches, 687
  in query criteria, 164–165
  reserved words and operators and, 518
  secondary indexes and, 487
  in sorts, 123, **135–137**
user names, on networks, **933**, 934
user-defined menu options. *See* menu options
Utilities submenu, System menu
  Custom option, 153, 934–935, 952
  Workshop option, 722, 754

V

.VAL files, 108, 118
ValCheck menu
  Clear submenu, 117
  Define submenu
    Auto submenu, 115–117
    Default option, 110
    HighValue option, 109–110
    LowValue option, 109–110
    overview of, 107–109
    Picture option, 110–114
    Required option, 114–115
    TableLookup submenu, 109, 605–608
ValCheck option, Tools/Delete submenu, 118, 403
validity checks, 87, **107–118**, 120. *See also* data entry
  advancing cursor to next field, **115–117**
  when field is filled, 116
  when Picture format is complete, 116–117

defining
  default values, 110
  lowest or highest acceptable value, 109–110
  required values, 114–115
deleting, **117–118**, 403
in Membership application example, **726–727**
for multiple tables, 551, **604–610**, 629
  AllCorrespondingFields option, 607–608
  defining, **605–608**
  JustCurrentField option, 606–607, 608
  overview of, **604–605**
  state abbreviations example, 610, *611*
  using tables with, 608–610, *609*
overriding, **118**
overview of, **107–109**
Picture formats
  defining, **110–114**
  defining acceptable values in, 113
  forcing entries in, 113–114
  literal values in, 112
Value dialog box, PAL, 832, *838*
Value option
  Image/Zoom submenu, 95–97
  PAL menu, 832, **838**, 859, 862
Value scripts, 838
values
  in PAL, **847**
  query criteria for
    exact values, 140, **158–160**, *159*
    inexact values, 140, 156, **161–165**
    ranges of values, 141, **166–168**
variables in PAL, 832, **848–850**
  assigning in PAL functions, 849
  assigning in PAL scripts, 849
  changing data type of, 832, **849–850**
vertical alignment settings, for reports, 197

INDEX

vertical bar (|), in saved queries, 692, *693*
video attributes, for forms, **297–298**
video configuration options, 900
Video Settings dialog box, Custom Configuration Program, 914, *954*, **958–960**. *See also* monitors; screens
  canceling and saving settings, 960
  Color Palette option, 959
  Color Settings option, 960–961
  Monitor Type options, 958–959
  Negative Colors option, 959–960
  Video "snow" option, 959
View dialog box, 62–64, *63*
ViewGraph submenu, Image/Graph submenu, 309, 313
viewing
  Clipboard, 676, *677*
  data on networks, 938–939
  field names for secondary indexes, 419–420
  file inventory, 417–418, *418*
  information about files, 391, **416–420**, 451
  memo fields, 50
  secondary indexes, 488
  table structures, 416–417, *417*
  a table's family, *419*, 488
views. *See* Field view; Form view; Table view
VisiCalc files, exporting and importing, 436

W

Wait option
  Overall menu, 326
  Setting menu, 230
Wait Workspace command, PAL, 700
waiting, avoiding on networks, **930–931**

"WARNING! Structure contains non-compatible field types" message, 427
While...EndWhile loops, in PAL scripts, 854
Who option, Tools/Info submenu, 936
wide tabular reports, 257–259, *257*, *258*
Width option, Setting/PageLayout submenu, 225
wildcard characters
  in DOS COPY command, 399
  in Find dialog box, 686, 687
  in Zoom dialog box, 32, 96, 97
Window option, System menu, 89
Windows. *See* Microsoft Windows
windows, **88–92**
  activating, 86, **89–90**, 118
  active window, **88**, *89*
  closing, 86, **91–92**, *92*, 119
  copying current editing window to a file, 681–682
  cycling through, 90
  maximizing and restoring, 86, **91**, 119
  moving, **90**, 119, 668
  opening multiple windows in Editor, 685
  sizing, 86, **90**, 119, 668
  switching between editing windows, 675
  tiling and cascading, 86, **91**, 119
word processors
  embellishing application documentation with, 819–820
  exporting reports to, **448–449**
  exporting text to, 683–684
  versus Paradox, 14
WordPerfect
  exporting text to, 683–684
  exporting to merge files, **439–445**
  printing structure of Paradox table, 440

  defining format of ASCII file, 440–441
  exporting Paradox data, 442
  preparing WordPerfect for imported file, 442–443
  creating primary merge file, 443–444, *444*
  performing the merge, 445
  importing merge files, 445–448, *447*
WordWrap option
  Editor Options menu, 679
  Form Design Field menu, 287–289
word-wrapping
  in Editor, **678–679**, *679*, 985
  in field masks on reports, **222–224**
  fields on forms, 274, **287–289**, *288*, 291, 293, **301**, 303
working directory, 23, **32–34**, 980. *See also* directories
Workshop option, System/Utilities submenu, 722, 754
Workshop program. *See also* applications
  Action Object Tools dialog box, *814*
  ActionEdit menu, 775
    Help Text option, 796
    Multi Action option, 769
  Application menu
    Close option, 811
    Directory submenu, 34, 53, 722, 758–759
    Edit option, 810
    Finish option, 815
    New option, 759
    Remove option, 811
    Test option, 809
  Borrow Multiple Actions dialog box, 774–775
  buttons and keyboard equivalents, **757**
  dialog boxes in, **756**
  Documentation Destination Selection dialog box, *816*
  Select Printer option, 816
  Documentation menu, 815–816

Documentation Printer Selection dialog box, 816–818, *817*
Documentation System Styles dialog box, 818–819, *818*
Edit: Multiple Actions dialog box, 770–771, *770*
Edit Application dialog box, *810*
Edit Session dialog box, **776–785**, *776*
  Add option, 776, 778
  EventProcs option, 777, 783
  Keys option, 777, 782
  overview of, **776–778**
  System Mode option, 778, 779
Edit Session-Table Information dialog box, 778–782, *779*
Execute PAL dialog box, 801
Form Selection dialog box, *781*
Help Screen dialog box, 797–800, *798*
  Cross-References area, 799
  Edit Text option, 798–799
  Edit XRef option, 800
  Test option, 800
Help screens, 758
Menu Definition dialog box
  Borrow button, 774
  creating and attaching actions to menu options, 771–772, *773*
  defining Help text, 797
  defining menu and submenu options, 766–767, *766*

renaming/editing menu options, 768
Menu Insert menu, 765–766
menu options, **754–758**, *755*, *756*
Multi-Action dialog box, 794–795, *794*
New Application dialog box, 759–762, *763*, 783, 785
Object Type dialog box, 771
OK/Cancel Object dialog box, 801–802, *802*
overview of, 712, **716–717**
ParadoxEdit menu, 812–813
Printer Setting dialog box, 789–790, *789*
Query By Example dialog box, **791–794**
  defining queries, 793–794, *793*
  overview of, 791–792, *791*
Remove Application dialog box, 811–812
Report Print dialog box, **786–789**, *787*
Report Selection dialog box, 787, *788*
Select: Help Display dialog box, 797
Select: Multiple Actions dialog box, 771–772, *772*
Select Table dialog box, 779, *780*
Session Event Procs dialog box, 783–785, *784*
Session Key Procs dialog box, 782–783, *782*
starting, 722, 750, **753–754**, *755*

Tools menu, 813–814
workstations, for Paradox on networks, 921–922
write locks, **923**
WriteBlock option, Editor File menu, 683–684
write-protecting tables, 411, 415–416
write-record locks, **925**

X

X-axis labels, 308, 311, 338
XCOPY command, DOS, 821–823
XCut option, Editor Edit menu, 674, 677
.XG file name extension, 399, 487
X-Y graphs, **321–322**, *323*

Y

.YG file name extension, 399, 487

Z

zeros, returning blank fields as, **518–519**, 604, **981–982**
zip codes, aligning, 224
Zoom feature, **93–97**
  in Help system, 31–32
  for searching
    records and fields, 94–95, 481
  text in memo fields, 97
  values in records, 95–97

Alan Simpson's Mastering Paradox 4.5 for DOS Companion Disk Coupon

If you want to use the example tables, forms, reports, and membership management applications presented in this book without keying them in yourself, you can send for a companion disk containing all the files (excluding the files that already came with your Paradox for DOS package). You can use each file as it is, or as a starting point in creating your own applications.

To purchase the disk, complete the order form below and return it with a check, international money order, or purchase order for $20.00 U.S. currency (plus sales tax if you are a California resident) to the address shown on the coupon. Or, use your VISA or MasterCard.

If you prefer, you can return the coupon without making a purchase to receive free, periodic newsletters and updates about Alan Simpson's latest books.

. . . .

Alan Simpson Computing
P.O. Box 945
Cardiff-by-the-Sea, CA 92007
Phone: (619) 943-7715
Fax: (619) 943-7750

☐ Please send the companion disk for *Mastering Paradox 4.5 for DOS*

☐ No disk, thanks, but please send free newsletters from Alan Simpson Computing

_____
NAME

_____   _____
COMPANY   PURCHASE ORDER NUMBER (IF APPLICABLE)

_____
ADDRESS

_____
CITY, STATE, ZIP

_____   _____
COUNTRY   PHONE NUMBER (REQUIRED FOR CHARGED ORDERS)

Check one:

☐ Payment enclosed
($20.00, plus sales tax for California residents),
made payable to *Alan Simpson Computing*

☐ Bill my VISA/MC

Card No. _____ Exp. Date _____

Check one disk size:

☐ 5¼" disk

☐ 3½" disk

. . . .

SYBEX is not affiliated with Alan Simpson Computing and assumes no responsibility for any defect in the disk or files.

FREE CATALOG!

Complete this form today, and we'll send you a full-color catalog of Sybex Computer Books.

Please supply the name of the Sybex book purchased.

_____

How would you rate it?

_____ Excellent   _____ Very Good   _____ Average   _____ Poor

Why did you select this particular book?

_____ Recommended to me by a friend
_____ Recommended to me by store personnel
_____ Saw an advertisement in _____
_____ Author's reputation
_____ Saw in Sybex catalog
_____ Required textbook
_____ Sybex reputation
_____ Read book review in _____
_____ In-store display
_____ Other _____

Where did you buy it?

_____ Bookstore
_____ Computer Store or Software Store
_____ Catalog (name: _____)
_____ Direct from Sybex
_____ Other: _____

Did you buy this book with your personal funds?

_____ Yes   _____ No

About how many computer books do you buy each year?

_____ 1-3   _____ 3-5   _____ 5-7   _____ 7-9   _____ 10+

About how many Sybex books do you own?

_____ 1-3   _____ 3-5   _____ 5-7   _____ 7-9   _____ 10+

Please indicate your level of experience with the software covered in this book:

_____ Beginner   _____ Intermediate   _____ Advanced

Which types of software packages do you use regularly?

_____ Accounting   _____ Databases   _____ Networks
_____ Amiga   _____ Desktop Publishing _____ Operating Systems
_____ Apple/Mac   _____ File Utilities   _____ Spreadsheets
_____ CAD   _____ Money Management   _____ Word Processing
_____ Communications   _____ Languages   _____ Other _____
                                                         (please specify)

Which of the following best describes your job title?

_____ Administrative/Secretarial   _____ President/CEO

_____ Director   _____ Manager/Supervisor

_____ Engineer/Technician   _____ Other _____
                                              (please specify)

Comments on the weaknesses/strengths of this book: _____

_____

_____

_____

_____

Name _____

Street _____

City/State/Zip _____

Phone _____

PLEASE FOLD, SEAL, AND MAIL TO SYBEX

SYBEX, INC.
Department M
2021 CHALLENGER DR.
ALAMEDA, CALIFORNIA USA
94501

SEAL

Main Features of the Paradox Screen

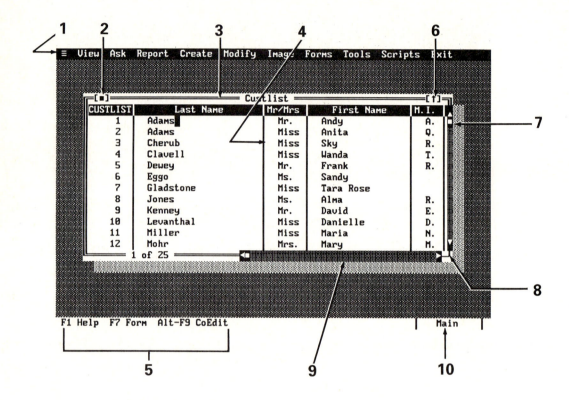

1. **Menu Bar** (Chapter 2)

    Mouse: Click any menu name (or the ≡ symbol for the System menu).

    Keyboard: Press F10 and the first letter of menu name, or highlight menu name with arrow keys and press ↵. (Press Alt-spacebar to open the System menu.)

2. **Close/Cancel** (Chapter 5)

    Mouse: Click to close window. To save changes first, press F2.

    Keyboard: Choose ≡ ➤ **C**lose. To save changes first, press F2.